ATONEMENT, JUSTICE, AND PEACE

Atonement, Justice, and Peace

*The Message of the Cross
and the Mission of the Church*

Darrin W. Snyder Belousek

WILLIAM B. EERDMANS PUBLISHING COMPANY

GRAND RAPIDS, MICHIGAN / CAMBRIDGE, U.K.

Published 2012 by
Wm. B. Eerdmans Publishing Co.
2140 Oak Industrial Drive N.E., Grand Rapids, Michigan 49505 /
P.O. Box 163, Cambridge CB3 9PU U.K.

Printed in the United States of America

18 17 16 15 14 13 12   7 6 5 4 3 2 1

Library of Congress Cataloging-in-Publication Data

Belousek, Darrin W. Snyder, 1969-
Atonement, justice, and peace: the message of the Cross and the mission of the church /
Darrin W. Snyder Belousek.
p.   cm.
ISBN 978-0-8028-6642-4 (pbk.: alk. paper)
1. Atonement.   2. Mission of the church.   3. Christianity and justice.
4. Peace — Religious aspects — Christianity.   I. Title.

BT265.3.B45   2012
232′.3 — dc23

2011025647

www.eerdmans.com

Contents

Preface

Near the end of his recent masterful survey of theories of atonement, theologian Peter Schmiechen comments concerning the contemporary church:

> It is difficult to have confidence if one does not know what to proclaim regarding Christ. Thus at the heart of the churches' struggle to find their identity and mission are the Christological questions posed by the life, death, and resurrection of Jesus. When ordained and lay leaders are not clear about atonement, there can be no confidence regarding vocation, ministry, or the future of the church.[1]

I agree.

This book studies the biblical theology of the cross with a view toward the mission of the church in the world. Accordingly, we aim to draw out the implications of the gospel of "redemption in Christ Jesus" (Rom 3:24) for our calling as Christians to pursue the "harvest of justice" that "is sown in peace by those who make peace" (Jas 3:18). We seek to understand both how God does justice and makes peace through the saving cross of Christ and the relevance of God's justice-doing and peacemaking through the cross for Christian action concerning contemporary issues of justice and peace. Beginning from Paul's message of the cross of Christ and the Gospel narratives of Jesus' ministry of teaching and healing, death and resurrection, this book addresses such questions as: Does the cross make sense in terms of retribution? What is the message of the cross concerning economic justice? Concerning capital punishment? The War on Terror? Inter-ethnic/inter-religious conflict? Christian disunity?

This book addresses itself primarily to Protestant Christianity, to both its

---

1. Peter Schmiechen, *Saving Power: Theories of Atonement and Forms of the Church* (Grand Rapids, MI: Eerdmans Publishing, 2005), p. 345.

evangelical and its mainline streams. We are concerned here with two opposite tendencies among contemporary Christians: passion for the message of salvation through Christ crucified disconnected from justice-doing and peacemaking in the name of Jesus, and passion for justice-doing and peacemaking disconnected from both the name of Jesus and the message of salvation through Christ crucified. This book thus addresses two distinct audiences within the church: those who are committed to proclaiming and living the gospel of Christ crucified, but do not see that message as connected essentially to justice-doing and peacemaking in the name of Christ, and those who are committed to doing justice and making peace but do not see such social action as connected essentially to the cross of Jesus Christ. By seeking to show the inseparability of the gospel of Christ crucified and Christian action for justice and peace, this book challenges *both* the "conservative" and "liberal" wings of the contemporary church.

This book pursues three overarching, interweaving goals:

1. to reframe our thinking about the message of the cross within the biblical story of redemption, critiquing the popular theology of the cross within evangelical Christianity (viz., penal substitution) (Parts I and II),
2. to reorient our perception and thinking concerning justice and peace from the perspective of the cross, challenging the dominant "retributive paradigm" within Western culture and Christianity (Parts I and III), and
3. to recast our vision for the mission of the church as part of God's purpose of redemption through the cross and resurrection of Christ, developing a "cruciform paradigm" through which to imagine faithful action for justice and peace according to the pattern of Christ (Parts I and IV).

The common thread running through these goals is to reshape our thinking about, and reorient our perception of, the cross of Christ. This reshaping and reorienting take place against the background of a worldview or paradigm that is already assumed, perhaps unconsciously, in Christian thinking about and perception of the cross. The distinctive contribution of this book is to carefully examine the assumed worldview or paradigm that has framed theology of the cross within the evangelical stream of Protestant Christianity in particular and the majority tradition of Western Christianity in general.

By approaching atonement theology in this way, we bring the perspective of the philosopher to the conversation. Regarding the relation between the Bible and philosophy, J. Lawrence Burkholder has noted:

> There is a tendency among people today . . . to assume that the only legitimate and fruitful approach to reality is through the Bible. That the Bible is the ultimate authority, I would not challenge.

> However, the Bible is seldom, if ever, approached without presupposi-
> tions. They change from age to age. Frequently, they reflect quite uncon-
> sciously a framework of meaning and habits of thought that are supplied by
> the prevailing world view.[2]

The indispensable role of the philosopher within the church is to exercise and
sharpen our critical awareness of the framework of presuppositions within which
we make sense of both Word and world. The "prevailing worldview" that has
framed theology of the cross within evangelical Protestant Christianity in particular, and the Western tradition in general, is the paradigm that understands retribution to be the sum of justice and peace as well as the substance of God and nature. The core task of this book is thus to focus our attention on this "retributive
paradigm" and show how it has framed our reading of Scripture and thinking
about the cross, to challenge its presuppositions on biblical grounds, to shift our
thinking about and perception of the cross to a paradigm shaped by Scripture,
and to revision the mission of the church within that "cruciform paradigm." We
thus follow what Paul Gooch has characterized as a "Pauline approach" to doing
philosophy with "the mind of Christ": "not only articulate and defend beliefs
against skeptics and cultured despisers but also offer to Christian communities
the clarification, interpretation, and critical appraisal of their beliefs."[3]

While the primary readership for this book will be found among academic
audiences in colleges and seminaries, my hope is that this book will also find a
church-wide audience among scholars, clergy, and laity alike. My intent in this
book is to be both seriously evangelical and authentically ecumenical. Our
point of view is developed primarily from the exegesis of Scripture and is
guided strictly by the apostolic faith of the orthodox creeds. We engage exten-
sively with biblical scholars and theological writers across a wide latitude of
Protestant Christianity — Adventist, Anglican, Baptist, Lutheran, Mennonite,
Methodist, Presbyterian, and Reformed — as well as with Roman Catholic and
Eastern Orthodox authors. We also draw from and dialogue with ancient and
medieval Christian sources, including Irenaeus, Athanasius, Augustine,
Anselm, and Aquinas, as well as engage contemporary theologians, including
Karl Barth, Jürgen Moltmann, and Miroslav Volf. Along the way we have also
chosen popular writers — C. S. Lewis, Ron Sider, and Philip Yancey — as con-
versation partners. Such popular writers exercise considerable influence upon
Christian thinking, and their contributions to the conversation merit serious
consideration and careful critique.

2. "The Bible and Philosophy," in Edward Zuercher, ed., *Sum and Substance: Essays by
J. Lawrence Burkholder* (Goshen, IN: Pinchpenny Press, 1986), p. 39.

3. Paul W. Gooch, "Paul, the Mind of Christ, and Philosophy," in Paul K. Moser, ed., *Jesus
and Philosophy: New Essays* (Cambridge: Cambridge University Press, 2009), pp. 84-105, here
p. 103.

Throughout the book, we make use of varied modes of thinking and writing, including exegesis of Scripture texts; meditation on biblical narrative and poetry; considerations from church history and orthodox tradition; argument from theological doctrines and philosophical perspectives; considerations from culture, history, science, and politics; and reflection on communal experience. We thus appeal to the threefold authority of Scripture, tradition, and reason, with Scripture being the first and final authority.

Part I is a preparation for the remainder of the book, laying out the motivations, methods, and objectives for the entire study. Any study of atonement theology from an evangelical perspective will concern, first and foremost, the question of how to interpret Scripture. We thus articulate upfront our "guiding rules" for reading Scripture and interpreting the cross. Following this, we engage the prevailing worldview within which the majority tradition of Western Christianity has read Scripture concerning the meaning of the cross — the retributive paradigm. We contrast this retributive paradigm with the tradition of the Gospels and the Apostles and examine how it has shaped Christian thinking concerning atonement, justice, and peace down the centuries.

Part II takes up Goal 1, critiquing the conventional evangelical theology of the cross — the penal substitution doctrine of atonement — and reframing our understanding of the message of the cross within the biblical story of redemption. Sections A and B lay out the core claims of the penal substitution account of the cross, testing the assumptions and implications of penal substitution by extensive examination of the scriptural texts most frequently summoned in favor of penal substitution atonement. Section C offers a balanced appraisal of penal substitution, affirming those aspects of substitutionary atonement which we think indispensable to a biblical account of atonement but rejecting those aspects which we find incompatible with Scripture and orthodox tradition. We then develop an alternative view of substitution in atonement that is more coherent with the witness of Scripture and free of the problematic aspects of the penal theory.

In connection with this, we should clarify one point in advance: this book does not, nor is intended to, propose a novel theory of atonement or defend one of the historic theories over against all others. And this for two reasons. First, as John Driver has shown us, the biblical witness offers a manifold of motifs for understanding atonement — ten in all.[4] Theories of atonement, however, tend to select one such image of atonement around which to construct a framework of salvation that either neglects all other images or reduces the several images to the one image. Penal substitution is typically presented in one of these two ways, either as *the* theory of atonement or as the theory of atonement

---

4. John Driver, *Understanding the Atonement for the Mission of the Church* (Scottdale, PA: Herald Press, 1986).

that uniquely and adequately explains the entire range of biblical images. Second, the tendency of commentators (à la Gustaf Aulén) has been to reduce the Christian tradition to three theories — Christus Victor, penal substitution, and moral influence. And apologists for penal substitution often reduce the tradition further, to a single theory. As Peter Schmiechen has shown us, however, the Christian tradition has developed a panoply of theories of atonement, each with something positive to offer our understanding of atonement. Following Driver and Schmiechen, we seek to draw from the riches of both Scripture and tradition.

Part III takes up Goal 2, reorienting our thinking concerning justice and peace according to the cross of Christ. In Section A, we elaborate Paul's message in Romans of the justice of God revealed through the cross of Christ and go on to show that Jesus' teaching concerning justice in the Gospels reflects the justice of God revealed through the cross. We then examine the scriptural witness to God's character, covenant, and creation to show that they also testify with Christ's cross to God's justice beyond retribution for the sake of redemption. Section B addresses the specific issues of economic justice and capital punishment in light of the canon of Scripture, the life-ministry of Jesus, and the cross of Christ.

Sections C and D of Part III develop Goal 2 further, focusing on the cross and peace. Section C unfolds Paul's vision in Ephesians of the peace of God revealed through the cross of Christ, showing how the cross makes peace in the midst of hostility. Along the way, we consider the implications of the peace of the cross for the ways of war. Section D draws out the practical implications of the peacemaking way of the cross, including Jesus' ministry as told in Luke's Gospel; the imagination, spirituality, and community that are essential to Christian peacemaking; the dynamics of inter-ethnic and inter-religious hostility; and the problem of division and disunity among Christians.

Part IV summarizes and synthesizes our study by taking up Goal 3, recasting our vision for the mission of the church from the perspective of the biblical story of salvation and the redeeming cross of Christ. We first sketch the "big picture" of the redemptive purpose of God in relation to the cross of Christ and the mission of the church and then draw out implications for the ends and means of Christian mission in service of the gospel of Christ crucified. We then articulate a "cruciform paradigm" for envisioning Christian mission in the pattern of the cross of Christ.

Throughout the writing of this book, the Bible has been my greatest teacher. Yet I must give appropriate recognition to those who have taught me to read the Bible with care and without whom this project would not have proved possible. Several persons have also provided invaluable instruction, counsel, and encouragement during this project, and others have graciously read and helpfully commented on either all or part of this book. My thanks to: Mark

Baker, Laura Brenneman, John Driver, André Gingerich Stoner, Nancy Heisey, Alan Kreider, Jay Landry, Chris Marshall, Peter Martens, Ben Ollenburger, James Reimer, Mary Schertz, Willard Swartley, Perry Yoder, and Tom Yoder Neufeld. Thanks also to Jon Pott, Editor-in-Chief of Eerdmans Publishing, for accepting this book and supporting its publication and to John Simpson, my editor at Eerdmans, for his careful and helpful work on this book. Any errors within this book accrue only to my own account, of course. Thanks, finally, to my wife, Paula, for her patience and encouragement throughout this project.

DARRIN W. SNYDER BELOUSEK

Let the words of my mouth and the meditation of my heart
be acceptable to you, O LORD, *my rock and my redeemer.*

PSALM 19:14

Abbreviations of Modern Bible Translations

ESV   English Standard Version

KJV   King James Version

NAB   New American Bible

NASB   New American Standard Bible

NEB   New English Bible

NET   New English Translation

NIV   New International Version

NJB   New Jerusalem Bible

NRSV   New Revised Standard Version

TNIV   Today's New International Version

PART I

"We Proclaim Christ Crucified"

Rethinking the Message of the Cross

CHAPTER 1

The Telos and Genesis of This Book

1.1. What This Book Aims to Achieve

Does the cross make sense in terms of retribution? What is the message of the cross concerning economic justice? Concerning capital punishment? The War on Terror? Inter-ethnic/inter-religious conflict? Christian disunity? Before we can address these questions of justice and peace, however, we must first reorient ourselves to the cross of Christ. As the cross is understood by the atonement theology of evangelical Christianity — penal substitution — such questions make little sense because the cross so understood is largely irrelevant to such questions. And the reason for this is that penal substitution sees the cross from an assumed (and unexamined) viewpoint. We will critically examine that assumed view — the "retributive paradigm" — in Chapter 3.

This book, then, is effectively about achieving a change in worldview — or, if you will, a paradigm shift, a "Copernican Revolution" of sorts: rather than seeing the cross in terms of an assumed understanding of justice and peace, we seek to understand justice and peace from the perspective of the cross.[1] We seek, that is, to develop a "cruciform paradigm" for the church's mission of justice-doing and peacemaking (Parts III and IV). The necessary prerequisite to developing that paradigm will be to make a thorough examination of evangelical atonement theology — penal substitution — and the paradigm for understanding justice and peace upon which it is founded (Parts I and II).

Such questions concerning the connection of the message of the cross to practical matters of justice and peace are too seldom addressed by the church

---

1. N. T. Wright, *Surprised by Hope: Rethinking Heaven, the Resurrection, and the Mission of the Church* (New York: HarperCollins, 2008), similarly seeks a "paradigm change" from the biblical perspective of the resurrection.

for another reason. Within contemporary Christianity there is a yawning gap between two camps — those who are passionate about the gospel of salvation, and those who are passionate about the gospel of justice and peace. This divide is sometimes cast as an opposition between "evangelism" and "mission," or "salvation/faith" and "ethics/works," or "piety" and "activism."[2] These camps, which often coexist on the same Christian college campus or within the same congregation, can have difficulty speaking to and understanding one another, and can even be suspicious of the other's motivations. Each tends to see the other as having shortchanged or distorted the core message and true purpose of the gospel. Indeed, one might characterize this divide in terms of a (supposed) divergence between different gospels. Those that identify the Christian calling with "evangelism" emphasize a "Pauline" gospel that centers on the message of Christ crucified: "Christ died for our sins." Those that identify the Christian calling with "social activism" emphasize a "Jesus" gospel that centers on the good news of the kingdom: "the kingdom of God has come near; repent, and believe the good news." The tendency of "evangelical" Christians is to "spiritualize" the kingdom, while the tendency among "peace and justice" Christians is to "historicize" the cross. The disconnect between God's salvation through the cross of Christ and Christian action for justice and peace thus goes both ways: those passionate for the message of salvation through Christ crucified can miss (or dismiss) the ethical implications of the cross for doing justice and making peace in the name of Christ, and those passionate for justice and peacemaking for the cause of the kingdom can miss (or dismiss) the distinctive "cruciform" pattern of Christian ethics.

This divide diminishes the witness of the church to the fullness of the gospel.[3] Such a divide need not exist, thankfully. Evangelicals for Social Action and Sojourners have sought to bridge this divide among American evangelicals by taking the position that Christians can and should do both evangelism and mission, have both faith and works, be both pious and activist. The mission statements of both organizations illustrate this "both-and" thinking within evangelical Christianity. Evangelicals for Social Action "emphasizes *both* the transformation of human lives through personal faith *and* also the importance of a commitment to social and economic justice as an outgrowth of Christian faith"[4] Sojourners characterizes itself as "a committed group of Christians who work together to live a gospel life that integrates spiritual renewal *and* social

---

2. Cf. Dallas Willard, *The Divine Conspiracy: Rediscovering Our Hidden Life in God* (San Francisco: HarperSanFrancisco, 1997), pp. 35-55.

3. For a historical overview of the "growing dichotomy between evangelism and social action" within American evangelical Christianity during the twentieth century, see Pedrito U. Maynard-Reid, *Complete Evangelism: The Luke-Acts Model* (Scottdale, PA: Herald Press, 1997), pp. 17-45.

4. http://www.esa-online.org/Display.asp?Page=About (emphasis added).

justice."[5] Within worldwide evangelical Christianity, The Lausanne Movement also affirms "that evangelism *and* socio-political involvement are *both* part of our Christian duty."[6]

In my estimation, however, such "both-and" evangelical thinking is lacking an adequate theological bridge joining the two sides of the "both-and." In particular, the affirmation of Christian action for justice and peace is often independent of a biblical theology of the cross — why and how Christ died is disconnected from why and how Christians are called to do justice and make peace in the name of Christ.

The Lausanne Covenant (1974) and the Chicago Declaration of Evangelical Social Concern (1973) each reflect this inadequacy. Article 5 of The Lausanne Covenant, "Christian Social Responsibility," begins, "We affirm that God is both the Creator and the Judge of all people. We therefore should share his concern for justice and reconciliation throughout human society and for the liberation of people from every kind of oppression." But no mention is made of God as Redeemer or how God's redemption in Christ through the cross is relevant to the Christian concern for justice, reconciliation, and liberation. The Lausanne Covenant does mention the cross in Article 6, "The Church and Evangelism," stating that "a church which preaches the cross must itself be marked by the cross." Yet beyond the need to demonstrate love and honesty in both personal and institutional dealings, it says nothing concerning how being "marked by the cross" might entail a call for the church to do justice and make peace. The Chicago Declaration of Evangelical Social Concern does connect being freed from sin (salvation) to doing works of righteousness (ethics), but curiously omits the cross from its proclamation of the gospel: "We proclaim no new gospel, but the Gospel of our Lord Jesus Christ who, through the power of the Holy Spirit, frees people from sin so that they might praise God through works of righteousness."[7]

In his book *Complete Evangelism*, New Testament scholar Pedrito Maynard-Reid develops this "both-and" evangelical thinking: "such a dichotomy [between evangelism and social action] is false and unbiblical . . . when one recaptures the biblical worldview, true evangelism is a whole. It involves *both* personal *and* social components; both are equally valid without one holding priority over the other."[8] Yet his book also illustrates how the cross can be missing from attempts to join the two sides of the "both-and" within evangelical thinking. While Maynard-Reid places significant emphasis on the resurrection of Jesus and the sending of the Holy Spirit as crucial to the gospel mission, the cross is

---

5. http://www.sojo.net/index.cfm?action=about_us.mission# (emphasis added).

6. The Lausanne Covenant, Article 5, http://www.esa-online.org/Images/mmDocument/Declarations%20&%20Letters/The%20Lausanne%20Covenant.pdf (emphasis added).

7. http://www.esa-online.org/Images/mmDocument/Declarations%20&%20Letters/Chicago%20Declaration%20of%20Evangelical%20Social%20Concern.doc.

8. Maynard-Reid, *Complete Evangelism*, p. 13, emphasis added.

conspicuously absent from the model he develops based on the Luke-Acts narrative. He passes over the cross and atonement theology in two brief paragraphs:

> We miss Luke's point, however, if we attempt to impose a theology of atonement upon his work. Luke does not focus on an atonement theology as Paul does — a theology that some think is almost totally centered on the cross. Luke's theology is more wholistic as it treats reconciliation, repentance, and forgiveness.[9]

Maynard-Reid is correct in emphasizing the holistic character of Luke's vision of the gospel; and he is correct to observe that Paul's gospel is centered on the cross. We beg to differ, however, with his narrow assessment of Paul's vision of the gospel. As we will show in Chapters 19 and 27, the Pauline vision is also holistic, concerning a many-dimensional salvation, including reconciliation, repentance, and forgiveness as well as justice and liberation. As we will show in Chapter 30, moreover, the Luke-Acts narrative of Jesus' life-ministry can be read fruitfully from the perspective of Paul's depiction of the peacemaking cross of Jesus in Ephesians 2.

In his book *Good News and Good Works,* theologian Ron Sider also develops the "both-and" vein of evangelical thinking, but does so with attention to the connection between the cross of Christ and Christian social action.[10] Seeking to embrace "the fullness of God's salvation," Sider combines the three major historic theories of atonement — penal substitution, moral influence, and Christus Victor — into a "messianic model of the atonement" that constitutes (at least in part) the Christian motivation for social action.[11] I agree that the church needs a full-fleshed theology of salvation and a full-orbed vision for social action, with the cross at the center of both.

I do, however, find Sider's own thinking concerning the connection between salvation and social action to be less than adequate. Sider writes, "The messianic model integrates the insights of the moral, substitutionary, and classic views of the atonement."[12] Yet, the theological interrelation between these respective theories is not adequately clarified. Each theory would seem to function independently: one theory (penal substitution) tells us how our sins are forgiven through the cross of Jesus; another theory (moral influence) shows us Jesus, in his teaching and in his cross, as the ethical example we are to follow; and yet another theory (Christus Victor) tells us that the cross has freed us from the devil so as to render us capable of doing what Jesus' example shows us to do.

9. Maynard-Reid, *Complete Evangelism,* p. 110.
10. Ronald J. Sider, *Good News and Good Works: A Theology for the Whole Gospel* (Grand Rapids, MI: Baker Books, 1999).
11. Sider, *Good News and Good Works,* pp. 95-100, 145.
12. Sider, *Good News and Good Works,* p. 99.

Sider does not examine the presuppositions behind the three theories, moreover, to see whether they make for a coherent model or not; he simply asserts that "the three views complement each other."[13] As we will show in subsequent chapters, the penal substitution theory is based squarely on the logic of retributive justice; yet as we will also argue, Jesus, through both his teaching and his cross, shows us the just ways of God that transcend retribution for the sake of redemption. We thus find a significant tension, if not fundamental incompatibility, between the assumptions of penal substitution and the implications of moral influence and Christus Victor.[14]

As Sider acknowledges, furthermore, penal substitution theory is largely irrelevant to Christian discipleship:

> By itself, the substitutionary model largely ignores Christ's example of teaching and proclaiming the kingdom in Galilee, and his victory over the forces of evil during his life and at Easter. If one reduces the Atonement merely to Jesus' death for our sins, one abandons the New Testament understanding of the gospel of the kingdom and severs the connection between the Cross and discipleship. The result is the scandal of professing Christians whose sexual practices, business dealings, and political attitudes are no different from those of non-Christians.[15]

Not surprisingly, then, the three theories in Sider's atonement model do not contribute equally to the Christian motivation for social action: penal substitution is minimized while moral influence and Christus Victor are emphasized.[16] Given the disconnection between penal substitution and Christian discipleship, the rationale for maintaining that theory in an atonement model intended to link salvation and social ethics is unclear.[17]

The gap in contemporary evangelical Christianity — between salvation through the cross of Jesus Christ and Christian action for justice and peace —

---

13. Sider, *Good News and Good Works*, p. 98.

14. I thus concur with James Wm. McClendon, Jr., *Doctrine: Systematic Theology, Vol. II* (Nashville, TN: Abingdon Press, 1994), p. 213, emphasis original: "It seems clear that the several atonement accounts *cannot* simply be mixed together and baked in a single loaf" because the various historical theories of atonement make conflicting claims.

15. Sider, *Good News and Good Works*, p. 97. Cf. Willard, *Divine Conspiracy*, pp. 43-49.

16. Judging by devotion of page space, moreover, atonement theology would seem to be the *least* important of the several theological motivations for social action that Sider discusses — see *Good News and Good Works*, pp. 139-45.

17. Sider claims that penal substitution is indispensable, because "Without that understanding of the Cross, we either trivialize sin or despair of hope" (*Good News and Good Works*, p. 97). In response to such a claim, see Paul S. Fiddes, *Past Event and Present Salvation: The Christian Idea of Atonement* (Louisville: Westminster/John Knox, 1989), pp. 100-101. We think that the alternative understanding of atonement to be developed in this book neither trivializes sin nor despairs of hope.

still needs bridging, therefore. And this book aims to construct that theological bridge on a biblical basis.

1.2. How This Book Began

1.2.1. *Capital Punishment and Christian Conviction*

It was a personal encounter with the question of the death penalty through the mission work of my local congregation that gave birth to the pondering and searching that eventually resulted in this book. I have not always believed that the practice of capital punishment is contrary to the gospel of Jesus Christ. Like most Christians, I had grown up believing, as a default position, that the death penalty was God's will. The death penalty was not much discussed in my home or in my congregation, and there were few occasions for questioning it. The Old Testament commanded the death penalty, and so it was taught — assumed, really — that this is what ought to be done. Occasionally would someone ask, "The Old Testament prescribes the death sentence for adultery, disrespect for parents, breaking the Sabbath, etc., but we do not call for the death penalty for those sins, so why for murder?" To avoid this inconsistency, someone else would make reference to the dispensationalist interpretation of the Bible and say that, while we are no longer under the "dispensation of Moses," which commands the death penalty for many sins but applies only to Israel, we are still under the "dispensation of Noah," which commands the death penalty for murder and applies to all humanity (Gen 9:1-7). That is about as far as my thinking about the matter went until I read — *really* read — John 8:2-11 and thought to myself, What did Jesus say? After more readings and much reflection on what Jesus did say — "Let anyone among you who is without sin be the first to throw a stone" (John 8:7) — this Gospel story changed my mind and heart, convincing me that human beings have no right to execute a death sentence (see Chapter 24).

Although opposed to the death penalty for this reason, I did not take up an active witness to this gospel conviction until 1999. A capital murder trial was about to begin in our city and one of our pastors challenged our congregation to make a public witness. The Spirit moved me and others in the congregation to respond. Following this trial, an ecumenical coalition organized a Christian response to the increasing use of the death penalty by our local prosecuting attorney, a professing evangelical Christian. We circulated petitions, published opinion essays, did television and newspaper interviews, gave talks in congregations, held prayer vigils at times of capital trials and executions, organized panel discussions, and held prayer services to remember murder victims and their families. We debated with the prosecuting attorney on a Christian satellite TV network and met with him privately to discuss the issue. And after a pro-life

Catholic was elected prosecuting attorney but declined to take a public stance on the death penalty, we brought together Christian community leaders to share our concerns with him also.

Globally and nationally, the tide of public opinion has been turning steadily against capital punishment over the past half century, for legal and humanitarian reasons. Why, though, were we opposed to the death penalty on *gospel* grounds? After all, since the legal establishment of Christianity in the fourth century, the official church and the vast majority of Christians had believed in capital punishment as the divinely ordained way that society should deal with violent offenders.[18] A strong majority of American Christians continue to support the use of the death penalty.[19] What, then, would be our explanation to fellow Christians regarding why we *as Christians* would protest the death penalty? We could, of course, quote Jesus' ethical exhortations: "Let anyone among you who is without sin be the first to throw a stone" (John 8:7); or "You have heard that it was said, 'An eye for an eye and a tooth for a tooth.' But I say to you . . ." (Matt 5:38-39); or "All who take the sword will perish by the sword" (Matt 26:52). And these seemed (to us) to be reasons enough. Yet we also recognized that Christianity had long ago found various ways of circumventing many things Jesus had taught.

I thus realized that, to be persuasive to fellow Christians, especially those of evangelical conviction, such interpretation of Jesus' ethical teachings needed to be rooted in the distinctive and defining feature of the gospel — the message of Christ crucified. Hence, I became convinced that the deep answer concerning the death penalty must be found in connection with the cross of Jesus Christ. What, though, was the link between atonement theology and criminal justice? Having grown up in Baptist congregations, the only atonement theology to hand was the popular Protestant penal substitution doctrine. In those terms, the best answer I could come up with was this: if God himself had already punished Jesus with death upon the cross in our place to pay for our sins, then what right have we who have been saved by the cross to require that anyone else be put to death for his sins? It surely appeared a coherent answer, one that some evangelical Christians actually do find compelling.[20]

---

18. The definitive study of Christian thinking about capital punishment over the centuries is James J. Megivern, *The Death Penalty: An Historical and Theological Survey* (Mahwah, NJ: Paulist Press, 1997).

19. An anecdote: A jury in Raleigh, NC convicted a man of multiple murders but, due to two jurors set against the death penalty, could not achieve unanimity on a death sentence, settling instead for a life sentence. After the trial, one juror who supported a death sentence remarked: "We were in tears because we never got to tell the family that we wanted to give him death. We were a very intelligent, Christian-based jury" (Barry Saunders, "Sentence Wrenched 10 Jurors," *Raleigh News & Observer*, 27 April 2010, 1B). In her mind, evidently, "intelligent, Christian-based" thinking supports the use of the death penalty.

20. Cf. William C. Placher, "Christ Takes Our Place: Rethinking Atonement," *Interpretation*

Yet something about this answer, appealing to God's wrathful execution of retributive violence against Jesus as the reason for our *not* doing so to one another, did not ring true — precisely because it failed to understand the cross on its own terms, on Jesus' own terms. This way of explaining the connection between the cross and the death penalty depends on the very principle of retribution — justice requires that wrongdoing be "paid back" with retaliatory punishment ("eye for eye, tooth for tooth, life for life") — that justifies the death penalty, both in the Old Testament law and in the minds of so many Americans, including Christians. The logic of retribution, that is, underlies both penal substitution and capital punishment.[21] Jesus himself, however, explicitly renounces retributive thinking in Matt 5:38-39. Jesus expressly forbids his followers to return "like for like" — evil for evil, violence for violence — because retribution is not the way for the children of God (Matt 5:45). Because it is incompatible with what Jesus revealed about the character of God and the way of God's kingdom in his teaching to his disciples, it seemed clear to me that the principle of retribution could not do as a basis for understanding the connection between the cross and the death penalty (see Chapter 25).

Thus seeing the need to reexamine atonement theology, I began rethinking and re-searching the message of the cross. I soon received the essential insight — a "gestalt shift" in perspective — that would inspire the premise underwriting this book. Guided by the Gospel accounts, I began seeing the cross itself as a crime scene. Instead of seeing the cross as God's punishment of innocent Jesus in place of guilty humanity (per penal substitution), I saw the cross as humanity's murder of God in the person of Jesus. Instead of seeing the cross as the preordained *solution* to the problem of an angry God dealing with sinful mortals, I began seeing the cross as posing the *question* of how God-in-Christ would faithfully right the ultimate wrong in cosmic history — how God the wronged (in the person of Jesus) would "justify" and "reconcile" humanity the wrongdoer.

For sure, I am not the first to tread this path or seek new vision on these questions.[22] As I began my study of atonement theology, two books in particu-

---

53/1 (1999), 5-20, and Gardner C. Hanks, *Capital Punishment and the Bible* (Scottdale, PA: Herald Press, 2002), pp. 184-94.

21. Thus H. Wayne House, "Response: Unpersuaded," in H. Wayne House and John Howard Yoder, *The Death Penalty Debate* (Dallas: Word Publishing, 1991), pp. 185-86, argues that supporting capital punishment goes hand-in-hand with believing in penal substitution: to deny the death penalty is to undermine the penal substitution doctrine — and, hence, to affirm penal substitution is to support the death penalty — because both rest on a retributive foundation: "Justice demands payment for sin."

22. For another interesting account of an intellectual-spiritual journey from penal substitution toward a new understanding of atonement, see Brad Jersak, "Nonviolent Identification and the Victory of Christ," in Brad Jersak and Michael Hardin, *Stricken by God? Nonviolent Identification and the Victory of Christ* (Grand Rapids, MI: Eerdmans Publishing, 2007), pp. 18-53.

lar were quite helpful in breaking my thinking about the cross out of the narrow categories I had inherited from my childhood church experience. John Driver's survey of the various biblical atonement motifs in *Understanding the Atonement for the Mission of the Church* helped me see that the biblical writers make use of many images other than "substitution" to interpret the meaning of the cross.[23] This multiplicity of biblical motifs informs our articulation of a "cruciform paradigm" for Christian mission (Chapter 36). Mark Baker and Joel Green's *Recovering the Scandal of the Cross* helped solidify my sense that the cross should not necessarily make easy sense for us within our assumed categories of understanding the world.[24] The cross, Paul said, is a "stumbling block" *(skandalon)* to our natural thinking that should confound rather than confirm our preconceptions. We thus attend to how the popular Protestant atonement theology (penal substitution) conforms Christian thinking about the cross to the dominant paradigm for understanding justice and peace — and thus obscures the scandalous message of the cross.

Not long after this change of perspective on the cross, I discovered the ground-breaking work of writers that were promoting a "restorative justice" perspective as a gospel-grounded alternative to the dominant retributive perspective. Howard Zehr's *Changing Lenses* sought to achieve "a new focus for crime and justice"; and Christopher Marshall took us *Beyond Retribution* in search of "a New Testament vision for justice, crime and punishment."[25] This book, which seeks a paradigm shift in our perceiving, thinking, and doing concerning justice and peace, is indebted to both of these authors.[26]

1.2.2. The Disunity of the Church and the Cross of Christ

The fact of Christian disunity — the division of the church by lines of denominational demarcation, with the consequent disruption of Christian communion around a single table — has long been a personal matter. Growing up I witnessed how the gospel could be used (and abused) to divide "these" Christians from

---

23. John Driver, *Understanding the Atonement for the Mission of the Church* (Scottdale, PA: Herald Press, 1986).

24. Joel B. Green and Mark D. Baker, *Recovering the Scandal of the Cross: Atonement in New Testament and Contemporary Contexts* (Downers Grove, IL: InterVarsity Press, 2000).

25. Howard Zehr, *Changing Lenses: A New Focus for Crime and Justice,* 3rd ed. (Scottdale, PA: Herald Press, 2005); Christopher D. Marshall, *Beyond Retribution: A New Testament Vision for Justice, Crime, and Punishment* (Grand Rapids, MI: Eerdmans Publishing, 2001).

26. The views of nineteenth- and early twentieth-century theologians who also endeavored to rethink atonement theology and criminal justice together — John McCleod Campbell, R. C. Moberly, and Hastings Rashdall — are examined in Timothy Gorringe, *God's Just Vengeance: Crime, Violence and the Rhetoric of Salvation* (Cambridge: Cambridge University Press, 1996), pp. 204-16.

"those" Christians. I heard many a pastor, invoking Scripture out of context, proclaim that dividing the church and refusing communion with other Christians in the name of "separation" from "unbelief" and "darkness" (cf. 2 Cor 6:14-18) was not a human tragedy but a holy duty. My fundamentalist upbringing in independent congregations thus taught me to be as wary of ecumenism as of Communism — both were the works of the devil. As an adult, by the grace of God, I was wooed back into the fellowship of the church and relationship with Christ through the friendship of "evangelical" Catholics. Christian disunity had contributed to my alienation from a divisive church to which I could not reconcile myself, but Christian friendship beyond the denominational divide led me home. As a result, ecumenical peacemaking (as I call it) has become my life-long calling.

Out of this personal context I began asking concerning the biblical basis of ecumenism: Does the unity of the church actually matter to the gospel of Christ? In one of my earliest seminary courses, on the biblical foundations of peace and justice, our class was assigned a paper on the topic, "What implications does the cross have for peacemaking?" I took this as an opportunity to begin working out an answer.

After citing a couple key Pauline texts (Romans 5 and 2 Corinthians 5), I stated my thesis: "God has made peace with us by creating his church on earth in the resurrected body of the crucified Christ; it is therefore the mission of the church in the world to make peace in Christ's name by calling the world to reconciliation with God through conversion to Christ." From there I went on to develop the premise of the church's mission of peacemaking in the world — the ministry of reconciliation *within* the church itself. Unless the church is "making every effort to maintain the unity of the Spirit in the bond of peace," as Paul put it (Eph 4:3), its witness to the world of peace with God through Christ is compromised in both authenticity and effectiveness. And that is so, I argued, because disunity in the church frustrates the atoning (right-making, one-making) power of the cross among Christians. Ecumenism is the necessary correlate of evangelism, I concluded, for the gospel of Christ crucified concerns equally reconciliation with God and unity in Christ (cf. 1 Corinthians 1, Ephesians 2).

My professor commented: "This is a good paper, but extremely narrow in its focus and consequent assessment of the implications of the cross." Some ten years later, I still cannot but disagree. Because the cross is the both the keystone of Christian unity and the content of Christian mission, peacemaking in the name of Christ cannot be divorced from reconciliation within the body of Christ. Far from being "extremely narrow" in focus, the vision of the church unified through the cross of Christ encompasses the whole of the Christian vocation to be peacemakers in the world. To the contrary, it is a narrow vision of both the cross and the church to suppose that Christians can break down the walls of hostility that divide our world while ignoring the divisions that fragment the church (see Chapter 33).

CHAPTER 2

Interpreting the Cross:
Guiding Rules of a Cruciform Hermeneutic

For I decided to know nothing among you
except Jesus Christ, and him crucified.

1 CORINTHIANS 2:2

J. Lawrence Burkholder's remark, cited in the Preface, that "the Bible is seldom, if ever, approached without presuppositions," is apt to be kept in mind as we address the message of the cross. I do not claim to have discovered an absolute vantage point from which to read the message of the cross — I have not. My interpretation of the cross, as with any other, is founded upon certain presuppositions, some of which have already become evident. The aim is not to be free of presuppositions, which is not possible, but to be explicit and careful about one's presuppositions as far as is possible. The crucial question is not whether one's reading of Scripture makes presuppositions, but whether such presuppositions square with Scripture. We are thus unavoidably caught in a "hermeneutical circle" — we read Scripture with presuppositions that need to be justified according to Scripture. This need not prevent one from making a reasonable defense of an interpretation of Scripture, however. As long as this "circle" is big enough — as long as one's presuppositions find confirmation in Scripture independently of the particular texts whose meaning is in question — one avoids the real problem of logical circularity.

Our biblical study of the theology of the cross will be guided by three rules. These guiding rules, drawn primarily from the Gospel witnesses, find confirmation in the early apostolic literature and are consistent with the orthodox creed of the church. They also find adherence among biblical scholars and theologians across a wide range of the Protestant-Evangelical spectrum, from Anglican and Baptist to Lutheran and Mennonite to Methodist and Presbyterian. In what follows, we articulate these guiding rules and draw out some implications for our study of the cross. Effectively, these guiding rules point to the cross itself as the basis of epistemology in theology.[1]

2.1. Continuity and Consistency of Jesus' Life and Death

First, the cross of Christ is continuous and consistent with both the life-ministry and resurrection of Jesus. Jesus himself made this point explicitly and repeatedly. After Peter confesses Jesus as the Messiah (Mark 8:29), Jesus explains what it means to be the Messiah with his first "passion" prophecy. The text uses the Greek verb *dei* ("it is necessary") to emphasize the divine imperative of *both* his messianic calling and his messianic fate — God's Messiah is to be none other than a *suffering and crucified* Messiah (Mark 8:31). All of Jesus' passion prophecies, moreover, culminate in the resurrection, emphasizing the unity of life, death, and resurrection in Jesus' messianic vocation: the faithful and crucified Messiah is also to be a *risen* Messiah.[2]

So, too, the apostolic witness affirms that Jesus' life and death are woven together into a single tapestry hemmed by divine purpose (Acts 10:36-43; Rom 8:3-4; Gal 4:4-5; Phil 2:5-8). Paul proclaims, further, that Jesus' death is one with his resurrection, for both serve the same divine purpose and fulfill the same inspired Scripture (Rom 4:25; 1 Cor 15:3-4; 2 Cor 5:15; 1 Thess 4:14). And the Nicene Creed, consistent with the witness of the Evangelists and Apostles, emphasizes the integrity of Jesus life, death, and resurrection concerning God's purpose of salvation and work of redemption. Under the phrase, "For us humans and for our salvation," come not only the cross, but also Jesus' birth, resurrection, and ascension.[3]

This first rule finds ample support in contemporary scholarship. The in-

---

1. On the cross as criterion of interpretation of Scripture and knowledge of God in Paul's thinking, see Charles B. Cousar, *A Theology of the Cross: The Death of Jesus in the Pauline Letters* (Minneapolis, MN: Fortress Press, 1990), p. 35; Richard B. Hays, *Echoes of Scripture in the Letters of Paul* (New Haven, CT: Yale University Press, 1989), p. 191; and Michael J. Gorman, *Cruciformity: Paul's Narrative Spirituality of the Cross* (Grand Rapids, MI: Eerdmans Publishing, 2001), pp. 16-17.

2. All four Gospels give ample testimony to the unity of the life, death, and resurrection of Jesus: Matt 16:21-26; 17:22-23; 20:17-28; Mark 8:31-38; 9:30-37; 10:32-45; Luke 9:21-27; 9:44-45; 13:31-35; 17:25; 18:31-34; John 10:11-18; 12:23-36.

3. This emphasis on the unity of the life, death, and resurrection of Jesus, that the Incarnation as a whole was the locus of God's saving purpose and redeeming work, was a consistent theme in the early church. See Gustaf Aulén, *Christus Victor: An Historical Study of the Three Main Types of the Idea of Atonement* (New York: Macmillan Publishing, 1969); and H. E. W. Turner, *The Patristic Doctrine of Redemption: A Study of the Development of Doctrine during the First Five Centuries* (London: Mowbray & Co., 1952).

tegrity of messianic purpose in Jesus' life and death is a central thesis of Anglican New Testament scholar N. T. Wright.[4] "Why did Jesus die?" asks Wright. "Ultimately, because he believed it was his vocation." Wright concludes: "Jesus, then, went to Jerusalem not just to preach, but to die."[5] Mennonite biblical scholar Tom Yoder Neufeld, in his study of the New Testament witness to Jesus, sounds this same point: "The structure of the gospel narratives of the New Testament is intended to show that one does not fully appreciate the meaning of Jesus's death if one divorces it from his life, from his words and his deeds, or . . . from his resurrection."[6] In his study of Paul's story of redemption, Lutheran theologian David Brondos concludes that Paul understood the life, ministry, death, and resurrection of Jesus as an integral whole of mission in service of others: "For Paul, what Christ was seeking for others in his *death* was the same thing he had been seeking in his *life* of service. . . . What Jesus *died* for is the same thing he had *lived* for."[7]

As indicated already, this guiding rule will have significant implications for how we interpret the death of Jesus. Insofar as Jesus' life and death are unified in a single divine purpose, we cannot adequately understand Jesus' death in terms that are fundamentally incompatible with his life-ministry. We thus seek to interpret the cross in terms that are *consistent and coherent* with what Jesus taught and how he lived out his divine mission. The ministry and cross of Jesus comprise an integral revelation of the salvation of God — and give a common testimony to the saving righteousness of God.

The Synoptic Gospels attest uniformly that first and foremost in Jesus' messianic mission is proclamation and enactment of the kingdom of God (Matt 4:17, 23; 9:35; 12:28; Mark 1:14-15; Luke 4:43; 8:1; 9:11; 11:20; 17:21). And Jesus' teaching reveals that the kingdom of God is an upside-down kingdom: the poor, not the rich, are part-owners in the kingdom; the meek, not the proud, inherit kingdom land; those that hunger after justice, not those that hunger after power, are filled with the bounty of the kingdom; the merciful, not the vindictive, receive favor from the judge of the kingdom; the pure in heart, not the self-seeking, have special access into the royal courts; and the peacemakers, not the warriors, are adopted as children of the king (Matt 5:3-11). Jesus teaches by word and example, moreover, that kingship in God's kingdom is not about "lording it over" others and having oneself acclaimed with lofty titles, as in human kingdoms, but instead about humble and costly service, giving one's life

4. N. T. Wright, *Jesus and the Victory of God: Christian Origins and the Question of God*, Volume Two (Minneapolis: Fortress Press, 1996), pp. 540-611.

5. Wright, *Jesus and the Victory of God*, pp. 593, 609.

6. Thomas R. Yoder Neufeld, *Recovering Jesus: The Witness of the New Testament* (Grand Rapids, MI: Brazos Press, 2007), pp. 264-65.

7. David A. Brondos, *Paul on the Cross: Reconstructing the Apostle's Story of Redemption* (Minneapolis, MN: Fortress Press, 2006), pp. 75, 77, emphasis original.

for the sake of others (Mark 10:41-45; Luke 22:24-27). Finally, as Jesus testifies, the kingdom of God, in visible contrast to the empire of Rome and all other kingdoms "from this world," is not established by violent force, but through suffering love and truthful witness (John 18:33-38a).

In order to understand the cross *as the cross of Jesus Christ,* therefore, we seek to interpret the cross as a yet further — indeed, the definitive — revelation of God's upside-down kingdom. As Mennonite New Testament scholar Willard Swartley puts it, "Jesus crucified, his death, is *one* in meaning with Jesus' life. In both his life and death Jesus' way is God's upside-down kingdom."[8] Hence, we should be wary of any theology that would align the cross with "the kingdoms of this world."

A — perhaps *the* — distinctive feature of God's upside-down kingdom, as proclaimed and enacted by Jesus himself, is the renunciation of retribution as the founding principle of the justice-doing and peacemaking of God. Instead of returning harm for harm, injury for injury, evil for evil, "tit for tat," the way of God's kingdom renounces retaliatory resistance to evil and returns right for wrong, good for evil, seeking to overcome evil with good (Matt 5:38-48; Luke 6:27-38). Jesus sums up the renunciation of retribution in the kingdom of God by the formula known as the Golden Rule (Matt 7:12a): "In everything do to others *as you would have them do* to you." This kingdom imperative directly inverts the principle of retribution, which commands us to pay back others in kind ("like for like"): "do unto others *as they have done* to you." In contrast to the negative formulation of the Golden Rule received within the Jewish tradition (cf. Tob 4:15) and taught by the great Rabbi Hillel ("do *not* do to others what you would *not* want them to do to you"), moreover, Jesus' kingdom imperative commands us to take action to serve the good of others in all situations, doing right even to those who do us wrong and seeking peace even for the sake of our enemies. Both Paul and Peter, continuing Jesus' teaching, explicitly renounce retribution as a guiding principle for Christian action (Rom 12:9-21; cf. 1 Thess 5:15; 1 Pet 3:9).

Therefore, because the cross of Jesus Christ is the definitive revelation of the kingdom of God, and because renouncing retribution is essential to Jesus' proclaiming and enacting God's kingdom, any theology that interprets the cross of Jesus as the ultimate satisfaction of retribution obscures rather than reveals God's kingdom of justice and peace. That is, the cross interpreted in terms of satisfying the law of retribution is something other than *the cross of Jesus Christ.* We thus concur with Baptist theologian Paul Fiddes, who makes this point with respect to law in general:

---

8. Willard M. Swartley, *Covenant of Peace: The Missing Peace in New Testament Theology and Ethics* (Grand Rapids, MI: Eerdmans Publishing, 2006), p. 182, emphasis original.

As Jesus showed a sovereign freedom over the way of the law, so a doctrine of atonement must be free from any notion of a "transaction" which somehow satisfies the demands of a divine law code. It hardly makes sense that the Jesus who declined to give law any final importance and who was certified as being in the right about this when God raised him from among the dead, should have died as a means of satisfying law.[9]

In order to bring Jesus' life and death, his ministry and his cross, into coherence, so that together they comprise a single story and proclaim a single gospel, we seek to understand them *on the same terms,* the very terms that Jesus himself taught and practiced. The cross, as much as the teaching and practice of Jesus, overturns the law of retribution.[10]

2.2. Coherence between Christ and the Covenant

Second, the life, death, and resurrection of Christ complete the vision and fulfill the promises of God's covenant with Israel.[11] His proclamation of the kingdom of God, Jesus says, does not abolish but fulfills "the law and the prophets" (Matt 5:17-18); even the renunciation of retribution, as summed up in the Golden Rule, "is the law and the prophets" (Matt 7:12b). Jesus affirms, in his hour of suffering, that his death accords with and fulfills both Scripture and the will of God (Matt 26:39, 54, 56; Mark 14:21, 36; Luke 22:37, 42). And the risen Jesus teaches the disciples to interpret his life and death, his messianic vocation of suffering and glory, "according to the scriptures," in terms of "the law of Moses, the prophets, and the psalms" (Luke 24:25-27, 44-48). Peter thus preaches that through the suffering of Jesus, "God fulfilled what he had foretold through all the prophets" (Acts 3:18). Paul, maintaining the tradition he had received, likewise interprets the life, death, and resurrection of Jesus "in accordance with the scriptures" (1 Cor 15:1-4), as "attested by the law and the prophets" (Rom 3:21).

9. Paul S. Fiddes, *Past Event and Present Salvation: The Christian Idea of Atonement* (Louisville: Westminster/John Knox, 1989), pp. 47-48.

10. That being said, we do not presume that this guiding rule by itself constitutes refutation of the penal substitution doctrine of atonement, which does understand the cross as the satisfaction of the law of retribution. To reject penal substitution on the basis of an assumption of the inadequacy of its premises, which include the principle of retribution, would only beg the question. The penal substitution doctrine needs to be addressed on its own terms and critiqued with respect to the evidence of Scripture (see Part II below).

11. Our first two guiding rules taken together parallel the first two of three Pauline hermeneutical constraints discerned by Richard Hays in his study of Paul's reading of the Old Testament, *Echoes of Scripture in the Letters of Paul*, pp. 178-92: "the criterion of God's faithfulness to his promises" and the criterion that "the death and resurrection of Jesus [are] the climactic manifestation of God's righteousness."

"Christ," Paul says, "is the goal [*telos*] of the Torah [*nomou*]" (Rom 10:4, my translation), the One in whom "every one of God's promises is a 'Yes'" (2 Cor 1:20).

This, too, is a central thesis of Wright: Jesus' life and death, an integrated whole of messianic mission, are interwoven with Israel's history and God's purpose. For in and through Jesus Christ, God shows complete faithfulness to the covenant with Israel and ultimate victory over the powers of evil, both for the purpose of revealing YHWH as God and for the salvation of the world.[12] Swartley echoes Wright: "The cross, culminating Jesus' life and teaching, and the resurrection are the means of God's victory over evil, establishing Jesus as Savior and Lord."[13] Brondos argues similarly that Paul understands the life-ministry, death, and resurrection of Jesus to comprise a single mission intended by God to fulfill God's covenant promise of redemption: "for Paul, Jesus' coming, ministry, death, and resurrection are a unified whole and had a single objective: the redemption of God's people."[14] We should thus be wary of any atonement theology that would isolate the message of the cross of Christ from either the biblical story of God's redemption or the redemptive purpose of God's people.[15]

This second guiding rule, too, will have significant implications for how we interpret the life and death of Jesus as revealing God's justice-doing and peace-making. Because God fulfills the covenant with Israel in and through Christ, Jesus himself — his life, death, and resurrection — is the true meaning of the covenant. We should thus not fail to see how the life-ministry and cross of Jesus, however *new* they appear to us, nonetheless fulfill the core ideals of covenant justice and peace.

For example, when Jesus teaches us that God-human reconciliation is inseparable from human-human reconciliation (Matt 5:23-24; 6:12, 14-15), and when Paul exposits the meaning of the peacemaking cross of Jesus in similar terms (Eph 2:13-18), we should not be astonished to find that the Torah teaches us the same principle of peacemaking or atonement-making (Lev 6:1-7). By the same token, we should also not overlook the revelation of *grace* operating at the

---

12. Wright, *Jesus and the Victory of God*, pp. 540-611.

13. Swartley, *Covenant of Peace*, p. 183.

14. Brondos, *Paul on the Cross*, p. 76.

15. Ancillary to this second guiding rule is that we see no fundamental tension between the story of the cross told by the Evangelists and Apostles in the Gospels and Acts and the story of the cross told by Paul in his letters. We thus see no reason to pit Paul against Jesus (or against the Gospels) when interpreting the cross. On the relationship between Paul and Jesus, see Brondos, *Paul on the Cross*, pp. 67-77, 98-102; James D. G. Dunn, *The Theology of Paul the Apostle* (Grand Rapids, MI: Eerdmans Publishing, 1998), pp. 182-206; and N. T. Wright, *What Saint Paul Really Said: Was Paul of Tarsus the Real Founder of Christianity?* (Grand Rapids, MI: Eerdmans Publishing, 1997).

heart of the covenant — including the ritual sacrifices for atonement-making in Leviticus. Interpretations of Jesus' death in terms of satisfying retribution will obscure this essential point. If we interpret the cross as the fulfillment of the covenant (which we should), but also interpret the cross as the ultimate satisfaction of the law of retribution (mistakenly, we will show), then we will (mistakenly, we would argue) look for the law of retribution operating at the heart of the covenant. Inversely, if we interpret (mistakenly, we will show) the sacrifices for atonement in terms of the law of retribution, and then interpret the cross in terms of the sacrifices for atonement (which we should), then we will understand (mistakenly, we would argue) the salvation achieved through the cross as the satisfaction of retribution. That is, a (misguided) retribution-based atonement theology will dispose us toward a (mistaken) retribution-based understanding of the covenant, and vice versa. In that case we would obscure the divine grace that is at the root of and revealed by means of *both* the sacrifices for atonement and the cross of Jesus Christ. As we will show, when Paul proclaims in his exposition of the saving cross of Jesus Christ that, "by grace you have been saved through faith, and this is not your own doing; it is the gift of God — not the result of works" (Eph 2:8-9), he expresses essentially what the Torah already discloses through the Levitical sacrifices for making atonement.

Now, the coherence of Christ and covenant does not imply that there is only *continuity* between Christ and the covenant. The gospel accounts give evidence of both continuity and discontinuity ("You have heard that it was said . . . but I say to you . . ."). And in Paul's gospel, there is evident a tension between what came before (God's faithfulness in the past) and what we see through the cross (God's doing in the now). We do best to resist the temptation to resolve this tension in favor of the "old" or the "new" — to make the cross either repetition of, or divorced from, the past. Paul's signature phrase introducing the cross — "but now" (Rom 3:21; Eph 2:13) — is telling: he says neither "and now of course," as if the cross were simply repetition, nor "and now for something completely different," as if the cross were divorced from God's previous work.[16] This tension, it seems to me, is the mystery of the gospel — that in Christ through the cross, God remains faithful to the covenant by doing the unprecedented. Ironically, we have seen this before: "Do not remember the former things, or consider the things of old. I am about to do a new thing; now it springs forth, do you not perceive it?" (Isa 43:18-19). The "things of old" refer to God's mighty acts in the Exodus from Egypt (vv. 15-17); the "new thing" speaks of God's imminent action to liberate Israel from exile in Babylon (v. 14). God is thus free to act faithfully by doing the unprecedented.

---

16. Apologies here to both the Apostle Paul and Monty Python!

2.3. The Cross of Christ Reveals the Justice and Peace of God

Third, the life-ministry, cross, and resurrection of Jesus Christ together reveal "the justice of God" (Rom 1:17; 3:21) and "the things that make for peace" (Luke 19:42; cf. Rom 5:1; Eph 2:14-16; Col 1:20). Jesus Christ, Scripture says, is an "image *(eikōn)* of the invisible God" (Col 1:15; cf. 2 Cor 4:4), and the Son is "the exact imprint *(charaktēr)* of God's very being" (Heb 1:3). As "icon" and "character" of God, Jesus Christ images or expresses God to the world. An icon is a window onto the mystery of divine reality, a way of seeing or imaging the invisible God. The Incarnation is an icon of God that images the divine character to the world. The way of Jesus in the world — his teaching and healing, cross and resurrection — is thus a window onto God's characteristic way of being and acting.[17]

Developing how it is that the life-ministry, death, and resurrection of Jesus Christ reveal the characteristic justice-doing and peacemaking of God is the constructive task of this book and the major focus of Part III. Yet at the outset we can draw one implication from this guiding rule: if the life-ministry and cross of Jesus Christ together reveal to us the characteristic justice-doing and peacemaking of God, we cannot determine or fix in advance the character of God's justice and peace apart from the revelation through Jesus Christ. That is, while the Torah, prophets, and psalms do show truly the character of God's justice-doing and peacemaking, we must wait and see what Jesus Christ will reveal to know fully the character of God's justice and peace. The corollary implication is that we cannot assume beforehand that the life-ministry and cross of Jesus Christ will conform to our prior, natural human thinking about justice and peace. So, in seeking to answer the question of how the cross reveals "the justice of God" and "the things that make for peace," we should bracket out the expectation that we will see in the cross the confirmation of our common conceptions of justice and peace.

This latter point is crucial. We should not suppose that, because we are "Christian" rather than "Jew" or "Greek," the cross of Christ is no longer a "stumbling block" *(skandalon)* for us. If we approach "the message of the cross" from the human logic of wisdom and power, we will indeed find ourselves stumbling headlong over the divine "foolishness" of "Christ the power of God

---

17. That said, we must take care to avoid two errors here. First, we need to recognize that "icon" is a figure of speech and not to be taken literally. We must thus avoid reducing Jesus to something less than the incarnate Son of God. Second, while God is revealed in the life and teaching, death and resurrection of Jesus the incarnate Son, we must avoid reducing either the reality of God to the person of the Son or the revelation of God to the Jesus of history. The apostolic faith of the orthodox creeds affirms both that the God who is one being in three persons is more than Jesus and that the revelation of God continues in the Jesus of ascended present and eschatological future, the Jesus who now sits at the right hand of the Father and who will come again to judge the world.

and the wisdom of God" (1 Cor 1:18-25). This point, I should emphasize, applies to Christians on the "left" as much as to Christians on the "right" of the political spectrum. The all-too-common tendency among politically liberal Christians is to simply associate the cross with their causes and thus assume that followers of Christ in the way of the cross ought to work out their Christian discipleship through the approved forms of political engagement. This struck me especially when, on a Good Friday in the city where I was living at the time, a diverse group of Christians staged the "Economic Justice Way of the Cross" to conclude an annual Pilgrimage for Justice and Peace. The march, a version of the traditional stations of the cross, addressed such political issues as trade policy, health care, immigration reform, the death penalty, and the ongoing wars in Iraq and Afghanistan. For one participant, "the procession was a source of comfort because it confirmed her religious and political beliefs."[18] As I argue in this book, the cross does have something scandalous to say concerning matters of justice and peace, including the death penalty, war, and economic justice. But when the cross makes us comfortable because it confirms our prior political views, then we know that the cross has ceased to be a scandal, that it has ceased to speak to us the unsettling Word of God.

As long as our thinking remains shaped by the scheme of this age (whether "liberal" or "conservative"), our understanding of the cross will inevitably be conformed to the world's ideas of justice and peace (Rom 12:2). If we assume beforehand that the cross should conform to our prior thinking, then we risk removing the scandal of the cross and thus robbing the cross of its revelatory power — its power to speak a new word breaking us out of the scheme of this age. Instead, we need to "be transformed by the renewing of [our] minds" so that we are able to see how the cross confounds rather than confirms our all-too-human assumptions. And in order for our minds to be transformed by the revelation of the cross, our assumptions must stumble and our perception must be reoriented — we need to undergo a "gestalt shift" in our perspective on the cross.

How are we to make a "gestalt shift"? Here, again, we must not miss the significance of Paul's signature phrase, "But now. . . ." Paul is convinced that something surprising happens at the cross. Although God demonstrates characteristic faithfulness to the covenant promises, nonetheless through the cross God does something unexpected. Presbyterian New Testament scholar Charles Cousar writes: "The word of the cross reveals God as a free, sovereign God, not bound by human categories and expectations."[19] The cross is revelation pre-

---

18. Yonat Shimron, "Way of the Cross Calls for Changes," *Raleigh News & Observer,* 11 April 2009, 4B.

19. Cousar, *Theology of the Cross,* p. 35. Cf. Karl Barth, *The Epistle to the Romans,* trans. Edwyn C. Hoskyns (London: Oxford University Press, 1933), pp. 91-92.

cisely because it discloses God's ways in a manner beyond human comprehension. Methodist New Testament scholar Richard Hays writes of the reversal of perspective induced by Paul's message of the cross:

> Shifts are necessary because God's eschatological action is fraught with surprise: "God chose what is foolish in the world to shame the wise, God chose what is weak in the world to shame the strong" (1 Cor. 1:26-27). "The word of the cross" enacts such a sweeping reversal that it looks like nonsense to the world.[20]

The key for us, therefore, is to let ourselves to be surprised by the cross, to allow the cross to become a *skandalon,* a stumbling block in the path to understanding. This requires that we remain open to the possibility that the cross, as the revelation of God's ways, might upset our assumptions and induce a reversal of perspective. And to be ready for surprise and reversal is to let the cross become a *question* for us once again.

Anthony Bartlett writes: "The cross, if it means what Christians claim it means, should become always again a question to Christians, and thereby to Christianity itself."[21] Concerning the traditional Western "satisfaction" theology of atonement, he thus asks:

> Why is it so obvious that a violent death should "work" as a form of ultimate resolution? Why is that violence itself not an outrage, beyond any possible formal effect that theologians might apply to it? . . . The violence manifested in the cross poses itself the question of the human species and its capacity for relentless, abusive violence.[22]

---

20. Hays, *Echoes of Scripture,* p. 169. Hays comments further on how the cross brought about a reversal (one might say, "paradigm shift") in Paul's own reading of Scripture: "To see the unexpected interpretive consequences of this eschatological word of the cross, we need only consider the case of Paul's reading of Deut. 21:23 in Gal. 3:13. Scripture spoke the truth when it said, "Cursed is every one who is hanged upon a tree," but Paul now construes that truth in an ironic mode: by hanging upon the tree, Jesus became cursed in order that blessing might accrue to others. The eschatological *apokalypsis* of the cross has wrought an inversion of Paul's reading of the text."

21. Anthony W. Bartlett, *Cross Purposes: The Violent Grammar of Christian Atonement* (Harrisburg, PA: Trinity Press International, 2001), p. 2.

22. Bartlett, *Cross Purposes,* pp. 5-6. Bartlett here is writing concerning Anselm's "satisfaction" theory of atonement. He follows a recent trend in the theological literature that portrays Anselm's theory as implying that God's will is satisfied by violence because God demands that Jesus die to satisfy God's wrath. As I will explain in Chapter 3 and the Coda following Chapter 4, I dissent from this interpretation of Anselm — indeed, I find it a gross distortion. What Bartlett writes here, however, is more-or-less appropriate to Calvin's penal substitution theory, in which God's law requires Jesus' death as satisfaction for humanity's sins.

Our own study of atonement theology asks similar questions. Indeed, as mentioned above, the gestalt shift we are looking to achieve here is motivated by just this sort of question, whereby the cross becomes troubling for us, itself a question that upsets our categories and reorients our vision. If we attend to the human violence so evidently displayed in the cross of Jesus Christ, we recognize the immediate reality of the cross as the scene of a most obscene act — the human murder of God incarnate. The question thus arises: Far from resolving the problem of human sin, the murder of Jesus upon the cross magnifies the problem to the extreme; how, then, will God deal with humanity now? This very question, I am suggesting, provides a lens through which we might fruitfully read Paul when he writes of God's surprising salvation revealed through the cross of Jesus Christ, "But now. . . ." And this is the question that prompts and guides our studies of the relationship between the cross, justice, and peace: How does God's dealing with humanity's outrageous violence committed at the cross upon God-self in the person of Jesus reveal to us the characteristic justice-doing and peacemaking of God?

CHAPTER 3

<hr>

Questioning Our Normal Thinking:
The Retributive Paradigm

Do not be conformed to this world,
but be transformed by the renewing of your minds,
so that you may discern what is the will of God —
what is good and acceptable and perfect.

ROMANS 12:2

In order for the cross to reorient our perspective concerning God's justice and peace, it is necessary to bring into focus and call into question our normal way of thinking concerning justice and peace.[1] In order to "change lenses" and gain "a New Testament vision" on justice and peace — to achieve a "paradigm shift" — it is needful first to critically examine the retributive paradigm that governs our normal thinking and common practice and shapes the dominant tradition of atonement theology in Western Christianity.[2] This chapter is thus a preparation for the remainder of the book.

---

1. By "normal" thinking we intend the "default" mindset of human beings, the way of thinking that is so common (culturally near-universal) and habitual (psychologically in-grained) that it seems "natural," as if this were not only the right way but the only way to think.

2. My usage of the term "paradigm" and associated terminology (e.g., "anomaly") borrows from Thomas S. Kuhn's epoch-making work, *The Structure of Scientific Revolutions*, 2nd ed. (Chicago: University of Chicago Press, 1970). Kuhn, as well known, did not give a precise definition of "paradigm." I will use "paradigm" more-or-less interchangeably with "pattern," "worldview," and "perspective," thus emphasizing implicitly the essential connection between conception and perception, theory and observation. It was Kuhn, following upon the work of N. R. Hanson, who famously characterized revolutionary changes (or "paradigm shifts") in scientific thinking as changes in worldview and likened them to gestalt shifts in perception (*Structure*, pp. 111f.). This connection between shifts in thinking and shifts in seeing will prove fruitful for our studies.

3.1. The Retributive Paradigm³

Examining the retributive paradigm entails questioning the normal human convictions, held by many Christians, that doing justice in response to crime requires "repaying" the offender his "due" in punishment for the crime and that making peace in conflict justifies using force in return for force. But questioning the popular convictions that buttress Christian endorsement of retributive practices such as capital punishment and just war, I think, goes hand-in-hand with critically reexamining the penal substitution view of the cross. This popular doctrine sees the cross as the ultimate satisfaction of divine retribution: by his death, Jesus pays God the penalty due for humanity's sins to appease God's wrath so that God and humanity may be at peace.

3.1.1. One Principle, Four Models

What connects the rationale for capital punishment and just war, on the one hand, to the rationale for penal substitution, on the other hand, is a common core principle — retribution. Retribution as definitive of justice and necessary for peace underlies both support for capital punishment and just war and adherence to penal substitution.

The principle of retribution — in simple terms, repayment in kind — is the essential core of the retributive paradigm. The retributive paradigm is a worldview that understands retribution to be constitutive of the heart of reality — morality and society, nature and God. The theory of retributive punishment, the tradition of just war, and the doctrine of penal substitution are respective models of the retributive paradigm. Each of these applies the common core principle of retribution to a particular question: How ought society to deal with violations of the law?⁴ How ought nations to deal with breaches of the

3. A note about words is called for here. We tend to make a mental distinction between "retribution" and "retaliation," the former connoting justice dispensed according to the rule of law and being praised, the latter connoting "getting even" for personal purposes and being censured. While the latter may be morally dubious, by calling such behavior "retaliation" in ordinary discourse we obscure the inherent connection, linguistic and semantic, between "retribution" and "retaliation." According to the *Oxford English Dictionary,* "retaliate" has the same Latin root — *retaliare,* "to return in kind" — as the *lex talionis* ("law of retaliation"), which is the legal measure of just retribution: "eye for eye, tooth for tooth." Strictly speaking, retaliation is lawful retribution, retribution dispensed according to the *lex talionis.* There is thus no essential difference between retribution and retaliation, both of which concern the same basic idea of doing justice or making right by means of repayment, reciprocating deed for deed, or returning "like for like."

4. Cf. Howard Zehr, *Changing Lenses: A New Focus for Crime and Justice,* 3rd ed. (Scottdale, PA: Herald Press, 2005), pp. 63-94, and Christopher D. Marshall, *Beyond Retribution: A New Testament Vision for Justice, Crime, and Punishment* (Grand Rapids, MI: Eerdmans Publishing,

peace? How can sinners in the hands of an angry God be saved? Within these models, retribution is constitutive of justice, peace, and salvation, respectively: justice is done when criminals are repaid in pain for breaking the law; peace is restored when enemies are repaid with force for threatening international order; and sinners are saved when God punishes Jesus with death in their place to pay the penalty for sin.

Although the common practices of retributive violence come readily to mind, it is important to clarify here that retribution need not be violent. Some retributive practices are essentially violent (e.g., tribal blood vengeance), but other retributive practices may be employed as an alternative to violence (e.g., suing for compensation). Retribution and violence, while overlapping, are not equivalent and should not be conflated. It is crucial to note this in order for us to become aware of how far the practice of retribution extends.

While practices of retributive violence (viz., capital punishment and just war) will be a major concern of this book, our concern includes also the retributive paradigm in the economic arena. The principle of retribution entails not only "payback" in the negative sense of punishment — evil for evil, harm for harm; it entails also "payback" in the positive sense of reward — good for good, value for value.[5] One might think of paying a laborer a day's wages for a day's work, tipping a server a certain percentage on the amount of one's bill, paying a seller the going price for a product, or repaying a loan with interest. The principle of retribution thus underwrites an economy of exchange, giving to others in proportion as we receive from others. Within this paradigm, the just wage for a worker or the proper tip for a server or the fair price for a product or the fair rate of interest on a loan is determined, not by the respective needs of the traders, but rather by the market value of the labor, service, product, or loan — the price for which one could exchange that labor, service, product, or loan in a free market. Economic justice thus corresponds to the market equilibrium: the fair wage is the minimum a worker will accept in exchange for his labor, given the other opportunities available. Within the exchange economy, "what is due" to another is defined by "what the market will bear," even if that falls short of what that other needs to live. To pay anything in excess of "what is due" — so an employee can feed her children, say — would go beyond justice into generosity.[6]

2001), pp. 109-29, for examinations of the retributive paradigm in criminal justice. T. Richard Snyder, *The Protestant Ethic and the Spirit of Punishment* (Grand Rapids, MI: Eerdmans Publishing, 2001), examines the retributive spirit in American culture and traces its roots to Protestant theology and ethics.

5. For an insightful exploration of retribution — economic, judicial, and theological — focused around the notion of debt — financial, moral, and spiritual — see Margaret Atwood, *Payback: Debt and the Shadow Side of Wealth* (Toronto: House of Anansi Press, 2008).

6. Interestingly, there is an undercurrent of moral dissent from and quiet resistance to the dominant idea that economic justice is determined by market exchange — see Lisa Dodson, *The*

The exchange economy, then, is another model of the retributive paradigm. To the ethical question concerning the just measure that I ought to give to others, the model answers: only in exchange for and in proportion to what I receive from others. The message of the cross, however, exceeds our human expectations as shaped by the exchange economy of the retributive paradigm: God-in-Christ renders divine good in exchange for human evil. Indeed, the cross of Christ is at the same time the faithful demonstration of God's justice and the supreme instance of God's generosity: God justifies humanity "by his grace as a gift" (Rom 3:24). Rather than generosity exceeding justice in the economy of salvation, the justice and generosity of God converge in the cross of Christ.

Now, to be sure, there is nothing inherently sinful in economic exchange; the marketplace is not a "necessary evil." Fair trade in the marketplace, we may agree with the ancient wisdom, is honorable before God (Prov 11:1; 16:11); and the exchange of value for value can contribute to the common good of human society.[7] Nonetheless, we should recognize that the exchange of good for good is only the base practice of common humanity and the normal measure of economic justice, which falls short of the full measure of the "greater righteousness" of God's kingdom. As we will see, moreover, the exchange economy proves an inadequate model for understanding covenant justice: the justice of God — as evident in God's relationship with Israel, the sacrifices for atonement, and the parables of Jesus — exceeds the economy of exchange (Chapters 11, 20, 21, and 23).

The retributive paradigm may thus be represented by the diagram on page 28. At the center of the paradigm is the principle of retribution, which is the common core of the models of the paradigm. The four models — penal substitution, capital punishment, just war, and exchange economy — apply the core principle within the respective arenas of atonement theology, criminal justice, international relations, and economic activity.

3.1.2. Confirmation of the Paradigm

While there is no direct logical linkage from retribution in theology (penal substitution) to retribution in criminal justice (capital punishment) or interna-

---

Moral Underground: How Ordinary Americans Subvert an Unfair Economy (New York: The New Press, 2009).

7. As the financial crisis of 2008-2009 demonstrates, however, in order for economic exchange to serve the common good, self-interest cannot be the sole and sufficient principle of the marketplace. See my articles, "Greenspan's Folly: The Demise of the Cult of Self-Interest," *America: The National Catholic Weekly,* Vol. 200, No. 11 (March 30–April 6, 2009), 10-13, and "Market Exchange, Self-Interest, and the Common Good: Financial Crisis and Moral Economy," *Journal of Markets and Morality* 13 (Spring 2010), 83-100.

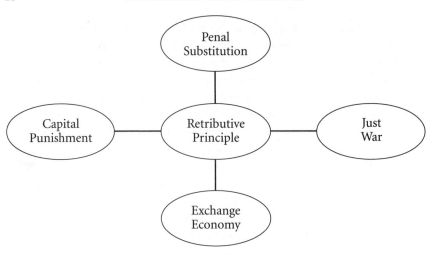

tional affairs (just war), that each of these is connected by a common principle would nonetheless lead one to expect correlations between belief in a retributive principle and support for retributive practices. The practical effect of the retributive paradigm on contemporary thinking should thus be empirically confirmable. Indeed, statistical evidence indicates a correlation between belief in retribution and support for capital punishment, on the one hand, and between belief in a retributive God and support for war, on the other hand.[8]

First, there is a strong connection between belief in retribution and the rationale for capital punishment in the popular American mind. Belief in retribution has consistently been the number one reason for popular support of the death penalty in the U.S. Polling data over a twenty-year period show that a near-constant 50% of those who support the death penalty for murder do so because they believe in "eye for eye, life for life" justice, or that murderers "get what they deserve" in the execution chamber. In 1997, research of American opinion showed that "Retribution ('a life for a life') has been a more popular reason than belief in deterrence since 1981. . . . Retribution is by far the most common reason given for favoring the death penalty."[9]

8. One might also inquire whether there are historical correlations between retribution in theology and retributive practices in penal justice or international relations. Timothy Gorringe, *God's Just Vengeance: Crime, Violence and the Rhetoric of Salvation* (Cambridge: Cambridge University Press, 1996), examines the relationship between Anselm's "satisfaction" theory of atonement and penal practice from the eleventh century to the nineteenth century. Anthony W. Bartlett, *Cross Purposes: The Violent Grammar of Christian Atonement* (Harrisburg, PA: Trinity Press International, 2001), considers the relationship between the thinking behind Anselm's "satisfaction" theory and the rationale for the Crusades.

9. See Phoebe C. Ellsworth and Samuel R. Gross, "Hardening of the Attitudes: Americans' Views on the Death Penalty," in Hugo Adam Bedau, ed., *The Death Penalty in America: Current*

Second, we also find empirical confirmation of a connection between retribution, theology, and war. The Baylor Religion Survey (2006) found correlations between personal images of God — whether an "Authoritarian" (angry, punitive) God or a "Benevolent" God, comprising 52.3% and 23.6% of evangelical Protestants, respectively — and views on moral and political issues. This study provides empirical evidence linking popular belief in a wrathful, retributive God — often associated with the penal substitution atonement doctrine — and popular support for justifying war. The Survey found that 45.0% of Americans in the general population believed at the time that the Iraq War was justified. Of believers in an "Authoritarian" God, 63.1% believe the Iraq War was justified, while 46.9% of believers in a "Benevolent" God believe the Iraq War was justified. Americans believing in an "Authoritarian" God are thus 34.5% more likely to believe that the Iraq War was justified than those believing in a "Benevolent" God and 40.2% more likely than the general population.[10]

3.2. Retributive Thinking in Christian Tradition: Justice

A co-requisite of rethinking the relation of the cross of Christ to retributive practices will be to make a thorough examination of the retribution-based penal substitution doctrine of atonement. Because penal substitution is held by many evangelical Christians to be "the biblical view," critical examination of this doctrine will require careful exegesis of the scriptural texts upon which it is founded. That is the primary task of Part II of the book. At present, we seek to examine the retributive paradigm as it has shaped Christian thinking about justice, peace, and atonement.

One might wonder why we begin our examination of the retributive paradigm with Greco-Roman philosophy rather than, say, the Old Testament. The theme of retribution, after all, is evident at many places in Scripture.[11] The reason is historical. Western Christian thinking concerning justice and peace has been shaped down the centuries by the writings of two great theologians, Augustine and Aquinas. And the thinking of Augustine and Aquinas on justice and peace was influenced substantially by Greco-Roman philosophy, especially Aristotle and Cicero.[12]

Controversies (New York: Oxford University Press, 1997), pp. 97-98. For polling data, see Ellsworth and Gross, p. 97, and the Gallup Poll data cited at http://www.clarkprosecutor.org/html/death/opinion.htm.

10. Baylor Institute for Studies of Religion, "American Piety in the 21st Century: New Insights to the Depth and Complexity of Religion in the US," September 2006, http://www.baylor.edu/content/services/document.php/33304.pdf, p. 39.

11. We will examine the theme of retribution in the Old Testament in Chapters 21 and 22.

12. Now, to avoid misunderstanding, I do not propose here the reactionary mindset of "Je-

3.2.1. Aristotle and Cicero: Retribution Is the Measure of Justice

According to Aristotle and Cicero, the natural law of justice is summed by the formula, "to do justice is to render to each what is due."[13] This notion of "what is due" implies what is earned, owed, or otherwise *deserved*. The word "due" thus carries a moral connotation: to render what is due is to render what is *merited,* however such merit is determined, whether by actions, contracts, laws, or some other measure. For Aristotle and Cicero, "what is due" is measured by the principle of retribution.[14]

Aristotle affirmed that retributive exchange — repayment in kind or rendering like for like, good for good and evil for evil — is the binding principle of civil society:

---

rusalem against Athens." Rather, I intend a critical engagement of Christian thought with Greek philosophy. Thus, I do not argue that, because Augustine and Aquinas turned to Greek philosophy more than Holy Scripture for their ideas of justice and peace, their thinking is therefore misguided solely on that account. (Nor do we suppose that, because their ideas of justice and peace were founded substantially upon Greco-Roman philosophy, Augustine and Aquinas were therefore misguided on other matters.) Greek philosophy was not, by far, mistaken about all things. We thus do not, by any means, oppose philosophy to either Scripture or Christianity. One can, as did Paul himself, recognize genuine wisdom within Greek philosophy (Acts 17:22-28) while at the same time critiquing it as falling short of the wisdom of God in Christ (1 Cor 1:18-2:16). Augustine also taught that Christians ought to "discriminate sensibly and carefully" among the theories of philosophers to find what is "consistent with our faith" and useful for "preaching the gospel" (*On Christian Teaching* 2.139-47). The Christian engagement with Greek philosophy thus calls for discernment, a careful sifting of ideas for what is and is not conformable to the gospel and profitable for the church. See Diogenes Allen, *Philosophy for Understanding Theology* (Atlanta: John Knox Press, 1985); Colin Brown, *Christianity and Western Thought: A History of Philosophers, Ideas & Movements. Volume I: From the Ancient World to the Age of Enlightenment* (Downers Grove, IL: InterVarsity Press, 1990); and Ronald H. Nash, *Life's Ultimate Questions: An Introduction to Philosophy* (Grand Rapids, MI: Zondervan, 1999).

13. Aristotle's theory of justice, formative for both Roman law and later Christian ethics, is found in his *Nicomachean Ethics,* V. Cicero's discussion of natural law justice is set forth in his dialogue on *The Laws,* in Book I of which he formulates the Greco-Roman idea of justice as "giving each his own." The classical theory of justice parsed the matter of "what is due" into two domains: commutative justice, concerning the reciprocal obligations owed by one person to another (in, for instance, a contract), and distributive justice, concerning the division of goods within society as a whole and the portion deserved by each person.

14. We thus observe and emphasize here that the very notion of "what is due" does not, of itself, entail retribution. While the Greco-Roman tradition, followed by the majority Christian tradition, did conceive of "what is due" in retributive terms, one can conceive of "what is due" in non-retributive terms. Indeed, as we shall see, the Greek philosopher Socrates and the early Christian thinker Lactantius each conceived of the "natural law" of justice in non-retributive terms (see Chapters 20 and 22 below). The classical formula — justice is to render "what is due" — is thus not itself problematic. Rather, it is the common understanding of "what is due" as essentially retributive that we question and challenge.

For it is by proportionate requital that the city holds together. Men seek to return either evil for evil — and if they cannot do so, think their position mere slavery — or good for good — and if they cannot do so there is no exchange, but it is by exchange [like for like] that they hold together.[15]

In popular practice, the philosophical principle by which "the city holds together" was taken to mean "to render good to friends and evil to enemies."[16] The popular ideal of a free citizen was of one who is able to bestow benefits on his friends and take vengeance on both his own enemies and his friends' enemies.[17] Aristotle applied the retributive paradigm to the arena of personal relationships. He analyzed friendship as an economy of exchange, a reciprocity between persons maintained by an exchange of "goods." The friend loves the other for the sake of the good — whether pleasure, utility, or virtue — that he receives from the other; and the love of friendship endures as long as each gives to the other in equality (or proportion) as he receives from the other.[18]

3.2.2. *Jesus and the Apostles: Love Is the Measure of Justice*

The Greco-Roman natural law theory contrasts with the tradition handed down to the early church from Jesus and the Apostles. In the Sermon on the Mount, Jesus renounces retribution/retaliation, both the philosophical principle (justice is to return "like for like," rendering good for good and evil for evil) and the popular practice (justice is to render good to friends and evil to enemies). By renouncing retribution both in principle and in practice, Jesus makes clear that the politics and economics of God's kingdom, in contrast with that of Greco-Roman society, is not based on retribution.[19]

15. Aristotle, *Nicomachean Ethics*, V, 5 (1132b34-1133a2). Citation from the W. D. Ross translation, in Richard McKeon, ed., *The Basic Works of Aristotle* (New York: Random House, 1941). One might wonder whether there is an alternative to retributive exchange as a moral basis for civil society. In *Civility: Manners, Morals, and the Etiquette of Democracy* (New York: Basic Books, 1998), Stephen L. Carter argues that civil society is based on shared sacrifice: "Civility . . . is the sum of the many sacrifices we are called to make for the sake of living together. . . . We should make sacrifices for others not simply because doing so makes social life easier (although it does), but as a signal of respect for our fellow citizens, marking them as full equals, both before the law and before God" (p. 11). While this leaves room for retributive practices (say, punishment of those who deny the equality of others), Carter's rethinking of the social contract in terms of shared sacrifice opens the possibility for social ethics to move beyond the retributive paradigm.

16. Plato, *Republic*, I, 331-32.

17. Cf. Plato, *Gorgias*, 456-57.

18. See *Nicomachean Ethics*, VIII and IX.

19. Jesus' teaching of non-retaliation had (quasi) parallels within the Jewish tradition — see Gordon M. Zerbe, *Non-Retaliation in Early Jewish and New Testament Texts* (London: Continuum, 1993).

Teaching the full righteousness of the law (Matt 5:17-20), Jesus first rejects retribution/retaliation in principle. Citing the Torah, Jesus teaches that retribution/retaliation is not the full measure of covenant justice: "You have heard that it was said, 'An eye for an eye and a tooth for a tooth.' But I say to you, Do not resist an evildoer . . ." (Matt 5:38-42; Luke 6:29).[20] The *lex talionis*, which Jesus invokes and then rejects, measured out retribution — restitution for personal injuries, punishment for serious crimes — within the Covenant Code (Exod 21:23-25; Lev 24:19-20; Deut 19:21). Jesus thus renounces retribution/retaliation concerning not only private relationships but also the legal practice of the covenant community.[21]

The examples Jesus gives — turning the other cheek, giving the cloak, and going the second mile — all illustrate the point of not returning "like for like" to those who treat us unjustly or do evil against us: turning the other cheek is not to strike back; giving the cloak also is not to counter-sue; going the second mile is not to counter force with force.[22] Instead of doing to others *as they have done* to us, according to the *lex talionis*, Jesus commands us to act according to a better law, "Do unto others *as you would have them do* unto you" (Luke 6:31). So, Jesus counsels action that demonstrates how I would want to be treated by another that I had wronged — respectfully, generously, mercifully.[23]

Having renounced the philosophical principle of retribution, Jesus goes on to renounce the popular practice of retribution as well:[24] "You have heard that it was said, 'You shall love your neighbor and hate your enemy.' But I say to you, Love your enemies" (Matt 5:43-44a), "do good to those who hate you" (Luke 6:27-28).[25] If we do good only to those who do good to us, to our friends and

20. L. John Topel, *Children of a Compassionate God: A Theological Exegesis of Luke 6:20-49* (Collegeville, MN: Liturgical Press, 2001), concerning Luke 6:27-30: "In all of these [injunctions] there is a sharp reversal of the *lex talionis*, and indeed of any principle of retaliation" (p. 157).

21. See Dorothy Jean Weaver, "Transforming Nonresistance: From *Lex Talionis* to 'Do Not Resist the Evil One,'" in Willard M. Swartley, ed., *The Love of Enemy and Nonretaliation in the New Testament* (Louisville, KY: Westminster John Knox Press, 1992), 32-71.

22. Jesus' prohibition against retaliation does not counsel passivity in the face of evil, for these positive commands instruct one how to take action in response to evildoing. Cf. Weaver, "Transforming Nonresistance," pp. 54-57, and Walter Wink, "Neither Passivity Nor Violence: Jesus' Third Way (Matt. 5:38-42 par.)," in Swartley, *Love of Enemy and Nonretaliation*, 102-25.

23. Topel, *Children of a Compassionate God*: "There is no strict retribution in Jesus' Golden Rule, since the Christian is not responding to the prior act of another but is discerning what should be his or her own prior act toward another. Nor is there . . . mitigated reciprocity in which one acts in such a way as to evoke a corresponding benevolent action from another, for in that case the Golden Rule should read "what you intend, or expect" which is not what the Greek text conveys" (p. 156).

24. The formula is not explicitly "love your friends and hate your enemies." But it does put "neighbor" and "enemy" into opposition, so that "neighbor" here is implicitly equivalent to "friend."

25. As his teaching on non-retaliation concerns both interpersonal and communal justice,

those who love us, Jesus teaches, then we have not actually fulfilled the righteousness that God desires. For retribution — doing good only in return for good, doing good to friends only — is merely the base ethic of common humanity, which even sinners and Gentiles follow (Matt 5:46-47; Luke 6:32-34).[26] Drawing from the fount of Hebrew wisdom (Prov 25:21-22), Jesus taught his disciples instead to do good to all, even enemies, even those who do evil, which is the way of reward in God's kingdom (Matt 5:46; Luke 6:35-36).[27]

Jesus goes on to teach his disciples kingdom practices that transcend the retributive practices of the exchange economy. Lending to only those from whom one expects repayment, Jesus says, is the common practice of human economy: "Even sinners lend to sinners, to receive as much again." In the kingdom economy, we are to lend regardless of prospect of repayment: "lend, expecting nothing in return" (Luke 6:34-35).[28] Likewise, Jesus taught his followers to bestow benefits (e.g., a dinner), not upon friends or neighbors who might repay the favor, but upon those who, because of their condition or circumstance, are not in a position to reciprocate (Luke 14:12-14). Such lending and giving that transcend economic exchange are rewarded with God's blessing.[29]

While Jesus' teaching explicitly renounces repaying evil with evil, which characterizes the retributive violence of capital punishment and just war, he

---

Jesus' teaching concerning love of enemies concerns national enemies and the enemies of God as well as personal enemies — see Topel, *Children of a Compassionate God*, pp. 142-43.

26. Aristotle represents the common ethic in rejecting outright the very idea of loving enemies or evildoers: "But if one accepts another man as good, and he turns out badly and is seen to do so, must one still love him? Surely it is impossible, since not everything can be loved, but only what is good. What is evil neither can nor should be loved" (*Nicomachean Ethics* IX, 3, 1165b13-15).

27. That we should do good to our enemies as well as friends is not unique to the Hebrew wisdom tradition, but finds precedent in sixth-century B.C. Greek poets and philosophers according to Diogenes Laertius, *Lives of Eminent Philosophers* (Cambridge, MA: Harvard University Press, 1972). The poet Cleobulus counseled that we do good to our enemies, in like manner as we do to our friends, in order to make friends of our enemies: "we should render a service to a friend to bind him closer to us, and to an enemy in order to make a friend of him." Cleobulus's counsel, however, was rooted, not in love of others and faithfulness to God, but rather in self-interest: "For we have to guard against the censure of friends and the intrigues of enemies" (*Lives*, 1.6.91; Vol. I, p. 95). Similarly, the philosopher Pythagoras counseled his fellows "to behave one to another as not to make friends into enemies, but to turn enemies into friends" (*Lives*, 8.1.23; Vol. II, p. 341). Still, one does not find, as far as I am aware, any counsel to *love* enemies or evildoers, not even in Socrates.

28. Topel, *Children of a Compassionate God*, comments on Luke 6:32-34, that this text, which comprises "a series of three contrasts with the way of sinners (responding in kind to others' generous treatment), implicitly rejects a morality of exchange underlying a *do ut des* ["I give so that you give"]" (p. 157).

29. By pointing his disciples toward divine reward for earthly deeds, Jesus does affirm God's sovereign prerogative of retribution. We will examine retributive justice in relation to divine judgment in Chapter 21.

does not condemn repaying good for good.[30] Giving and receiving good in kind is not inherently sinful, therefore; but neither is exchanging good for good of ultimate account in the kingdom economy. Thus, Jesus sends his disciples with the instruction to receive hospitality, "for the laborer deserves to be paid" (Luke 10:7; cf. Matt 10:10). At the same time, he instructs them that the goods of the kingdom — healing and peace — are not for exchange: "You received without payment; give without payment" (Matt 10:8). The kingdom is a gift economy that transcends the exchange economy of the marketplace.

As important as it is to see *what* Jesus taught, it is at least as important to recognize *why* Jesus taught his disciples to transcend the practice of retribution. To go beyond the common practice, to extend love to enemies as well as friends, Jesus says, is to act in the way that befits one who would be a child of God: "Love your enemies . . . *so that* you may be children of your Father in heaven" (Matt 5:44-45; cf. Luke 6:35). And practicing love-beyond-retribution is befitting a child of God because that is how God acts toward humanity, transcending retribution by giving good to both the good and the evil alike (Matt 5:45; Luke 6:35). The covenant community is to transcend retribution, therefore, because in doing so it bears witness to the way of God in the world. For Jesus, ethics is grounded in theology: the children of God are to act according to God's own righteousness and mercy (Matt 6:33; Luke 6:36). Jesus' teaching reflects the pattern of the Holiness Code. The general exhortation, "You shall be holy, for I the LORD your God am holy" (Lev 19:2), heads a long list of instructions, including the prohibitions of bearing hatred against and taking vengeance upon a neighbor (vv. 17-18). To love the neighbor and renounce vengeance are actions befitting the life of holiness; to transcend retribution is to be holy as God is holy — or, as Jesus put it, to "be perfect . . . as your heavenly Father is perfect" (Matt 5:48).[31]

The Apostles Peter and Paul, remaining true to Jesus' teaching, both instructed the early church not only to renounce retaliation and retribution but also to seek the good of evildoers and enemies (Rom 12:9–13:10; 1 Pet 2:11–3:12). Paul both renounces and inverts the practice of retribution: "Do not repay any-

30. Concerning the "reciprocity code," Nicholas Wolterstorff, "Jesus and Forgiveness," in Paul K. Moser, ed., *Jesus and Philosophy: New Essays* (Cambridge: Cambridge University Press, 2009), 194-214, thus observes: "Jesus's attitude toward the first aspect, that if someone does a favor, one owes him roughly equal favor in return, is deflationary acceptance. . . . Jesus's attitude toward the second aspect, that if someone does evil to you, then an equal evil is due him, is flat out rejection. Jesus's followers are not to return evil for evil" (p. 200).

31. The Covenant Code sanctions retribution by way of the *lex talionis* (Exod 21:23-25), and Jesus testifies that his teaching fulfills rather than abolishes "the law and the prophets" (Matt 5:17). Yet, as we will show (Chapters 21 and 25), the Torah and Prophets witness that the *lex talionis* does not ultimately fulfill God's will for the covenant community. Thus, by teaching the covenant community to transcend retribution, Jesus does fulfill "the law and the prophets."

one evil for evil," but instead "overcome evil with good" (Rom 12:17, 21). He further counsels that this goes beyond the fellowship of believers ("one another"): "See that none of you repays evil for evil, but always seek to do good to one another *and to all*" (1 Thess 5:15). Paul thus regarded non-retaliation as governing the entirety of Christian life, both inside and outside the covenant community. Elsewhere, he gives examples of non-retaliation in practice: "When reviled, we bless; when persecuted we endure; when slandered we speak kindly" (1 Cor 4:12b-13a).[32] Peter taught likewise: "Do not repay evil for evil or abuse for abuse; but, on the contrary, repay with a blessing" (1 Pet 3:9). The Greek word "evil" *(kakos)* used in these texts means wrong, harm, or injury. Paul and Peter thus exhort the early church: Do not pay back harm for harm, or return injury for injury; instead, do good to all, repaying evil with good. This apostolic teaching not only echoes Jesus, but also draws from the same fount of Hebrew wisdom (cf. Prov 20:22; 24:29).

The reason Christians should renounce retribution, according to Paul, is both theological and ethical. In Romans 12, Paul's statement of non-retaliation heads a list of three pairs of related injunctions, each of which contains a prohibition and an exhortation:

> Do not repay anyone evil for evil, but do whatever you can to live in peace with all (vv. 17-18);
> Do not avenge yourselves, but do good for your enemies (vv. 19-20);
> Do not be overcome by the power of evil, but overcome evil by the power of good (v. 21).

At the center of this list, Paul gives us the theological motivation for non-retaliation: "Beloved, never avenge yourselves, but leave room for the wrath of God; for it is written, 'Vengeance is mine, I will repay, says the Lord'" (Rom 12:19, citing Deut 32:35). First, then, Christians are to renounce retribution because retribution belongs to God: to claim the right of retribution for oneself is to usurp God's prerogative.[33]

Paul's instruction to leave retribution to God is bracketed by an appeal to the supreme command, that we are to love one another (Rom 12:9-10; 13:8-10). Love, Paul argues, is our highest obligation — we owe nothing to others except to love (13:8) — and love transcends retribution to fulfill the law: "Love does no wrong *(kakos)* to a neighbor; therefore, love is the fulfilling of the law" (v. 10). Retribution pays back evil *(kakos)* for evil *(kakos)*, but love does no evil *(kakos)* to anyone. Paying back harm for harm, returning injury for injury, thus runs

---

32. That Paul includes explicit teaching of non-retaliation in letters to three different churches indicates that it is an essential element of his ethic.

33. We will address the divine prerogative of retribution in Chapter 21.

counter to the covenant law of love; for loving one's neighbor as oneself forbids doing harm or injury, not even in exchange for harm or injury done. Paul's teaching thus parallels the Torah, which likewise puts taking vengeance and loving neighbor in opposition: "You shall not take vengeance . . . but you shall love your neighbor as yourself" (Lev 19:18).[34] Love, not retribution, therefore, is the supreme fulfillment of the covenant. Second, then, Christians are to re-nounce retribution because retribution runs contrary to the law of love.[35]

Whereas Paul points back to the Torah, Peter points us to Christ as the rea-son to renounce retaliation (1 Pet 2:11–3:12). Peter's overall instruction — "Con-duct yourselves honorably among the Gentiles" (2:12) — follows a chiastic ("X") structure:[36]

> All, accept the authority of human institutions (2:13-17, general injunction)
>> Slaves, accept the authority of masters (2:18-20, specific injunction)
>>> Christ, the example in suffering (2:21-25, hymn)
>> Wives, accept the authority of husbands
>> Husbands, honor wives (3:1-7, specific injunction)
> All, renounce retaliation and seek peace (3:8-12, general injunction)

At the center of this instruction, Peter states that the renunciation of retaliation is definitive of the Christian calling because it is an imitation of Christ himself:

> For to this you have been called, because Christ also suffered for you, leaving you an example, so that you should follow in his steps. . . . When he was abused, he did not return abuse; when he suffered, he did not threaten; but he entrusted himself to the one who judges justly. (2:21, 23)

Jesus' suffering for us is also an example for us, Peter says; and of all the aspects of Jesus' passion that he might have pointed to as an example, Peter emphasizes Jesus' renunciation of retaliation. Indeed, Peter gives threefold emphasis to Christ's refusal to retaliate: neither did he abuse in return for abuse, nor did he threaten in return for suffering; instead of avenging himself, he yielded to God's just judgment (2:23).[37] Jesus thus practiced at the cross what he preached on the

---

34. Paul's teaching in Romans 12 also finds an important narrative precedent in 1 Samuel 24, where David forges the opportunity to take vengeance upon his pursuer and persecutor Saul.

35. For a more in-depth analysis and extensive discussion of Paul's teaching of non-retaliation in Romans 12, see Gordon Zerbe, "Paul's Ethic of Nonretaliation and Peace," in Swartley, *Love of Enemy and Nonretaliation*, pp. 177-222. Our reading of Paul's ethic follows the "mediating" position described by Zerbe.

36. See Mary H. Schertz, "Nonretaliation and the Haustafeln in 1 Peter," in Swartley, *Love of Enemy and Nonretaliation*, pp. 258-86.

37. Schertz argues that v. 23 is the structural center of the Christological hymn in 1 Pet 2:21-24.

Mount, giving us the perfect example: we are not to return evil for evil, but instead are to turn from evil, do good, and seek peace (3:11); and by renouncing retaliation, we "live for righteousness" (2:24). The cross of Christ, then, is the supreme instance of non-retaliation, which all Christians are called to imitate; indeed, non-retaliation in the way of the cross is the purpose of our calling in Christ and the way of blessing from God (3:9). Christians are to renounce retaliation and pursue peace in all relationships with non-Christians ("among the Gentiles"), including relationships with political institutions and authorities (2:13).[38]

Both Paul and Peter instruct the church to renounce retaliation in response to evil. And both make clear that Christians are to practice non-retaliation toward those outside the church ("to all," "among the Gentiles"), especially enemies. While Paul roots renunciation of retribution in the Torah, Peter bases his argument on Christ. There is no tension here; for Christ himself, Paul proclaimed, is the goal of the Torah (Rom 10:4).[39] Both Paul and Peter, moreover, rest their respective arguments ultimately on trust in God's judgment, of which Christ on the cross is the perfect example.

3.2.3. The Early Church: Continuity with Jesus and the Apostles

The teaching of Jesus and the Apostles against retribution is continued in the teaching of Ignatius, third Bishop of Antioch. In an epistle written en route to martyrdom in Rome (c. AD 110), Ignatius counsels the Christians at Ephesus to renounce retribution in their dealings with their enemies, echoing the words of Jesus, Paul, and Peter: "Meet their animosity with mildness, their high words with humility, and their abuse with your prayers. But stand firm against their errors, and if they grow violent, be gentle instead of wanting to pay them back in their own coin" (Ignatius, *Ephesians* 10:2).[40]

The consistent teaching of Jesus, the Apostles, and the early church Fathers is reflected in the *Didache,* a late first-century manual for instructing candidates for baptism. The first section presents two ways — "the way of life" and "the way of death" — and exhorts catechumens to choose the former and forsake the latter (cf. Deut 30:15-20). The "way of life" is summarized by the two great commandments — love of God and love of neighbor — and the Golden Rule (*Didache* 1:1-4). And the very first thing that the catechumen "may learn from these words" is the teaching that we should love enemies and renounce re-

---

38. Schertz points out that Christian non-retaliation in 1 Peter is intended also to have a missionary appeal (cf. 2:12; 3:1-2, 14-17).

39. See also Zerbe, "Paul's Ethic of Nonretaliation and Peace," pp. 202-3.

40. Maxwell Staniforth and Andrew Louth, trans., *Early Christian Writings* (London: Penguin Books, 1987), p. 64.

taliation, doing good to those who do evil to us. In so teaching, the *Didache* warns against "the carnal appetites of the body" — implying that the instinct for retribution springs from the "desires of the flesh" that "war against the soul" (1 Pet 2:11). After presenting the contrasting "way of death," the first section ends with an exhortation: "Take care that nobody tempts you away from the path of this Teaching, for such a man's tuition can have nothing to do with God" (*Didache* 6:1).[41]

Athenagoras, a late second-century Greek philosopher who converted to Christianity, kept the teaching of Jesus, the Apostles, and the early church Fathers. In his *Plea for the Christians*, Athenagoras contrasted Christian practice and principle with the Greco-Roman norm. Christian doctrine, as evident in practice, both argues against the law of retribution and proclaims the law of love:

> What, then, are those teachings in which we are brought up? "I say unto you, Love your enemies; bless them that curse you; pray for them that perse-cute you; that ye may be the sons of your Father who is in heaven, who causes His sun to rise on the evil and the good, and sends rain on the just and the unjust." Allow me here to lift up my voice boldly in loud and audi-ble outcry, pleading as I do before philosophic princes . . . who of them have so purged their souls as, instead of hating their enemies, to love them; and, instead of speaking ill of those who have reviled them (to abstain from which is of itself an evidence of no mean forbearance), to bless them; and to pray for those who plot against their lives? On the contrary, they never cease with evil intent to search out skillfully the secrets of their art, and are ever bent on working some ill, making the art of words and not the exhibition of deeds their business and profession. But among us you will find uneducated persons, and artisans, and old women, who, if they are unable in words to prove the benefit of our doctrine, yet by their deeds exhibit the benefit aris-ing from their persuasion of its truth: they do not rehearse speeches, but ex-hibit good works; when struck, they do not strike again; when robbed, they do not go to law; they give to those that ask of them, and love their neigh-bours as themselves.[42]

Near the end of his *Plea*, Athenagoras explicitly rejects the human law of retri-bution as inadequate for Christian discipleship. Christian practice is account-able to divine law, which measures justice by love and thus calls us to transcend retribution:

41. *Early Christian Writings*, p. 193.

42. Athenagoras, *A Plea for the Christians*, XI, in Philip Schaff, *The Ante-Nicene Fathers, Vol. II: Fathers of the Second Century* (Grand Rapids, MI: Christian Classics Ethereal Library, 2004).

For our account lies not with human laws, which a bad man can evade (at the outset I proved to you, sovereign lords, that our doctrine is from the teaching of God), but we have a law which makes the measure of rectitude to consist in dealing with our neighbour as ourselves. . . .[43]

. . . for it is not enough to be just (and justice is to return like for like), but it is incumbent on us to be good and patient of evil.[44]

Athenagoras echoes both Jesus and Paul: covenant justice is not opposed to love; for to love the neighbor as oneself, including the enemy, is to fulfill covenant justice. Retribution, returning "like for like," fails to sum up covenant justice for it falls short of the law of love, which calls us to return good for both good and evil alike. Retribution in the positive sense, returning good for good, is not evil, but "it is not enough" — the full measure of justice goes beyond retribution. Athenagoras concludes by repudiating all practices of violence — including war, capital punishment, gladiatorial games, abortion, and infanticide — as contrary to the law of love.[45]

This apologetic is echoed in the second-century *Epistle to Diognetus*, which famously depicts Christians as "resident aliens" in the world (5:5). While living under the law of the land, and so posing no threat to Rome, Christians demonstrate that their true citizenship is in heaven by transcending the law of retribution through the practice of love: "They obey the prescribed laws, but in their private lives they transcend the laws. They show love to all men — and all men persecute them. . . . They repay calumny with blessings, and abuse with courtesy" (5:10-11, 15).[46]

Likewise, Tertullian, founder of the Latin tradition of Christian thought, defends Christians against accusations of being "enemies of the empire" by appealing to the Christian norm of non-retaliation. Christians pose no threat to Rome, Tertullian argues in his early third-century *Apology*, because Christians are obligated to love their enemies and do no injury to anyone, not even in return for injury. He writes: "If we are enjoined, then, to love our enemies, as I have remarked above, whom have we to hate? If injured, we are forbidden to retaliate, lest we become as bad ourselves: who can suffer injury at our hands?"[47] By retaliating against evildoers, one not only disobeys the teaching of Christ that we love our enemies, but also becomes like the evil one retaliates against: retaliating against evil turns oneself into an evildoer.

43. Athenagoras, *A Plea for the Christians*, XXXII.
44. Athenagoras, *A Plea for the Christians*, XXXIV.
45. Athenagoras, *A Plea for the Christians*, XXXV.
46. *Early Christian Writings*, pp. 144-45.
47. Tertullian, *Apology*, XXXVII, in Philip Schaff, *The Ante-Nicene Fathers, Vol. III: Latin Christianity: Its Founder, Tertullian* (Grand Rapids, MI: Christian Classics Ethereal Library, 2006).

The teaching of Jesus, the Apostles, and the early church Fathers is continued by the third-century *Apostolic Tradition*. The *Apostolic Tradition* lays down rules of church order, including ordination of bishops, elders, and deacons; acceptable occupations for church members; initiation of new believers; celebration of communion; and the practice of daily prayer in the home. It is the guidelines for baptism and church membership that are of interest to us. These are clear in *excluding* from the ranks of the catechumens, and so barring from baptism and membership, persons engaged in specific occupations deemed immoral or impious: pimps and prostitutes, idol-makers and idol-worshippers, magicians and astrologers. In this list are those serving in certain official positions:

> A soldier under authority shall not kill a man. If he is ordered to, he shall not carry out that order; nor shall he take the oath. If he is unwilling, let him be rejected. He who has the power of the sword, or is a magistrate of a city who wears the purple, let him cease or be rejected. Catechumens or believers who want to become soldiers should be rejected, because they have despised God. (*Apostolic Tradition* 16:9-11)[48]

By excluding from the church those responsible for enacting state policies of retributive violence — magistrates, executioners, and soldiers — the *Apostolic Tradition* maintains in practice the teaching of Jesus and the Apostles.

The early church took the teaching of Jesus and the Apostles so seriously that potential converts to Christianity were expected to practice that teaching before joining the church or having been taught the Sermon on the Mount. Alan Kreider comments:

> This may seem severe and legalistic to us today, even perverse. How could a community rebuff people as potential members for not living according to the standards of the group *before* they had been taught? But the early Christian catechists were attempting not so much to impart concepts as to nurture communities whose values would be different from those of conventional society. Christian leaders assumed that people did not think their way into a new life; they lived their way into a new kind of thinking.[49]

The early church recognized that inhabiting a new way of thinking (indeed, a new way of living) is essential to full reception of the teaching of Jesus and genuine conversion to the way of the cross. Potential converts to Christianity were

48. Geoffrey J. Cumming, *Hippolytus: A Text for Students*, 2nd ed. (Cambridge: Grove Books, 1987), p. 16. The *Apostolic Tradition* is thought to have been written by Hippolytus, presbyter of the church at Rome.
49. Alan Kreider, *The Change of Conversion and the Origin of Christendom* (Harrisburg, PA: Trinity Press International, 1999), p. 23, emphasis original.

coming for baptismal instruction having their thinking already conformed to the scheme of the age. In order to be ready to receive the teaching of Jesus that his followers renounce retribution and love enemies, their minds needed to be renewed through the adoption of new habits of character and conduct. Evidently, the rule set forth in the *Apostolic Tradition* was still in effect a century later and was applied even to the emperor Constantine. Despite his "conversion" in AD 312 and his legalization of Christianity in 313, Constantine was not baptized and admitted to communion until he was near death, in 337. In the process, the ecclesiastical authorities required him to submit himself to catechesis in the way of Jesus and thus to reject the purple and the sword of imperial authority — and so renounce retribution and violence — as a condition of membership in the body of Christ.[50]

3.2.4. Augustine and Aquinas: Back to Aristotle and Cicero

When we come to Augustine in the late fourth century, we find an ambivalence of mind — both the affirmation that love is the true measure of justice, that the duty to "render what is due" is fulfilled in the love of God and neighbor, in continuity with Jesus and the Apostles,[51] and the argument, at least in certain contexts, that retribution is the proper measure of justice, in line with Aristotle and Cicero. The teaching of the early church that Christians are to renounce retribution in principle and practice, as we have seen, was founded upon the Sermon on the Mount. In his commentary on the Sermon on the Mount, accordingly, we can observe Augustine's ambivalence.

Augustine comments that Jesus' teaching implicitly contrasts three levels of response to an evil or injury: the normal instinct of humanity, which is to inflict a greater evil in return for a lesser evil; the "lesser righteousness" of the Pharisees, which returns evil for evil according to the *lex talionis* ("eye for eye, tooth for tooth"); and the "greater righteousness" of the kingdom, according to which, as Augustine says, "no evil at all should be inflicted in return for an evil."[52] Augustine then argues that, while Jesus taught the renunciation of retribution "for the purpose of perfecting the disciples," nonetheless the "middle course" of exact retribution "holds a certain place." For, compared to excessive vengeance, it requires restraint and thus, to a degree, expresses virtue (moderation or self-control). Although it does not reach to the "very highest develop-

50. Kreider, *Change of Conversion*, pp. 33-37.

51. Cf. Augustine, *City of God*, XIX, 14, 21, 24. See Carol Harrison, *Augustine: Christian Truth and Fractured Humanity* (Oxford: Oxford University Press, 2000), pp. 210-11.

52. Augustine, *Our Lord's Sermon on the Mount, According to St. Matthew*, I.XIX, in Philip Schaff, *The Nicene and Post-Nicene Fathers, Series I, Volume VI* (Grand Rapids, MI: Christian Classics Ethereal Library).

ment of mercy," and although "perfect peace is to have no wish at all for such vengeance," to return evil in exact measure for evil, Augustine says, is an "incomplete, by no means severe, but merciful justice."[53]

Having argued that exact retribution is a moral virtue, Augustine goes on to argue that Jesus' teaching allows his disciples to deal out retribution under certain conditions.[54] "Nor are we thus precluded from inflicting punishment [Latin *vindicta*]" in return for injury, Augustine says, as long as it is done out of compassion, for the sake of the sinner's correction, and without vengeful desire on the part of the one inflicting the punishment. The authority to punish falls to the one "to whom, in the natural order of things, the power is given."[55]

Augustine's qualification of Jesus' teaching has practical implications. Having argued that retributive punishment, even if inconsistent with the "greater righteousness," is nonetheless justified by "the natural order of things," Augustine is able to uphold the moral code of the ancient household. This code established a hierarchy of relationships — husbands over wives, parents over children, masters over slaves — and sanctioned retributive punishment to maintain that order.[56] In *City of God*, Augustine states that nature grants the head of household the authority and obligation to reprimand the disobedient "by a word, or by a blow, or any other kind of punishment that is just and legitimate, to the extent allowed by human society" in order to restrain sin and restore the "domestic peace."[57] Because the household is "a small component part

53. Augustine, *Sermon on the Mount*, I.XIX, 56-57. As we noted above, there is nothing essentially contrary to the gospel in positive retribution, returning good in measure for good. Augustine, however, also affirms negative retribution, returning evil in measure for evil, as compatible with Christian discipleship — which is what is under question here.

54. Reformed philosopher Nicholas Wolterstorff, "Jesus and Forgiveness," follows in the Augustinian tradition, arguing that although Jesus rejects retribution he permits retributive punishment. As Wolterstorff correctly observes (pp. 198-202), Jesus rejects retribution outright by rejecting the *lex talionis*. It then follows, as Wolterstorff acknowledges, that Jesus rejects retributive punishment: "Jesus, it seems clear, is instructing his followers to reject retributive punishment" (p. 204). Nonetheless, like Augustine, Wolterstorff maintains that Jesus was not so strict in rejecting retribution: "Jesus was saying: retributive punishment is not required — permitted but not required" (p. 208). Wolterstorff's interpretation of Jesus' teaching is logically incoherent: if Jesus categorically prohibits retribution in the negative sense, then he prohibits all retributive practices that return evil for evil — including retributive punishment.

55. Augustine, *Sermon on the Mount*, I.XX, 63. One can thus see a parallel between Augustine's criteria of just punishment and the classic criteria of just war, taken over from Greco-Roman philosophy (discussed below): just cause, right intention, and proper authority. Augustine also qualifies "love your enemies" to allow for killing the enemy in war, as long as it is done for the neighbor's protection and without hateful intention (see Chapter 28 below).

56. The classic discussion of the household code is Aristotle, *Politics*, I.

57. Augustine, *City of God*, XIX, 16, trans. Henry Bettenson (London: Penguin Books, 2003), p. 876.

of the city" and the "domestic peace contributes to the peace of the city," Augustine argues, "Consequently it is fitting that the father of a household should take his rules from the law of the city, and govern his household in such a way that it fits in with the peace of the city."[58] According to Augustine, then, the common rules of human justice ("the law of the city"), not the "greater righteousness" of the heavenly kingdom, sets the moral standard of disciplinary practice in the Christian household.[59]

Augustine's view represents a significant shift in Christian apologetics. To "seek the peace of the city" is, for sure, consistent with the teaching of the prophets, Jesus, and the Apostles (Jer 29:7; Luke 19:42; Rom 12:18; 1 Pet 3:11). But whereas Athenagoras and Tertullian had argued that Christians pose no threat to the *pax Romana* because they have renounced retribution and are forbidden from returning evil for evil to anyone, Augustine argues that Christians should maintain the *pax Romana* by practicing retribution within their own households.[60] In the shift from Athenagoras and Tertullian to Augustine, then, the authority of "natural law" has supplemented — and, to some degree, supplanted — the authority of Jesus for Christian ethics.[61]

To an even greater degree than Augustine, Aquinas oriented his thinking about justice more according to the theory of Aristotle and Cicero than the tra-

58. Augustine, *City of God,* XIX, 16, p. 876.

59. On the background and development of Augustine's views on domestic order, especially how it reflected Roman practice and was conformed to the Platonist hierarchical view of things, see John M. Rist, *Augustine: Ancient Thought Baptized* (Cambridge: Cambridge University Press, 1994), pp. 211-13. Rist observes that, although Augustine protested the abuses of domestic authority, he affirmed that such were "abuses of an underlying proper order" (p. 213). Augustine even went so far as to affirm that, although contrary to God's original intention in creation, "the condition of slavery is justly imposed on the sinner" according to the natural order of things. The practice of slavery, Augustine thus argued, accords with the natural law: "But it remains true that slavery as a punishment [for sin] is also ordained by that law which enjoins the preservation of the order of nature" (*City of God,* XIX, 15, pp. 874-75). Concerning Augustine's views on slavery, see Rist, *Augustine,* pp. 236ff.

60. Harrison, *Augustine,* pp. 211-13, argues that Augustine's view was in line with previous apologetic stretching back to the New Testament, only that Augustine pointed out for the first time "how much a *necessary* compromise" a law-abiding life in support of the civic order actually involves (p. 213, emphasis original). In *City of God,* XIX, however, Augustine does more than simply point out how far the peace of the empire falls short of the peace of the kingdom. For he counsels Christians not only to obey civic law in public affairs but also to adopt Roman standards of moral discipline in domestic affairs. The Christian household has thereby become, effectively, a micro-colony of the empire.

61. I do not object outright to natural law ethics; in fact, I affirm the basic premise of natural law — that the natural order is a moral order, that God has ordained certain ends in the nature of things (though I do challenge the common understanding of natural justice as essentially retributive: see Chapter 22 below). I do object, however, to Augustine's qualification of covenant law by natural law such that Jesus' teachings for the discipleship community are diluted into the common ethic of the civil community.

dition of Jesus and the Apostles.[62] In the *Summa Theologiae*, Aquinas formulates the definition of justice in deliberate parallel to Aristotle ("the Philosopher"):

> And if anyone would reduce it to the proper form of a definition, he might say that "justice is a habit whereby a man renders to each one his due by a constant and perpetual will"; this is about the same definition as that given by the Philosopher, who says that "justice is a habit whereby a man is said to be capable of doing just actions in accordance with his choice."[63]

Aquinas later sums up the nature of justice according to the classical formula: "the proper act of justice is nothing else than to render each one his own."[64] As to what is required "to render each one his due" in matters of criminal justice, Aquinas again adheres to Aristotle and Cicero: retribution.

Concerning criminal justice, retribution requires the offender be "paid back in kind," with the proviso of equivalence (or proportionality) between the crime and the punishment. The principle of retribution finds no clearer expression than Cicero's statement in *The Laws:* "If a person transgresses any of these rules, the penalty shall fit the crime. . . . In this way each offender is to be paid back in his own coin — violence being punished by death or exile, greed by a fine, improper canvassing by disgrace."[65]

Aquinas, following Aristotle and Cicero, argues that criminal justice requires retribution, punishment "according to the equality of repayment." We can follow Aquinas's reasoning from the principle of retributive justice to the practice of retaliatory punishment in the *Summa Theologiae*. In *Summa Theologiae* II-II, Question 61, Aquinas develops his definition of justice and applies it to particular matters. In Article 1, he distinguishes commutative justice from distributive justice, the former dealing with relations person-to-person and the latter dealing with relations person-to-community. In Article 2, he defines commutative justice

---

62. Augustine acquired the notion of "natural law" from Stoic philosophy through his reading of Cicero (cf. Augustine, *Confessions,* III, vii, and Cicero, *Republic,* III). To see the substantial extent to which Aquinas's thinking about justice was indebted to Greco-Roman philosophy, one need only look at the citations in his discussion of the nature of justice in the *Summa Theologiae* (II-II, Q. 58). Of sixty-two citations over twelve articles, Aquinas cites Greco-Roman philosophers forty-six times (Aristotle 38, Cicero 7), church Fathers twelve times (including Augustine and Anselm), and Scripture four times. Concerning how to understand justice, then, Aquinas preferred Greco-Roman philosophy over biblical teaching by a ratio of more than ten-to-one! Even if we consider Scripture and tradition together, Aquinas preferred Aristotle and Cicero by more than two-to-one.

63. Thomas Aquinas, *On Law, Morality, and Politics* (Indianapolis, IN: Hackett Publishing, 1988), p. 145 (*Summa Theologiae* II-II, Q. 58, A. 1), citing Aristotle, *Nicomachean Ethics,* V, 5.

64. Thomas Aquinas, *On Law,* p. 162 (*Summa Theologiae* II-II, Q. 58, A. 11). Here, Aquinas follows Augustine, *City of God,* XIX, 21.

65. Cicero, *The Laws,* III, 11, 46, in *The Republic and The Laws,* trans. Niall Rudd (Oxford: Oxford University Press, 1998), pp. 154, 167.

in the context of economic exchanges: "it is necessary to equalize thing with thing, so that the one person should pay back to the other just so much as he has become richer out of that which belonged to the other. The result is that there will be equality according to the 'arithmetical mean.' . . ." In Article 3, he brings criminal matters, arising from injury done by one to another person or to another's property, under commutative justice. After detailing various criminal actions (murder, robbery, slander, etc.), he sums up what justice requires: "In all these actions, . . . the mean is taken in the same way according to the equality of repayment." The implication is clear: criminal justice requires "equality of repayment" — "paying back" the wrongdoer "in kind."[66] Criminal justice thus entails retributive punishment according to the *lex talionis*, which measures back to the offender a proportional evil — harm for harm, injury for injury.

3.2.5. The Retributive Paradigm in Atonement Theology

The retributive paradigm is evident, not only in Christian thinking about justice in matters of household order and criminal punishment, but also in Christian thinking about justice in relation to atonement.[67] One can see the retributive paradigm operating in Anselm's *Cur Deus Homo*. Concerning the necessity of the Incarnation, this classic text sets forth the understanding of the cross of Christ as the "satisfaction" of God. Peter Schmiechen outlines "the basic logic that drives the argument" in *Cur Deus Homo*:

> If sin has violated the honor of God, and if God must maintain the divine honor since it represents both God per se and God's purposes for the creation, then we are faced with an either/or: either humankind must be punished or God must save humankind. . . . But . . . further reflection on God's honor leads to the conclusion that there really is only one choice: God must complete the divine purpose and save humankind. This leads to the next step: if there is to be remission for sin, there must be satisfaction. Now since the option of punishment has been ruled out and God is to pursue the only real option of completing the divine purpose, satisfaction must take the form of the restoration of creation, which is also to say, restoring or paying back the honor of God.[68]

66. Quoted from Aquinas, *On Law*, pp. 167, 170. Aquinas's reasoning here closely parallels Aristotle's views on "rectificatory" (or "corrective" or "remedial") justice in *Nicomachean Ethics*, V, 4.

67. Concerning the significant role of the Greco-Roman tradition in the atonement theology of Western Christianity, see Colin E. Gunton, *The Actuality of Atonement: A Study of Metaphor, Rationality, and the Christian Tradition* (Grand Rapids, MI: Eerdmans Publishing, 1989), pp. 83-113.

68. Peter Schmiechen, *Saving Power: Theories of Atonement and Forms of the Church* (Grand Rapids, MI: Eerdmans Publishing, 2005), pp. 198-99.

Why does Anselm think that "if there is to be remission of sins, there *must* be satisfaction"? Let us examine Anselm's argument that "satisfaction" for human sin requires compensation — "repayment" — to God's honor. Anselm sets up his argument by framing the God-human relationship within the retributive paradigm — specifically, commutative justice.[69] Within this paradigm, Anselm defines what it is to sin according to the classic formula, that justice is to render to each what is owed: "If an angel or a man were always to render to God what he owes, he would never sin. . . . Then, to sin is nothing other than not to give to God what is owed to him."[70] What creatures owe to God, and what God demands from creatures, is to render God honor by subjection to God's will. "Someone who does not render to God this honour due to him is taking away from God what is his, and dishonouring God, and this is what it is to sin."[71] To disobey God's will is to dishonor God, which requires that "satisfaction" be made to God by means of recompense: "Therefore, everyone who sins is under an obligation to repay to God the honour which he has violently taken from him, and this is the satisfaction which every sinner is obliged to give to God."[72] In keeping with the retributive paradigm, Anselm invokes the criterion of proportionality: to make satisfaction to God for sin, "recompense ought to be proportional to the magnitude of the sin."[73]

Why, though, cannot God "pass over" sin and act unilaterally to restore sinners to right relationship without human recompense to divine honor? Not because God is incapable of doing so, Anselm replies, but because doing so would not be "fitting" for God to do. God *can* do all things, but this is something that God *must* not do. Why not? Anselm argues: sin cannot be let go without either compensation or punishment, for then there would be no distinction between innocence and guilt, which is "unfitting" for God to allow; moreover, to let the guilty go unpunished would effectively be to reward sin, which also would be "unfitting" for God, who dispenses reward to humanity according to the requirements of law.[74] Here, again, we see the retributive paradigm: the necessity of making satisfaction to God for sin is premised upon the requirement of retribution.

69. Anselm assumes the retributive paradigm without argument. It may be that he believed that the biblical portrayal of the God-human relationship fit the retributive paradigm. As we will show in Chapters 10, 11, 20, and 21, however, God's covenantal relationship with Israel is not governed strictly by retributive justice, not even in the cultic sacrifices for atonement-making, as is commonly supposed.

70. Anselm, *Why God Became Man*, I, 11, trans. Janet Fairweather, in Brian Davies and G. R. Evans, eds., *Anselm of Canterbury: The Major Works* (Oxford: Oxford University Press, 1998), p. 283.

71. Anselm, *Why God Became Man*, I, 11, p. 283.

72. Anselm, *Why God Became Man*, I, 11, p. 283.

73. Anselm, *Why God Became Man*, I, 20, p. 303.

74. Anselm, *Why God Became Man*, I, 12. Anselm offers no argument why this should be so.

How, then, are sinners to make recompense to God? Anselm argues that no amount of penitential action — prayer, fasting, charity — can do because any such act of obedience would only render to God the honor we *already* owe and thus cannot be offered as recompense.[75] To make satisfaction for sin thus requires humans to offer God *more* than obedience, which is humanly impossible. With humans unable to make satisfaction and the principle of retribution requiring either punishment or satisfaction, God is left with two options: either punish humanity for its sin, or else provide another means of satisfaction. Punishment, because it would put an end to humanity, is no real option at all, for then God would have abandoned his work of creation and so failed to remain faithful to his own purpose, which is surely unfitting for God.[76] So, God must provide another means of satisfaction, an alternative way for humanity to repay God's honor. This prompts the question: because sinners cannot repay God's honor, how is humanity to make satisfaction to God by recompense for sin? Anselm answers, by no other means than the God-Man: none but a human being *ought* to make satisfaction to God, but none other than God *can* make satisfaction, such that satisfaction for sin cannot be made except by the God-Man.[77] Atonement for the sins of humanity by means of satisfaction to God, therefore, necessitates the Incarnation. And Jesus, who is both fully God and fully human, is capable of rendering complete obedience to God's will through his life and death and thus making satisfactory recompense to God's honor on humanity's behalf. According to Anselm, then, the obedient life and death of Jesus the God-Man satisfies the moral debt that humanity owes to God on account of its disobedience, where the requirement of satisfaction presupposes the logic of retribution.

As Schmiechen observes, Anselm employs two notions of divine honor, corresponding to differing notions of what is "fitting" — and thus necessary — for God.[78] In one aspect, the divine honor pertains to God's very nature, an honor "which God maintains with perfect justice" by either imposing punishment or requiring satisfaction for disobedience.[79] What is "fitting" for God in this sense is what accords exactly with the requirement of retribution, such that

---

75. Anselm, *Why God Became Man*, I, 20, p. 303: "When you are rendering to God something which you owe him, even if you have not sinned, you ought not to reckon this to be recompense for what you owe him for sin." Anselm here distinguishes between rendering what is owed and making recompense for sin: the need for recompense arises from failure to render what is owed, such that rendering what is *now* owed cannot suffice as recompense for failure to render what *had been* owed (e.g., paying this month's rent does not make up for missing last month's rent).

76. Anselm, *Why God Became Man*, I, 19 and II, 4-5. Cf. Schmiechen, *Saving Power*, p. 206.

77. Anselm, *Why God Became Man*, II, 6.

78. Schmiechen, *Saving Power*, pp. 203-6.

79. Schmiechen, *Saving Power*, p. 203.

retribution constitutes what is "fitting" (so necessary) for God concerning justice. Anselm thus considers it unthinkable that God might deal with sin in any manner inconsistent with the principle of retribution: because it is God's nature to be just, how God deals with sin must "fit" with that nature. But this begs the question: what does God's just nature require? Anselm assumes that God's choice, to "fit" his just nature, must accord with what retribution requires. It is that assumption which reflects the retributive paradigm — and which we call into question.

In another aspect, the divine honor concerns "God's unswerving faithfulness to this purpose [viz., God's own design in creation] and the mutual obligations between God and humanity."[80] What is "fitting" for God in this sense is to remain faithful to the purpose that God has willed — to complete God's own purpose in creation, which has fallen into sin and needs restoration. We quite agree with this sense of what is "fitting" for God: it is necessary that God — whose very character is faithfulness, truth, and steadfast love — remain faithful, true, and steadfast in that which God has willed and purposed. Indeed, we affirm this idea as part of our own understanding of the necessity of the cross (Chapter 18). It is the other notion of divine honor — that it would be "unfitting" for God to deal with sin by any means other than what retribution requires — which we reject. As we will see, Scripture does not reveal either a divine character or a covenant relationship that is essentially or necessarily retributive (Chapter 21).

The retributive paradigm is operative also in the Protestant penal substitution doctrine.[81] Consider evangelical Anglican theologian John R. W. Stott's thinking about the justice of God in relation to the cross of Christ. In his defense of penal substitution, Stott wisely counsels against making rational presuppositions about justice:

80. Schmiechen, *Saving Power*, p. 204.
81. Although related by a common tradition of atonement theology within the retributive paradigm, the satisfaction theory (per Anselm) and the penal substitution theory (per Calvin) need to be kept distinct and should not be conflated. The two theories not only have different legal backgrounds (see James Wm. McClendon, Jr., *Doctrine: Systematic Theology, Vol. II* [Nashville, TN: Abingdon Press, 1994], pp. 203-8) but also understand the function and purpose of Christ's death in different terms. Schmiechen summarizes this difference: "penal substitution does rest entirely on the idea of violation of the Law, the requirement of punishment, and Christ dying and thereby paying the price for our salvation. . . . What Christ did, according to Anselm, has nothing to do with punishment but *restitution* of God's honor" (*Saving Power*, pp. 196-97, emphasis original). Whereas Anselm frames the problem in terms of the human obligation to repay a debt of honor to God on account of sin, Calvin frames the problem in terms of the divine requirement to punish humanity with death on account of sin. These are, then, different theories: "satisfaction of divine honor" (Anselm) ≠ "propitiation of divine wrath" (Calvin).

We must watch our presuppositions, therefore. It is perilous to begin with any *a priori*, even with a "God-given sense of moral justice" which then shapes our understanding of the cross. It is wiser and safer to begin inductively with a God-given doctrine of the cross, which then shapes our understanding of moral justice.[82]

We agree wholeheartedly with Stott's counsel here. Yet Stott seems to have neglected his own counsel when he comes to his chapter on "The revelation of God," where he writes of the justice of God.[83] In expositing the justice of God, Stott does not begin with the revelation of the cross, as we might expect, but rather with the classic problem of evil as presented in the biblical wisdom writers (e.g., Job). The classic problem of evil — "Why do the wicked prosper? Why do the righteous suffer?" — is premised upon the human assumption that divine justice is necessarily retributive: the righteous deserve prosperity and the wicked deserve suffering; therefore, the prosperity of the wicked and the suffering of the righteous is evidence that God has failed (or has yet) to do justice. Likewise, Stott assumes without question that God's justice is necessarily satisfied in retribution — in judgment that redresses "imbalances of justice" by meting out "just deserts," reward in exchange for righteousness, punishment in exchange for sin. He then interprets the justice of the cross according to this presupposed principle of retribution.

In his entire discussion, Stott not once considers the possibility that God's justice might not necessarily be retributive. "It is inconceivable," he writes, that God should fail to do justice by executing retribution, that God should forgive sins without punishment to satisfy what retribution requires.[84] The cross, in his interpretation of Rom 3:21-26, thus becomes the logical answer to the problem of unsatisfied divine retribution:

> By his past forbearance toward sinners God had created a problem for himself. . . . If God does not justly punish sin, he would be "unjust to himself." . . . So, although in his forbearance he temporarily left sins unpunished, now in justice he has punished them, by condemning them in Christ. He has thus demonstrated his justice by executing it. . . . Because of his past appearance of injustice in not punishing sins, he has given a present and visible proof of justice in bearing the punishment himself in Christ.[85]

Despite his own counsel, Stott has gotten things backward: instead of viewing the problem of evil from the perspective of the cross, he interprets the cross ac-

82. John R. W. Stott, *The Cross of Christ* (Downers Grove, IL: InterVarsity Press, 1986), pp. 104-5.

83. Stott, *Cross of Christ*, pp. 207-12.

84. Stott, *Cross of Christ*, p. 211.

85. Stott, *Cross of Christ*, p. 211.

cording to the unexamined notion of retributive justice that is presupposed by the problem of evil.[86]

It is the same with Leon Morris, evangelical New Testament scholar and proponent of penal substitution, when he discusses "the righteousness of God" in Rom 3:21-26. Morris is correct that "The cross demonstrates the righteousness, the justice of God." But as to what this "justice of God" is, Morris does not ask — and thus does not look to the cross of Christ to reveal the justice of God to us. Evidently, Morris assumes that he knows what God's justice must look like and that Paul must have agreed with him:

> Paul . . . is saying that the way God saves sinful man accords with what is right . . . the question that worried Paul was . . . "How could God be righteous if he *did* forgive?" Often and often people had sinned. You would expect that a just God would punish them. That is what justice means.

Morris presupposes that Paul thinks the just ways of God necessarily accord with "what is right" as defined by what retribution requires, which is simply "what justice means." On his view, therefore, the cross does not *reveal* God's justice but *reflects* back what "you would expect" — "the cross represents the paying of the penalty for sin."[87] As viewed by penal substitution, therefore, the cross of Christ confirms the retributive paradigm. We need to be wary of the assumption that the justice of God demonstrated through the cross of Christ should simply confirm what "you would expect."[88]

3.3. Retributive Thinking in Christian Tradition: Peace

3.3.1 Pax Romana: *Victory over the Enemy*

Our Greco-Roman inherited thinking, forged in the fires of empire past, understands peace as the achievement of military victory. "Peace and security" (the imperial slogan) is the outcome of a war in which the emperor and his army de-

---

86. We will address the classic problem of evil in Chapter 22.

87. Leon Morris, *The Atonement: Its Meaning and Significance* (Downers Grove, IL: InterVarsity Press, 1983), pp. 194-95.

88. I do not claim that this settles the argument concerning atonement theology. Although I object to any atonement theology that interprets the cross in terms that are fundamentally at odds with the teaching of Jesus (Chapter 2 above), and although penal substitution is premised on the principle of retribution, which Jesus himself explicitly renounced, it does not follow that penal substitution is therefore incorrect. Such an argument by counter-assumption would only beg the question. Whether penal substitution stands or falls is to be decided not *a priori* but *a posteriori* — not by testing its logical consistency with an alternative principle, but by testing its assumptions and implications against the evidence of Scripture (see Part II below).

feat the enemies threatening the empire and brings them into subjection. The victorious emperor is heralded by the people as "peacemaker" and "savior of the world." This connection between imperial peace and military victory is evident in the fact that the altar of peace of Caesar Augustus, who restored "peace and security" to the empire by defeating rivals to the throne, was built on the field of Mars: the peace of empire is won on the field of battle.[89] "Peace and security," then, is the achievement of enemy-defeating violence. Paul exposed the imperial "peace and security" as a false hope of salvation, subject to imminent judgment: "For you yourselves know that the day of the Lord will come like a thief in the night. When they say, 'There is peace and security,' then sudden destruction will come upon them" (1 Thess 5:2-3).[90]

3.3.2. Cicero, Augustine, and Aquinas: The "Just War"

The rhetoric of the *pax Romana,* together with the "natural law" of retributive justice, underwrites the classic tradition of "just war." According to Cicero, the prime goals of just war are avenging the honor and defending the "peace and security" of the empire.[91] The state is justified in avenging itself against and exacting punishment upon enemies through war, not only to preserve the peace, but simply to save the state. Cicero says in *The Republic* that, in contrast with a person, "the death of a state is never natural." It is thus imperative that the state be defended from demise; for to allow a state to dissolve would be "contrary to nature." Indeed, for the state to be destroyed would be as if "this whole world were to collapse and pass away." Because the eternal existence of the state is a requirement of natural law — "a state should be organized in such a way as to last for ever" — not only is any threat to the safety of the state a just cause for war, but the health of the state must be defended at all costs lest the state suffer death. The violence necessary to "secure the peace" is thus justified by the moral imperative of imperial survival: just war is the salvation and peace of the eternal empire.[92]

89. Cf. Klaus Wengst, *Pax Romana and the Peace of Jesus Christ* (Philadelphia: Fortress Press, 1987), pp. 11-54. Wengst writes (p. 11): "So the first thing that we must note is that the Pax Romana is a peace which is the political goal of the Roman emperor . . . and is brought about and secured by military actions through the success of his legions."

90. Concerning the imperial rhetoric of peace in relation to the peace of Christ, see Ulrich Mauser, *The Gospel of Peace: A Scriptural Message for Today's World* (Louisville, KY: Westminster/John Knox Press, 1992), pp. 84-89, and Erich Dinkler, "*Eirene* — The Early Christian Concept of Peace," in Perry B. Yoder and Willard M. Swartley, eds, *The Meaning of Peace: Biblical Studies,* 2nd ed. (Elkhart, IN: Institute of Mennonite Studies, 2001), pp. 80-89.

91. Cicero's influential views on *bellum justum* are excerpted in Arthur F. Holmes, ed., *War and Christian Ethics: Classic Readings on the Morality of War* (Grand Rapids, MI: Baker Books, 1975), pp. 24-31.

92. Cicero, *Republic,* III, 34, in *The Republic and The Laws,* p. 69. Cicero did develop rules of

The just war is thus a Roman idea that Western Christianity adopted and adapted, beginning with Augustine and culminating with Aquinas.[93] This was a clear departure from the teaching of Jesus and the tradition of the Apostles: for the first three centuries of the church, there was an explicit consensus among orthodox theologians that Christians ought not participate in warfare on account of obedience to Christ. Indeed, Christians were derided by their pagan detractors for their refusal to serve in the military.[94]

In *City of God*, Augustine takes over the idea of just war directly from Cicero.[95] That said, a few qualifications are in order. Augustine does maintain the Ciceronian view that natural law sanctions state violence to secure public order, but at the same time he expresses serious misgivings about even the justified use of violent force by public officials.[96] And, although Augustine does hold that war is justifiable, he does not think that war is desirable, much less a moral end in itself. He argues that no one makes war for war's sake, for everyone, even one who wages war, desires and seeks peace: "Indeed, even when men

---

"just war" with the intent of curbing the "excesses" of imperial warfare, yet his just war theory effectively grants absolute value to the state and thus only serves to justify the violence of empire.

93. The evident pagan origins of the just war tradition belie recent statements by proponents of the War on Terror, such as Jean Bethke Elshtain, that "the origins of just war thinking lie in Christian theology" ("International Justice as Equal Regard and the Use of Force," in Wes Avram, ed., *Anxious about Empire: Theological Essays on the New Global Realities* [Grand Rapids, MI: Brazos Press, 2004], p. 134.) Elsewhere, Elshtain comments that "The origins of this tradition are usually traced from St. Augustine's fourth-century masterwork, *The City of God*" (*Just War against Terror: The Burden of American Power in a Violent World* [New York: Basic Books, 2003], p. 50). This is correct, given the qualifier "usually." For the majority tradition wishing to gloss "just war" as an essentially Christian idea, the history begins with Augustine; for the minority tradition wishing to get to the actual roots of just-war thinking, the history begins with pagan philosophy. Regarding the Greco-Roman origins of just-war thinking and its later adoption and adaptation by Christianity, see Roland H. Bainton, *Christian Attitudes toward War and Peace: A Historical Survey and Critical Re-Evaluation* (Nashville, TN: Abingdon Press, 1960), pp. 33-43, 85-100; James Turner Johnson, *The Quest for Peace: Three Moral Traditions in Western Cultural History* (Princeton, NJ: Princeton University Press, 1987), pp. 47-66; and Lisa Sowle Cahill, *Love Your Enemies: Discipleship, Pacifism, and Just War Theory* (Minneapolis, MN: Fortress Press, 1994), pp. 55-95.

94. See Jean-Michel Hornus, *It Is Not Lawful for Me to Fight: Early Christian Attitudes towards War, Violence, and the State* (Scottdale, PA: Herald Press, 1980), and Bainton, *Christian Attitudes toward War and Peace*, chapter 5. The consensus was held among theologians both East (Irenaeus, Athenagoras, Origen) and West (Justin Martyr, Tertullian, Minucius Felix, Lactantius). As Bainton observes, this theological consensus was not universally practiced: there is evidence of Christian participation in the Roman military beginning in the late second century and increasing through the third century.

95. Augustine, *City of God*, XXII, 6. Augustine's views on just war are excerpted from various writings in Holmes, *War and Christian Ethics*, pp. 61-83. For a nuanced discussion of Augustine's view, see Cahill, *Love Your Enemies*, pp. 55-80.

96. See Rist, *Augustine*, pp. 226, 231-36.

choose war, their only wish is for victory; which shows that their desire in fighting is for peace with glory. For what is victory but the conquest of the opposing side? And when this is achieved, there will be peace."[97] Now, while Augustine's argument reflects the Roman rhetoric that war makes peace, Augustine was in no way naïve to suppose that the *pax Romana* was a peace in the true sense. Indeed, he makes clear a few pages later that the imperial peace by dominion over others is opposed to God's peace and so hardly worth the name.[98] Nor was Augustine taken in by the "imperial theology" of Eusebius that the success of the empire was the salvation of the church and humanity. A major theme of *City of God* is that the empire, although of some temporal good, is still fallen and cannot usher in the kingdom of God.[99]

Nonetheless, despite his ambivalence toward both war and empire, Augustine makes the case for Christian participation in just wars to defend an imperial peace. Christians have a duty to obey the law and defend the peace because the *pax Romana* is both necessary and useful to the mission of the church in the world.[100] The "natural order which seeks the peace of mankind" authorizes the emperor to wage war; hence, the imperial peace is just cause for war. The Christian soldier who fights a just war under imperial authority both performs his civic duty and acts righteously under God's will, such that he is blameless before God.[101] Several centuries later, Aquinas would complete the trajectory of this thinking: Christian participation in just wars is not sinful.[102]

What, then, is the moral essence of a just war? Following Cicero, Augustine and Aquinas state that underwriting just war is the retributive principle. Cicero held that retribution against enemies and saving the empire constitute the only just cause for war: "No just war can be waged except for the sake of punishing or repelling an enemy."[103] Echoing Cicero, Augustine argues first that war itself is not inherently evil; the evil of war lies not in the killing but in various excesses that the ancient philosophers called moral vices: "What is the evil in

97. Augustine, *City of God*, XIX, 12 (p. 866).

98. Augustine, *City of God*, XIX, 12 (pp. 868-69).

99. See Harrison, *Augustine*, pp. 202-9, and Rist, *Augustine*, pp. 216-28.

100. Augustine, *City of God*, XIX, 17, 26. On this, see Harrison, *Augustine*, pp. 218-19. Augustine's argument echoes the pastoral counsel of the Apostles: "I urge that supplications, prayers, intercessions, and thanksgivings be made for everyone, for kings and all who are in high positions, so that we may lead a quiet and peaceable life in all godliness and dignity" (1 Tim 2:1-2). Notice, however, the substantial shift from the Apostles to Augustine: from "Pray for the emperor" to "Defend the empire."

101. Augustine, *Reply to Faustus the Manichaean*, XXII, 75, in Philip Schaff, *The Nicene and Post-Nicene Fathers, Series I, Vol. IV: The Writings against the Manichaeans and against the Donatists* (Grand Rapids, MI: Christian Classics Ethereal Library).

102. Aquinas, *Summa Theologiae*, II-II, Q. 40, Art. 1.

103. Cicero, *Republic*, III, 35 (p. 69).

war? . . . The real evils in war are love of violence, revengeful cruelty, fierce and implacable enmity, wild resistance, and the lust of power, and such like."[104] As long as the warrior exercises self-control and avoids excess, warfare can be virtuous.[105] Augustine then states that the purpose of a just war is to deal out retribution for such evildoing: "and it is generally to *punish* these things, when force is required to *inflict the punishment* that, in obedience to God or some lawful authority, good men undertake wars."[106] Augustine thus understood just war as a punitive activity serving a moral purpose, a logical extension of the natural prerogative of the state to deal out retribution against evildoers, enemies, and rebels in order to secure the peace. In the *Summa Theologiae* Aquinas defines three criteria for just war: "proper authority," "just cause," and "right intention." Quoting Augustine, he defines "just cause" for war explicitly in terms of the moral purpose of retributive punishment:

> Secondly, a just cause is required, namely, that those who are attacked, should be attacked *because they deserve it* on account of some fault. Wherefore, Augustine says, "A just war is wont to be described as one that *avenges wrongs,* when a nation or state *has to be punished,* for refusing to make amends for the wrongs inflicted by its subjects, or to restore what it has seized unjustly."[107]

In the classic tradition from Cicero to Augustine to Aquinas, then, a just war is essentially a retributive war that "avenges wrongs" and "inflicts punishment" on evildoers.[108]

104. Augustine, *Reply to Faustus,* XXII, 74. Aquinas, *Summa Theologiae,* II-II, Q. 40, Art. 1, follows suit, citing this text to identify the evil in warfare with "wicked intention."

105. We thus observe a striking parallel between Augustine's view of punishment and his view of war: the retributive element in each, despite being contrary to the gospel, is not inherently sinful; rather, what makes punishment or war sinful is vice or excess that corrupts the moral purpose of dealing just deserts.

106. Augustine, *Reply to Faustus,* XXII, 74, emphasis added.

107. Aquinas, *Summa Theologiae,* II-II, Q. 40, Art. 1, in *On Law,* p. 221, emphasis added. Francisco Suarez (seventeenth century) follows Thomas in defining "just cause" for war in terms of retribution — punishment of wrongdoing. Suarez's writing on "just war" is excerpted in Holmes, *War and Christian Ethics,* pp. 199-225; see esp. pp. 205-7.

108. Recently, there has arisen a debate among scholars concerning the proper understanding of "just war." Some, citing the U.S. Catholic Bishops' 1983 pastoral letter *The Challenge of Peace* and 1993 reflection "The Harvest of Justice Is Sown in Peace," contend that "just war" is essentially *defensive* war, premised on a "presumption of nonviolence." Others, looking back to the classical tradition, contend that "just war" is premised on a "presumption for justice." The exchange between Paul J. Griffiths and George Weigel, "Just War: An Exchange," *First Things* 122 (April 2002), 31-36, is representative of this debate, with Griffiths taking the former position and Weigel the latter. Concerning the classical tradition from Cicero to Augustine to Aquinas, Weigel is correct: "just war" is essentially *retributive* war, premised on the presumption that the state is justified in avenging its honor against its enemies and dealing out punishment upon

3.3.3. Pax Americana: *Victory over the Enemy*

The ancient imperial way of thinking about peace arcs across the centuries through Christendom into the present time of the War on Terror. In his sermon at Washington National Cathedral on September 14, 2001, President Bush announced his intent to wage war against al-Qaeda and terrorists worldwide, pledging to "answer these attacks and rid the world of evil." The bombing of Afghanistan was meant to avenge or pay back ("answer") the terrorist attacks of 9/11. Addressing the nation and Congress on September 20, 2001, President Bush declared war in terms of executing retribution upon the enemies of America: "Our grief has turned to anger, and anger to resolution. Whether we bring our enemies to justice, or bring justice to our enemies, justice will be done." Later in his address, the President characterized a military response to the terrorist attacks in explicitly punitive terms: "The civilized world is rallying to America's side. They understand that if this terror goes unpunished, their own cities, their own citizens may be next."[109] The President's words echo those of Cicero, Augustine, and Aquinas: the War on Terror was to be a just war in the classic sense, an essentially retributive war — intended, first and foremost, to avenge harm and punish evildoing.

The dominant idea of "peace through victory" has shaped the post-9/11 rhetoric concerning the War on Terror. According to its architects and apologists, this war aims to establish the *pax Americana,* a new age of global "peace and security" to be won by the strength of America through victory over the enemy — variously named "terrorists," "terrorism," or, abstractly, "terror" — that threatens civilization.[110] In President Bush's remarks on 6 November 2001, we find a clear example of the rhetoric of *pax Americana:*

> No group or nation should mistake America's intentions: We will not rest until terrorist groups of global reach have been found, have been stopped, and have been defeated. . . . No nation can be neutral in this conflict, because no civilized nation can be secure in a world threatened by terror. . . . The war

---

those that act to harm it. The recent recasting of "just war" as premised upon a "presumption of nonviolence" is a departure from the classical tradition.

109. http://www.whitehouse.gov/news/releases/2001/09/20010920-8.html.

110. The age of *pax Americana,* an age of American global dominance — militarily, politically, and economically — has been unapologetically promoted by the Project for the New American Century. Several of the self-styled "neo-conservatives" associated with the PNAC advised, officially and unofficially, the Bush Administration in the forming of its "Bush Doctrine" of pre-emptive war. See the PNAC's 1997 "Statement of Principles" (http://www.newamericancentury.org/statementofprinciples.htm), its 2001 letter to President Bush concerning the war on terrorism (http://www.newamericancentury.org/Bushletter.htm), and its 2002 memorandum on the "Bush Doctrine" (http://www.newamericancentury.org/defense-20020130.htm).

against terrorism will be won only when we combine our strengths. . . . With your help, our vision of peace and freedom will be realized. . . .[111]

In his letter prefacing the National Security Strategy of 2002, President Bush echoed the imperial slogan: "In the new world we have entered, the only path to peace and security is the path of action." In a document that sets forth a policy of acting against "emerging threats before they are fully formed," "action" denotes primarily military action. In the list of "tools" in the national "arsenal" for fighting the War on Terror, President Bush lists "military power" first, ahead of "better homeland defenses, law enforcement, intelligence, and vigorous efforts to cut off terrorist funding."[112] The "only path to peace and security" is the path of conquest of America's enemies: "America's intentions" are to seek out and "defeat" terrorist groups around the globe. "Peace and security" in the "age of terrorism" thus necessitates and justifies preemptive war against any and all "enemies of civilization" as the first line of defense (the "Bush Doctrine"). We see a common thread running through the *pax Romana* rhetoric of the ancient emperors and the *pax Americana* rhetoric of President Bush:[113] securing peace justifies and necessitates complete victory over the enemies threatening the empire/nation; and victory is achieved through overwhelming strength — military might — that defeats and destroys the enemy.[114]

111. President George W. Bush, Remarks to the Warsaw Conference on Combating Terrorism, November 6, 2001: http://www.whitehouse.gov/news/releases/2001/11/20011106-2.html.

112. President George W. Bush, "The National Security Strategy of the United States of America," reprinted as an appendix in Avram, *Anxious about Empire*, pp. 187-215.

113. Neo-conservative supporters of the new *pax Americana* would prefer the term "hegemony" rather than "empire" to characterize their vision of American global dominance. See Kimberly Kagan, "Hegemony, Not Empire: How the Pax Americana Differs from the Pax Romana," *The Weekly Standard*, vol. 7, issue 33, May 6, 2002. The disanalogies between ancient Rome and modern America that Kagan mentions notwithstanding, the foreign policy shaped by the "Bush Doctrine" does share a vision of "peace and security" in common with the Roman Empire. Kagan's 2002 attempt to differentiate the *pax Americana* from the *pax Romana* was largely belied by the 2003 U.S. invasion and subsequent occupation of Iraq. For a non-ideological and unapologetic declaration and defense of American *imperium* without borders, see Robert D. Kaplan, "Imperial Grunts," *The Atlantic Monthly*, October 2005, http://www.theatlantic.com/doc/200510/kaplan-us-special-forces. Kaplan also produced a film for PBS, "Inside America's Empire," http://www.pbs.org/weta/crossroads/about/show_inside_americas_empire.html.

114. We should note here that a change of administration in the U.S. government does not necessarily mean a change in either rhetoric or goals: "We will not apologize for our way of life, nor will we waver in its defense, and for those who seek to advance their aims by inducing terror and slaughtering innocents we say to you now that our spirit is stronger and cannot be broken. You cannot outlast us, and we will defeat you" (President Barack H. Obama, Inaugural Address, January 20, 2009).

3.3.4. Pax Christi: *Dying for the Enemy*

The way of the cross is a stumbling block to the dominant idea of the age — whether the ancient age of *pax Romana* or the contemporary age of *pax Americana* — concerning "the things that make for peace." For the peacemaking cross of Jesus Christ stands in stark contrast to the "peacemaking" violence of empire. Caesar makes peace by war that conquers the enemies of the empire. Christ makes peace by love that dies for the enemies of God. At the cross, instead of achieving salvation and peace by defeating and destroying human enemies, Jesus saves humanity by willingly and humbly, in obedience to God, suffering death at his enemies' hands.

To those who associate "peace" with "strength" and "victory," the voluntary, non-retaliatory, other-cheek-turning cross of Jesus Christ must surely appear as "weakness" and "foolishness" (1 Cor 1:18-25). As if to confirm this very point, someone wrote in a recent letter to a local newspaper:

> What is there to gain by turning the other cheek to those who embrace what is evil? Terrorists have no desire to live in peace with anyone who will not bow to their will. If we turn the other cheek to those who fill their lives with the things of evil, then we only display weakness and ignorance. However, if we prohibit them from striking us, by means of superior force, technique, or strategy, then they scurry away. . . .[115]

While it may be noble to die for the salvation of the empire/nation, there is nothing virtuous or honorable in "turning the other cheek" and thereby potentially accepting death at the hands of the enemy; to do so would only let evil win the battle and thus "display weakness and ignorance." Imperial peace, *real* peace, is made by striking one's enemies first with "superior force" — preemptive war! In the worldly mind-set of *pax Romana* and *pax Americana,* to allow oneself to be struck down by the enemy rather than striking down the enemy, as does Jesus, is the ultimate weakness and stupidity, antithetical to the "peacemaking" that "saves" the empire/nation. Indeed, not only does Jesus die voluntarily at his enemies' hands, but Jesus actually dies *for* his enemies (Rom 5:6-10). This was a scandal to the Greco-Roman philosophical ideal of dying voluntarily only for "one's own" — family or friends, city or country (cf. v. 7).[116]

115. Tony Guthrie, "U.S. Can't 'Turn the Other Cheek' to Terrorists," *The Elkhart Truth,* p. A4, November 25, 2006.

116. Martin Hengel, *The Atonement: The Origins of the Doctrine in the New Testament* (Philadelphia: Fortress Press, 1981), pp. 6-18, compares and contrasts the New Testament witness to Jesus' death "for us" with Greco-Roman examples of vicarious, voluntary deaths. Socrates testified before the jury that he would die in obedience to God and for the good of Athens rather than commit injustice or abandon philosophy to save his life. But not even the noble Socrates makes a virtue of dying for one's enemies (cf. Plato, *Apology*).

If we are to see the cross of Jesus Christ as the powerful revelation of God's way of peacemaking, therefore, it will be necessary to achieve another "gestalt shift" that overcomes the dominant way of thinking about peace. We need to allow the cross to reveal the unexpected: the peacemaking of God that gains victory over evil, not through overwhelming violence, whether retaliatory or preemptive, against human enemies, but through suffering love that destroys enmity and reconciles enemies.

CHAPTER 4

A Biblical Vocabulary for Salvation, Justice, and Peace

God rose up to establish judgment,
to save all the oppressed of the earth.

PSALM 76:9

The effect of righteousness will be peace.

ISAIAH 32:17

4.1. Justice and Peace Are Big Words

In order that our seeing and thinking about justice and peace be transformed by the revelation of the cross, our language, too, must be transformed. Our words "justice" and "peace" inherited through the Greco-Roman tradition are too small to encompass God's justice and peace revealed through "the law and the prophets" as well as the life and death of Jesus Christ. In common usage, "justice" can mean as little as "payback," without any attention to the needs of the individuals concerned (e.g., dignity, protection, and provision) or the quality of relationships of those between whom "justice" is done (whether merciful and faithful), much less the overall rightness of the "just" situation (e.g., systemic matters of power and resource distribution). Similarly, "peace" can mean as little as "absence of war" or "cessation of conflict," without any attention to the well-being of those that are "at peace" (e.g., bodily and spiritual health) or to the presence of justice between those who are "at peace" (whether in right relationship), much less to the wholeness of the "peaceful" situation (e.g., the flourishing of community life). Thankfully, the biblical words for "justice" (He-

59

brew *mišpāt* and *ṣᵉdāqāh*, Greek *dikaiosynē*) and "peace" (Hebrew *šālôm* and Greek *eirēnē*) do comprise all these meanings, and more.[1]

Christopher Marshall observes how righteousness, justice, and peace, taken together, name the holistic relationship that God wills for his covenant people:

> To be righteous is to be faithful to the law of the covenant-keeping God and thus to treat fellow members of the covenant community with justice. To be unrighteous is to act in ways that break the covenant. The central concern of biblical law was the creation of *shalom,* a state of soundness or "all-rightness" within the community. The law provided a pattern for living in covenant, for living in *shalom.* Specific laws were considered to be just, not because they correspond to some abstract ethical norm or reflected the will of the king or protected the welfare of the state, but because they sustained *shalom* within the community.[2]

Perry Yoder also observes that *shalom* is the basic biblical word that encompasses the Bible's holistic vision of salvation, justice, and peace. *Shalom* is the name for the situation that is "all-right," in which everything is "as it ought to be." *Shalom* includes the presence of physical well-being as well as the absence of physical threats, the presence of social justice as well as the absence of political oppression, the presence of integrity as well as the absence of deceit.[3]

4.2. Righteousness and Justice Belong Together

Not only are our common words "justice" and "peace" too small, but the categories in which we employ these terms are often too narrow. Protestant ethics has tended to draw a sharp distinction between personal ethics and social justice, such that personal behavior and social issues are considered as belonging to separate spheres and as judged according to different standards. Accordingly, one hears a distinction made between "righteousness" and "justice," the former connoting *personal* righteousness and the latter *social* justice. Our usual discourse thus tends to consider moral uprightness (integrity, honesty, loyalty, etc.) as one thing, "putting things right" in response to injustice (say, discrimination, exploitation, or oppression) as quite another. Assuming such a distinc-

---

1. See Perry B. Yoder, *Shalom: The Bible's Word for Salvation, Justice, and Peace* (Nappanee, IN: Evangel Publishing House, 1987); Willard M. Swartley, *Covenant of Peace: The Missing Peace in New Testament Theology and Ethics* (Grand Rapids, MI: Eerdmans Publishing, 2006), pp. 27-52, esp. pp. 30 and 41; and Chris Marshall, *The Little Book of Biblical Justice: A Fresh Approach to the Bible's Teachings on Justice* (Intercourse, PA: Good Books, 2005), pp. 10-21.

2. Christopher D. Marshall, *Beyond Retribution: A New Testament Vision for Justice, Crime, and Punishment* (Grand Rapids, MI: Eerdmans Publishing, 2001), pp. 47-48.

3. Yoder, *Shalom,* pp. 10-23.

tion, one can be righteous within one's person while ignoring the demands of justice from one's neighbor. This might then be followed by the observation that the New Testament speaks almost exclusively about "righteousness" — such that the teaching of Jesus and exhortations of Paul are said to commend only maintaining righteousness (moral integrity) in personal conduct but not seeking justice in the social arena. Here we can be misled by traditions of translation that have narrowed the meaning of biblical words to fit our modern worldview, which is characterized by a relatively sharp distinction between private and public spheres. The biblical world and its words, however, do not segregate personal life and social life into separate spheres.

In the biblical worldview, in contrast to the Greco-Roman worldview, righteousness/justice is both a personal and a relational concept.[4] James Dunn:

> In the typical Greek worldview, "righteousness" is an idea or ideal against which the individual and individual action can be measured. Contemporary English usage reflects this ancient mind-set when it continues to use such expressions as "Justice must be satisfied." In contrast, in Hebrew thought "righteousness" is a more relational concept — "righteousness" as the meeting of obligations laid upon the individual by the relationship of which he or she is part.[5]

Personal righteousness is thus inseparable from covenantal relationship. Marshall:

> . . . the Hebrew idea of righteousness is *comprehensively relational.* It is not a private attribute that an individual can have on her or his own, independent of anyone else. It is something that one has specifically in one's relationships as a social being. Righteousness is, at heart, the fulfillment of the demands of a relationship, whether this relationship is with other human beings or with God. For this reason, righteousness language frequently appears in covenant-making contexts, for "covenant" was Israel's term for a committed relationship. Righteousness in this setting is the wholehearted loyalty of both parties to the demands of the covenant relationship.[6]

God, of course, is the ultimate One who "does justice" and "keeps faith" — as both maker of heaven and earth and maker of covenant — by fulfilling his obli-

---

4. For general background of "righteousness" in the biblical canon, see K. L. Onesti and M. T. Baruch, "Righteousness, Righteousness of God," in Gerald F. Hawthorne, Ralph P. Martin, and Daniel G. Reid, eds., *Dictionary of Paul and His Letters* (Downers Grove, IL: InterVarsity Press, 1993), pp. 827-37.

5. James D. G. Dunn, *The Theology of Paul the Apostle* (Grand Rapids, MI: Eerdmans Publishing, 1998), p. 341.

6. Marshall, *Beyond Retribution,* p. 47, emphasis original.

gations toward the oppressed and poor, the prisoner and the blind, the lowly and the stranger, the widow and the orphan (Ps 146:5-9). God, therefore, *is* the Righteous One. Again, Dunn:

> For the righteousness of God, in line with the understanding of "righteousness" above, denotes God's fulfillment of the obligations he took upon himself in creating humankind and particularly in the calling of Abraham and the choosing of Israel to be his people. . . . It should be equally evident why God's *righteousness* could be understood as God's *faithfulness* to his people. For his righteousness was simply the fulfillment of his covenant obligation as Israel's God in delivering, saving, and vindicating Israel, despite Israel's own failure.[7]

Thus, whereas Greco-Roman justice measures the righteousness of an individual or action against a mathematical standard,[8] biblical justice measures the righteousness of an individual or action against God: God's faithful and true acts of covenant loyalty and steadfast love are the measure of righteousness.[9]

The Hebrew words *mišpāt* and *ṣᵉdāqāh* — usually translated "justice" ("judgment" in the KJV) and "righteousness," respectively — are often paired together in biblical poetry, showing that the personal and the social, the ethical and the political, are inseparable in the covenant context (cf. Pss 33:5; 36:6; 72:1-2; Isa 1:21, 27; 5:7; 9:7; 11:4; 16:5; 28:17; 32:16; 56:1; 59:9, 14; Jer 22:13, 15).[10] The Psalms proclaim that "righteousness *(ṣᵉdāqāh)* and justice *(mišpāt)*" together comprise a single "foundation of [God's] throne" (Ps 97:2) and that the God who has "executed justice *(mišpāt)* and righteousness *(ṣᵉdāqāh)*" on behalf of Israel is the Holy One worthy of praise and worship (Ps 99:3-5). Likewise, Isaiah depicts justice and righteousness not only as the foundation of God's rule (Isa 9:7) but also as the expression of God's holiness: "But the LORD of hosts is exalted by justice *(mišpāt),* and the Holy God shows himself holy by righteousness *(ṣᵉdāqāh)*" (Isa 5:16). And the Holy God, Isaiah declares, expects his covenant people to manifest the same holy character of justice and righteousness in its community life: "For the vineyard of the LORD of hosts is the house of Is-

---

7. Dunn, *Theology of Paul,* p. 342, emphasis original.

8. Cf. Aristotle, *Nicomachean Ethics,* V, who defines justice by arithmetic and geometric ratios.

9. The relational, covenantal aspect of righteousness was gradually lost in translation as *ṣᵉdāqāh* was rendered in Greek by *dikaiosynē,* which was then rendered in Latin by *iustitia,* resulting in a notion of righteousness limited to legal justice (giving each his due). See Onesti and Baruch, "Righteousness, Righteousness of God," pp. 828-29.

10. On the *hendiadys* "righteousness and justice" in Hebrew Scripture, see Moshe Weinfeld, *Social Justice in Ancient Israel and in the Ancient Near East* (Jerusalem: Magnes Press, 1995), pp. 25-44. As Weinfeld shows, "righteousness and justice" is the task of both the individual and the king (pp. 45-56 and 215-30).

rael, and the people of Judah are his pleasant planting; he expected justice *(mišpāt)*, but saw bloodshed; righteousness *(ṣᵉdāqāh)*, but heard a cry" (Isa 5:7). Amos, too, declared that the divine character is to be reflected in the community life of the covenant people, whom he calls to return to the way of the Lord by doing justice and righteousness: "But let justice *(mišpāt)* roll down like waters, and righteousness *(ṣᵉdāqāh)* like an ever-flowing stream" (Amos 5:24).

The Greek translation of the Old Testament typically translated the Hebrew *mišpāt* with the Greek *krisis* or *krima* ("judgment") and *ṣᵉdāqāh* with *dikaiosynē*. Not surprisingly, therefore, modern New Testament translations tend to translate *dikaiosynē* as "righteousness" with the intended meaning of moral integrity or uprightness. Yet, *dikaiosynē* is also the Greek word for "justice." In *The Republic,* Plato could use *dikaiosynē* to name both the "perfectly righteous person," who is upright in all ways and possesses a soul in harmony with itself, as well as the "perfectly just city," which is ordered rightly in all aspects for the good of all citizens. For Plato, *dikaiosynē* is the characteristic excellence ("virtue," *aretē*) of *both* the good soul and the good city.[11] This one Greek word, then, can include both the social and the personal dimensions of ethics, both *mišpāt* and *ṣᵉdāqāh* — "putting things right" and moral integrity. So we should not restrict the meaning of *dikaiosynē* in the New Testament to merely personal moral integrity. We may thus read the beatitudes, "Blessed are those who hunger and thirst for *justice,* for they will be filled. . . . Blessed are those who are persecuted for the sake of *justice,* for theirs is the kingdom of heaven" (Matt 5:6, 10).[12]

Paul's expression "righteousness of God" *(dikaiosynē theou),* which we will often render as "justice of God," also includes both God's personal integrity and God's justice-doing.[13] Paul thinks of the justice of God against the background

11. Plato, *Republic,* IV.

12. Now, it does not follow that "righteousness" and "justice" are both implied by every instance of *dikaiosynē* in the New Testament. Sometimes "righteousness" in a narrower sense is the intended meaning. In Matt 3:15, Jesus instructs John to baptize him, "for it is proper for us in this way to fulfill all righteousness *(dikaiosynē)."* Here *dikaiosynē* evidently means something like "doing what is proper, or according to what is prescribed, or things done in the right way." In other places *dikaiosynē* can mean "righteousness" in the sense of Torah observance. That, evidently, is what Jesus means when he says, "Unless your righteousness *(dikaiosynē)* exceeds that of the scribes and Pharisees, you will never enter the kingdom of heaven" (Matt 5:20; cf. vv. 17-19). Later, Jesus describes "the righteousness of the scribes and Pharisees" when preaching in the temple: "Woe to you, scribes and Pharisees, hypocrites! For you tithe mint, dill, and cumin, and have neglected the weightier matters of the law: justice *(krisis)* and mercy and faithfulness" (Matt 23:23). The implication is that "righteousness" in the sense of strict legal observance falls short of the justice God desires. The righteousness after which we are to hunger and thirst (Matt 5:6) includes doing justice and mercy for the poor and afflicted.

13. See the helpful discussions in: Dunn, *Theology of Paul,* pp. 340-45; N. T. Wright, *What Saint Paul Really Said: Was Paul of Tarsus the Real Founder of Christianity?* (Grand Rapids, MI: Eerdmans Publishing, 1997), pp. 95-111; Enrique Nardoni, *Rise Up, O Judge: A Study of Justice in*

of "the law and the prophets" (Rom 3:21).[14] Accordingly, "righteousness of God" refers to both God's characteristic loyalty or truth (God's faithfulness, reliability, and trustworthiness) and God's "putting things right" (God's action to oppose evil and do justice to bring about the salvation he has promised).[15] "Righteousness language in the Hebrew Bible," as Chris Marshall emphasizes, "is thus *action* language as well as relational language."[16]

Both of these aspects of God's righteousness are linked to God's steadfast love and saving grace, which is quite different from our common way of thinking about God and justice. Within the retributive paradigm, one thinks of grace as a substitute for (or the opposite of) justice: if to do justice is to render the penalty "due," then to be gracious toward another is to withhold the penalty "due." The penal substitution doctrine of atonement thus understands grace as substituting for justice in correlation with Jesus substituting for us through the cross: God dispenses grace to us instead of the justice that is our due by dispensing our just due to Jesus instead, punishing him for our sins in our place. In this way, God is both gracious (withholding the penalty of sin due to us) and just (dispensing the penalty of sin upon Jesus instead of us) through the cross. Paul, however, declares that God's justice not only includes grace but is manifested precisely in grace: God does justice concerning us (we are "justified" — *dikaioumenoi*), not according to what we deserve, but "by his grace as a gift" (Rom 3:24). Far from the grace of God being a substitute for the justice of God, God's act of justice in working redemption through Christ *is* an act of grace: God does justice by means of grace.[17] That God does justice by means of, not instead of, grace entails that the justice of God cannot be understood simply according to the retributive paradigm. Thus, Marshall: "The justice of God is not primarily or normatively a retributive justice or a distributive justice but a restorative or reconstructive justice, a saving action by God that recreates *shalom* and makes things right."[18] Similarly, Richard Hays: "The witness of the Law and the Prophets to the righteousness of God is not merely, as Christians have sometimes strangely sup-

the Biblical World (Peabody, MA: Hendrickson Publishers, 2004), pp. 266-70; and A. Katherine Grieb, *The Story of Romans: A Narrative Defense of God's Righteousness* (Louisville: Westminster John Knox, 2002), pp. 20-25. Concerning the various debates in Christian history over how to interpret "the righteousness of God" in Paul, see Onesti and Baruch, "Righteousness, Righteousness of God."

14. Cf. Richard B. Hays, *Echoes of Scripture in the Letters of Paul* (New Haven, CT: Yale University Press, 1989), pp. 34-83.

15. We will examine God's justice in relation to covenant loyalty in Chapter 21.

16. Marshall, *Beyond Retribution*, p. 50, emphasis original.

17. Cf. Onesti and Baruch, "Righteousness, Righteousness of God," p. 831. Likewise, Marshall, *Beyond Retribution*, p. 50: "God's justice and God's mercy stand, significantly, in parallel, not in opposition."

18. Marshall, *Beyond Retribution*, p. 53; cf. Yoder, *Shalom*, pp. 34-37.

posed, a witness concerning a severe retributive justice; rather, it is a witness concerning God's gracious saving power."[19]

4.3. Justice and Peace Belong Together

Our common usage also segregates "justice" and "peace" into distinct categories. For us "justice" and "peace" tend to pull in opposite directions, such that we sometimes think "justice" must be sacrificed in order to "make peace," or vice versa. In the biblical world, to the contrary, these words are intimately related: there can be no peace without justice/righteousness, and vice versa (cf. Isa 9:7; 60:17; Pss 72:7; 85:10).[20]

Isaiah proclaims that the fruit of justice and righteousness is peace: "Then justice *(mišpāt)* will dwell in the wilderness, and righteousness *(ṣᵉdāqāh)* abide in the fruitful field. The effect of righteousness *(ṣᵉdāqāh)* will be peace *(šālôm)*, and the result of righteousness *(ṣᵉdāqāh)* quietness and trust forever" (Isa 32:16-17). Likewise, knowing the way of peace requires walking the way of justice: "The way of peace *(šālôm)* they do not know, and there is no justice *(mišpāt)* in their paths. Their roads they have made crooked; no one who walks in them knows peace *(šālôm)*" (Isa 59:8). Zechariah proclaimed similarly that justice is the substance of peace: "render in your gates judgments *(mišpāt)* that are true and make for peace *(šālôm)*" (Zech 8:16).

The New Testament also connects justice and peace. While Isaiah and Zechariah proclaimed that peace is the fruit of justice, James teaches that the inverse is true, that justice is the fruit of peacemaking: "And a harvest of justice *(dikaiosynē)* is sown in peace *(eirēnē)* by those who make peace *(eirēnēn)*" (Jas 3:18). Paul links justice and peace together in relation to the saving work of God through the cross of Jesus Christ: "Therefore, having been put right *(dikaiōthentes)* by faithfulness we have peace *(eirēnēn)* with God through our Lord Jesus Christ" (Rom 5:1, my translation). Paul also sees justice and peace as characteristic of God's reign: "For the kingdom of God is not food or drink but justice *(dikaiosynē)* and peace *(eirēnē)* and joy in the Holy Spirit" (Rom 14:17).

4.4. Salvation, Justice, and Peace Belong Together

Protestant thinking, following a sharp distinction between "grace" and "works," has tended to separate salvation (soteriology) from ethics. Accordingly, Protestant categories have tended to segregate "salvation" from "justice" and "peace":

19. Hays, *Echoes of Scripture*, p. 52.
20. Cf. Yoder, *Shalom*.

receiving salvation by grace through faith is one thing, working for justice and peace quite another. Yet, again, the biblical world and its words show an intimate connection between the salvation (Hebrew *yᵉšûʿāh*, Greek *sōtēria*) of God and the justice/righteousness and peace of God (cf. Pss 71:15; 85:8-11; 98:2; Isa 51:4-6; 60:17-18).

Two important examples are found in Isaiah. The prophet, surveying the ruins of Jerusalem, receives a vision of a messenger who proclaims the time for God to return to Zion to redeem his people and establish his kingdom: "How beautiful upon the mountains are the feet of the messenger who announces peace *(šālôm)*, who brings good news, who announces salvation *(yᵉšûʿāh)*, who says to Zion, 'Your God reigns'" (Isa 52:7). The gospel of God *is* peace and salvation. Later the prophet, surveying a situation of oppression, violence and bloodshed, sees a people who do not know the way of peace because there is no justice in the land (Isa 59:1-8). The prophet then looks in hope for justice from God: "Therefore justice *(mišpāt)* is far from us, and righteousness *(sᵉdāqāh)* does not reach us. . . . We wait for justice *(mišpāt)*, but there is none; for salvation *(yᵉšûʿāh)*, but it is far from us" (Isa 59:9, 11). A third important example is found in Jeremiah, whose prophecy of the messianic age places the "justice and righteousness" of God in parallel with the salvation and security of God's people: "In those days and at that time I will cause a righteous Branch to spring up for David; and he shall execute justice *(mišpāt)* and righteousness *(sᵉdāqāh)* in the land. In those days Judah will be *saved (yāšaʿ)* and Jerusalem will live in safety" (Jer 33:15-16a). Isaiah similarly envisioned God's people being saved by means of justice and righteousness: "Zion shall be redeemed by justice *(mišpāt)*, and those in her who repent, by righteousness *(sᵉdāqāh)*" (Isa 1:27).

Luke's Gospel follows the prophetic pattern of linking the salvation of God, fulfilled though the Messiah, with words and images of justice and peace. Mary's song "rejoices in God my Savior *(sōtēr)*," who acts to invert unjust orders on behalf of the poor and oppressed (Luke 1:47, 52-53). The canticle of Zechariah praises God for raising up a "Mighty Savior *(sōtēr)*," whose redemption enables us to "serve [God] . . . in holiness and righteousness *(dikaiosynē)*" and who will "guide our feet into the way of peace *(eirēnē)*" (1:69, 73, 79). Jesus twice manifests God's saving power — by forgiving sin and healing disease — and proclaims God's peace: "Your faith has saved *(sesōken)* you; go in peace *(eirēnē)*" (7:50; 8:48).[21] And after Zacchaeus has shown mercy to the poor and

21. Bible versions often render the exact same Greek sentence in these two texts *(hē pistis sou sesōken se — poreuou eis eirēnēn)* with different translations of the Greek verb *sesōken:* "saved" in 7:50 but "made whole" (KJV), "made well" (NRSV), or "healed" (NIV) in 8:48. The root verb *sōzō* means both "save" and "heal," but the variation in translation obscures the evident emphasis in Luke that forgiveness of sin and healing of disease are signs of a single messianic salvation that brings God's peace to people.

done justice for the those he has wronged, Jesus proclaims, "Today salvation *(sōtēria)* has come to this house" (19:9).

Paul, too, follows the prophetic pattern linking God's salvation to God's justice and peace. His opening declaration in Romans explicitly links together the salvation and justice of God: ". . . the gospel is the power of God for salvation *(sōtēria)*. . . . For in it the justice of God *(dikaiosynē theou)* is revealed . . ." (Rom 1:16-17). "Here God's righteousness and the gospel (God's saving work in Christ) are virtually synonymous."[22] Paul goes on in Romans to announce that the justice of God is made manifest "through the redemption that is in Christ Jesus" (3:21-24). Paul also invokes Isaiah 59 at Ephesians 6,[23] placing justice, peace, and salvation in order as essential elements of "the armor of God" which the faithful are to take up in their holy resistance against evil: "Stand therefore, . . . and put on the breastplate of righteousness *(dikaiosynē)*. As shoes for your feet put on whatever will make you ready to proclaim the gospel of peace *(eirēnē)*. . . . Take the helmet of salvation *(sōtēria)* . . ." (Eph 6:14-15, 17).

To bridge this gap between the comprehensive and interrelated meanings of the biblical words on the one hand and the narrow meaning of our common words and the restrictive categories of our inherited thinking on the other, we will supplement or qualify our ordinary words "salvation," "justice," and "peace" to add the biblical dimensions of meaning: "saving justice," "covenant justice," "liberating justice," "redemptive justice," "saving peace," "reconciling peace," "enemy-loving peace," "cruciform peace."

---

22. Onesti and Baruch, "Righteousness, Righteousness of God," p. 832.

23. Regarding the connection between Isaiah 59 and Ephesians 6, see Thomas R. Yoder Neufeld, *Ephesians* (Believers Church Bible Commentary; Scottdale, PA: Herald Press, 2002), pp. 308-10.

CODA

The Cross, Atonement, and Nonviolence

As is evident already and will become clearer by the end of this book, shifting to a cruciform paradigm of Christian mission leads us to renounce violence in Christian justice-doing and peacemaking. But we must be careful not to get matters in the wrong order: the cross comes before nonviolence. The cross is not merely the historical outcome of Jesus choosing nonviolence in the face of the evil powers of this world; nor is it only a symbol of the nonviolent way of Christian discipleship. The cross is more than nonviolence. The cross of Christ reveals the way that God does justice and makes peace through acts of costly faithfulness for the salvation of humanity.

Theologian J. Denny Weaver proposes a theology of the cross premised upon the ethic of nonviolence.[1] The aim of Weaver's project is twofold: to expose the violence at the heart of the traditional theory of atonement that has dominated Christian thinking and show how that theory implicitly sanctions violence in various social contexts, and to develop an alternative theory of atonement premised upon nonviolence, which he calls "narrative Christus Victor." The key historical part of his argument is that the shift from the "Christus Victor" atonement theology of the patristic period to the "satisfaction" atonement theology of the medieval period paralleled the "Constantinian shift" in the church during the fourth century and after — a shift from a marginal church to a dominating church, from a church persecuted to a persecuting church, from a church committed to peace to a church carrying out crusades. That is, Weaver's argument goes, the theological shift regarding atonement went hand-in-hand with an ethical shift — from principled pacifism to just war — which in turn reflected the ecclesiological shift begotten by the (unholy) synthesis of church and empire, the "church triumphant." Weaver also argues

---

1. J. Denny Weaver, *The Nonviolent Atonement* (Grand Rapids, MI: Eerdmans, 2001).

that the ecumenical councils of Nicaea and Chalcedon, by importing Greek philosophical formulas into the Christian creed to express orthodox Christology, also facilitated the shift in atonement theology.[2] Reversing this ecclesiological shift entails reversing the shift in the church's thinking about both ethics and salvation in order to recover the purer — more biblical, truer to Jesus — perspective of the early church. Hence Weaver's retrieval of the ancient "Christus Victor" theory of atonement — a theology of salvation, he argues, that fits both a pacifist ethic and a humble ecclesiology.

Weaver's arguments and theory of atonement comprise a substantive contribution to contemporary theology and merit serious consideration. As is clear already, I strongly sympathize with one of the main thrusts of his book. Weaver is right in challenging Christians to become conscious of the ways in which we have uncritically adopted the unredeemed patterns of this world — especially concerning violence — into our theology and ethics. I also quite agree with his emphasis on the need to "keep salvation ethical," to avoid divorcing salvation from ethics. Nonetheless, I have four concerns with Weaver's "nonviolent atonement" — rhetorical, ethical, theological, and historical.[3]

"Nonviolent Atonement": Rhetorical Critique

One may reasonably ask of Weaver's argument: What is the rationale for shifting backward in our thinking from post-Constantinian, post-Nicene Christianity to pre-Constantinian, ante-Nicene Christianity? Weaver assumes that the early church was essentially right — about Jesus, about ethics, and about salvation — and the medieval church went astray. One might find this a plausible argument on its face and readily agree with it, and some Christians do. But what if one does not already share Weaver's perspective? Those Christians thinking from the latter side of the "Constantinian shift" will, quite reasonably, want to be convinced regarding why they should change their thinking.[4]

Unfortunately, such convincing is not on Weaver's agenda. Weaver sets his "narrative Christus Victor" theory against the background of the cosmic warfare of good and evil as depicted in Revelation.[5] Weaver then sketches the main storyline of the Gospels, which "demonstrates that the narrative of Jesus as dis-

2. Weaver, *Nonviolent Atonement*, pp. 81-96.

3. My thanks to J. Denny Weaver for extensive email correspondence in the summer and fall of 2010, in which he provided helpful clarifications of his view concerning several of the issues discussed below. My critique of his view reflects the substance of that correspondence as well as the material in his book.

4. Cf. Hans Boersma, *Violence, Hospitality, and the Cross: Reappropriating the Atonement Tradition* (Grand Rapids, MI: Baker Academic, 2004), pp. 154-58, who is skeptical of Weaver's "Constantinian Fall" model of church history.

5. Weaver, *Nonviolent Atonement*, pp. 20-33.

played in the Gospels fits within the universal and cosmic story of the confrontation of reign of God and rule of Satan depicted in Revelation."[6] What, though, of the major premise that defines his theological perspective on atonement, the ethical principle of nonviolence, the validity of which he assumes beforehand and which then guides his exegesis of Scripture? Where one might have expected an argument, Weaver gives the reader presumption:

> My discussion . . . makes clear that this atonement motif [narrative Christus Victor] *presumes* nonviolence and is in fact meaningless apart from that *presumption.* . . . The book provides an alternative reading of the history of doctrine that is an extension of the biblical interpretation that *presumed* nonviolence.[7]

Weaver, moreover, begins the concluding summary of his main argument with this claim: "At the most obvious level, it is apparent that the story of Jesus depicted in the Gospels is a story of nonviolence and nonviolent resistance."[8] Proceeding to summarize his main argument, Weaver again makes reference to "the nonviolent assumption" and "an assumption of nonviolence." In other words, his argument goes, the major premise of the argument is self-evidently true — it is "obvious," "apparent" to anyone who has ever read the Gospels. The raison d'être of Weaver's book, however, belies this claim: for most of seventeen centuries (post-Constantine) it has been anything but "obvious" or "apparent" to the majority of Christians that "the story of Jesus in the Gospels is a story of nonviolence." Were it actually self-evident to any reasonable reader that nonviolence is the essence of the Gospel story, it is unlikely that the very shifts in Christian polity, ethics, and theology that concern Weaver would have taken place — such that the majority of Christians would still subscribe to a pacifist ethic and a "Christus Victor" theology, thus obviating his book! Ironically, then, Weaver's account of atonement theology premised on a "presumption of nonviolence" will be least convincing rhetorically for those readers (one might expect) he would most want to persuade.[9]

---

6. Weaver, *Nonviolent Atonement*, pp. 34-46.
7. Weaver, *Nonviolent Atonement*, p. 13, emphasis added.
8. Weaver, *Nonviolent Atonement*, p. 96.
9. Even the "choir" to whom Weaver is preaching (viz., Anabaptists/Mennonites) has been less than convinced by his "nonviolent atonement" perspective. See: Christopher D. Marshall, "Atonement, Violence and the Will of God: A Sympathetic Response to J. Denny Weaver's *The Nonviolent Atonement*," *Mennonite Quarterly Review* 77 (2003); Gerald W. Schlabach, "J. Denny Weaver, *The Nonviolent Atonement*," *Conrad Grebel Review* 21 (2003), 112-15; David Eagle, "Anthony Bartlett's Concept of Abyssal Compassion and the Possibility of a Truly Nonviolent Atonement," *Conrad Grebel Review* 24 (2006), 66-81; and Peter W. Martens, "The Quest for an Anabaptist Atonement: Violence and Nonviolence in J. Denny Weaver's *The Nonviolent Atonement*," *Mennonite Quarterly Review* 82 (2008), 281-311.

For sure, Weaver's account is coherent. But this should not surprise: if one presumes a principle of nonviolence, interprets the Bible consistently on that premise, and develops an atonement theology based on that biblical interpretation, then this "nonviolent atonement" theology will indeed confirm the validity of reading Jesus' life and judging church history according to nonviolence. In short, per the quotation above, Weaver's nonviolence-presuming atonement theology is premised upon a nonviolence-presuming scriptural exegesis — which will be convincing only to those that already agree with the initial presumption of nonviolence. Weaver's method of interpreting the cross thus parallels John Stott's method (Chapter 3 above), even though they articulate diverging theologies of the cross. Whereas Stott presumes the principle of retribution as the premise of his theology and reads the cross in a way that reflects back retribution (penal substitution atonement), Weaver presumes the principle of nonviolence as the premise of his theology and reads the cross in a way that reflects back nonviolence.[10]

"Nonviolent Atonement": Ethical Critique

Weaver premises his atonement theology on the ethical principle of nonviolence. Yet, as we have shown (Chapter 3), the ethical teaching of the New Testament is not nonviolence, but non-retaliation — and not non-retaliation only, of course, but also love of enemy and love of the poor. Strictly speaking, Jesus taught his disciples not to resist evildoers by retaliating and spelled out that non-resistance in examples of refusal to retaliate (Matt 5:38-41). Strange as it may seem, especially considering that the prophets repeatedly denounce "those who store up violence *(ḥāmās)*" (Amos 3:10) and condemn violence as sin along with oppression and robbery (cf. Isaiah 59; Jeremiah 22; Ezekiel 7; Habakkuk 1-2), nowhere does either Jesus or any of the Apostles teach, "Do not use violence." Following Jesus, Peter and Paul consistently teach non-retaliation, "Do not repay evil with evil" (Rom 12:17; 1 Thess 5:15; 1 Pet 3:9).

Now, what is the difference between non-retaliation and nonviolence? If I refuse to retaliate, if I do not resist evildoers by mirroring their own actions, am I not being nonviolent? Yes, to practice non-resistance/non-retaliation is to be nonviolent, but the inverse is not necessarily true: one can be nonviolent and

10. Of course, no method is completely bias-free. In order to avoid begging the question too egregiously, and so to keep the conversation open to those readers that might not agree initially with the conclusions toward which the arguments are moving, we will need to choose the beginning point of our study carefully. So, when critiquing the penal substitution doctrine of atonement in Part II, I will take the questions to be asked, the claims to be investigated, and the texts to be considered primarily from the writings of those that defend penal substitution.

still retaliate, for there are nonviolent ways of retaliating.[11] For example, I may refrain from retaliating violently against an enemy by not harming his person or property, but I can still retaliate nonviolently by a lawsuit. The first-century Jewish philosopher Philo of Alexandria interpreted the Torah's injunction against taking vengeance (Lev 19:18a) in just such terms, that one should not take the *lex talionis* into one's own hands but rather should seek retribution (financial compensation) through the legal process by the hand of the judge.[12]

Jesus' renunciation of retaliation is thus a more restrictive, more radical ethic than nonviolence. More restrictive because to renounce violence is to renounce only violent means of retaliating against evil — which leaves open nonviolent means of retaliation. Non-resistance calls us to renounce all means of retaliation, violent and nonviolent. More radical because to renounce retaliation goes to the root of the problem — the human desire for vengeance. Non-resistance leaves vengeance where it rightly belongs, with God alone (Deut 32:35; Prov 20:22; Rom 12:19).

Of course, I do not intend to suggest that the ethic of Jesus and the Apostles is somehow compatible with the practice of violence. As Paul would say, "No way!" *(mē genoito).* The way of the cross and the way of the sword are irreconcilable (see Chapter 28 below).[13] The New Testament condemns all manner of evil human practices — impiety *(asebeia),* injustice *(adikia),* and lawlessness *(anomia)* (cf. Matt 7:23; Rom 1:18; 6:19; Tit 2:12; Heb 1:9; 1 John 3:4) — that the prophets associated with violence *(ḥāmās)* and thus effectively condemns the violence by which such evil is pursued.[14] Nor do I mean to imply that an ethic of nonviolence is incompatible with New Testament teaching — far from it. Nonviolent action in response to evil is not necessarily retaliatory, of course; there are many non-retaliatory nonviolent means of responding to evil. Indeed, Jesus' three examples in his teaching can be interpreted as models of such action.[15] And Paul, while calling the church to renounce retaliation against evildoers, commissions the church to holy resistance against all forms of evil (see Chapter 35 below).

But we should understand that the New Testament teaching of the renun-

---

11. Weaver obscures this point. He includes non-resistance as one pole of the spectrum of "nonviolence" (*Nonviolent Atonement,* pp. 8-9), thus sliding over the substantive distinction that Jesus himself makes in his own teaching between retaliatory and non-retaliatory responses to evil.

12. Gordon M. Zerbe, *Non-Retaliation in Early Jewish and New Testament Texts* (London: Continuum, 1993), pp. 60-66.

13. See also Ronald J. Sider, *Christ and Violence* (Scottdale, PA: Herald Press, 1979), pp. 15-39.

14. The Hebrew word meaning "violence" *(ḥāmās)* is translated variously in the Septuagint (LXX) as "injustice" *(adikia),* "impiety" *(asebeia),* or "lawlessness" *(anomia).* This might explain why the Greek word meaning "violence" *(bia)* seldom appears in the New Testament.

15. Cf. Walter Wink, *Engaging the Powers: Discernment and Resistance in a World of Domination* (Minneapolis: Fortress Press, 1992), pp. 175-93.

ciation of retribution/retaliation goes deeper than the ethic of nonviolence. Insofar as we recognize the connection between what Jesus taught and how he
died, this makes a difference for understanding the cross. To characterize the
cross as "nonviolent," while correct as far as it goes, does not reveal the depths
of God's loving action in Christ on behalf of those who were sinners and enemies of God. As Ron Sider has put it, more than simply a witness to the weakness and folly of the sword, "the cross is the ultimate demonstration that God
deals with his enemies through suffering love."[16] Through the cross, God-in-
Christ does not simply refrain from dealing violently with human sinners.
More than this, God's gracious action in Christ through the cross, by which we
are justified and reconciled, renounces retaliation for the sake of God's covenant loyalty and justice, which seek the redemption of sinners beyond retribution for sin. The cross of Christ thus demonstrates, not simply nonviolence, but
God's retribution-transcending, sinner-redeeming, enemy-reconciling love,
justice, and peace. I thus concur with Willard Swartley:

> The issue of violence and nonviolence in relation to atonement may function
> as an ethical decoy that lures us from speaking what is most important about
> atonement: through the cross God *and* Jesus Christ in self-donation make
> peace between humans and God and between humans and humans.[17]

We might restate the point thus: Weaver is surely correct to recognize the
problem of violence in atonement theology. But the appropriate answer to
atonement theologies that imply that we are saved by violence (e.g., penal substitution) is not simply to assume that we are saved by nonviolence. For, insofar
as Jesus' death is evidently violent, such an assumption may leave us unable to
say anything positive regarding the redemptive value of the cross itself —
which, in fact, is Weaver's position: the death of Jesus on the cross is a deficit in
the economy of salvation. By presuming nonviolence as the answer to violence
in atonement theology, we may make the cross a stumbling block to ourselves,
such that we fail to see how God-in-Christ acts redemptively in response to human violence, not despite the cross, but (as Paul says) *through the cross*.[18]

An interpretation of the cross shaped by a "presumption of nonviolence"
might also miss (or dismiss) the "violence" of God's own action through the
cross. As we will see (Chapter 25), Paul depicts God's just act of forgiveness
through the cross of Christ with a startling image that is explicitly violent: God

16. Sider, *Christ and Violence*, p. 33.

17. Willard M. Swartley, *Covenant of Peace: The Missing Peace in New Testament Theology
and Ethics* (Grand Rapids, MI: Eerdmans Publishing, 2006), p. 183, n. 13, emphasis original.

18. I do not, therefore, employ "nonviolence" as a presupposed, primitive category for
naming and analyzing the salvation, justice, and peace of God revealed through the life, death,
and resurrection of Jesus.

crucifies both our transgressions and the legal demands against us (Col 2:13-14). And as we will see (Chapter 29), Paul depicts Jesus' peacemaking, reconciling work through the cross using explicitly violent images: Jesus *destroys* dividing walls and *murders* hostility (Eph 2:14-16). Beginning from a "presumption of nonviolence," one might tend to neglect the potential significance of such imagery. While the violent imagery of the cross needs to be appropriated carefully to avoid abuse, it should not be ignored. Instead of downplaying and devaluing such imagery, we place these images at the center of a cruciform paradigm of justice-doing and peacemaking. Indeed, as we will show (Chapter 25), the image of God "crucifying" the sinner-condemning law is revelatory for thinking about the implication of the cross of Christ for the practice of capital punishment. In addition, as we will show (Chapter 30), the image of Jesus' "hostility-murdering" cross is exegetically fruitful concerning the Gospel story; for one can instructively interpret Luke's narrative of the life-ministry, death, and resurrection of Jesus as a campaign of "murdering hostility."[19]

"Nonviolent Atonement": Theological Critique

My fundamental theological divergence from Weaver concerns whether the cross of Christ itself is revelatory of God's salvation or not — that is, whether the suffering and death of Jesus Christ were in some sense necessary, and whether they accomplished anything for the salvation of humanity, or not. Weaver himself denies that this is so:

> Asking who needs the death of Jesus or what the death of Jesus accomplishes for narrative Christus Victor brings a revealing point to the foreground . . . it [the death of Jesus] accomplishes nothing for the salvation of sinners, nor does it accomplish anything for the divine economy.[20]

As we emphasized in our guiding rules (Chapter 2), we affirm that the suffering and death of Jesus were integral to his messianic mission, necessary for fulfilling God's purpose in redeeming humanity from the power of sin and gaining victory over death. And as we will see (Part III), Paul depicts the cross of Jesus Christ as God's way of establishing justice and making peace — a decisive accomplishment for the salvation of humanity. It is God's distinctive revelation of salvation through the cross of Jesus Christ that shapes the Christian ethical mandate and model for justice-doing and peacemaking (Part IV).

---

19. Although I approach the question from a different angle and do not necessarily endorse his conclusions, I do share with Boersma, *Violence, Hospitality, and the Cross,* the goal of reappropriating rather than rejecting outright the violence of the cross.

20. Weaver, *Nonviolent Atonement,* p. 72.

"Nonviolent Atonement": Historical Critique

One further divergence between my view and Weaver's needs emphasis. As is evident from my first guiding principle for interpreting the cross, I diverge from Weaver concerning how to assess the orthodox faith of the apostolic church as expressed through the ecumenical councils of Nicaea, Constantinople, and Chalcedon. Weaver views the abstract formulas used to define the doctrines of the Trinity and the Incarnation in the creed of Nicaea-Constantinople ("one essence, three persons") and definition of Chalcedon ("fully God and fully human") as philosophical diversions from the gospel narrative that served imperial politics and led the medieval church to diverge from the teachings of Jesus and so sanction violence in its theology (atonement) and ethics (war). He thus sees Nicene-Chalcedonian Christology as enabling and facilitating the problem of violence in Christian tradition and so an obstacle to addressing that problem.[21] I view Nicaea and Chalcedon differently, as a faithful continuation of the New Testament and an essential (but not exhaustive) expression of Christian faith.[22]

Concerning Weaver's view on the history of doctrine, I would make four comments. First, constitutive of Weaver's negative appraisal of Nicaea and Chalcedon is his observation that the creedal formulations of Christian faith, having abstracted from the historical particularity of the Gospel narratives, are lacking in ethical content and so allow the church to separate Christ from ethics and join the sword to the cross: "The abstract categories 'man' and 'God' in these formulas allow the church to accommodate the sword and violence while still maintaining a confession about Christ at the center of its theology."[23] True, the ontological categories of the creedal formulas say nothing explicitly concerning either the moral character of God (e.g., that God is holy and just) or the ethical norm for believers (viz., that we ought to follow Christ); but it does not follow that the creedal tradition is devoid of normative substance. In fact, far from separating Christ from ethics, Nicene-Chalcedonian Christology makes a profound normative claim: if the Son is "True God from True God" and "became human" in Jesus (Nicaea), who himself is thus "Truly God and Truly human"

21. See Weaver, *Nonviolent Atonement*, pp. 92-96.

22. Concerning the historical development, biblical basis, and practical implications of the Nicene Creed, see Luke Timothy Johnson, *The Creed: What Christians Believe and Why It Matters* (New York: Doubleday, 2003). That the Nicene Creed was not an exhaustive expression of the catholic faith was the conviction of the Cappadocian bishops (Basil of Caesarea and Gregory of Nyssa), who vigorously supported and substantially contributed to the Trinitarian theology of the Nicene Creed: see Rosemary Jermann, "The Fourth-Century Cappadocian Witness," in *Faith to Creed: Ecumenical Perspectives on the Affirmation of the Apostolic Faith in the Fourth Century*, S. Mark Heim, ed. (Grand Rapids, MI: Eerdmans Publishing, 1991), pp. 83-94.

23. Weaver, *Nonviolent Atonement*, p. 94.

(Chalcedon), then Jesus is the ontologically universal and historically unique revelation of what God intended humans to be as "the image of God" and so how one is to live truly as a human being.[24] I thus find Nicene-Chalcedonian Christology to be not only fully compatible with a peace ethic but also instrumental in critiquing the role of violence in atonement theology.[25]

Second, Weaver's contention that Nicene-Chalcedonian Christology reflects imperial politics does not fit the historical facts. Although Constantine convened and presided at the Council of Nicaea, it does not follow that the Nicene Creed reflects either Constantine's theological convictions or his political agenda (viz., to ensure imperial unity by means of ecclesial unity). At that time, in fact, it was those of the Arian party (e.g., Eusebius) who enjoyed Constantine's favor and the adversaries of Arianism and defenders of orthodoxy (e.g., Athanasius) who suffered the empire's wrath. The Council rejected the pro-Arian creed drawn up by Eusebius, such that the decidedly anti-Arian formulas of the Nicene Creed — that the Son is "True God from True God, begotten not made, one in being with the Father" — reflect not the view of the emperor but the consensus of the bishops.[26] It was Arian Christology, moreover, that was amenable to the civil religion of the Roman Empire, which divinized and worshiped its emperors; for Arianism, which viewed Christ not as the eternal Son of God but as a created being of demi-god status, would have allowed the emperor to claim the same status as Christ. By affirming that the Son is eternally one and equal with the Father, a claim no emperor could match, orthodoxy not only faithfully maintained the apostolic tradition but also effectively safeguarded Christian worship from imperial manipulation. Insofar as the Nicene Creed is explicitly anti-Arian, therefore, it is effectively anti-"Constantinian."[27]

Third, Weaver's thesis that Nicene-Chalcedonian Christology enabled and

---

24. Cf. Roberta C. Bondi, "The Fourth-Century Church: The Monastic Contribution," in *Faith to Creed*, pp. 60-82.

25. I thus share the view of A. James Reimer, "Trinitarian Orthodoxy, Constantinianism, and Theology from a Radical Protestant Perspective," in *Faith to Creed*, pp. 129-61.

26. Weaver's view is based implicitly on the argument that, because the Council of Nicaea was convened by Constantine, the outcome of the council was not due to the guidance of the Holy Spirit, such that the Trinitarian orthodoxy of the Nicene Creed is only a human construct and thus lacks universal authority for the church. Weaver follows John Howard Yoder: "The doctrine is not supernatural truth. . . . It is not learning which the Holy Spirit gave to the Council Fathers of Nicaea, *because* these were bishops assembled from the whole world at the invitation from the Roman Emperor. It is valid because it reflects the serious struggle of men, within their language and their culture, with their commitment to an absolute God and to a normative Jesus" (quoted from Reimer, "Trinitarian Orthodoxy," p. 140, emphasis added). The Yoder-Weaver argument, insofar as it attempts to refute a claim (viz., that the Nicene Creed teaches divine truth) on the basis of its history (viz., the Council of Nicaea had human origins), is guilty of the genetic fallacy and so lacks logical force.

27. Cf. Reimer, "Trinitarian Orthodoxy," pp. 136-43, 156-59.

facilitated the "Constantinian shift" in the West is confounded further by the fact that one does not find a parallel development in the East. First, concerning salvation, Irenaeus and Athanasius each argued (before and after Constantine and Nicaea, respectively) for the doctrines of the Trinity and Incarnation as jointly necessary to an adequate doctrine of salvation: we are saved by Jesus, but only God can save, so God must include Jesus and Jesus must be both divine and human.[28] Far from sanctioning violence, Irenaean and Athanasian soteriology argues that God redeems humanity in Christ without violence and thus offers a viable alternative to the Western mode of atonement thinking, an alternative preserved within Eastern Orthodox theology.[29] Second, concerning ethics, unlike the Western Catholic tradition, the Eastern Orthodox tradition did not develop a "just war" theory that would sanction killing in warfare. Whereas prior pastoral practice (evident from Basil, bishop of Caesarea, in the fourth century) had judged even defensive killing for a just cause as sinful and so requiring penance,[30] during the Crusade era the Western Catholic tradition began to distinguish war from sin: waging a "just war" (i.e., under legitimate authority, for just cause, with right intention), Aquinas argued, is not sinful.[31] Although not strictly pacifist, the Eastern Orthodox tradition maintained that war, which is the reciprocation of evil for evil, belongs essentially to the realm of sin such that killing in war is inherently sinful and requires penance.[32] While

28. Weaver ignores both Irenaeus and Athanasius. Regarding the importance of Nicene theology for patristic soteriology and an adequate theory of atonement, see Peter Schmiechen, *Saving Power: Theories of Atonement and Forms of the Church* (Grand Rapids, MI: Eerdmans Publishing, 2005), pp. 178-92, 349-52. Schmiechen states: "Incarnation and Trinity are simultaneously the presupposition and the consequence of the proclamation that Jesus is the Christ, our Lord and Savior" (p. 350).

29. See Kallistos Ware, *The Orthodox Way*, rev. ed. (Crestwood, NY: St. Vladimir's Seminary Press, 1995).

30. The post-Constantine church thus did not simply sanction war. In correspondence with fellow bishop Amphilochius, Basil argued that all killing in warfare, because intentional even if defensive, is murder, no less than the purposeful destruction of an unborn child by abortion: "Soldiers who inflict death in war do so with the obvious purpose not of fighting, nor chastising, but of killing their opponents" (*Letter* 188, VIII). Basil counseled that exclusion from Eucharist for three years would be an appropriate penance for those who kill in war, even if the war is fought "on behalf of chastity and true religion" (*Letter* 188, XIII). That this practice of assessing penance for killing in war survived until the Crusades, see Roland H. Bainton, *Christian Attitudes toward War and Peace: A Historical Survey and Critical Re-Evaluation* (Nashville, TN: Abingdon Press, 1960), p. 109.

31. Aquinas, *Summa Theologiae*, II-II, Q. 40, Art. 1.

32. See John McGuckin, "Nonviolence and Peace Traditions in Early and Eastern Christianity" (2005), accessible online at http://incommunion.org/?p=335; Allyne L. Smith, Jr., "Pacifism in Eastern Orthodoxy," in Gabriel Palmer-Fernandez, *Encyclopedia of Religion and War* (London: Taylor & Francis, 2004), pp. 113-18; and Stanley Harakas, "The Morality of War," in Joseph J. Allen and Philip Saliba, eds., *Orthodox Synthesis: The Unity of Theological Thought* (Crestwood, NY: St. Vladimir's Seminary Press, 1981), pp. 67-94. For an alternative perspective, see Alexander F. C.

both Western Catholic and Eastern Orthodox traditions maintained Nicene-Chalcedonian Christology, therefore, they diverged on both the theology of atonement and the ethics of war. This fact, that the Eastern Orthodox tradition held to Nicene-Chalcedonian Christology but yet maintained a "nonviolent" atonement theology and did not sanction killing in warfare, undercuts Weaver's thesis that it was creedal orthodoxy itself that led the church to abandon peace and sanction violence in theology and ethics.[33]

Fourth, Weaver presents "satisfaction" atonement as representing the sanction of violence in the theology of Christendom. Unfortunately, Weaver begins his presentation by conflating Anselm's satisfaction theory with Calvin's penal substitution theory, projecting the substance of the latter onto the language of the former:

> Satisfaction atonement assumes that the sin of humankind against God has earned the penalty of death, but that Jesus satisfied the offended honor of God on their behalf *or* took the place of sinful humankind and bore their punishment *or* satisfied the required penalty on their behalf.[34]

Weaver writes here as if the three phrases conjoined by "or" connote the same idea — but they do not. While we have presented the atonement theologies of Anselm and Calvin as each premised on the logic of retribution, we have also made clear the distinction between them — and will continue to differentiate the two theories (Chapters 3 and 6). Whereas Calvin does understand Christ's death as a substitute punishment to pay the divine penalty, Anselm understands Christ's satisfaction of God's honor by perfect obedience as an alternative to divine punishment. This distinction makes a major difference for Weaver's argument against Anselm and for "nonviolent atonement." Both theories understand atonement as the "satisfaction" of divine justice. The contrast can be seen by asking: What is the objective at which God's justice aims in

---

Webster, "Justifiable War in Eastern Orthodox Christianity," in Paul F. Robinson, ed., *Just War in Comparative Perspective* (Farnham, UK: Ashgate Publishing, 2003), pp. 40-61.

33. In addition to this historical counterexample to Weaver's thesis, we might consider also a hypothetical counterexample. Suppose that the Council of Nicaea, rather than including abstract formulas concerning the divinity of the Son had instead included Jesus' teachings of non-retaliation and love of enemies in the Creed: would that have prevented the accommodation of just war theory in the Western church? Not likely, and for the same reasons that just war thinking became possible within Christian tradition in the first place. As we have seen already (Chapter 3) and will see further (Chapter 28), Augustine was able to accommodate just war to Christian ethics, not by ignoring the Sermon on the Mount, but by qualifying and reinterpreting it. The same would have been done with Jesus' teachings, I would suggest, even had they been placed in the Nicene Creed. Weaver's contention that the Nicene Creed was a causal factor in the "Constantinian shift" thus seems to me a case of misplaced blame.

34. *Nonviolent Atonement*, p. 3 (emphasis added).

atonement? Whereas God's justice does aim at Jesus' death in Calvin's theory, for it is precisely Jesus' death in humanity's place that satisfies God's justice, that is not so in Anselm's theory: God's justice aims at the restoration of God's honor (and, ultimately, creation's order), which aim is satisfied by Jesus' obedience to God's will on humanity's behalf. Thus, whereas there is explicit divine violence in Calvin's theory, for God the Father punishes God the Son, there is no actual divine violence in Anselm's theory: God is satisfied, not by a penalty of death, but by the restitution of obedience. It thus seems to me that Anselm's theory, while belonging to the "retributive paradigm," is not essentially incompatible with "nonviolent atonement."[35]

---

35. The requirement of satisfaction in Anselm's theory is derived from the logic of retribution, but retribution does not require violence. There are nonviolent retributive practices, such as debt repayment and just compensation, which is precisely what is involved in Anselm's theory (see Chapter 3 above).

"Christ Died for Us"

The Cross, Atonement, and Substitution

• •

Penal Substitution

Historical and Narrative Questions

CHAPTER 5

The Penal Substitution Doctrine of Atonement

The dominant understanding of the death of Jesus within evangelical Protestant Christianity is the doctrine of penal substitution atonement.[1] Indeed, some apologists for penal substitution hold that this doctrine is essential to evangelical Christianity. J. I. Packer, a prominent evangelical Anglican theologian, observes that penal substitution "is a distinguishing mark of the worldwide evangelical fraternity."[2] Baptist New Testament scholar Thomas Schreiner puts the point a bit more sharply: "The theory of penal substitution is the heart and soul of an evangelical view of the atonement."[3] The implication is that any

1. For a clear summary of penal substitution and how this thinking interprets the biblical canon, see Charles E. Hill, "Atonement in the Old and New Testaments," in Charles E. Hill and Frank A. James III, eds., *The Glory of the Atonement: Biblical, Theological and Practical Perspectives* (Downers Grove, IL: InterVarsity Press, 2004), pp. 23-31. For a portrayal of penal substitution as the centerpiece of Christian theology, see Steve Jeffery, Michael Ovey, and Andrew Sach, *Pierced for Our Transgressions: Rediscovering the Glory of Penal Substitution* (Wheaton, IL: Crossway Books, 2008), pp. 100-148. For a nonpartisan overview of the atonement debate within evangelical theology, see Roger E. Olson, *The Westminster Handbook to Evangelical Theology* (Louisville: Westminster John Knox Press, 2004), pp. 149-51.

2. J. I. Packer, "What Did the Cross Achieve? The Logic of Penal Substitution," in J. I. Packer, *Celebrating the Saving Work of God: The Collected Shorter Writings of J. I. Packer* (Carlisle, UK: Paternoster Press, 1998), I, pp. 85-123, here p. 85. The doctrine of penal substitution atonement was also one of the "five fundamentals" that defined the early twentieth-century Christian fundamentalist movement in the U.S. and Britain. The five fundamental doctrines were: inerrancy of Scripture, virgin birth and deity of Jesus Christ, substitutionary atonement, bodily resurrection of Jesus, and premillennial second coming of Christ. See R. A. Torrey, ed., *The Fundamentals: A Testimony to the Truth* (Los Angeles: Bible Institute of Los Angeles, 1917), accessible online at http://www .xmission.com/~fidelis.

3. Thomas R. Schreiner, "Penal Substitution View," in James Beilby and Paul R. Eddy, eds., *The Nature of the Atonement: Four Views* (Downers Grove, IL: InterVarsity Press, 2006), pp. 67-98, here p. 67.

view of the atonement that questions or challenges penal substitution is simply *un*evangelical, or at least lacking in evangelical "heart and soul." And, in a recent apologetic for penal substitution, Steve Jeffery, Michael Ovey, and Andrew Sach declare that penal substitution is essential not only to evangelical theology, but to the gospel itself: "This understanding of the cross of Christ stands at the very heart of the gospel." They thus find it incredulous that dissenters from penal substitution should consider themselves Bible-believing Christians: "The more disturbing thing is that some of the more recent critics of penal substitution regard themselves as evangelicals, and claim to be committed to the authority of Scripture."[4] In the eyes of its apologists, then, to dissent from penal substitution is to dissent from Scripture itself.

5.1. The Essence of the Doctrine[5]

Packer states the doctrine in straightforward terms, indicating both the substitutionary character of Jesus' death and the penal function of that substitution: Jesus "secured my immunity from judgement by bearing on the cross the penalty which was my due."[6] Schreiner defines penal substitution in similar terms:

> The Father, because of his love for human beings, sent his Son (who offered himself willingly and gladly) to satisfy God's justice, so that Christ took the place of sinners. The punishment and penalty we deserved was laid on Jesus Christ instead of us, so that in the cross God's holiness and love are manifested.[7]

4. Jeffery et al., *Pierced for Our Transgression*, pp. 21, 25.

5. Before we begin to examine a particular doctrine of atonement, we must first make an observation about this English word "atonement." Unlike the language of justification ("right-making"), reconciliation ("one-making"), or peacemaking, "atonement" is *not* a biblical word. It is, it would appear, a made-up word, coined in the sixteenth century in the English language. Its literal etymology is "at-one-ment" — which intentionally connotes reconciliation. The English word "atonement," therefore, has no precedents in any other language; we cannot trace prior usage in, say, Hebrew or Greek or Latin, because that prior usage simply does not exist. It thus means neither more nor less than whatever meaning we give it by our usage (say, by using "atonement" to translate the Hebrew *kipper*). This was brought home to me personally in 2005 when I was delivering a Palm Sunday meditation to the congregation of the Lithuanian Free Christian Church in Klaipeda, Lithuania. I said "make atonement" and the translator, a pastor who is fluent in English and received his theological training in English, said to me, "We don't have that word." He suggested "make peace" as a translation; after recovering from momentary disorientation, I agreed, as that is effectively the meaning I had intended. Recognizing this should give us caution and hopefully prevent us from quibbling over the "meaning" of the word "atonement."

6. Packer, "What Did the Cross Achieve?" p. 106.

7. Schreiner, "Penal Substitution View," p. 67.

We might sketch penal substitution atonement more fully as follows: God, who is righteous and holy, must satisfy his wrath against sin by punishing sinners with death; but God, who is also merciful, provides sinners an escape from divine wrath and retribution by ordaining and accepting Jesus' sacrificial death as punishment in their place. On the cross Jesus suffered in our place the death penalty that God had decreed as just retribution for our sins; in this way, Jesus propitiated God's righteous wrath and satisfied God's absolute justice, thereby making it possible for God to forgive the sins of humanity in accord with God's law. Evangelical Anglican scholar and preacher John R. W. Stott sums up the doctrine by the formula, "satisfaction through substitution."[8]

5.2. Key Elements of the Doctrine

5.2.1. Satisfaction of Justice

We first lay out several accounts of the penal substitution doctrine of atonement by some of its major apologists. We begin with the account of Charles Hodge, a leading late nineteenth-century American Presbyterian theologian.[9] Hodge's systematic account emphasizes two major premises of penal substitution, which concern God's justice and holiness: a holy God can have no part with sinners unless justice is satisfied, and a just God must mete out retributive punishment for sin. Hodge states that God cannot forgive sin "without a satisfaction to justice," and God's justice "renders it necessary that the righteous be rewarded and the wicked punished."[10] God's justice "demands the punishment of sin. If sin be pardoned it can be pardoned in consistency with the divine justice only on the ground of a forensic penal satisfaction."[11]

How, then, can sinners be pardoned their sins if God's justice necessitates punishment for sin? Only by Jesus' suffering and death on the cross in their place, which God designs in order to appease divine wrath and satisfy divine

8. John R. W. Stott, *The Cross of Christ* (Downers Grove, IL: InterVarsity Press, 1986), p. 159.

9. Charles Hodge, *Systematic Theology* (Grand Rapids, MI: Eerdmans Publishing, 1940). For a fuller exposition and critical examination of Hodge's systematic account of penal substitution, see Joel B. Green and Mark D. Baker, *Recovering the Scandal of the Cross: Atonement in New Testament and Contemporary Contexts* (Downers Grove, IL: InterVarsity Press, 2000), pp. 140-50; and Peter Schmiechen, *Saving Power: Theories of Atonement and Forms of the Church* (Grand Rapids, MI: Eerdmans, 2005), pp. 103-19.

10. Hodge, *Systematic Theology*, vol. 2, pp. 492 and 490 respectively. Hodge himself prefers to call this God's "vindicatory" justice, in distinction from the retributive justice administered by civil authorities (pp. 489-90). Yet, rewarding the righteous and punishing the wicked is the very substance of retributive justice as understood by classical, medieval, and modern philosophers.

11. Hodge, *Systematic Theology*, vol. 2, p. 488.

justice. Jesus thus suffers by the hand of God the punishment of death that was due to us for our sin:

> They were divine inflictions. It pleased the Lord to bruise Him. He was smitten of God and afflicted. These sufferings were declared to be on account of sin, not his own, but ours. He bore our sins. The chastisement of our peace was on Him. And they were designed as an expiation, or for the satisfaction of justice. They had, therefore, all the elements of punishment. . . .[12]

That is, God punishes Jesus as a "forensic penal substitution." Hodge thus summarizes:

> Hence the plan of salvation which the Bible reveals supposes that the justice of God which renders the punishment of sin necessary has been satisfied. Men can be pardoned and restored to the favour of God . . . because the penalty due to us was laid on Him [viz., Christ]. It is clear therefore, that the Scriptures recognize the truth that God is just, in the sense that He is determined by His moral excellence to punish all sin, and therefore that the satisfaction of Christ which secures the pardon of sinners is rendered to the justice of God. Its primary and principal design is neither to make a moral impression upon the offenders themselves, nor to operate didactically on other intelligent creatures, but to satisfy the demands of justice; so that God can be just in justifying the ungodly.[13]

The linchpin of the logic of penal substitution, as Hodge emphasizes, is the principle of retributive justice: "There is no force in this argument unless there is a necessity for the punishment of sin."[14] Peter Schmiechen thus aptly observes regarding Hodge's account: "in penal substitution it is the demand of legal justice that drives the entire theory."[15]

---

12. Hodge, *Systematic Theology,* vol. 2, p. 517.

13. Hodge, *Systematic Theology,* vol. 2, pp. 492-93. I. Howard Marshall, *Aspects of the Atonement: Cross and Resurrection in the Reconciling of God and Humanity* (London: Paternoster, 2007), writes: "It is easy for opponents of penal substitution to present the matter as though it is only because of the cross that God is prepared to abandon his wrath and forgive sinners. Certainly this is a frequent criticism of the doctrine. Yet I am not aware that any responsible defenders of the doctrine take this point of view, and if there were, I would side with their critics" (p. 54). Whatever criteria Marshall uses to define a "responsible defense" of penal substitution, this is in fact the very view of Charles Hodge: no forgiveness of sin without penal satisfaction of God's wrath; and no satisfaction of God's wrath without the penal death of Jesus in place of sinners; therefore, no abandonment of wrath and forgiveness of sinners by God without the cross of Christ. What Marshall himself actually thinks of Hodge I do not know, as he does not discuss Hodge in his book.

14. Hodge, *Systematic Theology,* vol. 2., p. 492.

15. Schmiechen, *Saving Power,* p. 103.

J. I. Packer's account of penal substitution also makes clear that this doctrine is premised squarely on the requirements of retributive justice: "Now we ... bring in the word 'penal' to characterize the substitution we have in view. To add this 'qualifier' ... is to anchor the model of substitution (not exclusively, but regulatively) within the world of moral law, guilty conscience, and retributive justice."[16] Packer echoes Hodge, underscoring both the centrality of legal retribution to the doctrine of atonement and the notion that the principle of retribution is rooted in God's own character: "the retributive principle has [God's] sanction, and indeed expresses the holiness, justice and goodness reflected in his law."[17] This major premise of penal substitution — that in a moral universe governed by a just God, sin requires retributive punishment and forgiveness is possible only on the ground of penal satisfaction — is emphasized in William Hordern's presentation of the early twentieth-century "fundamentalist" view:

> It would be unjust for God to forgive sins lightly and let bygones be bygones while the consequences of a man's sin live on and continue to injure others. Man has sinned and, in a moral universe, he ought to pay for his sin. Therefore, in his love and mercy, God sent his only begotten Son into the world. Jesus led a sinless life and did not deserve to die, but he voluntarily accepted death in order that he might save men. His death becomes a substitutionary atonement. He suffered the penalties of man's sin in order that the justice of God might be appeased and man allowed to go free.[18]

Now, what is this "retributive principle" that enjoys God's sanction and which underwrites the penal substitution doctrine? This principle of justice has been handed down through the majority Western tradition. The classical Greco-Roman tradition, the medieval Christian tradition, and the modern philosophical tradition agree with common opinion that retribution for wrongdoing entails imposing punishment on the wrongdoer as penalty for his wrongdoing. This punishment is intended, as the word "retribution" literally implies, to "repay" the wrongdoing to the wrongdoer — pain for pain, harm for harm, injury for injury. Justice as retribution is done when the wrongdoer is paid back "in kind" (see Chapter 3 above). In penal substitution thinking, the principle of retributive justice is upheld by the decree of God: sin deserves penalty, and the penalty for sin is the punishment of death. The substitutionary death of Christ fulfills its saving function precisely by being a penal satisfaction of divine retribution: upon the cross, Christ suffers in place of sinners the God-imposed punishment of death for sin.

16. Packer, "What Did the Cross Achieve?" p. 105.
17. Packer, "What Did the Cross Achieve?" p. 109.
18. William E. Hordern, *A Layman's Guide to Protestant Theology*, rev. and exp. ed. (New York: Macmillan, 1968), p. 60.

Recently, New Testament scholar I. Howard Marshall has offered a revisionist defense of penal substitution that seeks to distance the doctrine from this tradition of thinking about retributive justice. In discussing how to understand the nature of judgment and penalty, Marshall questions whether proportionate suffering serves justice:

> It does not do any good to the victim or others affected by the crime. . . . Nor is it clear how proportionate suffering by the offender undoes the offence . . . it is impossible to believe that God needs to make people suffer in the same way as they have caused others to suffer . . . in order that he might gain some kind of self-satisfaction or upholding of an abstract principle of justice. Popular usage . . . often thinks of retribution as the imposition of proportionate suffering on the person who has caused others to suffer or simply broken the law. It is this element that seems dubious.[19]

He articulates an alternative vision of retributive justice without the notion of "exacting some penalty that is judged to involve suffering that is proportionate to the sin."[20]

> Retribution should be understood to mean the action taken against offenders in order to uphold justice, to restrain evildoers, to undo so far as may be possible the effects of the offence, and, where the evildoer is irreformable, to exclude that person from the community and its benefits.[21]

This view, he thinks, is better suited to both human community and the biblical God:

> In this way we may be able to progress to a better understanding of what human justice ought to achieve, and equally a better understanding of the nature of divine justice. Judgement on wrongdoing and wrongdoers is concerned with the upholding of righteousness by the community or its ruler(s), the exclusion in one way or another of those who reject its moral standards, making restitution for the effects of sin where this is possible, and the restoration of penitent and repentant wrongdoers.[22]

Marshall thus seeks to reform penal substitution by revising the principle of justice that underwrites that doctrine; and he revises this principle by redefining "retribution" so that justice retains the retributive principle but without the "dubious element" (viz., imposing punishments of proportionate suffering).

19. Marshall, *Aspects of the Atonement*, p. 28.
20. Marshall, *Aspects of the Atonement*, p. 30.
21. Marshall, *Aspects of the Atonement*, p. 32.
22. Marshall, *Aspects of the Atonement*, p. 33.

I am quite sympathetic to Marshall's argument that such an alternative view of justice would better serve both human practice and theological understanding, and I affirm this direction of his thinking concerning atonement. But this cannot honestly be called "retribution" without divesting that word of its literal meaning. And to downplay the notion of proportionate suffering as "popular usage" of the term "retribution" is hardly convincing — it is central to the Western tradition of thinking about justice, from Aristotle to Cicero to Augustine to Aquinas to Kant. Moreover, if the necessity that justice impose punishments of proportionate suffering be removed from the retributive principle, as Marshall suggests, then the necessity that Christ suffer the punishment of death to pay the penalty for sins and so satisfy the principle of justice is also removed — and the logic of penal substitution is undermined. Recall Hodge: "There is no force in this argument unless there is a necessity for the punishment of sin."[23] To pursue such an alternative vision of justice, therefore, is to pursue an alternative understanding of atonement.

5.2.2. Propitiation of God

We turn next to Roger Nicole, a twentieth-century Reformed Baptist theologian:

> Moved by his immeasurable love to humankind, the Triune God, Father, Son and Holy Spirit, devised a marvelous plan to bring deliverance for a race of rebellious sinners who are born in iniquity, inclined toward evil and who transgress every day and in several ways his holy commandments. God designed to save from the midst of this sin-cursed race a great multitude of sinners, who were in no way deserving of this grace.
>
> To accomplish this, the Son, who is consubstantial with the Father and the Holy Spirit, did not insist in retaining his eternal glory, but he assumed a complete and sinless human nature, consubstantial with ours except for sin. He thus entered into humanity and united himself in the deepest manner with an innumerable number of sinners, taking on himself the guilt and punishment due for all their sins and providing them with his own immaculate righteousness before the divine tribunal. This effected the propitiation of the triune God's anger against the sinners; the reconciliation of God to us and us to God; the substitutionary sacrifice needed for expiation of sin; the redemption of guilty debtors enslaved to sin; and the ultimate victory over

---

23. I thus doubt that many penal substitution apologists would concur with Marshall on this point. Cf. Jeffery et al., *Pierced for Our Transgressions*, pp. 249-61, who defend a traditional understanding of retributive justice as necessary to the biblical view and so essential to penal substitution.

the enemies of our soul and the predicament of our broken relationship with God.[24]

Here we see another salient feature of the penal substitution doctrine — the primary effect of Jesus' death is "propitiation of the triune God's anger against the sinners" and the secondary effect is "the reconciliation of God to us and us to God."

J. I. Packer also gives primary place to propitiation in his explanation of Jesus' death: "Jesus knew on the cross all the pain, physical and mental, that man could inflict and also the divine wrath and rejection my sins deserve; for he is there in my place making atonement for me."[25] Under the heading "Propitiation," Packer states that "Here we reach the real heart — the heart of the heart, we may say — of Christianity." Like Nicole, Packer then spells out the meaning of the cross in terms that emphasize propitiation as the primary purpose and effect of the cross, reconciliation as secondary.

> The cross of Christ has many facets of meaning. As our sacrifice for sins, it was *propitiation,* that is, a means of quenching God's personal penal wrath against us by blotting out our sins from his sight. . . . As our propitiation, it was reconciliation, the making of peace for us with our offended, estranged, angry Creator.[26]

Nicole and Packer, in emphasizing propitiation as primary, reconciliation as secondary, state another implicit aspect of penal substitution: the purpose of the cross is, first, not to reconcile humanity to God, but rather to reconcile God to humanity. For God, angry at humanity on account of sin, is "estranged" from humanity (Packer); thus, the cross must achieve, first, "the reconciliation of God to us" and, second, "us to God" (Nicole).

5.3. Penal Substitution in Popular Theology

Penal substitution thinking is rooted deeply in the evangelical heart and mind and is manifest in various ways in popular theology. Dietrich Bonhoeffer, the German-Lutheran pastor-theologian whose life, death, and writings have inspired many:

> Jesus died the death of the godless; he was stricken by God's wrath and vengeance. His blood is the blood which God's righteousness required for the

24. Roger Nicole, "Postscript on Penal Substitution," in Hill and James, eds., *Glory of the Atonement,* p. 452.

25. J. I. Packer, *I Want to Be a Christian* (Wheaton, IL: Tyndale House Publishers, 1977), p. 59.

26. Packer, *I Want to Be a Christian,* p. 60.

transgression of his commandments. . . . God's vengeance is extinguished [upon Jesus] . . . who was stricken by God's vengeance for our salvation.[27]

John F. MacArthur, Jr., a Calvinist pastor-author popular among American evangelicals:

> Here's what was happening on the cross: God was punishing His own Son as if He had committed every wicked deed done by every sinner who would ever believe. And He did it so that He could forgive and treat those redeemed ones as if they had lived Christ's perfect life of righteousness.[28]

Mark Dever, a Baptist pastor, has championed penal substitution in *Christianity Today* as "the dominant Atonement imagery used in the Bible," stating that "substitution [is] the center and focus of the Bible's witness to the meaning of Christ's death." He summarizes:

> our main problem is God's righteous wrath against us for our sinfulness, which puts us in danger of eternal punishment. . . . Christ's perfect sacrifice for our sins is necessary to satisfy God's righteousness. Christ's death bore a divine penalty that we deserved. By taking our penalty upon himself, God satisfied his own correct and good wrath against us.[29]

In these popular accounts, we see again the key elements of penal substitution: that the "main problem" needing to be solved by the cross is "God's righteous wrath against us for our sinfulness" (Dever); that God himself intentionally inflicts upon Jesus the divine vengeance in place of humanity (Bonhoeffer, MacArthur, and Dever); that God's doing so was required by God's justice on account of human disobedience (Bonhoeffer and Dever) and was the necessary prerequisite so that God could forgive sins (MacArthur).

Although originating within the Calvinist tradition, this doctrine has become popular even within the Mennonite-Anabaptist tradition. In an article in *The Mennonite,* theologian Ted Grimsrud challenged a basic premise of penal substitution — a wrathful God who must be appeased before he can show mercy to humanity:

> The overall message tells us that the God of the Old Testament is a God of love, a God who seeks to bring salvation to the world. The Old Testament God saves straight out of God's love. The Old Testament does not, in its overall message, tell us that God's holiness and perfection prevent God from sim-

---

27. Dietrich Bonhoeffer, *Meditating on the Word,* trans. and ed. David M. Gracie (Cambridge, MA: Cowley Publications, 2000), pp. 82-83.

28. John F. MacArthur, Jr., *The Murder of Jesus* (Nashville: Word Publishing, 2000), p. 219.

29. Mark Dever, "Nothing but the Blood," *Christianity Today,* May 2006, pp. 29-33.

ply offering forgiveness and salvation; neither does the Old Testament in its overall message portray God as a God of wrath who requires sacrificial violence to balance the scales of justice in order to save. . . . God does not come in wrath in the end. God comes in suffering, persevering love. Justice for this God is about healing, not about retribution.[30]

A reader took issue with this, asserting implicitly that Grimsrud had denied the basic truth of Christian faith, and then repeated the basic elements of penal substitution:

If this is true, then why did Christ have to die? Grimsrud's statement is not true, and I am surprised to see it in print in a Christian publication. The God I serve is a holy God who cannot tolerate sin. The wages of sin is death. But the God I serve is also the God who loved me so much that he was willing, in Jesus Christ, to take my punishment. He couldn't just pretend my sin didn't exist; the punishment needed to be paid. He paid the price of my sin.[31]

For many folks in the church pews, the penal substitution doctrine of atonement provides the only possible and acceptable answer to the question, "Why did Jesus die?"[32]

Interestingly, penal substitution holds such a firm grip upon popular belief that Bart Ehrman, biblical scholar and erstwhile believer turned skeptical agnostic, still maintains that penal substitution is "the Christian understanding of atonement."[33] Citing a few Pauline texts, Ehrman characterizes Paul's view of atonement in a manner that many an evangelical believer would find familiar: "For Paul there is a relatively simple formula for how God provides eternal salvation for his people: sin leads to punishment; Christ took the punishment upon himself; therefore, Christ's death can atone for the sins of others." This theory neatly answers the perennial question: "Why is it that Jesus has to suffer and die? Because God has to punish sin."[34]

30. Ted Grimsrud, "Mercy, Not Retribution," *The Mennonite,* September 6, 2005, pp. 14-15.

31. *The Mennonite,* Readers Say, October 4, 2005, p. 4.

32. In an article in the same publication, I challenged another aspect of penal substitution thinking — its interpretation of sacrificial atonement as vicarious punishment to satisfy retribution: "The sacrifices of atonement [as found in Leviticus] evidently did not function according to the logic of retribution. The theory that Christ died as an atoning sacrifice *as payment of penalty to God,* therefore, does not accord with the Scriptures" (Darrin W. Snyder Belousek, "Once for All: Freeing Sacrificial Atonement from Retributive Justice," *The Mennonite,* April 7, 2009, pp. 12-14). An online reader commented that I had made an "attack on the historic and Biblical doctrine of penal substitutionary atonement" and denounced my view as belonging "with the unbelieving world" (http://www.themennonite.org/issues/12-9/articles/Once_for_all).

33. Bart D. Ehrman, *God's Problem: How the Bible Fails to Answer Our Most Important Question — Why We Suffer* (New York: HarperOne, 2008), p. 83.

34. Ehrman, *God's Problem,* pp. 84-85.

Given its prevalent place in evangelical thinking, whenever penal substitution is questioned controversy is sure to follow. Consider the controversy that has followed William P. Young's popular novel *The Shack*.[35] While affirming the necessity of the cross of Christ ("there was no plan B," says the character representing God the Father) and speaking of the cross as God's act of reconciliation, *The Shack* declines to explain further that reconciliation in "properly evangelical" terms — divine punishment of sin by the substitutionary death of Jesus. One reviewer thus writes that *The Shack* has shortchanged the gospel: "We are left with an incomplete gospel. . . . It is a gospel message that says nothing of how we may be saved from the sin that pollutes us."[36]

Within mainstream evangelical Christianity, then, any way of thinking about the cross of Christ other than penal substitution is not only false, but almost un-Christian. Dever implies that to challenge penal substitution is tantamount to rejecting any need for the cross: "In fact, there have always been a few Christians who question whether we need the Atonement, including, in recent years, some evangelicals who have challenged the dominant understanding of Christ's death on the Cross as the substitute for our sins."[37] And MacArthur declares that those offering any view of the cross other than penal substitution are "liberals, cultists, and pseudo-Christian religionists."[38]

5.4. Critiquing Penal Substitution

Before we proceed with our critical examination of penal substitution, I want to emphasize an important point. While I am critical of *penal* substitution, I do not necessarily reject the idea of *substitutionary* atonement per se, but rather object to certain versions of it. I affirm, in accordance with the apostolic witness, that Christ's death was sacrificial ("he offered himself"), vicarious ("for us"), atoning ("for sins"), and necessary to God's work of salvation ("the Messiah must suffer"). For biblical and theological reasons, I diverge from penal substitution on each of these points and seek to articulate an alternative view that is better grounded in Scripture and more consistent with the Creed. My goal, then, is not simply to critique penal substitution but to offer a constructive alternative for understanding the gospel proclamation, "Christ died for us."

Penal substitution apologists are warranted, I think, in the complaint that critics all too often consider either naïve or extreme versions of the doctrine,

35. William P. Young, *The Shack* (Los Angeles: Windblown Media, 2007). I offer no defense of this novel or its theology, but refer to it here only to illustrate the point.

36. Tim Challies, *A Reader's Review of* The Shack, accessible at http://www.challies.com/media/The_Shack.pdf.

37. Dever, "Nothing but the Blood."

38. MacArthur, *The Murder of Jesus*, p. 219.

which are dismissed easily — and for good reasons. In order to avoid drawing a caricature or jousting with a "straw man," I will examine penal substitution on its own terms, drawing the claims for examination from apologetic writings by several of its best known and most competent proponents. And in order to avoid, as much as possible, biasing my investigation, I will often follow an inductive method when dealing with Scripture. In testing the claims of penal substitution, the evidence for consideration will be drawn entirely from Christian tradition, its Scripture, creeds, and apostolic writings. And this evidence will be interpreted on the presuppositions of Christian faith, not by any assumed critical method or philosophical system. In the end, I agree with Packer that "knowledge of God's action in Christ's death" cannot be gained solely on the basis of empirical (historical) evidence or metaphysical theory, but rather "is *faith-knowledge:* by faith we know that God was in Christ reconciling the world to himself." Indeed, knowledge of salvation through Christ is "knowledge of a *mystery,* the mystery of the living God at work."[39]

---

39. J. I. Packer, "What Did the Cross Achieve?" p. 88, emphasis original. In this we do not oppose faith to reason, but affirm simply, following in the tradition of the Scholastic philosophers (cf. Thomas Aquinas, *Summa Contra Gentiles,* I.3-8), that some of the truths concerning God are not comprehensible by reason — and thus, that, as with the doctrines of the Trinity, creation, and Incarnation, the doctrine of the atonement cannot be fully understood through natural categories or rational theory.

CHAPTER 6

═══════

The Apostolic Faith Taught by the Early Church

For us humans and for our salvation . . .
he was crucified under Pontius Pilate. . . .

THE NICENE CREED

6.1. Penal Substitution: Orthodox Doctrine?

To question penal substitution is to challenge what many Christians have held to be not only "the faith of our fathers and mothers" but also "the faith of the Apostles." In the early twentieth century, the penal substitution doctrine of atonement was set forth within evangelical Christianity as one of five "fundamentals" of Christian faith, along with the inspiration and inerrancy of Scripture, the virgin birth and deity of Christ, and the bodily resurrection and imminent return of Christ. The essay on "The Atonement" in *The Fundamentals* states in the first paragraph that penal substitution is rooted in the apostolic faith as expressed in the orthodox creeds: "All the great historic creeds which set forth the atonement at any length set forth a substitutionary atonement."[1]

---

1. Franklin Johnson, "The Atonement," vol. III, ch. 5 of R. A. Torrey, ed., *The Fundamentals: A Testimony to the Truth* (Los Angeles: Bible Institute of Los Angeles, 1917). *The Fundamentals* is accessible online at http://www.xmission.com/~fidelis and at http://classic-web.archive.org/web/20030101082327/http://www.geocities.com/Athens/Parthenon/6258/fundcont.htm. Interestingly, *The Fundamentals* makes conflicting statements on the relation of penal substitution to the creeds. In vol. III, ch. 6, "At-One-Ment by Propitiation" by Dyson Hague, we read: "With regard to the writers and writings of the primitive church in the Ante-Nicene and the Post-Nicene era, it may be said, broadly speaking, that the atonement is presented by them as a fact, with its saving and regenerative effects. The consciousness of the primitive church did not seem to be alive to the necessity of the formation of any particular theory of the atonement."

Frank James echoes this view, claiming that "historic orthodox Christianity" is founded upon a doctrine of penal substitutionary atonement.[2] And Mark Dever claims that, in the debate over penal substitution, "At stake is nothing less than the essence of Christianity."[3]

Despite such claims, there is not now, nor ever was, an *orthodox* doctrine of atonement, strictly speaking. The early church Fathers, in defining orthodox Christianity ("the essence of Christianity") via ecumenical creeds according to the apostolic tradition, did not tie authentic faith to any one explanation of the saving effect of Jesus' death. Indeed, the ancient creeds do not articulate any specific doctrine of atonement at all.

6.2. The Apostolic Faith of the Ecumenical Creeds

6.2.1. *The Earliest Deposit and Development of the Faith*

The earliest creedal formulas of the church, representing the first "deposit" of the apostolic faith, appear within the canon of Scripture. Several such formulas are found in 1 Timothy, which exhorts church leaders to "keep the faith" handed down from the Apostles and to teach in accord with only "sound doctrine." The doctrine to be taught in the churches is distilled into several creedal formulas, three of which concern the saving significance of Jesus' ministry. The first affirms that the purpose of the Incarnation was the salvation of sinners: "The saying is sure and worthy of full acceptance, that Christ Jesus came into the world to save sinners" (1 Tim 1:15).

The second affirms both Christ's mediating role between God and humanity and Christ's human nature, as well as the self-giving manner of Christ's life-ministry and death: "there is one God; there is also one mediator between God and humankind, Christ Jesus, himself human, who gave himself a ransom for all" (1 Tim 2:5-6). This last phrase, "who gave himself a ransom for all," closely parallels Jesus' own characterization of his life-mission in Mark 10:45, which will receive careful attention in Chapter 9. Suffice it for now to say that this language — "ransom" *(antilytron)* — does not suggest either a sacrifice offered for

2. Frank A. James III, "General Introduction," in Charles E. Hill and Frank A. James III, eds., *The Glory of the Atonement: Biblical, Theological and Practical Perspectives* (Downers Grove, IL: InterVarsity Press, 2004), p. 15. James states that "historic orthodox Christianity" rests upon the doctrine of "vicarious atonement." As such, we agree — that Christ died "for us" is the ancient apostolic faith reflected in the orthodox creeds. But as to the vicarious character of this "for us," James narrows the idea of vicarious atonement to penal substitution (pp. 15-16): "The atonement is further complicated by the idea of substitution. How can a just God permit the innocent to substitute for the guilty?"

3. Mark Dever, "Nothing but the Blood," *Christianity Today,* May 2006, pp. 29-33.

sin or a punishment suffered for a crime, but rather the price paid to redeem a slave or release a captive. Keeping in mind that "Christ Jesus came into the world to save sinners," the imagery here suggests that, through his life and death, Christ Jesus gave himself in order to set all sinners free from captivity or slavery to sin.

The third proto-creedal formulation in 1 Timothy articulates "the mystery of our religion" and proclaims further Jesus' "vindication," presumably referring to his resurrection: "He was revealed in the flesh, vindicated in spirit, seen by angels, proclaimed among Gentiles, believed in throughout the world, taken up in glory" (1 Tim 3:16).

Such proto-creedal formulas are found also in the epistles of the early bishops, the first stage of development of the original deposit of apostolic faith. The letters of Ignatius, third bishop of Antioch, include several formulas of faith, some of which refer to the death of Christ. In *Ephesians* 18 Ignatius writes in creedal form with reference to baptism about "the Cross which so greatly offends the unbelievers, but is salvation and eternal life for us": "Under the divine dispensation, Jesus Christ our God . . . was born, and He submitted to baptism, so that by His Passion He might sanctify water."[4] In *Trallians* 9 Ignatius formulates the faith in a form that anticipates the Apostles' Creed, stating simply concerning Jesus' passion: "He was verily persecuted in the days of Pontius Pilate, and verily and indeed crucified, and gave up the ghost in the sight of all heaven and earth and the powers of the nether world."[5] Again, in *Smyrnaeans* 1 Ignatius presents a creedal formula that refers to Jesus' death with reference to his resurrection: ". . . [He was] truly pierced by nails in His human flesh (a Fruit imparting life to us from His most blessed Passion), so that by His resurrection He might set up a beacon for all time to call together His saints and believers . . . in the one body of His Church." Ignatius continues in the next chapter: "All this He submitted to for our sakes, that salvation might be ours."[6] In his creedal formulas Ignatius thus clearly affirms that Jesus' death was vicarious ("for our sake") and salvific (bringing salvation and life through baptism and resurrection), yet there is no suggestion here of a specific doctrine of atonement, let alone the penal substitution doctrine.

The second- and early third-century writings of Justin, Tertullian, and Irenaeus also contain proto-creedal formulations that continue the development of the deposit of faith begun in the apostolic writings of the first century. In his *Apology,* Justin includes numerous creedal formulas, many of which refer to Jesus' death and most of which simply confirm the fact of his death — "He was crucified" — without speaking in any terms concerning the meaning of his

4. *Early Christian Writings* (London: Penguin, 1987), pp. 65-66.
5. *Early Christian Writings*, p. 81.
6. *Early Christian Writings*, p. 101.

death.[7] Likewise with the creedal formulas found in the writings of Tertullian, which confirm the historical fact of Jesus' death in various terms — "[he] was nailed to the cross," "[he was] crucified under Pontius Pilate," "He suffered, He died and was buried, according to the Scriptures" — without elaborating in any terms the meaning of Christ's death.[8] In his *Against Heresies* and other writings, Irenaeus, bishop of Lyon, presents several creedal formulations of the apostolic faith, some lengthy. Concerning the death of Jesus, his shorter formulas affirm simply that Christ "suffered" and "died" while one of his longer formulas says that Christ "suffered for us and rose for us." Some of the longer formulas expand on the significance of Jesus' suffering and death with reference to the Incarnation and its purpose for humanity's salvation: "Who was made flesh for our salvation"; "he was made man among men . . . in order to abolish death and show forth life and produce a community of union between God and man."[9] It is thus clear that Irenaeus's creedal formulas affirm that Jesus' death was vicarious ("for us") and salvific ("for our salvation"). Yet, not only does Irenaeus not articulate anything that might be associated with the penal substitution doctrine, his creedal formulas identify the saving work of Jesus not with the cross alone but with the entire Incarnation.

6.2.2. Creedal Formulation of the Apostolic Faith

The ecumenical creeds articulated by the church Fathers in subsequent centuries explicitly mention Jesus' death, but they speak of its saving purpose in concise language using general terms.[10] The Apostles' Creed, originating in the second century as the confessional formula in the Roman Rite of initiation by baptism, set forth the basic belief required for church membership.[11] But it says not one word regarding the meaning of Jesus' death — only that "he suffered under Pontius Pilate, was crucified, died, and was buried." The Creed of Nicaea-Constantinople, originating with the Council of Nicaea (325) and finalized by the Council of Constantinople (381), formulates the doctrine of the Trinity concerning the "one being" *(homoousios)* of God the Father and God the Son.[12] Concerning the death of God the Son, however, it says only that the Son "for us

---

7. J. N. D. Kelly, *Early Christian Creeds*, 3rd ed. (London: Continuum, 2006), pp. 70-76.

8. Kelly, *Early Christian Creeds*, pp. 82-88.

9. Kelly, *Early Christian Creeds*, pp. 76-80.

10. Concerning the ecumenical creeds (or "symbols") of the early church, see Philip Schaff, ed., *Creeds of Christendom, with a History and Critical Notes*, vols. I and II (1877), and Kelly, *Early Christian Creeds*.

11. Hippolytus, *Apostolic Tradition* 21. Concerning the role of early creedal formulas in baptism and initiation, see Kelly, *Early Christian Creeds*, pp. 30-61.

12. We shall refer to this by the common shorthand, "Nicene Creed."

humans and for our salvation . . . came down from heaven, and was incarnate by the Holy Spirit of the virgin Mary, and was made human; and was crucified also for us under Pontius Pilate; He suffered and was buried. . . ."[13] The Definition of Chalcedon, affirmed at the Council of Chalcedon (451), formulates the doctrine of the Incarnation. It does not address the death of Christ, but does address the salvation of humanity. Rather than the cross being the locus of God's work of salvation, however, the Definition of Chalcedon affirms that the Incarnation itself was "for us and for our salvation." Jesus Christ, it says, was "begotten before all ages of the Father . . . and in these latter days, for us and for our salvation, born of the Virgin Mary. . . ." And the Athanasian Creed (fifth century) says simply that Jesus "suffered for our salvation."

Now, to attend to a question which we will deal with in depth and detail below in relation to Paul (in Chapter 16) but which might arise in the reader's mind at this point concerning the Nicene Creed: When the Creed says that Christ "was crucified for (hyper) us," what does this "for us" mean? For our sake? On our behalf? In our place? The Greek preposition *hyper* (with the genitive, as is the case here) usually means "for the sake of" or "on behalf of," but it could also take the meaning "in place of." Which is intended here? To answer this question, we might consider context. This phrase occurs in the Creed in the midst of a single, long sentence (in Greek) that begins with the phrase, "For (dia) us humans and for (dia) our salvation." The Greek preposition *dia* (with the accusative, as is the case here) takes the meaning "for sake of" or "on account of," but not "in place of." Context thus suggests that we read "for us" in the Creed as "for our sake." This reading gives the widest latitude of interpretation: the Creed's affirmation — that Christ "was crucified for our sake" — is compatible with all the historic theories of atonement that have been proposed and defended down the centuries of the church.

The ecumenical creeds confess clearly and consistently the vicarious character and saving purpose of the suffering and death of Jesus, that Jesus suffered and died "for us" and "for our salvation." None of these truly orthodox formulations of the apostolic faith, however, commit any Christian believer to any particular explanation of either the vicarious character or the saving efficacy of Jesus' death. In what sense Christ died "for us" and "for our salvation" — whether Jesus' vicarious death is one of "substitution" or "representation," and whether Jesus' death ransoms us from the devil, pays our sin-debt to God, or provides us with a perfect moral example — is not the subject of creedal definition. Moreover, none of the seven ecumenical councils ever pronounced definitively on the meaning of the phrases "for us" and "for our salvation" in the Nicene Creed. One can, therefore, deny the core claims of the penal substitution

---

13. See Luke Timothy Johnson's excellent discussion of this article of the Nicene Creed in *The Creed: What Christians Believe and Why It Matters* (New York: Doubleday, 2003), pp. 136-75.

doctrine of atonement — concerning propitiation of God's wrath and satisfaction of God's retribution by the substitution of Christ in place of sinners — all the while professing faith according to the ecumenical creeds of the apostolic church.[14] Hordern thus summarizes the historical situation left by the early formulation of Christian orthodoxy:

> Christianity teaches that God has performed a sacrifice, in and through Jesus, which has brought God and man back into fellowship with each other. But the problem arises: What did God do? Paul is clear that Jesus' death was central, but he gives no clear explanation. The Church never held a council on this doctrine, as it did on the Trinity and the nature of Christ. *No one doctrine has been held from the beginning, and hence it is difficult to speak of the orthodox position.*[15]

This is acknowledged by some apologists for penal substitution. Frank James:

> It may surprise modern Christians to learn that there is no single prevailing Christian view of the atonement. While orthodox Christians have, over the course of time, settled on a general consensus on the Trinity, on the deity of Christ and his two natures, and on salvation by grace, convergence on the atonement has been more elusive. To be sure many doctrinal divergences and nuances plague Christianity, but it is somewhat surprising that no single theory of the atonement predominates, given the fact that so many in church history have dubbed it the central doctrine of Christianity.[16]

Not only did the orthodox creeds and ecumenical councils not define a doctrine of atonement, but theological development during the patristic period produced a variety of ideas concerning how Christ achieved redemption.[17] Mi-

---

14. That is, the debate over atonement theology need not be church-dividing precisely because it is not a matter of creedal confession but rather a matter of theological explanation of what the creed affirms. To deny any one theory of atonement is not to deny the creed itself, which would put church unity into question. Steve Jeffery, Michael Ovey, and Andrew Sach, *Pierced for Our Transgressions: Rediscovering the Glory of Penal Substitution* (Wheaton, IL: Crossway Books, 2008), pp. 216-17, in defending penal substitution against its critics, do make the debate over atonement theology a church-dividing issue, however: "differences over penal substitution ultimately lead us to worship a different God and to believe a different gospel." Effectively, they raise penal substitution to creedal status.

15. William E. Hordern, *A Layman's Guide to Protestant Theology,* rev. and exp. ed. (New York: Macmillan, 1968), p. 25, emphasis added.

16. Frank A. James III, "The Atonement in Church History," in *Glory of the Atonement,* p. 209. We agree, of course, with James's statement here but find it to conflict with his earlier statement (cited above) in the same volume that "historic orthodox Christianity" rests on a doctrine of penal substitution atonement (pp. 15-16).

17. Concerning the diversity of understanding of the doctrine of atonement during the patristic period of creedal formulation, see H. E. W. Turner, *The Patristic Doctrine of Redemption:*

chael Winter comments on the state of atonement theology at the close of the patristic period (fifth century): "whereas the Fathers agreed that Christ had saved the human race from sin and its consequences, there was no unanimous tradition as to how this momentous achievement was brought about."[18] Surprisingly, to the modern mind, the patristic theologians did not focus on Christ's death alone as the necessary and sufficient achievement of redemption. Indeed, some patristic writers viewed the Incarnation itself as the achievement of redemption.[19] Such a "holistic" view of redemption is reflected in the Nicene Creed: the phrase "For us humans and for our salvation" heads a lengthy list comprising a single (Greek) sentence that includes Jesus' birth and life, suffering and death, resurrection and ascension.

6.3. The Protestant Faith of the Reformation Confessions

6.3.1. From Anselm to Calvin: Descent with Modification

The elevation of a particular doctrine of atonement to the status "article of faith" is a relatively late occurrence in the history of Christianity. Drawing on the Western/Latin tradition from Augustine to Anselm, the confessions, catechisms, and canons of the Protestant Reformation defined a doctrine of atonement specifically in terms of "satisfaction" or "penal substitution."[20] Before looking at these documents, we note the distinction between the medieval and modern versions of atonement theology.

Although the medieval and modern doctrines of atonement are both framed within the retributive paradigm, it is important not to conflate "satisfaction" (per Anselm) with "penal substitution" (per Calvin). The fundamental difference is that Anselm thinks of retribution in relation to a code of honor, while Calvin thinks of retribution in relation to a system of law.[21] This funda-

---

A Study of the Development of Doctrine during the First Five Centuries (London: Mowbray & Co., 1952).

18. Michael Winter, *The Atonement* (Collegeville, MN: Liturgical Press, 1995), p. 59.

19. Winter, *Atonement*, pp. 38-59.

20. Elements of "satisfaction" atonement thinking begin to appear in the patristic writers of the Latin West, beginning with Tertullian — see Turner, *Patristic Doctrine of Redemption*, pp. 102-13. The atonement theologies of Luther and Calvin are examined in Timothy George, "The Atonement in Martin Luther's Theology," and Henri Blocher, "The Atonement in John Calvin's Theology," pp. 263-78 and 279-303, in *Glory of the Atonement*. Interestingly, although Luther did not speak primarily of "satisfaction" and Calvin did not speak only of "penal substitution" to articulate their respective theologies of atonement, the confessions and catechisms of the Protestant Reformation do define the doctrine of atonement almost exclusively in such terms.

21. Regarding the differences between Anselm and Calvin, especially their different legal backgrounds, see James Wm. McClendon, Jr., *Doctrine: Systematic Theology, Vol. II* (Nashville,

mental difference entails a further difference regarding how each theory understands the "debt" of sin "owed" by humans and, hence, how that "debt" is to be
"repaid" to God.[22] While Anselm's medieval honor-code mindset thinks of that
debt as an obligation to a person's honor and of making satisfaction for dishonoring another as an *alternative* to punishment,[23] Calvin's modern law-system
mindset thinks of that debt as an infringement of the law and of satisfaction for
breaking the law as *requiring* punishment. Thus, whereas in Anselm's thinking
satisfaction is distinguished from penalty, in Calvin's thinking satisfaction is
equated with penalty.[24]

Together, these differences entail yet a further difference between Anselm
and Calvin concerning how each understands the salvation of humanity from
sin. Fiddes:

> *Cur Deus Homo?* asks Anselm: why did God become man? He answers: be-
> cause only man *must* pay the debt of honour, and only God *can* pay it.
> Anselm rejects a view of "penal substitution"; Christ is not punished in our
> place, but releases us *from* punishment *through* satisfaction. When, however,
> later on in the Reformation period, the Roman view of criminal law as a su-
> preme principle had been re-established in society, replacing feudal law,
> there could be no alternative to punishment if the law were infringed. The
> only satisfaction that could be offered to outraged justice *was* punish-
> ment. . . . In the act of atonement Christ pays the debt to justice by bearing

TN: Abingdon Press, 1994), pp. 203-8, and Peter Schmiechen, *Saving Power: Theories of Atonement and Forms of the Church* (Grand Rapids, MI: Eerdmans, 2005), pp. 194-99.

22. Anselm's theory, especially, employs the common financial metaphor of sin as a debt-
obligation. Concerning the implications and difficulties of this metaphor, see Douglas A.
Campbell, *The Deliverance of God: An Apocalyptic Reading of Justification in Paul* (Grand Rapids,
MI: Eerdmans Publishing, 2009), pp. 50-55. As Margaret Atwood, *Payback: Debt and the Shadow
Side of Wealth* (Toronto: House of Anansi Press, 2008), pp. 59-67, has shown, the notion of sin-
debt and redemption from or atonement for sin by substitutionary payment of debt has a pre-
Christian history.

23. It is often observed by commentators that Anselm took his notion of "satisfaction"
from the medieval church's system of penance. Anselm, a Benedictine monk, may also have
drawn his notion of "satisfaction" as an alternative to punishment from the sixth-century *Rule
of Benedict*. The *Rule* provides the opportunity for monks to "obtain pardon" for their faults by
amending their ways and "making satisfaction" in order to avoid the punishment of excommu-
nication, which is reserved as a measure of last resort (cf. *Rule* XXIII–XXX). Satisfaction as an
alternative to punishment is evident in ch. V of the *Rule,* concerning obedience: "if the disciple
obeys with an ill will and murmurs . . . he will incur the punishment due to murmurers, unless
he amend and make satisfaction."

24. Schmiechen, *Saving Power,* pp. 37-45, argues that Calvin's view in the *Institutes of the
Christian Religion* is not, overall, one of "retributive atonement." Nonetheless, in Calvin's view
satisfaction for sin requires punishment and sacrifice for sin functions as a vicarious punishment — i.e., retributive justice operates at the core of Calvin's logic of atonement.

the necessary punishment instead of humankind. The Son offers himself as a substitutionary victim on whom the penalty of God the Father falls.[25]

One might also frame this difference in terms of sacrifice. In Anselm's thinking, Christ offers his life in obedience to God on behalf of humanity, thereby satisfying God's honor and saving humanity from God's punishment. In Calvin's thinking, Christ sacrifices himself by undergoing punishment from God in place of humanity, thereby satisfying God's law and saving humanity from God's punishment. While in Anselm's theory, sacrifice averts punishment, in Calvin's theory, sacrifice *is* punishment.[26] The relationship between the medieval Anselmian view and the modern Calvinist view, we might thus say, is one of "descent with modification."

6.3.2. Satisfaction

Several Reformation documents articulate the Protestant doctrine of atonement in terms of satisfaction.[27] The Lutheran Augsburg Confession (1530): "their [humans'] sins are forgiven for Christ's sake, who, by His death, has made satisfaction for our sins" (Article IV). The Reformed Heidelberg Catechism (1563) follows suit: "Why was it necessary for Christ to humble himself even 'unto death'? Answer: Because with respect to the justice and truth of God, satisfaction for our sins could be made no otherwise, than by the death of the Son of God" (Question 40). Similarly, the Westminster Confession (1646): "Christ, by his obedience and death, did fully discharge the debt of all those that are thus justified, and did make a proper, real, and full satisfaction of his Father's justice in their behalf" (XI). Notice the emphasis on Christ's obedience and the absence of any mention of Christ undergoing punishment, reflective of Anselm's thinking, in which satisfaction is an alternative to punishment.

25. Paul S. Fiddes, *Past Event and Present Salvation: The Christian Idea of Atonement* (Louisville: Westminster/John Knox, 1989), pp. 97-98 (cf. pp. 96-104).

26. Accordingly, as we will see in Chapter 10, the penal substitution viewpoint interprets the sacrifices for sin in the Levitical cult as a form of vicarious punishment: the sacrificial animal bears the penalty of death for sin in place of the sinner. The equation between sacrifice and punishment is evident throughout the discussion of "The Satisfaction of Christ" in the Reformed theologian Charles Hodge's *Systematic Theology*, vol. 2, ch. 7.

27. The confessions, catechisms, and canons of the Protestant Reformation can be found online at http://www.reformed.org/documents/index.html and http://www.ondoctrine.com/20catech.htm.

6.3.3. Penal Substitution

Other Reformation documents articulated the Protestant doctrine of atonement in penal substitution terms. Calvin's Geneva Catechism on "The Doctrine of Christ" (1545):

> He died to discharge the penalty due by us, and in this way exempt us from it. But as we all being sinners were obnoxious to the judgment of God, he, that he might act as our substitute, was pleased to be sisted in presence of an earthly judge, and condemned by his mouth, that we might be acquitted before the celestial tribunal of God.

The Dutch Reformed Canons of Dort (1618-19) follow suit. In the "Second Main Point of Doctrine" concerning "Christ's Death and Human Redemption through It," Article 1 on "The Punishment Which God's Justice Requires" is followed with Article 2 on "The Satisfaction Made by Christ," which states:

> Since, however, we ourselves cannot give this satisfaction or deliver ourselves from God's anger, God in his boundless mercy has given us as a guarantee his only begotten Son, who was made to be sin and a curse for us, in our place, on the cross, in order that he might give satisfaction for us.

Likewise, the English Baptist Confession (1689): Christ "underwent the punishment due to us, which we should have borne and suffered" and so "has fully satisfied the justice of God" (VIII). Notice here penalty and punishment as the means of satisfaction, reflecting Calvin's thinking, in which satisfaction is equated with punishment.[28]

6.3.4. Beyond "Mere Christianity"

Luke Timothy Johnson comments on the contrast between the ancient ecumenical creeds and the Protestant Reformation statements concerning "essential" Christianity:

---

28. All the essential elements of the penal substitution doctrine are formulated in Calvin's *Institutes of the Christian Religion*, II. That the doctrine of penal substitution atonement, in its modern form, originates within Calvin's thought and the ensuing Reformed tradition raises the question whether penal substitution requires commitment to Calvinist theology. Jeffery et al., *Pierced for Our Transgressions*, pp. 268-78, argue at length that defending penal substitution is inseparable from upholding the "TULIP" system of Calvinist belief (total depravity, unconditional election, limited atonement, irresistible grace, and preservation of the saints).

The brief explanatory phrase "for us . . . and for our salvation" [in the Nicene Creed], furthermore, refrains from elaborating any theory of sin (original or otherwise) or any theory of atonement or election. In this respect, the Nicene-Constantinopolitan Creed is clearly superior to later confessions, which enter into elaborate discussions of such points (e.g., the Calvinist Westminster Confession of 1646, chaps. 6–10). Such reticence is liberating in at least two ways. First, it draws believers' attention away from themselves and toward the gracious act of God. Second, it allows the full complexity of Scripture on all these points to remain open for new meaning.

The creed tells us what is absolutely essential: God acts in the world for the sake of humans and to save them. The "how" and any further inquiry into the "why" remain unstated because they are (ultimately) unknowable and unnecessary.[29]

This position is paralleled by C. S. Lewis in *Mere Christianity*. Lewis is careful to distinguish between the essential doctrines of Christian orthodoxy — "mere Christianity" — and all theories of atonement, including penal substitution. In making this distinction, he states what I think to be precisely the right point:

The central Christian belief is that Christ's death has somehow put us right with God and given us a fresh start. Theories as to how it did this are another matter. A good many different theories have been held as to how it works; what all Christians are agreed on is that it does work. . . . *Theories about Christ's death are not Christianity:* they are explanations about how it works. . . .

We are told that Christ was killed for us, that His death has washed out our sins, and that by dying He disabled death itself. That is the formula. That is Christianity. That is what has to be believed. Any theories we build up as to how Christ's death did all this are, in my view, quite secondary: mere plans or diagrams to be left alone if they do not help us, and, even if they do help us,

29. Johnson, *Creed*, p. 318. Regarding why the Protestant confessions do indulge in detail, John Meyendorff, "The Nicene Creed: Uniting or Dividing Confession?" in S. Mark Heim, ed., *Faith to Creed: Ecumenical Perspectives on the Affirmation of the Apostolic Faith in the Fourth Century* (Grand Rapids, MI: Eerdmans Publishing, 1991), observes: "theological affirmations (or exclusions) contained in the various Protestant *Confessions* had a motivation greatly different from the rationale of ancient creeds. The Confessions were meant to replace the teaching magisterium of the medieval Latin church, and they were also aimed at listing all the essentials of the faith: by accepting those essentials one became eligible for sacramental communion and church membership. There was a concern for truth, certainly, but also a polemical intent and a desire to distinguish between 'essentials' and 'nonessentials'" (p. 16, emphasis original). This may help explain why some apologists for penal substitution (e.g., Jeffery et al., *Pierced for Our Transgressions*, pp. 216-17) seek to make atonement into a church-dividing issue.

not to be confused with the thing itself. All the same, some of these theories are worth looking at.[30]

He then proceeds, as do we, to consider the penal substitution doctrine of atonement.[31]

6.4. Penal Substitution as a Theological Model

Lewis's distinction between the orthodox doctrine that Jesus died "for us" and "for our salvation" and various theories of atonement will be important to keep in mind. Penal substitution is often called a (or *the*) "doctrine" of atonement — or, simply, penal substitution is effectively equated with "the atonement."[32] But this gives the (false) impression that it is of equal status to the orthodox doctrines set forth in the ancient creeds. In actuality, penal substitution is only one among many explanatory theories or "theological models" of the saving effect of the cross of Christ — and a relatively recently formulated one at that.[33] From this point on, we thus shift terminology and refer to the penal substitution *theory* or *model* of atonement to help us remember this point.

J. I. Packer himself recognizes penal substitution's status as a theological model analogous to scientific models: "As models in physics are hypotheses formed under the suggestive control of empirical evidence to correlate and predict phenomena, so Christian theological models are explanatory constructs formed to help us know, understand and deal with God, the ultimate reality."[34]

---

30. C. S. Lewis, *Mere Christianity* (London: HarperCollins Publishers, 1977), pp. 53-55, emphasis added.

31. Lewis himself seems to have had a liking for the "Christus Victor" view of the patristic period, as evidenced by his prominent and dramatic use of that motif in *The Chronicles of Narnia, Book Two: The Lion, the Witch, and the Wardrobe* (New York: HarperCollins, 1994), pp. 156-66. Concerning this motif in Lewis, see Gregory A. Boyd, "Christus Victor Response," in Beilby and Eddy, *Nature of the Atonement*, pp. 99-105.

32. The title of a recent compilation of apologetic essays favoring penal substitution — *The Glory of the Atonement* — gives the distinct impression that penal substitution is assumed to be equivalent to "the atonement."

33. Schmiechen, *Saving Power*, surveys and critiques various theories of atonement. Whereas Gustav Aulén argued that there are only three historic theories of atonement (Christus Victor, satisfaction/substitution, and moral influence), and penal substitution apologists maintain that there is only one historic theory, Schmiechen demonstrates that Christian tradition has developed some ten theories of atonement down the centuries.

34. J. I. Packer, "What Did the Cross Achieve? The Logic of Penal Substitution," in J. I. Packer, *Celebrating the Saving Work of God: The Collected Shorter Writings of J. I. Packer* (Carlisle, UK: Paternoster Press, 1998), I, pp. 85-123, here p. 93. Packer goes on to distinguish a three-tier hierarchy of models in Christian theology: biblical models (word-pictures taken from Scripture — e.g., kingdom of God), dogmatic models (defined through the formation of the

Subsequently, he calls penal substitution "a conceptual instrument for conveying the thought that God remits our sins and accepts our persons into favor not because of any amends we have attempted, but because the penalty which was our due was diverted onto Christ."[35] We think this an apt analogy: analogous to the hypotheses and constructions used to predict and explain empirical data in the sciences, penal substitution is a constructive hypothesis intended to explain various scriptural data concerning atonement and the cross.[36]

Acknowledging that penal substitution is an explanatory model, a "conceptual instrument" or constructive hypothesis, carries implications. First, as with all models of atonement, penal substitution is to be distinguished, not only from the creeds, but also from Scripture itself; therefore, we must be careful not to confuse the explanation with the evidence it is intended to explain. One can question the truth of penal substitution as an explanation of Scripture concerning atonement and the saving significance of Jesus' death while nonetheless maintaining full faith in the biblical message. Second, that penal substitution is a theological model in analogy with scientific models implies not only that it is a hypothetical-constructive aid to human understanding but also that it is *fallible* and, hence, *tentative*. Just as scientific models are always potentially in need of revision or even rejection in the face of new or anomalous evidence, so also we might need to revise or even reject penal substitution in favor of a better explanation on a more careful review of the scriptural evidence.[37]

Although any atonement model will be a human construction, our theological construction is not without constraint. The "basic truths" Marshall identifies as "essential to a New Testament theology of salvation" do constrain adequate models of atonement:

1. We are saved from the consequences of our sins by the grace of God and not by anything that we ourselves do.
2. In the death of Jesus, the Father and the Son are acting together in love. . . .

---

creeds — e.g., Trinity), and interpretive models (designed to defend and explain the faith — e.g., penal substitution).

35. Packer, "What Did the Cross Achieve?" p. 105.

36. Concerning models in science and theology, see Alister E. McGrath, *Science and Religion: An Introduction* (Oxford: Blackwell Publishing, 1999), pp. 144-76, and Ian G. Barbour, *Religion and Science: Historical and Contemporary Issues* (San Francisco: HarperSanFrancisco, 1997), pp. 106-36.

37. Here I diverge from McGrath, *Science and Religion*, pp. 163-64, who maintains that theological models, unlike scientific models, are not validated empirically. Those theological models that Packer calls "interpretive models," including penal substitution, not only can be, but surely must be, validated empirically by the "data" of Scripture and selected according to the best "empirical fit." For such models, as explanations of Scripture, are not simply "given" by revelation but are constructed by the human mind and thus must be tested for truth against revelation.

3. The decisive element in our salvation is . . . the death and resurrection of Jesus.

4. This death is the death of one who is, at one and the same time, the Son of God and the sinless human being. . . .

5. It follows that the incarnation was an essential condition for the saving action.

6. The salvation secured by the death and resurrection of Jesus becomes effective through the work of the Holy Spirit and through the faith of the recipient.

7. The main results of the atonement are, negatively, to deliver us from the guilt and power of sin and, positively, to restore us to a right relationship with God with all that involves.[38]

Yet, even these "basic truths" do not uniquely constrain the construction of a model of atonement; they are insufficient to determine a biblical theology of salvation. Marshall himself states: "Any doctrine of the death of Jesus must conform to or incorporate these basic points. . . . However, this basic core of beliefs leaves unanswered just how the death of Jesus is the means of salvation."[39] Scriptural evidence and creedal formulas thus "underdetermine" atonement theology.[40] Precisely because penal substitution is an explanatory model, and so is underdetermined by the scriptural evidence it is intended to explain, therefore, it cannot be argued that penal substitution is indispensable to a biblical theology of the cross that is consistent with the constraints of Christian orthodoxy.[41]

---

38. I. Howard Marshall, *Aspects of the Atonement: Cross and Resurrection in the Reconciling of God and Humanity* (London: Paternoster, 2007), pp. 9-10.

39. Marshall, *Aspects of the Atonement*, p. 10.

40. Theology thus shares the "problem of underdetermination" with science: empirical data and logical rules do not uniquely determine either a theory of nature or a theory of atonement.

41. Packer does not draw the conclusion to which his own analogy between scientific and theological models leads and in the end seems to say that penal substitution is indispensable. He concludes by quoting A. M. Hunter: ". . . We are not fond nowadays of calling Christ's suffering 'penal' or of styling him our 'substitute'; but can we avoid using some such words as these to express Paul's view of the atonement?" Packer gives this rejoinder: "Well, can we? And if not, what follows? Can we then justify ourselves in holding a view of the atonement into which penal substitution does not enter? Ought we not to reconsider whether penal substitution is not, after all, the heart of the matter? These are among the questions which our preliminary survey in this lecture has raised. It is hoped that they will receive the attention they deserve." "What Did the Cross Achieve?" p. 123. Although Packer seems to leave the question open to further investigation, the way he has put the matter seems to hedge the question in favor of the indispensability of penal substitution for understanding Paul's view of the cross.

CHAPTER 7

The Message Proclaimed by the
Evangelists and Apostles

This man, handed over to you according to
the definite plan and foreknowledge of God,
you crucified and killed by the hands of those outside the law.
But God raised him up, having freed him from death,
because it was impossible for him to be held in its power.

ACTS 2:23-24

7.1. Penal Substitution: Apostolic Preaching?

While the early church did not declare any one theory of atonement as ortho-dox doctrine, atonement for sin by penal substitution might nonetheless have been central to the earliest message of the Evangelists and Apostles. John Stott claims that penal substitution was indisputably the faith of the Apostles: "we should accept the direct statement of Christ and His apostles, that He bore our sins, understanding that phrase in its biblical meaning that He underwent the penalty of our sins for us."[1] Is that so? Was penal substitution, in fact, "the di-rect statement of Christ and His apostles"?

The question being asked is not whether the earliest message of the Evan-gelists and Apostles proclaims that Jesus died "for us" and "for our salvation" as the Nicene Creed affirms. As Martin Hengel has shown, the earliest tradition of the church understood Jesus' death as sacrificial ("he gave himself"), atoning ("for our sins"), and vicarious ("for us" or "for many").[2] It does not follow,

---

1. John R. W. Stott, *Basic Christianity* (Grand Rapids, MI: Eerdmans Publishing, 1966), p. 97.
2. Martin Hengel, *The Atonement: The Origins of the Doctrine in the New Testament* (Phila-delphia: Fortress Press, 1981).

however, that the earliest accounts of the Evangelists and Apostles depict Jesus'
death as a penal substitution. A careful inductive examination of the earliest
passion narrative (Mark) and the earliest apostolic preaching (Acts) finds a
story of the cross different from penal substitution.

Central to the penal substitution model is that it places God in the role of
causative agent in the death of Jesus. If we ask by whose plan and whose power
Jesus was punished with death, penal substitution answers, "God." Recall Mac-
Arthur: "Here's what was happening on the cross: God was punishing His own
Son. . . ." Or Bonhoeffer: ". . . he [Jesus] was stricken by God's wrath and vengeance." Or Hodge: "He [Jesus] was smitten of God and afflicted." The penal
substitution model thus maintains that God fulfills his plan of salvation for humanity by acting to put Jesus to death on the cross.

The further implication of the penal substitution model is that, because Jesus' death alone is necessary and sufficient to propitiate God's wrath, the resurrection would seem inconsequential for salvation, an inessential part of the
story. Because Jesus' death by itself satisfies God's vengeance, and because satisfying God's vengeance is "the main problem" to be solved by the cross, the resurrection seems just an epilogue or footnote to the drama of salvation as depicted by the penal substitution model.[3]

That the resurrection is inessential and inconsequential for salvation in the
penal substitution model is evident in the systematic lack of attention paid to the
resurrection in accounts and defenses of penal substitution. This is apparent in
Roger Nicole's lengthy account of atonement (quoted above), in which one finds
no mention or even allusion to the resurrection. In summarizing his systematic
exposition of the logic and meaning of penal substitution, J. I. Packer lists nine
"ingredients in the evangelical model of penal substitution" — in which the resurrection is nowhere to be found. Indeed, item five in his list underscores the
cross as the sole and sufficient means of salvation: "Christ's death for me is my
sole ground of hope before God."[4] This deficit concerning the resurrection in

3. In a 450-page book on the single topic of atonement, Charles E. Hill and Frank A. James
III, eds., *The Glory of the Atonement: Biblical, Theological and Practical Perspectives* (Downers
Grove, IL: InterVarsity Press, 2004), which is an evangelical apologetic for penal substitution,
the index contains only four references to resurrection, and all appear in a single essay on Paul
(Richard Gaffin, "Atonement in the Pauline Corpus"). Stunningly, in the essay by Royce Gordon
Gruenler, "Atonement in the Synoptic Gospels and Acts," there is only a single mention of the
resurrection, in the penultimate paragraph, as if an afterthought.

4. J. I. Packer, "What Did the Cross Achieve? The Logic of Penal Substitution," in J. I.
Packer, *Celebrating the Saving Work of God: The Collected Shorter Writings of J. I. Packer* (Carlisle,
UK: Paternoster Press, 1998), I, pp. 85-123, here pp. 120-21. Packer does address this criticism,
that the substitutionary view makes the resurrection unnecessary, as follows (p. 102):
". . . Christ's saving work has two parts, his dealing with his Father on our behalf by offering
himself in substitutionary satisfaction for our sins, and his dealing with us on his Father's behalf
by bestowing on us through faith the forgiveness which his death secured, and it is as important

penal substitution is apparent also in the recent book by Jeffery et al., who defend penal substitution on this point, claiming that it "is entirely at home with the resurrection of Jesus."[5] Whether penal substitution is "at home" with the resurrection is not the point. And that they miss the point — that, on penal substitution terms, the resurrection is inessential and inconsequential for salvation — is evident in their supporting observations, none of which concern the propitiation of God, the satisfaction of retribution, or the forgiveness of sin, which comprise the heart of the matter according to penal substitution.

The cross is the sum and substance of God's work, penal substitution claims, leaving the resurrection as inessential and inconsequential.[6] The Evangelists and Apostles, we shall see, tell the story differently. Indeed, that God had raised Jesus was so important to their message that the Apostles made it the marker of their witness. Before ascending into heaven, Jesus says of the Apostles, "you will be my witnesses" (Acts 2:8). To what were the Apostles to be witnesses? When selecting a replacement for Judas, Peter states that they should select "one of the men who have accompanied us during all the time that the Lord Jesus went in and out among us," who now "must become a witness with us to his resurrection" (1:21-22). Then at Pentecost, Peter proclaims to the crowd: "This Jesus God raised up, and of that all of us are witnesses" (2:32). And, again, when depicting the communal life of the early church, the narrator observes, "With great power the apostles gave their testimony to the resurrection of the Lord Jesus" (4:33). Indeed, when Paul is arrested in Jerusalem and brought to trial before both the Jewish council and the Roman governor, he testifies repeatedly that he is on trial, not on account of the cross of Christ, but on account of his hope in Christ concerning "the resurrection of the dead" (23:6; 24:15;

---

to distinguish these two parts as it is to hold them together. For a demonstration that part two is now possible because part one is finished, and for the actual implementing of part two, Jesus' resurrection is indeed essential, and so appears as an organic element in his work as a whole." But Packer neither explains why the resurrection is necessary to demonstrate that "part two is now possible because part one is finished"; nor does Packer explain how the resurrection is essential to "the actual implementing of part two." Moreover, his list of nine "ingredients" seems in tension with his statement of "part two." Earlier (p. 102), Packer states that the resurrection is essential for "bestowing on us through faith the forgiveness" of sins. But later (p. 121), Packer states that saving faith is given through Christ's death: "My faith in Christ is God's own gift to me, given in virtue of Christ's death for me: i.e. the cross procured it." Furthermore, in the remaining twenty pages of his presentation of penal substitution atonement after he stresses that the resurrection is essential to God's saving work, there is no further mention, much less treatment, of the resurrection. And in his collection of writings, *Celebrating the Saving Work of God*, there is not a single essay on the topic of the resurrection!

5. Steve Jeffery, Michael Ovey, and Andrew Sach, *Pierced for Our Transgressions: Rediscovering the Glory of Penal Substitution* (Wheaton, IL: Crossway Books, 2008), p. 213.

6. I. Howard Marshall, *Aspects of the Atonement: Cross and Resurrection in the Reconciling of God and Humanity* (London: Paternoster, 2007), duly notes this deficit in penal substitution thinking and offers a welcome consideration of the role of resurrection in the atonement.

26:6-8). While in no way downplaying the cross, the apostolic message placed a special emphasis on the resurrection, which thus deserves an adequate accounting in our atonement theology.

7.2. The Earliest Passion Narrative

7.2.1. *Jesus Was Crucified by Humans to Satisfy Humans, Not God*

The scriptural witnesses attest uniformly that Jesus was put to death by *human* agency for *political* purposes, not as the outworking of a divine conspiracy orchestrated from heaven in which human beings are accidental actors or incidental characters.[7] All four Gospels agree that Jesus was condemned by Roman authority under a political charge (Mark 15:18; Matt 27:37; Luke 23:2-3, 37; John 19:19), as the result of a conspiracy of the Jewish nation-temple leadership with the Roman authority (Mark 14:53–15:39; Matt 26:57–27:54; Luke 22:54–23:49; John 18:12–19:30).[8] He was accused of rebellion and insurrection (Luke 23:2-5) and was executed in a manner reserved for rebels and insurrectionists, for those who upset the *pax Romana*.[9] Mark's passion narrative, the earliest written account of Jesus' death, moreover, makes it clear that Pilate passed a death sentence on Jesus with the intention of appeasing the crowd: "So Pilate, *wishing to satisfy the crowd,* released Barabbas for them; and after flogging Jesus, he handed him over to be crucified" (Mark 15:15). Luke's account, based on careful investigation of eyewitness sources (Luke 1:2-3), confirms Mark's account, emphasizing repeatedly that Jesus was crucified to satisfy humans, not God:[10]

7. Thomas R. Yoder Neufeld, *Recovering Jesus: The Witness of the New Testament* (Grand Rapids, MI: Brazos Press, 2007), p. 252: "To focus on Jesus's death as solely God's act reduces the historical persons we encounter in the story of Jesus' death to playing little more than bit parts in a drama in which God is the only real actor. That is exactly how the gospel writers do not tell the story."

8. Cf. Yoder Neufeld, *Recovering Jesus*, pp. 247-50.

9. Cf. Yoder Neufeld, *Recovering Jesus*, pp. 242-43. As to *why* Rome would have executed Jesus as a rebel and the Jewish leadership would have sought as much, see N. T. Wright, *Jesus and the Victory of God: Christian Origins and the Question of God, Vol. 2* (Minneapolis: Fortress Press, 1992), pp. 540-52, and Joel B. Green, "The Death of Jesus and the Ways of God: Jesus and the Gospels on Messianic Status and Shameful Suffering," *Interpretation* 52/1 (1998), 24-37, here pp. 26-30.

10. Some may want to dispute that this text from Luke is evidence to the point. Many scholars of previous generations read Luke's Gospel as an apologetic by a Gentile author for the Roman Empire. Thus, Luke's account that Pilate three times declares Jesus innocent and tries to release him (Luke 23:13-22) would seem to deflect responsibility for Jesus' death from the Romans to the Jews. Even if this interpretation of Luke's Gospel, which has been challenged by recent scholarship, were correct, the textual emphasis on Pilate acting to satisfy the crowd in crucifying Jesus is present already in the earlier account of Mark, a Jewish author, who, writing soon after the siege and destruction of Jerusalem, owed nothing to Rome.

But they kept *urgently demanding* with loud shouts that he should be crucified; and *their voices prevailed.* So Pilate gave his verdict that *their demand*
should be granted. He released [Barabbas] and he handed Jesus over *as they
wished.* (Luke 23:23-25)

The Gospels are clear: Pilate puts Jesus to death "to satisfy the crowd," because of "their demand." There is nothing in the Gospel accounts depicting
God putting Jesus to death to satisfy his vengeance, or even humans putting Jesus to death to appease God's wrath. Rather, the Gospel accounts are consistent
in stating that Jesus is crucified, not by God's design to satisfy God's demands,
but by human design to satisfy human demands. Unless we are to suppose that
the shouts of the crowds ("Crucify him!") express God's desire and that the
judgment of Pilate executes God's will, we are led by the Gospel accounts to
conclude that the penal substitution model is off the mark.

In fact, there is not a single verse in all the New Testament stating that God
punished Jesus or that God put Jesus to death — no text that places God in the
role of causative agent in the death of Jesus. The closest one finds is where Paul
writes that God "did not withhold his own Son, but gave him up *(paredōken)*
for all of us" (Rom 8:32). Elsewhere Paul states that Jesus was "handed over"
(paredothē) to death (Rom 4:25) without specifying the agent doing the handing over. Let us assume that God is the implied agent in this text as well (cf.
"was raised for our justification"). Does God's "giving up" or "handing over"
Jesus then imply that God put Jesus to death?

To answer this question, let us examine some further evidence. The verb
Paul uses is that used repeatedly by Mark to speak of Jesus being betrayed to the
authorities who will kill him. Jesus says that he is to be "betrayed" *(paradidotai)*
to be killed by human hands (Mark 9:31); and when Judas arrives at the garden,
Jesus says, "the Son of Man is betrayed *(paradidotai)* into the hands of sinners"
(Mark 14:41). Mark uses the same verb to say that the Sanhedrin "handed over"
(paredōkan) Jesus to Pilate (Mark 15:1), and that Pilate "handed over"
(paredōken) Jesus "to be crucified" (Mark 15:15). In Mark's account, it is clear that
humans are doing the handing over and the killing. In Acts, Luke states that Jesus
was "handed over" *(ekdoton)* to be "crucified and killed by the hands of those
outside the law" (Acts 2:23). Even if we think that God is doing the "handing
over" here, it is nonetheless clear that human hands are doing the killing.

That God "gave up" Jesus (Rom 8:32) does not, therefore, imply that God is
the one who put Jesus to death; that God "surrendered" Jesus to death does not
place God in the role of causative agent in Jesus' death. Indeed, Paul uses this
same verb to speak of Jesus' relation to his own death. Jesus, Paul states several
times, "surrendered himself" *(paredōken eauton)* to death for us (Gal 2:20; Eph
5:2, 25). Surely we are not to understand Paul as saying that Jesus, by "surrendering himself," was the causative agent in his own death, that Jesus crucified

himself. Rather, Paul means to say that Jesus "gave himself," that Jesus freely offered himself in death for our sake (cf. Gal 1:4; 1 Tim 2:6; Tit 2:14). As the Gospels witness, Jesus died voluntarily, not against his will, but also not by his own
hand. Jesus, the Good Shepherd, does not spare his own life but rather exposes
himself to danger for our sake, to the extent of laying down his life to rescue his
sheep from death (John 10:11-18). Likewise, Paul says, God did not spare the life
of his own Son in extending himself to rescue us from all that threatens to separate us from God (Rom 8:31-39).

7.2.2. Jesus' Passion Culminates in Resurrection

Not only does the penal substitution model not fit the details of the Gospel accounts of Jesus' death, but it also overlooks, and thus effectively downplays, a
repeated emphasis of the good news — the resurrection. In the Synoptic Gospels, the resurrection of Jesus is hardly inconsequential to the meaning of the
rest of the story: none of the Gospels end at the cross. Indeed, every "passion"
prophecy that Jesus himself utters in all three Synoptic Gospels points to the
resurrection as the culmination, the dramatic climax, of the passion. The passion of the Messiah culminates in resurrection by God:

> See, we are going up to Jerusalem, and the Son of Man will be handed over to
> the chief priests and the scribes, and they will condemn him to death; then
> they will hand him over to the Gentiles; they will mock him, and spit upon
> him, and flog him, and kill him; and after three days *he will rise again*. (Mark
> 10:33-34)[11]

7.3. The Preaching of the Apostles: Peter

7.3.1. "You Crucified"

The basic story told in the Synoptic Gospels is paralleled in the early preaching
of Peter and Paul. Peter's very first sermon on Pentecost confirms the witness of
the Evangelists. Although Jesus surrenders himself obediently to the will of
God, letting himself be "handed over" rather than resisting arrest, he was nonetheless killed by human hands through human hostility: "this man . . . you crucified and killed by the hands of those outside the law" (Acts 2:22-24). Peter
preaches that Jesus is crucified, not by the hand of God to satisfy his law, but
"by the hands" of outlaw humanity. In his subsequent preaching, Peter repeatedly emphasizes human agency and responsibility in Jesus' death:

---

11. Cf. Mark 8:31; 9:31; Matt 16:21; 17:23; 20:19; Luke 9:22; 18:32-33.

". . . God has made him both Lord and Messiah, this Jesus whom *you cruci-fied*" (Acts 2:36);

"But *you rejected* the Holy and Righteous One and asked to have a mur-derer given to you, and *you killed* the Author of life . . ." (3:14-15);

". . . by the name of Jesus Christ of Nazareth, whom *you crucified . . .*" (4:10);

". . . Jesus, whom *you had killed* by hanging him on a tree" (5:30);

"*They put him [Jesus Christ] to death* by hanging him on a tree . . ." (10:39).

7.3.2. *"But God Raised Him Up"*

Peter's Pentecost preaching, moreover, confirms that, although God allowed hu-man purposes hostile to the divine will to be carried out in the death of Jesus, God's purpose was fulfilled through raising Jesus from death to life: "you cruci-fied and killed . . . *but God raised him up,* having freed him from death, because it was impossible for him to be held in its power" (Acts 2:22-24). Peter then repeats the same message at every opportunity. As often as Peter emphasizes human agency and responsibility for the death of Jesus, he further highlights God's agency and purpose in raising Jesus from death and exalting him to glory:[12]

". . . *God has made* him both Lord and Messiah, this Jesus whom you cruci-fied" (2:36);

". . . the *God* of our ancestors *has glorified* his servant Jesus, whom you handed over . . . you killed the Author of life, *whom God raised from the dead* . . ." (3:13-15);

". . . Jesus Christ of Nazareth whom you crucified, *whom God raised* from the dead" (4:10);

"The *God* of our ancestors *raised up Jesus,* whom you had killed by hanging him on a tree. *God exalted him* at his right hand as Leader and Sav-ior . . ." (5:30-31);

"They put him to death by hanging him on a tree, *but God raised him . . .*" (10:39-40).

Robert Tannehill comments on this distinctive pattern in Peter's preaching:

> Peter speaks not only of what God did through Jesus but also of what "you" did, namely, reject and kill God's Messiah. . . . Peter's sermons in Jerusalem constantly emphasize the sharp contrast between the hearer's role in denying and killing Jesus and God's vindicating act of resurrection. . . . The contrast-

12. Concerning this distinctive pattern of Peter's preaching in Acts 2–5, see Robert C. Tannehill, *The Narrative Unity of Luke-Acts: A Literary Interpretation* II: *The Acts of the Apostles* (Minneapolis: Fortress Press, 1990), pp. 33-42, 48-79.

ing pattern of speech used by Peter . . . emphasizes the conflict between the actions of the audience and God.[13]

7.4. The Preaching of the Apostles: Paul

7.4.1. "The Wisdom of This Age" against "the Wisdom of God"

We find the same pattern in Paul's speeches — a sharp contrast between the intentions and actions of humans and the intentions and actions of God. In his very first sermon, Paul confirmed the apostolic message — that Jesus was killed by human agents for human purposes: "Even though they found no cause for a sentence of death, they asked Pilate to have him killed" (Acts 13:28). Later, Paul again imputed responsibility for the death of Jesus, not to God, but to "the rulers of this age," who "crucified the Lord of glory" because of their ignorance of "God's wisdom" (1 Cor 2:6-8).

The logical implication of this latter text must not be overlooked; for it cuts directly against the claim central to penal substitution. The penal substitution model states that Jesus was executed precisely in order to fulfill a plan of salvation predestined by God, which implies that Jesus' execution was ultimately according to the divine wisdom. Paul states the opposite in this text.

The full text states: "But we speak God's wisdom, secret and hidden, which God decreed before the ages for our glory. None of the rulers of this age understood this; for if they had, they would not have crucified the Lord of glory" (1 Cor 2:7-8). Paul does more here than attribute agency and responsibility for the death of Jesus to "the rulers of this age." Paul's statement — "if they had understood God's wisdom, they would not have crucified Jesus" — entails logically that, because they did crucify Jesus, they did not understand God's wisdom. Paul's statement thus implies further that the human agents responsible for crucifying Jesus acted, not only in ignorance of, but also *contrary* to God's wisdom: *if* they *had* understood God's wisdom, they *would not* have crucified Jesus; thus, "the rulers of this age" crucified Jesus *against* the wisdom of God. That is, the crucifixion of Jesus by "the rulers of this age" did *not* fulfill God's ageless plan.

We must set Paul's statement in the context of his "message of the cross" to see the story he is telling. Paul's gospel proclaims "Christ the power of God and the wisdom of God" (1 Cor 1:24), which contrasts and conflicts with "the wisdom of this age [and] of the rulers of this age" (2:6). This conflict climaxes at the cross, where we see displayed the stark contrast between God's ageless wisdom and the wisdom of this age. God's power is revealed in the "weakness" of

13. Tannehill, *Narrative Unity of Luke-Acts*, II, pp. 34-35.

the cross (1:18–2:5), Christ's voluntary submission to the violent power of the world, while the power of this age is revealed in the violence wielded by the rulers against Christ. God's ageless wisdom is revealed by Jesus' "foolish" refusal to use violence and his undying trust in God's power, while the wisdom of this age is revealed by the rulers' "wise" trust in violence to put to death those that trouble their rule. By overcoming the violence of the world through the cross, Christ inverts wisdom and power: God's wisdom and power are displayed in what we mortals regard as "foolishness" and "weakness." The crucifixion of Christ by "the rulers of this age" reveals, not God's wisdom, but "the wisdom of this age." The clear implication of Paul's message of the cross is that Jesus' death by "the rulers of this age" was *not* according to "God's wisdom, secret and hidden . . . decreed before the ages." This divine wisdom, Paul writes, not only transcends the violent power of this world, but also outstrips the human imagination — it is "what no eye has seen, nor ear heard, nor the human heart conceived" (1 Cor 2:9, citing Isa 64:4).

7.4.2. "God Has Fulfilled by Raising Jesus"

Paul's early preaching also emphasizes the conflict between human purposes carried through by crucifixion and God's purpose fulfilled by resurrection. Paul's first sermon: "Even though they found no cause for a sentence of death, they asked Pilate to have him killed. . . . *But God raised him* from the dead" (Acts 13:28, 30). Following this, Paul gives a clear statement of the apostolic message — which concerns, not Jesus being killed by human hands, but God fulfilling the covenant through the resurrection: "And we bring you the good news that what God promised to our ancestors he has fulfilled for us, their children, by raising Jesus" (vv. 32-33a). Again, notice carefully both what Paul has said and what he has not said. Paul does *not* say: the good news is that God has fulfilled his pre-ordained plan by bringing about Jesus' death so he could pour out the divine wrath on him instead of us. Paul *does* say: the good news is that God has fulfilled his promised redemption "for us" precisely "by raising Jesus." As does Peter, Paul contrasts human and divine action and intention: ". . . the residents and leaders of Jerusalem . . . fulfilled those words by condemning him . . . what God promised . . . he has fulfilled . . . by raising Jesus" (vv. 27, 32-33). By crucifying Jesus, humans fulfilled the prophets; but by raising Jesus, God fulfilled his promise. According to Paul's first sermon, Jesus' death by human design fails to thwart God's plan, which God acts to bring to completion by raising Jesus (cf. 24:15; 26:6-8).[14]

From the beginning, then, Paul saw the resurrection as essential to God's

---

14. Cf. Tannehill, *Narrative Unity of Luke-Acts*, II, pp. 167-70.

saving activity in Jesus. In the epistles, Paul continues to emphasize the resurrection as integral to God's redeeming work. Indeed, throughout his letters, Paul speaks of God raising Jesus from the dead no less than eleven times in various contexts.[15]

In one place, Paul declares the resurrection to be essential to the completion of our redemption in Christ: "It [righteousness] will be reckoned to us who believe in him who raised Jesus our Lord from the dead, who was handed over to death for our trespasses and was *raised for our justification*" (Rom 4:24-25). Humanity's being put right with God, Paul says, is dependent not only on Christ having died for our sins but also on Christ having been raised by God. In another place, Paul declares that the death of Jesus itself, apart from the resurrection, was insufficient for salvation, even for forgiveness of sins. Without the resurrection, Paul says, God's work is incomplete and thus our faith is pointless — such that we would be neither redeemed from sin nor freed from death. In the same letter where Paul begins, "I decided to know nothing among you except Christ, and him crucified" (1 Cor 2:2), and goes on to proclaim the gospel that "Christ died for our sins" (15:3), he then writes, "If Christ has not been raised, your faith is futile and you are still in your sins" (v. 17). Logically, this latter statement entails that the resurrection of Jesus is essential to both God's redeeming us from sin and our trusting God for salvation: our faith in God is empty, for we remain in sin and thus under death, *unless* Jesus has been raised. Paul's two claims — that Jesus "was raised for the sake of our justification" (Rom 4:25) and that without Christ's resurrection we "are still in [our] sins" (1 Cor 15:17) fit together: were Jesus not raised, we would remain in sin and without faith; hence, the resurrection is necessary for us to be freed from sin and right with God.[16]

"Paul's point," I. Howard Marshall notes, "is the crucial one that the death [of Christ], by itself, is not sufficient to deal with sins. . . . Here, then, it is made absolutely clear that the death of Jesus would have no saving efficacy apart from his resurrection."[17] Charles Cousar's comment on 1 Corinthians 15 sees the same implication:

> Though the gospel announces that Christ died "for our sins" (v. 3), a denial of Jesus' resurrection . . . prohibits forgiveness from being actualized (v. 17). . . . Thus Jesus' resurrection obviously carries saving significance . . . the resurrection of Jesus is a constituent event in the saving action of God. The juxtaposition between "Christ died for our sins" (15:3) and "if Christ has

15. Rom 4:24; 6:4; 8:11; 10:9; 1 Cor 6:14; 15:15; 2 Cor 4:14; Gal 1:1; Eph 1:20; Col 2:12; 1 Thess 1:10.

16. On the significance of these texts for atonement theology, see Marshall, *Aspects of the Atonement*, pp. 80-97.

17. Marshall, *Aspects of the Atonement*, p. 70.

not been raised, you are still in your sins" (15:17) leaves no doubt about the indispensable role of both crucifixion and resurrection for salvation.[18]

N. T. Wright elaborates on the linkage between the resurrection of Jesus and the forgiveness of sins in the thinking of Paul:

> The crunch comes in verse 17: if the Messiah isn't raised, then your faith is futile *and you are still in your sins.* In other words, with the resurrection of Jesus a new world has dawned in which forgiveness of sins is not simply a private experience; it is a fact about the cosmos. Sin is the root cause of death: if death has been defeated, it must mean that sin has been dealt with. But if the Messiah has not been raised, we are still in a world where sin reigns supreme and undefeated so that the foundational Christian belief, that God has dealt with our sins in Christ, is based on thin air and is reduced to whistling in the dark.[19]

Cousar goes on to note other Pauline texts that link the resurrection to salvation (2 Cor 5:15; Rom 4:24-25; 8:34) and draws the conclusion: "One is left with the profound impression that Jesus' resurrection, alongside the crucifixion, plays a decisive role in the drama of salvation."[20]

We can see, therefore, that the penal substitution model, insofar as it grounds forgiveness of sins on the all-sufficiency of Jesus' death, cannot adequately account for Paul's emphasis on the resurrection as integral and indispensable to God's salvation, including the forgiveness of sins. John Stott's treatment of the resurrection is indicative of the inadequacy of penal substitution on this point. Stott does recognize the emphasis on the resurrection in the early apostolic preaching and literature.[21] And we agree: "Although they [the apostles] emphasized it [resurrection], it would be an exaggeration to call their message an exclusively resurrection gospel."[22] That being said, however, Stott subsequently limits the significance of the resurrection. He treats the resurrection in one section on "The Victory in Christ" in a chapter on "The Conquest of Evil."[23] In his account, "the resurrection was *the conquest confirmed and an-*

18. Charles B. Cousar, *A Theology of the Cross: The Death of Jesus in the Pauline Letters* (Minneapolis, MN: Fortress Press, 1990), pp. 94, 96. Cousar observes further that the confessional formula in Rom 10:9 refers only to the resurrection: "if you confess with your lips that Jesus is Lord and believe in your heart that God raised him from the dead, you will be saved." Our salvation, this implies, hinges on the resurrection as much as the death of Jesus. See also Marshall, *Aspects of the Atonement*, pp. 70-71.

19. N. T. Wright, *Surprised by Hope: Rethinking Heaven, the Resurrection, and the Mission of the Church* (New York: HarperCollins, 2008), p. 247, emphasis original.

20. Cousar, *Theology of the Cross*, p. 98.

21. Cf. Stott, *Cross of Christ*, pp. 32-35.

22. Stott, *Cross of Christ*, p. 35.

23. Stott, *Cross of Christ*, pp. 235-39.

nounced," the victory of Christ having already been won completely at the cross.[24] The resurrection, then, serves only to ratify the victory of the cross, to declare "the divine reversal of the human verdict," but is not effectively integral to Christ's dealing with sin and victory over evil.[25]

Stott's account thus makes the resurrection objectively unnecessary to Christ's saving work. For that the cross alone was sufficient, as he makes clear:

> Of course the resurrection was essential to confirm the efficacy of his death, as his incarnation had been to prepare for its possibility. But we must insist that Christ's work of sin-bearing was finished on the cross, that the victory over the devil, sin, and death was won there, and that what the resurrection did was to vindicate the Jesus whom men had rejected, to declare with power that he is the Son of God, and publicly to confirm that his sin-bearing death had been effective for the forgiveness of sins. . . . This is the implication of Romans 4:25. . . .
>
> . . . The resurrection did not achieve our deliverance from sin and death, but has brought us an assurance of both.[26]

The resurrection does not achieve anything for our salvation, Stott claims, but only brings us assurance of salvation. Yet, as we have seen, Paul says otherwise: had Christ *not* been raised, we would still be in our sins and thus subject to death (1 Cor 15:17). Not the cross alone, therefore, but the resurrection also was essential to Christ achieving our deliverance from sin and death. Marshall, furthermore, points out the obvious weakness in such an interpretation of Rom 4:25 as Stott offers:

> it is very odd to make confession of belief in the raising of Jesus the ground of salvation [implied in Rom 10:9], if his resurrection is merely the guarantee that his death for us was effective [Stott's view]. Rather, we would have expected that what was necessary, as the actual divine basis for our salvation, was belief in the fact that Jesus died for our sins.[27]

It is evident that without substantial revision penal substitution cannot comprehend Paul's message that the resurrection is essential to God's work of salvation through Christ.[28]

---

24. Stott, *Cross of Christ*, p. 235, emphasis original.

25. Stott, *Cross of Christ*, p. 35.

26. Stott, *Cross of Christ*, pp. 238-39.

27. Marshall, *Aspects of the Atonement*, p. 85.

28. Not only Paul, but a number of the early Christian writers, especially in the Eastern/Greek tradition, emphasized the essentiality of the resurrection in salvation, a point often lost on Western readers. The comment of Jaroslav Pelikan, *The Christian Tradition: A History of the Development of Doctrine* I: *The Emergence of the Catholic Tradition (100-600)* (Chicago: Univer-

What, then, does Paul mean by saying that Christ "was raised for our justification" (Rom 4:25)? A plausible (but surely partial) answer is that Paul's soteriology in Romans is concerned not only with our being *reckoned right* before God (vv. 1-8, 22-24) but also with our being *made righteous* in our life with God (5:19).[29] The overarching theme of Romans is "the gospel of God" concerning Jesus Christ, which is intended by God "to bring about the obedience of faith." Paul sounds this theme at the beginning and end of his letter (1:1-4; 16:25-27). This gospel, which is "the power of God for salvation" and reveals "the righteousness of God" (1:16-17), not only assures us that by faith we have been reckoned right with and reconciled to God through the death of Jesus Christ (3:21-26; 5:1-11), but also insists that the death and resurrection of Jesus Christ has freed us from slavery to sin and its end in death (5:12–6:23). And God's work of redemption in Christ, Paul says, serves a further purpose — *so that* "we too might walk in newness of life" (6:4), *so that* "the just requirements of the law might be fulfilled in us" (8:4). Full justification, in Paul's view, is *both* a status of right standing before God by faith in Christ *and* a life of right acting by walking faithfully in the way of God through the Spirit of the risen Christ (8:4-30). In Paul's soteriology, "the righteousness of God" fulfilled in us *is* "the obedience of faith," with emphasis on both "obedience" and "faith." The purpose of Christ's death and resurrection for our sake was *both* to bring us to God *and* to bring about the life of righteousness in us, to free us *from* slavery to sin *for* service of God (6:17-18, 22). (Peter echoes this double theme in 1 Pet 2:24; 3:18.) And for this purpose, the death of Christ, though "once for all," is insufficient; resurrection to new life is also necessary (cf. Rom 6:1-11).[30]

7.5. The Preaching of the Apostles: "According to the Plan of God"

We have yet to consider a further, essential aspect of the early apostolic narrative of the cross — that Jesus submitted to death and was raised by God "according to the definite plan and foreknowledge of God" (Acts 2:23). In emphasizing human

---

sity of Chicago Press, 1989), seems apropos of the penal substitution view: "Yet when a modern Western Christian turns to the Christian writers of the second and third centuries for their understanding of salvation in Christ, it is neither their attention to the teachings and example of Christ (which he may, rather superficially, identify with Protestant liberalism) nor their preoccupation with the passion and death of Christ (which he may, with some justification, see as an ancestor of the orthodox doctrine of the vicarious atonement), but their emphasis on the saving significance of the resurrection of Christ that he will find most unusual" (p. 149).

29. Cf. Marshall, *Aspects of the Atonement*, p. 88.

30. This leads directly to the question of how we participate in Christ's death and resurrection so that we also might indeed be dead to sin and alive to God: through baptism now, Paul says (Romans 6), and through resurrection later (1 Corinthians 15). We will address this question regarding baptism in Chapter 17.

agency and purpose in Jesus' death in contrast with divine agency and purpose in Jesus' resurrection, the Apostles and Evangelists did not believe that the cross was outside God's "plan of salvation."[31] Indeed, Peter and Paul make clear that they understand Jesus' death and resurrection as being in accord with God's purpose of redemption. Peter: "In this way God fulfilled what he had foretold through all the prophets, that his Messiah would suffer" (3:18). Paul: "they fulfilled those words [of the prophets] by condemning him . . . what God promised . . . he has fulfilled . . . by raising Jesus" (13:27, 32-33). It does not follow, however, that God's plan of salvation is necessarily that supposed by the penal substitution model — that God planned the Incarnation and so orchestrated history just so Jesus could be put to death on the cross to pay the penalty for sins. Let us again consider how Peter and Paul tell the story of the cross in their early sermons and how the early Christian community included the story of the cross in their prayers.

7.5.1. Jesus Dies by Human Injustice

When Peter and Paul present the passion of Jesus in their early preaching, they consistently depict the human act of putting Jesus to death in unambiguously evil terms, as an unrighteous deed, an *outlaw* act *against* God's servant:

> "this man . . . you crucified and killed *by the hands of those outside the law*" (Acts 2:23).
> ". . . Jesus, whom you *handed over and rejected* in the presence of Pilate, though he had decided to release him. But you *rejected the Holy and Righteous One* and asked to have a murderer given to you, and you *killed the Author of life* . . ." (3:13-15).
> ". . . Jesus, whom you had killed *by hanging him on a tree*" (5:30).
> "They put him to death *by hanging him on a tree* . . ." (10:39).
> "Even though they found *no cause for a sentence of death,* they asked Pilate to have him killed" (13:28).

And when the early Christian community gathers to pray in praise and thanksgiving for the release of Peter and John from prison, they refer to the death of Jesus in similar terms: "For in this city, in fact, both Herod and Pontius Pilate, with the Gentiles and the peoples of Israel, gathered together *against your holy servant Jesus,* whom you anointed . . ." (4:27). Jesus was put to death, the apos-

---

31. Yoder Neufeld, *Recovering Jesus,* p. 250: "It turns out, however, that in the view of the early followers of Jesus such analysis [of who killed Jesus, and why] cannot possibly fully explain the *meaning* of Jesus's death. . . . While depicting Jesus's death as the result of the miscarriage of justice, as a result of human treachery and callousness, the evangelists also all assert that Jesus's death was in some sense God's deed."

tolic story goes, by a life-destroying act of human lawlessness that not only put God's anointed one on a cross but also put him under a divine curse (cf. Deut 21:22-23). The apostolic witness could not be clearer in naming Jesus' death at human hands by crucifixion as a willful act of human evildoing.

7.5.2. God's Action Reverses Human Evildoing

At the same time, Peter and Paul underscore that the human ignorance and lawlessness that rejected Jesus and put him to death neither precluded God's foreknowledge, nor escaped God's judgment, nor thwarted God's purpose: God's plan was not to be undone or outdone by human evildoing. The execution of Jesus was indeed a human act of violent rebellion against God's reign. Nonetheless Jesus' rejection and death were encompassed by God's promise and purpose, which God acts faithfully to bring to fruition by raising Jesus from the dead. By raising Jesus, God exalts Jesus to preeminent position, thus rendering vain the plans of the rulers and peoples who conspired to overthrow God's kingdom and signaling that such rebellion is subject to imminent judgment. By raising Jesus, God lifts up the one cast down by humanity and sets him into the place of honor, demonstrating steadfast love by vindicating his servant.

Accordingly, the preaching of Peter and Paul and the prayers of the early Christian community patterned their story of the cross after Psalms 2 and 118:

> *Peter:* "Rulers of the people and elders . . . let it be known to all of you, and to all the people of Israel, that this man is standing before you in good health by the name of Jesus Christ of Nazareth, whom you crucified, whom God raised from the dead. This Jesus is 'the stone that was rejected by you, the builders; it has become the chief cornerstone' . . ." (Acts 4:8-12, citing Ps 118:22).

> *Community:* "Sovereign Lord, . . . it is you who said by the Holy Spirit through our ancestor David, your servant: 'Why did the Gentiles rage, and the peoples imagine vain things? The kings of the earth took their stand, and the rulers have gathered together against the Lord and against his Messiah.' For in this city, in fact, both Herod and Pontius Pilate, with the Gentiles and the peoples of Israel, gathered together against your holy servant Jesus, whom you anointed, to do whatever your hand had predestined to take place" (Acts 4:27-28, citing Ps 2:1-2).

> *Paul:* "My brothers, you descendants of Abraham's family, and others who fear God, to us the message of this salvation has been sent. Because the residents of Jerusalem and their leaders did not recognize him or understand the words of the prophets that are read every sabbath, they fulfilled those very words by condemning him. . . . But God raised him

from the dead. . . . And we bring you the good news that what God promised to our ancestors he has fulfilled for us, their children, by raising Jesus; as also it is written in the second psalm, 'You are my Son; today I have begotten you'" (Acts 13:26-33, citing Ps 2:7).

Having foreseen from heaven what the rulers and peoples of earth had conspired to do "against the LORD and his anointed," God derides and humiliates them by raising and exalting the very one they had humiliated and destroyed. To their dismay, God has not only turned their evil conspiracy against them but has also turned their evil done in ignorance of God's plan to serve God's own redemptive purpose. For God has taken "the stone that the builders rejected" and made him "the chief cornerstone."

The apostolic story of the cross is thus a story of divine reversal and redemption of human evil — a story of God bringing righteousness from sin, vindication from injustice, life from death. In this story, the resurrection of Jesus is both essential and consequential to God's work of addressing and undoing evil. I. Howard Marshall:

> . . . the resurrection is . . . God's action, which undoes what evil human beings and the devil sought to accomplish by putting Jesus to death. They thought that, by putting him to death, they could bring his work to an end and discredit his message. The resurrection is the event in which God undoes what they have done through overcoming death and its effects.[32]

In raising Jesus, God, by his power and grace, has turned human death-dealing lawlessness — indeed, the greatest lawlessness imaginable: "you killed the Author of life" — into fulfillment of God's life-giving covenant promise (Acts 2:39; 13:32). Tannehill, in reference to Peter's speech at Pentecost, comments:

> The two themes of human responsibility and divine sovereignty may seem to conflict, but both are necessary to produce the ironic view of Jesus' death that is typical of Luke-Acts. The residents of Jerusalem and their rulers, blind to God's purpose, act to rid themselves of Jesus and are responsible for their actions, but this very act contributes to God's purpose of enthroning Jesus as Messiah. . . . God's transcendence is displayed in the world where a surprising grace or a surprising justice appears that transcends, and may contradict, human intentions and powers. The Pentecost speech is primarily the disclosure to its audience of God's surprising reversal of their intentions, for their rejection has resulted in Jesus' exaltation as Messiah, Spirit-giver, and source of repentance and forgiveness.[33]

32. Marshall, *Aspects of the Atonement*, p. 75.
33. Tannehill, *Narrative Unity of Luke-Acts*, II, p. 37.

Through cross and resurrection, God not only redeems the suffering of his servant, but also invites change of life ("repentance") and offers forgiveness of sin, "the gift of the Holy Spirit," and "times of refreshing" — even to those who have rejected God's servant and conspired against God's reign, and all "in the name of Jesus" the crucified and risen One (Acts 2:37-39; 3:19-26; 5:31; 10:43; 13:38-39).[34] As Yoder Neufeld observes, this demonstrates God's love for enemies and passion for reconciliation:

> Viewing the story of Jesus's death as both the story of *human* injustice and an act of *God* leads us to the heart of the theological significance early followers of Jesus saw in his death. In the view of the evangelists the great miracle of the cross is nothing less than God transforming the most intense expression of human rebellion against God into God's own act of reconciliation toward those very same rebels. It is the ultimate expression of God's ingenious and persistent love for God's own enemies.[35]

The risen Jesus further commissions the apostles to be "my witnesses," to go forth "to the ends of the earth" as witnesses to resurrection and to proclaim good news, including forgiveness of sin and healing of life in the name of the crucified and risen Christ (Luke 24:47-48; Acts 1:8, 22; 2:32; 3:15; 4:2, 33; 5:32; 10:39).[36] The apostolic ministry of proclaiming the gospel "to the nations," a mission made possible by the resurrection of Jesus, was as indispensable to God's "plan of salvation" as was Jesus' death.[37]

7.5.3. Human Sin, Divine Providence

Now, to anticipate a possible objection, we note here that there is no contradiction in saying both that Jesus surrenders to death by his choice *according to* God's will and that Jesus is killed by human hands *against* God's will. The apostolic message repeatedly affirms two things: (1) God allows Jesus to suffer and die — Jesus is "handed over" or "surrenders himself" to his human captors and

---

34. Morna D. Hooker, *Not Ashamed of the Gospel: New Testament Interpretations of the Death of Christ* (Grand Rapids, MI: Eerdmans Publishing, 1994), p. 91: "Three points are made: first, 'you' (the audience, i.e. the Jews) are responsible for his death having handed him over to Pilate with the demand that he crucify him; second, God raised him from the dead — in confirmation of which, appeal is made, either to scripture or to the apostles as witnesses; third, in his name, forgiveness and salvation are now offered to those who repent."

35. Yoder Neufeld, *Recovering Jesus*, p. 258, emphasis original.

36. Recognizing this point helps address Marshall's comment (*Aspects of the Atonement*, pp. 75-76) concerning the question of how the resurrection of Jesus is related to the salvation of sinners in Acts.

37. Cf. David A. Brondos, *Paul on the Cross: Reconstructing the Apostle's Story of Redemption* (Minneapolis, MN: Fortress Press, 2006), pp. 46-48.

executioners according to God's will; and (2) Jesus suffers and dies at the hands of humans acting in rebellion against God's will. Both aspects of the cross, human and divine, fulfill the Scriptures: the people fulfill the words of the prophets by condemning Jesus to death, and God fulfills his promise to the ancestors by raising Jesus from the dead (Acts 13:27, 32-33). These two sides of the apostolic message are mutually consistent and consistent with the sovereign freedom of God and the relative freedom of humans. That God *permits* the violence against Jesus on the cross does *not* entail either that God *performs* that violence or that the human performance of that violence *pleases* God's will. Thus, from the fact that God (in Christ) *consents* to the cross it does *not* necessarily follow that God *causes* the death of Jesus. A sovereign God is free to allow humans to act in ways that are contrary to God's will (i.e., sinful) but are nonetheless comprehended by God's foreknowledge and providence.[38] And the apostolic witness, in both Gospels and Acts, is clear in depicting the crucifixion of Jesus as a human act of willful murder — sin.

It is not necessary that God act to put Jesus to death, or even dictate Jesus' death by others' doing, in order that the cross be comprehended by God's knowledge and further God's purpose. For it is not necessary that all cosmic events be due directly to the immediate agency of God for all things to be subject to God and serve the good that God has willed. It is possible for God's will to be expressed in both permissive and active ways with respect to the same divine purpose and cosmic event: God knowingly permits Jesus to be killed (divine freedom allows human sin), but God acts powerfully to vindicate Jesus (divine providence turns historical evil to ultimate good).[39] God's sovereign knowledge, freedom, and power to turn historical evil to ultimate good remain intact regardless of human ignorance or intention. Divine providence does not nullify human freedom; nor does human freedom trump divine providence: we are free to do evil as God permits, but God remains always free to overrule human evil and use it for the divine good intended from the foundation of the world.[40]

38. Cf. Augustine, *City of God*, XI.18, XII.23, and XIV.11, 27.

39. From the Calvinist perspective, everything that happens in the cosmos is the express intent of God's will and the immediate effect of God's power (see Calvin, *Institutes of the Christian Religion*, I.16). From that perspective, it is impossible that any event, much less the cross, be both according to God's will (in one aspect) and against God's will (in another aspect), as we suggest here is the witness of the apostles concerning the cross.

40. Cf. James Wm. McClendon, Jr., *Doctrine: Systematic Theology, Vol. II* (Nashville, TN: Abingdon Press, 1994), pp. 181-82. This brief discussion must pass over the centuries-long debate within Christianity concerning the compatibility of divine foreknowledge/providence and human freedom, a question on which Christians have diverged. Calvin himself denied compatibility: divine foreknowledge/providence entails that human freedom is impossible (*Institutes of the Christian Religion*, II.5). For a recent and interesting contribution to that debate on the side of compatibility, see Kirk R. MacGregor, *A Molinist-Anabaptist Systematic Theology* (Lanham, MD: University Press of America, 2007).

Peter Martens aptly characterizes Jesus' death as a case of "providential irony":

> [H]is killing could advance two entirely differing agendas, of his actual killers on the one hand, who thought that they were terminating Jesus and his ministry, and on the other hand, of God and Jesus, who were able to use this death to advance an entirely different agenda, the salvation of the human race.[41]

Such irony is evident in John's account of how the scheming of the religious and political leaders against Jesus for their own purpose would, in their ignorance and without their intention, serve God's purpose of saving the people (John 11:47-53). We might say here that the cross of Christ is the ultimate fulfillment of the ancient wisdom: "The LORD brings the counsel of the nations to nothing; he frustrates the plans of the peoples. The counsel of the LORD stands forever" (Ps 33:10-11); "The human mind may devise many plans, but it is the purpose of the LORD that will be established" (Prov 19:21).

According to the way the Apostles and Evangelists actually tell the story, Jesus' death was planned by human agents to punish a putative evildoer and was intended precisely for him, not as a divine punishment in place of others. Jesus was crucified according to the worldly wisdom and plan of "the rulers of this age," not God's wisdom and plan; and his death was intended to appease "the crowd," not God. The consistent pattern of the apostolic message — "you crucified and killed him, but God raised him up" — is clear: neither God's purpose nor action put Jesus to death; while human purpose and action worked death by crucifixion, God nonetheless fulfills his covenant promise and eternal plan through resurrection.[42]

---

41. Peter W. Martens, "The Quest for an Anabaptist Atonement: Violence and Nonviolence in J. Denny Weaver's *The Nonviolent Atonement*," *Mennonite Quarterly Review* 82 (April 2008), 281-311, here p. 302.

42. As Brondos observes, the earliest accounts of Jesus' death do not so much as raise, much less answer, the question *why* Jesus' death was necessary to fulfill God's plan, but only state that it was so and invite us to accept that message by faith. He writes (citing Matt 19:26; Mark 14:36; Luke 1:37, 18:22): "There seems to be no answer in the Gospels and Acts to questions such as this, other than that there was a divine plan foretold in the Scriptures that had to be carried out. Of course, it might be argued that the first Christians believed that there was something in God's nature or the nature of the created order that left God no alternative but to let his Son be crucified if the world was to be saved. This is the claim made by most of the later stories of redemption . . . particularly those that revolve around the notions of satisfaction and penal substitution: it was impossible for God to forgive sins without Jesus' death. Yet no such claim is found in the Gospels or Acts, either explicitly or implicitly; instead, the Jewish view that nothing is impossible for God is consistently upheld" (*Paul on the Cross,* p. 51).

CHAPTER 8

Paul's Story of the Cross

God proves his love for us in that
while we still were sinners Christ died for us . . .
while we were enemies,
we were reconciled to God through the death of his Son. . . .

ROMANS 5:8, 10

We have seen that Paul's earliest preaching of the cross (and resurrection) follows the received pattern of the apostolic account first proclaimed by Peter at Pentecost. What, though, we might wonder, about Paul's own, mature thinking about the cross? We will now compare the penal substitution model to Paul's distinctive story of the cross as presented in his epistles.[1] And we will make the case that penal substitution departs at several points from the Pauline story of God's redemption through the cross of Christ.

8.1. Penal Substitution: Sinners in the Hands of a Wrathful God

Penal substitution frames the meaning of the cross of Jesus by this question: What is to be done for human sinners in the hands of a wrathful God? Framed thus, penal substitution points to propitiation of God, in Packer's words, as "the real heart — the heart of the heart, we may say — of Christianity." Dever thus presents the "main problem" addressed by the cross as "God's righteous

---

1. For a more extensive treatment of Paul's story of God's redemption through the cross of Christ, see David A. Brondos, *Paul on the Cross: Reconstructing the Apostle's Story of Redemption* (Minneapolis, MN: Fortress Press, 2006).

wrath against us for our sinfulness" — such that the cross achieves first and foremost the propitiation of God: "By taking our penalty upon himself, God satisfied his own . . . wrath against us." Similarly, Nicole: "This [Jesus' death] effected the propitiation of the triune God's anger against the sinners."

The primary emphasis of penal substitution on propitiation provides us with two questions as we examine whether this model of atonement is confirmed by Paul's story of the cross: Does Paul frame the cross by the wrath of God and depict Jesus' death as the propitiation of God? Does Paul depict God as alienated from humanity and thus in need of reconciliation to humanity before humanity can be reconciled to God?

8.2. The Cross of Christ: The Propitiation of God, or the Redemption of Sinners?

8.2.1. The Penal Substitution View

Our first question is this: Does Paul frame the cross by God's wrath and depict Jesus' death as propitiation of God? As Nicole and Dever each tell the salvation story of the cross, the "main problem" to be dealt with at the cross is the wrath of God; and thus the primary purpose and effect of Jesus' suffering and death is the propitiation of God's wrath. Penal substitution thinking thus frames the cross of Christ by the question of the wrath of God, so that the divine-wrath-propitiating cross of Christ is the logical answer to this question: How can sinful humanity under divine wrath be saved?

8.2.2. What Paul Says in Romans

By contrast, Paul frames the cross, not by the problem of God's wrath, but by the demonstration of God's righteousness/justice through covenant faithfulness. And as Paul tells the story, at the heart of God's saving purpose through the cross of Christ is the gracious redemption of sinners, not the propitiation of wrath. We have arranged and highlighted Rom 3:21-26 below (generally on the basis of the NRSV) to illustrate this point:

(A) But now, apart from law, *the justice of God* has been disclosed and is attested by the law and the prophets, *the justice of God through the faithfulness of Jesus Christ* for all who believe.
  (B) For there is no distinction, since *all have sinned* and fall short of the glory of God;
    (A) they are now *justified*

(C) *by his grace* as a gift, *through the redemption* that is in Christ Jesus, whom God presented a mercy seat through faithfulness in his blood.

(A) He did this *to show his justice,*

(B) because in his forbearance he had passed over *the sins previously committed;*

(A) it was *to prove at the present time that he himself is just* and that he *justifies* the one who has the faith of Jesus.

This concentric contour makes visible the following pattern of Paul's story:[2]

justice/sin/justice/grace-redemption/justice/sin/justice.

And this pattern shows us four things.

First, at the center of Paul's story stands the cross of Christ (C), by which God graciously presents Jesus as "mercy seat" to fulfill God's purpose of redeeming humanity from sin. Although Paul does not mention the cross itself, the references of "through faithfulness" and "in his blood" clearly allude to Jesus' faithfulness-unto-death. Second, the main frame (A) of Paul's story, which frames not only the gracious gift of God through the redeeming cross of Christ (C) but also the sins of humanity (B), is God's faithful action in Christ to demonstrate covenant righteousness/justice. God demonstrates righteousness/justice in faithfulness to the covenant by graciously justifying all those having faith.[3] Third, the main frame (God's justice) and center (God's grace and Christ's cross) of Paul's story are directly connected. The sinner-redeeming cross of Christ is none other than the faithful demonstration of God's covenant righteousness/justice and gracious gift to humanity. *The cross of Christ thus reveals that the justice of God is redemptive in purpose and gracious in means:* God's justice accomplishes redemption of sinners; and God accomplishes redemptive justice by grace. Again, note the contrast with penal substitution, according to which God's justice accomplishes propitiation of God by satisfying retribution for sin on Jesus. And fourth, in Paul's story, God's faithful demonstration of covenant justice/righteousness (A) through the cross of Christ (C) frames, not the problem of God's wrath, but the situation of human sin (B). The redemptive purpose of the cross of Christ is thus to redress and rectify the situation of human sin (justification), not to resolve the problem of divine wrath (propitiation).

2. The "concentric" or "chiastic" (X) pattern of this text is typically Pauline and characteristic of biblical literary structure. Concerning chiastic patterns and contouring of biblical texts, see Mary H. Schertz and Perry B. Yoder, *Seeing the Text: Exegesis for Students of Greek and Hebrew* (Nashville, TN: Abingdon Press, 2001), pp. 46-65.

3. Regarding God's justice as covenant faithfulness in Romans 3, see Richard B. Hays, *Echoes of Scripture in the Letters of Paul* (New Haven: Yale University Press, 1989), pp. 46-54.

Paul thus depicts the covenant justice of God as being demonstrated through the *faithfulness* of Jesus Christ, for the sake of *redemption* of humanity from sin, by means of God's *grace* manifest in the cross of Christ. Insofar as we regard Rom 3:21-26 as the heart of Paul's gospel of salvation, then the "heart of the heart" of the story of the cross, according to Paul, is God's gracious redemption in Christ Jesus (v. 24).[4] Paul, then, does not depict the cross of Christ as the propitiation of God, but as the fulfillment of God's redemptive purpose by grace through the faithfulness of Jesus.

8.2.3. The Canonical Background to Paul's Story

The Greek word Paul uses at the heart of his story of the cross to express "the redemption *(apolytrōsis)* that is in Christ Jesus" (Rom 3:24) is telling of how he imagines salvation through the cross. Derived from the verb *lytroō*, "redeem" or "release" or "set free," the noun *apolytrōsis* suggests freedom from bondage — the redemption, liberation, or deliverance of a prisoner from slavery. Paul uses this word throughout his letters to depict the salvation of God through Jesus Christ, a salvation of cosmic scope and redemptive purpose:

> We know that the whole creation has been groaning in labor pains until now; and not only the creation, but we ourselves, who have the first fruits of the Spirit, groan inwardly while we wait for adoption, the *redemption (apolytrōsin)* of our bodies (Rom 8:22-23).
>
> "He is the source of your life in Christ Jesus, who became for us wisdom from God, and righteousness and sanctification and *redemption (apolytrōsis)*" (1 Cor 1:30).
>
> "In him we have *redemption (apolytrōsis)* through his blood, the forgiveness of [or release from] our trespasses according to the riches of his grace that he lavished on us" (Eph 1:7-8a).
>
> "He has rescued us from the power of darkness and transferred us into the kingdom of his beloved Son, in whom we have *redemption (apolytrōsis)*, the forgiveness of [or release from] sins" (Col 1:13-14).
>
> "He it is who gave himself for us that he might *redeem* us *from (lytrōsētai ... apo)* all iniquity and purify for himself a people of his own who are zealous for good deeds" (Tit 2:14).

4. Although "justification" is surely a prominent concept in Paul's story of salvation in Romans 2–5, Paul deliberately places it into the broader context of God's action to liberate and redeem his people in faithfulness to the covenant, beginning in ch. 3 and continuing in subsequent chapters (beyond ch. 5, there are only two further references to justification, in 8:30 and 33). Cf. I. Howard Marshall, *Aspects of the Atonement: Cross and Resurrection in the Reconciling of God and Humanity* (London: Paternoster, 2007), pp. 121-22.

Morna Hooker aptly comments, "The language here reminds us . . . of God's re-demption of his people at the Exodus."[5]

This Greek word that Paul uses to tell of "the redemption that is in Christ Je-sus" ties his message of the cross into the overarching story of God's redemption. At the beginning of his Gospel, Luke uses another form of the same verb "re-deem" *(lytroō)* to proclaim God's salvation accomplished through the Savior-Messiah: "Blessed be YHWH the God of Israel, for he has come to and accom-plished redemption *(epoiēsen lytrōsin)* for his people and has raised up a mighty savior for us . . ." (Luke 1:68-69, my translation). Zechariah goes on to sing that, with the coming of the Savior-Messiah, God "has shown the mercy promised to our ancestors and remembered his holy covenant" by fulfilling the promise to free his captive people "from our enemies and from the hand of all who hate us" (Luke 1:71-75). The mission goal of the Savior-Messiah is to "accomplish re-demption," to liberate God's people in fulfillment of covenant promise.

Now, in speaking of God "looking upon" his people in bondage to a hostile power, "remembering" his promise of redemption to the ancestors, and acting to bring about deliverance from captivity, Zechariah's canticle echoes the exo-dus story:

> After a long time the king of Egypt died. The Israelites groaned under their slavery, and cried out. Out of the slavery their cry for help rose up to God. God heard their groaning, and *God remembered his covenant* with Abraham, Isaac, and Jacob. *God looked upon the Israelites,* and God took notice of them. (Exod 2:23-25)

After sending Moses to Egypt to be his agent of liberation (Exod 3:10), YHWH gives Moses this message for the people: "Say therefore to the Israelites, 'I am the LORD, and I will free you from the burdens of the Egyptians and deliver you from slavery to them. I will *redeem* (LXX *lytrōsomai*) you with an outstretched arm and with mighty acts of judgment" (6:6). Following the destruction of the Egyptian army, Moses and the Israelites sing a song to YHWH, their salvation, "In your steadfast love you led the people whom you *redeemed* (LXX *elytrōsō*)" (15:13). When Moses later instructs Israel to remember that God, acting out of his steadfast love and faithfulness, has saved them from captivity and slavery, he says: "It was because the LORD loved you and kept the oath that he swore to your ancestors, that the LORD has brought you out with a mighty hand, and *re-deemed* (LXX *elytrōsato*) you from the house of slavery, from the hand of Pha-raoh king of Egypt" (Deut 7:8). And when in corporate worship the people of

---

5. Morna D. Hooker, *Not Ashamed of the Gospel: New Testament Interpretations of the Death of Christ* (Grand Rapids, MI: Eerdmans Publishing, 1994), p. 26. Cf. Luke Timothy Johnson, *Reading Romans: A Literary and Theological Commentary* (Macon, GA: Smyth and Helwys Pub-lishing, 2001), p. 56.

Israel recite the story of God's salvation, they continue to express God's act in the same terms: "With your strong arm you *redeemed* (LXX *elytrōsō*) your people, the descendants of Jacob and Joseph" (Pss 77:15; cf. 74:2; 78:42; 106:10; 107:2).

Centuries later, when Isaiah announces good news of salvation — hope for return from exile and restoration of Jerusalem — he uses this same verb "redeem" *(lytroō)*. Isaiah's message of hope rests on God's original act of salvation in Israel's history by which the Israelites were liberated from slavery and constituted as God's people: "But now thus says the LORD, he who created you, O Jacob, he who formed you, O Israel: Do not fear, for I have *redeemed* (LXX *elytrōsamēn*) you; I have called you by name, you are mine" (Isa 43:1). Isaiah further prefaces his vision for the restoration of peace to Jerusalem (52:7-10) using this same word to depict the city's deliverance by God's action. The city of Zion was "sold" into captivity when YHWH allowed it to fall to the Babylonians, but now YHWH will redeem the holy city from its bondage: "Shake yourself from the dust, rise up, O captive Jerusalem; loose the bonds from your neck, O captive daughter Zion! For thus says the LORD: You were sold for nothing, and you shall be *redeemed* (LXX *lytrōthēsesthe*) without money" (vv. 2-3). Isaiah thus sees God's saving action to return Israel from exile and restore Jerusalem in freedom as the renewal of the story of redemption begun with the exodus and continued through the covenant. Envisioning Israel returned and Jerusalem restored, Isaiah thus says: "They shall be called, 'The Holy People, The *Redeemed* (LXX *lelytrōmenon*) of the LORD'; and you shall be called, 'Sought Out, A City Not Forsaken'" (62:12).[6]

The exodus story of God's redemption of Israel is the canonical framework for Paul's story of God's redemption through the cross of Jesus Christ. The penal substitution model takes the cross out of the canonical story of Paul's account and places it within an abstract logical scheme of sin, wrath, and retribution, such that the cross of Christ is interpreted as providing the penal satisfaction necessary and sufficient to resolve the problem of God's wrath toward sinners. The logic of atonement implicit in the penal substitution model makes perfect sense on its own terms, quite apart from and irrespective of the history of God's saving work through redemption of his covenant people. Paul, however, sets his story of the cross in Rom 3:21-26 within the canonical narrative of Israel's redemption. His choice of language in v. 24 — like the historical psalms, the prophecy of Isaiah, and the canticle of Zechariah — recalls *the* formative story of salvation in Israel's consciousness, the exodus.[7] Seen against its

6. The Greek citations here refer to the Septuagint (LXX), the ancient Greek translation of the Old Testament, read in synagogues throughout the Jewish Diaspora and used by Paul and other New Testament writers.

7. Cf. James D. G. Dunn, *The Theology of Paul the Apostle* (Grand Rapids, MI: Eerdmans Publishing, 1998), pp. 227-28.

canonical backdrop, the purpose of the cross of Christ is fulfillment of God's promise of redemption — begun with exodus from slavery, continued through covenant, renewed in return and restoration from exile, consummated through cross. Thus, David Brondos:

> for Paul the ultimate goal or purpose for which Christ gave up his life in obedi-
> ence to God was the redemption of God's people, of whom Jewish and Gentile
> believers . . . now form part. . . . According to Paul, Jesus had been sent by
> God as his agent to bring about the promised redemption, and it was to this
> that he had dedicated himself in life and death.[8]

In setting forth "the redemption that is in Christ Jesus" in Romans, moreover, Paul continues telling the story in terms of slavery and liberation, captivity and release.[9] In Romans 6, Paul describes us as having been enslaved to sin, subject to the dominion of death, helpless to redeem ourselves from captivity to a hostile power. But God has graciously provided a means of release from our slavery to sin and deliverance from our domination by death — through the redeeming death and resurrection of Jesus Christ.[10] And in Romans 8, Paul brings this narrative of redemption in Christ to consummation with the liberation of humanity "from the law of sin and of death" and the coming liberation of the creation "from its bondage to decay" and its "groaning in labor pains" under the curse of sin, even "the redemption of our bodies" (Rom 8:1-3, 18-25).[11]

8.2.4. Two Objections

The penal substitution apologist might want to interject a couple questions here. First: "But don't the demonstration of God's justice and the redemption of sinners require propitiation of God's wrath by penal satisfaction? After all, Paul spends the first two chapters in Romans depicting God's wrath against humanity because of their sins." Second: "Didn't you just remove the wrath of God from Paul's story of the cross by a subtle retranslation? Didn't Paul actually say that God presents Jesus as a "propitiation" (cf. KJV, NASB)? And doesn't that im-

---

8. Brondos, *Paul on the Cross*, p. 74, emphasis original.

9. On the cultural background of Paul's language, see Johnson, *Reading Romans,* pp. 106-9.

10. Cf. John Driver, *Understanding the Atonement for the Mission of the Church* (Scottdale, PA: Herald Press, 1986), pp. 171-72.

11. We thus see that the broader canonical framework of Paul's story of redemption in Christ Jesus, as depicted in Romans, is the "Fall" of humanity, by which sin entered the cosmos and all creation came under the dominion of death (5:12-14), and God's action to liberate humanity and all creation from the curse of sin and death (8:1-39). On Genesis 1–3 as the background story for Paul in Romans, see A. Katherine Grieb, *The Story of Romans: A Narrative Defense of God's Righteousness* (Louisville, KY: Westminster John Knox Press, 2002), pp. 56-83.

ply that Paul himself did see the point of Jesus' death as the propitiation of God's wrath?" The first question assumes that God's wrath upon sin must necessarily be satisfied by retributive punishment. The second question concerns a key Greek word in Rom 3:25, *hilastērion,* which we have rendered "mercy seat." We will address these two questions at length in Chapters 12 and 14 respectively.

8.3. The Cross of Christ:
The Reconciliation of God, or the Reconciliation of Sinners?

8.3.1. The Penal Substitution View

Now our second question: Does Paul depict God as being alienated from humanity and thus in need of reconciliation to humanity before humanity can be reconciled to God? According to the penal substitution model, insofar as the main problem is God's wrath and the primary purpose of the cross is to appease God, the cross achieves first, not the reconciliation of humanity to God, but the reconciliation of God to humanity. Roger Nicole: "This [viz., the death of Jesus] effected the propitiation of the triune God's anger against the sinners; the reconciliation of God to us and us to God."[12] God, angry toward us on account of sin, must first be reconciled to us before we can be reconciled to God; hence the need for God's wrath to be propitiated by Jesus' death as the prior condition of all else. Packer: "As our propitiation, it [viz., Jesus' death] was reconciliation, the making of peace for us with our offended, estranged, angry Creator."[13] Not only is God "offended" and "angry" at humanity on account of sin, but God is "estranged" from humanity. Packer and Nicole follow Calvin in depicting a just God "at enmity" with, and needing reconciliation to, sinful humanity: "God . . . was our enemy until he was reconciled to us by Christ" (*Institutes* II.16.2); "God, at the very time when he loved us, was hostile to us until reconciled in Christ" (*Institutes* II.17.2).[14]

Having said this, Calvin himself immediately observed that speaking of God as the enemy of humanity needing reconciliation by Christ's death creates "an appearance of contradiction" (*Institutes* II.16.2). As Calvin well knew, it is God's own love for us that is demonstrated in Christ's death "while we were still sinners . . . while we were enemies" (Rom 5:8, 10). Calvin thus set about to "explain the difficulty" of how God both loved us and was our enemy at the same

---

12. Roger Nicole, "Postscript on Penal Substitution," in Charles E. Hill and Frank A. James III, eds., *The Glory of the Atonement: Biblical, Theological and Practical Perspectives* (Downers Grove, IL: InterVarsity Press, 2004), p. 452.

13. J. I. Packer, *I Want to Be a Christian* (Wheaton, IL: Tyndale House Publishers, 1977), p. 61.

14. John Calvin, *Institutes of the Christian Religion,* trans. Henry Beveridge.

time.[15] Our concern here is not a contradiction within Calvin's thinking, but rather the coherence of his view, maintained by penal substitution, with the witness of Scripture in the letters of Paul. We ask: Is this how Paul depicts God in the act of reconciliation through the cross, as a hostile party at enmity with humanity and thus in need of being reconciled to humanity by Christ?

Before we proceed, we note that there is a point of orthodoxy looming over this discussion. Consider Schmiechen's summary of Calvin's view: "Sin has alienated God from God's very creation, a separation so severe that it cannot be overcome without judgment and punishment."[16] One wonders how the Incarnation — the union of God and creation in the divine-human person, Jesus — was possible in the first place. We may put the argument this way: if God were alienated from the creation by sin, and God could not overcome that alienation and be reconciled with the creation except by the punishment of sin in the death of Jesus, then it follows that God could not have been reconciled with the creation until the cross; but, if God could not have been reconciled with the creation prior to the cross, then God could not have overcome the alienation by sin and been united with the creation through the Incarnation; yet, according to the orthodox teaching of the church, God *did* unite with the creation through the Incarnation. At least one of the premises must be mistaken, therefore: either God was not alienated from the creation by sin, or God could reconcile the creation fallen into sin by means other than punishment, or both. In our view, both premises are mistaken: sin alienates humanity from God, not God from humanity (the present chapter); and God is able to, and in fact does, reconcile sinners without need of punishment (Chapters 10, 11, and 12 below).

8.3.2. What Paul Says in Ephesians

There is no doubting that sinful humanity, living in depravity and perversity, and thus being under divine judgment, has alienated itself from God — and so stands in need of reconciliation to God. That is precisely the situation Paul describes in Rom 1:18-32 (to be examined carefully in Chapter 12 below). In Ephesians 2, Paul tells essentially the same story. The human predicament — prior to the peacemaking, reconciling work of the cross — is characterized by our living "in the passions of our flesh, following the desires of flesh and senses." In this condition, "we were by nature children of wrath, like everyone else" (Eph 2:3).

---

15. Concerning Calvin's internal wrestling on this point, see Peter Schmiechen, *Saving Power: Theories of Atonement and Forms of the Church* (Grand Rapids, MI: Eerdmans, 2005), pp. 42-45.

16. Schmiechen, *Saving Power*, p. 43, citing *Institutes* II.16.

Our obedience to "the flesh" rather than God revealed that we were under God's wrath. Being disobedient "children of wrath," we experienced God's wrath through the destructive and deathly consequences of our obedience to sin: "You were dead through the trespasses and sins in which you once lived" (v. 1). Living in obedience to sin and thus under the judgment of death, humanity is alienated from and needs reconciliation to God.

Now, as penal substitution tells the story of the cross, Christ reconciles God and humanity because his death propitiates God's wrath/enmity against humanity. Paul's depiction of Christ's work of reconciliation, however, tells a different story. The purpose of the cross, Paul says, is to make peace between hostile human parties, Jew and Gentile, by reconciling them to one another and, together, to God. The primary effect of the cross is thus the destruction of division and hostility, both inter-human hostility and human hostility against God. Jesus "is our peace," for

> in his flesh he has made both groups into one and has broken down the dividing wall, that is the hostility between us . . . that he might create in himself one new humanity in place of the two, thus making peace, and might reconcile both groups to God in one body through the cross thus putting to death that hostility in himself. (Eph 2:14-16)

The cross thus addresses, not the problem of divine wrath, but the situation of *human hostility,* which is "put to death" in Jesus' body through the cross. It is not God who extinguishes his own enmity toward humanity upon Jesus' body at the cross, but instead Jesus who *in his flesh, in himself,* extinguishes human hostility, hostility toward one another and toward God. Rather than Jesus' death extinguishing divine enmity against human beings and reconciling God to humanity, Paul's story is that Jesus "puts to death" human hostility in himself through the cross because of God's desire to reconcile humanity, both within itself and to God. There is nothing in this story, as Paul tells it, of God being at enmity with and needing to be reconciled to humanity.

In order that Paul's story might fit their model, penal substitution apologists attempt to portray the enmity in Eph 2:14-16 as a *mutual* enmity, not only between Jew and Gentile, but also between God and humanity. That is, "the hostility" *(tēn echthran)* of which Paul speaks, they say, is human enmity toward one another, human enmity toward God, *and* God's enmity toward humanity.[17] They thus read this text to say that Jesus' death, by "putting to death that hostility in himself," propitiates God's wrath.[18] Their interpretation does not square

---

17. Cf. Marshall, *Aspects of the Atonement,* pp. 105, 113, 118.

18. Cf. John R. W. Stott, *The Cross of Christ* (Downers Grove, IL: InterVarsity Press, 1986), pp. 197-98; and J. I. Packer, "The Atonement in the Life of the Christian," in Hill and James, eds., *The Glory of the Atonement,* pp. 409-25, here p. 416.

with the Greek text, however. By juxtaposing "the hostility" *(tēn echthran)* and "the dividing wall" *(to mesotoichon tou phragmou)*, the deliberate intent of Paul's wording is to relate "the hostility" to "the dividing wall." This dividing wall separates "the both" *(ta amphotera)* or "the two" *(tous duo)*, which are to be made into "one new humanity" *(hena kainon anthrōpon)* in Christ. The clear implication is that by "the hostility" Paul speaks of an enmity between two groups of human beings, caused and symbolized by "the dividing wall" that separates them, which are to be reconciled by Christ to God "in one body." The penal substitution interpretation of "the hostility" in Ephesians 2 as including God's enmity toward humanity, therefore, reads into the text the model's own presuppositions.

8.3.3. *What Paul Says Elsewhere*

Packer's depiction of God as "estranged" from humanity, and Nicole's depiction of God as needing to be reconciled to humanity, run directly contrary to what Paul says elsewhere concerning the cross and reconciliation. Nowhere does Paul depict God as being alienated from and needing to be reconciled to humanity; it is always and only humanity that is alienated from and needing to be reconciled to God. And that because, Paul emphasizes, it is always and only humanity that has proved false and broken covenant, never God. "All have sinned and fall short of the glory of God" (Rom 3:23); nonetheless, God remains steadfast in love and faithfulness toward humanity: "What if some were unfaithful? Will their faithlessness nullify the faithfulness of God? By no means! Although everyone is a liar, let God be proved true" (vv. 3-4a).

God, ever faithful and true, is neither "estranged" from nor in any need of being reconciled to humanity, contrary to the penal substitution model. Indeed, God is the one who acts faithfully to reconcile faithless humanity to himself through the faithfulness of Jesus Christ. Paul says this clearly and repeatedly. Here are three texts, in which the agent of reconciliation is God-in/through-Christ, the bearer of hostility and recipient of reconciliation is humanity, and the one to whom humanity is reconciled is God:

> "For if while *we were enemies, we were reconciled to God* through the death of his Son, much more surely, having been reconciled, will we be saved by his life. But more than that, we even boast in God through our Lord Jesus Christ, through whom *we have now received reconciliation*" (Rom 5:10-11).
>
> "All this is from God, *who reconciled us to himself* through Christ . . . that is, God was in Christ *reconciling the world to himself* . . ." (2 Cor 5:18-19).
>
> "For in him [Christ] all the fullness of God was pleased to dwell, and

through him God was pleased to *reconcile to himself all things,* whether
on earth or in heaven, by making peace through the blood of his cross.
And *you who were once estranged and hostile* in mind, doing evil deeds,
he has now reconciled in the body of his flesh through death, so as to
present you holy and blameless and irreproachable before him" (Col
1:19-22).

Contrary to penal substitution, Paul does not depict God as "estranged" from
and "hostile" toward humanity (Packer) and thus needing to be reconciled to
humanity (Nicole). Indeed, Paul depicts the situation in opposite terms, that
humanity is "estranged" from and "hostile" toward God and needing to be reconciled to God, not the other way around: "And *you* who were once *estranged*
and *hostile* in mind . . . he has reconciled in his body of flesh through death"
(Col 1:21).[19] Nor does Paul state that, while loving us, God was our enemy (as
Calvin claims). Again, Paul declares just the opposite, that even while *we* were
enemies with God, *God* nonetheless *loved* us: "God proves his love for us in that
. . . while we were enemies . . ." (Rom 5:8, 10).[20]

How penal substitution misreads Paul's message of reconciliation is evident in I. Howard Marshall's interpretation of the Romans 5 text cited above.
Marshall follows Calvin and reads here a mutual enmity between God and humanity: "The enmity is best understood as mutual. But, despite his enmity,
God, in his love acted to provide a means whereby sin and its consequences
could be canceled, and he could treat people as friends rather than enemies; this
involved Christ dying for them."[21] As Marshall sees it, God has to deal first with
his own enmity before he can deal with humanity's sin. God's enmity thus
stands in the way of humanity's reconciliation, such that God is the primary
obstacle to right relationship: God has to overcome himself first, as it were, in
order to reconcile humanity. As Marshall depicts it, the major conflict in the
drama of reconciliation is internal to God, a conflict between God's enmity and
God's love in which love wins out so that humanity can be saved.

The drama of divine-human reconciliation as Paul tells it, however, is a
story of God's love overcoming humanity's enmity through Christ's cross. The
major conflict at the heart of the drama is not God-the-enemy against God-the-

19. Cf. S. E. Porter, "Peace, Reconciliation," in Gerald F. Hawthorne, Ralph P. Martin, and
Daniel G. Reid, eds., *Dictionary of Paul and His Letters* (Downers Grove, IL: InterVarsity Press,
1993), pp. 695-99, here p. 698.

20. Thus Hooker, *Not Ashamed of the Gospel,* p. 27 (emphasis original): "it is *we* who are
reconciled to *God* and not *God* to *us:* the gospel is not about placating an angry God, but about
an appeal to wayward men and women to be reconciled to a loving Father." See also Brondos,
Paul on the Cross, pp. 139-44, and D. M. Baillie, *God Was in Christ: An Essay on Incarnation and
Atonement* (New York: Scribner's, 1948), pp. 184-89.

21. Marshall, *Aspects of the Atonement,* p. 104.

lover. Nor does Paul depict the drama as a confrontation between the wrath of God and the love of Christ; for, as D. M. Baillie points out, Paul declares that the cross of Christ by which humanity is reconciled is itself the demonstration of the love of God.[22] Rather, the conflict is humanity-the-enemy against God-the-lover, which God acts to resolve by reconciling humanity through the cross. Paul thus portrays the drama of reconciliation by setting up a clear contrast between God's love for humanity, demonstrated through the cross, and humanity's enmity toward God, overcome through the cross: "God proves his love for us in that while we still were sinners Christ died for us . . . while we were enemies, we were reconciled to God through the death of his Son . . ." (Rom 5:8, 10).[23]

Some penal substitution apologists recognize this textual evidence yet insist on the penal substitution view anyway. Leon Morris acknowledges that "the New Testament writers always speak of *man* as being reconciled, never God," and admits that speaking of God as needing and receiving reconciliation "goes beyond that of the New Testament." Despite the clear biblical witness, Morris insists that thinking of the cross as the resolution of God's hostility toward humanity is essential to a biblical doctrine of atonement: "We cannot get a glimmering of an understanding of what the New Testament understands by Christ's atoning work unless we see that God is hostile to every evil thing and every evil person."[24] We do not dispute that God is opposed to evil and that dealing with evil is central to the saving work of God through the cross. But we do dispute that God is at enmity with and thus in need of being reconciled to humanity.

To sum: By placing primary emphasis on divine wrath, and by making the propitiation of God the primary effect of the cross, the penal substitution model places God in a position of alienation from and hostility toward humanity and thus in the position of needing to receive reconciliation through the cross. And that implication of penal substitution directly contradicts Paul's story of the reconciling cross of Christ.

---

22. Baillie, *God Was in Christ*, p. 186.

23. William C. Placher, "Christ Takes Our Place: Rethinking Atonement," *Interpretation* 53/1 (1999), 5-20, p. 16, places the emphasis in reconciliation in the proper place: ". . . focusing on God's need to be reconciled to us gets things backwards, from the New Testament standpoint. For Paul, it is we who need to be reconciled to God, not the other way around. God's love endures; it is our sin that has broken our relationship with God; it is we who like sheep have gone astray. The barriers that have to be broken down in reconciliation were built from our side. God does not have to be wooed back to loving us, for while we were yet sinners Christ died for us."

24. Leon Morris, *The Atonement: Its Meaning and Significance* (Downers Grove, IL: InterVarsity Press, 1983), pp. 137-38.

CHAPTER 9

===

Jesus' Understanding of His Own Death

For the Son of Man came not to be served but to serve,
and to give his life a ransom for many.

MARK 10:45

9.1. The Biblical Jesus

We consider now Jesus' own understanding of his death. Here we examine, not some "historical Jesus" reconstructed speculatively through critical methods, but the only real Jesus of history available to us, the Jesus to whom the canonical Gospels bear witness in faith.[1] Every scholarly quest for the "historical Jesus" makes various presuppositions about history, truth, and reality that, to some degree, predetermine the "Jesus" that is "discovered" in the ancient sources.[2] By setting down in advance criteria for deciding which evidence is authentic and relevant and how it is to be interpreted, one delimits *a priori* the possible historical figures which "Jesus" might be seen to fit. The result is that how Jesus himself understood his life and death is effectively decided apart from the evidence of Scripture so that Scripture is read to fit a pre-figured "Jesus." Yet such presuppositions by which the evidence is to be judged are themselves open to question. The implication is that "historical Jesus" scholars must

---

1. Cf. Luke Timothy Johnson, *The Real Jesus: The Misguided Quest for the Historical Jesus and the Truth of the Traditional Gospels* (New York: HarperCollins Publishers, 1996).

2. For three recent examples, see: Paula Fredriksen, *From Jesus to Christ: The Origins of the New Testament Images of Jesus* (New Haven: Yale University Press, 1988); E. P. Sanders, *The Historical Figure of Jesus* (London: Penguin Books, 1993); and John Dominic Crossan, *Jesus: A Revolutionary Biography* (San Francisco: HarperSanFrancisco, 1994).

either rationally justify their presuppositions (an inevitably circular task) or make rationally unjustified ("faith") commitments. There is thus no disentangling "the Jesus of history" from "the Christ of faith": any reconstruction of the former will be dependent upon commitments regarding the latter (whether orthodox or heterodox).[3]

In our study, we make an orthodox faith commitment, assuming no skepticism concerning the authenticity and relevance of the various sayings of Jesus concerning his death as attributed by the canonical Gospels. And if we begin from the premise of faith rather than skepticism, then, precisely because the risen Jesus instructed his disciples how to interpret his death with respect to the Scriptures (Luke 24:26-27, 44-45), we should expect Jesus' own understanding to be reflected in the Gospel accounts.[4]

9.2. Necessary, but Why and for What?

Jesus, the Synoptic accounts tell us, speaks repeatedly of his coming suffering, death, and resurrection (Mark 8:31; 9:31; 10:33-34; pars. in Matthew and Luke). These passion-resurrection prophecies make evident that Jesus understands his suffering, death, and resurrection as integral to his God-appointed, Spirit-anointed mission of proclaiming and inaugurating the kingdom.[5] These prophecies also reveal that Jesus recognizes a certain necessity in his suffering, death, and resurrection: "The Son of Man must *(dei)* undergo great suffering, . . . and be killed, and . . . be raised" (Luke 9:22; cf. Mark 8:31; Matt 16:21). Together these prophecies reveal that Jesus sees resurrection, not death, as the culmination of his divine purpose; that he is to be raised, Jesus says, is just as necessary as that he is to die.[6] The Garden scene further makes evident that Jesus

3. Cf. N. T. Wright, *The Meaning of Jesus: Two Views* (San Francisco: HarperSanFrancisco, 1999), and James D. G. Dunn, *A New Perspective on Jesus: What the Quest for the Historical Jesus Missed* (Grand Rapids, MI: Baker Academic, 2005). For a critique of "historical Jesus" scholarship concerning the question of Jesus' self-understanding of his death, see Scot McKnight, *Jesus and His Death: Historiography, the Historical Jesus, and Atonement Theory* (Waco, TX: Baylor University Press, 2005), pp. 3-101.

4. One might argue, following the method of "form criticism," that the canonical Gospels are historical sources, not for Jesus himself, but for the early Christian proclamation of Jesus. While I agree that we cannot disentangle faith from history in any examination of Jesus, and that the canonical Gospels witness to how the early church proclaimed its faith in Jesus, it does not follow that the canonical Gospels do not witness also to Jesus himself. To suppose that a faith account of Jesus is thereby lacking in historical authenticity seems to me a false dichotomy. Cf. D. M. Baillie, *God Was in Christ: An Essay on Incarnation and Atonement* (New York: Scribner's, 1948), pp. 46-47, 54-58.

5. N. T. Wright, *Jesus and the Victory of God: Christian Origins and the Question of God, Vol. 2* (Minneapolis: Fortress Press, 1992), pp. 574-76.

6. McKnight, *Jesus and His Death*, writes (p. 225), "In the passion predictions it is made

understands his imminent suffering and death as according to God's will (Mark 14:36; pars. in Matthew and Luke). And the risen Jesus recounts his suffering, death, and resurrection as a fulfillment of the Scriptures (Luke 24:26-27, 44-46).

As Joel Green observes, that Jesus understands his suffering and death in relation to God's purpose and providence, and that his disciples fail to understand this (Mark 8:27-33; 9:30-32), entails a revision of human thinking about the will and ways of God:

> Jesus' passion predictions . . . locate Jesus' suffering and death within the divine plan and so call for a transformation in the way humanity is to understand the ways of God. From this new vantage point, divine mission and divine status are correlated with and not denied by humiliation, rejection, suffering, and death. From Jesus' perspective, then, his impending crucifixion is itself an interpretive act by which the will of God is to be disclosed.[7]

The implication of a to-be-crucified Messiah is that we can no longer associate God's plan of salvation with human notions of glory and power, which Jesus himself resisted in the wilderness and had to refute among his followers (Matt 4:1-11; 20:17-28). Nonetheless, none of these sayings of Jesus concerning the necessity of his death actually tell us anything of how he understands the *meaning* of his death — whether vicarious ("for us") or not, atoning ("for sin") or not and, if so, in what sense.[8]

When addressing these questions, we need to distinguish the question of how Jesus understood his death from the question of how the early church understood Jesus' death. We cannot assume that Jesus' self-understanding will necessarily reflect the understandings of his death developed subsequently within the early church. Because Paul understood Jesus' death as a Passover sacrifice, or because John and the writer of Hebrews each understood Jesus' death as an atoning sacrifice, it does not follow that Jesus himself also did so. We should thus be careful not to project upon Jesus' self-understanding expectations derived from later interpretations. We need, that is, to allow Jesus to have his own view of his life and death and to allow the Gospel accounts to reveal Je-

---

clear that death for Jesus is not a tragedy but the *telos* of his mission." While agreeing with the first part of that statement, it seems to me that the second part overlooks two things: of the nine "passion" prophecies across the three Synoptic Gospels, all but one (Luke 9:44) culminate with resurrection; and the Greek construction of Mark 8:31 (pars. Matt 16:21 and Luke 9:22) implies that the necessity *(dei)* of which Jesus speaks applies to his resurrection as much as to his suffering and death. This evidence suggests to me, not only that death and resurrection are "tightly interwoven" in Jesus' mind, as McKnight observes (pp. 229-30), but also that Jesus saw *resurrection* as the *telos* of his mission.

7. Joel B. Green, "The Death of Jesus and the Ways of God: Jesus and the Gospels on Messianic Status and Shameful Suffering," *Interpretation* 52/1 (1998), 24-37, here pp. 33-34.

8. Cf. McKnight, *Jesus and His Death*, pp. 155-56, 238-39.

sus' own witness concerning himself. With respect to the penal substitution model, we need to ask: Does Jesus understand his impending death as a substitute penalty for human sin? Does Jesus understand the suffering he is about to undergo as the vengeance of God poured out on himself in place of sinners? We will address these questions by examining a few key texts in the Synoptic Gospels where Jesus himself does disclose something of how he understands his own life and death.[9]

9.3. The Transfiguration

The Transfiguration (Mark 9:2-8 and pars. in Matthew and Luke) is not typically considered in connection with the question of the meaning of Jesus' suffering, death, and resurrection. Yet it seems to be of crucial significance since in it Jesus himself receives a revelation concerning the purpose of his divine vocation. Anticipating the ordeal awaiting him in Jerusalem, Jesus converses with Moses and Elijah. In the accounts of both Mark and Matthew we are left wondering as to the content of their conversation, but Luke's account tells us that they "were speaking about his departure *(exodos)*, which he was about to accomplish at Jerusalem" (Luke 9:31).

Luke sets this moment at the crucial juncture in his narrative of Jesus' mission.[10] Just prior to this, Peter has confessed that Jesus is the Messiah (Luke 9:18-20) and Jesus has explained that his messianic vocation entails suffering, death, and resurrection: "The Son of Man must undergo great suffering . . . and be killed, and on the third day be raised" (v. 22). The Transfiguration takes place "about eight days after these words" (v. 28). And just after the Transfiguration, "When the days drew near for him to be taken up," Jesus "set his face to go to Jerusalem" (v. 51). So between Jesus' first passion prophecy and his resolve to journey toward Jerusalem, "the city that kills the prophets" (13:34), where he will be "taken up," Jesus speaks with Moses and Elijah concerning his approaching "exodus" in Jerusalem. Clearly, by the "exodus" of Jesus, we are intended to think of his suffering, death, resurrection, and ascension.

Not only the language of "exodus," but also the presence of Moses and Elijah and the mountain locale of the Transfiguration recall the holy mountain Sinai-Horeb. It was at Sinai-Horeb that YHWH revealed the Torah to Moses and made a covenant with Israel (Exodus 19–24) and that Elijah took refuge un-

9. Concerning Jesus' understanding of his death in the Fourth Gospel, see Morna D. Hooker, *Not Ashamed of the Gospel: New Testament Interpretations of the Death of Christ* (Grand Rapids, MI: Eerdmans Publishing, 1994), pp. 94-111, and John T. Carroll and Joel B. Green, *The Death of Jesus in Early Christianity* (Peabody, MA: Hendrickson Publishers, 1995), pp. 82-109.

10. Robert C. Tannehill, *The Narrative Unity of Luke-Acts: A Literary Interpretation.* Vol. 1: *The Gospel according to Luke* (Philadelphia: Fortress Press, 1986), pp. 219-32.

der YHWH's protection from his enemies (1 Kings 19). With respect to Israel's Scripture traditions, the "faith location" of the Transfiguration is in the wilderness where God delivers his people, reveals his law, instructs his servant, and protects his prophet.[11] This conjunction of "exodus" and "mountain" provides Jesus with the narrative frame of reference for understanding his own suffering, death, and resurrection — the story of the original exodus.

According to Luke's Gospel, therefore, Jesus understands his suffering, death, and resurrection as a new and climactic chapter of the story of God's original work of redemption, by which he had saved Israel and covenanted with his people. Jesus thus understands his own suffering, death, and resurrection as making a "new exodus" and a "new covenant" (cf. Luke 22:20). Through him, God is opening a new way of liberation from captivity for humanity, a new relationship between God and humanity that leads to righteousness and life. Thus Hooker: "Jesus' death, then, is seen by Luke as a new Exodus, a great redemptive act whose results will presumably be parallel to those achieved by the Exodus from Egypt."[12]

This narrative also provides Luke the frame for understanding the necessity of Jesus' suffering and death. As Luke Timothy Johnson has argued, the final word from the heavenly voice on the mountain of Transfiguration, "listen to him" (Luke 9:35), "cannot be anything but a deliberate allusion to Deut 18:15 as Luke reads it, and certifies Jesus not only as God's Son and the chosen servant, but as the 'prophet like Moses.'"[13] This inference is confirmed by Peter's citation of this text with direct reference to Jesus in Acts 3:22-23 as well as Stephen's citation of this text in his recounting of the career of Moses as background for the ministry of Jesus (7:35-40). As Luke presents him, then, Jesus is the "prophet like Moses" whom God has "raised up" — both figuratively at his birth and now literally at his resurrection (cf. Luke 1:68-69; Acts 2:22-24, 32-36) — to bring about the redemption of his people. As Johnson also argues, the pattern set with Moses — who proclaimed God's word to Israel, which caused division within Israel and rejection of Moses by Israel, resulting in his suffering and alienation from Israel but concluding with vindication from God — is the pattern according to which Luke tells the story of Jesus.[14] The biblical pattern

11. Joseph A. Fitzmyer, S.J., *The Gospel According to Luke (I–IX)* (Anchor Bible; Garden City, NY: Doubleday, 1981), pp. 794-95. Concerning the echoes of Exodus in Luke's account of the Transfiguration, see Willard M. Swartley, *Israel's Scripture Traditions and the Synoptic Gospels: Story Shaping Story* (Peabody, MA: Hendrickson Publishers, 1994), pp. 87-91.

12. Hooker, *Not Ashamed of the Gospel*, p. 80. Cf. Carroll and Green, *Death of Jesus in Early Christianity*, p. 68, and Wright, *Jesus and the Victory of God*, pp. 650-51.

13. Luke Timothy Johnson, *The Gospel of Luke* (Collegeville, MN: Liturgical Press, 1991), p. 156.

14. Luke Timothy Johnson, *Living Jesus: Learning the Heart of the Gospel* (San Francisco: HarperSanFrancisco, 1999), pp. 161-72.

of prophetic ministry in God's service — inaugurated with Moses, fulfilled in Jesus, imitated by Stephen, and continued with the Apostles — includes rejection and suffering (cf. Luke 2:34-35; 11:47-51; 12:49-53; Acts 7:51-60; 5:41; 9:15-16). Thus it is that Jesus explains to the disciples from Scripture why it was necessary for the Messiah to suffer by "beginning with Moses and all the prophets" (Luke 24:26-27). As Luke understands it, then, Jesus' suffering and death fulfills the biblical pattern of God's prophet, who suffers rejection by the people and receives vindication from God in the service of God's purpose of redemption.

9.4. The "Ransom" Saying

In Mark's Gospel, following both his Transfiguration and his third prophecy of passion and resurrection, Jesus speaks of the purpose of his mission in terms of a servant who gives his life for others: "For the Son of Man came not to be served but to serve, and to give his life a ransom for many *(lytron anti pollōn)*" (Mark 10:45). This saying is found in the parallel passage in Matthew (20:25-28) but not in Luke (22:24-27).

9.4.1. The Penal Substitution View

John Stott connects the "ransom" saying with the Suffering Servant in Isaiah 53, with v. 10 — "When you make his life an offering for sin . . ." — the key link. The implication is that Jesus intends by this saying to identify himself as the Suffering Servant. Stott thus reads the "ransom" saying to imply that Jesus understands his death in terms of penal substitution: Jesus dies with the intention of bearing the penalty of sin in place of others.[15] Stott's interpretation, a common view, is questionable on two grounds.

First, it is not nearly so clear as Stott asserts that Mark 10:45 is linked to Isaiah 53. That question is open to debate and has generated substantial scholarly discussion.[16] Lest the point here be misunderstood, the question is not whether

15. John R. W. Stott, *The Cross of Christ* (Downers Grove, IL: InterVarsity Press, 1986), pp. 146-47.
16. See McKnight, *Jesus and His Death,* pp. 159-239; Otto Betz, "Jesus and Isaiah 53," Morna Hooker, "Did the Use of Isaiah 53 to Interpret His Mission Begin with Jesus?" and Rikki Watts, "Jesus' Death, Isaiah 53, and Mark 10:45: A Crux Revisited," in William H. Bellinger, Jr. and William R. Farmer, eds., *Jesus and the Suffering Servant: Isaiah 53 and Christian Origins* (Harrisburg, PA: Trinity Press International, 1998), pp. 70-87, 88-103, and 125-51; Peter Stuhlmacher, "Isaiah 53 in the Gospels and Acts," in Bernd Janowski and Peter Stuhlmacher, eds., Daniel P. Bailey, trans., *The Suffering Servant: Isaiah 53 in Jewish and Christian Sources* (Grand Rapids, MI: Eerdmans Publishing, 2004), pp. 147-62; and Alberto de Mingo Kaminouchi, *"But It Is Not So among You": Echoes of Power in Mark 10:32-45* (London: T&T Clark, 2003), pp. 142-46.

the Gospel writers or Jesus himself understood his life and death as fulfilling the Suffering Servant prophecies. That much is clear. There are four explicit citations of Isaiah 53 in the Gospels and Acts with reference to Jesus (Matt 8:17; Luke 22:37; John 12:38; Acts 8:32-33). Matthew interprets Jesus' ministry of healing in this way: "He took our infirmities and bore our diseases" (Matt 8:16-17; citing Isa 53:4a). And Jesus interprets the manner of his death, that he would die the death of a rebel, likewise: "And he was counted among the lawless" (Luke 22:37; citing Isa 53:12b). The Synoptics also make a number of implicit allusions to the Suffering Servant in the passion narratives, especially concerning Jesus' being "betrayed" or "handed over" (*paradidomai;* cf. Isa 53:6, 12).[17]

The question here, rather, is whether Jesus intends to identify himself with the Suffering Servant of Isaiah 53 by his "ransom" saying. He does invoke the Servant figure of Second Isaiah as the mandate of his mission (Luke 4:18-21; Isa 61:1-2). And the spirit of the "ransom" saying does reflect the Servant theme — one giving his life on behalf of, and for the sake of, many. We cannot, however, simply infer from the various circumstantial evidence that Jesus therefore intends to identify himself as the Suffering Servant by speaking of himself as "a ransom for many." That would be to read the Suffering Servant into the "ransom" saying rather than to link the "ransom" saying to the Suffering Servant, thus getting the logic backward and so begging the question. We need to begin with the textual evidence of the "ransom" saying.

The textual evidence linking Mark 10:45 specifically to Isaiah 53 is mixed, however, insufficient in my view to warrant a confident conclusion that by the "ransom" saying Jesus surely intends to identify himself with the Suffering Servant. Isaiah 53 does speak of the Servant making "many" righteous and bearing the sin of "many" (vv. 11-12), as well as the Servant's "life" being offered (53:10). Yet examination of the key verse, v. 10, shows no evident link to Mark 10:45. The key word in the saying, *lytron* ("ransom"), does not appear in the Greek version of Isa 53:10; the Greek text reads *peri harmatias* ("concerning sin"), a possible allusion to the "sin offering." Nor does "ransom" appear in the Hebrew version of Isa 53:10; the Hebrew text reads *'āšām,* which designates the "guilt offering," not a ransom *(kōpher).* Kaminouchi comments concerning this disconnect between Mark 10:45 and Isa 53:10:

> the LXX never translates ['āšām] as [lytron], and indeed, they are different concepts: ['āšām] comes from the ritual world and designates the sacrifice offered for sin. [Lytron], however, comes from the world of slavery, where it denotes primarily the price paid to liberate a slave and only secondarily is

---

17. See Joel Marcus, "The Old Testament and the Death of Jesus: The Role of Scripture in the Gospel Passion Narratives," in Carroll and Green, *Death of Jesus in Early Christianity,* pp. 213-18.

used in a religious context to signify offering for the expiation of a sin or for the release of a vow.[18]

While Jesus speaks of himself as a servant, furthermore, he identifies himself in Mark 10:45 as "Son of Man," in which one might hear an echo of Daniel 7 (cf. Mark 14:62) rather than see an allusion to Isaiah 53. If Jesus does intend to identify himself here with the Suffering Servant, why then does he identify himself as "Son of Man" rather than "Servant of the Lord"? The interpretation of the "ransom" saying as Jesus' self-identification with the Suffering Servant thus generates an unexplained anomaly.[19]

Second, Stott assumes that the Suffering Servant in Isaiah 53 is properly interpreted as a penal substitute. As we will show in Chapter 13, however, not only do the details of the Song of the Suffering Servant not require a penal substitution reading, but the Song lends itself to interpretation in terms other than penal substitution. Thus, even if one does see a textual link between the "ransom" saying and Isaiah 53, one cannot simply infer that "ransom" equals "penal substitute" as Stott does.

9.4.2. The Text and Context of the Saying

To interpret Jesus' "ransom" saying, we need to begin, neither with Isaiah 53 nor with presuppositions about Jesus and the Suffering Servant, but with the text in Mark 10:45. The saying is a parallel extension of the phrase "not to be served but to serve." Thus, "to give his life a ransom for many" elaborates the meaning of "to serve." Jesus' giving himself "a ransom for many" expresses both the end and means of his divine mission to "serve" others.[20] The common view among many Christians is that Jesus came into the world just so that he might die ("cradle-cross" theology), but that view is seriously questionable. Jesus himself sums up his mission thus: "The Son of Man came to seek out and to save the lost" (Luke 19:10). Even if one were to limit Jesus' saving work to his death, that would still leave Jesus' work of "seeking" through his life-ministry. That "the Son of Man came . . . to serve . . . to give his life" thus need not be taken in reference to Jesus' death only. Because serving others comprises Jesus' entire ministry, we may say here that not only Jesus' death but his *whole life*, including teaching and healing, cross and resurrection, is a min-

18. Kaminouchi, *"But It Is Not So among You,"* p. 143; concerning the Hellenistic background of *lytron*, see pp. 147-51.

19. One might conjecture here that, by the "ransom" saying, Jesus intended to merge the Son of Man figure from Daniel with the Servant figure from Isaiah. Cf. Wright, *Jesus and the Victory of God*, p. 598.

20. Cf. Hooker, *Not Ashamed of the Gospel*, p. 55.

istry of service. Jesus gives *himself* for others — all his living, dying, and rising is the "ransom for many."

We should notice also the "for" that begins the "ransom" saying. This "for" links this saying to the foregoing discussion between Jesus and his disciples, which concerns the connections between kingdoms, rulers, greatness, and suffering (Mark 10:35-45). After Jesus announces his passion and resurrection a third time (vv. 33-34), James and John approach Jesus and request positions of privilege and power when Jesus enters his glory (vv. 35-36). They are correct to connect the coming of God's kingdom with Jesus' passion, for Jesus has taught them that his identity as the Messiah is integrally linked to rejection, suffering, death, and vindication (8:27-33). But they do not yet understand that what is true for the Master is true for the disciples — the way of the kingdom and of glory, for both Jesus and his followers, is none other than the way of the cross, patient endurance of suffering and humble submission to death (10:38-39; cf. 8:34; 14:36).[21] When the other disciples realize what James and John have asked of Jesus, they become angry (10:41). Theirs is the anger of envy; for the disciples still see each other as rivals for "first" or "greatest" in the kingdom (cf. 9:33-35). By their rivalry they fail to understand that the kingdom which Jesus inaugurates is not a kingdom in which a "first" or "great" one dominates all others, not like that lorded over by Caesar (10:42). Instead, in the kingdom of God, the "first" and "great" one is found in the position of "last" and "least," the position of "slave of all" (vv. 43-44). And that one is none other than Jesus himself, who gives his life in suffering service for others (v. 45). Jesus' giving himself "a ransom for many," therefore, both contrasts the way of God's reign with the way of human domination and identifies the way of lordship with the way of servanthood.[22]

9.4.3. The Meaning of "Ransom"

Having read this saying in its immediate context, let us next expand on the sense in which the life of Jesus the Servant might be understood as "a ransom for many." What does this word "ransom" (Greek *lytron*, Hebrew *kōpher*) signify? In its primary usage, the *lytron/kōpher* referred to neither a sacrifice for sin nor a punishment for transgression, but a price of release or a price of return.[23]

21. Cf. Timothy J. Geddert, *Mark* (Believers Church Bible Commentary; Scottdale, PA: Herald Press, 2001), pp. 249-51.
22. Cf. Carroll and Green, *Death of Jesus in Early Christianity*, p. 31.
23. Because "ransom" *(kôpher)* derives from the same root *(kāphar)* as "atonement" *(kipper)* in Hebrew, one might be tempted to think that "ransom" implies sacrifice. Or one might think that *kôpher* and *kāphar* share a common root and thus a common meaning, "to cover." However, one cannot simply infer the meaning of the piel stem *kipper* from the meaning of its

The primary social context of the *lytron/kōpher* was neither the altar of sacrifice nor the court of law, but the marketplace or the battlefield; and the implied beneficiary of the *lytron/kōpher* is neither sinner nor transgressor per se, but a slave or captive. The *lytron/kōpher* is that which is given in exchange for freedom or deliverance, the price of manumission or means of *redemption (lytrosis)*.[24] A key example of this is found in a prophetic text concerning God's redemption of Israel from exile: "I give Egypt as your ransom *(kōpher)*, Ethiopia and Seba in exchange for you" (Isa 43:3). In this light, we might see Jesus' life given "a ransom for many" as the God-provided means of releasing "many" from slavery and captivity to a hostile power: Jesus the Servant is Israel's new way of redemption. For Jesus to say that he came to serve and so to "give his life a ransom for many" is thus to say that the life of service in the way of the cross is the way of liberation — release from sin — and freedom from oppression in the redeemed community.[25]

In the Hebrew Scriptures the *lytron/kōpher* could also signify the price of saving one's life from death. In Num 35:31 the *lytron/kōpher* signifies a substitute penalty for the death of a murderer. Far from underwriting a penal substitution interpretation of Jesus' "ransom" saying, however, this text repudiates the very notion of penal substitution: taking a "ransom" for murder is absolutely prohibited — "a murderer must be put to death." In Exod 30:11-16, the *lytron/kōpher* is the price one would pay to YHWH to "ransom" one's life and thereby avoid the "plague" of God's wrath. This ransom was no offering for sin or penalty for transgression, but a poll tax for the support of the sanctuary, payable by all adult males whether rich or poor when they were registered for military service. In Ps 49:7-9, the *lytron/kōpher* signifies a price one would pay to God to secure eternal life, "that one should live on forever and never see the grave." Eternal life is not possible for us, however, for "no ransom avails for one's life, there is no price one can give to God for it." We mortals cannot provide what is needed to secure our lives against death, "For the ransom of life is costly, and can never suffice." But God will redeem or ransom one's life from the grave (Ps 49:15).[26] In this light, we might see

---

qal root *kāphar* ("to cover"), much less can one simply infer a meaning for *kōpher* from *kipper* or vice versa. Hebrew words often change meaning from root to stem.

24. C. S. Mann, *Mark* (Anchor Bible; Garden City, NY: Doubleday, 1986), p. 415. Concerning the Greek and Jewish backgrounds of "ransom" and "redemption," see Kaminouchi, *"But It Is Not So among You,"* pp. 147-51, and Leon Morris, *The Atonement: Its Meaning and Significance* (Downers Grove, IL: InterVarsity Press, 1983), pp. 107-18.

25. Cf. Kaminouchi, *"But It Is Not So among You,"* pp. 151-55.

26. James H. Waltner, *Psalms* (Believers Church Bible Commentary; Scottdale, PA: Herald Press, 2006), p. 249, also connects "ransom" in Psalm 49 to Jesus' "ransom" saying at Mark 10:45. There is no sense in Psalm 49 that "ransom" has anything to do here with the psalmist's sin or transgression. Psalm 49 is a wisdom psalm, not a lament or confession. As Waltner comments, the point here is that "There is no buying one's way out of dying" (p. 247).

Jesus' life given "a ransom for many" as the God-provided way of rescuing us mortals from the power of death and granting us immortality with God.

Now, one might want to read in this expression, "ransom for many" *(lytron anti pollōn)*, the notion of substitution, pointing to the Greek preposition *anti*, which carries the meaning of "exchange" — "this for that" (Latin, *quid pro quo*). That is precisely the meaning of *anti* in those texts where Paul instructs the church to renounce the world's practice of retributive justice: "Do not repay anyone evil [in exchange] for *(anti)* evil" (Rom 12:17; cf. 1 Thess 5:15). Is Jesus the "ransom," therefore, a substitute?

This question has generated some discussion in recent literature. McKnight has argued against a substitutionary interpretation of this text:

> The notion of ransom is a price paid in order to rescue someone from some hostile power. . . . What is unobserved by the substitutionary theory advocates is that the ransom cannot be a substitute, as we might find in theologically sophisticated language: where death is for death, and penal judgment is for penal judgment. Here we have a mixing of descriptions: a ransom for slaves. Jesus, in Mark's language, does not become a slave for other slaves. He is a ransom for those who are enslaved. The difference ought to be given careful attention. To be a substitute the ransom price would have to take the place of another ransom price or a slave for another slave, but that is not what is involved here. What we have is a ransom price and slaves, and the price is paid so the slaves can be liberated. The ransom is the price paid to the hostile power in order for the captives to be liberated. The ransom does not become a substitute so much as the *liberating price*. . . . The ransom, in this case, is not that Jesus "substitutes for his followers *as a ransom*" but that he ransoms by being the price paid in order to rescue his followers from that hostile power. The notion is one of being Savior, not substitution. The best translation would be that Jesus is a "ransom *for the benefit* of many."[27]

Jeffery et al. have critiqued McKnight's view:

> McKnight's point is that when a sum of money is paid in order to redeem a slave, that money does not become a slave — it is still money. Thus those who find substitution in this text are guilty of a category error.
>
> McKnight is mistaken, however, for the ransom in this case is not money but a life given up in death. This is precisely a substitute, for this life given up in death does take the place of other lives, which would have been given up in death. The substitute (Christ's death) and the thing substituted for (our deaths) are drawn from the same category.[28]

27. McKnight, *Jesus and His Death*, p. 357, emphasis original.
28. Steve Jeffery, Michael Ovey, and Andrew Sach, *Pierced for Our Transgressions: Rediscovering the Glory of Penal Substitution* (Wheaton, IL: Crossway Books, 2008), p. 71, n. 91.

Jeffery et al., however, simply presuppose the penal substitution view —
Christ's death in place of our deaths — and impose that view on the "ransom"
saying rather than deriving the notion of substitution from the "ransom" saying, thus begging the question. There is no doubt that, presupposing penal substitution, one can fit the "ransom" saying to the theory, but the question is
whether the "ransom" saying itself implies substitution.

I hope here to add some clarity to the question. The phrase "ransom for
(*anti*) many" does imply the notion of exchange ("this for that"), which is the
common meaning of *anti*. We need to distinguish carefully, however, between
exchange and substitution; although *anti* can connote substitution (we will examine this in more detail in Chapter 15), substitution is not necessarily present
in every case of exchange. Exchange and substitution are not identical categories: every substitution is an exchange ("this for that"), but not every exchange
is a substitution ("this in place of that"); the category of exchange thus subsumes the category of substitution — that is, substitution is a sub-category of
exchange. It is this distinction, I think, that McKnight should have emphasized
and which Jeffery et al. apparently miss.[29] And in making this distinction, it is
role or function, not class of object, that matters, a point that McKnight's discussion obscures.

One mode in which X might substitute for Y is when X acts in place of Y so
as to fill the role or serve the function of Y. In this sense, a substitute fills the
role or serves the function of that for which it is exchanged, whether it belongs
to the same class or not; but this is not necessarily the case in every instance of
exchange. Consider an example involving things of different classes. Exchanging money for a good or service does not substitute one thing for ("in
place of") another, not because the things exchanged belong to different classes,
but rather because the things exchanged serve different functions. If I purchase
a cup in a shop, the proprietor and I make an exchange — my money for her
cup — but the money does not substitute for ("take the place of") the cup: it
does not function as a cup, nor can it be inventoried as a cup, much less sold as
a cup. But, now, if I go to use the cup to drink and accidentally break it, I may
substitute my cupped hands in place of the broken cup to drink: a cup and
cupped hands serve the same function.

Consider, then, two examples involving things of the same class — human
beings. Take, first, the example of exchange in the story of Joseph. Judah has
pledged Jacob that he will bear responsibility for returning Benjamin to his father (Gen 43:8-9). When, the brothers having gone back down to Egypt,
Benjamin is found with Joseph's cup in his sack and Joseph claims Benjamin for

29. I. Howard Marshall, *Aspects of the Atonement: Cross and Resurrection in the Reconciling
of God and Humanity* (London: Paternoster, 2007), p. 47, also mistakenly equates a ransom price
with a substitute and thus imputes the idea of penal substitution to the "ransom" saying.

his slave, Judah pleads with Joseph to let the boy go and take him as his slave instead: "please let your servant remain as a slave to my lord in place of (Hebrew *taḥat*, Greek *anti*) the boy" (44:33). In this case, Judah not only proposes an exchange — himself for Benjamin — but also pledges a substitution: he will serve as Joseph's slave in place of Benjamin. We might say that Judah "ransoms" Benjamin from slavery by substituting himself for Benjamin in Joseph's service. But consider, second, an exchange of prisoners in wartime. Each side exchanges a prisoner with the other side — this man for that man — but the prisoners exchanged are not substitutes for each other: neither "takes the place" of the other by serving as prisoner of his own side. Rather than substituting one prisoner in place of another, the prisoner exchange releases both prisoners — each one is a "ransom" for the other.

While every ransom is an exchange, not every ransom is a substitution, because not every exchange is a substitution. Ransom might involve substitution, therefore, but not necessarily. One could see Jesus as "ransom for many" in analogy with the case of Judah and Benjamin: Jesus substitutes himself for us in slavery to gain our freedom. Such analogy, however, prompts the theologically awkward question: Into whose service does Jesus place himself in exchange for us? The devil's? By sinning we do "sell" ourselves into slavery to sin (John 8:34; Rom 6:16-23) and so, we might say, into the devil's service. But then the devil would seem to gain rights over Jesus on account of our sin, as Joseph gained rights over Judah. Or does Jesus place himself in *God's* service in exchange for us? But Jesus is already God's servant, and we were not God's servants: that, after all, was the problem! Better, then, that we think of Jesus as ransom simply in terms of exchange, not substitution. So we might say concerning Jesus our "ransom" — he gives his life, not as a substitute in place of our lives, but in exchange for our freedom, to secure our release from captivity to sin and death.[30]

9.4.4. The Canonical Background of the Saying

Finally, let us place Jesus' speaking of his life as "a ransom for many" into canonical context. Although the textual evidence linking the "ransom" saying specifically to Isaiah 53 is inconclusive, the appropriate background for the "ransom saying" is most likely Second Isaiah. Isaiah 40–55 is replete with the language of ransom/redemption. Isaiah repeatedly uses "ransom" in parallel with "redemption" to recall God's past work of salvation to release Israel from slavery in Egypt

---

30. I thus concur with Geddert, *Mark*, p. 252: "a full doctrine of substitutionary atonement can hardly be claimed for this verse [Mark 10:45]. The word *ransom (lutron)* emphasizes liberation more than substitution."

and thus to depict Israel's return from exile in Babylon as God's present work of salvation exceeding that of the past (Isa 35:8-10; 43:1-7, 14-21; 51:9-11; 52:1-12). Accordingly, Isaiah calls God "the Redeemer of Israel" and calls the people saved by God "the redeemed" or "the ransomed of the LORD." Although such language does not appear explicitly within any of the Servant songs, the motif of ransom/redemption is closely associated with the first Song and appears prominently in the second Song. After the first Song has introduced the Servant figure, whose mission is to "bring forth justice to the nations" (42:1-4), YHWH goes on to declare that he has called his covenant people Israel "in righteousness" to be "a light to the nations, to open the eyes that are blind, to bring out the prisoners from the dungeon, from the prison those who sit in darkness" (vv. 6-7). The release of prisoners from captivity, of course, is the very epitome of "ransom." If we see the Servant as Israel's representative "to the nations," then by this conjunction we can see "ransom" as integral to the Servant's mission. This fits well with the second Song, in which YHWH assigns the Servant the task of returning Israel to YHWH and restoring the remnant of Israel (49:5-6). The second Song is similarly followed by God's declaration of "a day of salvation" in which God will release Israel from captivity, return the people from exile, and restore the nation (vv. 7-26).

So, by his "ransom" saying, Jesus evidently links his suffering, death, and resurrection with the prophecies in Second Isaiah concerning God's purpose to ransom Israel from captivity and return Israel from exile. Second Isaiah, in turn, links God's present purpose to redeem Israel from captivity/exile with both God's past action to deliver Israel from slavery and the ministry of the Servant of YHWH. This Servant, perhaps seen as Israel's representative, is chosen and commissioned by God to restore the exiles of Israel and to release the prisoners of the nations. In canonical context, therefore, Jesus' "ransom" saying likely connects his life-service "for many" through suffering, death, and resurrection to the exodus from slavery, the return from exile, and the Servant's mission of restoration for Israel and justice "to the nations."[31]

All this fits well with the Markan context for Jesus' "ransom saying." Mark's account of Jesus' life and death, as evident from its structure and language, is consciously guided by Isaiah's vision of the return of Israel from exile as God's new exodus (Isaiah 40–55). Just as God led Israel from exile by "the Way of the Lord," so now Jesus is the new manifestation of the "Way of the Lord" by which God will lead his people to redemption (40:3; 42:16; 43:16, 19;

---

31. Cf. Wright, *Jesus and the Victory of God*, pp. 588-91, 601-4. Wright comments: "I suggest, then, that Isaiah 40–55 as a whole was thematic for Jesus' kingdom announcement. His work is not to be understood in terms of the teaching of an abstract and timeless system of theology, not even of atonement-theology, but as the historical and concrete acting out of YHWH's promise to defeat evil and rescue his people from exile, that is, to forgive their sins at last" (pp. 603-4).

48:17; Mark 1:2-3).[32] Not by happenstance, then, does Mark place Jesus' "ransom" saying at the culmination of that narrative section most emphatically marked by "the Way of the Lord" motif and deliberately shaped by Israel's Scripture tradition concerning the exodus (Mark 8:27–10:52).[33] As Morna Hooker appropriately observes, therefore, the "ransom" saying depicts Jesus' death as "the saving action by which God establishes his new people . . . a saving act parallel to the Exodus and Return."[34] The significance of the "ransom" saying in Mark's Gospel thus converges with the significance of the Transfiguration event in Luke's Gospel: Jesus sees himself as God's new exodus, the way by which God will do a new and climactic work of salvation, liberating many from captivity and (re-)creating his covenant community.

9.4.5. Ransom: A Price Paid?

If we wonder what "price" God has "paid" to ransom Israel from captivity in Babylon, the prophet tells us — none: "For thus says the LORD: You were sold for nothing, and you shall be redeemed without money" (Isa 52:3). God need not "pay" any "price" to anyone to redeem his people; for the "ransomed of the Lord" are liberated by God, not by an exchange between God and some other power. God may elect to use Cyrus as a human instrument to "set my exiles free" from captivity; but Cyrus will do so "not for price or reward" (45:13). Had God paid Cyrus a ransom price in exchange for Israel's freedom, then this transaction would have been worked by the will of two parties — in which case Israel's freedom would have depended not only upon God but also upon Cyrus. God pays no ransom price in exchange for Israel's freedom, for God alone is the Savior of Israel. As was creation, so also redemption is the work of God's sovereign will and power (vv. 1-17).

This is important for our thinking of Jesus giving "his life a ransom for many." God's work of redemption in Christ is *costly* to God: we have been "ransomed . . . with the precious blood of Christ" (1 Pet 1:18-19; cf. Rev 5:9).[35] It does not follow, nor should we think, however, that God thus secures our redemption by a transaction, that God has literally paid a price in the coinage of Jesus' blood in exchange for us. For, again, such thinking prompts the theologically awkward question: To whom has God paid this price? The devil? Then the devil

32. Cf. Joel Marcus, *The Way of the Lord: Christological Exegesis of the Old Testament in Mark* (Louisville, KY: Westminster/John Knox Press, 1992), and Watts, "Jesus' Death, Isaiah 53, and Mark 10:45," pp. 128-31.

33. Cf. Swartley, *Israel's Scripture Traditions and the Synoptic Gospels*, pp. 96-115.

34. Hooker, *Not Ashamed of the Gospel*, p. 56. Cf. Green, "The Death of Jesus and the Ways of God," pp. 31-32.

35. Cf. Hooker, *Not Ashamed of the Gospel*, p. 126.

would seem to have rights equal to God's, implying that God is less than sovereign. To God-self? Then it would appear that God is the oppressor from whom we needed to be liberated rather than the Redeemer who saves us. Leon Morris comments aptly on Jesus as "ransom" for humanity:

> . . . in the New Testament there is never any hint of a recipient of the ransom. In other words we must understand redemption as a useful metaphor which enables us to see some aspects of Christ's great saving work with clarity but which is not an exact description of the whole process of salvation. We must not press it beyond what the New Testament tells us about it. To look for a recipient of the ransom is illegitimate.[36]

9.5. The Last Supper

Jesus' last meal with his disciples before his death is depicted in the Synoptic Gospels as a commemoration of the Passover (Mark 14:12-16 and pars. in Matthew and Luke). During the meal, Jesus says that the bread of blessing that is broken and the cup of thanksgiving that is poured out signify his own body and blood, given for others. Here we will focus on Jesus' saying over the cup, which connects his life and death ("blood") to God's covenant: "This is my blood of the covenant, which is poured out for many" (Mark 14:24). Matthew's account follows Mark's but adds "for the forgiveness of sins" (Matt 26:28). Luke's account also links Jesus' life and death ("blood") to God's covenant but adds that this is a "new" covenant: "This cup that is poured out for you is the new covenant in my blood" (Luke 22:20).[37] What does Jesus mean by this saying?

9.5.1. The Penal Substitution View

Gruenler interprets the "cup" saying as connecting Jesus' death ("blood") to the sacrifices for sin in the Levitical cult.[38] He then interprets the "cup" saying as implying that Jesus understands his death as an atonement for sin in the penal substitution sense.[39] The penal substitution model claims that Jesus' blood ef-

---

36. Morris, *The Atonement*, p. 129.

37. The Lukan account of the Last Supper has significant variants in the ancient manuscripts. See Bruce M. Metzger, *A Textual Commentary on the Greek New Testament*, 2nd ed. (Stuttgart: United Bible Societies, 2002), pp. 148-50.

38. Not all penal substitution apologists link the Last Supper to the Levitical cult — e.g., Jeffery et al., *Pierced for Our Transgressions*, who correctly identify the links to Passover and covenant. We will consider their view below.

39. Royce Gordon Gruenler, "Atonement in the Synoptic Gospels and Acts," in Charles E. Hill and Frank A. James III, eds., *The Glory of the Atonement: Biblical, Theological and Practical*

fects forgiveness because God's justice requires bloodshed in order for sins to be forgiven and Jesus' death satisfies God's justice by paying the penalty for sins in his blood.

Gruenler's interpretation is questionable on three grounds. First, it does not fit the actual context and language of the text. The narrative context links the Last Supper, not to the Levitical cult, but to the Passover. As we will see below, moreover, Jesus' own words link the cup ("blood"), not to the Levitical cult, but to the covenant-making ceremony at Sinai (Exodus 24) as well as to the prophets (Jeremiah, Zechariah, and possibly Isaiah).[40] Gruenler's interpretation effectively assumes that "blood" has the singular significance of atonement by blood per the Levitical cult, mixing Passover blood and covenant blood with atoning blood into an all-purpose "blood" that avails for the forgiveness of sins.[41] In this common view, "blood" and "forgiveness of sins" necessarily refer to the Levitical cult, especially the Day of Atonement (cf. Lev 17:11). As McKnight reminds us, however, that is a fundamental mistake: "Christian theology tends to blur the distinct functions of blood in the Old Testament. Not every use of blood was atoning and forgiving. . . . *Pesah* blood, covenant blood, and atoning blood are three different kinds of blood."[42] The sacrifices offered in the covenant ceremony, accordingly, were not sin offerings but rather burnt offerings and peace offerings (Exod 24:5).

Second, Gruenler's interpretation, linking the cup ("blood") to the Levitical cult, generates an anomaly needing explanation. Throughout his ministry, Jesus largely bypassed the temple. Although he directed the healed leper to present himself to the priest and make a purification offering (Mark 1:40-44), Jesus offered forgiveness of sins, apart from sacrifice and bloodshed. He forgave sins on his own authority, conditional not upon sacrifice but upon repentance and faith, mediated not by blood but by his own word, claiming that the divine prerogative of forgiveness belongs to himself (2:1-12). As Daniel Antwi has observed, by his personal ministry of divine forgiveness Jesus effectively assumed the atoning function of the temple cult into himself:

> The Synoptic presentation of Jesus and his mission as the one who has the power *(exousia)* to forgive sins gives ample reason to propose that by his

Perspectives (Downers Grove, IL: InterVarsity Press, 2004), pp. 94ff. Cf. Hill, "Atonement in the Old and New Testaments," pp. 28-29 in the same volume.

40. The phrase "the blood of the covenant" *(dam-habrît)* appears only in Exod 24:8, with an echo in Zech 9:11, "blood of my covenant" *(dam-bᵉrîtēk)*, but never in Leviticus. Kevin J. Vanhoozer, "The Atonement in Postmodernity: Guilt, Goats and Gifts," in *Glory of the Atonement*, p. 398, also mistakenly connects the "cup" saying to the Temple cult despite the fact that Jesus' words point elsewhere.

41. Morris, *The Atonement,* also seems to conflate the blood of the covenant sacrifice and the blood of the sin sacrifice (cf. pp. 36, 41).

42. McKnight, *Jesus and His Death,* p. 285.

words and actions Jesus was, by implication, *identifying his role with that of the hitherto given institution for atonement.* . . . That is to say, Jesus was declaring that he embodied in himself that which constituted the means of atonement hitherto known to the people only through the cult.[43]

Jesus understood his words and deeds to be the atoning action of God ministered directly through his very person, such that divine forgiveness of sins was presently available to God's people through his ministry, apart from temple and cult. Why, then, would Jesus think of his death in terms of the temple cult, as the shedding of blood necessary for sins to be forgiven by God, when his own prior words and deeds had *already* proclaimed and enacted divine forgiveness of sins, implying that such was no longer required?[44]

Jesus, moreover, taught that mercy and love are "much more important" than all the sacrifices of the temple (Matt 9:13; 12:7; Mark 12:28-34) — indeed, that in himself "something greater than the temple is here" (Matt 12:6). And during his final week, Jesus pronounced judgment upon the temple for its corruption and injustice (Mark 11:15-17) and prophesied that it would fall to destruction (Mark 13:1-2). Why, then, if he had declared sacrifice to be of lesser importance than mercy, if his own ministry had *already* rendered the temple obsolete concerning forgiveness of sins, and if the temple itself was corrupt and doomed, would Jesus link the meaning of his death to the sacrificial cult of the temple? Jesus, rather, explicitly links the significance of his suffering and death

43. Daniel J. Antwi, "Did Jesus Consider His Death to be an Atoning Sacrifice?" *Interpretation* 45/1 (1991), 17-28, p. 27, emphasis original. We do not agree, however, with the conclusion that Antwi goes on to draw from this, that Jesus thus understood his death as an atoning sacrifice per the Temple cult. At no time during his ministry does Jesus state, implicitly or explicitly, that his authoritative power to forgive sin derives (ex post facto) from his (yet to be accomplished) death. Rather, Jesus announces his authority to forgive based on his identity/status (Mark 2:10). And that was precisely the issue for his religious critics: "Why does this fellow speak in this way. It is blasphemy! *Who* can forgive sins but God alone" (2:7). The issue for all involved was not whether a proper sacrifice had occurred such that forgiveness could be offered, or that this pronouncement of forgiveness had occurred apart from the Temple. Rather, the issue concerned the status of the one pronouncing forgiveness, which all agreed only God could rightly do. The priest at the Temple could pronounce forgiveness only as the representative of God. By claiming authoritative power to forgive sin, Jesus was thus claiming himself to be no less than God's executive agent, that he was able and authorized to do what only God could do, which spurred the scribes to charge him with blasphemy. Jesus' claim of authoritative power to forgive sin, exercised prior to and hence apart from his death, was thus dependent not on his death but on his person, his relation to God (cf. Mark 1:11). The appropriate inference here, therefore, is that Jesus understood himself as assuming the atoning function of the Temple cult, thus obviating sacrifice and bloodshed as the means of obtaining divine forgiveness, which was presently available to the people through his very person.

44. In Chapter 11 we will examine whether in the Old Testament bloodshed was necessary for forgiveness of sin. There we will challenge the view, expressed by Antwi, that prior to Jesus atonement for sin had been available to the people of Israel only through the Temple cult.

to the Passover and the covenant. Neither the original Passover observance nor the covenant-making ceremony was a function of the temple. Indeed, both preceded construction of the sanctuary, consecration of the priesthood, and institution of the sacrificial rites.[45] By announcing the end of the temple and declaring himself to have assumed and surpassed the cult, Jesus implies that he himself inaugurates a new era for the people of God, a way of life that *already* transcends the temple.[46]

It is imperative to keep in mind here that how Jesus himself understood his death and how his followers understood his death are two different questions. There is no doubt that an early tradition of the church understood Jesus' death as a sacrificial offering that effects the expiation (removal or cleansing) of sins. Whereas Hebrews, Paul, and John each use the cultic language of "offering" (*prosphora*) or "sacrifice" (*thysia*) or "atoning sacrifice" (*hilasmos*), Jesus himself never spoke of his death in such terms. Had Jesus understood his death as an atoning sacrifice, why did he not use the cultic language to say so? The text under consideration, we would argue, neither supports nor contradicts that early Christian understanding, but rather projects a different dimension of the meaning of Jesus' death. When interpreting Jesus' death, we must be careful neither to collapse its manifold of meaning into a singularity, nor to superimpose the view of Jesus' followers onto Jesus himself.

Third, even if Gruenler were correct to connect the "cup" saying to the Levitical cult, the penal substitution view assumes that the sacrifices for sins were intended to propitiate God and satisfy retribution. As we will show in Chapter 11, however, the penal substitution interpretation of the Levitical cult is not supported by the scriptural evidence. We thus seek to interpret how Jesus' "blood of the covenant" is "for the forgiveness of sins" without presupposing that Jesus' death was intended as a penal substitution.

9.5.2. The Passover Context

We will take our cue for interpreting Jesus' "cup" saying, not from a presupposed and preferred doctrine of atonement, but from the Gospel accounts themselves. The Synoptic Gospels present the Last Supper with two overlapping layers of significance. By his own words and actions, Jesus links his suffering and death — not to the Levitical sacrifices, not even to the Day of Atone-

45. Alternatively, one might argue that, insofar as the Passover sacrifice had been subsumed into the Temple cult by the first century, by assuming the Temple cult into himself Jesus also assumes the cultic function of the Passover sacrifice into himself. Either way, Jesus declares that the locus of God's atoning action is no longer the Temple and its cult, but himself, his words and deeds.

46. Cf. Wright, *Jesus and the Victory of God*, pp. 246-74, 320-68, 405-28.

ment — but rather to the Passover and to the covenant. We should not find this surprising, given that Passover and covenant are central events in Israel's history and are linked closely by a common story of salvation: God's redemption of Israel from Egypt, commemorated by the Passover observance, leads to God's covenanting with Israel at Sinai, sealed by the covenant sacrifice (Exodus 1–24). Israel's liberation from Pharaoh's slavery through Passover (Exodus 12) is correlated to Israel's commitment to serve YHWH at Sinai (Exodus 24), as Propp comments: "Exodus 24 may in fact be read as the mirror image of the *Pesaḥ*. The blood ritual in Exodus 12 initiates Israel's freedom; the blood ritual of Exodus 24 terminates it. Released from involuntary servitude to Pharaoh, Israel voluntarily enters Yahweh's servitude."[47] It is thus quite appropriate and significant that Jesus' "cup" saying should link the event of Passover and the blood of covenant. At the Last Supper, Jesus merges the exodus story of salvation with the story of his own suffering, death, and resurrection.[48] We will consider the Passover and covenant motifs in turn.

All four Gospels and Paul connect Jesus' death to Passover. But we must take care here to observe that they do so in different ways. In none of the Gospel accounts does Jesus ever actually identify himself with the Passover lamb. In the Synoptic accounts of the Last Supper, Jesus interprets the bread and wine of the Passover meal as symbols of his own imminent suffering and death, his body to be broken and his blood to be poured out. But Jesus does not identify himself with or otherwise link himself to the Passover lamb.[49] John's passion narrative also connects Jesus to the Passover lamb in an indirect, if dramatic, fashion: Jesus is crucified at the same time as the lambs are being slaughtered (John 19:14, 31).[50] Paul does directly identify Jesus with the Passover lamb: "our paschal lamb *(pascha)*, Christ, has been sacrificed" (1 Cor 5:7).

In any case, the Passover lamb, we must keep in mind, was not a sacrifice for sins, being neither a sacrifice (strictly speaking) nor for sins.[51] In its origin,

47. William H. C. Propp, *Exodus 19–40* (Anchor Bible; New York: Doubleday, 2006), p. 309.

48. Wright, *Jesus and the Victory of God*, pp. 554-59.

49. In John's Gospel, of course, the Last Supper takes place the evening before the day of preparation for the Passover — and thus is not a Passover meal. There is thus much scholarly debate over whether the Synoptic tradition or John's account is historically accurate on this point. Most scholars think that the Synoptic tradition is historically accurate, and we follow that majority view here. For an argument in favor of John's account, see McKnight, *Jesus and His Death*, p. 370.

50. John's Gospel also has John the Baptist say of Jesus, "Here is the lamb of God, who takes away the sin of the world" (John 1:29). *Which* lamb John intends here, whether the Passover lamb or some other, and whether John the Evangelist intends the same lamb to which John the Baptist was referring, however, is unclear and the subject of much debate. See: McKnight, *Jesus and His Death*, pp. 369-71; Hooker, *Not Ashamed of the Gospel*, pp. 97-98; and Raymond E. Brown, *The Gospel According to John (i–xii)* (Anchor Bible; Garden City, NY: Doubleday, 1966), pp. 58-63.

51. C. J. den Heyer, *Jesus and the Doctrine of Atonement* (Harrisburg, PA: Trinity Press International, 1998), pp. 19, 59-60, 102-6.

the Passover observance was not a sacrificial function of the priestly office or the temple cult (Exodus 12). The institution of the Passover observance preceded construction of the sanctuary, consecration of Aaron, and institution of the cult; and the instructions for the Passover observance are independent of sanctuary, priest, and cult. The original ritual was focused around family and home: the Passover lamb was slain not by the priest but by the family head; it was not offered on the temple altar but was eaten at the family table; and its blood was not poured out at the base of the temple altar but smeared on the doorposts and lintel of the family home.[52] The Passover event itself concerned, moreover, not remission of sins, but aversion of destruction and redemption from slavery. The connection of the cup ("blood") to forgiveness of sins, therefore, evidently has nothing to do with Passover per se.

Regarding the significance of the Passover context for the meaning of Jesus' suffering and death, let us consider Jesus' own words. First, Jesus takes elements of the Passover meal, bread and wine, and says of them, "This is my body . . . for you. . . . This is my blood . . . for many."[53] By these words, Jesus invests the elements of bread and wine with redemptive significance — they now signify redemption through himself for his disciples ("for you") as well as for all Israel and all humanity ("for many"). In the post-exodus tradition, the unleavened bread is called "the bread of affliction (*'onî*)" (Deut 16:3). This was a deliberate echo of the exodus story, where YHWH says to Moses, "I have observed the misery (*'onî*) of my people who are in Egypt . . . and I have come down to deliver them . . ." (Exod 3:7-8). By identifying the "bread of affliction" with his body given for others, Jesus identifies his death with the suffering of God's people. This suggests that Jesus understands the death he is about to undergo as a redemptive sharing in the suffering of his people: as then God had observed his people in affliction and acted to redeem them, so now Jesus is acting to redeem God's people by sharing with them in their affliction and dying on their behalf.[54] According to rabbinic tradition, the unleavened bread signifies the suddenness of redemption and the four cups of wine signify the four verbs depicting God's act to redeem Israel from Egypt (Exod 6:6-7).[55] Jesus' symbolic interpretation of the material el-

---

52. Later developments in Jewish tradition do show increasing involvement by the priests and a central role for the Temple by the first century. See McKnight, *Jesus and His Death*, pp. 243-58.

53. This "saying" is a composite of Mark 14:22-24; Matt 26:26-28; and Luke 22:19-20.

54. The motif of righteous suffering, including redemptive suffering, has an extensive background, both canonical and extracanonical: Psalm 22, Isaiah 40–55, Wisdom 2-6, 2 Maccabees, and 4 Maccabees. Cf. Wright, *Jesus and the Victory of God*, pp. 579-604. Concerning redemptive suffering and Jesus' death, he concludes: "There was, then, no such thing as a pre-Christian Jewish version of (what we now think of as) Pauline atonement-theology. . . . Jesus, therefore, was not offering an abstract atonement theology; he was identifying himself with the suffering of Israel" (p. 592).

55. Nahum N. Glatzer, ed., *The Passover Haggadah* (New York: Schocken Books, 1989), pp. 8-9.

ements of the Passover meal in reference to himself, his own body and blood to be broken and poured out for others, thus suggests that he understood his suffering and death as the present realization of God's work of redemption through the original Passover event: Jesus is the new exodus.[56]

Second, Jesus' saying concerning the bread and cup, "Do this in remembrance of me" (Luke 22:19; cf. 1 Cor 11:23-25), evokes the primary purpose of the Passover festival — to remember God's work of salvation, which is the historical origin of Israel's life as God's people. YHWH had instructed Moses and Aaron:

> This shall mark for you the beginning of months; it shall be the first month of the year for you. . . . This shall be a day of remembrance for you. You shall celebrate it as a festival to the LORD; throughout your generations you shall observe it as a perpetual ordinance . . . for on this very day I brought your companies out of the land of Egypt. (Exod 12:2, 14, 17)

Likewise, the Apostles, following Jesus, instructed the early Christians to proclaim God's salvation worked through Jesus by remembering his death in the Eucharist: "For as often as you eat this bread and drink the cup, you proclaim the Lord's death until he comes" (1 Cor 11:26). The early Christians celebrated the Eucharist with the same sense that the ancient Israelites commemorated the Passover, the same sense in which Jesus himself had celebrated the Last Supper and had instructed his disciples to commemorate his own death — as a remembrance of God's gracious work of redemption.

Now, some penal substitution apologists have endeavored to frame the Passover itself as an instance of penal substitution. Jeffery et al.: "the Passover lamb functioned as a penal substitute, dying in the place of the firstborn sons of the Israelites, in order that they might escape the wrath of God."[57] They follow Stott: "in the original Passover in Egypt each paschal lamb died instead of the family's first-born son, and the first-born was spared only if a lamb was slain in its place."[58] Insofar as one sees Jesus as a Passover lamb, if it is in fact correct that the Passover lamb was intended as a penal substitute, then this would lend substantial support to the penal substitution model.[59]

This claim, that the Passover lamb was intended as a penal substitute, however, generates a logical problem. If the Passover lamb functioned as a penal

---

56. Cf. Wright, *Jesus and the Victory of God*, pp. 559-63; McKnight, *Jesus and His Death*, pp. 278-83.

57. Jeffery et al., *Pierced for Our Transgressions*, p. 34.

58. Stott, *Cross of Christ*, p. 72.

59. Cf. Jeffery et al., *Pierced for Our Transgressions*, pp. 38-41. As we observed above, such a claim is complicated by the fact that Jesus never identifies himself with the Passover lamb, but only with the bread and wine. Jeffery et al. note this anomaly (p. 39, n. 9), but offer no explanation.

substitute for the firstborn sons of the Israelites, the former dying in place of the latter, then there must have been a one-to-one correspondence between each lamb slain and each life spared. Jeffery et al. claim that there was indeed a "one-to-one correspondence between the life of a son and the life of a lamb."[60] But the text itself makes clear that this was not necessarily so. "If a household is too small for a whole lamb," then *two* families were to share *one* lamb; in that case, "the lamb shall be divided in proportion to the number of people who eat of it" (Exod 12:4). This division of the lamb confounds the logic of substitution. For if the lamb functioned as a penal substitute, it would follow that dividing the lamb "in proportion to the number of people" would also divide the substitutionary value of the lamb between the households. (Otherwise, if the substitutionary value of the lamb were indivisible, one lamb could have functioned as a penal substitute for all the firstborn sons, which was evidently not the case.) Thus, if each lamb substituted for the life of one firstborn son, as Jeffery et al. and Stott claim, then where two families shared one lamb only half the life of the first-born son of each family would have been saved from God's wrath — which makes no sense.

Interpreting the Passover lamb as a penal substitute, moreover, generates an unexplained anomaly. If the Passover lamb spared the lives of the firstborn sons of the Israelites because it satisfied the wrath of God, as Jeffery et al. maintain, then the obvious question arises: Why was God wrathful against the firstborn sons of the Israelites? Of what transgression were they guilty? Being firstborn? Being born in Egypt? Being born into slavery? The text gives no indication that God is wrathful against the Israelites or their firstborn sons. To the contrary, God's wrath and judgment is manifestly directed toward Egypt, Pharaoh, and Egypt's gods. The biblical narrative makes clear that YHWH intends this last plague "upon Pharaoh and upon Egypt" (Exod 11:1) and that by this plague YHWH is executing judgment "on all the gods of Egypt" (12:12).[61]

---

60. Jeffery et al., *Pierced for Our Transgressions*, p. 37.

61. Jeffery et al., *Pierced for Our Transgressions*, p. 38, try to avoid this anomaly by appealing to Ezek 20:4-10, in which YHWH declares to Ezekiel that he would "pour out my wrath upon [Israel] and spend my anger against them in the midst of the land of Egypt" because the people had defiled themselves "with the idols of Egypt" (vv. 7-8). Two comments. First, the Ezekiel text says nothing about the Passover lamb, much less uses God's wrath against Israel's idolatry as rationale for the Passover lamb. Second, the Ezekiel text makes clear that God withholds his wrath against Israel and acts to deliver Israel from bondage, not because Israel has propitiated God by the death of the Passover lamb or anything else, but simply "for the sake of my name" (v. 9). Ezekiel's testimony to God's redemption of Israel from Egypt thus does not fit the penal substitution model.

9.5.3. The Covenant Connection

The Synoptic tradition of the Last Supper, as well as Paul (1 Cor 11:25), connects Jesus' death also to the covenant. Jesus' saying over the cup echoes the ceremony of covenant ratification at Mount Sinai. Jesus' words, "this is my blood of the covenant *(to haima mou tēs diathēkēs)*" (Matt 26:28), reflect the words of Moses to the people concerning the sacrificial blood that seals the covenant, "See the blood of the covenant (LXX *to haima tēs diathēkēs*) that the LORD has made with you" (Exod 24:8). As Moses sprinkled the blood of the covenant on the people (Exod 24:8), so Jesus gives the cup of his "blood" to his disciples to drink (Matt 26:27).

Jesus' "cup" saying thus connects his suffering and death to the exodus from slavery and ratification of covenant. As with Luke's account of the Transfiguration, the "faith location" of the Last Supper in the Synoptic tradition is the grand story of God's salvation in Israel's history. As exodus and covenant were the fountain and foundation of Israel's faith and community, so Jesus' life, death, and resurrection were the origin of the faith and community of the early Christians. The suffering, death, and resurrection of Jesus is the new Passover; Jesus himself is the new exodus and the new covenant, God's way of redemption from slavery, restoration to righteousness, and renewal of life.[62]

What, though, about the connection of blood to forgiveness of sins in Jesus' "cup" saying? As argued above, Jesus "cup" saying does not refer to the Levitical cult. And the Passover context of the Last Supper does not connect blood and forgiveness of sins, but rather blood and liberation from slavery. In the Last Supper, it is Jesus' reference to covenant that provides the connection between the cup ("blood") and forgiveness of sins. The covenant sacrifice itself did not effect remission of sins, of course — it sealed the exclusive relationship of love and loyalty between God and his people (Exod 24:7-8). Why, then, if Jesus says that the cup is "my blood of the covenant," does he say that his blood is "poured out for many for the forgiveness of sins" (Matt 26:28)?

Forgiveness of sin, healing of disease, and redemption of life were the primary blessings of God's covenant, expressions of God's steadfast love and covenant loyalty (cf. Exod 20:5-6). The psalmist sings in praise of these "benefits" of God's covenant: "Bless the LORD, O my soul, and do not forget all his benefits — who forgives all your iniquity, who heals all your diseases, who redeems your life from the Pit, who crowns you with steadfast love and mercy" (Ps 103:2-4). Now, after his resurrection and prior to his ascension, Jesus instructs his disciples that, in fulfillment of the Scriptures, "repentance and forgiveness of sins is to be proclaimed in his name to all nations" (Luke 24:47). And, beginning from Pentecost,

---

62. In this, we concur more or less with Stott, *Cross of Christ*, pp. 68-72, the "less" concerning Stott's force-fitting of the Passover into the penal substitution model.

the Apostles do proclaim repentance and forgiveness of sins "in the name of Jesus" to both Jews and Gentiles (Acts 2:38; 3:19-20; 4:12; 5:31; 10:43; 13:38-39). More than that, the Apostles heal the sick and raise the dead by the power of Jesus' name (3:1-16; 4:5-12, 29-30; 9:32-42). Through the apostolic witness and ministry, therefore, God was offering the "benefits" of the covenant — forgiveness of sin, healing of disease, and redemption of life — to anyone who would repent and believe "in the name of Jesus." In covenant with Israel, God had provided for forgiveness of sin and cleansing of impurity through the Levitical rites. No longer would God's covenant blessing be accessible only through the Temple and only to Israel. As God had offered these covenant "benefits" to Israel apart from the Temple in Jesus himself through his ministry (cf. Luke 4:31-41; 5:17-26; 6:6-11; 7:1-17, 36-50; 8:26-56, etc.), so now through Jesus' death, resurrection, and exaltation God was continuing to offer these "benefits" freely to all "in the name of Jesus."

Tannehill comments (with reference to Acts):

> The ruling power of Jesus is saving power. Through the enthroned Messiah benefits are "poured out" or "given" to the Messiah's people. The presentation of this in the Acts speeches suggests continuity with the saving work of Jesus during his previous ministry, for the beneficial power that Jesus then showed to the limited number of people who encountered him will now be offered to all. Thus the Spirit, which rested on Jesus but not on his followers during his preresurrection ministry, has been poured out on others by the exalted Jesus (2:33), and this benefit will be extended to new groups as the mission expands. Repentance and release of sins are associated with Jesus' exaltation in a similar way, for God "exalted" Jesus "at his right hand to give repentance to Israel and release of sins" (5:31). These gifts will be offered universally. . . . This is an extension of Jesus' work during his earthly ministry, in which release of sins had a central place.
>
> . . . Thus we may say that God saves by establishing through Jesus the messianic reign which is the time of salvation promised Israel in Scripture, a time of salvation that the Gentiles may share. Jesus is Savior as the ruling Messiah, who, in fulfillment of the promise to David, mediates the benefits of God's rule. The Spirit, repentance and release of sins, and salvation through Jesus' name are all part of these benefits.[63]

Jesus' life, death, and resurrection are the foundation of a new relationship between God and humanity, the fountain of a new offer of God's grace, in which the benefits of God's covenant — forgiveness of sin, healing of disease, and redemption of life — are extended to all humanity, to anyone who will repent and believe "in the name of Jesus."

Accordingly, Jesus says his life poured out for others and offered up in

---

63. Tannehill, *Narrative Unity of Luke-Acts, Vol. Two,* pp. 39-40.

death is "the new covenant in my blood" (Luke 22:20; cf. 1 Cor 11:25). Jesus' "cup" saying in Luke echoes two prophetic oracles from the exilic period that promise return from exile, renewal of covenant, and restoration of the people. First, by speaking of "new covenant" *(kainē diathēkē),* Jesus echoes Jeremiah, who declared that God had promised to make a "new covenant," the first "benefit" of which is forgiveness of sins:

> The days are surely coming, says the LORD, when I will make a new covenant (LXX *diathēkēn kainēn*) with the house of Israel and the house of Judah. It will not be like the covenant that I made with their ancestors when I took them by the hand to bring them out of the land of Egypt — a covenant that they broke, though I was their husband, says the LORD. But this is the covenant that I will make with the house of Israel after those days, says the LORD: I will put my law within them, and I will write it on their hearts; and I will be their God, and they shall be my people. No longer shall they teach one another, or say to each other, "Know the LORD," for they shall all know me, from the least of them to the greatest, says the LORD; for I will forgive their iniquity, and remember their sin no more. (Jer 31:31-34)

Second, by speaking of "new covenant" in connection with his "blood of the covenant," Jesus echoes Zechariah,[64] who linked the blood of the covenant directly with God's deliverance of the exiles: "As for you also, because of the blood of my covenant with you, I will set your prisoners free from the waterless pit. Return to your stronghold, O prisoners of hope; today I declare that I will restore to you double" (Zech 9:11-12). The "blood of my covenant" (LXX *haimati diathēkēs*) between God and Israel is a sign of hope of redemption from captivity and a promise of restoration to freedom.[65]

Jesus' "cup" saying at the Last Supper, therefore, connects his suffering and death, as symbolized in the elements of the Passover meal, not only to exodus from slavery and ratification of covenant, but also to return from exile and renewal of covenant. Jesus thus understands himself to be the one through whom God intends to fulfill the prophecies of return, renewal, and restoration for his people Israel.[66] And by connecting his suffering, death, and resurrection to Is-

---

64. Cf. Marcus, "The Old Testament and the Death of Jesus," pp. 218-20.

65. Marcus, "The Old Testament and the Death of Jesus," pp. 213-18, argues also that the phrases "poured out" and "for many" in Jesus' "cup" saying link it to the song of the Suffering Servant (cf. Isa 53:12). I am not convinced of this connection. Even so, if Jesus' "cup" saying does allude to the Suffering Servant, it does not follow that Jesus' words at the Last Supper support a penal substitution view of the cross any more than the fourth Servant song itself requires a penal substitution interpretation in the first place (see Chapter 13 below). Concerning the various possible Old Testament background texts for the "cup" saying, see also McKnight, *Jesus and His Death,* pp. 284-92.

66. Cf. Green, "The Death of Jesus and the Ways of God," p. 32.

rael's return from exile and God's renewal of covenant, Jesus again connects himself to forgiveness of sins. As N. T. Wright has argued, the prophets of Israel's exile, whose message shaped Jesus' self-understanding, proclaimed that YHWH would forgive the sins of Israel, return Israel from exile, and renew covenant with Israel as a single act of salvation (cf. Isaiah 52–55, Jeremiah 31–33, and Ezekiel 36–37).[67] He writes:

> Forgiveness, in other words, is not simply one miscellaneous blessing which will accompany covenant renewal. Since covenant renewal means the reversal of exile, and since exile was the punishment for sin, covenant renewal/ return from exile *means* that Israel's sins have been forgiven — and vice-versa.[68]

Insofar as Jesus understands himself to be the fulfillment of these prophecies, for him to proclaim "the new covenant in my blood" is thus to proclaim both "release from captivity and return from exile" and "the forgiveness of sins in my name." In this way, then, Jesus' self-offering of his life, body and blood, as "a ransom for many" inaugurates a "new covenant" that is "for the forgiveness of sins."

9.6. Jesus: New Exodus and New Covenant

Here we see that the Lukan Transfiguration account, the Markan "ransom" saying, and the Synoptic Last Supper tradition converge, conjointly revealing Jesus' own understanding of his suffering, death, and resurrection. In these texts, Jesus consciously and consistently links his suffering, death, and resurrection to the ancient story of God's salvation of Israel — redemption from slavery, return from exile, and ratification/renewal of covenant. According to the Synoptic Gospels, therefore, Jesus understands his death and resurrection as inaugurating a new exodus and a new covenant "for many" — a new way of redemption that extends God's salvation from Israel "to the nations" (cf. Isa 42:1 4; 49:1 6).[69]

Finally, we note, Jesus' "cup" saying also has eschatological overtones. Having said that the cup is "my blood . . . poured out for many," Jesus speaks in anticipation of feasting in God's kingdom: "Truly I tell you, I will never again drink of the fruit of the vine until that day when I drink it new in the kingdom of God" (Mark 14:25; cf. Matt 26:29; Luke 22:18). The Last Supper not only

67. Wright, *Jesus and the Victory of God,* pp. 268-74.
68. Wright, *Jesus and the Victory of God,* p. 269.
69. None of this in any way implies, much less need be understood in terms of, penal substitution. Cf. Vanhoozer, "The Atonement in Postmodernity," pp. 396-401.

points back to the exodus from slavery and the return from exile, therefore, but also looks forward to the coming in full of the kingdom of God. Indeed, as N. T. Wright has argued, the prophets envisaged the return of Israel from exile and the return of YHWH as King as inextricably linked (cf. Zech 9:9-12) — and Jesus saw both being inaugurated by his death and resurrection.[70] The eschatological banquet, envisioned by prophets (Isa 25:6-10) and proclaimed by Jesus (Matt 8:11-12; Luke 14:15-23), would be the great in-gathering of many peoples into God's salvation. The cup is both symbol of Jesus' death and sign of the coming kingdom. Jesus' death, as his preaching (Mark 1:14-15; Matt 4:17; Luke 4:43), announces the imminent and irresistible arrival of God's reign "on earth as in heaven."[71]

We might represent the results of this chapter by the following diagram:

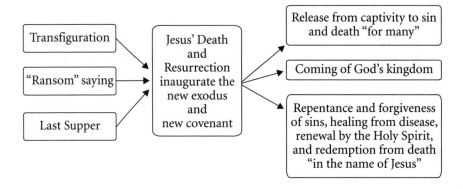

70. Wright, *Jesus and the Victory of God*, ch. 13.
71. Cf. McKnight, *Jesus and His Death*, pp. 328-34.

•   •

Penal Substitution

Exegetical and Theological Questions

CHAPTER 10

Sacrificial Atonement — Propitiation and Retribution?

Thus he shall make atonement for the sanctuary,
because of all the uncleannesses of the people of Israel,
and because of their transgressions, all their sins.

LEVITICUS 16:16A

10.1. The Penal Substitution View

There is no doubt that an early tradition of the Christian community understood Jesus' death as a sin offering, "a sacrifice of atonement for the sins of the
people" (Heb 2:17). Indeed, the Letter to the Hebrews depicts Jesus' self-offering
as the final sacrifice: "Christ had offered for all time a single sacrifice for sins"
(Heb 10:12; cf. 7:27; 9:12, 24-26). Peter Schmiechen observes: "sacrifice provided
the early Christians with an image from their authoritative tradition and practice for interpreting Jesus' death and resurrection. Since the image itself was
drawn from cultic rituals dealing with sin and forgiveness, it was a natural way
to see in Jesus an atoning event."[1] The penal substitution model thus, appropriately, interprets Jesus' death as an atoning sacrifice for sins — and, hence, sets
the cross against the background of the Levitical cult.

By emphasizing appeasement of God's wrath as the major point of Jesus'
death and primary effect of the cross, however, penal substitution makes an assumption — that sacrificial atonement is to be understood essentially in terms
of *propitiation,* appeasing or placating God's wrath upon sinners. J. I. Packer:
"The cross of Christ has many facets of meaning. As our sacrifice for sins, it was

1. Peter Schmiechen, *Saving Power: Theories of Atonement and Forms of the Church* (Grand
Rapids, MI: Eerdmans Publishing, 2005), pp. 35-36.

propitiation, that is a means of quenching God's personal penal wrath against us by blotting out our sins from his sight."[2] Entwined with this is another assumption — sacrificial atonement appeases divine wrath because sacrifice for sin satisfies God's required *retribution* for sin. Again, Packer:

> How did Christ's death make peace? By being a *propitiation,* an offering appointed by God himself to dissolve his judicial wrath against us by removing our sins from his sight. . . . How did the Savior's self-sacrifice have this propitiatory effect? By being a vicarious enduring of the *retribution* declared due to us by God's own law . . . — in other words, by *penal substitution.*[3]

Penal substitution thus assumes, following Calvin, that atoning sacrifice functioned as a vicarious punishment of human sinners for the sake of propitiating divine wrath.

Penal substitution interprets the death of Jesus in terms of atoning sacrifice, as is appropriate, but because the model assumes that atoning sacrifice served the purpose of propitiation of wrath by means of satisfaction of retribution, we thus want to examine the sacrificial rituals of atonement-making in Leviticus to see whether or not the evidence of Scripture bears out the assumptions of penal substitution. In questioning the penal substitution view of sacrificial atonement, we do *not* question the background conviction motivating that view. Penal substitution is motivated by the conviction that God is holy and just; and a holy and just God cannot forgo dealing with sin and sinners without compromising personal integrity: a holy God cannot dwell in the midst of an unclean people; and a just God cannot let sin be. The question then is: How will a holy God maintain relationship with a people made unclean by sin? How will a just God deal with the sins of a people who are to be holy as God is holy? Penal substitution not only sees sin, and God's wrath provoked by sin, as a barrier to relationship between God and humanity, but also claims that this barrier can be removed through divine forgiveness only if the prior condition of retributive justice has been satisfied. So John Stott: "Sin and wrath stand in the way. God must not only respect us as the responsible beings we are, but he must also respect himself as the holy God he is. Before the holy God can forgive us, some kind of 'satisfaction' is necessary."[4] According to Leviticus, God ordains sacrificial atonement as the means of maintaining relationship between a holy and just God and a sinful and un-

2. J. I. Packer, *I Want to Be a Christian* (Wheaton, IL: Tyndale House Publishers, 1977), p. 60, emphasis original.

3. J. I. Packer, "The Atonement in the Life of the Christian," in Charles E. Hill and Frank A. James III, eds., *The Glory of the Atonement: Biblical, Theological and Practical Perspectives* (Downers Grove, IL: InterVarsity Press, 2004), 409-25, here p. 416, original and added emphasis.

4. John R. W. Stott, *The Cross of Christ* (Downers Grove, IL: InterVarsity Press, 1986), p. 110.

clean people.[5] Penal substitution thus interprets atoning sacrifice as the punishment of sin for the satisfaction of retribution, which propitiates God and restores relationship between God and humanity.

We agree that the key question behind atoning sacrifice concerns the relationship between a holy and just God and a sinful and unclean humanity — and that Leviticus concerns how a holy and just God deals with sin and sinners by means of sacrifice. We aim to demonstrate, however, that atoning sacrifice in Leviticus has nothing to do with either propitiating God or satisfying retribution. We ask: Does an interpretation of these sacrificial rituals in terms of propitiating wrath and satisfying retribution make sense of the evidence? More specifically: Are the sacrifices directed at God-self? Is the effect of the sacrifices the propitiation of God's wrath? Is the death of the sacrificial victim intended as a satisfaction of retribution? Is the sacrificial victim a penal substitute?[6]

Now, it may concern some readers that we do not begin here with a theory of sin and sacrifice, whether a theological theory (e.g., von Rad or Eichrodt)[7] or an anthropological theory (e.g., Girard).[8] The reason is straightforward. If we were to adopt a deductive approach and interpret sacrifice in Leviticus by an assumed theory, our interpretation would be only as convincing as the theory we have assumed; and that theory would itself be convincing only insofar as it is warranted by relevant scriptural evidence. To justify our choice of theory, that is, we would need to appeal to scriptural evidence. A deductive approach would thus beg the question of how to interpret atoning sacrifice. So we take an inductive approach, laying out the textual evidence in need of explanation.[9] In this way, we test the claims of penal substitution against the scriptural evidence rather than against another rational reconstruction of that evidence.[10]

5. Cf. Steve Jeffery, Michael Ovey, and Andrew Sach, *Pierced for Our Transgressions: Rediscovering the Glory of Penal Substitution* (Wheaton, IL: Crossway Books, 2008), p. 43.

6. The results of the inquiry in this chapter have been presented previously in summary form in "Once for All: Freeing Sacrificial Atonement from Retributive Justice," *The Mennonite*, April 7, 2009, 12-14.

7. Gerhard von Rad, *Old Testament Theology*, vol. 1: *The Theology of Israel's Historical Traditions*, trans. D. M. G. Stalker (Edinburgh: Oliver and Boyd, 1962), pp. 250-79; Walther Eichrodt, *Theology of the Old Testament*, vol. 1, trans. J. A. Baker (Philadelphia: Westminster Press, 1961), pp. 101-77.

8. René Girard, *Violence and the Sacred*, trans. Patrick Gregory (Baltimore: Johns Hopkins University Press, 1977).

9. Regarding the reading of the scriptural evidence, I am grateful to Prof. Perry Yoder for clarifying remarks concerning atonement and the sacrificial rituals in Leviticus, presented in a guest lecture in Prof. Mary Schertz's seminar on atonement at Associated Mennonite Biblical Seminary in the fall of 2005.

10. The comment by Eichrodt, *Theology of the Old Testament*, p. 141, is apt for our investigation: "the Old Testament nowhere gives us a direct exposition of the meaning of this worship [viz., ritual sacrifice]; it is possible to arrive at various conclusions *a posteriori*, but never with more than a certain degree of probability. The certainty with which judgments are at times ex-

10.2. Propitiation of Wrath

If the rituals of sacrificial atonement concern propitiating God's wrath, *then* we would reasonably expect the object of the rituals (i.e., the recipient of action) to be God. That is, *if* the purpose of atoning sacrifice is to appease God, *then* the action of the ritual would be directed toward God. Therefore, *if* the textual evidence shows *otherwise*, that the sacrificial rituals are directed toward any object other than God, *then* sacrificial atonement does *not* concern propitiation. This would seem a crucial test for penal substitution. What does the textual evidence show?

10.2.1. Sin and Guilt Offerings

Let us consider first the various rituals of atonement by means of sin and guilt offerings described in Lev 4:1–6:7. Here we find that various conditions require "making atonement" *(kipper)*[11] by sacrificial offering, and various procedures and offerings are specified, depending on: (1) the identity of the offender (whether a priest, the whole congregation, a ruler, or an ordinary person: 4:3-35), (2) the material resources of the worshipper (the poor may sacrifice pigeons or turtledoves instead of a goat or sheep, and the poorest may make a grain offering instead of an animal sacrifice: 5:7-13), and (3) the nature of the offense — whether a transgression creates harm or loss that must be healed or restored, the "guilt offering" *('āšām)* (5:14–6:7), or not, the "sin offering" *(ḥaṭṭā't)* (5:1-13). We will examine these two sacrificial rituals separately.

There are a number of features common to all sacrificial rituals involving sin offerings (4:1–5:13), including: (1) the sin offering is only for unintentional sins (4:2, 13, 22, 27), (2) the offender lays a hand upon the head of the sacrificial animal before it is slaughtered (4:4, 15, 24, 29, 33 — *except* for a grain offering), (3) the offender confesses the sin committed (5:5), (4) the priest puts some of the blood from the sacrificial animal on the horns of the altar, pouring out the remaining blood at the base of the altar (4:7, 17-18, 25, 30, 34; 5:9 — *except* for a grain offering), and (5) there is a concluding formula of absolution — "Thus the priest shall make atonement [*kipper;* LXX *exhilasetai*] on your behalf for the sin that you have committed, and you shall be forgiven" (4:35b; cf. 4:20b, 26b, 31b; 5:10b, 13a). Notice that the ritual of sin offering does *not* specify that *any* blood be applied to the sinner. The sacrificial blood is applied *only* to the altar. What is applied to the sinner is *forgiveness*.

---

pressed on this point and on the subject of the whole pattern of development of the idea of sacrifice is usually in inverse proportion to what the available evidence will bear."

11. The verb *kipper* is the piel stem of *kāphar*, meaning "to cover" (as in, "cover with pitch" — cf. Gen 6:14). But we cannot simply infer the meaning of *kipper* from the meaning of the qal stem of the verb.

The ritual of guilt offering (5:13–6:7) differs in important ways from the ritual of sin offering: (a) it covers both unintentional transgressions (5:14-19) and intentional transgressions (6:1-7),[12] (b) all offenders must bring a ram "or the equivalent" (5:18; 6:6), and there seems to be no provision for poverty cases, (c) there is no specification that the transgressor lay a hand upon the head of the sacrificial animal, (d) the blood of the sacrificial animal is to be poured out at the base of the altar (cf. 7:2) but there is no specification that blood be applied to the horns of the altar,[13] and (e) instead of confessing, the offender compensates the injured party by making restitution and paying a penalty of one-fifth more (5:16; 6:5). Nonetheless, the ritual of guilt offering concludes with a similar formula of absolution: "The priest shall make atonement [*kipper;* LXX *exhilasetai*] on your behalf before the LORD, and you shall be forgiven for any of the things that one may do and incur guilt thereby" (6:7; cf. 5:18b).

If attention were restricted to only the evidence regarding the sin offering, and if one were to disregard the obvious exceptions (see Chapter 11 below), one might be able to construct a coherent interpretation of atonement in these sacrificial rituals in terms of propitiation and penal substitution. For example, the offender placing a hand on the sacrificial animal might be taken as a ritual identification with the animal as a "substitute penalty" in place of the offender, and the blood placed on the horns of the altar might be taken as appeasing divine wrath. But these features of the ritual of sin offering are conspicuously ab-

---

12. It is often observed by commentators that there is no provision for making atonement for intentional transgressions of the law by sacrificial means — intentional transgressions must be dealt with by criminal punishment (typically the death penalty). The basis for such claims is Numbers 15, which provides supplementary material to the cultic law in Leviticus. As does Leviticus, this text prescribes the sin offering for unintentional sins committed by either the congregation or individuals (Num 15:22-29). But "whoever acts high-handedly . . . affronts the LORD," and for that there is no sacrificial remedy — "such a person shall be utterly cut off and bear the guilt" (vv. 30-31). To emphasize the point, an incident is recalled of someone breaking the Sabbath by gathering sticks — at YHWH's instruction, he is taken outside the camp and stoned to death (vv. 32-36). This text would seem to recognize only two categories of wrongdoing — unintentional sin, remedied sacrificially, and intentional transgression, requiring punishment, leaving no possibility of dealing with intentional transgression by sacrificial means. The text itself, however, does not draw a distinction between unintentional and intentional actions, but between sinning unintentionally and acting "high-handedly" — i.e., arrogantly, in deliberate defiance of God and his law. These extremes leave room for intentional transgressions that are not committed "high-handedly" and which thus can be remedied by sacrificial means. This supplementary text, moreover, makes no mention of the guilt offering, which in Leviticus does provide sacrificial remedy for at least some intentional transgressions of the law — e.g., deceit, robbery, fraud, and giving false testimony, each of which is a violation of the Decalogue and implies intentionality.

13. A supplementary instruction states, "The guilt offering is like the sin offering, there is the same ritual for them" (7:7). So, one might infer that manipulation of the blood at the altar was intended if not stated. Similarly regarding the laying of the hand on the sacrificial animal.

sent from the ritual of guilt offering — and yet the ritual of guilt offering effects atonement and forgiveness the same as the ritual of sin offering. Already, then, we see that atonement-making in the Levitical sacrifices is not linked necessarily with either a ritual sign of penal substitution or with ritual manipulation of blood to propitiate God (if that is even the correct interpretation of these aspects of the ritual of sin offering).

10.2.2. Other Atonement Rituals

Much more evidence, however, must be taken into account before we draw any further inferences regarding the significance of these atonement rituals. As part of the seven-day ritual to consecrate Aaron and his sons, YHWH instructs Moses: "Also every day you shall offer a bull as a sin offering for atonement *(kipper)*. Also you shall offer a sin offering for the altar, when you make atonement *(kipper)* for it, and shall anoint it, to consecrate it" (Exod 29:36). Later, after giving specifications for the altar, YHWH gives instructions for the high priest: "Once a year Aaron shall perform the rite of atonement *(kipper)* on [the altar's] horns. Throughout your generations he shall perform the atonement *(kipper)* for it once a year with the blood of the atoning sin offering. It is most holy to the LORD" (30:10). Following the prescription of the sacrificial rituals, Moses does what God prescribes, making a "sin offering" on behalf of the altar: "Thus he consecrated it, to make atonement *(kipper)* for it" (Lev 8:14-15). From the penal substitution perspective, these verses leap out as anomalous: Why make atonement on behalf of the *altar?* If the purpose of making atonement by sacrifice is to appease God and offer a substitute penalty for sin to satisfy divine retribution, why do this for the altar? What sin has it committed (even unintentionally)? Why would YHWH be wrathful toward the very altar he has just ordained for the tabernacle?

When we turn to the Day of Atonement ritual, this anomaly persists:

> He shall slaughter the goat of the sin offering that is for the people and bring its blood inside the curtain, and do with its blood as he did with the blood of the bull, sprinkling it upon the mercy seat and before the mercy seat. Thus he shall make atonement *(kipper)* for the sanctuary, because of the uncleannesses of the people of Israel, and because of their transgressions, all their sins; and so he shall do for the tent of meeting, which remains with them in the midst of their uncleannesses. No one shall be in the tent of meeting from the time he enters to make atonement *(kipper)* in the sanctuary until he comes out and has made atonement *(kipper)* for himself and for his house and for all the assembly of Israel. Then he shall go out to the altar that is before the LORD and make atonement *(kipper)* on its behalf, and shall take

some of the blood of the bull and of the blood of the goat, and put it on each of the horns of the altar. He shall sprinkle some of the blood on it with his finger seven times, and cleanse it and hallow it from the uncleannesses of the people of Israel. (Lev 16:15-19)

Integral to the Day of Atonement ritual is making atonement on behalf of both the sanctuary and the altar. The same questions arise: Why? What offense have they committed? How could the sanctuary or altar have transgressed and so provoked God's wrath?[14] What could it mean to satisfy retribution on behalf of places or things?

The anomaly grows when we consider atonement rituals concerning cleansing or purification (Leviticus 12–15). Childbirth (12:6-8), leprosy (14:10-32), and bodily discharge (15:13-15, 25-30) all require making atonement *(kipper)* by blood sacrifice. In each case, the worshipper offers a burnt offering and a sin offering, and the priest makes atonement on her or his behalf. Again, why? Neither childbirth, nor leprosy, nor seminal emission, nor menstruation is sin; none of these are transgressions against the covenant.[15] Why — if, in fact, making atonement propitiates God by satisfying retribution — is God wrathful against a woman for having given birth or a man for having a skin lesion? These sacrificial rituals make no sense in terms of penal substitution.

10.2.3. An Alternative Approach to Sacrificial Atonement

It would seem, then, that the penal substitution model is inadequate to explain the textual evidence concerning the several sacrificial rituals of atonement-making — sin and guilt offerings, consecration of the altar, the Day of Atonement, and purification rituals. To make sense of all the evidence, a different approach is needed. We will begin with atonement for purification from un-

---

14. Jeffery et al., *Pierced for Our Transgressions*, p. 47, attempt to find God's wrath in the Day of Atonement ritual on the basis that Lev 16:1 mentions the deaths of Aaron's sons, who died when offering "unholy fire" on the altar (Leviticus 10). This is a weak case, for two reasons. First, that story itself makes no mention of God's wrath, only that Aaron's sons were consumed by "fire . . . from the presence of the LORD" (10:1-2). One might see this fire as a display of God's wrath, but that is an inference, and one not obviously supported by the text, which implies that the consuming fire is a manifestation of God's holiness (v. 3). Second, the mention of the death of Aaron's sons in Lev 16:1 does not concern the purpose of the Day of Atonement ritual, but rather its timing: Aaron is "not to come just at any time into the sanctuary . . . so that he may not die" (v. 2). And again, as in Leviticus 10, the concern is not that God's wrath will strike him, but rather that unless Aaron enters the inner sanctum in the right way at the right time (cf. v. 3), God's holy presence will consume him: "for I appear in the cloud upon the mercy seat."

15. Jeffery et al., *Pierced for Our Transgressions*, pp. 43-44, effectively blur the distinction between sin and uncleanness.

cleanness, for the altar, and for the sanctuary. In each of these cases, the text makes clear that the effect of making atonement is cleansing from impurity so that what is atoned for by blood sacrifice, and so purged of impurity, can be separated from uncleanness and consecrated to YHWH ("hallowed" or "made holy"). This interpretation can then be extended to sin and guilt offerings.

Concerning purification from childbirth, leprosy, or bodily discharge, we find:

> He shall offer it before the LORD, and make atonement *(kipper)* on her be-half; then she shall be clean *(ṭāhēr)* from her flow of blood (Lev 12:7).
>
> Then the priest shall make atonement *(kipper)* on his behalf before the LORD: the priest shall offer the sin offering, to make atonement *(kip-per)* for the one to be cleansed *(ṭāhēr)* from his uncleanness *(ṭum'āh)*. Afterward he shall slaughter the burnt offering and the grain offering on the altar. Thus the priest shall make atonement *(kipper)* on his be-half and he shall be clean *(ṭāhēr)* (14:18b-20).
>
> The priest shall offer one for a sin offering and the other for a burnt offer-ing; and the priest shall make atonement *(kipper)* on her behalf before the LORD for her unclean discharge *(ṭum'āh)* (15:30; cf. v. 15).

Notice that in the atonement rituals for purification the standard formula of absolution found in the rituals of sin and guilt offering, "Thus the priest shall *make atonement* on your behalf for the sin that you have committed, and you shall *be forgiven*" (4:35b), is replaced with a parallel formula: "the priest shall *make atonement* on her behalf, and she shall *be clean*" (12:8b; cf. 14:20b). The text then summarizes the rituals of atonement for purification, emphasizing cleansing and separation: "Thus you shall *keep the people of Israel separate from their uncleanness (ṭum'āh),* so that they do not die in their uncleanness *(ṭum'āh)* by defiling my tabernacle that is in their midst" (15:31). The effect of making atonement is purgation from uncleanness; and the purpose is that what is so purged may be kept separate from uncleanness.

Concerning the altar at its consecration, we find: "Seven days you shall make atonement *(kipper)* for the altar, and *consecrate* it, and the altar *shall be most holy;* whatever touches the altar shall become holy" (Exod 29:37). The ef-fect of making atonement for the altar is that it is purged from uncleanness, so that it may be consecrated and so "shall become holy," separated unto YHWH (cf. Ezek 43:26).

Concerning the sanctuary and the altar on the Day of Atonement, we find:

> Thus he shall make atonement *(kipper)* for the sanctuary, because of the uncleannesses *(ṭum'ōt)* of the people of Israel, and because of their trans-gressions, all their sins; and so he shall do for the tent of meeting, which re-

mains with them in the midst of their uncleannesses *(ṭum'ōt)*. No one shall be in the tent of meeting from the time he enters to make atonement *(kipper)* in the sanctuary until he comes out and has made atonement *(kipper)* for himself and for his house and for all the assembly of Israel. Then he shall go out to the altar that is before the LORD and make atonement *(kipper)* on its behalf. . . . He shall sprinkle some of the blood on it . . . and *cleanse it and hallow it from the uncleannesses (ṭum'ōt)* of the people of Israel. (Lev 16:16-19)

Notice, first, that the ritual to "make atonement for the sanctuary" (v. 16) is occasioned by the need to make a "sin offering . . . for the people" (v. 15). The need for making atonement for the sanctuary and altar on the Day of Atonement is "because of the uncleannesses of the people of Israel, and because of their transgressions, all their sins" (v. 16). The implication here is twofold: first, the sins and transgressions of the people generate uncleanness; and, second, the people's sin- and transgression-generated uncleanness contaminates the holy precincts, even the inner sanctum, of the tabernacle.

The tabernacle is God's place of dwelling among his people and of meeting with his priest. The sins and transgressions of the people pollute the house of God. Hence the need for a God-ordained ritual means to deal with sin and transgression in order to remove pollution from God's house, lest God reject the sanctuary because of uncleannness. The ordinary sin and guilt offerings provide the means of removing sin and pardoning guilt and so prevent contamination of the tabernacle. Yet, some sins and transgressions might not get dealt with by the ordinary means, such that priests and people remain unclean and pollution accumulates in the sanctuary. Unless dealt with in a regular manner, the accumulating pollution might occasion a crisis in the community's covenant relationship with God (cf. Lamentations 1–2).[16] Hence the need for a God-ordained annual ritual for cleansing the priests and the inner sanctum, the sanctuary, and the entire people by means of the bull (Lev 16:6-14), the slaughtered goat (vv. 15-19), and the exiled goat (vv. 20-22) respectively.

Notice, also, that the sanctuary is cleansed by the priest only once he himself has been cleansed and that the people are excluded from the sanctuary during the ritual of cleansing. This is precisely because the sanctuary "remains with them in the midst of their uncleannesses." In order for the priest to cleanse the sanctuary from the pollution generated by the people's sins and transgressions, the priest himself must first be cleansed and the unclean people must be excluded from the sanctuary (Lev 16:16-17). The purpose of making atonement for the sanctuary and altar on the Day of Atonement is thus "to cleanse it and hallow it from the uncleannesses of the people," to clean God's house and keep

---

16. Cf. Jacob Milgrom, *Leviticus 1–16* (Anchor Bible; New York: Doubleday, 1991), pp. 253-61; John H. Hayes, "Atonement in the Book of Leviticus," *Interpretation* 52/1 (1998), 5-15; pp. 12-13.

it holy. Again, therefore, we find that the effect of atonement is cleansing from uncleanness; and the purgation effected by atonement makes it possible for what is purged to be consecrated — separated unto YHWH.[17]

10.2.4. Counter-Arguments

Now, as we have observed, pollution within the holy precincts is offensive to God and, left to accumulate, might provoke God's wrath with calamitous consequences for the covenant community. The rituals of atoning sacrifice, performed with regularity, then, prevent the people from falling under the wrath of God. Thus, YHWH says to Aaron and his sons: "You yourselves shall perform the duties of the sanctuary and the duties of the altar, so that wrath may never again come upon the Israelites" (Num 18:5). One might thus argue that the sacrificial system for dealing with sin, transgression, and impurity did serve the purpose of propitiating God. True, God's holiness and presence required removal of uncleanness from within the sanctuary and from among the priests and people. And, yes, the sacrificial rituals, by providing a God-ordained means of dealing with uncleanness, did serve preventively to avert God's wrath, to avoid a crisis in which YHWH the Holy One might reject the sanctuary or even eject the people from the land. Yet *averting* God's wrath by removing uncleanness and *appeasing* God are not the same thing. The crucial difference here lies in the *object* of the *kipper* (atonement-making) rites: if the purpose were to appease God, then the object of ritual action would be God; but the sacrifices are not directed at or enacted upon God.[18]

Rather, the *kipper* rites are directed at the uncleanness and enacted upon

17. Thus Milgrom, rejecting the traditional rendering "sin offering," argues that "purification offering" is the more accurate translation of the Hebrew *ḥaṭṭā't* — because the same ritual concerns both sin and uncleanness and effects purification of places and things as well as forgiveness of people: "To my knowledge, all versions and translations, old and new, render the *ḥaṭṭā't* sacrifice as 'sin offering.' This translation is inaccurate on all grounds: contextually, morphologically, and etymologically. The very range of the *ḥaṭṭā't* in the cult gainsays the notion of sin . . . the *ḥaṭṭā't* is prescribed for persons and objects who cannot have sinned. . . . 'Purification offering' is certainly the more accurate translation" (*Leviticus*, p. 253). Also Hayes, "Atonement in the Book of Leviticus."

18. Two stories in the Torah and one in the historical books do link the verb *kipper* and propitiation: Numbers 16, Numbers 25, and 2 Samuel 21. The incidents related in these stories, however, do not involve any cultic rituals of blood sacrifice for sin and purification — and thus do not tell us anything concerning how to interpret those sacrificial rituals. In two of these incidents, moreover, God's wrath is propitiated by means other than bloodshed. In Numbers 16, it is Aaron's offering of incense, not a blood sacrifice, that appeases God's wrath and stops the plague (Num 16:46-48). And in 2 Samuel 21, the "offering" that pleases God, rights wrong, and brings healing to the land is not the killing of Saul's sons but the faithful acts of honoring the dead by the mother Rizpah and King David (2 Sam 21:14).

(or on behalf of) that which has become unclean (whether sanctuary, altar, priests, or people) in order to remove that uncleanness from God's holy presence. Indeed, far from God being the object of action in the sacrificial ritual, God is the (implied) subject of action, the one who acts through the ritual (mediated by priest and sacrifice) to remove uncleanness. As von Rad observes, one can see the *kipper* rites as God's own action to save the community from crisis: "What was effected in expiation was that in both cases, with persons and objects alike, Jahweh removed the baneful influence of an act. He broke the nexus of sin and calamity. . . . Expiation was thus not a penalty but a saving event."[19]

What, though, one might ask, about the sacrifices being a "pleasing odor to the LORD" — does not that imply that sacrifice was intended to propitiate God? Thomas Schreiner contends that "this image indicates that they [viz., sacrifices] satisfy God's wrath, that they appease his anger."[20] Is that correct?

First, it is not only the sin offering that is described as "a pleasing odor to the LORD" (Lev 4:31), but also the burnt offering, the grain offering, and the well-being offering (1:9, 13, 17; 2:2, 9; 3:5, 16). While the burnt offering was "acceptable in your behalf as atonement for you," nowhere are the grain and well-being offerings said to be occasioned by sin or required for transgression or to effect atonement. Thus, it is far from obvious that these latter sacrifices were offered with the intention of propitiating God's wrath. In Numbers, moreover, concerning the ritual of redemption of the firstborn, it is specified that the firstborn of "clean" animals — cows, sheep, and goats — may not be redeemed, but must be sacrificed. The priests may eat the flesh, but the blood must be sprinkled on the altar and the fat must be burned on the altar "for a pleasing odor to the LORD" (Num 18:17-18). Again, there is no indication that such a "pleasing odor" has anything to do with propitiating God. Indeed, why would God be wrathful toward a firstborn animal? The redemption of the firstborn did not concern propitiation of God, but rather was intended as a reminder to Israel that God had redeemed its people from slavery (Exod 13:1-2, 11-16).

Because all these sacrificial rituals are said to produce "a pleasing odor to the LORD" (using the same Hebrew wording — *rêaḥ-nîḥôaḥ layhwāh*), it would seem that one cannot give a consistent interpretation of this "pleasing odor" as a propitiation of God. And because the "pleasing odor" is not obviously a propitiation of wrath in these other sacrificial rituals, it is far from clear that the "pleasing odor" of the sin offering concerns propitiation. Contrary to Schreiner's claim, therefore, there is no obvious, much less necessary, connection of the "pleasing odor" of sacrifice to propitiating God.

19. Von Rad, *Old Testament Theology*, 1, p. 271.
20. Thomas R. Schreiner, "Penal Substitution View," in James Beilby and Paul R. Eddy, eds., *The Nature of the Atonement: Four Views* (Downers Grove, IL: InterVarsity Press, 2006), pp. 67-98, here p. 83.

Stephen Finlan, citing Gen 8:21, also argues that the "pleasing odor" of sacrifice implies the pacification or mollification of an angry God: "Noah's sacrifices assuaged God's wrath."[21] After the floodwaters recede, Noah makes a burnt offering on an altar, in response to which YHWH pledges "in his heart" to "never again curse the ground because of humankind . . . nor . . . ever again destroy every living creature as I have done." This text does indicate that the "pleasing odor" of the burnt offering induces a change in YHWH's intention, such that YHWH pledges never to do again what he had done previously. Two comments. First, the connection of this sacrifice to the Levitical cult is not clear. It may be that the writer here intends to connect Noah to Moses and Aaron and the tabernacle, but that can be at most a matter of speculation. Second, the flood narrative indicates that God brought on the flood to destroy life, not out of holy wrath against human evildoing (which "was great in the earth"), but rather out of heart-felt regret and sorrow for his own having created a humankind whose heart is inclined toward evil (Gen 6:5-7; cf. 8:21).[22] The "pleasing odor" of Noah's offering, rather than assuaging God's wrath, would seem to assuage God's remorse.

Second, from the fact that these offerings are "pleasing" to God it does not follow that this necessarily involves propitiation in the sense of placating an angry deity. The odor from, say, the burnt offering might "please" God, not by appeasing God's wrath, but by being a sign of the obedience that God desires: God is pleased, not because his wrath has been appeased, but because the worshipper has shown obedience. This might be the source of the sensibility among the prophets that "to obey is better than sacrifice" (1 Sam 15:22). When the people seek to "please" God by offering sacrifice rather than rendering obedience, the prophets denounce this as an abuse of the cult and an offense to God: burnt offering is no substitute for loyalty, righteousness, and justice (Isa 1:10-20; Jer 7:21-23; Hos 6:6; Amos 5:21-24; Mic 6:6-8). Thus understood, the odor from the burnt offering pleases God as a sign of the substance of covenant relationship; but absent covenant loyalty, righteousness, and justice, such sacrifice offends God.

10.3. Retribution for Sin

Our second question for examination in light of the textual evidence is this: In addition to purification, does making atonement *(kipper)* for sin in the Levitical sacrifices have to do with satisfying retribution or compensating God

21. Stephen Finlan, *Problems with Atonement: The Origins of, and Controversy about, the Atonement Doctrine* (Collegeville, MN: Liturgical Press, 2005), p. 12, quoting Douglas M. L. Judisch.

22. Note that Gen 6:5-8 and 8:20-22 derive from the same (older) source tradition of the flood narrative.

or offering a substitute penalty for sin? Emile Nicole argues that it does: "in *kip-per* rites, purification cannot be disconnected from compensation: through compensation given to God, purification and forgiveness were granted."[23] This "compensation" made to God for sin would be the sacrifice offered by the sinner: the offender offers the sacrifice as compensation to God, the offended party, and the purpose of the compensatory offering is to satisfy God's retribution for sin and thereby to propitiate wrath. Does this fit the evidence?

10.3.1. Sin and Guilt Offerings

Consider, first, the ritual of guilt offering (Lev 5:14–6:7). In this case, the offending party, having caused injury to or taken property from the offended party, is required to pay damages plus a penalty: "you shall make restitution . . . and add one fifth" (5:16; cf. 6:5). Thus, according to the Levitical ritual, making reparation for wrongdoing does involve a kind of retributive justice — the offender makes "proportional compensation" to the offended. Such compensation, however, was not punishment. Hayes comments: "The basic principle operative in Israelite laws dealing with injured parties was restitution. That is, the concern of Israelite law was for restoration of the victim to the status prior to the wrong rather than the *punishment* of the offender."[24] Such restitution, moreover, did not involve the guilt offering itself. While comprising a single ritual, reparation is a two-stage process: *first* one makes right with the neighbor by restitution (6:4-5), *then* matters are put right with God by sacrifice (vv. 6-7); indeed, the latter cannot proceed until the former is completed. The financial compensation to the neighbor is thus distinct from the sacrificial offering to God which follows: restitution is rendered to the injured party, not to God.[25] Rather than rendering compensation, offering sacrifice concerned restoring relationship

23. Emile Nicole, "Atonement in the Pentateuch," in Hill and James, *Glory of the Atonement*, p. 48.

24. Hayes, "Atonement in the Book of Leviticus," p. 11, emphasis original.

25. One might want to say here that restitution to the neighbor is an indirect means of repayment to God: we repay God by repaying the neighbor. In a sense, that is true: because obeying God entails doing right by one's neighbor, wronging the neighbor offends God and so requires righting relationship with God as well as neighbor; making restitution to the neighbor thus renders obedience to God by fulfilling the just ordering of the covenant community that God has ordained. Restitution to the neighbor should not be regarded as repayment to God, however, for two reasons. First, regarding restitution to the neighbor as repayment to God would effectively convert the neighbor into a proxy for God and thereby diminish the reality and significance of the injury done to, and thus the covenant rights of, the neighbor. To the contrary, it would seem the very point of requiring restitution prior to sacrifice to recognize the rights of the neighbor. Second, were restitution to the neighbor repayment to God, it is evidently insufficient — a sacrifice is still required.

with God, just as making restitution concerned restoring relationship with the neighbor. The entire ritual of the reparation offering thus concerned restoration of right relationship.[26]

Perhaps, though, the ram offering is to be understood as compensation or penalty paid to God, who is the ultimate party injured when humans commit wrongdoing against one another in transgression of God's law (cf. Lev 6:2). Let us now include the sin offering, in which financial reparation is not made. Can we give a consistent interpretation of both sin and guilt offerings as compensation made or penalty paid to God to satisfy retribution? *If* the sin and guilt offerings were intended to satisfy retribution by making compensation or paying penalty for sin and transgression, where the sacrificial victim serves as a substitute for the sinner, per the penal substitution model, *then* one would expect logically, based on the law of retribution, that the *compensation* or *penalty* would be proportional to the *sin* or *transgression*. That is, *if* the principle of retribution governs the sin and guilt offerings, *then* we should find proportionality between the magnitude of the sin or transgression and the magnitude of the compensation or penalty — the worse the sin or transgression, the greater the penalty required to compensate for it. Thus, *if* the sin and guilt offerings were the offender's payment of a compensatory penalty to God, *then* one should expect that, the more severe the sin or transgression committed, the more valuable or costly the animal slaughtered. This would seem to be a crucial test for penal substitution. What does the textual evidence show?

Contrary to what one would expect given the assumptions of penal substitution, the details concerning the sin and guilt offerings in Leviticus 4–6 show clearly and consistently that the value of the animal slaughtered in the sin and guilt offerings does not vary at all with *which* sin or transgression was committed. In fact, the material nature of the sin or transgression is not even a factor in either sacrificial ritual.

Regarding the sin offering, the value of the animal sacrificed varies, not with the sin needing atonement, but the *social status* and *financial means* of the one *who* sins:

> if the "anointed priest" sins, then he is to offer a bull, the most valuable animal (Lev 4:3-13);
>
> if the "whole congregation of Israel" is in error, then also a bull is to be offered (vv. 13-21);
>
> if a "ruler" or "elder" sins, then the sinner is to offer a male goat, which is less in value than a bull (vv. 22-26);
>
> if "anyone of the ordinary people" does wrong, then the sinner is to offer a female goat or a female sheep, which is less in value than a male be-

26. Cf. Hayes, "Atonement in the Book of Leviticus," pp. 11-12.

cause in any herd female breeding stock will be more abundant than
male breeding stock (4:27–5:6);

if, however, a layperson cannot afford a goat or sheep, then either two
turtledoves or two pigeons are to be offered (5:7-10);

if a layperson cannot afford even that, then a grain offering is acceptable
(vv. 11-13).

The inference is that, because the offering does not vary in proportion to the
sin, the sacrifice is not a compensatory penalty for sin. Moreover, recalling that
the object of atoning sacrifice is not God but the sin itself — and so sin-
induced pollution in the holy place — one also observes in the textual evidence
that *where* the blood from the sacrifice is applied and sprinkled in the holy
place (to cleanse it from pollution) depends, again, *not* upon which *sin* was
committed, but only upon *who* committed the sin.[27]

Now, one might point out here two aspects of the biblical understanding of
sin that are evident in the sin offering: sin is not only an individual, private af-
fair, but implicates the covenant community to one degree or another; and, because of the social aspect of sin, the seriousness or weightiness of a sin is a function of the social position of the sinner: the higher the sinner's position, the
greater the communal implication. A sin committed by a priest or elder thus
carries more serious social consequences than a sin by a layperson: the sins of
the priests or elders threaten to undermine the moral order of the whole community. In making atonement for such sins, therefore, a more valuable animal
must be sacrificed and the sacrificial blood must be applied to more places in
the holy precincts. One might then argue that, in this way, there is "proportionality" between the sin and the sacrifice. This is not the kind of proportionality
pertaining to the law of retribution, however, which concerns strictly the relation between the act itself and the penalty for the act, irrespective of individual
identity (to which justice is "blind").[28]

Regarding the guilt offering, the offering required is a ram irrespective of
the guilt-incurring act committed. Whether one has transgressed concerning
"any of the holy things of the LORD" (Lev 5:15), or done "any of the things that
by the LORD's commandments ought not to be done" (v. 17), or transgressed
"against the LORD by deceiving a neighbor" (6:2), the sacrifice is the same in
each case — an unblemished ram "or its equivalent" (5:15, 18; 6:6). The infer-

27. On the relationship between the physical location of blood cleansing and the social position of the sinner, see Milgrom, *Leviticus*, pp. 257-58, and Hayes, "Atonement in the Book of
Leviticus," p. 8.

28. As Von Rad, *Old Testament Theology*, 1, pp. 263-66, points out, the modern understanding of the relation of sin (crime) and penalty (punishment), in which sin is distinguishable and
separable from penalty, thus allowing determination of an equality or proportionality between
them, is foreign to the thinking evident in the Old Testament.

ence is that, because the sacrifice does not vary with the transgression, there is no proportionality of sacrifice and transgression — and, hence, the sacrifice is not a compensatory penalty.

To summarize: Despite Nicole's claim that in the atonement *(kipper)* rituals "purification cannot be disconnected from compensation," the textual evidence does not exhibit the connection between sin or transgression and sacrifice that would be expected if Nicole were correct, if the sin and guilt offerings were intended as payment of compensation. Because the sin and guilt offerings do not vary at all in proportion to the sin or transgression committed, the Levitical rituals of sacrificial atonement do not follow the logic of retribution and so do not make sense as a compensatory penalty to God to satisfy retribution. We conclude, therefore, that, contrary to the penal substitution model, atoning sacrifice was not intended as a compensatory penalty.[29]

10.3.2. Counter-Arguments

What, though, one might ask, about the ritual gesture whereby the offender lays a hand on the head of the animal offered (Lev 4:4, 15, 24, 29, 33)? John Stott points to this as certain proof that the sacrificial victim was a penal substitute:

> By laying his hand(s) on the animal, the offerer was *certainly* identifying himself with it and "solemnly" designating "the victim as standing for him" . . . having taken his place, the substitute animal was killed in recognition that the penalty for sin was death, its blood . . . was sprinkled, and the offerer's life was spared.[30]

Emile Nicole echoes Stott: "there can be *no doubt* that by this gesture the animal was presented as a substitute for the human being who offered it."[31] Jeffery et al. likewise claim that "such an interpretation is inescapable."[32] Leon Morris is more cautious, but defends the same position: "It is not easy to see what the laying on of hands means if there is no symbolic transfer to the animal which was to die of the sins being confessed" — that is, if the sacrificial victim does not die as a penal substitute.[33] This gesture parallels that of the high priest during the

---

29. I. Howard Marshall, *Aspects of the Atonement: Cross and Resurrection in the Reconciling of God and Humanity* (London: Paternoster, 2007), p. 44, acknowledges that "the specific vocabulary of penalty does not seem to be associated with" sacrifice, but maintains nonetheless that a sacrifice can be considered a penalty because it involves a cost. We will address the element of cost in sacrifice in the next chapter.

30. Stott, *Cross of Christ*, p. 137, emphasis added.

31. Nicole, "Atonement in the Pentateuch," p. 44, emphasis added.

32. Jeffery et al., *Pierced for Our Transgressions*, p. 49.

33. Leon Morris, *The Atonement: Its Meaning and Significance* (Downers Grove, IL: InterVarsity Press, 1983), p. 47.

ritual of the Day of Atonement, who lays both of his hands on the head of the live goat and confesses over it all the sins of Israel, so as to put all those sins on the head of the goat before it is exiled into the desert (Lev 16:20-22). Does this not prove that sacrificial atonement is penal substitution?

When all the textual evidence is taken into account, however, it is doubtful whether the ritual gesture of the offender laying a hand on the head of the sacrificial animal can be interpreted consistently as signifying that the offering is a penal substitute for the offender. The very same ritual gesture occurs in both the burnt offering (Lev 1:4) and the offering of well-being (3:2), using the same formula as for the sin offering *(wᵉsāmak yādô ʿal rōʾš)*. It is plausible to see ritual identification happening in these cases, but neither of these rituals essentially implies any obvious sense of wrath being propitiated, retribution being satisfied, compensation being given, or penalty being paid. The burnt offering, a continual offering day and night that is reduced to ashes on the altar, would seem to signify the whole-life, perpetual service that Israel owes to YHWH as his people (cf. 6:8-13). The offering of well-being is said to be offered either in thanksgiving or as a votive offering or as a free-will offering (7:12, 16; cf. 27:9-13). Such an offering could be made in thanksgiving for YHWH's act of deliverance from death at the hands of one's enemies (cf. Ps 56:12-13), but this is not at all the same as being spared a death justly deserved under the law. In the cases of the burnt and the well-being offerings, therefore, there is no obvious sense that the one presenting the sacrificial animal does so "in place of" forfeiting his life as a penalty for sin or transgression. Indeed, in these cases, there is no indication at all that sin is necessarily concerned, much less transferred from sinner to substitute.

But, now, if the same ritual gesture does not signify penal substitution in the burnt and well-being offerings, then we cannot honestly be sure whether it signifies penal substitution in the sin offering. So it reads far too much into the ritual act of laying hands on the sacrificial victim to take it as unequivocal evidence for a penal substitution interpretation of the rituals of atonement: such an interpretation fits half the evidence (concerning sin offerings and the Day of Atonement) and conflicts with the other half (concerning burnt offerings and offerings of well-being). While Nicole's claim, "Laying on of the hand necessarily entails some kind of identification,"[34] is plausible, it far exceeds what the varied evidence warrants to infer with certainty (as do Stott, Nicole, and Jeffery et al.) that the sacrificial victim was a penal substitute. We are thus warranted in keeping to a minimal interpretation of this ritual act: laying a hand on the head of the sacrificial animal identifies the animal as belonging to the one offering it for sacrifice. Such a gesture is by no means insignificant, for the sacrificial animal must belong to (be "from the flock" of) the one who offers it.[35]

34. Nicole, "Atonement in the Pentateuch," p. 44.
35. My thanks to Perry Yoder for pointing this out.

To the ritual gesture of identification, Morris adds the claim that "The animal was killed by the worshipper" in support of a penal substitution interpretation. He elaborates:

> But for animals [i.e., excluding birds] it was certainly the worshipper who performed the act of killing (Lv. 1:3-5; 3:1-2, *etc.*). In this way he gave symbolic expression to his recognition that his sin merited the severest punishment. He himself performed the act which set forth the truth that he deserved death.[36]

Morris is correct in observing that the instructions for the various sacrifices consistently direct the one bringing the offering to slaughter the animal, using the repeated formula "and he shall slaughter. . . ." But, as Morris cites, this is true of both the burnt and well-being offerings as well as the sin and guilt offerings, each using the same wording *(wᵉšāḥaṭ).*[37] In the burnt and well-being offerings, as noted above, the animal sacrifice has nothing obvious to do with penal substitution. So, we reach a conclusion similar to that concerning the ritual gesture of placing a hand on the head of the sacrificial animal: because the worshipper slaughtering the animal does not signify penal substitution in the cases of burnt and well-being offerings, and because the same formula is used in all cases, we cannot honestly be sure that it signifies penal substitution in the sin and guilt offerings. In the face of such varied evidence, Morris's view is less than compelling.

10.4. Sacrificial Atonement — Purification and Separation

Our inductive study of the textual evidence of the Levitical cult warrants the inference that making atonement *(kipper)* via blood sacrifice does not concern sin and guilt only (but also contracted impurity), and does not at all concern propitiating God or satisfying retribution. If, as penal substitution claims, the primary effect of atoning sacrifice were propitiation of God's wrath, then logically the object of the ritual act would invariably be God. Yet the textual evidence shows consistently that the object of atonement-making is never God, nor even the sinner per se (atonement is made "on behalf of" the sinner), but always the sin or the sin-induced pollution or the uncleanness itself. Indeed, as von Rad argues, we might well see God (represented by the priest) as the implied primary actor in the *kipper* rites:

---

36. Morris, *The Atonement*, pp. 47-48.

37. Actually, the Hebrew text leaves ambiguous who is doing the slaughtering in the guilt offering: "*they* shall slaughter . . ." (Lev 7:2). But it is plausible to interpret this consistently with the other rituals, especially in light of the instruction, "The guilt offering is like the sin offering; there is the same ritual for them" (v. 7).

Accordingly, the one who receives expiation is not Jahweh, but Israel: Jahweh is rather the one who acts, in averting the calamitous curse which burdens the community . . . although the priest actually performs the actions for expiation, in the last analysis it is Jahweh himself who effects or refuses expiation.[38]

And if, as penal substitution claims, atoning sacrifice propitiates God by satisfying retribution, then logically the sacrifice offered to make atonement would vary in proportion to the "magnitude" or seriousness of the sin committed. Yet the textual evidence shows consistently that the sacrifice does not vary at all according to the sin.[39]

The evidence of Scripture suggests instead that sacrificial atonement deals with uncleanness — generated through sin, guilt, or contracted impurity — that threatens to pollute the holy place, things, and people of God. Rather than propitiation of God's wrath or payment of penalty to God, atoning sacrifice was the God-provided means by which God-self acted to remove sin, guilt, and impurity and so cleanse pollution from the holy place, things, and people that are consecrated to God's service.[40] This is true of both the purification rituals (Lev 15:31) and the atonement rituals (16:33).[41] The inference that better explains the scriptural evidence is that atonement-making by ritual sacrifice effects *purgation* (cleansing or expiation) for the purpose of *separation* (consecration or sanctification).[42] Such cleansing and consecration are necessary for a sinful, unclean people to maintain communion with a holy God; for only that which is made holy can be in contact with the holy, and only that which has been purified can be made holy.[43] In this way, we can see the sacrificial rituals for making atonement as serving the overarching imperative of holiness (cf. Lev 19:2; 20:22-26).[44]

38. Von Rad, *Old Testament Theology*, p 270.

39. I thus disagree with Eichrodt, *Theology of the Old Testament*, pp. 159-60, that the expiatory rites of the Levitical cult were aimed at propitiating God's wrath and making compensation to God.

40. The cleansing of pollution (purification of the sanctuary) and forgiveness of sin (atonement on behalf of persons) are closely connected in the sacrificial ritual — see Hayes, "Atonement in the Book of Leviticus," pp. 9-10.

41. I thus concur with von Rad, *Old Testament Theology* (pp. 272-79), that in the Old Testament worldview the primary categories are clean and unclean, holy and profane, which subsume the rituals of sacrificial purification and atonement-making.

42. Cf. Marshall, *Aspects of the Atonement*, pp. 124-25. Marshall is peculiar among penal substitution apologists in that he does not understand sacrificial atonement in relation to propitiation and retribution but rather expiation, purification, and sanctification.

43. My thanks to Perry Yoder for this point.

44. One can, of course, question whether this interpretation of sacrificial atonement-making in the Levitical cult is itself adequate to *all* the textual evidence. We recognize, with Milgrom, that "No single theory embraces the entire complex of sacrifices" (*Leviticus*, p. 49) and, with Eichrodt, that at most only "a certain degree of probability" is possible in this matter

We thus return to the beginning point and find that this conclusion from Leviticus fits very well with how Hebrews depicts the death of Jesus in terms of the Levitical cult. The writer portrays Jesus as the merciful and faithful high priest in God's service who became human "to make a sacrifice of atonement for the sins of the people" surpassing all previous sacrifices (Heb 2:17; cf. 9:23–10:18). How, though, is the key term "to make atonement" *(hilaskesthai)* understood in this letter? Evidently, the writer understands atoning sacrifice within the Levitical cult in terms of expiation, the removal or cleansing or purification of sin (cf. Heb 9:13-14, 22-23; 10:1-4). Likewise, the writer understands the function of Jesus' self-offering to be that of a sacrifice for sins on our behalf that brings about the removal of or purification from sin: "he has appeared once for all at the end of the age to remove sin by the sacrifice of himself" (9:26b; cf. 10:11-12); "When he had made purification for sins, he sat down at the right hand of the Majesty on high" (1:3). The purpose of Christ's atoning sacrifice, accordingly, is understood in terms of purification from sin for the sake of making holy a people set apart for God's service: "the blood of Christ, who through the eternal Spirit offered himself without blemish to God, [will] purify our conscience from dead works to worship the living God" (9:14); "And it is by God's will that we have been sanctified through the offering of the body of Jesus Christ once for all. . . . For by a single offering he has perfected for all time those who are sanctified" (10:10, 14).[45] Jesus' atoning sacrifice, as presented in Hebrews, thus concerns cleansing from sin (purification) for the sake of separation unto God (sanctification).[46] Not once does Hebrews suggest, much less state, that God's wrath must be appeased, that retribution demands payment for sin, or that Jesus offers himself to propitiate God or satisfy retribution.[47]

Let us, then, summarize our view: atonement-making is the righteous work of a holy God maintaining covenant relationship with a sinful, unclean people. It is God's work, not ours. God does not cleanse pollution and forgive sin in response to sacrifice; rather, sacrifice is God's way of making atonement.

(*Theology of the Old Testament,* p. 141). We thus cannot say that this is the "best" interpretation possible — further study of the textual evidence may yield a better interpretation yet. Nonetheless, our inductive study of the evidence has ruled out (with a high degree of probability, I think) some possibilities as inadequate accounts — viz., explanations of atoning sacrifice in terms of propitiation and retribution.

45. Concerning how Jesus' death as a sacrifice for sins "once for all" can be effective "for us" in the present, see Paul S. Fiddes, *Past Event and Present Salvation: The Christian Idea of Atonement* (Louisville: Westminster/John Knox, 1989), pp. 75-82.

46. Cf. Richard D. Nelson, "'He Offered Himself': Sacrifice in Hebrews," *Interpretation* 57/3 (2003), 251-65, here pp. 259-60. Nelson provides an in-depth discussion of how Jesus' work of atonement-making in Hebrews is understood in relation to the Levitical cult.

47. The lack of textual evidence notwithstanding, Simon J. Kistemaker, "Atonement in Hebrews," in Hill and James, *Glory of the Atonement,* pp. 163-75, insists on interpreting "atonement" in Hebrews in terms of propitiation of wrath.

In atoning sacrifice, God is the primary actor, not humans; sacrifice atones, not because it "satisfies" God, but because God acts thorough it to make atonement. It is a common mistake to get the cause-effect relationship backward and think that sacrifice is the cause and atonement the effect — and thus to think that sacrifice acts on God to effect atonement, making God the medium of the process. God is the actor, the atonement-maker, sacrifice is the medium: God acts to cleanse and forgive sinners by removing sin and pollution through sacrifice, thereby restoring covenant relationship. Divine justice is done here, but it is restorative justice, not retributive justice.

In arriving at this conclusion, that sacrificial atonement concerns purification for the purpose of sanctification, we purposely have *not* speculated concerning how the sacrificial rituals "work" to effect purification, or by what "mechanism" uncleanness is expiated and sins are forgiven. And the reason is simple, yet profound: at work within the sacrificial rituals is God-self, the Holy One to whom belongs the power and prerogative to forgive sin, purify his people, and consecrate them for himself. Von Rad's observation is apt: "While the Old Testament is very full of allusions to the divine activity wherever it becomes effective among men, and full too of the most intensive address and of 'revelation,' there is a realm of silence and secrecy in respect to what God works in sacrifice."[48] By distinguishing between *what* atoning sacrifice *does*, which is revealed, and *how* atoning sacrifice *works*, which is left mysterious, we recall Moses' final address to Israel: "The secret things belong to the LORD our God, but the revealed things belong to us and to our children forever" (Deut 29:29).[49]

---

48. Von Rad, *Old Testament Theology*, 1, p. 260.

49. We might look to the understanding of the atonement within contemporary cultures that continue to practice sacrificial rituals to provide insight into what it is that atoning sacrifice is believed to accomplish. See David W. Shenk, *Justice, Reconciliation and Peace in Africa*, rev. ed. (Nairobi: Uzima, 1997), and Gwinyai H. Muzorewa, "Salvation through the Sacrifice of God's Firstborn Son," in Mark D. Baker, ed., *Proclaiming the Scandal of the Cross: Contemporary Images of the Atonement* (Grand Rapids, MI: Baker Academic, 2006), pp. 163-71.

CHAPTER 11

Forgiveness of Sin: Not without Bloodshed?

Indeed, under the law almost everything is purified with blood,
and without the shedding of blood there is no forgiveness of sins.

HEBREWS 9:22

11.1. The Penal Substitution View

We have shown that sacrificial atonement, as evident in both Leviticus and Hebrews, concerns not penal satisfaction — propitiating God and satisfying retribution — but purification from uncleanness for separation unto God. Still, one
might ask: Does not the Bible require bloodshed as the prior condition of forgiveness of sin? The penal substitution model certainly maintains that God
cannot forgive sin unless blood is shed by sacrificial or penal means. Charles
Hodge: "If sin be pardoned it can be pardoned in consistency with divine justice only on the ground of a forensic penal satisfaction." J. I. Packer also affirms
"the need for penal satisfaction as a basis for forgiveness."[1] Packer goes on to say
that to question the need for penal satisfaction as the prerequisite of forgiveness
"is 'naturalistic' criticism, which assumes that what humanity could not do or
would not require, God will not do or require either. Such criticism is profoundly perverse, for it shrinks God the creator into the image of the human
creature. . . ."[2] Far from being "perverse," we will show to the contrary that not
only do both the Levitical sacrificial rites and God's redeeming actions reveal

---

1. J. I. Packer, "What Did the Cross Achieve? The Logic of Penal Substitution," in J. I.
Packer, *Celebrating the Saving Work of God: The Collected Shorter Writings of J. I. Packer* (Carlisle,
UK: Paternoster Press, 1998), I, pp. 85-123, here p. 114.
2. Packer, "What Did the Cross Achieve?" p. 114.

that penal satisfaction is not a prerequisite of forgiveness of sin, but also that maintaining that it is effectively shrinks the abundant mercy of God into the narrow requirements of law.

The text usually cited in support of the penal substitution view is Heb 9:22b, "without the shedding of blood there is no forgiveness of sins." This text would appear to state that bloodshed is *sine qua non* of forgiveness: if blood is not shed, whether by sacrifice or by punishment, sins cannot be forgiven. So Hodge: "Without the shedding of blood (i.e., without vicarious punishment) there is no remission. This is recorded, not merely as a fact under the Mosaic dispensation, but as embodying a principle valid under all dispensations."[3] Similarly, Stott:

> This Old Testament background helps us to understand two crucial texts in the letter to the Hebrews. The first is that "without the shedding of blood there is no forgiveness" (9:22). . . . No forgiveness without blood meant no atonement without substitution. There *had* to be life for life or blood for blood.[4]

As Stott indicates, Heb 9:22 refers to the Levitical system of atoning sacrifice. Morris thus comments on the sacrificial rites: "Nobody who came thoughtfully to God by the way of sacrifice could be in any doubt but that sin was a serious matter. It could not be put aside by a light-hearted wave of the hand but required the shedding of blood."[5]

Heb 9:22 is usually cited only in part, however. The full text reads, "Indeed, under the law almost everything is purified with blood, and without the shedding of blood there is no forgiveness of sins." The partial quotation excludes the crucial qualifications, "under the law" and "almost everything." Absent these qualifications, the fragment of Heb 9:22 cited as a prooftext for penal substitution would appear to be a universal and unalterable law of justice that governs divine mercy: God cannot forgive sinners unless retribution for sin is satisfied by bloodshed. The evidence of Scripture, however, shows not only that such a "law" did not actually govern the Levitical sacrifices for sin, but also that no such "law" governs God's sovereign prerogative of mercy.

3. Charles Hodge, *Systematic Theology* (Grand Rapids, MI: Eerdmans Publishing, 1940), vol. 2., pp. 491-92.

4. John R. W. Stott, *The Cross of Christ* (Downers Grove, IL: InterVarsity Press, 1986), p. 138, emphasis added.

5. Leon Morris, *The Atonement: Its Meaning and Significance* (Downers Grove, IL: InterVarsity Press, 1983), pp. 50-51.

11.2. Exceptions under the Law

Let us begin with the qualification "almost everything." According to the Levitical code (Leviticus 4:1–6:7), the rituals of sin and guilt offering typically — but not always — require sacrificial bloodshed. There is an exception in the sin offering: in cases of extreme poverty when the offender cannot afford even two turtledoves or two pigeons, a grain offering is accepted, atonement is made by the priest, and sin is forgiven (Lev 5:11-13). According to the Levitical code itself, it is possible and permissible that sin be forgiven without animal sacrifice. Even "under the law," then, bloodshed was not strictly necessary as a prior condition of forgiveness; God graciously provided for exceptions.[6]

The penal substitution apologist might be tempted here either to ignore or to downplay this acceptance of exceptions. Morris ignores it: "In a sacrifice the blood must be manipulated in prescribed ways and part or all of the animal must be burnt on the altar. All this speaks of the necessity for death [i.e., blood], nothing less, if sin is to be put away."[7] Emile Nicole downplays it: "The provision of mere grain as sin offering (Lev. 5:11-13) must be put back into proper perspective. It was an exception among exceptions!"[8] If we consider it carefully, however, this "exception among exceptions" reveals the grace of God at work at the heart of the sacrificial system.

11.2.1. Atonement-Making Is All from God, Not Us

First, the immediate implication of the acceptability of exceptions is that the law is not to be used to exclude anyone from God's mercy, not even the poorest of the poor. By no means is it ever the divine intent that the law become a barrier preventing anyone from being reconciled to God. The corollary is that forgiveness does not depend in any way on the status of the sinner, but solely and completely on God's status as God. God forgives our sin, not because of who we are or what we offer, but because of who God is, "a God merciful and gracious"

---

6. One may add to this exception the observation (made to me by Perry Yoder) that, in the ritual for the Day of Atonement, God also deals with sin without bloodshed by means of the scapegoat. The live goat, which is exiled to the wilderness rather than sacrificed on the altar, bears upon itself and thus carries away "all the iniquities of the people of Israel, and all their transgressions, all their sins" (Lev 16:20-22).

7. Morris, *The Atonement*, p. 67. This statement comes after a lengthy argument that "blood = death." Morris's book contains no citation of Lev 5:11-13.

8. Emile Nicole, "Atonement in the Pentateuch," in Charles E. Hill and Frank A. James III, eds., *The Glory of the Atonement: Biblical, Theological and Practical Perspectives* (Downers Grove, IL: InterVarsity Press, 2004), p. 45.

(Exod 34:6-7). Atonement-making is, in truth, all from God, not from us. Thus Paul: "All this is from God . . ." (2 Cor 5:18).[9]

11.2.2. Sacrificial Atonement Is Divine Gift, Not Divine-Human Exchange

Second, as we have shown (Chapter 10), it is evident that the sacrifice offered to God is not proportional to, and hence not compensation for, the sin committed. The corollary is that the worshipper should not think that one's offering "buys" forgiveness for sin. The exceptions to the rule make this clear: whether the worshipper offers a lamb or a goat or two pigeons or two turtledoves or two quarts of flour, atonement is made and sin is forgiven, regardless of the "exchange value" of the "commodity" offered. Making atonement by sin offering, therefore, does not work according to the rules of the marketplace; atonement is not a "transaction" made according to the "going rate" for forgiveness of sin. At least some penal substitution apologists do characterize atonement-making as a market transaction. Thus, Emile Nicole: "The *normal rate* for an ordinary member of the community was a female lamb or goat."[10] Such language depicts the priests (representing God) setting "rates" for forgiveness just as sellers set the price for this or that commodity — which suggests that the only difference between the marketplace and the holy place is the kind of goods being traded.

The Temple was not to be a place where humans procure divine goods at market prices but rather the place of divine gift-giving.[11] That a goat or turtledoves or wheat are equally acceptable to God as a sin offering entails that no one can boast that the value of one's offering or the goodness of one's labor merited God's mercy. Or, conversely, that God accepts equally the offering of an animal or birds or grain means that rich and poor may boast equally in being forgiven, each boasting solely in God's grace. Because all life is given by God in creation, whatever sacrifice humans offer — whether animal or birds or grain — reflects the original grace of God. Even animal sacrifice is not divine-human exchange: "the blood that makes atonement" (Lev 17:11) already belongs to God (Gen 9:4-5), and God has no need for blood (Ps 50:7-15). Any sacrifice that humans might offer is always already God's gift to them and so cannot satisfy God's need.

9. This point — that it is "all from God" — is emphasized repeatedly by D. M. Baillie, *God Was in Christ: An Essay on Incarnation and Atonement* (New York: Scribner's, 1948).

10. Nicole, "Atonement in the Pentateuch," p. 45, emphasis added.

11. Indeed, that humans had perverted God's place of showing mercy to humanity into a marketplace for human trade in divine goods was the motivation behind Jesus' "cleansing" of the Temple (John 2:16): "Take these things out of here! Stop making my Father's house a marketplace!"

By examining the exception to the rule of the sin offering, we learn two important truths concerning sacrificial atonement: sacrifice for sin is God's gift to us, not our payment to God; and, correspondingly, making atonement is God's doing for our sake, not our doing for God's satisfaction. The Hebrew text of Lev 17:11 makes both truths explicitly and emphatically clear: "For the life itself of the flesh is in the blood, *and I myself (wa'ǎni) have given it to you* upon the altar to make atonement *for your lives;* for it is the blood, by means of the life, that makes atonement."[12] Jay Sklar comments aptly: "As in the New Testament, then, God shows his grace not only by granting forgiveness, but by providing sinners with the means of forgiveness to begin with."[13] God is the sole and sufficient provider for our lives in every regard, providing even the means of dealing with our sins; God the Creator, who gives life to all creatures, is also God the Redeemer, who cleanses and forgives sins by means of his generous gift. *The underlying premise of the sacrificial system, therefore, is nothing other than God's grace.*

This is directly pertinent to thinking about forgiveness of sins through Christ. Jesus freely offers himself in obedience to God as a sacrifice for sins on our behalf (Heb 5:7-10; 7:27; 9:24-28; 10:10-14). But his atoning death is not our payment *to God* in exchange for being spared the penalty of sin (per penal substitution). For Jesus himself is God's personal gift *to us* (John 3:16; Gal 1:4; 2:20; 1 John 5:11), and we cannot possibly repay God with his own gift! Jesus is the One whom God graciously provides for the sake of our salvation, the One through whom God extends mercy and forgives sins in order to cleanse us from impurity and reconcile us to himself. This is the very idea expressed by Paul in his message of the cross: Jesus' life and death, signified and offered "in his blood," is God's gracious gift for our justification and faithful action for our redemption (Rom 3:24-25). God's gracious initiative to justify and redeem sinners precedes any attempt from our side to "make things right" with God by sacrifice.

Atonement-making for sin, therefore, is God's gracious act on our behalf, not our attempt to compensate and satisfy God. Indeed, humans cannot possibly compensate God for sin by offering as a sacrifice what already belongs to God. In this regard, we agree with Anselm's point that human beings cannot make compensation to God for sin by acts of obedience, for in doing so we only render what already belongs to God.[14] Whereas Anselm uses this as the logical leverage necessitating that Christ the God-Man make atonement for sin by compensation to God on humanity's behalf, however, we see this as the *reductio ad absurdum* of the very notion of making atonement for sin by human com-

---

12. Translation by Jay Sklar, "I Myself Have Given," in Gary D. Pratico and Miles V. Van Pelt, *Basics of Biblical Hebrew: Grammar,* 2nd ed. (Grand Rapids, MI: Zondervan Publishing, 2007), p. 78, emphasis added. The Hebrew text emphasizes God as the giver of the means of making atonement by using the first person pronoun, which is not required grammatically.

13. Sklar, "I Myself Have Given," p. 78.

14. Anselm, *Cur Deus Homo* I.20.

pensation to God. The difference lies in Anselm's presupposition that the God-human relationship is regulated by the law of retribution (see Chapter 3 above), which we think is precisely what is called into question by both the cult of sacrifice and the cross of Christ.

Forgiveness, therefore, is divine gift, not to be gained through market trade, blood in exchange for mercy. For it is God-self who all-sufficiently provides both "the blood that makes atonement" and the mercy that forgives sins. The exception proves the rule: God's grace cannot be bought! We thus agree with Hans Boersma that God's covenantal relationship with Israel, even as expressed in the sacrificial cult, and hence as fulfilled in the cross of Christ, is not to be understood on the basis of a "strict economy of exchange."[15] So, when Paul writes, "For by grace you have been saved through faith, and this is not your own doing; it is the gift of God" (Eph 2:8), he affirms nothing other than the divine grace operating at the heart of the sacrificial system. As with the cultic rites of atoning sacrifice, so with Jesus' death: the sacrifice that atones for sins is not our payment to God for God's satisfaction, but God's gift to us for our sake. The "economy" of atonement is thus not an economy of exchange, premised on the principle of retribution, but rather an economy of grace, flowing from the generosity of God.

11.2.3. *The Cost of Forgiveness Is Borne by God, Not Us*

Third, that the law makes an *exception* for the poor *to* offer sacrifice for sin rather than *exempting* the poor *from* sacrifice implies that atonement-making is bound up with sacrifice — and thus that forgiveness of sins both requires participation by the sinner and is costly to God. The sin offering is always attended by a confession (cf. Lev 5:5).[16] In atonement-making, what is required on the part of the sinner — no matter what the sin or who the sinner — is not compensation to God but confession of sin. The act of confession before the priest, acting on behalf of both humanity and God, acknowledges the sinner's need for forgiveness from God and recognizes God's power, prerogative, and presence to forgive sins. To confess sin — which honors covenant relationship, acknowledging both disobedience against God and need of reconciliation to God — is in a way the sinner's true sacrifice, the humble offering of oneself to God (cf. Pss 25:4-12; 50:23; 51:17; Hos 6:6; Joel 2:12-13; Mic 6:8).[17]

15. Hans Boersma, *Violence, Hospitality, and the Cross: Reappropriating the Atonement Tradition* (Grand Rapids, MI: Baker Academic, 2004), pp. 153-79.

16. Although this is not explicitly stated, the guilt offering also would seem to require an acknowledgment of guilt: "when you have sinned and realize your guilt . . ." (Lev 6:4).

17. Cf. Baillie, *God Was in Christ*, p. 198: "If we use the terminology of an ancient sacrificial system, we should remember that in the last analysis the only offering we can make to God is the offering of ourselves in faith and love."

Yet, as noted above, because the forgiveness of sins is not a function of what is sacrificed, it is evident that God's forgiveness of sins does not depend in any way on human offerings. Concerning what makes atonement for sin, therefore, neither the human offering sacrifice nor the human-offered sacrifice is of supreme significance. While human participation is required, what matters supremely is God's gracious action, which precedes any human action. The corollary is that the cost of forgiving sins is borne entirely on God's part. God's forgiveness of sin is the first characteristic expression of God's own steadfast love and covenant loyalty (Exod 34:6-7; Ps 103:3); and faithful action is costly to the One who keeps faith in spite of all (cf. Psalms 105–107, 136; Hosea).

Forgiveness of sin *is* costly. We thus agree with Morris's observation that "An essential element in the sacrificial approach was the element of cost."[18] But we do not agree that the "cost" of forgiveness is "covered" by humans, who "pay the price" of God's mercy by offering God a compensatory sacrifice. One might argue that the cost of forgiveness is borne by the sinner because he is required to sacrifice an animal (or birds or grain) to be forgiven. Yet, as observed above, the sacrificial animal offered by humans is God's creature, the life of which (in the blood) already belongs to God. The original sacrifice of the atonement ritual, therefore, is made from *God's* side: it is God's own gift of life, released by the death of the sacrificial animal, that is poured out on the altar. Rather than forgiveness being the effect of human sacrifice to God, therefore, forgiveness is, in a real sense, *the sacrifice that God offers* on behalf of and for the sake of humans. Again, it is not really humans who make atonement by offering sacrifice, but God (represented by the priest) who makes atonement on our behalf. Thus, offering a sacrifice of atonement for sins signifies, not that God forgives sins in "exchange" for our "compensation" to God, but rather that forgiveness is costly to God, that God willingly bears the burden of our sins as the cost of covenant faithfulness.[19]

We thus find substantial consistency between Old and New Testaments concerning sacrifice, atonement, and forgiveness: it is the work of God's grace, through and through. While agreeing with D. M. Baillie that in the New Testament we encounter "the idea of an atonement in which *God alone bears the cost*," in which "it is God Himself that makes the sacrifice,"[20] we would argue that such was true also of sacrificial atonement in the Old Testament.[21] We thus concur with I. Howard Marshall:

18. Morris, *The Atonement,* p. 51.

19. Regarding atoning sacrifice as the costliness of divine forgiveness, cf. Baillie, *God Was in Christ,* pp. 171-79.

20. Baillie, *God Was in Christ,* pp. 175, 177, emphasis original.

21. We thus find greater agreement with what Baillie writes later: "There has never been an age when it would have been true to say that God was not carrying the load of sins of His people and thus making atonement and offering forgiveness" (*God Was in Christ,* p. 192).

When the New Testament speaks of divine forgiveness, we have to understand it as requiring no restitution or retribution from the sinner, but as resting on something that God in his mercy has done to make it possible. . . .

In the New Testament . . . God, who provided the path of sacrifice in the Old Testament, now intervenes to provide a new offering, himself dying in the person of the Son who has united himself with humanity. This is the offering which will deal with sin. . . . The conferral of forgiveness costs the sinner nothing, but it costs God everything.[22]

Atoning sacrifice, whether through cult or cross, signifies that our sins are forgiven solely by God's grace — that the costly consequences of our sins are absorbed entirely into God's mercy. As Baillie says of atonement in the New Testament, we would thus say of atonement in the Old Testament: "God's forgiveness . . . outruns all human attempts at expiation, because the expiation is made in the heart and life of God Himself."[23]

11.3. Mercy beyond the Law

The penal substitution apologist might still want to maintain that, exceptions allowing bloodless sacrifice notwithstanding, the overall intent of the Levitical cult is that forgiveness requires bloodshed — indeed, that atonement-by-blood is the God-ordained way of dealing with sin (Lev 17:11). Thus, Emile Nicole: atonement-by-blood is "a general principle underlying the whole OT sacrificial system."[24]

11.3.1. God under Law?

This is where the qualification "under the law" in Heb 9:22 matters. The sin offering prescribed by the Levitical code was Israel's God-ordained means of dealing with sins; but it does not follow that God is restricted to such means of dealing with sins. Ordaining a ritual means of atonement-making does not entail that God cannot deal with sin *directly*, apart from mediation through priest and sacrifice. Is God "under the law," *bound* by the Levitical code? Can God forgive sin *only* under the prescribed atonement rituals? Reading Heb 9:22 per penal substitution, as requiring bloodshed as the necessary prior condition of sins being forgiven, entails that God is "under the law" and so is not free to forgive

---

22. I. Howard Marshall, *Aspects of the Atonement: Cross and Resurrection in the Reconciling of God and Humanity* (London: Paternoster, 2007), pp. 50-51.

23. Baillie, *God Was in Christ*, p. 178.

24. Nicole, "Atonement in the Pentateuch," p. 44.

sin "apart from law." For if God cannot forgive sin except as regulated "by law" then there must be a "higher law" that regulates God's mercy: God may not forgive sin without penal satisfaction (recall Hodge).

That is also the view articulated by Anselm in *Cur Deus Homo*. Anselm argues that God cannot forgive sin unless satisfaction to justice is made — that God cannot "forgive a sin out of mercy alone." Anselm's reasoning is that such would not be "fitting" for God to do. God's freedom is bounded by what it is "fitting" for God: "For the term 'freedom' relates only to the freedom to perform what is advantageous or fitting." And what is "fitting" for God's freedom is defined by the necessity that God govern everything under his dominion by the law of retribution: "it is not fitting for God to forgive a sin without punishment" because "it is not fitting for God to allow anything in his kingdom to slip by unregulated." Anselm thus sums up the argument: "In consequence of this reasoning, if it is not fitting for God to do anything in an unjust or unregulated manner, it does not belong to his freedom or benevolence or will to release unpunished a sinner who has not repaid to God what he has taken away from him."[25] That is, Anselm concludes, God may not show mercy in an "unregulated" or unlawful way, and hence God cannot forgive sin unless compensation for sin has been paid. God, then, is free to forgive only within the bounds of the law of retribution.

We will test this claim — that God's freedom to forgive sins is restricted by law such that God may not have mercy unless retribution has been satisfied by bloodshed — against Scripture. And we will show that the canon of Scripture — Torah, Prophets, Psalms, and Gospels — bears manifold witness to God doing just what the logic of satisfaction and penal substitution says God cannot or would not do: dealing with (cleansing and forgiving) sin "apart from law," apart from sacrificial or penal bloodshed.

Now, in defense of penal substitution, Jeffery et al. have argued that the law of justice that limits the mercy of God is not an external constraint on God's will. Rather, the law requiring bloodshed as the prerequisite of forgiveness is intrinsic to God-self: "The standard of justice on which basis Christ was punished in our place is not external to God, but *intrinsic* to him; it is a reflection of his own righteous, holy character."[26] If this be so, then for God to require sacrifice or impose punishment as the prior condition of forgiving sins is simply for

---

25. Anselm, *Cur Deus Homo*, I.12, trans. Janet Fairweather, in Brian Davies and G. R. Evans, eds., *Anselm of Canterbury: The Major Works* (Oxford: Oxford University Press, 1998), pp. 284-86. We have noted before, but it bears repeating, that we must be careful not to conflate Anselm's satisfaction theory of atonement with the Calvinist penal substitution model, even though both are framed within the retributive paradigm.

26. Steve Jeffery, Michael Ovey, and Andrew Sach, *Pierced for Our Transgressions: Rediscovering the Glory of Penal Substitution* (Wheaton, IL: Crossway Books, 2008), p. 301, emphasis original.

God to act in accord with his own character, for God to be God. But conversely, if this be so, then were God to make any exception to this intrinsic standard of justice and forgive sin "apart from law," God would compromise his very integrity and fail to be God. If this law is intrinsic to God, and if God be God, then there can be no exceptions to the law. Again, we shall see, Scripture testifies to God doing what penal substitution advocates say the intrinsic law of God's character strictly forbids him doing, forgiving sin without bloodshed. Whether penal substitution depicts this law of justice as an external constraint on God or as the intrinsic character of God, Scripture testifies otherwise.

11.3.2. Forgiveness apart from Law: Torah

We begin with the original sins of humanity in Genesis. The story of Adam and Eve leaves us no doubt that "quick and sure" death is the divinely ordained punishment for disobeying God's command (Gen 2:16-17). Surprisingly, God suspends the law-prescribed death sentence and spares their lives when they disobey, choosing instead to deal with humanity's first sin by other means. God does banish Adam and Eve from the garden and lets their labor and survival be difficult as consequence for their sin. Yet God nonetheless provides for their protection in the harsh conditions of exile, making sturdy leather garments to replace their flimsy fig-leaf tunics (3:16-24).[27]

Now the biblical fact that Adam and Eve do *not* die "in the day" that they sin as God had threatened (Gen 2:17), and thus the biblical fact that God does *not* satisfy the demand of God's own law by imposing the death penalty on Adam and Eve, generates an awkward question: Has God broken his own law? Has God proved himself untrue? This awkward question has led many interpreters down the centuries to suppose that, by threatening Adam "you shall die," God must have meant a "death" other than (or in addition to) natural death: if God did not punish Adam and Eve with natural death on that day, then it must be that God punished them with "spiritual" death.[28] We do not wish at all to deny the spirituality of human life, that we are physical-spiritual beings and so can be "dead" spiritually as well physically (cf. Rom 7:23 24; 8:4 8; Eph 2:1). It is anything but obvious, however, that such spiritual death is what is

27. A popular interpretation of this story is that God sacrificed the animals to make atonement by blood for Adam and Eve's sin and then used the skins to make clothing for them. The leather clothing was to be a reminder to them of the "price" of their sin. The story is thus read as confirming the penal substitution model of atonement. There is nothing in the text itself, however, to support such an interpretation. The text says merely, "And the LORD God made garments of skins for the man and for his wife, and clothed them" (Gen 3:21). There is neither mention of nor reference to sacrifice. Taking this text at its face, God's purpose was to provide protective clothing for them.

28. E.g., Augustine, *City of God* XIII.12.

meant in Genesis 2–3, where "death" quite evidently means death in the natural sense — a return to the ground, a dissolution of the body into the stuff of earth (Gen 3:19). The rationale for a non-literal reading of "death" in 2:17 is thus not the text itself but the need to preserve the necessary legal linkage between sin and penal death, the assumption that sin requires a penalty of death ("death" in some sense) to satisfy the just wrath of God.[29]

An alternative reading of the story would be that not only do Adam and Eve have a choice whether to obey God or not, but also God has a choice whether to impose a penalty of death for disobedience or not. And the story makes clear that God chooses to override his own judgment of death for sin. God's choosing to deal with humanity's first sin by other than the death-demanding law would thus demonstrate that God is free to break the legal linkage between sin and death. That God decrees and, in the very first instance, transcends his own law implies that God's justice and mercy cannot be bound by any law, that God remains free to be just and merciful as he chooses.

God goes on to demonstrate that sovereign freedom even further when dealing with the first murder one chapter later. If there is any sin deserving a penalty of death, it is "murder with malice aforethought" (as the law books put it). And that is how Cain does away with his brother Abel (Gen 4:5, 8). Yet God punishes Cain's sin with exile, not death, and, having spared Cain's life, places a mark of protection on him precisely in order to prevent his blood from being shed by other humans as retribution for his sin (vv. 9-16). The Bible bears witness from the very beginning, therefore, to God's direct and merciful dealing with human sin without sacrificial or penal bloodshed.

The epiphany on the holy mountain further reveals God's mercy unbound by law. The divine name — "I am who I am" or "I will be who I will be" (Exod 3:14) — not only speaks the supremacy of deity over nature and history, but also declares the sovereignty of divine mercy and grace above law and ritual. Moses requests that God show himself, and God grants this request: "I will make all my goodness pass before you, and will proclaim before you the name, 'YHWH'; and I will be gracious to whom I will be gracious, and will show mercy on whom I will show mercy" (33:18-19). The divine self-revelation declares that God's grace and mercy are matters of divine freedom of will, unbounded by any law. The very name (YHWH) reveals God's gracious and merciful character, God's freedom to forgive sins transcending the limits of law-prescribed action. God's self-revelation to Moses on the holy mountain, therefore, implies that God's forgiveness is subject only to God's sovereign will.

The historical books provide a striking example of God's grace and mercy without bounds. After Solomon has dedicated the Temple as a "house for the name of the LORD," God appears to Solomon, saying:

---

29. That would seem to be the case in Jeffery et al., *Pierced for Our Transgressions*, pp. 118-21.

I have heard your prayer, and have chosen this place for myself as a house of sacrifice. When I shut up the heavens so that there is no rain, or command the locust to devour the land, or send pestilence among my people, if my people who are called by my name humble themselves, pray, seek my face, and turn from their wicked ways, then I will hear from heaven, and will forgive their sin and heal their land. (2 Chron 7:12-14)

God accepts Solomon's dedicatory prayer and chooses the Temple dedicated in God's name as "a house of sacrifice." Yet, concerning what will turn away God's wrath (expressed through drought, devastation, and pestilence) provoked by the people's sins and elicit God's mercy and forgiveness, God prescribes not sacrifice, but humility, prayer, and repentance. God's merciful will to forgive the people's sins is not premised on sacrifice and hence not on bloodshed. Rather, solely on account of his name will God have mercy on and forgive the sins of "my people who are called by my name."

11.3.3. Forgiveness apart from Law: Prophets

The Prophets also proclaim God's forgiveness of sins, solely on account of God's own steadfast love and abundant mercy. Indeed, Isaiah begins with a personal testimony to God's power and will to make atonement, to purge from sin and uncleanness, apart from sacrificial bloodshed (Isa 6:1-7). God calls Isaiah by a vision in the temple: Isaiah sees "the Lord sitting on a throne, high and lofty." The seraphim attending God sing "Holy, holy, holy is the LORD" while the Temple shakes and fills with smoke. Overwhelmed by God's holiness and power, Isaiah laments, "Woe is me! I am lost, for I am a man of unclean lips, and I live among a people of unclean lips; yet my eyes have seen the King, the LORD of hosts." Isaiah the sinner expects to perish in God's presence ("Woe is me! I am lost"), but God acts graciously to restore Isaiah's life for the sake of God's people (cf. vv. 8-13). A seraph brings a live coal from the altar, touching it to Isaiah's lips: "Now that this has touched your lips, your guilt has departed and your sin is blotted out *(kipper)*." God's atonement for Isaiah's sin is mediated not by a bloody sacrifice but by a burning coal.[30]

Elsewhere we hear God say again and again through his prophets that he will have mercy and make atonement — act to forgive and cleanse and heal and re-

---

30. One might infer here that, because the burning coal is taken from the altar, animal sacrifice is implied — and, hence, that Isaiah's sin is purged by bloodshed. However, the seraph's saying emphasizes the coal itself — ". . . *this* has touched your lips . . ." — not the coal's having contact with blood from an animal sacrifice. The coal here mediates God's purgative power apart from sacrificial bloodshed. Indeed, the text deliberately emphasizes God's presence and power in excess of the Temple and its rituals (Isa 6:1-4).

store Israel from its sins — neither on account of Israel's righteousness nor by means of blood sacrifice, but on account of God's holy name and by means of God's holy power. Isaiah announces to the people: "I, I am He who blots out your transgressions for my own sake, and I will not remember your sins" (Isa 43:25). Jeremiah declares God's consoling word of steadfast love and abundant mercy to an unfaithful and unjust people: "I will heal. . . . I will restore. . . . I will cleanse them from all the guilt of their sin against me, and I will forgive all the guilt of their sin and rebellion against me" (Jer 33:6-8). Ezekiel proclaims God's purifying and restoring word to an unclean people living in exile because they have profaned the name of God and defiled their homeland by bloodshed and idolatry:

> It is not for your own sake, O house of Israel, that I am about to act, but for the sake of my holy name, which you have profaned among the nations to which you came. I will sanctify my great name. . . . I will take you from the nations . . . and bring you into your own land. I will sprinkle clean water on you, and you shall be clean from all your uncleannesses, and from all your idols I will cleanse you. (Ezek 36:22-25)

And Hosea speaks God's word of steadfast love to an unfaithful people: "I will heal their disloyalty, I will love them freely, for my anger has turned from them" (Hos 14:4).

God pledges to act faithfully and mercifully, without any requirement of sacrificial bloodshed as a prior condition. The prophets thus depict God exercising sovereign prerogative and power, prerogative of mercy to forgive sin and power of holiness to purge uncleanness, unbound by any law, even the Levitical code.[31]

11.3.4. Forgiveness apart from Law: Psalms

There are also numerous texts in the Psalms that praise or petition God precisely because God forgives sin solely on account of God's abundant mercy and steadfast love or for God's own name's sake, without any prerequisite of sacrificial bloodshed (e.g., Psalms 6, 25, 32, 40, 103, and 130). Psalm 51 is a prime example.[32]

---

31. And not even bounded by God's covenant with Israel. Clement, bishop of Rome, interpreted the prophetic ministry of Jonah as God's offer of forgiveness of sin to Gentiles (Assyrians) apart from the covenant, by means of repentance and intercession rather than sacrifice: "When, after Jonah had proclaimed destruction to the people of Nineveh, they repented of their sins and made atonement *(exilasanto)* to God with prayers and supplications, they obtained their salvation, notwithstanding that they were strangers and aliens to him" (1 *Clement* 7:7). Maxwell Staniforth and Andrew Louth, trans., *Early Christian Writings* (London: Penguin Books, 1987), p. 26.

32. For exegetical purposes I accept the traditional interpretation of Psalm 51 as David's confessional prayer after being convicted of his sin by the prophet Nathan (as set forth in the

David is guilty of adultery and murder (2 Samuel 11); and the law demands death, penal bloodshed, for both crimes — there is no provision for making atonement by blood sacrifice for such sins (cf. Exod 21:12-14; Lev 20:10; 24:17-21; Num 34:30-34). David thus stands in need of deliverance from death. Acknowledging his sin and recognizing his need for salvation, David pleads God's mercy, appealing to God's steadfast love: "Have mercy on me, O God, according to your steadfast love; according to your abundant mercy, blot out my transgressions. Wash me thoroughly from my iniquity, and cleanse me from my sin" (Ps 51:1-2). By petitioning God to expunge his transgression and cleanse *(ṭāhēr)* him from his sin, David appeals directly to God to make atonement on his behalf. Accordingly, he confesses that God's judgment on his sin is justified (v. 4). And he knows what the prophets have proclaimed, that bringing a burnt offering in place of obedience would offend rather than please God, that sacrifice is no substitute for righteousness (v. 16; cf. 1 Sam 13:8-14; 15:10-31). David thus petitions God to deal directly with his sins, to expunge his sins, cleanse him from pollution, and restore him to right relationship: "Hide your face from my sins, and blot out all my iniquities. Create in me a clean heart, O God, and put a new and right spirit within me" (Ps 51:9-10). And he presents his own humility as his offering before God: "The sacrifice acceptable to God is a broken spirit; a broken and contrite heart, O God, you will not despise" (v. 17).

In all this, even though the sin of bloodshed has been committed and the law demands (penal) bloodshed, there is not one declaration that God cannot make atonement for (forgive and cleanse) David's sins without (sacrificial) bloodshed. The only reference to cultic purgation *(ḥaṭṭaʾ)* and purification *(ṭāhēr)* is metaphorical, a petition for God to cleanse the sinner with hyssop to render him clean of sin's pollution: "Purge me with hyssop, and I shall be clean; wash me, and I shall be whiter than snow" (v. 7). This prayer thus attests God's own power (symbolized by the hyssop) to purge us from sin without bloodshed, God's free will to deal directly with sin "apart from law."[33]

---

psalm's superscript). For an alternative interpretation that extends its meaning beyond that traditional setting, see Kathryn L. Roberts, "My Tongue Will Sing Aloud of Your Deliverance: Praise and Sacrifice in the Psalms," in Stephen Breck Reid, ed., *Psalms and Practice: Worship, Virtue, and Authority* (Collegeville, MN: The Liturgical Press, 2001), pp. 99-110.

33. Bruce K. Waltke, "Atonement in Psalm 51," in Hill and James, *Glory of the Atonement*, pp. 51-60, suggests that the reference to purgation with hyssop recalls the purification ritual for lepers in Leviticus 14 (p. 58). This ritual would be performed when, on examination of the leprous person who had been living outside the camp, the priest found that the disease had healed. The ritual involved mixing blood from a slaughtered bird into a vessel of fresh water, dipping the hyssop branch into the water-blood mixture, and sprinkling it seven times on the one who is to be cleansed of leprosy (cf. Lev 14:2-7). Thus, Waltke claims, David's petition for purification does entail sacrificial bloodshed. If Waltke is correct that David's petition for purgation by hyssop in Ps 51:7 alludes to this ritual, then he is surely correct in stating that David's appeal to this ritual is "ad hoc" (p. 58): obviously, David was not diseased with leprosy and sin is not to be

11.3.5. Forgiveness apart from Law: Gospels

The witness of the Torah, Prophets, and Psalms continues in the Gospels. The Synoptic narrative introduces John the Baptist as the last prophet, who "prepares the way" for the coming of the messianic age of salvation (Matt 3:3; Mark 1:2-3; Luke 3:4-6). At the annunciation of his birth, the angel tells Zechariah that John "will turn many of the people of Israel to the Lord their God" (Luke 1:16); and at his birth, Zechariah sings that John will "go before the Lord to prepare his ways, to give knowledge of salvation to his people by the forgiveness of their sins" (Luke 1:76-77). The heart of John's prophetic ministry, therefore, is to call the people to repentance (Matt 3:2; Luke 3:7-14) and proclaim the forgiveness of sins. Indeed, John goes out to the Jordan River "proclaiming a baptism of repentance for the forgiveness of sins" (Mark 1:4; Luke 3:3; cf. Matt 3:5-6). Prior to Jesus, through the prophetic ministry of John, therefore, God was forgiving sins by means of repentance and washing with *water* — apart from the Temple and its law-prescribed sacrifices, without need of blood.

God's offering of forgiveness of sin apart from sacrifice and bloodshed continues in the ministry of Jesus, only more radically. All the Gospel accounts depict Jesus repeatedly (and scandalously!) announcing and enacting the divine prerogative of mercy. Jesus proclaims forgiveness to all and forgives the sins of those who come to him seeking mercy (Mark 2:1-12 par. Matt 9:1-8 and Luke 5:17-26; Luke 7:36-50; John 8:1-11). Whereas John had offered washing with water as the means of signifying repentance and receiving forgiveness, Jesus forgives sin on his own authority and on account of the recipients' faith. His forgiveness surpasses that offered through John: Jesus not only forgives sins apart from the Temple and sacrifice, without any requirement of bloodshed,

---

equated with disease in the Levitical cult. But the discrepancy between Psalm 51 and Leviticus 14 goes further; for the ritual of purgation by hyssop did not even complete the process of cleansing, much less effect forgiveness of sin or suffice for making atonement. The purgation ritual with hyssop signaled the beginning of a process by which the petitioner would be cleansed from pollution, a process involving washing of clothes, shaving of hair, and bathing of body (Lev 14:8-9). Moreover, to complete the full process of cleansing from pollution and restoration to the community after healing from leprosy, the petitioner must yet bring both a guilt offering and a sin offering so that the priest can "make atonement on his behalf" (vv. 10-20). Thus, if David's petition for purgation by hyssop does allude to the purification ritual for lepers, as Waltke suggests, it is of no use to David in his situation; for the full process still requires blood (guilt and sin) sacrifice to make atonement, and the law makes no provision for atonement by blood sacrifice for David's sin and guilt. Thus, if David's petition does allude to the purification ritual in Lev 14:4-7, then the efficacy of this petition for the sake of forgiveness of his transgression and cleansing of his sin depends entirely on God's grace, not any (implied) sacrificial shedding of blood. This is supported by the fact that David's petition for purgation by hyssop in Ps 51:7 mentions neither water nor blood. The purgation for which David petitions God is to be effected directly by God's purifying action, symbolized by and effected through the hyssop.

but does so directly, mediated only by his own word. That, of course, is precisely how God announced forgiveness to Israel through the prophets: "I will forgive. . . ." Jesus also tells a parable implying that God's mercy and forgiveness can be mediated by prayer and penitence, apart from sacrifice, apart from water, apart even from Jesus' word. The contrite tax collector prays simply, "God, be merciful to me, a sinner," and Jesus announces that "this man went down to his home justified" (Luke 18:13-14).[34] Through the ministry of Jesus, then, God was exercising sovereign authority to forgive sin freely, "apart from law."[35] *Prior to Jesus' death on the cross, therefore, the shedding of blood was not required as the necessary condition of God forgiving sin.*[36]

11.3.6. God Is Free to Forgive

The Scriptures bear manifold witness — from the story of Genesis to the cult in Leviticus to the message of the Prophets and Psalms to the ministries of John and Jesus — that God does not need bloodshed or sacrifice in order to have mercy on sinners and forgive sins.[37] How, then, to interpret Heb 9:22, "without the shedding of blood there is no forgiveness of sins"? Clearly, Heb 9:22 does not set forth a "universal law" regulating divine forgiveness in "all dispensations" (per Hodge). For all the evidence from Scripture demonstrates that God can and does act freely to forgive sin and cleanse iniquity "apart from law," without requiring sacrificial bloodshed as a prior condition. As Morna Hooker observes, therefore, "it has to be remembered that there were plenty of Jews who experienced God's forgiveness in other ways; it would be foolish to assume, on the basis of this remark, that God 'could not' forgive sins unless Christ had died."[38] All this indicates that we read Heb 9:22 in light of its two crucial qualifications, "under the law almost everything. . . ." We thus concur with Brondos:

> In Heb 9:22, therefore, the author is simply making an observation concerning how purification and forgiveness were obtained according to the stipula-

34. That this parable is set in the Temple does not imply that sacrifice is assumed. Jesus says only, "Two men went up to the temple *to pray* . . ." (Luke 18:10).

35. Cf. Michael Winter, *The Atonement* (Collegeville, MN: Liturgical Press, 1995), pp. 88-90.

36. Concerning the connection between the death of Jesus and the forgiveness of sins, see Chapter 9 above.

37. Morris, *The Atonement*, pp. 57-79, observes that atonement-making does happen apart from the Temple and sacrifice, but considers only cases involving the death of a person or animal and so does not acknowledge the substantial body of evidence of God making atonement and forgiving sin without bloodshed.

38. Morna D. Hooker, *Not Ashamed of the Gospel: New Testament Interpretations of the Death of Christ* (Grand Rapids, MI: Eerdmans Publishing, 1994), pp. 117-18.

tions of the old covenant, rather than arguing about what was possible or impossible for God to do. He does not write that under the law everything *must* be purified with blood, nor that without the shedding of blood there *cannot* be forgiveness of sins, but that the law (that is, according to the commandments regarding sacrifices) *almost* everything is purified with blood (but not *everything*), and the rites stipulated there aimed at procuring atonement or forgiveness prescribe the shedding of blood as part of the expiatory rite.[39]

Noticing that the statements in Heb 9:22 are formed in the *indicative* mood, rather than the imperative, we can put the point simply: this text is *descriptive* of the Levitical cult, not prescriptive and not so restrictive of God's sovereign freedom to forgive sin and cleanse impurity. According to the witness of Scripture, the sovereign God remains free to exercise the divine prerogative of mercy, free to forgive sins unbound by any law, whether external to God's will or intrinsic to God's character.

39. David A. Brondos, *Paul on the Cross: Reconstructing the Apostle's Story of Redemption* (Minneapolis, MN: Fortress Press, 2006), pp. 54-55.

CHAPTER 12

God's Wrath: Requiring Penal Satisfaction?

For the wrath of God is revealed from heaven
against all ungodliness and wickedness
of those who by their wickedness suppress the truth.

ROMANS 1:18

12.1. The Penal Substitution View

God is free to forgive sin as God wills, the penal substitution apologist might concede, but does not God's wrath upon sinners nonetheless need to be satisfied? Was not that, after all, the very necessity of Christ's death, to satisfy God's wrath so that God could forgive sin? J. I. Packer states that the cross of Christ was "a means of quenching God's personal penal wrath against us. . . ."[1] Elsewhere, Packer writes that Christ's death, as propitiation of God, was intended "to dissolve his judicial wrath against us. . . ."[2] I take it that Packer intends "personal penal wrath" to be synonymous with "judicial wrath." Packer thus emphasizes three distinct aspects of God's wrath: it is personal, an expression of God's character; it is penal or judicial, requiring satisfaction by means of retributive punishment; and it is directed "against us." One finds similar depictions of God's wrath in the writings of other penal substitution apologists. Mark Dever emphasizes all three aspects: God's wrath is an expression of his charac-

---

1. J. I. Packer, *I Want to Be a Christian* (Wheaton, IL: Tyndale House Publishers, 1977), p. 60.

2. J. I. Packer, "The Atonement in the Life of the Christian," in Charles E. Hill and Frank A. James III, eds., *The Glory of the Atonement: Biblical, Theological and Practical Perspectives* (Downers Grove, IL: InterVarsity Press, 2004), pp. 409-25, here p. 416.

ter ("God's righteous wrath . . ."), is directed against human beings (". . . against us for our sinfulness"), and is penal, requiring satisfaction by punishment ("By taking our penalty upon himself, God satisfied his own . . . wrath against us"). Jeffery et al. emphasize two aspects: "He is not merely angry at 'sin' in an abstract, impersonal sense . . . it is towards *sinners* that his wrath is directed."[3] As does Stott: God's wrath is an expression of God's character — God's "holy reaction to evil" — and requires penal satisfaction.[4]

The understanding of God's wrath as personal, penal, and "against us" provides the logical linkage between the wrath of God and the cross of Christ within the penal substitution model. Because God's wrath is personal, an expression of God's character, God cannot tolerate sin without compromising his own integrity; because God's wrath is penal, God's wrath can be satisfied only by means of retributive punishment; and because God's wrath is against us on account of our sins, God can express his wrath provoked by sin only by executing retributive punishment upon sinners. Forgiving sinners, therefore, requires satisfaction of God's wrath by execution of retributive punishment upon a substitute for sinners; it is thus necessary that Christ die as a penal satisfaction in place of sinners. This can be compacted into a syllogism: human sin provokes divine wrath; divine wrath requires penal satisfaction; therefore, human sin requires penal satisfaction, such that divine forgiveness of human sin requires penal substitution. Our question is whether or not Scripture gives evidence supporting this syllogism.

To address this question, we will review God's wrath as revealed in the Old Testament and then as understood by Paul. There are several sub-questions to examine here: Is the wrath of God as displayed in the Old Testament *personal* (an expression of God's character) or impersonal? If personal, is it manifest directly by divine intervention or worked out indirectly through the natural course of events, or both? If personal and direct, is God's wrath *penal* in nature, requiring retributive punishment as satisfaction? And is God's wrath directed against human beings themselves? Finally, does Paul understand the wrath of God in such terms — as personal, penal, and "against us"?

3. Steve Jeffery, Michael Ovey, and Andrew Sach, *Pierced for Our Transgressions: Rediscovering the Glory of Penal Substitution* (Wheaton, IL: Crossway Books, 2008), p. 289, emphasis original. For more on the wrath of God within the penal substitution model, cf. Richard Gaffin, "Atonement in the Pauline Corpus," in Charles E. Hill and Frank A. James III, eds., *The Glory of the Atonement: Biblical, Theological and Practical Perspectives* (Downers Grove, IL: InterVarsity Press, 2004), pp. 150-53.

4. John R. W. Stott, *The Cross of Christ* (Downers Grove, IL: InterVarsity Press, 1986), pp. 103, 106, 110.

12.2. The Old Testament Witness to God's Wrath

12.2.1. God's Personal Wrath

The Scriptures do reveal God's wrath as personal, an expression of God's character.[5] And God's wrath is manifest in various ways, both directly (by divine intervention) and indirectly (through the course of events). We will attend here to the wrath of God manifest directly and return later to the wrath of God revealed indirectly.

The personal wrath of God "against us" — wrath as an expression of God's character and directed against human beings — is evident in many biblical texts. In the Psalms, God's wrath or anger is sometimes depicted as being upon an individual person (Pss 6:1; 38:1; 88:16; 102:10), other times as directed toward entire nations or peoples (Pss 2:4-5, 12; 21:9; 78:31; 89:46; 106:23, 40), and yet other times as directed toward humanity in general (Pss 90:7-11; 110:5). Examples of God's personal wrath in the wisdom, narrative, and historical books include God's wrath upon humanity in general (Job 14), against the enemies of Israel (Exod 15:7; 1 Sam 28:18), against Israel for national disobedience (Exod 32:10; Num 11:33; 2 Kgs 22:13, 17; 2 Chron 34:21; 36:16), against Israel and Judah for the transgressions of evil kings (2 Kgs 21:6, 15; 23:26), and against particular individuals or groups within Israel (Numbers 16; 2 Sam 6:7; 2 Chron 12:12; 19:2). The prophets Isaiah and Jeremiah (along with other prophets) depict God's wrath upon Israel and upon the nations because of idolatry, violence, injustice, and oppression (Isa 5:25; 9:9-21; 10:1-4; 14:4-6; 30:27-28; 59:15b-19; Jer 2:35; 3:5; 4:4; 6:11; 7:29-30), and also upon the mass of humanity for its evildoing (Isa 13:6-16; 63:1-6). The Old Testament, then, gives ample witness to God's personal wrath upon humans on account of evildoing.

12.2.2. Is God's Personal Wrath Necessarily Penal Wrath?

The Torah, Prophets, and Psalms thus all testify to the personal wrath of God "against us." It does not follow from this, however, that this wrath of God is necessarily *penal* wrath — provoked by sin and requiring punishment as satisfaction — as the penal substitution model claims. Whether that is so or not

---

5. Several different Hebrew words are translated as "anger," "wrath," "rage," or "fury," and we do not attempt to distinguish them here. For a fuller exposition of YHWH's anger/wrath, see John Goldingay, *Old Testament Theology*, vol. II: *Israel's Faith* (Downers Grove, IL: InterVarsity Press, 2006), pp. 138-42. As Goldingay observes (cf. pp. 136-38), anger or wrath is not God's only or necessarily first response to human sin. The prophets also speak of God "hiding" or "withdrawing" from his people when they have turned away from him to sin.

must wait on what Scripture will show. And we will find that the evidence of Scripture is mixed on this question.

First, regarding what provokes God's personal wrath, we do not find a consistent cause. In nearly all circumstances, it appears that God's personal wrath expresses judgment on sin and transgression (i.e., evildoing). But in at least one incident, God's personal wrath was expressed with deadly consequence on account of inadvertent contact with the holy (2 Sam 6:6-7; 1 Chron 13:9-10) — for a cause other than sin. During the procession to bring the ark of covenant to Jerusalem, the ark was jostled, and one of the attendants steadied the ark with his hand. "The anger of the LORD was kindled against Uzzah; and God struck him there because he reached out his hand to the ark; and he died there beside the ark" (2 Sam 6:7). The explanation for God's wrath is unclear in the Hebrew text and does not appear in the Greek version, leaving the meaning of the text in dispute. Tradition has thus generated various interpretations, which appear in various translations: "for his error" (KJV), or "for his negligence" (NET), or "for his irreverent act" (NIV). But the text itself does not state that Uzzah's action was sinful. Uzzah, then, suffers death by God's wrath, but apparently not on account of having sinned. The text implies that holy things of YHWH are off limits unless approached by those divinely ordained, in a regular manner, at the times appointed because YHWH's holiness is deadly to mortals (cf. Lev 10:1-2; 16:1-2; Num 4:15).

Second, and more important, regarding what turns away God's personal wrath on account of evildoing, we again do not find a consistent cause but a diversity of causes. Sometimes God's wrath is satisfied in retributive punishment (Num 16:20-35; 2 Kgs 17:7-18; Isa 66:15; Zeph 1:7-18; Ps 78:49-51, 56-64). Yet other times God's personal wrath on account of evildoing is turned away by other than penal means. Sometimes it is turned away by human actions, including prophetic or priestly intercession (Exod 32:7-14; Num 11:1-3; Numbers 14; Deut 9:15-21; Ps 106:23) or offering of incense (Num 16:41-50), the righteous zeal of one acting on behalf of God (Num 25:1-13), the transgressor's humility (2 Chron 32:24-26; Zeph 2:1-3; 3:11-13) or confession (Psalm 32), and the nation's prayer and repentance (2 Chron 7:13-14; Jer 4:1-4; Jonah 3). And many times God's wrath is turned away by God-self for his name's sake or because of his great mercy (Isa 12:1; 48:9-11; 57:16-19; Jer 3:12-14; Ezek 20:7-9, 13-14, 21-22; 36:16-32; Dan 9:15-19; Hos 14:4; Pss 6:4; 78:38; 85:1-3; 106:45).

The evidence of Scripture thus does *not* warrant the conclusion that God's personal wrath is *necessarily* penal wrath. God's personal wrath is not provoked only by evildoing but also by inadvertent contact with the holy, and what turns away God's personal wrath on account of evildoing is not necessarily punishment but also intercession, zeal, confession, repentance, and God's own mercy. The personal wrath of God against sinners thus does not necessarily require penal satisfaction; God does not necessarily require punishment as satisfaction for sin. God's personal wrath, therefore, does not display the consistency and invariability required to play the logical role assigned to it by the penal substitution model. For its manifold expression in various circumstances does not exhibit a necessary linkage between sin (provocation) and punishment (satisfaction), contrary to what penal substitution assumes. The personal wrath of God cannot be reduced to the middle term of a syllogism between sin and punishment, as penal substitution would have it. As revealed by Scripture, God's personal wrath eludes human domestication by logical formulas and resists a rational reconstruction under the law of retribution.[6] This should warn us against making any generalizations concerning God's wrath.[7]

12.3. The Pauline Witness: "The Wrath of God" in Romans 1

When we turn to Paul, we find that his references to the wrath of God are also too varied to allow generalization.[8] Paul does refer to God's personal wrath upon the disobedient (Rom 1:18, 2:5; Eph 5:6; Col 3:6). Some of his references to God's wrath characterize humanity's situation in sin until now (Rom 1:18; Eph 2:3; 1 Thess 2:16); others point to future judgment, a "day of wrath" yet to come (Rom 2:5; 5:9; Eph 5:6; Col 3:6; 1 Thess 1:10; 5:9). Only two of Paul's references to God's wrath refer explicitly to penal consequences — one concerning wrath in the present and judgment executed by governing authorities (Rom 13:4), and one concerning wrath in the future and judgment to be executed by God (Rom 2:5-11).

Because the penal substitution model depicts the cross of Christ as the solution to the problem of God's personal penal wrath upon sinners, the question for us concerns whether Paul connects God's wrath concerning the human sin-situation to the cross in such terms — personal, penal, and "against us" — or not. And it is not at all obvious that Paul links God's wrath concerning human sin to the cross in the way that the penal substitution model assumes. The key text to consider here, of course, is Rom 1:18: "For the wrath of God *(orgē tou*

---

6. As further evidence that God's wrath is beyond rational explanation, one has only to review the sequence of stories in Numbers 11–12, in which the diverse appearances of God's wrath have neither consistent cause nor consistent resolution and thus cannot be comprehended by a logical formula linking sin, wrath, and punishment.

7. So Leon Morris, *The Atonement: Its Meaning and Significance* (Downers Grove, IL: InterVarsity Press, 1983), claims, "There is a consistency about God's wrath in Scripture" (p. 153). His claim is twofold: first, "one thing and one thing alone aroused God's anger, and that was sin" (p. 154); second, "God's wrath is not put away by some human activity . . . its removal is due to none less than God himself" (p. 157). As we have seen, the evidence of Scripture confounds Morris's generalization on both counts.

8. For further discussion, see G. L. Borchert, "Wrath, Destruction," in Gerald F. Hawthorne, Ralph P. Martin, and Daniel G. Reid, eds., *Dictionary of Paul and His Letters* (Downers Grove, IL: InterVarsity Press, 1993), pp. 991-93.

theou) is revealed from heaven against all ungodliness and wickedness of those who by their wickedness suppress the truth" (NRSV).

12.3.1. The Penal Substitution View

The penal substitution model reads the opening statement of Paul's argument in Rom 1:18-32, that humanity in sin is under the wrath of God, as setting the stage for the introduction of the cross of Christ in 3:21-26. God's wrath and Christ's cross are counterpoints in the drama of salvation: God's wrath necessitates Christ's death as penal satisfaction for sin, and Christ's death suffices to propitiate God's wrath. The cross is the necessary and sufficient solution to the problem of human sinners under God's wrath. Thus, Schreiner: "The line of argument in Romans 1:18–3:20 provokes us to ask how God's wrath can be averted. We discover in Romans 3:25 that God's wrath has been satisfied or appeased in the death of Christ."[9] If we examine Romans 1 carefully, however, the text does not actually read the way that penal substitution assumes.

12.3.2. What Paul Says: "Wrath upon All Impiety and Injustice"

First, while the "wrath" of which Paul speaks in Rom 1:18 is evidently personal ("the wrath *of God*"), it is *not* "against us." God's wrath, Paul writes, is "upon all impiety and injustice" *(epi pasan asebeian kai adikian)*. The way Paul actually puts it, the object of God's wrath is not human beings themselves, but their wicked ways and evil deeds, which is made clear by the Greek construction of the text. God's wrath is revealed against, not humanity itself, but the evildoing of humanity.

12.3.3. What Paul Says: "God Gave Them Up"

Recognizing that the wrath of God in Rom 1:18 is directed at evildoing rather than "against us," we can ask whether God's wrath "upon all impiety and injustice" might be interpreted in other than penal terms. As understood by penal substitution, "the wrath of God" is necessarily something external to the cause-effect order of creation, a judicial penalty imposed directly by divine intervention in the world. Thus, Jeffery et al.:

---

9. Thomas R. Schreiner, "Penal Substitution View," in James Beilby and Paul R. Eddy, eds., *The Nature of the Atonement: Four Views* (Downers Grove, IL: InterVarsity Press, 2006), p. 87. Cf. Jeffery et al., *Pierced for Our Transgressions*, p. 81.

[I]t is simply impossible to maintain that "God's wrath" in Romans (or indeed anywhere else) refers simply to the natural out-working of sin in human experience. It is rather his active, retributive response to sin, a judicial penalty, imposed in accordance with his personal righteous hostility to everything that is evil.[10]

We do not doubt God's power and freedom to actively intervene in the natural order, nor do we think it impossible that God might do so to execute judgment on human evildoing. But is this *necessarily* the means of God's judgment? And is that what Paul has in mind in Romans 1? Earlier, we asked whether God's personal wrath is manifest directly by divine intervention or worked out indirectly by the course of events, or both. Whereas penal substitution (per Jeffery et al.) insists that the former is the only mode of God's wrath and denies that the latter is even possible to consider, we think the answer is "both" — and that the latter is what Paul has in mind. Not only can we maintain an alternative view of "the wrath of God," but the textual evidence in Romans 1 gives us several clues pointing in that direction.

Paul describes the situation of sinful humanity under divine judgment in Rom 1:18-32 as one of denial leading to depravity. Having "suppress[ed] the truth" of God's immortality and power, even though these are evident to all through the cosmos God has created, humans "became futile in their thinking" and "exchanged the truth about God for a lie and worshiped and served the creature rather than the Creator" (1:18-25). That is, humanity denies the Creator by idolizing the creation; and from this idolatry humanity descends into ever-deepening depravity and ever-worsening perversity (vv. 26-32). In describing this situation, Paul says three times that "God gave them up" to falling further into the pit of sin by their own choice (vv. 24, 26, 28).[11]

It is this — God "giving up" human beings to the evil consequences of their own God-denying choices — that reveals "the wrath of God upon all impiety and injustice." The final consequence of humanity's descent into sin is the end pronounced by God from the beginning: those who choose sin as a way of life "are deserving of death" (Rom 1:32, my translation).[12] As Paul writes, "So what advantage did you then get from the things of which you are now ashamed? The end of those things is death" (6:21). Paul depicts the idea here with a financial metaphor, "the wages of sin is death" (v. 23), and elsewhere with an agricul-

---

10. Jeffery et al., *Pierced for Our Transgressions*, p. 80.

11. Jeffery et al., *Pierced for Our Transgressions*, pp. 77-80, conveniently neglect this thrice-repeated emphasis by Paul that "God gave them up."

12. The usual translation here is "deserve to die" (NRSV, NET). The Greek reads *hoi ta toiauta prassontes axioi thanatou eisin*, which may be translated as "the ones doing such things are deserving *(axioi . . . eisin)* of death *(. . . thanatou . . .)*." That is, death is the fitting or proper end of those who live a life of sin.

tural metaphor, those who sow sin reap corruption and death as their harvest (Gal 6:7-8). Either way, the point is the same: death is the end that befits a life of sin. The "wrath of God" as depicted by Paul in Romans 1 is thus manifest, not as an external penalty imposed directly by divine intervention, but rather in the outworking of sin to its own end in death.

Paul's depiction in Romans 1 of divine judgment upon human sin and the link between human sin and God's wrath is rooted in Israel's prayerbook. When Paul argues subsequently "that all, both Jews and Greeks, are under the power of sin" and hence that all humanity stands under God's wrath and judgment (Rom 3:1-20), he cites the Psalms no less than seven times. The Psalms depict God's wrath and judgment upon evildoing similarly to Paul's description in Romans 1. As Paul writes that "God gave up" humans to the consequences of their choices, so the psalmist has written of God concerning a disobedient nation: "But my people did not listen to my voice; Israel would not submit to me. So I gave them over to their stubborn hearts, to follow their own counsels" (Ps 81:11-12). God "hands over" human beings to receive the evil end of their own devising.

Humans suffering the eventual consequences of evil choices, as a manifestation of divine justice, is a common theme in the Psalter. Several psalms of lament express the desire that personal enemies or enemy nations fall under God's wrath and judgment. These psalms expect to see the judgment of God revealed when evildoers reap the evil they sow by injustice and violence rebounding against them and falling on their own heads. In this way, God's wrath is revealed, not directly by divine intervention, but indirectly as evil works itself out through the course of events to the downfall and destruction of evildoers. Consider Psalm 7, for example, concerning personal enemies:

> Rise up, O LORD, in your anger; lift yourself up against the fury of my enemies . . . you have appointed a judgment. . . . See how they conceive evil, and are pregnant with mischief. . . . They make a pit, digging it out, and fall into the hole that they have made. Their mischief returns upon their own heads, and on their own heads their violence descends. (Ps 7:6, 14-16)

When evildoers suffer the evil they have made, we see the "judgment" that God has "appointed." Similarly, Psalm 9, concerning the nations: "The nations have sunk into the pit that they have made; in the net that they have hid has their own foot been caught. The LORD has made himself known, he has executed judgment; the wicked are snared in the work of their own hands" (Ps 9:15-16). When nations reap the evil they have sown, God "has executed judgment." Such depictions of God's wrath and judgment are also found elsewhere in the Psalter (Pss 37:12-15; 57:6; 59:12-13; 69:22-25; 140:8-11).[13]

---

13. Goldingay interprets Psalm 94, which calls upon the "God of vengeance" to give the arrogant and wicked their just deserts (vv. 1-2), in similar terms. Whereas translations commonly

This understanding of divine wrath is also witnessed in the Prophets (cf. Obadiah 15; Zeph 1:14-18). Isaiah depicts God's wrath as God both "hiding his face" from a sinful people and "handing them over" to their sin so that the people are overcome by sin's consequences: "But you were angry, and we sinned; because you hid yourself, we transgressed. We have all become like one who is unclean . . . and our iniquities, like the wind, take us away . . . for you have hidden your face from us, and have delivered us into the hand of our iniquity" (Isa 64:5b-7). Fiddes thus comments:

> In fact when the prophets and psalmists think more personally about the relationship between God and his people, they speak of the divine judgement upon human beings in another way, in terms of his "giving up" people to the natural consequences of their own sin. It is characteristic of Hebrew thought to depict God as "hiding his face" from his disobedient people, or "letting them go." His righteous wrath against sin is worked out by his surrendering people to the way they themselves desire to tread.[14]

12.3.4. *The Wrath of God in Romans 1: An Alternative View*

Drawing on the Psalms, then, Paul depicts God revealing wrath upon sin by "giving up" rebellious humanity to sin so that the evil consequences of our chosen disobedience fall on our own heads, resulting in further depravity and perversity. Such wrath is not, as penal substitution would insist, an external penalty imposed directly by divine intervention in the natural order. It is manifest indirectly in the natural order through the outworking of one's evildoing to its end.[15]

---

read that God will "repay them for their iniquity and wipe them out for their wickedness" (v. 23 NRSV; cf. NIV), Goldingay argues that the more natural translation of the Hebrew text is that God repays the wicked by means of the consequences of their own wicked deeds: "he is bringing back their wickedness upon them; he will put an end to them through their evil doing" (*Israel's Faith*, p. 144; cf. pp. 607ff.).

14. Paul S. Fiddes, *Past Event and Present Salvation: The Christian Idea of Atonement* (Louisville: Westminster/John Knox, 1989), p. 92.

15. This discussion implicitly involves the philosophical question concerning divine action in the created order, which we cannot address at length here. Jeffery et al. are surely right to question an understanding of God's wrath that excludes God from the outworking of sin in death. They thus rightly reject the "false dichotomy" between "personal" and "impersonal" wrath, the idea that the operation of divine wrath in the natural order "excludes the possibility of any sort of personal response to evil on God's part" (*Pierced for Our Transgressions*, p. 78; cf. Fiddes, *Past Event and Present Salvation*, p. 93). Having rejected that false dichotomy, however, it does not follow that "the wrath of God" in Romans 1 must be seen as an external penalty imposed directly by divine intervention, as they insist. Their argument would seem to rest on another false dichotomy — that either an event is the directly intended, immediate effect of God's

Averting this divine wrath does not require penal satisfaction. Because it is manifest in the outworking of one's evildoing, one might avert this wrath and avoid sin's end by active repentance, turning from evildoing to doing right. Or, if one is already fallen, or about to fall, into the pit dug by one's own sin, averting the end of one's sin requires divine deliverance: "For evils have encompassed me without number; my iniquities have overtaken me. . . . Be pleased, O LORD, to deliver me; O LORD, make haste to help me" (Ps 40:12-13). Or both:

> There is no soundness in my flesh because of your indignation; there is no health in my bones because of my sin. For my iniquities have gone over my head; they weigh like a burden too heavy for me. . . . For I am ready to fall, and my pain is ever with me. I confess my iniquity; I am sorry for my sin. . . . Do not forsake me, O LORD; O my God, do not be far from me; make haste to help me, O Lord, my salvation. (Ps 38:3-4, 17-18, 21-22)

While there is no doubt that humanity caught in its own sin needs redemption, the "wrath of God" to which Paul refers in Romans 1 does not fit the penal substitution model, which requires penal satisfaction as the prior, necessary condition of redemption.

In reaching this conclusion, I concur with several previous studies. John Driver: "Romans 1:18-32 appears to describe precisely this type of manifestation of God's wrath in which the horrible consequences of disobedience to God

---

personal power, or else God is entirely excluded from the event. Between those extremes lies a middle position — the distinction, maintained by Augustine and Aquinas, between primary and secondary causation. (Concerning Augustine, see Ernan McMullin, "Natural Science and Belief in a Creator," in Robert J. Russell, William R. Stoeger, S.J., and George V. Coyne, S.J., eds., *Physics, Philosophy, and Theology: A Common Quest for Understanding,* 2nd ed. [Vatican City: Vatican Observatory Foundation, 1995], pp. 58-59; concerning Aquinas, see Alister E. McGrath, *Science and Religion: An Introduction* [Oxford: Blackwell Publishing, 1999], p. 105, and *Nature: A Scientific Theology,* vol. 1 [Grand Rapids, MI: Eerdmans Publishing, 2001], pp. 167-73.) On this view, God is the primary cause of all things, originating the cosmos in creation and upholding the natural order by his conserving power and concurring will; nonetheless, the causal structure of the natural order has a God-endowed sufficiency and so operates according to its God-created capacities without need for divine intervention. Natural events are not merely the occasions on which God acts to produce effects; rather, God is the primary cause of the created order within which events occur by secondary (natural) causes, which include human choices. When sin works itself out to its own end, the natural order is the secondary cause of such consequences; but God is still the primary cause of that natural order. One could thus see "God giving up" humanity to sin as God's personal choice *not* to actively intervene in the natural order of secondary causes and so to allow human beings to suffer the ensuing consequences of their sinful choices. The distinction between primary and secondary causation, characteristic of the Catholic tradition, is not necessarily inimical to the Calvinist thinking of Jeffery et al. Charles Hodge, the Reformed theologian, articulated a view of divine providence that recognizes secondary causation. See his *Systematic Theology* (Grand Rapids: Eerdmans Publishing, 1940), vol. I, part I, chapter XI.

come down on the heads of the evildoers."[16] Luke Timothy Johnson: "God's wrath therefore is the symbol for the destruction that humans bring on themselves by rebelling against the truth. . . . It is a retribution that results, not at the whim of an angry despot but as the necessary consequence of a self-distorted existence."[17] James Dunn: "This is the 'wrath of God': to grant humans their desires when their desires are lusts, to grant men and women their self-indulgent choices — and the consequences of those choices."[18] Green and Baker: "Sinful activity is the result of God's letting us go our own way — and this 'letting us go our own way' constitutes God's wrath."[19] And I. Howard Marshall: "God's judgement upon sin is the abandoning of sinners to a situation without him, so that they are left under the power of sin and false gods that cannot save, and the end result is death. That is the nature of judgement, in that God wills it to be so. It leaves sinners to their own sin."[20] We note also that even the penal substitution apologists Jeffery et al., their previous arguments to the contrary notwithstanding, eventually come to effectively affirm this same view: "in Romans 1:18-32 God responds in anger to people's sin by withdrawing his restraining hand and leaving them to it."[21]

12.4. "Standing in the Breach" — Bearing God's Wrath?

12.4.1. *The Penal Substitution View*

We have already referred to the intercessory ministry of Moses, whose prayer before God on behalf of others turns away God's wrath (Exod 32:7-14; Num 11:1-3; 14; Deut 9:15-21; Ps 106:23). The Old Testament examples of God's wrath being turned away by intercession merit closer attention — they provide a key analogy for understanding the prophetic and priestly ministry of Jesus as intercessor before God on behalf of humanity. Jesus "is at the right hand of God" and "indeed intercedes for us" (Rom 8:34); he is the "great high priest" who "always lives to make intercession for . . . those who approach God through him" (Heb 4:14-16; 7:25).

---

16. John Driver, *Understanding the Atonement for the Mission of the Church* (Scottdale, PA: Herald Press, 1986), p. 161.

17. Luke Timothy Johnson, *Reading Romans: A Literary and Theological Commentary* (Macon, GA: Smyth and Helwys Publishing, 2001), p. 33.

18. James D. G. Dunn, *The Theology of Paul the Apostle* (Grand Rapids, MI: Eerdmans Publishing, 1998), pp. 122-23.

19. Joel B. Green and Mark D. Baker, *Recovering the Scandal of the Cross: Atonement in New Testament and Contemporary Contexts* (Downers Grove, IL: InterVarsity Press, 2000), p. 55.

20. I. Howard Marshall, *Aspects of the Atonement: Cross and Resurrection in the Reconciling of God and Humanity* (London: Paternoster, 2007), p. 61.

21. Jeffery et al., *Pierced for Our Transgressions,* p. 262.

The penal substitution model interprets Jesus' intercessory role, of course, as one of substitution: Jesus stands "in our place" under God's wrath, bearing the penalty of death imposed upon us for our sins. According to this model, the intercessor functions to turn away God's wrath *from the sinners* by bearing that wrath *upon himself* through self-substitution. The question here is whether such a view of Jesus' intercession finds precedent in the examples of wrath-turning intercession in the Old Testament.

12.4.2. *"Standing in the Breach"*

Christoph Schroeder examines several texts where God's servant is depicted as "standing in the breach" to turn away God's wrath (Ps 106:23) and finds there a pattern of intercession other than that of the penal substitution model. He writes:

> There are texts concerning the interaction between God's wrath and a human representative that follow another logic than that of the model of satisfaction or the scapegoat theory. In these texts, the individual does not act as a passive scapegoat [an innocent substitute victim] for God's wrath. To the contrary, one person's active doing of justice within and in representation of the human community turns the divine wrath away. This is precisely what defines the relationship between God's wrath and the human representative expressed by the metaphor "to stand in the breach."[22]

The wrath-provoking "breach" needing repair is created by the covenant community's failure to do justice and righteousness. God's wrath thus expresses God's desire that righteousness and justice be done "on earth as in heaven." When God looks on his covenant community and sees unrighteousness and injustice rampant in the land, he searches the land to find one who will "stand in the breach" and do reparative justice on behalf of the community:

> The people of the land have practiced extortion and committed robbery; they have oppressed the poor and needy, and have extorted from the alien without redress. And I sought for anyone among them who would repair the wall and stand in the breach before me on behalf of the land, so that I would not destroy it; but I found no one. Therefore, I have poured out my indignation upon them; I have consumed them with the fire of my wrath; I have returned their conduct upon their heads, says the Lord GOD. (Ezek 22:29-31)

22. Christoph Schroeder, "'Standing in the Breach': Turning Away the Wrath of God," *Interpretation* 52 (1998), 16-23, here p. 18.

God's wrath is poured out when God sees unrighteousness and injustice in the community but there is "no intercessor" to intervene, to end injustice and put things right (cf. Ezekiel 13; Isa 59:15b-19). God's wrath is turned away when God finds the one who will intercede "on behalf of the land," who will "repair the wall" of righteousness and "stand in the breach" of justice. What saves the land and people from destruction, therefore, is not that someone bears God's wrath in place of others, but that someone does reparative justice on behalf of the covenant community. Indeed, the one who removes oppression and restores justice is called "the repairer of the breach" (Isa 58:9b-12).

12.4.3. Prophetic Intercession: The Ministry of Jeremiah

The special intercessory role of the prophet in turning away God's wrath is illustrated negatively in the ministry of Jeremiah. God looks at the city of Jerusalem and, having seen injustice running rampant in the streets and truth lying wounded in the public square, summons his prophet to search the city for one who will intervene on behalf of the many: "Run to and fro through the streets of Jerusalem, look around and take note! Search its squares and see if you can find one person who acts justly and seeks truth — so that I may pardon Jerusalem" (Jer 5:1). So Jeremiah searches the whole city but finds no one who keeps the law: all have broken the covenant (5:4-5; 6:9-13). No one else having been found to intervene, God instructs Jeremiah to preach in the temple, to denounce injustice, violence, and idolatry, and to warn the people to repent if they are to avoid disaster (7:1-15). God then instructs Jeremiah to refrain from interceding any further on behalf of the people, who have neither listened nor repented:

> As for you, do not pray for this people, do not raise a cry or prayer on their behalf, and do not intercede with me, for I will not hear you. . . . Is it I whom they provoke? says the LORD. Is it not themselves, to their own hurt? Therefore thus says the Lord GOD: My anger and my wrath shall be poured out. . . . (7:16-20)

That God instructs Jeremiah to stop interceding implies that Jeremiah has already been interceding. In a later lament to God, Jeremiah recalls his earlier intercession: "Remember how I stood before you to speak good for them, to turn away your wrath from them" (18:20). After the Babylonians had taken the national leadership into exile, Jeremiah would once again intercede, this time on behalf of the remnant in Jerusalem (ch. 42). And that God instructs Jeremiah twice more to refrain from interceding for the people (11:14; 14:11) makes evident both Jeremiah's persistence in intercession and the potential for prophetic intercession to turn away God's wrath.[23] In the absence of a prophet to intercede, God's unabated wrath will be poured out on account of the people's evildoing and impiety. God thus warns the nation: unless there is someone to "stand in the breach" and act with reparative justice on behalf of the people, wrath is surely coming: "Hear the word of the LORD, O house of David! Thus says the LORD: Execute justice in the morning, and deliver from the hand of the oppressor anyone who has been robbed, or else my wrath will go forth like fire, and burn, with no one to quench it, because of your evil doings" (21:11-12). Conversely, the prayerful, powerful intercession by the prophet on behalf of a sinful people repairs the breach, turning away God's wrath and saving the people from destruction.

12.4.4. Prophetic Intercession: The Ministry of Jesus

This special role of intercessor before God on behalf of the people is evident in the ministry of Jesus. In Luke's Gospel, we see Jesus following the prophetic pattern and fulfilling the role of the faith-keeping, justice-doing, truth-telling servant who intercedes on behalf of the people to avert the wrath of God. After Jesus has "set his face to go to Jerusalem" (Luke 9:51), he twice intercedes for Jerusalem, praying that it would turn from the path of violence and receive God's gift of peace, but warning of calamity to come if it does not (13:34-35; 19:41-44). Entering Jerusalem, Jesus intercedes a third time with a prophetic sign in the Temple, calling the leaders of the people to repent from their ways of injustice and restore right worship and righteous living among the people (19:45-46). The leaders do not heed the exhortation and warning of God's prophet, however, but instead seek to kill him (19:47; cf. 13:34).

Now, the nation-Temple leaders have done a dastardly deed — they have conspired against and taken the life of the Lord's anointed one. The crucifixion of Jesus has thus broken wide open the breach of justice in the covenant community. Although justified by the leaders of the people as violence necessary to save the nation and Temple from destruction (cf. John 11:47-53) and to uphold

23. Elmer A. Martens, *Jeremiah* (Believers Church Bible Commentary; Scottdale, PA: Herald Press, 1986), p. 75. Hermann Spieckermann, "The Conception and Prehistory of the Idea of Vicarious Suffering in the Old Testament," in Bernd Janowski and Peter Stuhlmacher, eds., Daniel P. Bailey, trans., *The Suffering Servant: Isaiah 53 in Jewish and Christian Sources* (Grand Rapids, MI: Eerdmans Publishing, 2004), pp. 1-15, has argued that Jeremiah is prohibited by God from taking up the prophetic role of intercessor (p. 11). In all three instances (7:16; 11:14; 14:11), however, the "do not" is formed with *'al-*, not *lô'*, which indicates that it is only a temporary injunction ("stop"), not an absolute prohibition ("you shall not"). That is, God is not denying Jeremiah the prophetic role of intercessor but only instructing him to not intercede further in this specific situation. Jack R. Lundbom, *Jeremiah 1-20* (Anchor Bible; New York: Doubleday, 1999), confirms this point: "Jeremiah is being told, 'do not pray at the present time,' not 'do not ever pray again'" (p. 474).

piety (cf. Mark 14:55-64; Matt 26:59-66), in truth this violent act of injustice and impiety puts the nation in danger of God's wrath (cf. Ps 2:4-6). But Jesus, the righteous servant of the Lord, takes the initiative to "stand in the breach," acting with reparative justice while nailed to the very instrument of his unjust death. Jesus, petitioning God's mercy, intercedes once more on behalf of the sinful nation whose leadership has betrayed God's covenant: "Father, forgive them; for they do not know what they are doing" (Luke 23:34). Jesus' act of prophetic-priestly intercession in death on behalf of many, and God's merciful offer of repentance and forgiveness "in the name of Jesus," repairs the breach of justice, thus turning away God's wrath and bringing healing and peace to all those who approach God through Jesus.

This might also be a way to understand Jesus' ministry of reconciliation as depicted by Paul in Rom 5:1-11. Jesus puts himself forward into the breach between humanity and God, intervening on behalf of the ungodly and sinful out of God's own love for those at enmity with him (vv. 6-8). At the cost of his life, the shedding of his own blood, Jesus acts with justice to repair and right the relationship, thus averting God's wrath (i.e., future judgment) upon humanity (v. 9) and reconciling humanity to God (vv. 10-11). Through the costly faithfulness of Jesus on our behalf, justice is done, we are put right ("justified") before God, and peace is restored (v. 1).[24]

After examining examples of intercessory, wrath-turning justice-doing (Ezek 22:30-31; Jer 5:1; Exod 32:11-13), as we have done here, Schroeder writes:

> How does one person's act save a whole people? The metaphor "to stand in the breach" gives a clear answer. Not by presenting oneself as a scapegoat, but by exposing oneself, by acting on behalf of others, by risking one's life for others is a people saved. Does God *need* a scapegoat? No. God's wrath is not directed against those who "stand in the breach." It is poured out when no one is willing to go up into the breach, when nobody is willing to act on behalf of others.[25]

The prophetic-priestly intercessor, rather than bearing God's wrath in place of sinners, turns away God's wrath by acting with faith and justice that repairs the breach. The wrath-turning intercession of God's servant on behalf of the people, as evident in the ministries of both Jeremiah and Jesus, therefore, does not fit the penal substitution model.

---

24. Concerning Jesus as intercessor for our reconciliation with God, see Michael Winter, *The Atonement* (Collegeville, MN: Liturgical Press, 1995), pp. 101-14.

25. Schroeder, "Standing in the Breach," p. 20.

CHAPTER 13

The Suffering Servant — a Penal Substitute?

But he was wounded for our transgressions,
crushed for our iniquities;
upon him was the punishment that made us whole,
and by his bruises we are healed.

ISAIAH 53:5

We have reached three conclusions in Chapters 10-12: atoning sacrifice concerns neither propitiation of wrath nor satisfaction of retribution, God's forgiveness is not necessarily conditional upon sacrificial bloodshed, and God's wrath does not necessarily require penal satisfaction. Nonetheless, it might be that God chooses to satisfy his wrath against sin through penal substitution — by executing retributive punishment on an innocent substitute. Apologists for penal substitution point to the Fourth Servant Song in Isaiah 52–53 as a key example of God making atonement for sin by penal substitution.[1]

13.1. A Significant Text: Canon within the Canon

The New Testament writers depict the life and ministry, suffering and death of Jesus in terms of the Suffering Servant, by both direct quotation (Matt 8:17; Luke 22:37; John 12:38; Acts 8:32-33; 1 Pet 2:21-25) and literary allusion.[2] One can

---

1. Cf. John R. W. Stott, *The Cross of Christ* (Downers Grove, IL: InterVarsity Press, 1986), pp. 145-49, and Steve Jeffery, Michael Ovey, and Andrew Sach, *Pierced for Our Transgressions: Rediscovering the Glory of Penal Substitution* (Wheaton, IL: Crossway Books, 2008), pp. 52-67.

2. For a survey of these references, see Joel Marcus, "The Old Testament and the Death of Jesus," in John T. Carroll and Joel B. Green, eds., *The Death of Jesus in Early Christianity* (Peabody, MA: Hendrickson Publishers, 1995), pp. 213-18.

argue that Isaiah 53 functioned as a "canon" or "rule of faith," not only for the early church as it recounted the life and death of Jesus, but for Jesus himself as he understood his own life and death.[3] So John Stott: "there is good evidence that his whole public career, from his baptism through his ministry, sufferings and death to his resurrection and ascension, is seen as a fulfillment of the pattern foretold in Isaiah 53."[4]

We quite agree with Stott on this point, but not necessarily with his view that it is "definite without doubt" that the Suffering Servant is a penal substitute.[5] Thomas Schreiner also thinks that Isaiah 53 is an open-and-shut case in favor of penal substitution: "The passage also teaches clearly and often that Christ Jesus died in the place of sinners, taking their penalty on himself."[6] So interpreted, Isaiah 53 would lend substantial support to penal substitution: because the New Testament writers depict the passion of Christ as fulfilling the Suffering Servant, if the Suffering Servant is a penal substitute, then it is plausible to conclude that the New Testament writers understood Jesus' death also to be a penal substitution. Jeffery et al. state the case with confidence:

> It seems obvious on first reading of the text that the Servant is portrayed as a penal substitute, willingly taking upon himself the sin and punishment of others, suffering in their place in accordance with God's will and under God's hand. And surely the many New Testament allusions to this passage establish beyond doubt that Jesus and the apostles understood Jesus' death in the same way.[7]

3. See William R. Farmer, "Reflections on Isaiah 53 and Christian Origins," in William H. Bellinger, Jr. and William R. Farmer, eds., *Jesus and the Suffering Servant: Isaiah 53 and Christian Origins* (Harrisburg, PA: Trinity Press International, 1998), pp. 260-80. Regarding how Isaiah 53 was interpreted by the early church, see Christoph Markschies, "Jesus Christ as a Man before God: Two Interpretive Models for Isaiah 53 in the Patristic Literature and Their Development," in Bernd Janowski and Peter Stuhlmacher, eds., Daniel P. Bailey, trans., *The Suffering Servant: Isaiah 53 in Jewish and Christian Sources* (Grand Rapids, MI: Eerdmans Publishing, 2004), pp. 225-323.

4. Stott, *Cross of Christ,* p. 146.

5. Stott, *Cross of Christ,* p. 147. Penal substitution apologists thus focus much of their attention regarding the Suffering Servant on one phrase in the final verse of the Song, "he bore the sin of many" (53:12c). This, they insist, can mean no otherwise than that the Suffering Servant is a penal substitute on whom is laid the legal penalty (death) for the sins of others. Cf. J. Alan Groves, "Atonement in Isaiah 53," in Charles E. Hill and Frank A. James III, eds., *The Glory of the Atonement: Biblical, Theological and Practical Perspectives* (Downers Grove, IL: InterVarsity Press, 2004), pp. 61-89. For an alternative reading of "sin bearing," see David A. Brondos, *Paul on the Cross: Reconstructing the Apostle's Story of Redemption* (Minneapolis, MN: Fortress Press, 2006), pp. 112-22.

6. Thomas R. Schreiner, "Penal Substitution View," in James Beilby and Paul R. Eddy, eds., *The Nature of the Atonement: Four Views* (Downers Grove, IL: InterVarsity Press, 2006), pp. 67-98, here p. 86.

7. Jeffery et al., *Pierced for Our Transgressions,* p. 52.

It is clear enough to me that the New Testament writers appeal directly and deliberately to the Song of the Suffering Servant in a twofold way: as a platform for proclaiming "the good news about Jesus" (Acts 8:30-35) and as a prophecy of righteous, redemptive suffering fulfilled in the life and death of Jesus (Matt 8:14-17; 1 Pet 2:21-25). It does not necessarily follow, however, that the New Testament writers thus understand Jesus' death as penal substitution. That would follow only if the Song itself understands the suffering of the Servant as penal substitution. And whether the case for the penal substitution view of the Suffering Servant is as obvious, clear-cut, and beyond doubt as it seems to Stott, Schreiner, and Jeffery et al. requires a careful re-reading of the text.

Several interpretive questions attend this text.[8] As with the other Servant Songs in Isaiah (42:1-4; 49:1-6; 50:4-9), the primary question concerns the Servant's identity: Is the Servant an individual person (God's prophet) or a collective personality (God's people)?[9] Both readings are possible for each of the four songs. While Christian tradition has tended to interpret the Servant as having an individual identity that is fulfilled in Jesus Christ, Jewish tradition has tended toward identifying the Servant with Israel as a people and setting the Songs' fulfillment against an eschatological horizon.[10] We will be concerned here not with the Servant's identity but with whether the pattern of the Servant's suffering and death as depicted in the Fourth Song fits the penal substitution model. As familiar by now, two claims lie at the core of the penal substitution model: (1) Jesus' death propitiates God's wrath upon sinners because (2) Jesus' death in place of sinners satisfies retribution for sin. The question here, then, is whether this is so of the Suffering Servant in Isaiah 53.

13.2. The Servant's Suffering: A Propitiation of God?

13.2.1. The Penal Substitution View

Let us consider, first, propitiation. The Song gives no indication that the suffering of the Servant is directed toward God as propitiation of wrath. There is not so much as a single allusion to, much less mention of, God's wrath in the entire Song, no suggestion that God is angry and needs to be appeased. However we

8. Cf. Henning Graf Reventlow, "Basic Issues in the Interpretation of Isaiah 53," in Bellinger and Farmer, *Jesus and the Suffering Servant,* pp. 23-38.

9. Cf. R. E. Clements, "Isaiah 53 and the Restoration of Israel," in Bellinger and Farmer, *Jesus and the Suffering Servant,* pp. 39-54. Hans-Jürgen Hermisson, "The Fourth Servant Song in the Context of Second Isaiah," in Janowski and Stuhlmacher, *The Suffering Servant,* pp. 16-47, argues that the Servant in all four songs should be understood as *both* the prophet himself and Israel as a people.

10. Marcus, "The Old Testament and the Death of Jesus," pp. 223-24.

interpret the Servant's ministry of suffering, it is thus far from obvious that it has anything to do with propitiating God. To interpret the Servant's suffering as propitiating God's wrath would require reading into the Song certain presuppositions that would only beg the question.

Schreiner, for example, cites Isa 53:10a, "it was the will of the Lord to crush him with pain," as proof positive that "In his death Christ satisfied the wrath of God."[11] Schreiner here makes two implicit assumptions: that "the will of the Lord" implies the wrath of God, and that what satisfies God's wrath is suffering. These assumptions are much less than obvious, especially considering that the context gives no indication of God's wrath. Even if we grant the assumption that this verse implies the wrath of God, to infer that the Servant's suffering satisfies God's wrath requires logically making the further assumption that God's wrath requires penal satisfaction. Far from proving the point, Schreiner's reading of the text presupposes the conclusion to be proved and thus begs the question; that is, instead of using the Suffering Servant text to support the penal substitution model, Schreiner reads the Suffering Servant according to penal substitution. Besides being logically circular, Schreiner's reading of the text is based on a false premise. As we have demonstrated (Chapter 12), the scriptural evidence does not support the claim that there is a necessary link between God's wrath and penal satisfaction. If the Suffering Servant is to lend support to the penal substitution model, therefore, that support must rest substantially on the penal aspect of the Servant's death.

13.2.2. An Alternative Reading

The Fourth Servant Song, moreover, suggests an alternative reading on this point. The Hebrew text of Isa 53:10a can also be translated to read that God "desires," or "delights," or "takes pleasure" in the Servant's suffering. This verb *(ḥāphēṣ)* used elsewhere in the Prophets speaks of God's desire for and delight in righteousness and justice done out of covenant loyalty and the pleasure that God takes in those who do as much (cf. Isa 56:4; Jer 9:23-24; Hos 6:6; Ps 147:10-11). Furthermore, the prophet Ezekiel declared also that God does not will the death of the wicked, that God is not pleased by the death of sinners for their sins: "As I live, says the Lord God, I have no pleasure *(ḥāphēṣ)* in the death of the wicked, but that the wicked turn from their ways and live" (Ezek 33:11; cf. 18:23). We might then ask: If God does not take any "pleasure" in the *just* punishment and death of the *wicked*, why would God take "pleasure" in the *unjust* punishment and death of the *righteous*? If it is not God's will that even sinners should die the death they deserve, why would it be God's will that his Servant

---

11. Schreiner, "Penal Substitution View," p. 86.

should die a death he does not deserve? We might thus infer: what God wills, and so what pleases God, is undying covenant loyalty and suffering for sake of righteousness and justice. God delights, not in the Servant's suffering itself, but in the Servant's willingness to suffer in service to the covenant and God's covenant people (Isa 53:10b-12).

Before turning to the penal aspect of the Servant's death, we must address another important point of translation. Most English translations of Isa 53:10b speak of the Servant's life being "an offering for sin" (KJV, NRSV) or "sin offering" (TNIV). These translations apparently follow the Greek text (LXX), which speaks of the Servant's life being given "concerning sin" *(peri harmatias)*, which might be interpreted as the formula for the "sin offering" in Leviticus.[12] The Hebrew word traditionally rendered as "sin offering" throughout the Torah is *ḥaṭṭā't*. But here the Hebrew text reads *'āšām*, which is rendered traditionally in the Torah as "trespass offering" (KJV) or "guilt offering" (NRSV, NASB, TNIV). The NASB is consistent in rendering *'āšām* as "guilt offering" both in the Torah and in Isa 53:10b.[13] Whichever translation we choose, however, neither propitiation nor retribution is necessarily implied. As we have demonstrated (Chapter 10), neither the sin offering *(ḥaṭṭā't)* nor the guilt offering *('āšām)* functioned as propitiation of wrath or satisfaction of retribution. We will consider below how translation of this verse might make a difference for interpreting the Servant's suffering and death.

13.3. The Servant's Death: A Penalty for Sin?

Let us consider, then, retribution. There is a penal aspect of the Servant's death. Having committed no violence or deceit for his own part, the Servant suffers a punishment of death that he does not deserve. The Suffering Servant is a victim of injustice, for he is wrongly condemned and innocently executed (Isa 53:7-9). But is his unjust execution intended as a penal substitution? Is he punished with death in place of others? Is his punishment intended to satisfy retribution?

---

12. Concerning the complex relations and various differences between the Hebrew and Greek versions of Isaiah 53, see David A. Sapp, "The LXX, 1QIsa, and MT Versions of Isaiah 53 and the Christian Doctrine of Atonement," in Bellinger and Farmer, *Jesus and the Suffering Servant*, pp. 170-92. For an alternative take on the same question, see E. Robert Ekblad, "God Is Not to Blame: The Servant's Atoning Suffering according to the LXX of Isaiah 53," in Brad Jersak and Michael Hardin, eds., *Stricken by God? Nonviolent Identification and the Victory of Christ* (Grand Rapids, MI: Eerdmans Publishing, 2007), pp. 180-204.

13. Joseph Blenkinsopp, *Isaiah 40–55* (Anchor Bible; New York: Doubleday, 2002), also translates "guilt offering" — cf. pp. 346, 351.

13.3.1. *"For Our Transgressions"*

The key verse in the Song is Isa 53:5. Most English translations say that the Servant is wounded and crushed "for" the transgressions and iniquities of the people (53:5a). How do we read this "for"? One might read it with a substitutionary sense, to mean that the Servant is put to death *in place of* or *instead of* others to pay the penalty for their sins, but the text itself does not say as much. One could also read this "for" to mean only that the Servant suffers and dies *on behalf of* or *for the sake of* others.

However one might interpret this "for" in English, consideration of the Hebrew and Greek texts of 53:5a leads to a different reading. We would translate the Hebrew text more accurately to read that the Servant is wounded and crushed "from" the iniquities and transgressions of others. The Hebrew preposition here is *min,* meaning "from" or "out of" in various senses, including "because of" or "by reason of." It does not have the meaning of substitution — "in place of" or "in exchange for."[14] Such a translation is supported by the Greek (LXX) text at 53:5a, which uses the preposition *dia* with the accusative case, meaning "because of" or "on account of." We should thus read Isa 53:5a to say that the Servant is "wounded because of our transgressions, crushed on account of our iniquities."[15] This alternative reading fits well with the text at 53:8, where the same Hebrew preposition is used to say that the Servant is put to death "out of" *(min)* an unjust trial, "from" *(min)* the people's transgression. We might thus translate: "As a result of an unjust trial he was taken away . . . he was . . . stricken because of the rebellion of my people."[16] I concur with Morna Hooker: "In other words, the Servant suffered *as a result of* the sins of others."[17] We will consider below how this alternative translation makes a difference for interpreting the Servant's suffering and death.

13.3.2. *Exclusive or Inclusive Place-Taking?*

Otfried Hofius has argued that that the Suffering Servant is an example of "exclusive place-taking" or substitution, but that the New Testament writers apply Isaiah 53 to Christ under the idea of "inclusive place-taking" or representation.[18] Thus, while rejecting the penal substitution view of the cross, Hofius

---

14. Thus, "A *min* B" implies here that B is the cause of A, that A happens as a result of B.

15. Blenkinsopp, *Isaiah 40–55,* p. 345. This is the reading chosen by the New English Translation — see the NET text note for Isa 53:5a.

16. Cf. NET translation and notes of Isa 53:8.

17. Morna D. Hooker, "Did the Use of Isaiah 53 to Interpret His Mission Begin with Jesus?" in Bellinger and Farmer, *Jesus and the Suffering Servant,* p. 96, emphasis original.

18. Otfried Hofius, "The Fourth Servant Song in the New Testament Letters," in Janowski

nonetheless argues that such is how we should read the Suffering Servant in Isaiah 53.[19] The crucial evidence for Hofius's substitutionary view of the Suffering Servant is the repeated emphasis in the Hebrew text that "*he* bore" the pains and sins of others (53:4a, 11b, 12c).[20]

The logic of Hofius's argument would seem to be this: while the people sin but do *not* suffer for their sins, the Servant, who does not sin, does suffer, but not for his *own* sins; taking the place of the people, the Servant suffers for their sins; the suffering they deserve has been transferred onto the Servant instead. Notice that, in order for this text to exemplify the logic of substitution, the Servant's suffering must be *exclusive* of the people: insofar as *he* suffers for their sins *in place of* them, *they* do *not* suffer. Jeffery et al., defending the penal substitution view based on Hofius's argument, emphasize this key point: "he experiences the punishment due to them, and they do not. Indeed, the sufferings experienced by the Servant are not shared by Israel precisely *because* he experienced them in their place, as their substitute."[21] The question here is not whether the Servant suffers the ill consequences of the people's sin — that he does so is quite clear in the text. The question, rather, is whether Servant suffers those consequences in place of the people — and, hence, whether the people are spared the consequences of their own sin. The penal substitution view of the Suffering Servant claims that the people do not suffer for their sins but are spared the suffering they deserve. If that proves not to be the case, if the people (as well as the Servant) *do* suffer the consequences of their own sin, then the Suffering Servant can*not* be an example of penal substitution.

Considering the first, and arguably the most important, of the places where the text emphasizes that "he" bore "our" suffering, "Surely he has borne our infirmities and carried our diseases" (53:4a). I think that Hofius perhaps misses something in the text. He appropriately calls attention to the emphasis in the Hebrew text on "he" but neglects the equal emphasis on "our" — it is *our* sicknesses that he bears, *our* diseases that he carries.[22] He thus overlooks a key point of ambiguity: How are we to interpret this "our"? Is it "our" suffering because it

---

and Stuhlmacher, *The Suffering Servant*, pp. 163-88. It is only the former, not the latter, thesis with which we take issue here. Regarding the latter, we are quite in agreement with Hofius.

19. Cf. Jeffery et al., *Pierced for Our Transgressions*, pp. 54-55.

20. Hofius, "The Fourth Servant Song," pp. 164-65.

21. Jeffery et al., *Pierced for Our Transgressions*, p. 56, emphasis original.

22. The emphasis on "he" in the text is observed by the use of the personal pronoun, which is not required grammatically. One does not find a parallel use of the possessive pronoun "our" in the text, however, because Hebrew lacks self-standing possessive pronouns, which appear only as pronominal suffixes. Nonetheless, there is a correlation in the text between use of the personal pronoun "he" (*hû'*) and use of the pronominal suffix "our" (*-ênû*), which produces rhyming in the poetic structures of 53:4a and 5a. This rhyming pattern, noticed only by reading aloud the Hebrew text, brings out the equal emphasis on "he" and "our."

is *due* to "us," anticipated as judgment coming to "us" — "ours" *de jure?* Or is it "our" suffering because it *afflicts* "us," having already fallen upon "us" — "ours" *de facto?* Or both — "ours" *de jure* and *de facto?* Hofius's argument presupposes the first reading: the Servant's suffering is the rightful due of the people, which falls on the Servant instead, sparing them the suffering they deserve.

The text of the Song, however, leaves this ambiguous, allowing for the possibility that "our" suffering is *both* a due judgment and a present reality. In that case, "we" have been bearing "our" sicknesses and carrying "our" diseases; the suffering that is "ours" by right has already fallen upon "us" in fact: "we" *are* suffering what "we" *deserve.* That the Servant bears "our" suffering on himself would thus imply that the suffering due to "us," which "we" are already experiencing as judgment for "our" sin, has now fallen on "him." The implication would then be that "he" *shares* in "our" suffering, that "he" suffers *with* "us" in the consequences of "our" sin. Exclusivity would apply here, not to suffering, but to guilt: "we" and "he" are both suffering, but only "we" deserve it.

How we interpret this ambiguity in the text depends in part on the implied background against which we read the Fourth Servant Song. Hofius's argument would seem to read the Servant's suffering against a background of the "prospering wicked" as portrayed in the biblical wisdom literature. These are the ones who do evil but are not suffering any ill consequences for it; instead, they are enjoying good health and abundant wealth (cf. Ps 73:3-12). On such a reading, the Servant suffers the ill consequences of sin that the wicked do *not* suffer — hence, the Servant suffers "in place of" the wicked, the consequences of their sins having been transferred to him.

The historical situation and canonical context of Second Isaiah — exile — suggests a different background, that of a people burdened under the weight of their own iniquity and bearing the wounds of their own transgressions.[23] Both the deuteronomic historian and the prophet Isaiah understood Israel's exile in Babylon as the consequence of the nation's sins (cf. Deut 4:25-31; 28:15-68; 2 Kgs 23:26-27; 24:3-4, 19-20; Isaiah 1; 40:1-2; 42:24). Now, were the Servant's death a penal substitution, such that he suffers in place of the people and dies to pay the penalty for their sins, we would expect that the people for whom he suffers and dies would not be suffering the consequences of their own sins; by the logic of substitution, those consequences would be transferred to the Servant instead, sparing the people the suffering they deserve. Were the Servant's suffering and death a penal substitution, therefore, we would expect the Servant to suffer exile in place of the people. To the contrary, the people *do* suffer exile for their owns sins, which reveals God's judgment upon his people. And having suffered exile as the consequence of their own sin, the people need redemption by God

---

23. Cf. Paul D. Hanson, "The World of the Servant of the Lord in Isaiah 40–55," in Bellinger and Farmer, *Jesus and the Suffering Servant,* pp. 9-22.

from the captivity into which their own sin has delivered them (cf. Isa 42:18-25; 43:25-28; 49:13, 24-26; 50:1; 51:21-23).

The Servant takes the part of his people in sin, bearing their burden on himself. He suffers with and on behalf of — indeed, as a result of — his people for the sake of their redemption (cf. Isa 40:11; 41:10, 13; 43:1-2, 22-24; 46:3-4). The Servant's suffering, therefore, is *redemptive* but *not exclusive* of the people. I thus concur with Hooker:

> . . . if we remember that the Servant was not the only person to be suffering, these statements read rather differently from the way in which they are normally interpreted. The so-called Servant did not escape suffering, even though he was innocent; on the contrary, he seems to have borne the brunt of the suffering. The suffering which he endured belonged by right to his people. What we have here is not "vicarious suffering," *if* by that we mean substitutionary suffering — the anomalous "exclusive place-taking" which is without parallel in Old Testament thought; rather we have an example of "*inclusive* place-taking" or what we in English normally term "representation."[24]

Such an alternative reading would lend itself naturally to the New Testament use of Isaiah 53 to interpret the life-ministry of Jesus. Jesus ministers by offering himself to the people's need for healing: "That evening they brought to him many who were possessed with demons; and he cast out the spirits with a word, and cured all who were sick. This was to fulfill what had been spoken through the prophet Isaiah, 'He took our infirmities and bore our diseases'" (Matt 8:16-17). Jesus heals the people by taking their part, taking upon himself the burden of ill from which they were suffering.

13.3.3 "Made Us Whole"

The Song says, further, that the punishment of the Servant effects peace *(šālôm)* and healing for the people (Isa 53:5b). The penal substitution view reads this to say that the Servant's punishment effects peace because his death has satisfied the requirements of retribution: payment for sin has been made by his death, and thus the people gain peace. The text does imply that peace is gained by the people as a result of the punishment endured by the Servant.[25] But the text does *not* say that the penal death of the Servant effects peace *because* retribution has been satisfied, *because* payment for sin has been made. Indeed, the Song says explicitly quite the opposite — that, far from satisfying retribution, the death

---

24. Hooker, "Did the Use of Isaiah 53 to Interpret His Mission Begin with Jesus?" p. 97, emphasis original.

25. The phrase, "punishment of our peace" (Isa 53:5b), is a genitive of result, "punishment that resulted in our peace" (see NET text note).

penalty executed upon the Servant is a "perversion of justice" (v. 8a). The Servant's death is an *unjust* punishment resulting from "an unjust trial" (NET).

If we are to conclude here that the Servant's suffering has brought healing and peace to the people because the Servant has been punished with death, then we must do so against the consistent witness of the prophets. The prophets agree: injustice is destructive, not productive, of peace (cf. Isa 32:17; 59:8-9; Jer 6:13-15); healing is the result, not of injustice, but of justice (cf. Isa 58:1-14; Jer 5:1). Unless we are to discount this testimony, we must understand the link between the punishment and death of the Servant and the healing and peace of the people in terms other than penal substitution.

One might thus give an alternative reading here, too: the Servant's punishment has brought peace to the people, not because it has satisfied justice (which it did not), but because it has brought their suffering to an end. How might this be? Perhaps in this: by seeing this righteous one suffer unjustly the death penalty that they themselves justly deserve, the people finally come to their senses and turn from iniquity. The Servant's death shocks the people's conscience (cf. Isa 52:14), bringing them to repentance; the Servant's righteous suffering turns the people from "our own way" to God's way (cf. 53:6). Such repentance leading to righteousness satisfies God's will: "As I live, says the Lord GOD, I have no pleasure in the death of the wicked, but that the wicked turn from their ways and live. . . . And when the wicked turn from their wickedness, and do what is lawful and right, they shall live by it" (Ezek 33:11, 19). This, then, might be what the Song means by saying, "The righteous one, my servant, shall make many righteous, and he shall bear their iniquities" (Isa 53:11b). The Servant "makes many righteous" by "bearing their iniquities" in that, by suffering unjustly the deathly consequences of their iniquity, he moves the people to confession and repentance, to forsake injustice and violence for righteousness and peace. And having forsaken their sin and turned to God, they no longer suffer the consequences, thus again enjoying peace (cf. Ps 34:11-14).

This alternative reading fits well with the most extensive — and, from the penal substitution view, most important[26] — citation of the Suffering Servant in the New Testament, 1 Pet 2:21-25. Echoing the Suffering Servant (Isa 53:7-9), Peter interprets Christ's suffering "for you" as "an example, so that you should follow in his steps" (1 Pet 2:21). Like the Suffering Servant, Christ had done nothing to deserve death — "He committed no sin, and no deceit was found in his mouth" (v. 22) — yet he was condemned and executed. He willingly suffered unjustly at the hands of sinners, enduring violent abuse without retaliation, trusting his vindication to God (v. 23). Christ thus bore the consequences of human sins upon himself, voluntarily taking our injustice and violence into his own body through the cross. His purpose in suffering the death of sinners was

26. Cf. Jeffery et al., *Pierced for Our Transgressions*, pp. 62-65.

to free us from sin that leads to death and enable us to live for righteousness: "He himself bore our sins in his body on the cross, so that, free from sins, we might live for righteousness" (v. 24a). And the suffering of Christ has freed us from sin by showing us the way of righteousness: "by his wounds you have been healed. For you were going astray like sheep, but now you have returned to the shepherd and guardian of your souls" (vv. 24b-25). Having witnessed Jesus' righteous suffering "for us," we are moved to repent, to turn from sin and back to God.[27]

We thus conclude: the Servant's suffering and death are *vicarious,* "for" others,[28] but it does not necessarily follow that they are substitutionary, "in place of" others. The Servant's suffering and death are also *redemptive* as much as they are vicarious, bringing healing and peace, but it does not necessarily follow that they are redemptive because retribution has been paid its due. While it is *possible* to read the Fourth Servant Song as confirming the penal substitution model, it is surely not *necessary* — or obvious.[29] To claim that it is "definite beyond doubt" that the Suffering Servant is a penal substitute, as does Stott, asserts far more than the text itself can warrant.[30]

13.4. Three Points of Interpretation

Before developing an alternative reading of the Suffering Servant, we need to consider carefully certain points in the text, beginning with the two items deferred above.

13.4.1. "We Accounted Him Stricken by God"

First is the translation of the preposition *min* in Isa 53:5a — "from" rather than "for." This translation is not only lexically accurate but also helps us to see more clearly this verse in relation to the preceding and succeeding verses. The preceding verses read,

27. I agree with Jeffery et al., *Pierced for Our Transgressions,* p. 97, that Christ's action "for us" as depicted in 1 Pet 2:21-25 is more than exemplary. As we will show (in Chapter 18 below), however, the "substitution" here is not the exclusive place-taking of penal substitution but rather the inclusive place-taking that Morna Hooker has termed "interchange."

28. Cf. Hermann Spieckermann, "The Conception and Prehistory of the Idea of Vicarious Suffering in the Old Testament," in Janowski and Stuhlmacher, *The Suffering Servant,* pp. 1-15.

29. So Jeffery et al., *Pierced for Our Transgressions,* pp. 52-61, while acknowledging several of the points made here, nonetheless maintain a substitutionary reading. That being said, the certainty with which they argue the case is much overstated.

30. Stott, *Cross of Christ,* p. 147.

> He was despised and rejected by others;
>> a man of suffering and acquainted with infirmity;
> and as one from whom others hide their faces
>> he was despised, and we held him of no account.
> Surely he has borne our infirmities
>> and carried our diseases;
> yet we accounted him stricken,
>> struck down by God, and afflicted. (vv. 3-4 NRSV)

These verses present us with contrasting and alternating perceptions of the Servant, set off by "surely" and "yet" in v. 4. "Surely," *'āchēn*, sets up a contrast and implies a truth told against what has been previously (and wrongly) thought or said. This contrast is subsequently strengthened by the use of the personal pronouns *hû'* ("he") and *'năḥnû* ("we"), which emphasize the alternation and opposition between what "we" thought of "him" and what "he" has actually done.

This contrast of perceptions characterizes the Song's middle section. The Song's beginning and final sections (52:13-15; 53:11b-12) speak in the voice of "I," YHWH, concerning "my servant." The middle section of the song (53:1-11a) speaks in the voice of "we," the people, concerning "him," the Servant. The contrasting perceptions of the Servant belong to "we," the people. As Janowski interprets the Song, this contrast sets into opposition the perspectives of the people "before" and "after" the revelation of YHWH's vindication of his Servant (53:1b): "surely" marks the "after" perspective, and "yet" marks the "before" perspective.[31] The news that YHWH has vindicated his Servant (52:13-15) astonishes the people, generating wonderment and inducing a gestalt shift in "our" perception (53:1a NET): "Who would have believed what we just heard?"

Before his vindication, the people denied the Servant's divine vocation — "we held him of no account" (53:3c) — and thus saw the Servant's suffering as divine affliction: he was "struck down by God" (v. 4b). After his vindication, the people now see the Servant's suffering as solidarity with the people: "surely," the Servant is "a man of suffering and acquainted with infirmity" (v. 3b), for he is the one who "has borne our infirmities and carried our diseases" (v. 4a). The "yet" in v. 4b shifts perspective from "after" back to "before," creating dissonance within "our" image of the Servant. The people see the same Servant before and after his vindication, but give opposite reasons for his suffering. Before his vindication, the people, having rejected the Servant

---

31. Bernd Janowski, "He Bore Our Sins: Isaiah 53 and the Drama of Taking Another's Place," in Janowski and Stuhlmacher, *The Suffering Servant*, pp. 48-74; see esp. pp. 60-65. Concerning the crucial verse, 53:4, he writes, "This unassuming sentence is one of the keys to understanding" the drama depicted in the Song (p. 60).

(v. 3a), saw their rejection as reflecting God's rejection and so projected God's judgment onto the Servant's suffering. After his vindication, the people see the Servant's suffering as a sharing in the people's suffering by virtue of his divine vocation (vv. 2-3). This contrast between "surely" and "yet" implies that the "before" image of the Servant is off the mark: "struck down by God" is how "*we* accounted him," but this is *not* the truth about the Servant's suffering as revealed by YHWH's vindication.

The next verse continues the contrast of perceptions:

> But he was slain from *(min)* our rebellion,
>   injured from *(min)* our transgressions. . . . (v. 5a, my translation)

As "yet" had done in the preceding verse, so "but" shifts perspective again, from "before" to "after" — from "our" mistaken accounting to the true accounting of the Servant's suffering.[32] Translating the preposition "from" helps the contrast between these opposing views stand out in clearer relief. Previously, "we accounted him . . . struck down by God," but that accounting had been off the mark — he was slain because of "us." Previously, "we" had wanted to believe that the Servant's suffering was God's judgment upon him, but he suffered as a result of "our" rebellion. By projecting God's judgment onto the Servant, "we" have tried to disburden ourselves of responsibility for the Servant's suffering. YHWH's vindication of his Servant, however, places responsibility where it truly lies: the Servant's suffering indicts, not "him," but "us."

This alternation of contrasting perceptions thus presents "us" with an uncomfortable truth that does not conform to the popular image of the Servant: "his" afflictions are not divine judgment, but human injustice; "he" is struck down, not by God, but by "us." The New English Translation does well to reflect these nuances in the text:

> He was despised and rejected by people,
> one who experienced pain and was acquainted with illness;
> people hid their faces from him;
> he was despised, and we considered him insignificant.
> But he lifted up our illnesses, he carried our pain;
> even though we thought he was being punished, attacked by God,
> and afflicted for something he had done.
> He was wounded because of our rebellious deeds,
> crushed because of our sins. . . . (Isa 53:3-5a NET)

---

32. In the Hebrew text, "yet" and "but" translate the usual conjunction *waw,* which can take various senses depending on context. Given the sharp contrast set up in 53:4, translating the conjunction here with the sense of opposition is appropriate.

Faced with the truth revealed by YHWH's vindication of his Servant, "we" are moved from self-justification to confession — that the Servant has suffered as a result of "our" injustice and rebellion, hence that "our" salvation (peace and healing) is the undeserved benefit of the righteous-doing of the very one "we" had despised and rejected:[33]

> . . . he endured punishment that made us well;
> because of his wounds we have been healed.
> All of us had wandered off like sheep;
> each of us had strayed off on his own path,
> but the LORD caused the sin of all of us to attack him. (vv. 5b-6 NET)[34]

Having recognized "our" guilt in the Servant's suffering and confessed responsibility accordingly, "we" can now see clearly and speak truly concerning the Servant: "he" has neither done wrong nor spoken falsely, but "he" has suffered and died by the oppression and injustice of others — indeed, from "our" sin and transgression (vv. 7-9).

Hooker comments concerning such an alternative reading as we have given here:

> If this is a correct interpretation, then what is being said in this chapter is, first of all, that the Servant suffers *as a result of the sins of others*. The onlookers thought him guilty, but now that he has been vindicated by God, they realize that he was innocent. He suffered, not because of his own sins, but because of theirs. If we forget our Christian presuppositions, and read the text in that light, it comes across in a new and interesting way. . . .[35]

What is "new and interesting" here is that the fourth Servant song shows how divine redemption confounds human reason and transcends human expectation. As Janowski points out, the "we" perspective is premised on the "action-consequences connection," which assumes that all suffering is punishment deserved for individual sin. In these verses (vv. 3-9), the moral calculus of the "we" breaks down; for the drama of redemption ruptures the logic of retribution.[36] The perspective of the "we" — "our" assumptions concerning God's justice

---

33. Janowski, "He Bore Our Sins," p. 60.

34. See the NET notes for these verses.

35. Hooker, "Did the Use of Isaiah 53 to Interpret His Mission Begin with Jesus?" p. 97, emphasis original.

36. Cf. Janowski, "He Bore Our Sins," pp. 63-64. Janowski makes his point here for the same reason we have above: "They now realize that the Servant's suffering was the consequence not of his actions but of their actions, the actions of others. This is indicated by the causative formulations with [*min*] in verse 5a: 'pierced *because of* our transgressions, crushed *because of* our iniquities'" (p. 64, emphasis original). See also pp. 49-54, 70-74.

and, hence, "our" accounting of the Servant's suffering — has been shaped by the retributive paradigm, which the Song exposes and critiques.

13.4.2. "Sacrifice of Reparation"

Second is the translation in Isa 53:10b — "guilt offering" rather than "sin offering." As we have seen (Chapter 10), the *'āšām* dealt with breaches of justice in the covenant community created by transgressions that cause harm and so incur guilt and require reparation (Lev 5:14–6:7). Making reparation for transgression required both restitution to the victim to repair the harm done and sacrifice to God to repair the covenant breach. One thus finds the NJB translating *'āšām* in the Torah as "sacrifice of reparation."

The use of *'āšām* in Isaiah 53 is evidently metaphorical: the Servant is not being depicted literally as a sacrificial victim offered on the temple altar.[37] What, then, might this mean? By speaking of the Servant's life as an *'āšām* — "sacrifice of reparation" — put forth by God, I suggest that the Song depicts the Servant's ministry as God's way of dealing with the people's guilt by "repairing the breach" of covenant justice created by their rebellion.[38] This recalls our discussion of "standing in the breach" (Chapter 12). We showed how the life-ministry of Jesus reflects the pattern of the faithful prophet who intercedes on behalf of the whole community by "stepping into the breach" to act with reparative justice. Might the Suffering Servant also fit this pattern? We think so and will elaborate this idea below.[39] In both cases, the Servant of the Lord "repairs the breach" at the cost of his own life. As Schroeder observes, ". . . stepping into the breach can include laying down one's life. But this has nothing to do with punishment by God."[40]

---

37. For another possible reading of *'āšām* here, see the NET notes to Isa 53:10.

38. Cf. Janowski, "He Bore Our Sins," pp. 67-69. Janowski also offers a non-sacrificial interpretation of v. 10, translating *'āšām* as "a means of wiping out guilt" with this gloss: "'Surrender of *one's own life* as a means of wiping out guilt' is therefore identical with 'taking over the consequences of *other's actions*.' As I see it, the expression about the vicarious 'bearing' of the guilt of others (v. 4a; cf. vv. 11b, 12b) means to say nothing more than this" (p. 69, emphasis original).

39. Jostein Ådna, "The Servant of Isaiah 53 as Triumphant and Interceding Messiah: The Reception of Isaiah 52:13–53:12 in the Targum of Isaiah with Special Attention to the Concept of the Messiah," in Janowski and Stuhlmacher, *The Suffering Servant*, pp. 189-224, argues that the Aramaic Targum version of Isaiah depicts the Suffering Servant as an intercessor on behalf of the people after the pattern of Moses (cf. pp. 214-22). Ådna concludes: "As the intercessor for Israel the Messiah does not hesitate to jump into the "breach" between sinners and God that resulted from their guilt" (p. 222).

40. Christoph Schroeder, "'Standing in the Breach': Turning Away the Wrath of God," *Interpretation* 52 (1998), 16-23, here p. 20.

13.4.3. God and the Servant

Finally, we need to attend to an overall pattern in the song. As we have seen already, the prophetic perspective of the song affirms that human evildoing is the direct cause of the suffering and death of the Servant. At the same time, the song presents the suffering and death of the Servant as *both* God's doing *and* the Servant's doing.[41] In this respect, the song portrays a "duality" of God and Servant:

A   God lays on the Servant the burden of the sins of others: "the Lᴏʀᴅ has laid on him the iniquity of us all" (Isa 53:6c);

A′ yet the Servant also takes on himself the burden of the sins of others: "he bore the sin of many" (vv. 11c, 12c).

B   The Servant suffers and dies according to the will of God: "it was the will of the Lᴏʀᴅ to crush him with pain" (v. 10a);

B′ yet the Servant also suffers and dies of his own willing: "he poured himself out to death" (v. 12b).

C   God puts forth the Servant's life as a "guilt offering" (v. 10b);

C′ yet the Servant himself also acts on behalf of those who are guilty: he "made intercession for the transgressors" (v. 12c).

The Hebrew text emphasizes this "duality" by using the same verb to depict the actions of both God and Servant. God chooses not to intervene in the people's rebellion to spare the Servant's life, but "lets" the consequences of the rebels' iniquity "strike" (*hiphgîaʿ; pāgaʿ* hiphil perfect) the Servant (v. 6c).[42] And the Servant, according to God's will, "interposes" (*yaphgîaʿ; pāgaʿ* hiphil imperfect)

---

41. Cf. Thomas R. Yoder Neufeld, *Recovering Jesus: The Witness of the New Testament* (Grand Rapids, MI: Brazos Press, 2007), pp. 254-56; Hermann Spieckermann, "The Conception and Prehistory of the Idea of Vicarious Suffering in the Old Testament," pp. 5-8.

42. The use of the hiphil (causative) stem of the verb is reflected explicitly in the NET translation, "the Lᴏʀᴅ *caused* the sin of all of us to attack him" (Isa 53:6c). The question for translation here is how to interpret the causation involved: How does God "cause" the consequences of the people's sin to fall on the Servant? Invoking a distinction from medieval philosophy (Augustine and Aquinas), we can ask whether this is primary or secondary causation: Does God directly impose the consequences of the people's sin on the Servant by an act of intervention, or let the consequences of the people's sin fall on the Servant through the course of events? The Hebrew grammar allows for either possibility: God "causes to attack" (NET) or God "lets strike" (my translation). It could be the former, but the latter makes good sense here: God chooses *not* to intervene to prevent the evil consequences of the people's injustice from striking down his Servant, but instead consents to let those consequences fall on the Servant and then acts to vindicate him. In this way, God's will is done by both secondary and primary causation — the people strike the Servant down, but God raises him up — just as in the case of Jesus (cf. Chapter 7 above).

himself between the rebels and the consequences of their iniquity, choosing to bear the people's sin upon himself (v. 12c).

Now, one might be tempted to infer here that God directly imposes a punishment of death upon the Servant in place of the people (per penal substitution). To read the text in that way would nullify the context, which, as we have demonstrated above, repeatedly emphasizes just the opposite: the popular accounting, that the Servant is "struck down by God," is wrong, for "we" have unjustly killed him (vv. 4b-5a, 8). Nonetheless, the text and its context do emphasize God's active role in this drama: God desires that the Servant interpose himself between the people and the consequences of their rebellion in order to deal with their guilt (vv. 10b, 12c); God lets the people's rebellion strike down the Servant (v. 6c); and thus the Servant suffers and dies according to God's will (v. 10a). It does not follow from this that God purposed to put his Servant to death, but rather that God desires that this righteous one intercede on behalf of the unrighteous many, even to the point of suffering himself the deathly consequences of others' sins.

Not only does the suffering and death of the Servant involve the will and action of both God and Servant, therefore, but the will and action of both are in perfect concord. The implication is important: neither does God act upon the Servant against his will, nor does the Servant direct his action toward God to change his will. The Servant is not God's "victim," and God is not "propitiated" by the Servant's death. The Servant is no powerless pawn of divine power, but a willing participant in God's purpose. Nor is the Servant a passive victim of human evildoing, but an agent of justice and peace in the face of injustice and violence. God and the Servant act in concert to deal justly with sin in order to bring about the healing of the people, repair of the covenant, and restoration of peace. The life and ministry, suffering and death of the Servant thus manifests a "two-sidedness" that will be paralleled in the life and ministry, suffering and death of Jesus.

13.5. An Alternative Reading of the Suffering Servant

13.5.1. Doing Justice and Making Peace at Cost to One's Life

With all this in mind, we can now offer an alternative reading of the Suffering Servant. Let's begin with the metaphorical depiction of the Servant's life as a "sacrifice of reparation" ('āšām) put forth by God (Isa 53:10b) and poured out by the Servant (v. 12b). This language suggests that the Servant offers his life to repair a breach of justice within the covenant community. As we have observed, the song narrates the story of the Servant against the implied background of a people in rebellion against God, a community on the brink of calamity or in the midst of collapse (cf. chs. 56–59).[43] Powerless to save themselves, the people are in dire need of redemption from the consequences of their sins. A community in crisis thus faces a crucial question: "What happens when a people is stumbling toward extinction under the burden of its sin-induced infirmities and diseases, and the traditional institutions of sacrifice and atonement have proven ineffectual to relieve them of their sin and guilt?"[44] The people cry to God for someone to intervene, and God calls his Servant to "step into the breach," to intercede on behalf of the covenant community, to right injustice and restore peace.

How, though, shall the Servant right injustice and restore peace? By punishing the transgressors with retribution and crushing the rebels with violence? Not this Servant of the Lord. Far from seeking to defeat and destroy the perpetrators of injustice and the enemies of peace, the Servant intercedes to save the very transgressors and rebels that have breached justice and violated peace (53:12c). Instead of dealing with the wicked by means of fraud and force (v. 9b), the very sins that have caused the breach, the Servant deals with them by peaceable means (v. 7b) intended to lead them onto the path of justice (v. 11b). Indeed, rather than acting against the people, the Servant suffers in solidarity with them, taking upon himself their affliction and oppression, the affliction and oppression they suffer because of their own rebellion and transgression (vv. 3-4a, 7a).

But the Servant's solidarity in suffering with the people for the sake of their redemption is very costly for the Servant. Through his intercession, the Servant gives up his life for others, "he pour[s] himself out to death" on behalf of a sinful people (vv. 8-9, 12b-c). The Servant intervenes to repair the harm done by the people's transgression, but he himself is injured by their transgression; the Servant intercedes to end the people's rebellion, but he himself is slain by their rebellion (vv. 4-5a). Not only does the Servant give his life for others, he dies at the hands of those for whom he gives his life; not only does the Servant die by an act of rebellion (v. 8), he dies a rebel's death (v. 12b).

Nonetheless, it is God's desire that the Servant intervene to do justice and make peace, even at the cost of his life. God delights in the Servant's willingness to act according to God's covenant and perform the righteousness that God desires; and God takes pleasure in the Servant's readiness to suffer and die on be-

43. Cf. Hanson, "The World of the Servant of the Lord in Isaiah 40–55," pp. 17-20.

44. Hanson, "The World of the Servant of the Lord in Isaiah 40–55," p. 18. As Perry Yoder has observed, during the Babylonian captivity it was impossible to offer sacrifices for sins because the Temple had been destroyed and the priests had been exiled. Thus, the sacrificial system cannot be said to have been "ineffectual," as Hanson writes, because sacrifice for sin was simply not being made. We would thus emend Hanson's comment here to read: "What happens when . . . the traditional institutions of sacrifice and atonement *are unavailable* to relieve them of their sin and guilt?"

half of others out of loyalty to God's covenant (v. 10). And it is through the Servant's self-sacrificial intercession that God's will for the covenant community is fulfilled (vv. 10c-11). Indeed, by means of the Servant's self-sacrificial intercession, the breach of injustice is healed and the peace of the people is restored (v. 5b). Hanson comments aptly:

> What is being described is not a scapegoat loaded with the iniquity of the people and then slaughtered capriciously as a substitute. Rather we encounter one who, having identified his human will with divine redemptive purpose, enters into solidarity with a people at their nadir point, in their guilt-ridden disease, and acts in partnership with God to break the bondage that is destroying them.[45]

Because of the Servant's justice-doing and peacemaking in faithfulness to and fulfillment of God's will, God honors and exalts the Servant, reversing the evildoing of humanity and demonstrating power before the nations (52:13-15; 53:11a, 12a).[46]

13.5.2. Parallels with Jesus

This reading of the Suffering Servant, we will all recognize, parallels closely the life-ministry, death, and resurrection of Jesus Christ as told in the Synoptic Gospels and Acts. Both the Servant and Jesus act according to God's will, doing justice and making peace in faithfulness to the covenant, at cost to their own lives (cf. Chapter 12 above).

Now, there is one sense in which the Servant suffers and dies "in place of" others. The Servant dies not only by the transgressions of the people against God's covenant, but the Servant dies wrongly condemned for the transgressions of which those who condemn him are themselves guilty. In this sense, the Servant bears the guilt and suffers the death belonging to the people (cf. Isa 53:4-9). There is here, too, a close parallel with Jesus. The chief priests and the high council condemned Jesus on charges of crimes against both Temple and nation and of blasphemy against God. Yet, in truth, it was they, the Temple-nation leadership, by their own policies of collaboration with Rome and oppression of the poor, that had corrupted the Temple, perverted the nation, and blasphemed God. Jesus, by his prophetic words and symbolic actions, had exposed their transgressions; and for that they sought his death. Jesus thus stood before his people, judged guilty for the very transgressions of which his judges

---

45. Hanson, "The World of the Servant of the Lord in Isaiah 40–55," p. 18.

46. As contemporary examples of this redemptive pattern of the Suffering Servant, consider Martin Luther King, Jr., and Oscar Romero.

were themselves guilty. His death thus bore the judgment belonging to others.[47] In neither case, however, is this penal substitution. God allows both the Servant and Jesus to be struck down by the injustice and violence of others. But God does not condemn either the Servant or Jesus, sentencing and putting them to death to pay the penalty for others' sins. In both cases, the texts tell us, this is entirely "our" doing: both the Servant and Jesus die by the wrongful judgment and sinful hands of "we" the people. The people counted both the Servant and Jesus "with the transgressors," but in both cases were entirely mistaken. Nevertheless, God acts to reverse evildoing and work redemption, vindicating both the Servant and Jesus for their righteousness and bringing healing and peace out of "our" injustice and violence.

Given the parallels, it is no wonder that the New Testament writers saw Jesus in light of the Suffering Servant and took cues and quotations from this prophetic-poetic text when narrating the passion of Christ.[48] Yoder Neufeld comments:

[H]ere we have a well from which one can draw for reflection on Jesus as a messiah who suffers on behalf of others. Further, we find here a source for the idea that Jesus's suffering and death brings healing and reconciliation to the very ones who have brought that suffering and death upon him.[49]

Our interpretation of the Isaiah 53, therefore, not only offers an alternative to penal substitution, but also shows how the justice-doing, peacemaking work of Jesus Christ can be seen to fulfill the prophetic vision of the Lord's Servant.

47. Cf. N. T. Wright, *Jesus and the Victory of God: Christian Origins and the Question of God, Volume Two* (Minneapolis: Fortress Press, 1996), pp. 547-52, 604-9.

48. Cf. John Driver, *Understanding the Atonement for the Mission of the Church* (Scottdale, PA: Herald Press, 1986), pp. 87-92, who interprets the Song of the Suffering Servant together with the other Servant songs regarding their significance for the Gospel narratives of Jesus.

49. Yoder Neufeld, *Recovering Jesus*, p. 255.

CHAPTER 14

Jesus — God's Sacrificial Victim?

They are now justified by his grace as a gift,
through the redemption that is in Christ Jesus,
whom God presented a mercy seat
through faithfulness in his blood.

ROMANS 3:24-25A

Our study of Isaiah 53 has shown that the popular interpretation of the Suffering Servant as a penal substitute is neither obvious nor necessary. In particular, we have shown that this song need not be read as depicting the Servant as God's sacrificial victim, put to death to propitiate God's wrath against the people on account of their sins. Still, the penal substitution apologist may want to interject here, does not Paul depict Jesus himself in just that way, as a penal substitute and propitiatory victim?

We thus return to the question deferred from Chapter 8, concerning Rom 3:24-25, "they are now justified by his grace as a gift, through the redemption that is in Christ Jesus, whom God put forward as a sacrifice of atonement *(hilastērion)* by his blood, effective through faith" (NRSV).[1] This text would seem to provide support for the penal substitution view that God purposed to make Jesus a sacrificial victim on the cross in order to propitiate divine wrath against sinners and pay the penalty due for sins.[2] Evidently, by speaking of Jesus as *hilastērion*, Paul alludes to the sacrificial ritual of the Day of Atonement. The

---

1. The crucial Greek text we are examining is . . . *Christō Iēsou, hon proetheto ho theos hilastērion dia pisteōs en tō autou haimati* . . . (Rom 3:24b-25a). I would translate: "Christ Jesus, whom God presented a mercy seat through faithfulness in his blood."

2. Cf. Steve Jeffery, Michael Ovey, and Andrew Sach, *Pierced for Our Transgressions: Rediscovering the Glory of Penal Substitution* (Wheaton, IL: Crossway Books, 2008), pp. 80-85.

high priest would sprinkle blood from the slaughtered goat on the *hilastērion* — the lid of the ark of covenant, in the inner sanctum — in order to make atonement for the people's sins and cleanse the sanctuary (LXX Lev 16:15-16).

14.1. The Debate: "Propitiation" or "Expiation"?

14.1.1. "Propitiation" v. "Expiation"

The Greek word *hilastērion* at Rom 3:25 has been translated traditionally "propitiation" (KJV, NASB), but increasingly in the twentieth century "expiation" (NAB, ESV). Translated either way, each word pictures Jesus' death as an atoning sacrifice. But there is no small difference between these interpretations, semantically and theologically.[3] Semantically, "propitiation" connotes "appeasing wrath" or "rendering merciful," while "expiation" connotes "removing guilt" or "wiping away sin." Thus, Morris: "Propitiation is a personal word; one propitiates a person. Expiation is an impersonal word; one expiates a sin or a crime."[4] This semantic distinction makes a theological difference.

"Propitiation" implies that the primary purpose of Jesus' death was to appease God and, hence, that Jesus' death was directed toward satisfying God. As propitiation, Jesus' death was, in the first place, for God's sake — God needed Jesus' death in order to be merciful without compromising holiness and justice. "Propitiation" thus suggests the image of a wrathful God that must be "satisfied" and rendered merciful by sacrificial bloodshed before he will forgive sins.

"Expiation," by contrast, implies that the primary purpose of Jesus' death was to deal with sin and, hence, that Jesus' death was directed toward removing sins. As expiation, Jesus' death was, in the first place, for our sake — we needed Jesus' death in order for our sin and guilt to be removed. "Expiation" thus suggests the image of a merciful God who gave Jesus for the sake of purifying humanity, not satisfying himself.

Another way to see the contrast between "propitiation" and "expiation" is to ask, What needs to be removed as the means of forgiveness? The "propitiation" view sees God's wrath as the primary barrier to forgiveness: God's wrath is the first thing needing removal if sin is to be forgiven. The "expiation" view focuses on the sin and its polluting effects as the primary matter to be dealt with concerning forgiveness: thus, the sin itself is the first thing needing removal in order that humans might be released from their sin.

3. Concerning the debate over how to translate *hilastērion*, see J. M. Gundry-Volf, "Expiation, Propitiation, Mercy Seat," in Gerald F. Hawthorne, Ralph P. Martin, and Daniel G. Reid, eds., *Dictionary of Paul and His Letters* (Downers Grove, IL: InterVarsity Press, 1993), pp. 279-84.

4. Leon Morris, *The Atonement: Its Meaning and Significance* (Downers Grove, IL: InterVarsity Press, 1983), p. 151.

14.1.2. The Claim for "Propitiation"

Penal substitution apologists, not surprisingly, show a strong preference for the traditional translation "propitiation," regarding "expiation" as an inaccurate, misleading, and revisionist reading of the text.[5] The chief commentator supporting the traditional view is C. E. B. Cranfield, who translates *hilastērion* as "propitiatory sacrifice" or "propitiatory victim." He thus reads Rom 3:25 in terms of penal substitution:

> God, because in His mercy He willed to forgive sinful men and, being truly merciful, willed to forgive them righteously, that is, without in any way condoning their sin, purposed to direct against His very own Self in the person of His Son the full weight of that righteous wrath which they deserved.[6]

Leon Morris insists on the traditional rendering of *hilastērion:* "There is no reason, either in the Greek Old Testament or in non-biblical Greek, for seeing it as meaning anything other than 'propitiation.'"[7] As we will show, Morris's claim notwithstanding, there is substantial reason based on the Septuagint for understanding *hilastērion* in terms other than those of the penal substitution model.[8]

5. Cf. John R. W. Stott, *The Cross of Christ* (Downers Grove, IL: InterVarsity Press, 1986), pp. 168-72; Royce Gordon Gruenler, "Atonement in the Synoptic Gospels," in Charles E. Hill and Frank A. James III, eds., *The Glory of the Atonement: Biblical, Theological and Practical Perspectives* (Downers Grove, IL: InterVarsity Press, 2004), pp. 90-105; D. A. Carson, "Atonement in Romans 3:21-26," in Hill and James, *Glory of the Atonement,* pp. 119-39; J. I. Packer, "What Did the Cross Achieve? The Logic of Penal Substitution," in J. I. Packer, *Celebrating the Saving Work of God: The Collected Shorter Writings of J. I. Packer* (Carlisle, UK: Paternoster Press, 1998), I, pp. 85-123, here p. 103; Morris, *The Atonement,* pp. 166-70; Leon Morris, *The Cross of Christ* (Grand Rapids, MI: Eerdmans Publishing, 1988), p. 6; Thomas R. Schreiner, "Penal Substitution View," in James Beilby and Paul R. Eddy, eds., *The Nature of the Atonement: Four Views* (Downers Grove, IL: InterVarsity Press, 2006), pp. 67-98, here p. 87; and Jeffery et al., *Pierced for Our Transgressions,* pp. 82-85.

6. C. E. B. Cranfield, *A Critical and Exegetical Commentary on The Epistle to the Romans,* vol. I (Edinburgh: T&T Clark, 1975), pp. 216-17. Cranfield's language, "propitiatory victim," reflects that of Calvin (cf. *Institutes of the Christian Religion,* II.12.4, II.16.6). Cranfield paints the picture of a God who is merciful toward us and willing to forgive our sin yet still needs his wrath appeased. This picture seems incoherent to me: if God is *already* merciful and willing to forgive, how is wrath a barrier to God's mercy that must be removed before sin can be forgiven? Why is propitiation necessary in the first place?

7. Morris, *The Atonement,* p. 167.

8. Morris argues subsequently that Paul must have meant "propitiation" in Rom 3:25 on the grounds that Paul's preceding argument in Romans 1–3 treats of sinful humanity under divine wrath: if the human situation before God has been changed by the death of Christ, it must therefore be because Christ's death has propitiated God's wrath (Morris, *The Atonement,* pp. 168-69; cf. Stott, *Cross of Christ,* p. 172, and Jeffery et al., *Pierced for Our Transgressions,* p. 84). This argument, however, begs the question examined above (Chapter 13) concerning the rela-

14.1.3. The Case for "Expiation"

How shall we translate *hilastērion*, "propitiation" or "expiation"? To decide the matter, we will consider use of the related verb *hilaskomai* and noun *hilasmos* in the New Testament, of which there are two instances of each, and compare those instances to precedents in the Greek Old Testament (LXX). "The crucial question," we agree with John Stott, "is whether the object of the atoning action is God or man. If the former, then the right word is "propitiation" (appeasing God); if the latter, the right word is "expiation" (dealing with sin and guilt)."[9] We will thus examine the New Testament usage of atonement language and the precedent usage in the LXX to see whether atoning action is directed toward God and his anger (propitiation) or humans and their sins (expiation).[10]

In Jesus' parable we hear the tax collector in the Temple praying, "God, be merciful to me *(hilasthēti moi)*, a sinner" (Luke 18:13). The tax collector petitions God with the second person passive imperative, implying that God, not the tax collector, is the intended initiator (subject) of the action of the verb *hilaskomai;* and the tax collector identifies himself, not God, as the intended recipient (object) of the action — "to me" *(moi).* The object of the action here is thus this human being, not God. The petition assumes, not that God must be rendered merciful by a propitiating human action, but that God is ready to show mercy to the contrite sinner. Because the atoning action is directed from God (initiator) to the tax collector (recipient), we might as well render this petition in the active voice, "God, make atonement for me, the sinner."

The usage of *hilaskomai* in Luke 18:13 is analogous to that in LXX Ps 78:9, "Help us, O God our Savior . . . forgive *(hilasthēti)* our sins *(hamartiais hymōn)* because of your name." Like the tax collector's prayer in the parable, this psalm petitions God to act with forgiveness of sins. As in Luke 18:13, the second person passive imperative implies that the addressee — God — is the intended initiator of the action of the verb *hilaskomai* and the petitioner — "us" — is the expected recipient. Thus, the subject of the atoning action is God, and the object is sins and sinners — thus, atoning action concerns expiation, not propitiation.

In Hebrews, we read that Jesus came "to make a sacrifice of atonement for the sins *(hilaskesthai tas harmatias)* of the people" (Heb 2:17), where the verb appears in the infinitive form. Here the direct object of the verb *hilaskomai* is "the sins" *(tas harmatias),* which appears in the accusative case. The atoning ac-

---

tionship between the wrath of God and the cross of Christ in the thought of Paul. For further critique of Morris's argument on this point, see Gundry-Volf, "Expiation, Propitiation, Mercy Seat," pp. 281-82.

9. Stott, *Cross of Christ*, pp. 169-70.

10. Gundry-Volf, "Expiation, Propitiation, Mercy Seat," p. 280: "The context will probably be determinative in each case in deciding whether *hilask-* implies propitiation or expiation."

tion that Jesus performs thus concerns "the sins," not wrath, and the stated recipient of the atoning action is "the people," not God. Again, we find that the
atoning action is initiated by God-in-Christ and directed toward the sins of humanity — and thus concerns expiation, not propitiation.

The usage of *hilaskomai* in Heb 2:17 is analogous to that in LXX Ps 64:4,
". . . lawless deeds *(anomiōn)* overpower us, but you make atonement for
(hilasē) our impieties *(asebeias)*." *Hilasē* is the second person future middle of
hilaskomai, the subject of which is implicitly God, to whom the psalm is clearly
addressed. The object of the verb is *asebeias* ("impieties"), which appears in the
accusative case and is parallel with *anomiōn* ("lawless deeds"). Thus, God is the
subject of the atoning action and sins are the object of that action — hence,
atonement-making here concerns God's action to expiate sin, not human action to propitiate God.

In John's first epistle, we read that Jesus "is the atoning sacrifice *(hilasmos)*
for our sins" (1 John 2:2; cf. 4:10). As to John's understanding of how Jesus'
death atones for our sins, he writes that Jesus' blood "cleanses us from all sins,"
that "If we confess our sins, he who is faithful and just will forgive us our sins
and cleanse us from all unrighteousness" (1:7, 9). Elsewhere, John writes that Jesus "was revealed to take away sins" (3:5). The effect of Jesus' death concerning
humanity's sins is to "cleanse" *(katharizō)* or "remove" *(airō)* sin — thus, Jesus'
death as an "atoning sacrifice" *(hilasmos)* functions as an expiation of sin, not a
propitiation of God.[11]

In LXX Ezek 44:27, *hilasmos* is used to translate Hebrew *hattā't*. We have
observed (Chapter 10) that in the Levitical cult *hattā't* denotes both the "sin offering" and the "purification offering" — and thus that there was really a single
offering for both sin and impurity, concerning removal of pollution. In Ezekiel
44, the *hilasmos* belongs to a ritual of purification: "They shall not defile themselves. . . . After he has come clean. . . . On the day he goes into the inner court,
to minister in the holy place, he shall offer his *hilasmos* . . ." (vv. 25-27). Whether
we translate *hilasmos* as "sin offering" or "purification offering" or "atoning
sacrifice," the Old Testament background is purification from sin, not propitiation of God, which fits well with the context in 1 John.

J. Ramsey Michaels has argued that *hilasmos* in 1 John has the sense of *both*
expiation and propitiation.[12] The evidence he presents for the latter is that John
writes of Jesus as our "advocate with *(pros)* the Father" in 2:1, the verse preceding that speaking of Jesus as "the atoning sacrifice *(hilasmos)* for our sins." That
Jesus is our advocate, he contends, "makes God the *object*, not the subject, of

---

11. Cf. Morna D. Hooker, *Not Ashamed of the Gospel: New Testament Interpretations of the
Death of Christ* (Grand Rapids, MI: Eerdmans Publishing, 1994), pp. 130-32.

12. J. Ramsey Michaels, "Atonement in John's Gospel and Epistles," in Hill and James, *Glory
of the Atonement*, pp. 112-16.

the reconciliation said to be taking place."[13] The Greek text does put "God" in the accusative case as the grammatical object of the preposition *pros*. The NIV interprets the text as does Michaels, translating this phrase "one who speaks *to* the Father in our defense," which makes God the object of Jesus' action on our behalf. The preposition *pros* need not imply that God is the recipient of the action of which Jesus is the agent, however — "to," "toward," "upon," or "against" are not the only options for translating *pros*. One could just as well render *pros* "with," in the sense of either "in accordance with" or "in company with." Indeed, "with" is how many translations render *pros* here (cf. NAB, NASB, NET, NJB, NRSV). Such a rendering of 1 John 2:1 fits well with what Paul writes, that "the Spirit intercedes for *(hyper)* the saints according to *(kata)* the will of God" (Rom 8:27). Both God the Son and God the Spirit intercede on our behalf in accord with and in company with God the Father.[14] As John emphasizes, Jesus' death to expiate sin is already an expression of God's love for us: "In this is love, not that we loved God but that he loved us and sent his Son to be the atoning sacrifice *(hilasmon)* for our sins" (1 John 4:10). There is thus simply no need for Jesus to propitiate God by sacrifice in order to render God merciful toward us; for the Incarnation of the Son reveals that God has loved us from the beginning and that God's love is the moving cause of the Son's death "for our sins."[15]

The New Testament usage of *hilaskomai* and *hilasmos*, consistent with its precedent usage in the Greek Old Testament, speaks consistently of God's atoning action in Christ directed toward sin on behalf of sinners, not human action directed toward God to satisfy God. The criterion for interpretation, Stott has said, "is whether the object of the atoning action is God or man." "Propitiation" indicates an action by humans directed toward God, and "expiation" indicates an action by God toward sin and sinners. According to Stott's own criterion,

---

13. Michaels, "Atonement in John's Gospel and Epistles," p. 114 (emphasis original). To understand the heavenly intercession of the Son on our behalf as the propitiation of the Father, as Michaels does, generates a significant problem of internal coherence for penal substitution. According to penal substitution, the primary purpose and effect of the death of Jesus was to propitiate the wrath of God on account of the sins of humanity. As is written elsewhere, because Christ is "a priest forever" in heaven, he "always lives to make intercession" and is thus "able for all time to save those who approach God through him" (Heb 7:24-25). Heavenly intercession on our behalf is thus the ongoing vocation of the risen and ascended Christ. So, if the purpose and effect of the Son's intercession is to propitiate the Father's wrath, then the Son is continually doing in heaven at the throne what was to have been fully accomplished on earth at the cross. The cross would thus seem to have been ineffective, or at least incomplete, in accomplishing its primary purpose of saving humanity from divine wrath. Michael's interpretation of 1 John 2:1-2, although given in defense of penal substitution, effectively undermines it.

14. We thus concur with I. Howard Marshall, *Aspects of the Atonement: Cross and Resurrection in the Reconciling of God and Humanity* (London: Paternoster, 2007), pp. 55-56, concerning how to understand the intercession of Son and Spirit with the Father.

15. Cf. D. M. Baillie, *God Was in Christ: An Essay on Incarnation and Atonement* (New York: Scribner's, 1948), pp. 184-89.

these texts uniformly favor "expiation" over "propitiation." Given the choice of translating *hilastērion* either "propitiation" or "expiation," therefore, "expiation" is preferable based on the textual evidence of both the New Testament and the Greek Old Testament. James Dunn summarizes well the case for preferring "expiation" to "propitiation" as a translation for *hilastērion:*

> Should we translate "expiation" or "propitiation"? The problem with the latter is that it invariably evokes the idea of appeasing God, whereas in Rom. 3.25 Paul explicitly states that it is God himself who provided the *hilastērion.* More to the point, Hebrew usage contrasts markedly with the common Greek usage on this precise point. Characteristically in Greek usage the human being is the active subject and God is the object: the human action propitiates God. But in Hebrew usage God is never the object of the key verb *(kipper)*. Properly speaking, in the Israelite cult, God is never "propitiated" or "appeased." The objective of the atoning act is rather the removal of *sin* — that is, either by purifying the person or object, or by wiping out the sin. Atonement is characteristically made "for" a person or "for sin." And it can be said that it is God himself who expiates the sin (or for the sin). Of course, the atoning act thus removes the sin which provoked God's wrath, but it does so by acting on the sin rather than on God. The imagery is more of the removal of a corrosive stain or the neutralization of a life-threatening virus than of anger appeased by punishment.[16]

That this conclusion differs from Leon Morris's reflects the difference in our starting points. Whereas we have based our interpretation on the New Testament and its Greek Old Testament precedents, Morris takes extracanonical, non-Christian Greek literature as the departure point and determining factor for interpreting *hilaskomai:* "As far as the general run of Greek literature is concerned, there cannot be the slightest doubt that the meaning is 'to propitiate.' ... This creates a presumption that it will be used in similar fashion in the New Testament."[17] Regarding Greek usage, Morris is undoubtedly correct. Why pagan ideas about the gods should create a "presumption" for Christian interpretation of Paul's idea of the God revealed in Jesus, however, is not at all obvious.

16. James D. G. Dunn, *The Theology of Paul the Apostle* (Grand Rapids, MI: Eerdmans Publishing, 1998), pp. 214-15. Cf. Gundry-Volf, "Expiation, Propitiation, and Mercy Seat," p. 282: "In summary, not 'propitiatory' but 'expiatory' is the more appropriate description of Christ's atoning death as a *hilastērion* since (1) expiation clearly fits the Pauline understanding of that death as God's own gracious initiative in love toward the ungodly ... as well as God's judgment against sin, (2) the idea of the appeasing of a wrathful God is in tension with Paul's understanding of Christ's death, (3) the context of Rom 3:25 does not require propitiation, and (4) the usage of the *hilask-* word group in the LXX suggests a development of meaning toward the connotation of expiation."

17. Morris, *The Atonement*, pp. 152-53.

To take our hermeneutical clues from Greek usage, as Morris argues, would seem to rest on the assumption that Paul intends his word usage to reflect the world of Greek religion.

Yet Paul himself critiques Greek religion on just this very point, appeasing the gods by sacrifice. The pagan worship of many gods whom humans appease by making sacrifices to idols, Paul says, offers nothing of value to belief in and service of the one true God (cf. 1 Cor 8:4-6). This point is driven home in Paul's speech to the Greek philosophers in Athens (Acts 17:16-31), in which he distinguishes between the customs of Greek religion and the truths of Greek philosophy. Citing Greek sources, Paul validates the philosophical idea of a universal God as the basis for critiquing the cultural practice of idolatry.[18] The philosophers are correct, Paul proclaims, that the God of the cosmos does not live in temples built by human hands and has no need to be served by human hands (vv. 24-25). Addressing a Greek audience and using Greek rhetoric, Paul thus appeals to Greek philosophy (Stoicism) in order to reject the popular notion of a god who is to be satisfied or propitiated by human action — a notion that the Hebrew Scriptures also reject.[19] The thrust of Paul's argument is that the human attempt to appease God by sacrifice is an inappropriate response to God founded on a false idea of God. Why, then, should we suppose that Paul's belief in God would be conformed to the very errors of Greek religion that he explicitly rejects?

That the Greek myths depict the gods as angry deities that must be placated lest they do harm to humanity is neither in question nor to the point here.[20] The New Testament canon, together with the Greek Old Testament, is

18. Cf. Colin Brown, *Christianity and Western Thought: A History of Philosophers, Ideas & Movements*, vol. 1: *From the Ancient World to the Age of Enlightenment* (Downers Grove, IL: InterVarsity Press, 1990), pp. 66-71. Lynn Allan Losie, "Paul's Speech on the Areopagus: A Model of Cross-Cultural Evangelism," in Robert L. Gallagher and Paul Hertig, eds., *Mission in Acts: Ancient Narratives in Contemporary Context* (Maryknoll, NY: Orbis Books, 2004), pp. 221-38, comments: "It was in the philosophical traditions of the Greco-Roman world, rather than in its religions, that Christian preachers could find a point of contact for the proclamation of the gospel. . . . The myths of the traditional gods were full of tales of corruption and intrigue . . . the philosophers thought profoundly about nature and the gods (or God). The purpose of their inquiries was not to gain access to or find ways to manipulate divine power through religious ritual, but to give guidance to people on how to live an ethical life that would be of benefit to society" (p. 225).

19. As we showed in Chapters 10 and 11, the sacrificial cult in Leviticus was intended for the sake of the people, not for the satisfaction of God — not to serve God's needs, but to deal with the people's sins and uncleanness. When the people viewed sacrifice as being for God's sake, then the cult became perverted, necessitating the reminder that God has no need of anything humans might offer (cf. Psalm 50).

20. In defense of interpreting *hilaskomai* according to its usage in Greek literature, Jeffery et al., *Pierced for Our Transgression*, p. 84, argue that *hilaskomai* "certainly does not import into the biblical notion of propitiation all of the objectionable pagan connotations of sinful human

the appropriate place to begin our inquiry into Paul's meaning; for Paul's letters do not simply belong to "the general run of Greek literature." And, given our findings, it would appear that Morris's "presumption" only obscures the evidence of both New and Old Testaments.[21]

14.1.4. But Not "Victim"

More recent translations avoid a choice between "propitiation" and "expiation," electing to translate *hilastērion* as "sacrifice of atonement" (NRSV, TNIV). Whether "propitiation," "expiation," or "sacrifice of atonement," we must be careful that our choice of translation does not make Jesus on the cross into God's sacrificial victim for sin. Penal substitution, at least, explicitly depicts Jesus as God's "propitiatory victim" (Cranfield), slaughtered by God to satisfy God's wrath. But what the penal substitution model makes explicit may be implicit in other translations also. Thus, John Toews:

> The word translated *sacrificial offering (hilastērion)* is best understood as a divinely ordered sacrifice for sin. . . . The word pictures Jesus as God's intended atonement sacrifice in analogy to the Jewish festival of atonement, the day on which God "wiped away" the accumulated sins of the people for the previous year.[22]

In Toews's mind, translating *hilastērion* as "sacrificial offering" suggests an analogy: as the high priest slaughtered the goat on the altar and sprinkled its blood upon the ark of covenant, so God slaughters Jesus upon the cross and spills his blood to atone for sins.

While Paul does depict Jesus' death in sacrificial terms, this analogy does not accurately represent what Paul has in mind in Rom 3:25. What is needed here is a careful distinction between Jesus' death being *sacrificial* and Jesus himself being a sacrificial *victim*. All the animals offered for sin and slaughtered on the altar were, properly speaking, *victims* — unknowing and unwilling, passive

---

beings seeking to appease the malice of a petulant deity." Such special pleading is unconvincing. If "propitiation" in penal substitution does not involve sinful humans appeasing an angry God by means of atoning sacrifice, then what is the controversy about? We might put the point this way: if penal substitution does not concern propitiation in the sense of appeasing divine anger, then why are apologists for penal substitution so insistent that *hilaskomai* must mean "propitiate"? It is precisely the element of human appeasement of divine anger within penal substitution, apart from Greek religion, that is the point in question.

21. For further critique of Morris's view on this question, see Gundry-Volf, "Expiation, Propitiation, Mercy Seat," p. 280.

22. John E. Toews, *Romans* (Believers Church Bible Commentary; Scottdale, PA: Herald Press, 2004), p. 104.

not participant, destined for death. Paul depicts the death of Jesus as quite the opposite. Jesus offers himself on the cross knowingly and willingly, participating actively in God's purpose: ". . . our great God and Savior, Jesus Christ. He it is who *gave himself* for us that he might redeem us . . ." (Tit 2:13b-14). More often than speaking of God "giving up" Jesus (Rom 4:25; 8:32), Paul speaks of Jesus "giving himself" out of love for us (Gal 1:4; 2:20; Eph 5:2; 5:25). And when Paul does speak of God "giving up" Jesus for sake of our salvation, this, too, expresses God's graciousness toward us, not God's intent to victimize Jesus to "satisfy" God-self. Indeed, in speaking of God presenting Jesus as *hilastērion* (Rom 3:25), Paul makes clear that this is "by [God's] *grace* as a *gift*" (v. 24a). David Brondos comments on such expressions in Paul's writings:

> God's love was revealed in his willingness to give his Son over to death, "delivering him up" so that his plan might be accomplished. The idea is not that God had his Son killed or crucified but that God "gave him over" or "delivered him up" in the sense of not intervening to save him from suffering at the hands of evildoers, and letting them put him to death on a cross.[23]

Michael Gorman notes similarly: "In all of these passages, Christ's self-giving and God's giving are interpreted, either implicitly or explicitly, as acts of love."[24]

Whether Paul presents the matter from Jesus' perspective or from God's perspective, he depicts Jesus' death "for us" as *gift*. Indeed, that Paul uses the same verb *(paradidōmi)* from both perspectives implies that he sees God's "giving up" and Jesus' "giving himself" as two aspects of a single divine self-donation. Paul's language thus contrasts with that of Cranfield, who in depicting Jesus as God's "propitiatory victim" writes of God the Father directing his wrath "against" God the Son. We distort Paul's intention, therefore, when we depict Jesus as God's "victim."

The point here is reinforced elsewhere. In John's Gospel, Jesus says, "I lay down my life in order to take it up again. No one takes it from me, but I lay it down of my own accord" (John 10:17-18). Hebrews also speaks consistently of Jesus "offering himself" (Heb 7:27; 9:14, 25-26), emphasizing the voluntary character of his sacrifice.[25] The biblical witness is clear: Jesus is no victim, destined for the slaughter, whose life is taken from him against his will. I thus concur with Peter Martens: "someone who intentionally, voluntarily and actively surrendered himself to death, as Jesus did, ought not to be considered a 'vic-

---

23. David A. Brondos, *Paul on the Cross: Reconstructing the Apostle's Story of Redemption* (Minneapolis, MN: Fortress Press, 2006), p. 71.

24. Michael J. Gorman, *Cruciformity: Paul's Narrative Spirituality of the Cross* (Grand Rapids, MI: Eerdmans Publishing, 2001), p. 85.

25. Cf. Richard D. Nelson, "'He Offered Himself': Sacrifice in Hebrews," *Interpretation* 57/3 (2003), 251-65, here pp. 257-58.

tim.'"[26] Insofar as we wish to speak of Jesus as "victim," then, doing so requires us to accept the paradoxical notion of a *willing* victim.

14.2. *Hilastērion* in Canonical Context

14.2.1. *The Usage of* Hilastērion *in the Septuagint*

Yet, the chief difficulty with the usual translation of Rom 3:25 — whether "propitiation," "expiation," or "sacrifice of atonement" — and the imagery and analogy it suggests is that it does not cohere with the canonical usage and significance of *hilastērion*.[27] As used elsewhere in the canon of Scripture, *hilastērion* does not actually refer to either the scapegoat (the live goat that bears away the sins of the people) or the sacrificial victim (the goat slaughtered on the altar to cleanse the sanctuary) in the Day of Atonement ritual. In order to interpret Paul's meaning in this text, we need to examine carefully the usage of *hilastērion* in the Greek Old Testament, the Septuagint (LXX).[28]

26. Peter W. Martens, "The Quest for an Anabaptist Atonement: Violence and Nonviolence in J. Denny Weaver's *The Nonviolent Atonement*," *Mennonite Quarterly Review* 82 (April 2008), 281-311, here p. 296.

27. Royce Gordon Gruenler, "Atonement in the Synoptic Gospels," asserts without argument that "Romans 3:21-26 . . . constitutes an integral sense unit within which *hilastērion* ("mercy seat/propitiation") must be defined" (*Glory of the Atonement*, p. 91). This view is questionable, if only for the fact that Rom 3:25 is the historically *last* usage of *hilastērion* in the biblical canon (assuming that Hebrews predates Romans); and it is reasonable to assume (in the absence of evidence or argument to the contrary) that later word usage should be understood (in part, at least) with reference to earlier usages. Moreover, Gruenler's claim implies that, insofar as *hilastērion* is to be understood solely in terms of its immediate context in Rom 3:21-26, its usage in v. 25 is effectively independent of the usage of *hilastērion* in the Torah. But that would create a disconnection between Jesus as *hilastērion* and the sacrificial system, which seems to run contrary to both what Paul intended and what the penal substitution model assumes.

28. Jaroslav Pelikan, *Whose Bible Is It? A Short History of the Scriptures* (New York: Penguin Books, 2005), p. 66: "The Septuagint should not be the only place to look for the meaning of a word in the Gospels or in Saint Paul, but it definitely must be the first place to look." Luke Timothy Johnson's caveat (*Reading Romans: A Literary and Theological Commentary* [Macon, GA: Smyth and Helwys Publishing, 2001], p. 57) concerning *hilastērion* in Rom 3:25 is thus appropriate at this point: "The reader should be neither surprised nor discouraged, but rather remember that the language of the nascent Christian movement was just in the process of being forged in Paul's letters, which are, in fact, the first evidence for this language, which used older terms in new combinations and with new referents. Paul's words may have been clear to his first readers because they shared his cultural context and something of the same experience. We, on the other hand, are left to the task of excavation, hoping at least to approximate Paul's intended meaning. I emphasize this because the one thing we must not do — especially in passages like this one that have been subjected to so much theological interpretation for centuries — is simply assume that the meanings later theological systems have assigned to Paul's words are the meanings he intended. Far better for us to achieve a "strange" reading that is more tentative, than an assured

The Septuagint uses *hilastērion* consistently throughout the Torah to refer specifically to the "mercy seat" (NRSV) or "atonement cover" (TNIV) or "atonement lid" (NET) — the lid of the ark of covenant (cf. Exod 25:22) in the inner sanctum of the tabernacle.[29] The Septuagint contains twenty-seven usages of *hilastērion*.[30] In twenty-one of twenty-seven usages, all found within the Torah, it is clear that *hilastērion* refers to the "mercy seat" and to neither a sacrificial victim nor the altar of sacrifice. The LXX Torah thus preserves a clear and consistent linguistic distinction between the "mercy seat" and the sacrificial victim slaughtered on the altar.[31] It is evident that *hilastērion* is a technical term within the LXX Torah used specifically to refer to the lid of the ark of covenant.[32] Moreover, this is precisely how the word *hilastērion* is used in Heb 9:5, the only other usage in the New Testament: to refer specifically to the "mercy seat" (NRSV, NET) or "atonement cover" (TNIV).[33]

---

reading that, because of its familiarity, teaches us nothing we did not already know." That being said, I find Johnson's own "excavation" of *hilastērion* does not go deep enough, because he uncovers this term in the Torah only in relation to the Day of Atonement ritual.

29. Greek *hilastērion* translates Hebrew *kapporet*, which Jacob Milgrom concludes is "Untranslatable, so far." He argues: "It can hardly be rendered 'mercy seat/throne' or 'cover' . . . either on etymological or semantic grounds: the verb *kipper* never implies mercy or cover; and the *kapporet* never served an expiatory or covering function. . . . But as the *kapporet* (rather than the cherubim or the ark) is the focal point of the purgation rite (*kipper*), perhaps it took its name from its function on the Day of Purgation" (*Leviticus 1–16* [Anchor Bible; New York: Doubleday, 1991], p. 1014). My purpose here is not to translate *hilastērion* (i.e., to find an adequate English equivalent for it), but rather to interpret its significance according to its usage. Thus, although I will generally follow the KJV-RSV-NRSV traditional rendering "mercy seat," I will leave this term in quotation marks to indicate that it represents, but does not necessarily translate, the Greek *hilastērion* and Hebrew *kapporet*.

30. Exodus, 13x; Leviticus, 7x; Ezekiel, 5x; and 1x each in Numbers and Amos.

31. Cf. Stephen Finlan, *Problems with Atonement: The Origins of, and Controversy about, the Atonement Doctrine* (Collegeville, MN: Liturgical Press, 2005), pp. 40-41.

32. The six doubtful cases are all found in the prophets: LXX Amos 9:1; Ezek 43:14, 17, 20. These texts refer to the altar but not to the ark. But in each of these doubtful cases it is clear that *hilastērion* refers to a concrete, inanimate object. In Amos 9:1, YHWH, standing beside the altar, instructs the prophet to "smite the *hilastērion*." In Ezek 43:14, 17, the prophet is shown a vision of the Temple, in which are described the dimensions of the altar with reference to the *hilastērion* (which, apparently, is understood to be a part of the altar). And in Ezek 43:20, the prophet is instructed to take blood from the burnt offering on the altar and to place it on the four horns of the altar and on the four corners of the *hilastērion*. It would appear, then, that the prophetic tradition in Israel, both before (Amos) and during (Ezekiel) the exile, viewed the *hilastērion* as part of, or at least closely connected to, the altar of sacrifice rather than the ark of covenant. Even so, in no case in the LXX, even where reference to the "mercy seat" is doubtful, does *hilastērion* ever refer to a sacrificial victim.

33. This linguistic evidence is acknowledged by Carson, "Atonement in Romans 3:21-26," who nonetheless prefers to interpret *hilastērion* as "propitiation." In his article, however, Carson does no textual exegesis on the significance of the *hilastērion* in the Torah (as we do below) to uncover the full canonical meaning of the term.

We may thus conclude confidently that, concerning the Day of Atonement ritual (Leviticus 16), *hilastērion* refers neither to the scapegoat bearing away the people's sins, nor to the goat slaughtered on the altar to cleanse the sanctuary, nor to the altar of sacrifice. As used in the LXX, *hilastērion* does not refer to a sacrificial offering at all. Within the LXX Torah, it refers specifically only to the "mercy seat," the lid of the ark of covenant, upon which is sprinkled the blood of the sacrificial victim. While connecting Christ and his death to the Day of Atonement, therefore, Paul's depiction of Christ as *hilastērion* does *not* identify Christ with *either* a sin-bearer or a sacrificial victim.

The textual evidence from the Torah thus undercuts the analogy implied by the usual translation of *hilastērion* and so calls into question the interpretation of Jesus as God's sacrificial victim that it implies. Both penal substitution and Toews's analogy (cited above) are thus off the mark. Contrary to the tradition, by depicting Jesus as *hilastērion,* Paul does *not* intend to say that Jesus is God's sacrificial victim for human sin — that God ritually slaughters Jesus on the cross, analogous to the high priest ritually slaughtering the goat on the altar, to make atonement for sin. This analogy also suffers from a common confusion. When linking the cross to the Day of Atonement, the tendency is to depict Jesus' death as the sacrificial death of a sin-bearer — and thus to connect Jesus to the scapegoat. But this completely confuses matters. There are two goats involved in the Day of Atonement ritual, between which the text makes a clear distinction (Lev 16:7-10): the sin-bearing animal (the scapegoat) is *not* sacrificed but exiled (vv. 20-22), and the sacrificial animal (the goat offered on the altar as a sin offering) does *not* bear sin but cleanses pollution (vv. 15-19). This common confusion is evident in Jeffery et al., who state that the scapegoat is "condemned to death."[34] To the contrary, the scapegoat is exiled, alive. In the Day of Atonement ritual, the sin-bearer is not a sacrificial victim, and the sacrificial victim is not a sin-bearer: there is no sacrifice of a sin-bearer. There is no thus connection between the scapegoat and the *hilastērion* — the blood sprinkled on the *hilastērion* is not that of the scapegoat, which is exiled, not sacrificed. In depicting Jesus as *hilastērion,* therefore, Paul does not intend to depict Jesus as the scapegoat.[35] Whatever conclusion we draw concerning Jesus' death and the Day of Atonement, we must avoid such confusion.

14.2.2. *The Significance of* Hilastērion *in the Torah*

Let us examine carefully the significance of the "mercy seat" *(hilastērion)* in the Torah. The veiled inner sanctum of the tabernacle is, first, the place where

---

34. Jeffery et al., *Pierced for Our Transgressions*, p. 50.
35. Nelson, "He Offered Himself," p. 252, observes similarly that Hebrews also makes selective use of the Levitical sacrificial system to understand the death of Jesus, "eliminating the scapegoat entirely."

God's holy presence dwells. YHWH says to Moses, "Tell your brother Aaron not to come just at any time into the sanctuary inside the curtain before the mercy seat (LXX *hilastēriou*) that is upon the ark, or he will die; for I appear in the cloud upon the mercy seat (LXX *hilastēriou*)" (Lev 16:2). For the high priest to enter behind the veil is to come into the sanctifying, terrifying presence of God; the inner sanctum hidden behind the veil is thus the "holiest" place provided by God for meeting (via a mediator) with his people.

The "holy of holies" — containing the ark of covenant, which is covered by the "mercy seat" — is, second, the place from which God delivers the divine word for the people in the presence of his prophet-priest. YHWH tells Moses: "You shall put the mercy seat (LXX *hilastērion*) on top of the ark; and in the ark you shall put the covenant that I shall give you. There I will meet with you, and from above the mercy seat (LXX *hilastēriou*) . . . I will deliver to you all my commands for Israel" (Exod 25:21-22). Later, once the ark is constructed and the tabernacle set up, we read of such a meeting: "When Moses went into the tent of meeting to speak with the LORD, he would hear the voice speaking to him from above the mercy seat (LXX *hilastēriou*) that was on the ark of the covenant from between the two cherubim; thus it spoke to him" (Num 7:89).

The "mercy seat" is, third, the place where God (represented by the priest) cleanses the sanctuary and reconciles the people on account of their transgressions:

> He shall slaughter the goat of the sin offering that is for the people and bring its blood inside the curtain . . . sprinkling it upon the mercy seat (LXX *hilastērion*) and before the mercy seat (LXX *hilastērion*). Thus he shall make atonement for the sanctuary, because of the uncleanness of the people of Israel, and because of their transgressions, all their sins; and so shall he do for the tent of meeting, which remains with them in the midst of their uncleannesses. (Lev 16:15-16)

The "mercy seat" within the inner sanctum is, therefore, the divinely set-aside place where God's holy presence (veiled by the cloud of incense) dwells among his people, where God speaks the divine word for his people through his prophet, and where God deals with the sins of his people through his priest, cleansing the sanctuary because of the people's uncleanness. All this comprises the canonical background of Paul's depiction of Jesus as God's "mercy seat" (*hilastērion*) in Rom 3:25.[36]

---

36. In further support of interpreting *hilastērion* at Rom 3:25 as "mercy seat," see Gundry-Volf, "Expiation, Propitiation, Mercy Seat," pp. 282-83.

14.2.3. Jesus as Hilastērion: God's Presence, Word, and Cleansing

In Rom 3:25 Paul proclaims that God puts forth, in a public display, Jesus as "mercy seat" (hilastērion). Paul's usage of hilastērion is obviously metaphorical: he does not mean to say that Jesus is, literally, God's new lid for the ark of the covenant. So, then, what might Paul mean? The Torah, as we showed above, provides the canonical background for interpreting Paul's meaning, and it gives the hilastērion a threefold significance for seeing Jesus as God's "mercy seat." First, Jesus is God's holy presence among the people, the place of meeting with God. Second, Jesus is God's anointed prophet through whom God speaks, the place where the people hear God's word. Third, Jesus is God's appointed priest through whom God exercises power to cleanse his people from sin, the place where God purges pollution from his holy presence caused by his people's sins. God thus presents Jesus to the world, Paul is saying, as the one in whom we meet the holy God "face-to-face" (revealed in human flesh rather than veiled by an incense cloud or fabric curtain), from whom we hear God's word, and through whom our sins are cleansed.

I thus concur with Joseph Fitzmyer, who, after rejecting the traditional interpretation that "God has set forth Christ as 'appeasing' or as 'a means of appeasing' his own anger or wrath," explicates hilastērion much as we have done here:

> But this interpretation of hilastērion [i.e., propitiation] finds no support in the Greek OT or in Pauline usage elsewhere. . . . Consequently, hilastērion is better understood against the background of the LXX usage of the Day of Atonement rite, so it would depict Christ as the new "mercy seat," presented or displayed by the Father as a means of expiating or wiping away the sins of humanity, indeed as the place of the presence of God, of his revelation, and of his expiating power.[37]

Fitzmyer also emphasizes the threefold significance of hilastērion: Jesus as God's holy presence, revelatory word, and atoning power. We thus can see that, while correct up to a point, even "expiation" or "the place and means of expiation" falls short as an interpretation of hilastērion; for it misses two of the three aspects of the word.[38] Driver puts it simply and accurately: "Jesus Christ in his

---

37. Joseph A. Fitzmyer, *Romans* (Anchor Bible; New York: Doubleday, 1993), pp. 349-50.

38. Cf. Hooker, *Not Ashamed of the Gospel*, p. 44, emphasis original: "It may well be that the answer is 'both', and that Jesus is here seen both as the atoning sacrifice *and* as the place where God and humanity are reconciled." As Perry Yoder observes, it is not quite correct to speak of the hilastērion as a "means" of expiation; for, strictly speaking, it is the hilastērion that receives the expiating blood — and, hence, that which is cleansed from sin-induced pollution (cf. Lev 16:15b). The hilastērion is thus the *object*, not the instrument, of expiation in the Day of Atonement ritual. The blood, rather, is the instrument that mediates God's expiating power (cf. Lev 17:11).

death for us has become God's mercy seat for humanity."[39] Similarly, Hengel: "Christ crucified . . . like the mercy-seat in the Holy of Holies . . . was the place where God's mercy was supremely manifested."[40]

14.3. Jesus: God's "Mercy Seat"

14.3.1. *"Through Faithfulness in His Blood"*

God's public presentation of Jesus as "mercy seat," Paul says in Rom 3:25, is made "through faithfulness in his blood" *(dia pisteōs en tō autou haimati)*. This double prepositional phrase expresses the means by which God presents Jesus as "mercy seat" for humanity. The phrase "through faithfulness" *(dia pisteōs)* echoes "through the faithfulness of Jesus Christ" *(dia pisteōs Jēsou Christou)* earlier in the text (v. 22).[41] The faithfulness through which God presents Jesus as "mercy seat" is thus primarily Jesus' own faithfulness — his fidelity to God and loyalty to covenant. Yet, I would suggest, this faithfulness has itself a dual aspect — Jesus' faithfulness reveals God's faithfulness. First, God presents Jesus as "mercy seat" by means of Jesus' publicly lived ministry, which he pursued faithfully in humble obedience unto death, even to the point of his blood being shed on a cross, the ultimate test of fidelity to God and loyalty to covenant (cf. Phil 2:8). That Paul adds "in his blood" to "through faithfulness" signifies that Jesus' faithfulness through all of life is made known and made full through the cross. In this aspect, "in his blood" signifies Jesus' entire life self-sacrificially given up in death. Jesus' whole life — a living sacrifice offered to God, in faithfulness unto death, on our behalf — is the means by which God presents Jesus as "mercy seat," by which God effects atonement for humanity.[42]

In turn, Jesus' faithfulness — his devotion to God in body and blood, life and death — reveals to the world God's own right-doing in fulfillment of covenant. Jesus' obedience to God unto death demonstrates to the world God's own righteousness, God's faithfulness in keeping his covenant promise of redemp-

---

39. John Driver, *Understanding the Atonement for the Mission of the Church* (Scottdale, PA: Herald Press, 1986), p. 155. See also Driver's extended discussion of atonement, expiation, and *hilastērion*, pp. 147-55 and p. 257n. 2.

40. Martin Hengel, *The Atonement: The Origins of the Doctrine in the New Testament* (Philadelphia: Fortress Press, 1981), p. 45, quoting Manson. Cf. C. J. den Heyer, *Jesus and the Doctrine of Atonement* (Harrisburg, PA: Trinity Press International, 1998), pp. 60-64.

41. Douglas A. Campbell, *The Deliverance of God: An Apocalyptic Reading of Justification in Paul* (Grand Rapids, MI: Eerdmans Publishing, 2009), p. 642.

42. Cf. Campbell, *The Deliverance of God,* p. 642 (emphasis original): "*This* [viz., the cross] is where God's purpose to have Christ function as [*hilastērion*] is effected; therefore, it is *by means of* this set of events and the narrative describing it that God's purpose of atonement is fulfilled. . . ."

tion: "He [God] did this to show his righteousness . . ." (Rom 3:25b).[43] That God's faithfulness is demonstrated and God's justice revealed "in [Jesus'] blood," therefore, signifies that the obedient life and self-sacrificial death of Jesus constitutes the means of God's righteous act of covenant faithfulness. God's justice-doing and faith-keeping for the redemption of sinners is thus costly to God. That God actively "put forward" Jesus as "mercy seat" for humanity at the cost of Jesus' life signifies that ultimately God himself willingly bears the burden of dealing justly with our sins.[44] Recalling our discussion of the relationship between sacrifice and forgiveness (Chapter 11), we see again that the sacrifice that makes atonement is God's own sacrifice: Jesus' life and death, offered on our behalf and on account of our sins, is God's sacrifice of covenant faithfulness.[45]

Putting it all together (Rom 3:24-26): Jesus' obedient life and self-sacrificial death ("through faithfulness in his blood") reveal that God has acted justly and graciously, at cost to God in the person of Jesus ("by his grace as a gift"), in order to put right ("justify") humanity in faithfulness to covenant for the sake of redemption, thereby demonstrating God's own righteousness ("to show his righteousness"). Katherine Grieb explicates Rom 3:25 in similar terms:

> When Paul uses this language [i.e., *hilastērion*] to speak of Jesus' death in Romans 3:25, he is saying that God put Jesus Christ forward as a way of deal-

43. Concerning the connection between God's justice and covenant faithfulness in Romans 3, see Richard B. Hays, *Echoes of Scripture in the Letters of Paul* (New Haven, CT: Yale University Press, 1989), pp. 46-54.

44. Such language depicting Jesus' death as the "price" or "cost" of God's redemption of humanity must be taken metaphorically, not literally. We must be very careful not to interpret Jesus' death as a "price" God "paid" *to* anyone or anything, as if God were under obligation to some higher principle (e.g., the principle of retribution) or in debt to some other power or personality (e.g., the devil) in the cosmos. A literal interpretation of the cross as the "price" or "cost" of salvation undermines God's sovereignty: God does not "owe" anyone for anything; no one has "rights" to anything that exclude God and which God must secure by an "exchange." God freely and willingly, not out of any external necessity or under any higher obligation, bears the burden of our sin and accepts the cost of our redemption through the life, death, and resurrection of Jesus Christ. Regarding Jesus' death as the "price" or "cost" of God's redemption, see the helpful discussion in Brondos, *Paul on the Cross*, pp. 144-49. He writes: "While the redemption of God's people thus 'cost' God something, since the 'price' both God and his Son 'paid' was the Son's death, this does not mean that this price was paid *to* someone, such as the devil or God himself. Instead, the idea is similar to that of an athlete who pays a high price to win a competition by making many sacrifices in order to prepare for that competition, or of the soldier or police officer who pays the ultimate price of his or her life to defend or protect someone else" (p. 147).

45. Gustaf Aulén, *Christus Victor: An Historical Study of the Three Main Types of the Idea of Atonement* (New York: Macmillan Publishing, 1969), observes that such a notion is attested in the patristic writers: "the idea is that sacrifice stands in the Divine Economy as the means whereby the Divine will-to-reconciliation realises itself, and which also shows how much it costs God to effect the Atonement" (pp. 57-58).

ing with the sins of Israel committed in breach of the covenant and with the sins of the world that resulted from the disobedience of Adam and Eve. Jesus Christ represents Israel and therefore also represents the world for which Israel was chosen to be God's servant. As the Anointed One, the Messiah, he is the designated representative of Israel (like the high priest; see Hebrews for a corresponding argument). Like the mercy seat, he is the place where God will deal with the covenant violations of Israel. Moreover, he is himself the sacrifice for sin. So Jesus Christ is the person who offers the sacrifice, the place where the sacrifice is performed, and the sacrifice itself. Because the death of Jesus Christ is God's action ("whom God put forward," 3:25) the faithful death of Jesus on the cross is also the manifestation (3:21) of God's covenant righteousness. . . . Jesus' sacrificial death is God's own act of covenant righteousness, which reveals God's love for Israel and for the whole world.[46]

The Synoptic Gospel passion narratives present us with a dramatic picture of Jesus as God's "mercy seat" — God's presence, word, and cleansing — presented publicly for the sake of humanity at precious cost to God. Hanging on the cross, having remained obedient unto death, to the point of having his body crushed and blood shed as visible testimony to whole-life devotion to God, Jesus manifests God's mercy by making atonement ("in his blood"!) on behalf of both Gentiles and Jews. He intercedes before God on behalf of the very ones that have sinned against him (and so against God) — "Father, forgive them; for they do not know what they are doing." (Luke 23:34) — and reconciles to God the repentant criminal executed alongside him — "Truly I tell you, today you will be with me in Paradise" (v. 43). In saying as much, Jesus faithfully fulfills God's merciful will for sinful humanity. And as he dies on the cross, displayed before the world, Jesus shows forth the holy presence of God among sinful humanity for all eyes to see: "And the curtain of the temple was torn in two, from top to bottom. Now when the centurion, who stood facing him, saw that in this way he breathed his last, he said, 'Truly, this man was God's Son'" (Mark 15:38-39; cf. Heb 10:19-22).

14.3.2. *Jesus Himself Is the "Mercy Seat"*

Notice that by saying that God put forth Jesus as *hilastērion*, Paul speaks not specifically of the cross, but of Jesus. Paul uses *hilastērion* to refer metaphorically, neither to an act of ritual slaughter nor to a sacrificial victim nor to a

---

46. A. Katherine Grieb, *The Story of Romans: A Narrative Defense of God's Righteousness* (Louisville: Westminster John Knox, 2002), pp. 40-41.

physical place or thing, but to Jesus himself, a flesh-and-blood person.[47] So David Brondos:

> A close look at Paul's words here [Rom 3:25-26], however, reveals that for Paul it is not Christ's death or blood per se that is the *hilastērion,* but *Christ himself,* "*whom* God put forward as a *hilastērion.*" This means that it is not an *event* that constitutes the *hilastērion,* but a *person.*[48]

For sure, the cross is God's most dramatic public display of Jesus as *hilastērion.* Following Brondos's clue that God's act of presenting Jesus as *hilastērion* does not refer to the event of Jesus' death per se, however, I think that we might see the Incarnation itself as God's faithful presentation of Jesus as "mercy seat": the living-and-dying-and-rising Christ is the accessible place where humanity meets God "face-to-face," hears God's word, and receives cleansing from sin. I would thus expand Grieb's interpretation: not only Jesus' passion, but his entire Incarnation — birth, ministry, death, resurrection, and ascension — is "God's own act of covenant righteousness, which reveals God's love for Israel and for the whole world." Paul means to say in Rom 3:25 that Jesus *himself* is the sacrificial offering of God, through whom God deals faithfully, justly, and graciously with our sins, righting and redeeming sinners at ultimate cost to God-self.

14.3.3. Jesus' Sacrifice, Our Sacrifice

It should thus be clear that we do not at all intend to deny or downplay Paul's depiction of Jesus' death using sacrificial imagery. As we have seen, in addition

---

47. That Paul should apply the term *hilastērion* to a person is peculiar but not without precedent. In the literature of the Maccabean martyrs, there is a metaphorical usage of *hilastērion* to describe the deaths of certain "devout ones" who offer themselves in self-sacrifice to Gentile persecutors on behalf of the Israelite nation to effect expiation of sins and purification of the people (4 Macc 17:22; cf. 2 Macc 7:30-38; 4 Macc 6:24-30). Regarding the New Testament depiction of Jesus as faithful witness (martyr) and its background in the Old Testament and Jewish literature, see Driver, *Understanding the Atonement,* pp. 115-28. Although 4 Maccabees was likely written contemporaneously with Paul, we note here that the narrative intention of 4 Maccabees is very different from that of Paul. The writer of 4 Maccabees explicitly uses Greek philosophy (Stoicism, especially), rather than the biblical narrative of divine redemption, to frame the suffering and deaths of the Jewish martyrs. By suffering for the sake of piety, the refrain repeats throughout the narrative, the martyrs demonstrate by their deaths that "reason is sovereign over the emotions" (4 Macc 1:1, 7-9, 13, 30; 6:31–7:3; 8:1; 13:1-3; 16:1; 18:2). The elder Eleazar is depicted as being a martyr for philosophy as much as for the law (5:22-24, 35). By their death in undying loyalty to God's law, the Jewish martyrs become consummate examples of true philosophy as well as of the true Israelite. Nonetheless, despite the differences, Paul's account of Jesus' sacrifice does stand in the same tradition of martryological narrative as the Maccabean account — cf. Campbell, *The Deliverance of God,* pp. 647-51.

48. Brondos, *Paul on the Cross,* p. 128.

to relating Jesus' death to the Day of Atonement (Rom 3:25), Paul describes Jesus' death in terms of both the Passover sacrifice (1 Cor 5:7) and the covenant sacrifice (11:25). Insofar as YHWH's deliverance of Israel from Egypt — commemorated in the Passover meal — and YHWH's covenant-making with Israel at Sinai — sealed by the covenant sacrifice — are the fountain and foundation of Israel's life as God's holy people, Paul thus understands Jesus' death as both a new redemption wrought by God and the foundation of a new covenant relationship with God. He describes Jesus' death, moreover, in terms that echo the burnt, grain, and peace offerings, "a fragrant *(euōdias)* offering and sacrifice to God" (Eph 5:2). The burnt offering (Leviticus 1), the grain offering (Leviticus 2), and the peace offering (Leviticus 3) were voluntary (free-will) sacrifices, offerings with thanksgiving and praise in a covenant of peace with God. The smoke from these sacrifices would rise as a "pleasing odor (LXX *euōdias*) to the LORD" (Lev 1:9b; 2:2b; 3:5b). Paul thus implies that Jesus offers himself as a free-will sacrifice to God, pleasing God by his lived devotion and obedient death. Jesus offers his whole life — out of love for us, on our behalf — with thanksgiving and praise in a covenant of peace with God.

So, likewise, Paul exhorts, we are to offer our lives in self-sacrificial love for one another: "Therefore be imitators *(mimētai)* of God, as beloved children, and live in love, as Christ loved us and gave himself up for us, a fragrant offering and sacrifice *(prosphoran kai thysian . . . euōdias)* to God" (Eph 5:1-2). Far from depicting Jesus as substituting for us and so taking our place in the sacrificial offering that is acceptable and pleasing to God, Paul depicts Jesus' life and death as both modeling for us the kind of sacrifice we are to offer to God and making the way for us to offer ourselves in sacrifice to God. We are called to imitate the sacrifice that Jesus himself offered, the offering of one's *own* life in love for others and obedience to God.

Indeed, that is precisely how the early church martyrs understood their own deaths, as imitation of Christ's sacrificial offering of himself to God on our behalf. Ignatius, bishop of Antioch and martyr (c. AD 110), wrote of his own coming martyrdom in the very terms Paul used to write of Jesus and to exhort the church. In his letter to the church at Rome, Ignatius speaks of his death as "a sacrifice *(thysia)* to God" in imitation of Christ's self-offering in death: "He who died for us is all that I seek; He who rose again for us is my whole desire. . . . Leave me to imitate *(mimētēn)* the Passion of my God" (*Romans* 4:2; 6:1, 3).[49] Similarly with Polycarp, Bishop of Smyrna, concerning his own martyrdom (c. AD 155). The memoir of his death depicts the martyr tied to his stake as "a noble ram taken out of some great flock for sacrifice *(prosphoran):* a goodly burnt-offering all ready for God" (*Martyrdom of Polycarp* 14:1). Just before he is

---

49. Maxwell Staniforth and Andrew Louth, trans., *Early Christian Writings* (London: Penguin Books, 1987), p. 87.

burned alive in the arena, Polycarp prays to God, offering his life as "a sacrifice *(thysia)* rich and acceptable" (v. 2). And, as the flames began to consume his body, the Christians who witnessed Polycarp's death were "aware of a delicious fragrance *(euōdias)*, like the odour of incense" (15:2).[50] Jesus' death was thus understood by the Apostle Paul and the early church Fathers, not as a substitutionary sacrifice, but as an exemplary sacrifice. Christ offered his life to God, not in our stead, but on our behalf so that we might offer our own lives in imitation of his self-offering for others.

50. *Early Christian Writings*, pp. 129-30.

CHAPTER 15

"One Died for All": In Our Place?

For the love of Christ urges us on,
because we are convinced that one has died for all;
therefore all have died.
And he died for all,
so that those who live might live no longer for themselves,
but for him who died and was raised for them.

2 CORINTHIANS 5:14-15

Still, the penal substitution apologist may ask, when Paul writes that "Christ died for us" (Rom 5:8) and "for our sins" (1 Cor 15:3), does he not intend to say that Jesus died *in our place,* that Jesus' death *substitutes* for our death justly deserved for sin?[1] Many Christians do take it for granted that Paul intends by this phrase to say that Christ died "in our place" as payment to God for sin. Paul writes further that Christ died for our sins "in accordance with the scriptures." *Which* "scriptures," whether the entire (Old Testament) canon or a specific text, Paul does not say.[2]

Early Christians, as we have seen, found manifold resources in the Scriptures for understanding Jesus' death. The Apostles appeal to the Psalms to interpret Jesus' death and resurrection as God's victory over rebellious powers — death and hell, rulers and nations (Acts 2:14-36; 4:24-30; 13:26-41). The Evange-

---

1. Cf. John R. W. Stott, *The Cross of Christ* (Downers Grove, IL: InterVarsity Press, 1986), p. 9; Thomas R. Schreiner, "Penal Substitution View," in James Beilby and Paul R. Eddy, eds., *The Nature of the Atonement: Four Views* (Downers Grove, IL: InterVarsity Press, 2006), pp. 67-98, here p. 92.

2. Nor, by the way, does Luke tell us which "scriptures" Jesus uses to teach his disciples about the suffering and death of the Messiah (Luke 24:26-27, 44-46).

lists cite the Suffering Servant in the prophet Isaiah to interpret the ministry
and death of Jesus as obedient service to God that brings healing and peace to a
people burdened by sin (Matt 8:16-17; Mark 10:45; Luke 22:37). And Hebrews
employs the sacrificial system in Leviticus to interpret Jesus' death as an atoning
sacrifice for sins (Heb 2:9-18; 9:11–10:18).

When reading Paul's gospel "that Christ died for our sins in accordance
with the scriptures," most Christians instinctively think of only either Leviticus or Isaiah 53.[3] As we have seen, both of these texts have been interpreted
popularly in terms of penal substitution. Many readers of Paul thus make the
(unconscious) inference that Paul must mean penal substitution when he
writes that "Christ died for our sins." But is that so? As we demonstrated, neither the Levitical cult (Chapter 10) nor the Suffering Servant (Chapter 13) requires a penal substitution interpretation and, indeed, are amenable to alternative readings. Thus, even if "Christ died for us" and "for our sins" do evoke
Leviticus or Isaiah 53, that does not entail a penal substitution meaning of Jesus' death.

We thus need to revisit the debate regarding how to understand the sense
in which Christ has died "for us." Here we seek to re-examine various arguments for the majority position within evangelical thinking that sees Paul's
phrase "one died for all" at 2 Cor 5:14 as a proof-text for penal substitution. The
crux of the debate, as we see it, is whether Paul understands Jesus' death "for us"
in the sense of *exclusive* or *inclusive* place-taking. We argue, contrary to the majority position, that 2 Cor 5:14 is a clear example of inclusive place-taking.

15.1. A Crucial Text for Penal Substitution

Penal substitution at its core comprises three interconnected affirmations:
(1) that Christ's death is a *substitution* for our deaths: Jesus died not only "for
our sake" (benefaction) or "on our behalf" (representation) but "in our place,"
(2) that Christ's substitutionary death saves us by being a *propitiation* of God's
wrath, and (3) that Christ's death propitiates God because it is a *satisfaction* of
divine *retribution* for sins.

Having addressed (2) and (3) in previous chapters, we now address (1).
Concerning Christ's substitutionary death, we consider specifically that characteristic phrase of the Pauline gospel, "Christ died for us."[4] That this formula is

3. Cf. William R. Farmer, "Reflections on Isaiah 53 and Christian Origins," in William H.
Bellinger, Jr. and William R. Farmer, eds., *Jesus and the Suffering Servant: Isaiah 53 and Christian
Origins* (Harrisburg, PA: Trinity Press International, 1998), pp. 260-80, here p. 277.

4. It seems likely that the origin of this phrase is pre-Pauline; for Paul, in affirming that
"Christ died for our sins," testifies that he is handing on a received tradition (1 Cor 15:3). Our
concern here, however, is with the meaning of the phrase, not its origin. Concerning the latter,

carried over into the Nicene Creed — "he was crucified for us under Pontius Pilate" — certainly places it at the center of atonement theology. There are several texts in which Paul speaks of Christ dying "for us" (or some variation).[5] We will focus on one key instance that is often cited as proof positive that Paul understood Christ's death as substitutionary: "For the love of Christ controls us, since we have concluded this, that Christ [lit. one] died for all; therefore all have died" (2 Cor 5:14 NET). Here, many have argued, Paul clearly intends to say that Christ died "in our place."[6]

Our aim is to examine and assess four arguments for this view, those by R. E. Davies,[7] M. J. Harris,[8] Harald Riesenfeld,[9] and Daniel Wallace.[10] And we will do so in three parts. First, we consider the phrase "for us": What does this mean? Second, we clarify the meanings of "substitution" and "representation," showing that the former is characterized by exclusive place-taking and the latter by inclusive place-taking. Third, we apply these results to the exegesis of 2 Cor 5:14, showing that substitution does not fit the Greek text, but that representation better fits the text.[11]

15.2. The Crucial Phrase: "For Us"

15.2.1. What "For"?

Does this phrase, "for us" (or "for all"), mean "for our sake" (benefaction), or "on our behalf" (representation), or "in our place" (substitution)? And what, if anything, are the differences among these interpretations?

The differences among meanings of "for us" *(hyper hēmōn)* turn on how

---

cf. Martin Hengel, *The Atonement: The Origins of the Doctrine in the New Testament* (Philadelphia: Fortress Press, 1981), pp. 33-39.

5. For a discussion of these several texts, see David A. Brondos, *Paul on the Cross: Reconstructing the Apostle's Story of Redemption* (Minneapolis, MN: Fortress Press, 2006), pp. 108-26.

6. Cf. Stott, *Cross of Christ*, p. 147.

7. R. E. Davies, "Christ in Our Place — The Contribution of the Prepositions," *Tyndale Bulletin* 21 (1970), 71-91.

8. M. J. Harris, "Appendix: Prepositions and Theology in the Greek New Testament," in *The New International Dictionary of New Testament Theology*, vol. 3, ed. Lothar Coenen et al. (Grand Rapids, MI: Zondervan, 1986), 1171-1215.

9. Harald Riesenfeld, *"hyper,"* in *Theological Dictionary of the New Testament*, vol. 8, ed. Gerhard Friedrich (Grand Rapids, MI: Eerdmans, 1972), 507-16.

10. Daniel B. Wallace, *Greek Grammar beyond the Basics: An Exegetical Syntax of the New Testament* (Grand Rapids, MI: Zondervan, 1996).

11. We note that, while 2 Cor 5:14 is a crucial text in the debate over penal substitution, that doctrine of atonement does not rise or fall on this one text, such that its loss as a "prooftext" for penal substitution does not of itself bring down the whole doctrine.

we interpret the preposition "for" *(hyper)*. The Greek preposition *hyper* has a wide semantic range, depending on case and context. Its possible meanings include (with the genitive, as is the case here):[12]

1. in some entity's interest: for, on behalf of, for the sake of,
2. the moving cause or reason: because of, for the sake of, for, and
3. denoting general content: about, concerning.

Each of these meanings makes sense in, and could be appropriate to, the specific text we are considering (2 Cor 5:14). This ambiguity is at the heart of the problem of interpretation, which Wallace acknowledges up front: "the case for a subtitutionary sense for [*hyper*] is faced with the difficulty that the preposition can bear several other senses that, on a lexical level, at least, are equally plausible in the theologically significant passages."[13] The wide range of meaning suggests choosing a preliminary translation that carries as many connotations as possible. This criterion recommends the translation "for." Because "for" itself has many meanings in English, however, that still prompts the question: What "for"? Atonement theology, to some extent, is the task of interpreting this "for."

Defenders of penal substitution have argued that in at least this one crucial text for atonement theology, 2 Cor 5:14, it is certain that *hyper* takes the sense of substitution ("in place of") rather than merely representation ("on behalf of") or benefaction ("for the sake of").[14] Substitution (or exchange) is the natural meaning of the Greek preposition *anti*.[15] This is the preposition used to formulate the *lex talionis* against which Jesus taught: "An eye [in exchange] for *(anti)* an eye and a tooth [in exchange] for *(anti)* a tooth" (Matt 5:38). We thus see both Paul and Peter use *anti* in their injunctions against retribution: "Do not repay anyone evil [in exchange] for *(anti)* evil" (Rom 12:17 NET; cf. 1 Thess 5:15; 1 Pet 3:9). Had Paul wanted to say clearly in Greek that Christ died "in our place," he could readily have used *anti*. We have seen that Jesus uses this preposition to depict himself giving his life as "a ransom for *(anti)* many" (Mark 10:45). Not once, however, does Paul write that Christ died *anti hēmōn;* he consistently uses *hyper* to say that Christ died "for us."

This point is acknowledged by Harris and Wallace.[16] Nonetheless, they argue that Koine Greek, the language of the New Testament, allowed a blurring of the sharp distinction in Classical Greek between *anti* (substitution, exchange)

12. Walter Bauer, et al., *A Greek-English Lexicon of the New Testament and Other Early Christian Writings*, 3rd ed. (Chicago: University of Chicago Press, 2000), pp. 1030-31.
13. Wallace, *Greek Grammar*, p. 383.
14. Cf. Wallace, *Greek Grammar*, p. 387.
15. Cf. Davies, "Christ in Our Place," pp. 72-81; Wallace, *Greek Grammar*, pp. 365-68.
16. Harris, "Prepositions and Theology," p. 1197; Wallace, *Greek Grammar*, p. 383.

and *hyper* (representation, benefaction) and, thus, that *hyper* takes on the additional meaning of substitution in the New Testament.[17] Wallace: "Throughout the Koine period [*hyper*] began to encroach more and more on the meanings of [*anti*] though never fully phasing it out."[18] This overlap of meanings, Harris contends, explains why Paul always uses *hyper*, never *anti*: "But why does Paul never say that Christ died *anti hēmōn* . . . ? Probably because the prep. *hyper*, unlike *anti*, could simultaneously express representation and substitution."[19]

Let us review the evidence for this overlap of meaning between *anti* and *hyper* in Koine Greek. "On behalf of the view that [*hyper*] has at least a substitutionary sense to it in passages dealing with the atonement,"[20] Wallace presents three main sources of evidence: extra-New Testament Greek texts from (a) the Greek translation of the Old Testament (Septuagint, LXX) and (b) Greco-Roman papyri; and an extra-Pauline New Testament text, (c) 1 Tim 2:6. After presenting this evidence, Wallace concludes that the Greek Old Testament and extra-New Testament Greek usage of *hyper* establishes a presumption in favor of reading Paul's phrase "Christ died for us" with a substitutionary sense: "In the least, in light of the well-established usage of substitution in Hellenistic Greek, there seems to be no reason not to adopt this nuance [viz., substitution] as part of the Pauline doctrine of the atonement."[21] In examining this evidence, we thus need to ask whether it does establish a presumption in favor of a substitutionary interpretation of "Christ died for us," as Wallace claims, or not.

15.2.2. *Substitutionary* Hyper: *Old Testament Examples*

Wallace cites two biblical texts in the Septuagint — Deut 24:16 and Isa 43:3-4 — in which, it is said, *hyper* clearly takes on a substitutionary sense.[22] Wallace cites Davies for "discussion" of these texts, but Davies himself only cites the texts as "clear uses of [*hyper*] with the meaning 'instead of'" and does not analyze them.[23]

The first text prohibits punishing parents for their children's sins and vice versa; each should die for his own sins. We translate (literally): "Fathers shall not be put to death for *(hyper)* their children and sons shall not be put to death

---

17. Cf. Wallace, *Greek Grammar*, pp. 383-88.

18. Wallace, *Greek Grammar*, p. 387.

19. Harris, "Prepositions and Theology," p. 1197.

20. Wallace, *Greek Grammar*, p. 383.

21. Wallace, *Greek Grammar*, pp. 388-89.

22. Wallace, *Greek Grammar*, p. 384; cf. Harris, "Prepositions and Theology," p. 1196. Wallace also cites an unpublished dissertation by B. K. Waltke, but we will consider here only published arguments.

23. Davies, "Christ in Our Place," p. 83. Davies and Wallace also cite Judith 8:12, but as this text does not bear theologically on atonement, we omit it here.

for *(hyper)* their fathers; each one in his own sins shall be put to death" (LXX Deut 24:16). Here one can make a reasonable case that *hyper* takes a substitutionary meaning: one may *not* put be put to death "in place of" — "for the sins of" — another.

The Torah thus restricts the death penalty so that only the guilty party may be punished. The upshot is that both collective and substitutionary punishment is forbidden in Israel's law. This carries implications for thinking about Christ's death. Those holding the view that God punishes Jesus with death in our place as a substitute for our sins, *and* that in so doing God fulfills the covenant law, have not taken this text seriously enough. The Torah unequivocally *prohibits* imposing the death penalty on a substitute victim; that is, penal substitution is *contrary* to covenant law. This point is reinforced in Exod 32:30-34, where, just after the covenant ceremony at Sinai, YHWH refuses Moses' offer to have himself blotted out from the covenant community in place of the people on account of their sins. YHWH says, "Whoever has sinned against me I will blot out of my book . . . when the day comes for punishment, I will punish them for their sin." YHWH thus explicitly rejects the idea of substitutionary punishment as the basis for covenant relationship. For the sake of logical consistency, therefore, penal substitution apologists must say further that, in justifying humanity by putting Jesus to death in place of humanity, God *violates* covenant law: humanity's law-breaking is put right by God's law-breaking, so that two wrongs add up to right![24]

The second text concerns God's salvation of Israel in Exile. We translate (literally):

> Because I am the LORD your God the Holy One of Israel, the One who saves you: I made an exchange for *(allagma)* you, Egypt and Ethiopia and Soene for you *(hyper sou)*; since you became precious in my sight, even glorified, I loved you and I will give many peoples for you *(hyper sou)* and rulers for *(hyper)* your head. (LXX Isa 43:3-4)

The first verse of this poetic text places *hyper* in parallel with *allagma*, "that which is given or taken in exchange; the price of a thing" (Liddell & Scott), thus effectively giving *hyper* the sense of a price of exchange. And the second verse extends this metaphor such that *hyper* signifies a head-price, the price of freedom. Here one can make a reasonable case that *hyper* takes on the sense of exchange, "this for that." Two points, however. First, as we have shown (Chapter 9), we need to distinguish between exchange and substitution, which are not identical: substitution is a sub-category of exchange. In this case, *hyper* signifies

---

24. Paul does say at Rom 3:21 that the righteousness of God is disclosed through the death of Jesus Christ "apart from law" *(choris nomou)*. But he does *not* say that God justifies sinners in Christ "against law" *(kata nomou)*.

exchange ("this for that"), but not (necessarily) substitution ("this in place of that"). Second, even as exchange, the sense of *hyper sou* ("for you") here has nothing to do with a penalty for sin or a punishment for crime. Instead, the prophet declares God's loving liberation of Israel from exile; the imagery is of captives ransomed and set free, not the vicarious punishment of an innocent substitute as a penalty for sin.

The LXX versions of these two texts do show that *hyper* could take the meaning of substitution (Deut 24:16) or exchange (Isa 43:3-4). At the same time, however, when taken to bear upon the question of the meaning of Christ's death "for us" in the New Testament, these texts offer mixed messages. Deut 24:16 is unequivocal in saying that substitutionary punishment is repugnant to God's covenant law, which would cut against penal substitution as a biblical idea. And Isa 43:3-4 depicts God's salvation of Israel in terms of ransom from captivity, which might favor a liberationist view of Christ's death and resurrection rather than penal substitution. These Old Testament examples, therefore, while establishing precedents for *hyper* taking the sense of substitution, do not establish a presumption in favor of a penal substitution interpretation of Christ's death "for us" in the New Testament, as Wallace claims they do.

15.2.3. *Substitutionary* Hyper: *Extra-Biblical Sources*

Davies, Wallace, and Harris also cite extrabiblical literature for examples of the use of *hyper* with the sense of substitution or exchange.[25] These examples are found in various legal and financial documents in which *hyper* is used in the same way that *anti* would have been used — to denote one person signing for ("in place of" or "in the name of") another person in a legal transaction (e.g., a sale or contract or will) or the price paid for ("in exchange for") something in a financial transaction (e.g., a bill of sale). We take at face value their respective assessments of this collective evidence, that it shows *hyper* being used with the meaning of substitution or exchange in Koine Greek.

It is not so obvious, however, that this evidence establishes a presumption in favor of a substitutionary interpretation of Christ's death "for us." Wallace's argument here would be that, because Greco-Roman legal and financial documents use *hyper* with the sense of substitution, it is reasonable to presume that Paul means "in our place" when he writes that Christ died "for us." The relevance of this evidence for interpreting *hyper* in New Testament texts concerning Christ's death is questionable, however. Although the extrabiblical evidence indicates that *hyper* could take the sense of substitution or exchange in the con-

---

25. Davies, "Christ in Our Place," p. 83; Harris, "Prepositions and Theology," p. 1197; Wallace, *Greek Grammar*, pp. 384-86.

text of Greco-Roman legal and financial documents, it does not follow that such should be so, much less is so, in the context of early Christian theological discourse. The meaning of *hyper* (as with other prepositions) is not only case-sensitive but context-relative. The preposition may be suitable to the meaning of substitution in some contexts, but not others. To infer that this evidence, drawn from transactions in the law court and the marketplace, establishes a presumption in favor of a substitutionary meaning of Christ's death "for us," as Wallace does, implies the prior assumption of a context of transaction for Paul's thinking about atonement. Wallace thus effectively *presumes* a transactional view of atonement — that the cross is a transaction between God and Christ-acting-in-our-place — and so begs the question.

15.2.4. *Substitutionary* Hyper: *A New Testament Example*

Davies and Wallace each cite 1 Tim 2:6 as an extra-Pauline New Testament text in which *hyper* is used with the sense of substitution: Christ "gave himself a ransom for all *(antilytron hyper pantōn)*."[26] Davies argues that *hyper* here "clearly . . . has a substitutionary meaning." This catechetical formula was likely derived from Jesus' own saying that he came as a servant to give himself "a ransom for many *(lytron anti pollōn)*" (Mark 10:45). As we have argued (Chapter 9), Jesus' "ransom" saying is understood better in terms of exchange than substitution: Jesus gives his life, not as a substitute slave "in our place," but "in exchange for" our freedom from captivity to sin and death. That the catechetical formula in 1 Tim 2:6 adds *hyper* to the original saying, and thus uses *hyper* in close connection with *anti,* does imply that *hyper* takes the meaning of exchange here. Seeing substitution in this text, as do Davies and Wallace, however, conflates substitution and exchange, which need to be carefully distinguished.[27] While reinforcing a liberationist view of how Jesus' death saves us, 1 Tim 2:6 does not establish a presumption in favor of a substitutionary interpretation of "Christ died for us."

We conclude, therefore, that while there is substantial evidence — in Old Testament Greek texts, in extra-New Testament Hellenistic Greek documents, and in at least one extra-Pauline New Testament Greek text — that *hyper* could and did take the meaning of substitution or exchange, this evidence fails to establish a presumption in favor of reading Paul's phrase "Christ died for us" as implying substitutionary atonement, contrary to what Wallace has claimed.

26. Davies, "Christ in Our Place," pp. 89-90; Wallace, *Greek Grammar,* p. 388.
27. Cf. Davies, "Christ in Our Place," p. 89: "The prefixed [*anti-*] reinforces the idea of substitution. . . ." Davies' comment slides over the difference between substitution and exchange by assuming that *anti* simply implies substitution.

15.2.5. *"Christ Died for Us": Substitution?*

Before proceeding in the argument, it is appropriate here to consider an important text for atonement theology, Rom 5:6-8, where Paul writes of Christ dying "for us" in two variations: "while we were still weak . . . Christ died for *(hyper)* the ungodly . . . while we were still sinners Christ died for us *(hyper hēmōn)*." Does Paul mean to say here that Christ died "for our sake" or "on our behalf," or that Christ died "in our place"?

Unlike the texts we have examined above, this use of *hyper* does not clearly imply substitution or exchange. Harris acknowledges this ambiguity, citing this text as one in which "it is difficult to determine whether or not the prep. denotes substitution."[28] Riesenfeld cites this text as a case where *hyper* takes the sense of "on behalf of" — Christ dies "for our sake" or "for our cause" such that his death "accrues to our favor."[29] Wallace, interestingly, does not cite this text at all in his argument in favor of substitution "as part of the Pauline doctrine of the atonement" based on usage of *hyper*.

Davies does make a case for reading *hyper* with a substitutionary sense in Rom 5:6-8. The basis for his argument is the contrast that Paul draws between what humans might do for one another but rarely would — "rarely will anyone die for *(hyper)* for a righteous person — though perhaps for *(hyper)* a good person someone might actually dare to die" (v. 7) — and what God has done for us in Christ to demonstrate his love to us. Davies argues:

> In his discussion of whether or not men would die for a righteous man or for a good man, it seems unlikely that Paul is speaking merely of dying for the sake of or for the cause of such a person, as many have been found who have been willing to lay down their lives in battle for the cause of a great hero, general or king. It seems more likely that Paul is speaking of dying in someone's place, which, he says, would be extremely rare and only likely in the case of a person of real "goodness."[30]

Whether it seems "likely" that Paul's expression "Christ died for us" implies substitution in this context, or not, depends on what kind of scenario one supposes that Paul has in mind here. Davies supposes here a scenario analogous to that at the end of Dickens's *A Tale of Two Cities,* in which Sydney Carton mounts the scaffold for Charles Darnay. In this literary example, Carton indeed dies "in place of" Darnay — an "unrighteous" man dies for a "righteous" man by taking his place at the guillotine; and if such a scenario is what Paul has in mind here, then his expression "Christ died for us" does imply substitution.

---

28. Harris, "Prepositions and Theology," p. 1197.
29. Riesenfeld, *"hyper,"* p. 509.
30. Davies, "Christ in Our Place," pp. 86-87.

Such a situation of one dying in place of another, we could thus read Paul as saying, happens quite rarely in human affairs, but now the absolutely unheard of has happened: Christ has died in place of the "ungodly" and "sinners."[31]

We might just as well suppose here a different narrative analogy of "dying for" another, however, the sort of narrative that Davies dismisses as "unlikely" — the noble action of sacrificing one's life "for the cause of" someone who is deemed worthy of such sacrifice. We could thus read Paul as saying that, as rarely as one finds among humans the nobility to sacrifice one's life for the sake of another deemed worthy, God has now outdone all human expectation by sacrificing his life through Christ for the sake of those who are certainly unworthy. Which scenario seems the "more likely" background of what Paul has in mind, furthermore, will depend in turn on one's prior theological disposition: if one is inclined to see substitution, one will deem "more likely" a scenario such as that in *A Tale of Two Cities,* etc. I thus think that this cannot serve as a "proof-text" for the question, whatever one's theological disposition; for such "proof" will inevitably be circular: how one interprets Christ's dying "for us" in Rom 5:6-8 will depend on what kind of scenario one supposes Paul has in mind in v. 7, and what kind of scenario one supposes Paul has in mind there will depend on one's prior theological disposition. The text is ambiguous; I thus concur with Harris's ambivalence.

15.3. Clarifying Substitution and Representation

As we have seen, arguments concerning atonement sometimes fail to distinguish between the concepts of exchange ("this for that") and substitution ("this in place of that"). This tendency, I would argue, results from a lack of clarity regarding the concept of substitution. In Chapter 9, we began to bring some clarity to the matter by distinguishing substitution from exchange: substitution is a sub-category (or specific kind) of exchange; thus, every substitution is an exchange, but not every exchange is a substitution. If I purchase a book from you, we make an exchange: my money for your book; if I later discover the book to be flawed, then I may come back to you and ask for a substitute book: a new book in place of the old book. Both transactions are cases of exchange, but only

---

31. Davies, "Christ in Our Place," p. 87. Davies adds to this the argument that the whole of Paul's argument up through Romans 5 concerns the need for humanity's salvation from the wrath of God, which Jesus' death "for us" accomplishes (cf. 5:9). God's wrath against us, therefore, is satisfied by Christ's death "in our place." But this argument presupposes the penal substitution view of the relation between God's wrath and human sin; the most Davies can argue in this way without begging the question, therefore, is that this text can be read consistently with the penal substitution view. We have argued (Chapter 12) that the wrath of God in Paul's argument in Romans can be given an alternative interpretation to the penal substitution view.

the latter is a case of substitution; for in the latter case, in contrast with the former, the things exchanged serve the same function — that is, the new book "takes the place of" the old book, but my money does not "take the place of" your book. An example of substitution in Scripture that helps clarify this distinction, we noted, is found in Genesis, where Judah offers himself as Joseph's slave in Benjamin's stead: "please let your servant remain as a slave to my lord in place of (Heb., *taḥat*; Gk., *anti*) the boy" (Gen 44:33). Judah offers to Joseph not only an exchange — himself for Benjamin — but a substitution: he will serve as Joseph's slave in Benjamin's place.

Such care needs to be taken also in distinguishing substitution ("in place of") from representation or intervention ("on behalf of" or "for the cause of"). As we find arguments conflating substitution and exchange, we also find arguments conflating or blurring the line between substitution and representation.

We find repeated the claim that representation implies substitution "in most cases." Davies claims, "a person doing or suffering something on behalf of someone is often doing it in his place. As G. B. Winer says, 'In most cases one who acts in behalf of another takes his place.'"[32] Wallace follows suit, quoting Winer via Robertson.[33] Harris, too, makes a similar claim: "To act on behalf of a person often involves acting in his place."[34] Such claims depict the category of representation as overlapping to a large degree with the category of substitution, such that "most cases" of representation lie within the category of substitution. We find also the converse claim that substitution implies representation. So, Harris: "a substitute represents."[35] Taken at face value, Harris's claim depicts substitution as a sub-category of representation: all cases of substitution lie within the category of representation. And J. I. Packer claims simply that, between substitution and representation, there is "a distinction without a difference."[36]

This tangle of claims that entangle the categories of representation and substitution calls for some clarity to be brought to the question. Our aim here will be not only to delimit the categorical relationship between substitution and representation, but also to discover characteristic features or essential criteria that define each category. While we agree with penal substitution apologists that one should not insist on a strict dichotomy between representation and substitution, nonetheless, for the sake of conceptual clarity and logical consis-

32. Davies, "Christ in Our Place," p. 82.

33. Wallace, *Greek Grammar*, p. 384.

34. Harris, "Prepositions and Theology," p. 1196.

35. Harris, "Prepositions and Theology," p. 1197.

36. J. I. Packer, "What Did the Cross Achieve? The Logic of Penal Substitution," in J. I. Packer, *Celebrating the Saving Work of God: The Collected Shorter Writings of J. I. Packer* (Carlisle, UK: Paternoster Press, 1998), I, pp. 85-123, here p. 98. Packer's claim is based entirely on entries found in the *Oxford English Dictionary*, but dictionary definitions cannot settle a philosophical question.

tency, we must avoid conflating the two categories. Both substitution and representation involve "doing for" another, but in distinct ways.

15.3.1. Substitution

Let us begin by defining the category of substitution, taking the place of another, in contrast with representation, acting on behalf of another. In order to do that, we focus on examples that are clearly cases of substitution but not representation.

In most cases in sport, a substitute does not represent. In baseball, player B may be substituted for player A, but player B does not then represent player A; player B, having taken the place of player A in the lineup and on the field, represents himself — whatever runs he scores, hits he makes, or errors he commits accrue to his own record. Consider substitute teaching: the substitute teacher takes the place of the regular teacher in the classroom, assuming her duties (taking attendance, giving the lesson, enacting discipline, etc.), but the substitute teacher does not represent the teacher for whom she substitutes. The substitute acts as if she were the rightful teacher of the class, but not as if she were the other teacher; the benefits of her having fulfilled the duties of teacher (say, pay and time) thus do not accrue to the other teacher, but to herself.

We find in these examples two essential characteristics of substitution. First, as we saw when distinguishing substitution from exchange in the case of Judah and Benjamin, the substitute fulfills the role or performs the function of the one for whom he or she substitutes. This feature, we will see, can also be found in cases of representation. Second, which is distinctive of substitution and will prove to be the crucial element, the substitute's action *excludes* the action of the one for whom he or she substitutes. Insofar as one player substitutes for another player in a sporting match, that other player himself does *not* play; insofar as one teacher substitutes for another teacher in the classroom, that other teacher herself does *not* teach. Indeed, were the first player himself to be playing in the match, or were the first teacher herself to be teaching the class, then there would simply be no substitution in either case. The logic of substitution, therefore, is the logic of exclusion: to act "in place of" another is to exclude that other from the action.

15.3.2. Representative Substitution

Some cases of substitutive action are cases of representative action. In some sports, a substituted player may represent the player whose place he takes. In hockey, for example, one player may serve out another player's (viz., the goalie's) penalty. In this case, by taking the place of the penalized player in the penalty box, the substituted player acts on behalf of the penalized player, serving his time as if he himself were the penalized player. Here, the benefits of the substitute's action accrue to the other player: the substituted player's time served in the penalty box both clears the other player of the penalty against him and frees him to continue playing.

The case of substitution from Dickens's *A Tale of Two Cities* also involves representation. When Carton mounts the scaffold for Darnay, Carton clearly substitutes for Darnay: he takes Darnay's place upon the scaffold, dying in his stead. And in so doing, Carton represents Darnay, acting on his behalf, dying as if he himself were Darnay. By dying in Darnay's stead, Carton spares Darnay's life, so that the benefit of Carton's death accrues to Darnay's advantage: death for Carton means life for Darnay. We may also consider Judah and Benjamin as a case of representative action. In offering to take the place of Benjamin, Judah agrees to act as if he himself were the one rightly subjected to servitude. By acting on behalf of Benjamin, the benefit of Judah's action accrues to Benjamin: slavery for Judah means freedom for Benjamin.

We may call such cases as these "representative substitution." In these three cases, we see both what characterizes substitution and what representation adds to substitution. Each case exhibits the distinctive characteristic of substitution — *exclusion*. The substitute player's serving in the penalty box excludes the other player from doing so; had the penalized player served his own penalty, there would have been no substitution. Carton's death *excludes* that of Darnay; had Darnay himself died on the scaffold, there would have been no substitution. Judah's entrance into Joseph's service excludes Benjamin's service; had Benjamin remained in Joseph's service, there would have been no substitution. And each case reveals a characteristic feature of representative action: a substitute represents the one for whom he or she substitutes when the action is undertaken on behalf of or in the name of the other such that the merits (or demerits) of his or her action accrue to the gain (or loss) of that other. This feature of other-benefaction is lacking in the cases of the substitute player and teacher. We might say that the representative "takes the part of" the one on whose behalf he or she acts, taking up the concern or cause of another as if his or her own but for the other's sake.

It is the hybrid category of representative substitution, I would argue, that best fits the logic of penal substitution. The very idea of penal substitution is precisely that Jesus functions in his death as a sin-bearer for humanity in such a manner that (a) his sin-bearing death is *exclusive* of those whose sins he bears (he bears our sins, we do *not*; he dies, we do *not*), but (b) the benefit of his sin-bearing death accrues to the account of those whose sins he bears "in their place" (he bears our sins, we thus are free from sins; he dies, we thus live). The question for examination below will be whether the text under consideration, 2 Cor 5:14, also fits this category.

15.3.3. *Representation*

Despite these cases of representative substitution, where the categories of substitution and representation overlap, representation remains distinct from substitution. In addition to implying other-benefiting action, cases of representation involve action on behalf of another which is not exclusive of the other's action but rather allows or implies inclusion of the other's involvement in the representative action. We consider separately cases of representation that allow or imply other-involvement.

Here are three cases in which acting on behalf of (in the name and for the benefit of) another *allows* the involvement of the other. An attorney representing a client in a criminal trial acts on behalf of his client, but neither does he take his client's place under legal judgment, much less on the witness stand, nor does his representative action exclude his client from participating in his own defense. A human rights advocate may act on behalf of the cause of some persons or groups, but such representative action does not exclude those persons or groups from cooperating with the advocate in their own cause. A priest or pastor may pray on behalf of, and so represent, a congregation before God, but his or her praying is not exclusive of others, who may participate in the prayer with their own contributions and affirmations ("Yes, Lord!" "Have mercy!" "Amen!").

Here are two cases in which action on behalf of another *implies* the involvement of the other. If I authorize an agent to negotiate a contract in my name, then the rights and obligations entailed in the contract negotiated are *mine* because I myself am entailed in the negotiation by the agent's action on my behalf. The agent functions as *my* agent precisely insofar as he or she *includes* myself by way of representation. Similarly regarding representative government. If I consent to a legislative authority (by, say, will of the majority), then the rights and responsibilities entailed in the laws so enacted are *mine* because I myself am included in the legislature's action by way of representation.

These examples reveal what essentially distinguishes representation from representative substitution. Whereas all cases of substitution (representative and non-representative) are characterized by *exclusion,* all cases of representation are characterized by *inclusion.* Representation, distinct from substitution, has an essentially *inclusive* aspect. In contrast with substitution, representative action "on behalf of" another allows the cooperative action, or implies the consensual involvement, of that other.[37] We might put the distinction this way: both representative substitution and representation involve identifying oneself with another, but, whereas such identification in substitutive action *excludes*

---

37. Cf. Stott, *Cross of Christ,* p. 276: "A 'representative' is one who acts on behalf of another in such a way as to involve the other in his action."

the other's participation, such identification in representative action *includes* the other's participation. Whereas the other-beneficiary aspect of representation is compatible with the other-exclusive aspect of substitution (representative substitution), the other-exclusive aspect of substitution is *in*compatible with the other-inclusive aspect of representation.

We may summarize our findings as follows:

Substitution: other-exclusive, self-benefiting action ("in place of")
Representative substitution: other-exclusive, other-benefiting action ("in place of" and "on behalf of")
Representation: other-inclusive, other-benefiting action ("on behalf of")[38]

Given that exclusion/inclusion is the crucial distinction here, one can view both substitution and representation as mutually exclusive sub-categories under the higher category of "place-taking." We see no problem in doing so, as long as the exclusion/inclusion distinction is kept clear: whereas substitution (both representative and non-representative) is *exclusive* place-taking, representation is *inclusive* place-taking. This implies logically that one and the same act of place-taking can*not* be *both* an instance of exclusive place-taking and an instance of inclusive place-taking. The categorical relationship between substitution and representation can thus be depicted:

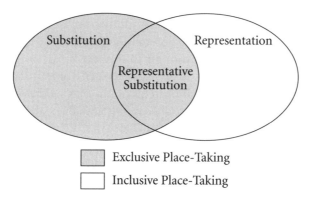

We thus see that the exclusion-inclusion distinction, which cuts across the overlapping categories of substitution and representation, is of crucial importance, distinguishing two different kinds of place-taking. Contrary to Packer's

---

38. "Representation" may not be the best word to express what we intend here, because it may not be adequate to say all that needs to be said concerning Christ's death "for us." But, as with the debate between "propitiation" and "expiation," it is the term, paired with "substitution," that frames the ongoing debate.

view, that we have here "a distinction without a difference," this distinction will make a crucial difference for our analysis of the text that is the primary concern of this chapter.

15.4. "One Died for All" — Substitution or Representation?

The upshot of the previous sections is that whether Paul's phrase "Christ died for us" implies substitution or not requires careful examination on a case-by-case basis — one cannot give a general argument either way. In each case where Paul writes that Christ died "for us," one must both demonstrate that the sense of substitution for *hyper* fits both text and context and test whether the case follows the logic of substitution or not. So, let us thus carefully examine 2 Cor 5:14. Paul writes: *hē gar agapē tou Christou synechei hēmas, krinantas touto, hoti eis hyper pantōn apethanen, ara hoi pantes apethanon.* We might translate literally (keeping the Greek word order): "For the love of Christ impels us, considering this, that one for all died, therefore all died."

This text is cited in standard reference works (e.g., *TDNT*) as one case where "the sense 'in the place of' is predominant."[39] This text is cited also in the standard lexicon of New Testament Greek (BDAG) as one instance where *hyper* takes the substitutionary meaning "in place of" or "instead of." This is the one text where Wallace himself is unequivocally certain that *hyper* "is used with a substitutionary force," contending that substitution "must be the sense" in this text.[40] And even some scholars who dissent from the penal substitution view affirm that Paul clearly means substitution in this text.[41]

Now, as far as I am aware, no apologist for penal substitution maintains that Christ acted as a mere substitute in his death, denying that Jesus died "on our behalf" or "for our sake." That, of course, is a fundamental affirmation of the Nicene Creed, that the incarnation of Christ was "for the sake of humanity and for the sake of our salvation." Rather, the majority evangelical view would seem to be that Jesus died as our representative substitute.[42] Thus, when it is claimed that 2 Cor 5:14 is clearly a case of substitution, I take it that "representative substitution" is meant. So, the question before us is whether this text presents a case of representative substitution. And we argue that it is not, but rather a clear case of representation.

39. Riesenfeld, "hyper," p. 513.

40. Wallace, *Greek Grammar*, esp. pp. 387-88.

41. E.g., Charles B. Cousar, *A Theology of the Cross: The Death of Jesus in the Pauline Letters* (Minneapolis, MN: Fortress Press, 1990), pp. 56, 77, citing Riesenfeld, "hyper."

42. Thus Murray J. Harris, *The Second Epistle to the Corinthians: A Commentary on the Greek Text* (Grand Rapids, MI: Eerdmans Publishing, 2005), p. 421: "He represented them by becoming their substitute." Cf. Packer, "What Did the Cross Achieve?"

15.4.1. Representation: Argument by (Dis-)Analogy

Harris argues on the basis of analogy with John 11:50 that *hyper* in 2 Cor 5:14 is used with the sense of substitution.[43] John 11:50 is also cited by others as a case of *hyper* taking the sense of substitution. Wallace states that "it is difficult to deny a substitutionary sense to [*hyper*]" there, again citing Davies.[44] Davies does state that John 11:50 is a "clear example" of "the preposition [*hyper*] where the meaning includes 'in the place of' as well as 'for the sake of.'"[45] But, again, Davies does not analyze the text, leaving us wondering what makes this a "clear example." Let us take a careful look at this text and Harris's argument for substitution there.

In John 11:50, Caiaphas says to the Sanhedrin, "You do not realize that it is more to your advantage to have one man die for *(hyper)* the people than for the whole nation to perish" (NET). Harris comments: "It is clear that *hyper* here denotes substitution, not simply benefit or representation, since Caiaphas remarks that such a death 'for the people' would ensure that 'the whole nation' did not perish. . . . That is, politically the death of the one . . . would be a substitute for the death of the many."[46] The death of "one man for the people" would spare "the people" from death: "the one" is to die and, because of his death, "the people" will live.

We agree with Harris here, for the usage of *hyper* in John 11:50 follows the logic of substitution: were "the one" *not* to die, then "the people" would perish; but were "the one" to die, then "the people" would *not* perish. That is, "the one" dies "for the people" if, and only if, "the people" do *not* die — and, hence, dies instead of "the people." The death of "the one" is *exclusive* of the death of "the people" — and, therefore, substitutionary. The death of "the one," moreover, is representative: he dies "on behalf of" or "for the sake" of "the nation," the benefit of his death accruing to the advantage of "the nation" for whom he dies. John 11:50, therefore, is a clear case of representative substitution.

But this representative substitution has nothing to do with penal substitution.[47] In Caiaphas's mind, Jesus' death will save the nation, not because Jesus will thus bear divine punishment for the nation's sins, but rather because his death will dissipate a dangerous movement and so avoid the empire destroying the nation in order to "keep the peace." It is the wrath of Rome, not the wrath of God, that Caiaphas fears and that Jesus' death will avert (John 11:45-48). In

---

43. Harris, "Prepositions and Theology," pp. 1196-97.
44. Wallace, *Greek Grammar*, esp. p. 387.
45. Davies, "Christ in Our Place," p. 85.
46. Harris, "Prepositions and Theology," p. 1197.
47. Steve Jeffery, Michael Ovey, and Andrew Sach, *Pierced for Our Transgressions: Rediscovering the Glory of Penal Substitution* (Wheaton, IL: Crossway Books, 2008), esp. pp. 75-76, distract the reader from this point by redirecting attention from the purpose of Jesus' death "for the people" to the substitutionary function of that death, thus avoiding the crucial question.

John's view, the purpose of Jesus' death "for the nation" was not to propitiate God, but rather to unify God's people, "to gather together into one the children of God who are scattered" (John 11:52 NET; cf. 12:20-33).

Harris goes on to compare John 11:50 and 2 Cor 5:14, concluding by analogy that *hyper* bears the sense of substitution in the latter text the same as the former:

> Very similar [to John 11:50] is the Pauline affirmation that "one died for all" . . . where . . . *hyper* is shown to bear a substitutionary sense by the inference Paul draws: "therefore all died" (2 Cor. 5:14). The death of Christ was the death of all, because he was dying their death. In becoming the object of divine wrath against human sin, Christ was acting vicariously, viz., *hyper hēmōn*, not only "on our behalf" or "with a view to our good" but "in our place."[48]

Hyper has a substitutionary sense in this text, Harris argues, by reason of the inference that Paul draws from the proposition "one for all *(hyper pantōn)* died" — "therefore all died."[49] The death of "one for all" in 2 Cor 5:14, Harris thus contends, is "very similar" to the phenomenon of representative substitution in John 11:50.

Harris's argument falls apart at this point, however, because precisely here the analogy fails. Recall that *hyper* takes a substitutionary sense in John 11:50 because the death of "the one" is *exclusive* of the death of "the people." Were 2 Cor 5:14 a case of representative substitution "very similar" to John 11:50, therefore, we would expect Paul's inference in 2 Cor 5:14 to exhibit the logic of substitution in the way that John 11:50 does. That is, by analogy, we would expect the text to read "one for all died, therefore all were *spared*" or "one for all died, therefore all were *exempted* from death" — that is, "one for all died, therefore all did *not* die." Yet, Paul infers quite the opposite: "one for all died, therefore all died." Reading *hyper* in 2 Cor 5:14 with the sense of substitution would render senseless what Paul literally says: if Christ died instead of all, then Christ and only Christ died, but Paul says, "all died." Shillington comments:

> If Paul means that Christ died "instead of" all, how can he then propose the consequence that *all died*. If he intends substitution, surely he would use a different word and say, "Christ died instead of all, therefore all did not have to die." Paul concludes otherwise. Christ's death draws *all* into his death so that they die with him. . . . This concept is quite different from substitutionary death.[50]

---

48. Harris, "Prepositions and Theology," p. 1197.

49. Likewise, Riesenfeld, *"hyper,"* p. 513: "in the . . . forensic expression *eis hyper pantōn apethanen* in v. 14 the sense 'in the place of' is predominant, as is shown by the development of the thought in the following clause: *ara hoi pantes apethanon*."

50. V. George Shillington, *2 Corinthians* (Believers Church Bible Commentary; Scottdale, PA:

Harris, in his own commentary on 2 Corinthians, recognizes this point: "When Christ died, all died; what is more, his death involved their death."[51] Yet Harris maintains that "When Christ died, he was acting both on behalf of and in the place of all human beings."[52] Harris fails to see the logical contradiction in what he is saying: if Christ's death "involved their death," then Christ did *not* die "in the place of all" — if Christ's death was *inclusive* of "all" (representative), then it could not have also been *exclusive* of "all" (substitutionary). Harris, it seems, would have it both ways — whether Jesus' death is all-exclusive or all-inclusive, it is substitutionary. He fails to distinguish between exclusive and inclusive place-taking, resulting in a contradictory conclusion.

In order to avoid such a contradiction and so maintain a substitutionary reading of the text, it seems one would have to argue that "died" takes two different senses, literal and non-literal, in the two clauses of v. 14b. For if the "one" and the "all" both died in the same sense, and the "all" died on account of the "one" having died, then the death of the "one" is inclusive of the death of the "all," in which case we have representation, not substitution. Now, that Jesus' literal death on the cross is in view here is clear; so, the non-literal sense of "died" would appear in the second clause: "one for all died (literally), therefore all died (non-literally)." For the substitutionary view to work, it seems one would have to read Paul as saying that, on account of Christ having died "in place of all," it is (only) *as if* "all died." Margaret Thrall comments:

> The "substitutionary" interpretation may hold good if v. 14c means "all are regarded as dead," are dead *de iure* on the basis of Christ's death . . . all are, juridically, regarded by God as having died. This would mean that, whilst Christ alone in actuality suffered the penalty for sin, all are regarded *as though* they had suffered themselves.[53]

As Thrall points out, not only is this not what Paul's text actually says, but also this diminishes the sense of reality of the death involved:[54] the "all" did die, but not really.

We conclude: insofar as Jesus' death "for the people" in John 11:50 *is* a case of representative substitution because it is other-exclusive, then by the same criterion Jesus' death "for all" in 2 Cor 5:14 is *not*. Paul's inference there, "one for all died, therefore all died," implies just the opposite of John 11:50, that the death

---

Herald, 1998), p. 123, emphasis original. Cf. Margaret E. Thrall, *A Critical and Exegetical Commentary on the Second Epistle to the Corinthians* (New York: Continuum, 1994), p. 409, and Frank J. Matera, *II Corinthians: A Commentary* (Louisville, KY: Westminster John Knox, 2003), p. 134.

51. Harris, *Second Epistle to the Corinthians*, p. 421.

52. Harris, *Second Epistle to the Corinthians*, p. 421.

53. Thrall, *Second Epistle to the Corinthians*, pp. 409-10.

54. Thrall, *Second Epistle to the Corinthians*, p. 410.

of "one for all" is *inclusive* of the death of "all." Contrary to Harris, therefore, making literal sense of the internal logic of 2 Cor 5:14 requires reading *hyper* there as signifying representation: "one *on behalf of* all died, therefore all died."

John 11:50 is a case of representative substitution: Jesus' death "for the nation" is both other-exclusive and other-benefiting. 2 Cor 5:14 is *not* a case of representative substitution, for it is not a case of substitution; and it is not a case of substitution because Jesus' death "for all" is not "all"-exclusive but "all"-inclusive. 2 Cor 5:14, in contrast with John 11:50, is a case of *representation*. We thus concur with Davies, to this extent: "The statement that one died for all with the consequence that all may be said to have died must certainly mean more than the fact that he died for their sake or with a view to their good. It means at least that he died as their Representative if not as their Substitute."[55] We have demonstrated, however, that the logic internal to the text itself rules out "substitute" in this case.

15.4.2. Representation: Argument from Immediate Context

Careful examination of 2 Cor 5:14 clearly favors reading *hyper* there with the sense of representation ("on behalf of"). We shall argue, further, that the case for reading *hyper* with the sense of representation is confirmed when that text is read in conjunction with v. 15 and in the context of the following verses.

2 Cor 5:15 reads: *kai hyper pantōn apethanen, hina hoi zōntes mēketi eautois zōsin alla tō hyper autōn apothanonti kai egerthenti.* We might translate literally (keeping the Greek word order): "and he for all *(hyper pantōn)* died, so that the ones who live might live no longer unto themselves but unto him who for them *(hyper autōn)* died and was raised." The question here is how to interpret Paul's two uses of *hyper* in v. 15 in conjunction with v. 14.

2 Cor 5:14-15, we should notice, has a distinctive parallel structure:[56]

```
                    one died for all
            therefore all died
    and             he died for all
                                    in order that those who live
                                    should live no longer      for themselves
                                    but [that they should live]  for him
            who died [for them]
    and     was raised [for them].
```

55. Davies, "Christ in Our Place," p. 87.
56. Adapted from Paul Barnett, *The Second Epistle to the Corinthians* (Grand Rapids, MI: Eerdmans Publishing, 1997), p. 292.

These parallels, I think, weigh on the side of reading *hyper* ("for") with a consistent sense throughout. Insofar as we have demonstrated that *hyper* takes the sense of representation ("on behalf of") in v. 14, the parallel structure weighs in favor of reading *hyper* with the sense of representation in v. 15 also. Still, to avoid begging the question, we should not assume that, because Paul uses *hyper* in parallel phrases in subsequent verses, the sense of *hyper* must be the same in both verses. For it may be that Paul shifts meaning between verses. We see Paul employ such a meaning-shift within a single verse in Rom 4:25, using the preposition *dia*: "[Christ] was handed over *on account of (dia)* our transgressions and was raised *for the sake of (dia)* our justification." Rather than resting our argument on the parallel structure of 2 Cor 5:14-15, we will examine carefully the syntactical relations that internally connect the two verses.

It seems that if *hyper* takes the sense of representation in "one for all died" in v. 14b, as we have demonstrated, then it does so in "he for all died" in v. 15a. And this for two reasons. First, the Greek formulation of these two phrases is identical — *eis hyper pantōn apethanen* and *hyper pantōn apethanen*. Second, there is a tight syntactical connection between the end of v. 14 — "one for all died, therefore all died" — and the beginning of v. 15 — "he for all died." These clauses are connected by the coordinating conjunction *kai* ("and"), which indicates here a continuation or repetition of thought. In both phrases, therefore, Paul intends to say the same thing with the same nuance. Insofar as we have demonstrated that *hyper* takes the sense of representation in v. 14b, we should thus read vv. 14b and 15a together: "we are convinced that one *on behalf of* all died; therefore all died. And he *on behalf of* all died. . . ."

Continuing to v. 15b, we see again that it makes most sense to read Paul's third use of *hyper* also as "on behalf of" rather than "in place of." And this, again, for two reasons. First, v. 15b connects to 15a via the subordinating conjunction *hina* ("so that"), which indicates that Paul intends v. 15b to express the purpose of what has been stated to be so in 15a. We thus expect that what Paul declares concerning Christ's death in the main clause — that Christ died "on behalf of all" — to be affirmed and amplified in the subordinate clause expressing the purpose of that which he has declared. A meaning-shift in *hyper* here would seem to change the flow of thought from main clause to subordinate clause.

Second, were *hyper* to shift meaning within v. 15 from "on behalf of" to "in place of," then Paul would end up saying that Christ "was raised in place of them." It would seem rather odd, to say the least, for Paul to say that Christ substitutes for us in the resurrection of the dead — as if Christ's resurrection were exclusive of the very ones for whom Christ died! Elsewhere, Paul speaks not only of Christ's resurrection as the "first fruits" of a resurrection in which all those who belong to Christ will share (1 Cor 15:20-23; cf. 2 Cor 4:14), but also of our having been "raised with Christ" (Eph 2:6; Col 2:12; 3:1). Evidently, Paul understands the resurrection of Christ as in some way *inclusive* of us, that Christ was raised "on our behalf" and "for our sake" (cf. Rom 4:25). In resurrection as well as death, Christ is our representative.

We have thus shown that 2 Cor 5:14-15 speaks coherently concerning Christ's death and resurrection when we interpret *hyper* consistently throughout with the sense of representation ("on behalf of"). Might one, nonetheless, give a coherent reading of these verses from a substitutionary perspective?

For the sake of argument, let us agree with Davies, and others, that *hyper* must mean "in place of" in Paul's expression "one died for all" at 2 Cor 5:14, contrary to what we have demonstrated. It would follow, for the reasons we explained above, that *hyper* must mean "in place of" in that same expression at v. 15a. What, then, of v. 15b? Even those who are certain that Paul means to say that Christ "died in place of all" in vv. 14 and 15a do not insist that *hyper* takes a substitutionary sense in v. 15b. Davies translates, "him who for their sakes *(hyper autōn)* died and was raised."[57] Riesenfeld, similarly, maintains that *hyper* shifts meaning from "in the place of" in v. 15a to "on behalf of" or "in favor of" in v. 15b.[58] Could one translate *hyper* in this instance as simply "for our sake"? Yes. The benefaction of Christ's death and resurrection, however, is connected essentially to his status as substitute or representative. Thus, even if one prefers to *translate* "for our sake," *hyper* would still *connote* here either "in our place" (which is problematic in this instance) or "on our behalf."

But notice the implication. Insofar as *hyper* takes the meaning "on behalf of" in v. 15b, it does so concerning *both* Christ's death and resurrection; for the Greek syntax conjoins both under the *single* prepositional phrase *hyper autōn* ("for them"). And insofar as Paul intends to speak of Christ's death as *inclusive* of ("on behalf of") "them" in v. 15b, it only makes sense to infer that Paul intends to speak of Christ's death as inclusive of ("on behalf of") "all" in vv. 14 and 15a. For if Paul were to say that Christ died "in place of all" in v. 15a and that Christ died "on behalf of them" in v. 15b, then he would be saying that Christ's death is both exclusive and inclusive of those for whom he died, which would be a contradiction in terms. Although it is possible that Paul might speak of Christ's death as exclusive of "us" in one text but as inclusive of "us" in another text, we should expect Paul to speak consistently in the same sentence.

The only way to avoid this contradiction from the substitutionary perspective would be to maintain that Paul intends a *double entendre* in v. 15b, that in this one instance *hyper* means *both* "in place of," concerning Christ's death, and "on behalf of," concerning Christ's resurrection. A *double entendre* is possible when a preposition can express distinct but related senses (e.g., *dia*, "through" and "by means of").[59] Harris remarks that "*hyper* ... could simultaneously ex-

57. Davies, "Christ in Our Place," p. 87.
58. Riesenfeld, "*hyper*," p. 513.
59. Cf. Harris, "Prepositions and Theology," p. 1177.

press substitution and representation"[60] — that is, we take it, *hyper* could express the notion of representative substitution ("in place of" and "for the sake of"). But could it express contrary notions, exclusion and inclusion, at the same time? And would Paul have intended such? As Harris himself comments, "care needs to be exercised in determining an intended *double entendre*,"[61] and neither Harris nor Riesenfeld claims that Paul intends such at 2 Cor 5:15b.

We thus conclude that 2 Cor 5:14-15 hangs together perfectly well if we interpret *hyper* consistently as "on behalf of" in all three instances: "we are convinced that one *on behalf of* all died; therefore all died. And he *on behalf of* all died so that the ones who live might live no longer unto themselves but unto him who *on behalf of* them died and was raised." Moreover, if one insists that *hyper* takes a substitutionary meaning ("in place of") in v. 14, then (by reason of the argument above) one should do likewise concerning v. 15a; and thus concerning v. 15b one must maintain that either (1) Paul speaks of Christ's resurrection as exclusive of those for whom Christ died, or (2) Paul commits a contradiction in speaking of Christ's death as exclusive and inclusive in the same sentence, or (3) Paul employs *hyper* with a *double entendre* to express contrary notions (exclusion and inclusion) in a single instance. None of these interpretive possibilities seems tenable. These difficulties confirm our argument that *hyper* takes the meaning of representation ("on behalf of") in both v. 14 and v. 15, which gives a consistent and coherent interpretation. We can depict these results as follows:

Hyper in v. 14	*Hyper* in v. 15a	*Hyper* in v. 15b	Implication
1. "in place of"	"in place of"	"in place of"	Christ's resurrection is exclusive of those for whom Christ died
2. "in place of"	"in place of"	"on behalf of"	Paul commits a contradiction in terms — Christ's death is both exclusive and inclusive of "all"
3. "in place of"	"in place of"	"in place of" (death) and "on behalf of" (resurrection)	One preposition expresses contrary notions (exclusion and inclusion) in a single instance
4. "on behalf of"	"on behalf of"	"on behalf of"	Consistent and coherent

15.4.3. Representation: Argument from Extended Context

We last consider, briefly, 2 Cor 5:14-15 in context of the verses following and ask whether they support the interpretation of Christ's death as inclusive — and so

60. Harris, "Prepositions and Theology," p. 1197.
61. Harris, "Prepositions and Theology," p. 1177.

representative — of those for whom Christ died. And we think they do so, in four ways.

First, Paul speaks of the relationship of those for whom Christ died and was raised to Christ himself as being "in Christ": "if anyone is in Christ *(en Christō)*, he is a new creation" (v. 17a NET). Salvation by Christ's death and resurrection results in one being "a new creation" by inclusion "in Christ."

Second, Paul follows this by speaking of God's reconciling action as also being accomplished "in Christ": "God was in Christ *(theos ēn en Christō)* reconciling the world to himself" (2 Cor 5:19). Here, "in" *(en)* may very well have a *double entendre*, both "in" (locative sense) and "by means of" (instrumental sense), considering that Paul has just said that God "reconciled us to himself through *(dia)* Christ" (v. 18). We may thus infer that, in order for "us" to be reconciled to God who "was in Christ," the "us" reconciled to God "through Christ" must then also be "in Christ." And insofar as God's reconciliation of "us" to himself is accomplished by Christ's death, it would follow that Christ's death is inclusive of "us" who are reconciled thereby to God.

Third, Paul goes on to speak of the "ministry of reconciliation" that God gives to those who are reconciled to God through Christ: "Therefore we are ambassadors for Christ *(hyper Christou)*, as though God were making His plea through us. We plead with you on Christ's behalf *(hyper Christou)*, 'Be reconciled to God!'" (2 Cor 5:20 NET). One can see here an implied parallel between Christ's death "for all" *(hyper pantōn)* in vv. 14-15 and our ministry "for Christ" *(hyper Christou)* in v. 20. We now act "on behalf of Christ" in calling the world to reconciliation with God through Christ as Christ acted "on behalf of all" to reconcile the world to God through his death; as Christ has acted as our representative, so now we act as Christ's representative. Taking up this God-given ministry of reconciliation is what it means for us to "live no longer for ourselves" but for Christ (v. 15b). Christ's death "for all" is no more exclusive of the "all" for whom Christ died than our ministry "for Christ" is exclusive of Christ, in whose name we call the world to be reconciled to God.

Fourth, Paul concludes his discussion of Christ's death by speaking of God making sinners righteous: "God made the one who did not know sin to be sin for us *(hyper hēmōn)*, so that in him *(en autō)* we would become the righteousness of God" (2 Cor 5:21 NET). Davies takes this text to be a patent example of substitution.[62] He argues that, because Paul has said earlier that God has not reckoned our sins against us (v. 19), it must be that God has reckoned them to Christ instead, such that Christ takes our place as the bearer of sin-guilt — hence, "made sin."[63] Paul, however, does not say as much here, and elsewhere he

---

62. Davies, "Christ in Our Place," pp. 88-89.

63. Paul's expression "made sin" — *epoiēsen hamartian* — is the subject of much discussion. The difficulty for interpretation lies in the fact that this compact expression appears no-

says, not that God has reckoned our sins to Christ, but that God has removed our sins from us and nailed them to the cross (Col 2:14).[64] Davies thus makes a non-trivial, question-begging interpolation in the text.

Even so, does this "for us" mean substitution? Which is to ask, is Christ who is made sin "for us" *exclusive* of "us" who would become righteousness? For sure, there is place-taking happening here, but not substitution, one "in place of" another. Rather, we have here what Hooker has aptly termed "interchange" — Christ becomes what we are so that we might become what Christ is.[65] This is not a simple exchange of places, but a mutually inclusive place-taking: Christ "being made sin" does not exclude us from being sinners (which we are, justified by grace); and we "becoming righteousness" does not exclude Christ from being the righteousness of God (which he forever is). Notice, further, that just as God acted "in Christ" *(en Christō)* to reconcile the world to himself (v. 19) so God accomplishes this interchange of sin and righteousness "in him" *(en autō)*. The Christ who is "made sin" is thus *inclusive* of those who "would become the righteousness of God." Christ "for us" — by which he is "made sin" and we "become righteousness" — thus *includes* we who would become God's righteousness "in Christ."

15.5. Christ Our Representative

All the evidence we have considered concerning 2 Cor 5:14 — in analogy with John 11:50, in conjunction with 2 Cor 5:15, and in context of 2 Cor 5:16-21 — uniformly favors reading Paul's phrase "one died for all" with the sense of representation: "one died on behalf of all." Christ's death and resurrection, Paul says, were *inclusive* of all humanity: in both death and resurrection, Christ is the human corporate representative.[66] Morna Hooker thus comments: "'For

---

where else in the biblical canon (as far as I know), such that there are no scriptural precedents by which one might try to understand what Paul might have meant. Some commentators see in it a reference to the scapegoat of the Day of Atonement ritual (Lev 16:20-22). Other commentators read it as Paul's shorthand for saying that God has made Jesus a "sin offering." (In light of the fact that the scapegoat is referred to as a "sin offering" *(peri hamartias)* in Lev 16:9, even though it is not actually sacrificed but exiled, these two views could be merged into one.) Along with Shillington, *2 Corinthians*, p. 135, we read this expression in its context as a statement of Christ's identification and solidarity with humanity in sin and death for the sake of reconciling humanity to God.

64. We will address this point further in Chapter 18.

65. Cf. Morna D. Hooker, *Not Ashamed of the Gospel: New Testament Interpretations of the Death of Christ* (Grand Rapids, MI: Eerdmans Publishing, 1994), p. 35; Cousar, *Theology of the Cross*, p. 79. We will develop this notion of "interchange" further in Chapter 18.

66. We must be careful here not to draw the inference that Christ, as corporate representative of humankind, is only universally human, but not particularly human — i.e., a particular

all' — that little word *huper* once again. What does this 'for all' mean? It means, says Paul, that all have died. *Christ died, not instead of the human race, but as their representative:* in some mysterious sense, the whole of humanity died on Calvary."[67]

Elsewhere, Paul depicts Christ as the human representative in relation to Adam.[68] As all were in some sense implicated in Adam's sin, and thus became sinners "in Adam," so all are included in Christ's obedience, and thus become righteous "in Christ":

> Therefore just as one man's trespass led to condemnation for all, so one man's act of righteousness leads to justification and life for all. For just as by the one man's disobedience the many were made sinners, so by the one man's obedience the many will be made righteous. (Rom 5:18-19)

"Adam" and "Christ" here are archetypes, respective representatives of the human choice for sin and consequent subjection to death, realized by Adam, and of the human potential for becoming righteous and receiving life, realized by Christ. What Paul says concerning Christ's obedience in life and death,[69] he says also concerning Christ's resurrection from the dead: "For since death came through a human being, the resurrection of the dead has also come through a human being; for as in Adam all die, so all will be made alive in Christ" (1 Cor 15:21-22). The death that came to all by identifying with Adam in sin (by all hav-

---

instance of universal humankind. While the Representative Human, Christ remains a particular human. For if one is human in any sense, one is *a* human. Moreover, we should not suppose that, as the Representative Human, Christ in his humanity differed in any essential respect from that of any other particular human. For such would run contrary to the orthodox doctrine of the Incarnation, according to which the incarnate Son, with respect to his humanity, is essentially the same as all other humans: Jesus is "truly God and truly Man" (Definition of Chalcedon; cf. D. M. Baillie, *God Was in Christ: An Essay on Incarnation and Atonement* [New York: Scribner's, 1948], pp. 85-93). How it can be that Christ, in his human particularity, represents humanity universally, Paul does not explain, of course, nor do we attempt a rational explanation — it is a truth of revelation to be accepted by faith.

67. Hooker, *Not Ashamed of the Gospel*, p. 36, emphasis original. Regarding how one might understand Christ as the corporate representative of humanity in death and resurrection, see James D. G. Dunn, *The Theology of Paul the Apostle* (Grand Rapids, MI: Eerdmans Publishing, 1998), p. 211, and John Driver, *Understanding the Atonement for the Mission of the Church* (Scottdale, PA: Herald Press, 1986), p. 106.

68. For a thorough examination of the Adam-Christ typology in Paul's thought, see Morna D. Hooker, *From Adam to Christ: Essays on Paul* (Cambridge: Cambridge University Press, 1990).

69. As emphasized by Richard B. Hays, "Made New by One Man's Obedience: Romans 5:12-21," in Mark D. Baker, ed., *Proclaiming the Scandal of the Cross: Contemporary Images of the Atonement* (Grand Rapids, MI: Baker Academic, 2006), pp. 96-102, Paul's emphasis here is not on Christ's death per se, but his *obedience*. It is thus by Christ's obedience, in life and death, that humanity is made new "in Christ."

ing chosen to sin — Rom 5:12) is reversed by the life that comes to all by identifying with Christ in resurrection (by means of faith and baptism — 6:4-5). We
might express the Adam-Christ typology in this way: what had been done by
and come to Adam, and which has subsequently been done by and come to all
humanity (viz., sin and death), has now been undone and outdone by God
through Christ for all humanity, so that all humanity might be remade by God
in Christ. Adam's disobedience is undone by Christ's obedience; death "in
Adam" is outdone by life "in Christ."

Finally, as Driver observes, the notion of substitution (exclusive place-
taking) is inadequate to capture all of what Paul says concerning Christ's death:
it is both too one-sided and too narrow.[70] Too one-sided, because substitution
neglects the two-sidedness of Christ's work: Christ acts both on behalf of God,
representing God to humanity, and on behalf of humanity, representing humanity to God. That is the sense in which we affirm that the divine-human being Jesus Christ is the "one mediator between God and humankind" (1 Tim
2:5). It would be false to say that Christ "substitutes" for God, taking God's
place and acting exclusively of God; for, as Paul emphasizes, "God was in Christ
reconciling the world to himself" (2 Cor 5:19). Representation, therefore, allows
us to express the two-sidedness of the one undivided divine work of salvation.
Too narrow, because substitution carries an individual emphasis: we think of
substitution as primarily an exchange between individuals — this one in place
of that one. Yet, Paul nearly always uses plural, corporate language when speaking concerning Christ's death "for" others. Only twice does Paul use singular
terms with an individual emphasis.[71] In every other instance, some fifteen
times, Paul uses plural language with a corporate emphasis.[72] This corporate
emphasis is reflected in the plural language used elsewhere in the New Testament concerning Christ's death "for" others.[73] Jesus is not the universal substitute, taking the place of each human one by one (exclusion), but rather our corporate representative, taking the place of all humanity at once (inclusion) —
"once for all" (Rom 6:10).

---

70. Driver, *Understanding the Atonement*, p. 108.

71. Namely: "one for whom Christ died" (Rom 14:15) and "the Son of God, who loved me
and gave himself for me" (Gal 2:20).

72. Namely: "for you" (1 Cor 11:24), "for us" (Rom 5:8; 2 Cor 5:21; Gal 3:13; Eph 5:2; 1 Thess
5:10; Tit 2:14), "for our sins" (1 Cor 15:3; Gal 1:4), "for many" (Rom 5:15, 19), and "for all" (Rom
5:18; 8:32; 2 Cor 5:14-15).

73. Namely: "for you" (Luke 22:19-20), "for us" (1 John 3:16), "for our sins" (1 John 2:2;
4:10), "for many" (Mark 10:45; 14:24; Matt 26:28), and "for all" (1 Tim 2:6).

CHAPTER 16

"God Was in Christ":
Propitiation, Reconciliation, and Trinitarian Theology

All this is from God,
who reconciled us to himself through Christ. . . .
God was in Christ
reconciling the world to himself. . . .

2 CORINTHIANS 5:18-19

There is a *semantic* distinction between saying "Christ in our place" (substitution) and saying "Christ on our behalf" (representation), but is there a *theological* difference? And, if so, does that theological difference make a *practical* difference? The answer to both questions, we aim to show in this and the next chapter, respectively, is Yes.

16.1. The Cross: God Divided against Himself?

16.1.1. The Penal Substitution View

The penal substitution model depicts Jesus as God's propitiatory victim and humanity's penal substitute. In so doing, this model depicts God the Father acting against God the Son — bruising and smiting him, striking him with vengeance, punishing him and shedding his blood. Again, Hodge: "It pleased the Lord to bruise him. He was smitten of God and afflicted." Bonhoeffer: "God's vengeance is extinguished [upon Jesus] . . . who was stricken by God's vengeance for our salvation." MacArthur: "Here's what was happening on the cross: God was punishing His own Son. . . ." And Cranfield: "God . . . purposed to direct against His very own Self in the person of His Son the full weight of that righteous wrath which they deserved." Effectively, these descriptions of the cross depict atonement being made by means of a violent intra-Trinitarian transaction: the first person of the Trinity, God the Father, punishes the second person of the Trinity, God the Son, to satisfy the first person.[1]

This language suggests a picture of the Triune God in which the Son is a "detachable person" of the Godhead — from whom the Father can separate himself and remove himself to a distance, over against whom the Father can stand, and upon whom the Father can act for his own sake, to satisfy himself. In penal substitution perspective, the cross involves the Father acting against or upon the Son and so reveals God divided against himself. The penal substitution model thus implies a Trinity comprising not only distinct but separable, even conflicting, persons — quite contrary to the ecumenical creedal affirmation of Nicaea and Constantinople.[2] The orthodox Trinity comprises three distinct but inseparable persons — Father, Son, and Spirit — who are "one in being" or "of the same essence" or "consubstantial" *(homoousion)*. That the creed affirms three distinct divine persons who are "one in being" entails that we should not think that any one person of the Trinity can be divided off from the others. Likewise, we should not think of the distinct divine persons as three individuated instantiations of a generic "divine substance" that can exist as independent beings. Trinitarian theology, that is, is *not* "tritheism."[3] Fiddes aptly observes: "One of the problems of a theory of penal substitution is that it depends for its logic upon a strong individualization of Father and Son as independent subjects, which makes it hard to speak of the one personal reality of a God who becomes vulnerable for love's sake within his creation."[4]

1. Some feminist critics have thus charged that penal substitution portrays the cross as an event of divine child abuse. See Rita Nakashima Brock and Rebecca Ann Parker, *Proverbs of Ashes: Violence, Redemptive Suffering, and the Search for What Saves Us* (Boston: Beacon Press, 2001), and J. Denny Weaver, *The Nonviolent Atonement* (Grand Rapids, MI: Eerdmans Publishing, 1999), pp. 122-56. For an apologetic response to such charges, see Steve Jeffery, Michael Ovey, and Andrew Sach, *Pierced for Our Transgressions: Rediscovering the Glory of Penal Substitution* (Wheaton, IL: Crossway Books, 2008), pp. 228-33.

2. Following Timothy Johnson, *The Creed: What Christians Believe and Why It Matters* (New York: Doubleday, 2003), pp. 46-49, 59, 307-9, I take the Nicene Creed as a "rule of faith," as a guide to the interpretation of Scripture and as a constraint on the construction of theological models. Appeal to a Trinitarian creedal formula as a "rule of faith" that guides scriptural interpretation and doctrinal development belongs to an ancient tradition reaching back to Augustine in the fourth century (*On Christian Teaching*, 3.2-5) and Irenaeus in the second century (*Against Heresies*, 1.10). On the relation of Scripture to creed in the early church, see E. Glenn Hinson, "The Nicene Creed Viewed from the Standpoint of the Evangelization of the Roman Empire," in *Faith to Creed*, ed. S. Mark Heim (Grand Rapids: Eerdmans, 1991), 117-28, here pp. 123ff.

3. Cf. Kallistos Ware, *The Orthodox Way*, rev. ed. (Crestwood, NY: St. Vladimir's Seminary Press, 1995), pp. 29-31.

4. Paul S. Fiddes, *Past Event and Present Salvation: The Christian Idea of Atonement* (Louis-

16.1.2. *What Paul Says*

In Ephesians, Paul depicts Jesus on the cross, not as the object of God's ven-geance, but as God's agent of reconciliation: Jesus is the one who acts through the cross to destroy dividing walls and murder human hostility in order to make peace between Jews and Gentiles and to reconcile both to God. Paul, however, is careful not to divorce Jesus' peacemaking work from God's atoning work. The peacemaking cross of Jesus (Eph 2:14-18) is the gracious gift of God for our salvation (v. 8). Jesus' dying is God's own doing to cleanse, forgive, and justify humanity, God's faithful act of covenant righteousness. By saying that God "puts forth" or "presents" Jesus as the "mercy seat" (Rom 3:25), Paul makes it clear that God is acting, *not upon or against* Christ to satisfy God-self, but *in and through* Christ to demonstrate God's justice by redeeming humanity from sin. This is reflected in Paul's consistent use of prepositions throughout his let-ters to depict the intimate relation between God's action and Jesus' action: God acts "in" *(en)* and "through" *(dia)*, but never "against" *(kata)* or "upon" *(epi)*, Jesus.[5]

Paul describes the relation between God's action and Jesus' action in these terms: "All this is from God, who reconciled us to himself through Christ . . . that is, God was in Christ *(theos ēn en christō)* reconciling the world to himself" (2 Cor 5:18-19). This intimate God-acting-in-Christ is transferred to those that are "in Christ," to whom God has entrusted the message of reconciliation, so that now God-acts-in-us and we thereby participate in God's work of reconcili-ation: "So we are ambassadors for Christ, since God is making his appeal through us; we entreat you on behalf of Christ, be reconciled to God" (v. 20). Jesus' death on our behalf, having reconciled us to God, therefore, enables us to entreat others "on behalf of Christ" to "be reconciled to God." According to Paul, God now acts "through us" just as God acted "through Christ" in order that the world might be reconciled to God. James Dunn comments:

> . . . God was involved in the act of reconciliation — "through Christ" (v. 18), "in Christ" (v. 19). . . . The imagery is not of God as an angry opponent hav-ing to be cajoled or entreated, but of God, the injured partner, actively seek-ing reconciliation. . . . If Christ is the representative of God in effecting the reconciliation ("God was in Christ"), the apostles are the representatives of God in proclaiming it ("God makes his appeal through us").[6]

ville: Westminster/John Knox, 1989), p. 108. Concerning the relation of Father and Son at the cross, see Fiddes's helpful discussion on pp. 90-94, 108-10.

5. See Rom 3:24; 5:1, 9-11; 6:23; 8:39; 2 Cor 5:19; Eph 1:10; 2:7; Col 1:20.

6. James D. G. Dunn, *The Theology of Paul the Apostle* (Grand Rapids, MI: Eerdmans Pub-lishing, 1998), pp. 229-30.

So, whereas penal substitution depicts the Son taking the place of humanity as the *object* of the Father's wrath and, hence, as the recipient of the Father's retribution, Paul portrays Jesus as the *agent* of God's reconciliation, the One who through his death and resurrection saves us from futile lives of sin and reconciles us to God (Rom 5:8-11), thereby enabling us to become agents of God's reconciliation.

16.1.3. Is There Really a Problem Here?

Jeffery et al. see no real problem here for penal substitution. They point out, correctly, that the distinction between the persons of the Trinity allows "that a particular action can be done *by* one person of the Trinity (the subject of the action) *to* another (the object)."[7] Thus the Father can give authority to the Son and the Son can give glory to the Father; the Father can be faithful to the Son and the Son can be obedient to the Father; the Father can show love toward the Son and the Son can show love toward the Father. This, they conclude, dissolves critics' claims concerning a division of the Trinity in the penal substitution model: "All this demonstrates that it is perfectly biblical for one person of the Trinity to perform an action *upon* another: no division of the Trinity is entailed."[8]

In making their argument, however, Jeffery et al. commit the classic "slippery slope" fallacy. For in moving from premise to conclusion, they make a subtle shift from "to" to "upon" as if between these two prepositions there is a distinction without any difference. Yet this shift in terms slides over distinctions that do matter here. Between one person relating *to* or acting *toward* another and one person imposing *upon* or acting *against* another there is a non-trivial difference. Thus one person giving instruction, honor, or love to, and these being received by, another is one thing; but one person imposing punishment upon or exercising vengeance against, and these being suffered by, another is quite something else. The former involve a relationship of mutuality between giver (subject) and recipient (object), but the latter imply a status of subjection of recipient (object) to giver (subject).

The Trinity, Jeffery et al. rightly emphasize, does involve a mutuality of relationship between distinct persons; there is within God's being a reciprocal relating of persons one to another. The Trinity is wholly incompatible, however, with subjection of one person to another. That the Son is "begotten" of, and the Spirit "proceeds" from, the Father, as the Nicene Creed says, in no way implies a subjection of the second and third persons to the first person of the Trinity, all three of whom are eternally co-equal and act in concert by the operation of a single

7. Jeffery et al., *Pierced for Our Transgressions*, pp. 130-31, emphasis original.
8. Jeffery et al., *Pierced for Our Transgressions*, p. 281, emphasis added.

will, as Augustine says.[9] The very concern under discussion here is that penal substitution does indeed portray one person of the Trinity (the Father) imposing upon or acting against another person of the Trinity (the Son) — and, hence, the subjection of Son to Father, contrary to Trinitarian theology: God the Father subjects God the Son to punishment of death in place of humanity.

Now Jeffery et al. might reply that the Father neither "imposes" a punishment upon nor "inflicts" death against the Son. The Son dies willingly in accord with the will of the Father. There is here, not subjection, but rather simply obedience. We quite agree that the Son "humbled himself and became obedient to the point of death" (Phil 2:8). The voluntary *kenosis* of Christ is not to be understood as the subjection of Son to Father within the Trinity. That Christ "did not regard equality with God as something to be exploited" for his own sake "but emptied himself" does not imply that the Son thereby became subjected to the Father for the Father's sake, but rather that Christ denied himself the privileges of deity and subjected himself to the conditions of humanity in sin and death for our sake, all the while retaining essential "equality with God" (vv. 6-7).

The penal substitution view of the death that Christ suffers for our sake, nonetheless, does imply that it is something imposed and inflicted by the Father upon and against the Son. As Jeffery et al. emphasize, it is essential to penal substitution that death be understood strictly as divine retribution for human sin, an external penalty imposed directly by God's action. Death, they insist, cannot be simply the consequence of sin according to natural causes, but rather is a punishment that God inflicts upon humanity by divine intervention in the created order.[10] Now, if penal substitution is to be a coherent model of atonement, then its explanation of the problem of sin and death (death = divine retribution for sin) and its explanation of how the cross resolves that problem (cross = penal satisfaction of divine retribution) must fit together exactly. In order that the cross resolve that problem, therefore, Jesus' death must be an exact substitution for our deaths. Insofar as Jesus dies in our place, per penal substitution, then in order for Jesus' death to substitute exactly for our deaths, death must fall on him in the very same way that it falls on humanity: not simply as the natural consequence of sin, but as the punitive action of God. Otherwise, were this not so, then either we would not have exact substitution, punishment (of one) in place of punishment (of all), in which case we could not be sure whether penal satisfaction had been actually accomplished, or else we would equivocate on the meaning of "substitution." On the penal substitution view, therefore, the cross must be God's own act of judgment exercised against Christ in our place, a punishment imposed by God upon Christ.

9. See Augustine, *On the Holy Trinity* I-II.
10. Jeffery et al., *Pierced for Our Transgressions*, pp. 118-23.

16.1.4. A Necessary Corrective to the Penal Substitution View

John Stott does recognize the theological difficulty here and offers a clarification:

> We must not, then, speak of God punishing Jesus or of Jesus persuading God, for to do so is to set them over against each other as if they acted independently of each other or were even in conflict with each other. We must never make Christ the object of God's punishment or God the object of Christ's persuasion, for both God and Christ were subjects not objects, taking the initiative together to save sinners.[11]

This clarification is intended to serve as a corrective to the penal substitution model:

> Any notion of penal substitution in which three independent actors play a role — the guilty party, the punitive judge and the innocent victim — is to be repudiated with the utmost vehemence. It would not only be unjust in itself but would also reflect a defective Christology. For Christ is not an independent third person, but the eternal Son of the Father, who is one with the Father in his essential being.[12]

We agree wholly with the thrust of Stott's statements here; and we likewise reject all language depicting God the Father exacting punishment upon or inflicting death against God the Son, which is contrary to both Paul's speaking of God-acting-in/through-Christ and, as Stott implicitly acknowledges, the Nicene Creed. Stott himself is not consistent on this point, however. Although he rejects language depicting God the Father acting against God the Son, Stott nonetheless endorses Cranfield's view (quoted above) that God the Father directs his wrath "against" God the Son to satisfy himself.[13]

This recalls our previous discussion (Chapter 14) concerning the propriety of depicting Christ as God's "victim." On account of the sacrificial character of Jesus' death, that Jesus voluntarily offers himself on our behalf as a sacrifice of atonement for sins (cf. Hebrews), we may speak of Christ as both "priest" and "sacrifice," as did the Western Latin Fathers.[14] In doing so, however, we must take care not to sever the giving act from the gift given, the one who offers from the offering made. The life of the Son given "for us" is not an offering sacrificed by a third party, but an offering made by the Son himself in accordance with the

11. John R. W. Stott, *The Cross of Christ* (Downers Grove, IL: InterVarsity Press, 1986), p. 151.

12. Stott, *Cross of Christ*, p. 158.

13. Stott, *Cross of Christ*, p. 134.

14. H. E. W. Turner, *The Patristic Doctrine of Redemption: A Study of the Development of Doctrine during the First Five Centuries* (London: Mowbray & Co., 1952), pp. 96-113.

Father's will. Augustine thus writes appropriately of Christ as being "in one both the offerer and the offering."[15]

We must also take care not to sever the action of God the Father from the action of God the Son — and so must never speak either of the Father acting "against" or "upon" the Son or of the Son "appeasing" the Father. Here, again, Augustine proves a good precedent. While he does agree that Christ's death "was made a sacrifice for sin,"[16] Augustine is careful *not* to say that the Father acts against the Son or that the Son's death appeases the Father's anger. Indeed, Augustine emphatically rejects the very idea, not only that the Son's death appeases the Father's anger, but that the Father cannot show mercy unless his anger be appeased first.

Augustine addresses this matter in a series of questions concerning Rom 5:8-10. He asks, "But what is meant by 'justified in His blood'? . . . And what is meant by 'reconciled by the death of His Son'?" He poses a possible response with a series of rhetorical questions that express a view akin to penal substitution:

> Was it indeed so, that when God the Father was wroth with us, He saw the death of His Son for us, and was appeased towards us? Was then His Son already so far appeased towards us, that He even deigned to die for us; while the Father was still so far wroth, that except His Son died for us, He would not be appeased? . . .

Augustine then refutes this view with further rhetorical questions that express the contrary view: "Pray, unless the Father had been already appeased, would he have delivered up His own Son, not sparing Him for us? Does not this opinion seem to be as it were contrary to that [which was just mentioned]?"[17] Augustine thus takes the view that, far from the Son's death being required to appease the Father, the Son's death could in no way have appeased the Father in the first place. For unless the Father had already been appeased toward us, unless the Father were already moved by his own love toward us and so already disposed toward our good, he would not have sent the Son into the world for our sake in the first place (cf. John 3:16; 1 John 4:10).[18] Indeed, Augustine emphasizes, contrary to the penal substitution view, no appeasement is necessary

15. Augustine, *On the Holy Trinity* IV.14, in Phillip Schaff, ed., *Nicene and Post-Nicene Fathers,* series I, vol. III (Grand Rapids, MI: Christian Classics Ethereal Library), p. 107.

16. Augustine, *On the Holy Trinity* IV.12; p. 104.

17. Augustine, *On the Holy Trinity* XIII.11; p. 237.

18. D. M. Baillie, *God Was in Christ: An Essay on Incarnation and Atonement* (New York: Scribner's, 1948), pp. 188-89 (emphasis original): "God's merciful attitude toward sinners is never regarded as the *result* of the process, but as its cause and source. It all took place because God so loved the world."

for the Father to show us mercy, "For He hath not in anger shut up His tender mercies."[19]

"Therefore," Augustine concludes, "together both the Father and the Son, and the Spirit of both, work all things equally and harmoniously."[20] Here Augustine restates the "principle of inseparable operation,"[21] which defines (in part) the orthodox doctrine of the Trinity: "the Father, and the Son, and the Holy Spirit, as they are indivisible, so work indivisibly."[22] There is not, nor can be, any degree of division within the Triune God. This was the consistent view among the orthodox theologians, both East and West. Gregory of Nyssa, a Greek Father and contemporary of Augustine:

> All that the Father is we see revealed in the Son; all that is the Son's is the Father's also; for the whole Son dwells in the Father, and he has the whole Father dwelling in himself. . . . The Son who exists always in the Father can never be separated from him, nor can the Spirit ever be divided from the Son who through the Spirit works all things. . . . It is impossible to envisage any kind of severance or disjunction between them: one cannot think of the Son apart from the Father, nor divide the Spirit from the Son.[23]

Consistency with orthodox Trinitarian theology thus places a significant constraint on models of atonement: there can be no dividing or separating God the Father from God the Son, much less setting one person of the Trinity upon or against another.

16.1.5. What Remains of Penal Substitution?

All this being said, it is now unclear what remains of the heart of the penal substitution model — propitiation and retribution. The cross is necessary for sal-

19. Augustine, *On the Holy Trinity* XIII.12; p. 238.

20. Augustine, *On the Holy Trinity* XIII.11; p. 238. Augustine's expression "the Spirit of both" reflects the Western-Latin tradition of Trinitarian theology, which depicts a "double procession" of the Spirit from both the Father and the Son. The Eastern Orthodox tradition maintains the "single source" view, that the Son is "begotten" of the Father and the Spirit "proceeds" from the Father. See Ware, *Orthodox Way*, pp. 32, 91-92. The contested *filioque* ("and the Son") was added later to the Nicene Creed by the Latin West without ecumenical affirmation by the Greek East. Concerning this controversy, see Johnson, *Creed*, pp. 228-31. Nonetheless, Augustine's point here that the internal unity and harmony of the Trinity admits of no division or conflict between the distinct persons is affirmed equally in Eastern Orthodox theology. See Jaroslav Pelikan, *The Christian Tradition: A History of the Development of Doctrine*, vol. 2: *The Spirit of Eastern Christendom (600-1700)* (Chicago: University of Chicago Press, 1989), pp. 77-78.

21. Cf. Jeffery et al., *Pierced for Our Transgressions*, pp. 129-30.

22. Augustine, *On the Holy Trinity* I.4; p. 23.

23. Gregory of Nyssa, *On the Difference between Essence and Hypostasis*, quoted from Ware, *Orthodox Way*, p. 31.

vation, according to penal substitution, precisely because God's wrath is real and requires propitiation by penal satisfaction; and the cross effects atonement because Christ's death is real and actually accomplishes propitiation of wrath because it actually satisfies divine retribution. But if, as Stott says (and I agree), we must never "speak of God punishing Jesus" or "make Christ the object of God's punishment," then it is not at all clear how one is to say, without equivocating, that on the cross Jesus bears in our place the penalty of death for sin required by God. If Jesus bears God's punishment for sin in our place, but God does not really punish Jesus and Jesus is not really the object of God's retribution, then is Jesus really punished in our place, and is God's retribution actually satisfied? And if, as Stott says (and again I agree), we must never speak of "Jesus persuading God" or make "God the object of Christ's persuasion," then it is not at all clear how one is to say, without equivocating, that on the cross Jesus in our place has appeased the wrath of God against us. If Jesus takes our place under God's wrath, but Jesus does not really appease God and God is not really the object of Jesus' propitiating death, then does Jesus really appease God, is God's wrath actually propitiated?

It may be theologically unorthodox for the penal substitution apologist to *speak* in such terms, but it nonetheless seems logically necessary that one *think* in such terms if penal substitution is to make sense.[24] Stott's attempt to clarify terms and reform the penal substitution model in a manner consistent with orthodox Trinitarian theology seems to have emptied the cross of Christ of its objective content as the propitiation of God's wrath and the satisfaction of God's retribution — and, hence, has put into jeopardy the very logic of penal substitution. This leaves doubtful whether one can both retain the substance of penal substitution and maintain consistency with Trinitarian theology — a mere change of terminology will not suffice.[25] I. Howard Marshall has sought to do

24. Cf. Fiddes, *Past Event and Present Salvation,* pp. 108-9, and Peter Schmiechen, *Saving Power: Theories of Atonement and Forms of the Church* (Grand Rapids, MI: Eerdmans Publishing, 2005), pp. 319-20.

25. One might propose that a way to avoid this difficulty for penal substitution is to appeal to the divine-human nature of Jesus and say that God punishes Jesus in his humanity but not his deity, so that God's punishment is directed at Jesus qua human but not Jesus qua God. But this generates two substantial problems of its own. First, it would imply that it is only Jesus qua human, not Jesus qua God, who substitutes for humanity under God's wrath and judgment. But that would undermine the essential point that Stott himself so clearly emphasizes — atonement is made by God's self-substitution (*Cross of Christ,* pp. 149ff.). Second and more seriously, this proposal, by dividing Jesus' humanity from his deity, implies that Jesus comprises two separable persons, one human and one divine, that co-inhabit a single body. But this runs afoul of the orthodox doctrine of the Incarnation, according to which the incarnate Son is "a single undivided person who is God and man at once" (Ware, *Orthodox Way,* p. 71). As the Definition of Chalcedon states, the church confesses "one and the same Christ, Son . . . in two natures . . . indivisibly, inseparably . . . concurring in one Person and one Substance, not parted or divided

just that, retain the substance of penal substitution while revising it in accord with Trinitarian theology.[26] Whether his revision is successful, we will consider below. We note here that Marshall does so by revising the model's notions of judgment and penalty in a way that other apologists for penal substitution (e.g., Jeffery et al.) might find unacceptable.

16.2. The Cross: God Alienated from Himself?

16.2.1. The Penal Substitution View

Our doubt is confirmed when considering the penal substitution interpretation of Jesus' utterance from the cross, "My God, my God, why have you forsaken me?" (Mark 15:34). Stott maintains that this is "a cry of real dereliction" and, hence, that in Jesus' suffering and death on the cross "an actual and dreadful separation took place between the Father and the Son."[27] This separation between Father and Son happens, penal substitution says, because at the cross Jesus both bears the sins of all humanity and suffers the penalty for those sins in place of humanity, both of which are necessary in order for Jesus to satisfy divine retribution as the universal penal substitute. The Father, whose justice requires this punishment for sin but whose holiness can have nothing to do with sin, must separate himself from the sin the Son bears and so must separate himself from — and, hence, "turn his back" on or "hide his face" from — the sin-bearing Son.

To speak of "an actual and dreadful separation" between God the Father and God the Son suggests, again, the picture of a Trinity comprising not only distinct but separable persons, such that Father and Son can each exist and act apart from the other. In this situation, the Son's express desire in his darkest hour is for his Father's presence, for which he cries out. But the Father refuses his Son's request and denies his presence to his Son in his hour of peril for the sake of the Father's own integrity. The will of the Son and the will of the Father, unified in the garden and the trial, now seem to have diverged at the cross.[28] Ac-

---

into two persons, but one and the same Son . . ." (Philip Schaff, *Creeds of Christendom*, vol. II [Grand Rapids, MI: Christian Classics Ethereal Library], pp. 94-97).

26. I. Howard Marshall, *Aspects of the Atonement: Cross and Resurrection in the Reconciling of God and Humanity* (London: Paternoster, 2007), pp. 52-67. Cf. David H. McIlroy, "Toward a Relational and Trinitarian Theology of Atonement," *Evangelical Quarterly* 80/1 (2008), 13-22.

27. Stott, *Cross of Christ*, p. 81.

28. In defense of penal substitution, one might want to propose here that it is only Christ's human will that expresses the desire for his Father's presence at the cross and that Christ's divine will agrees with the dereliction and separation, such that Father and Son remain divinely united in will. Yet, such a solution would only shift the division, from within God's essential be-

cording to penal substitution, therefore, the cross separates Father and Son, such that accomplishing the work of salvation alienates the Son from the Father. Stott, recognizing the tension between this interpretation and Trinitarian theology, writes later of the "conviction that Father and Son cannot be separated, especially when we are thinking about the atonement. . . ."[29] Yet, according to Stott, that is precisely what the cross does, separates and alienates Father and Son. Where Stott sees one statement — "an actual and dreadful separation . . . between the Father and the Son" — being "balanced" by another statement — "Father and Son cannot be separated" — I see incoherence.[30]

Other penal substitution apologists, seeing this problem, have sought to blunt its implications. Jeffery, et al., sensing the tension between penal substitution and Trinitarian theology, attempt to avoid the idea of the Trinity being sundered at the cross by downplaying the language of "forsakenness" from literal claim to metaphorical reference: "the language of 'abandonment' or 'forsakenness' is a metaphorical way of referring to divine judgment."[31] Although put forth in defense of Stott's account, their suggestion that Christ utters only a metaphor from the cross is precisely the view that Stott himself repudiates. Stott insists — and the penal substitution model requires, he says — that we take Christ's cry literally as naming a "real dereliction" by God and an "actual separation" from God; a merely metaphorical reading will not do, in Stott's view.

I. Howard Marshall's view of the separation and alienation of Christ from God on the cross takes the problem to the extreme. As we have already observed (Chapter 3), Marshall revises the notion of God's judgment on sin, downplaying the notion of retributive punishment by infliction of proportionate suffering. God's judgment on sin, Marshall maintains, is manifested ultimately in the sinner's *exclusion* from God:

> To disobey God and rebel against him is to break the personal relationship with God, and thus in a sense to cut oneself off from him. Thus it is appropriate for God to respond to those who cut themselves off from him by excluding them from his kingdom. Final judgement is the execution of such a penalty after God, in his mercy, has provided a way of salvation that has been persistently refused and rejected.[32]

---

ing to within Christ himself, such that Christ's two wills (divine and human) are put in opposition. Such a view would be contrary to the orthodox doctrine of the Incarnation, which teaches that Christ's two wills, divine and human, are *both* in perfect concert with the will of God the Father. Cf. Ware, *Orthodox Way*, pp. 71-73.

29. Stott, *Cross of Christ*, p. 157.
30. Stott, *Cross of Christ*, p. 82.
31. Jeffery et al., *Pierced for Our Transgressions*, p. 72.
32. Marshall, *Aspects of the Atonement*, p. 33.

The ultimate penalty for sin is personal alienation from God, created by one's own sin but made permanent by execution of God's judgment. It is that eternal consequence of sin, more than death itself, that Christ our substitute bears in our place: "the central act [of salvation] can be regarded as God doing something in Christ that involves Christ's death while bearing our sins. This is the painful consequence of our sins, and it saves us from that painful consequence of exclusion from the kingdom of God."[33] On the cross, therefore, Christ not only bears the wrath of God and the consequences of our sin in death but also suffers the ultimate penalty for sin, "eternal exclusion" from God's presence.[34]

While we are appreciative of Marshall's rethinking of divine judgment in relation to atonement, especially his focus on both the relational reality of sin and the restorative aim of justice, we find the direction that Marshall takes here in thinking about the cross to be deeply problematic. Let us take his view on its own terms and see where it leads. Because sin is itself a break of relationship with God, the ultimate penalty for sin would be permanent personal alienation or eternal exclusion from God; it is this ultimate penalty that Christ has suffered in our place on the cross. Inasmuch as the cross is the penalty of sin borne by Christ in our place, it is effectively a break of relationship within God, between God the Son and God the Father. And because that break of relationship bears the ultimate penalty for sin, the cross marks a permanent separation or alienation within God: God the Son is cut off forever from God the Father by the penalty for sin that the Son bears as substitute for humanity. Having suffered the ultimate penalty of sin in place of sinners, Christ is excluded eternally from God.

That, I think, is the conclusion to which Marshall's view leads logically — and, clearly, it is unacceptable theologically: the orthodox Trinity is eternally unified. In order to maintain both Marshall's view and Trinitarian theology, it appears that we would need to take his talk of Christ suffering "eternal exclusion" metaphorically (per Jefferies et al.). Although such an interpretation seems plausible enough, it risks emptying penal substitution of its objective content. For, again, will a metaphorical punishment do within the penal substitution model? How does a metaphorical punishment propitiate divine wrath and satisfy divine retribution? We thus continue to doubt whether the penal substitution view can both retain its substance and be brought into coherence with Trinitarian theology.

16.2.2. The Testimonies of the Psalms, Jesus, Hebrews, and Paul

To think that the cross separates Father from Son is at odds also with the testimony of the psalms that Jesus cites from the cross as well the testimonies of Je-

---

33. Marshall, *Aspects of the Atonement*, pp. 51-52; cf. p. 130, n. 34.
34. Marshall, *Aspects of the Atonement*, p. 91, n. 56.

sus himself concerning his relationship as Son to his Father, of Hebrews to the ministry of Christ, and of Paul to the coworking of God and Christ in the cross.

The popular idea that God "turns his back" on or "hides his face" from Jesus at the cross is countered by the very psalm text that Jesus cites to express his identification with sinners. The psalmist praises God precisely because, despite his cry of dereliction, God has *not* forsaken his servant or turned his back on him: "For he did not despise or abhor the affliction of the afflicted; he did not hide his face from me, but heard when I cried to him" (Ps 22:24). This implication of the presence of God to Christ on the cross is reinforced by the other psalm text that Jesus cites at the moment of his death: "Father, into your hands I commit my spirit" (Luke 23:46; Ps 31:5a). By confidently commending his life into God's hands, Christ affirms the faithful presence of God in his very moment of death: if the Son were truly derelict and absolutely alone on the cross, abandoned and forsaken by his Father, as Stott says, how then could the Son die by giving his life into his Father's hands? Indeed, this psalm likewise affirms God's faithful presence to those who fear that God has abandoned them in their affliction: "I had said in my alarm, 'I am driven far from your sight.' But you heard my supplications when I cried out to you for help" (Ps 31:22). In the midst of suffering the "God-forsaken" death of sinners, Jesus cites the psalmist to express the faith that God is faithful to redeem (cf. vv. 5b, 7-8), that God does not nor ever would abandon his Servant.

Jesus testifies both to the unity of Father and Son — "The Father and I are one" (John 10:30) — and to the mutual indwelling ("coinherence") of Father and Son — "I am in *(en)* the Father and the Father is in *(en)* me" (14:10). The night before his death, Jesus tells his disciples that they will forsake him, but says, "Yet I am not alone because the Father is with me" (16:32). As John's Gospel gives no indication that the unity and mutual indwelling of Father and Son, or the constant presence of Father with Son, are in any way disrupted by the cross, it seems reasonable to assume that these hold as true at Jesus' death as much as during Jesus' life. Indeed, as Luke Timothy Johnson observes, the Son is intimately united with the Father through the mutual love between Father and Son and the Son's obedience to the Father's will (cf. 14:10, 31; 15:9, 15; 17:4).[35] The cross is the ultimate demonstration of the intimate unity of Father and Son; the Son does not die alone, because the Father was "in him" and "with him." It thus would contradict Jesus' own testimony to conclude, as does Stott, that "In the darkness, however, he was absolutely alone, being now also Godforsaken."[36]

Hebrews confirms the testimony of both the psalmist and Jesus. Hebrews is

---

35. Luke Timothy Johnson, *Living Jesus: Learning the Heart of the Gospel* (San Francisco: HarperSanFrancisco, 1999), p. 189.

36. Stott, *Cross of Christ*, p. 82.

intently concerned with the incarnate life and sacrificial ministry of Jesus on behalf of those with whom "he shared the same things" (Heb 2:14). Jesus not only shared the lot of suffering with humanity, but also was made "perfect through sufferings," "learned obedience through what he suffered," and earned the crown of glory and honor "because of the suffering of death" (2:9-10; 5:8). Where, we might ask, was God in the midst of Jesus' suffering? Was the Son perfected through suffering as the pioneer of salvation apart from the presence and participation of the Father? Did the Son learn obedience through suffering without the oversight and instruction of the Father? Was the Son crowned with glory and honor because he suffered in abandonment by the Father? The writer indicates the nearness of God in the suffering of Jesus: "In the days of his flesh, Jesus offered up prayers and supplications, with loud cries and tears, to the one who was able to save him from death, and he was heard because of his reverent submission" (5:7). Jesus suffered death in obedient submission to God; and for that very reason "he was heard" when he prayed for God's salvation. It is usual and appropriate to associate these "prayers and supplications . . . loud cries and tears" with Jesus' agony in the garden. There is nothing in the text, however, that prevents us from including here Jesus' prayers and cries from the cross — that God not forsake him (Mark 15:34), that God forgive his executors and persecutors (Luke 23:34), that God receive his life (Luke 23:46). In all these prayers, "he was heard." And Jesus was heard precisely because God was with Jesus in his death on the cross.

Paul, as we have observed already, also testifies that God acts "in" and "through" the death of Christ to bring about reconciliation. In Pauline perspective, far from separating Father from Son, the cross unites Father and Son in one purpose of making peace: "God was in Christ *(theos ēn en Christō)* reconciling the world to himself" (2 Cor 5:19); "For in *(en)* him all the fullness of God was pleased to dwell, and through *(dia)* him God was pleased to reconcile to himself all things, whether on earth or in heaven, by making peace through *(dia)* the blood of his cross" (Col 1:19-20). If "God was in Christ" in the sense that "all the fullness of God was pleased to dwell in Christ," and this is as true in Jesus' death as in his life, then "the fullness of God" dwelled "in Christ" on the cross. Paul's witness to salvation, including the cross, as the single work of an undivided Father and Son acting in concert for the sake of reconciling the world, would also seem to be invalidated by the penal substitution model.

16.2.3. An Unfaithful Father?

By his cry from the cross — "My God, why have you forsaken me?" — Jesus, as Jürgen Moltmann says, "is laying claim upon the faithfulness of his Father to himself, the Son who has taken his part."[37] To interpret the cross as the event in which God the Father actually forsakes God the Son — a "real dereliction," in Stott's words — would thus imply further that the cross represents the Father's refusal of his Son's claim and, hence, the failure of the Father to remain faithful to the Son. If the Son were truly "derelict" at the cross — "absolutely alone," in Stott's words — then it can only be because he has been left derelict, not only by his companions, but also by his Father. Per penal substitution, God, the same as humanity, abandons Jesus to his fate on the cross; God flees the scene as do the disciples (Mark 14:50) or at least stands "looking on from a distance" as do the women (15:40). That God had abandoned his Son was, actually, the inference drawn by the onlookers who derided Jesus: "He trusts in God; let God deliver him now, if he wants to; for he said, 'I am God's Son'" (Matt 27:43).

Attempting to preempt this implication, Stott claims that Christ's God-forsakenness on the cross was by mutual consent between Father and Son: "whatever happened on the cross in terms of 'God-forsakenness' was voluntarily accepted by both."[38] At first glance, this seems to save the appearances: the Father remains faithful to the Son, for the Son consents to the Father's absence. Yet, Stott insists that Jesus' cry is one of "real dereliction": Jesus is left "derelict" by all, even God. How, though, can one *consent* to be abandoned or forsaken by another? If I consent to your taking leave of me, then I have not been forsaken by you and you have not abandoned me — we have merely parted; I am left alone, but not derelict. Being forsaken or abandoned implies that the forsaken or abandoned party has *not consented* to the situation. What Stott says here to save the appearances thus makes no sense. It, moreover, puts the lie to the question in Jesus' cry, "Why have you forsaken me?" The question, taken as Stott interprets it, implies that the Son has actually been forsaken by the Father; but in truth, given what else Stott says, the Father does not forsake the Son because the Son has *consented* to die alone. Stott's view thus generates an unacceptable dilemma: either God has proved unfaithful or Jesus has cried falsely; if Jesus cries of "real dereliction," then he dies alone not by consent, in which case God proves unfaithful; but if Jesus dies alone by consent, then he is not really "derelict," in which case his cry of "real dereliction" proves false.

Moltmann, noting that Paul writes both of God "surrendering" Jesus and Jesus "surrendering" himself, says similarly: "This deep community of will between Jesus and his God and Father is now expressed precisely at the point of their deepest separation. . . . In the cross, Father and Son are most deeply separated in forsakenness and at the same time are most inwardly one in their sur-

37. Jürgen Moltmann, *The Crucified God: The Cross of Christ as the Foundation and Criticism of Christian Theology*, trans. R. A. Wilson and John Bowden (New York: Harper & Row, 1974), p. 150.

38. Stott, *Cross of Christ*, p. 151; cf. p. 81.

render."[39] And the same criticism applies: if Father and Son have equally willed this separation, then there is no real "abandoning" or "forsaking" of Son by Father; if the Son has consented to be abandoned to death by his Father, then the Son's cry, "Why have you forsaken me?" is without both sense and truth.

16.2.4. An Absent God?

If Jesus dies "absolutely alone," as Stott puts it, then the cross signifies the absence of God in the midst of Jesus' suffering and death. Now, Stott does rightly affirm the presence of God in Christ and thus the suffering of God in Christ through the cross: salvation through the cross is the work of God-in-Christ.[40] Yet an incoherence remains in Stott's view. If God was suffering in Christ upon the cross, then what sense are we to make of the claim that Christ died "absolutely alone" — indeed, what sense are we to make of Christ's cry of "real dereliction"? If Christ was in fact derelict, then God was not present and so could not suffer in Christ; and if God was in fact present in Christ's suffering, then Christ was not derelict. Stott cannot have it both ways as he wishes.

Moltmann, similarly, wants to say *both* that God "was himself active with his own being in the dying Jesus and suffered with him" and so was not "absent in the godforsakenness of Jesus," *and* that "The cross of the Son divides God from God to the utmost degree of enmity and distinction."[41] If God really suffers with the dying Jesus on the cross, then the cross does not divide Father from Son "to the utmost degree." Where Moltmann sees "paradox," I see incoherence — which Moltmann himself projects onto the Godhead: the cross "was a deep division in God himself, in so far as God abandoned God and contradicted himself, and at the same time a unity in God, in so far as God was at one with God and corresponded to himself."[42] In Moltmann's view, the cross reveals contradiction within God's own being. Moltmann is correct that "To comprehend God in the crucified Jesus . . . requires a revolution in our concept of God."[43] We thus cannot believe any longer in the god of classic theism — a static god that neither knows the suffering of humanity nor can be moved by love to save humanity. Yet we do not follow Moltmann in asserting a God who divides, abandons, and contradicts himself.

If Jesus were absolutely isolated from God — if the Son were divided from the Father "to the utmost degree" — in his suffering on the cross, then the passion of Christ would fail to reveal the love of God, contrary to the witness of

---

39. Moltmann, *Crucified God*, pp. 243-44; cf. pp. 241-44.
40. Stott, *Cross of Christ*, pp. 156-58, 329-37.
41. Moltmann, *Crucified God*, pp. 190, 192, 152.
42. Moltmann, *Crucified God*, p. 244.
43. Moltmann, *Crucified God*, p. 152.

both Paul (Rom 5:8) and John (1 John 4:9-10). Indeed, if God were absent from Christ at the cross, then the cross of Christ would not reveal God at all, except in the negative, as a God who absents himself from suffering and death. But that the cross of Christ reveals God is at the heart of New Testament Christology: Christ crucified, Paul says, is "the power of God and the wisdom of God" (1 Cor 1:24). Based on the Philippians hymn (Phil 2:6-11), the Gospel of John, and the Revelation of John, Richard Bauckham concludes that, far from God being "hidden," the Sovereign God makes himself openly visible in the cross:

> Briefly to recapitulate the testimony of the three New Testament witnesses we have studied to the effect of recognizing the crucified Jesus as belonging to the identity of God: Here God is seen to be God in his radical self-giving, descending to the most abject human condition, and in that human obedience, humiliation, suffering and death, being no less truly God than he is in his cosmic rule and glory on the heavenly throne. It is not that God is manifest in heavenly glory and hidden in the human degradation of the cross. The latter makes known who God is no less than the former does.[44]

Ironically, then, despite the intentions of both Stott and Moltmann, their views appear to empty the cross of its most powerful and pertinent message to a world groaning still in sin and death — that God has not abandoned the world to its despair but has come near in Christ and borne our sin and sorrow "with us" and "for us," that "God was in Christ" on the cross "reconciling the world" at the very nadir of the world's weakness and shame.

We thus need to understand Jesus' cry from the cross (Mark 15:34) in accord with that message. If God *has* abandoned Jesus to suffer and die alone on the cross, then the silence of the cross, the absence of a word from God to vindicate Jesus against his accusers and persecutors, signifies that God abandons the innocent victims to their fate at the hands of their torturers and murderers. If, to the contrary, God has *not* abandoned Jesus, then the silence of the cross signifies God's self-humiliated *presence* in the degradation of the cross, that God has voluntarily assumed the shameful weakness of the condemned, that God participates personally in the solitary suffering of the executed. The awful silence of the cross, the troubling absence of a word from God, signifies that God dwells with the degraded and broken, the tortured and executed in their "God-forsakenness" — indeed, that God consents to take their part and has done so to the uttermost. Jesus' cry from the cross finds a silent sky precisely because God is *already* fully present in and with him at the cross. The silence of the cross, therefore, signifies, not the absence of God, but that hung on the cross is God-self, that "Truly this man was God's Son!" as the centurion testified (Mark

44. Richard Bauckham, *God Crucified: Monotheism and Christology in the New Testament* (Grand Rapids, MI: Eerdmans Publishing, 1998), p. 68.

15:39). The cross of Christ thus ratifies the announcement from heaven at the baptism and transfiguration, that Jesus is the Son of God (1:11; 9:7). The cross of Christ, even in its silence, *is* the word of God.

16.3. The Scandal of the Cross: A Crisis for Theology

That the centurion knows the presence of God through the cross of Christ implies that our knowledge of God must conform to the revelation of the cross — and not the converse. The cross of Christ, even and especially in its silent "forsakenness," reveals to the world who God truly is. The cross thus occasions a crisis for theology:

> The silence of God in the cross produces a crisis in our knowledge of God; in the face of this scandal we can no longer project God from human ideas of power and glory, envisaging him as the supreme case of a human ruler, the ultimate and immutable cause of our mutable world.[45]

The silence of the cross is the absence of God, therefore, only insofar as we project onto the cross human presuppositions of the nature of deity. The silence of the cross is the absence of God only insofar as we expect to see in Jesus Christ the ideal god of Greek philosophy, who is immune from and indifferent to suffering within the cosmos.[46] The silence of the cross is the absence of God only insofar as we expect to see in Jesus Christ a lord of the cosmos resembling the lord of the empire, who vindicates himself and vanquishes his enemies by violence. The silence of the cross is the absence of God, that is, *unless* the scandal of the cross is true — that through the cross of Christ, God has chosen unto himself and taken upon himself what the world in its wisdom deems foolish, weak, low, despised, and of no account, the way of suffering and death, for the sake of our salvation (1 Cor 1:27-28). God-in-Christ has chosen the folly, weakness, and nothingness — the "God-forsaken" silence — of the cross by which to reveal his wisdom, power, and presence; and it is only by this silence, this nothingness, that we come to know the mystery of God who saves us in "Christ crucified" (2:1-2).

The death of Jesus is thus that event through which God enters most fully into the broken reality of human existence estranged from and hostile toward God, existence characterized as "in sin" and "under death." The cross figures the hopeless existence of a humanity that has forsaken God through sin and stands

---

45. Fiddes, *Past Event and Present Salvation,* pp. 194-95.

46. Even in the exodus story, YHWH responds personally to the suffering of his people and sets about to save them from their oppression (Exod 2:23-25; 3:7-10). Cf. Ware, *Orthodox Way,* pp. 63-64.

under God's judgment of death — an existence which in truth is, and hence which Jesus on the cross really experiences and thus expresses as, "God-forsaken."[47] Jesus on the cross voluntarily identifies with humanity in its alienation from and judgment under God; and because "God was in Christ," God, through the person and cross of Christ, consents to and participates in that human alienation and divine judgment for the sake of our reconciliation. God-in-Christ "journeys into the far country" of human alienation, even to the furthest point of suffering death, in order to return alienated humanity to God. By Christ taking the part of humanity separated from God by sin and standing under judgment of death, God draws into himself through the person and cross of Christ the breach between God and humanity brought about by sin and death in order to heal that breach.[48]

Now, although God participates in human alienation through the person and cross of Christ, we must not think that by this God becomes alienated from himself, that the cross alienates the Father in heaven from the Son on earth. For that would imply that the cross stands between an estranged Father and Son who must then be reconciled. That is precisely Moltmann's view: "The cross stands between the Father and the Son in all the harshness of its forsakenness."[49] So, Father and Son, alienated by the cross, must be reconciled by the resurrection: "The cross of the Son divides God from God to the utmost degree and distinction. The resurrection of the Son abandoned by God unites God with God in the most intimate fellowship."[50] To the contrary, the cross stands between a faithful God and an estranged world; and God reaches out in Christ through the cross to the world in order to reconcile the world to himself. The resurrection, moreover, is not God's self-reconciliation, but God's victory in Christ over the powers of sin, death, and hell (Acts 2:24-31; 1 Cor 15:12-28, 54-57; Rev 1:17-18).

It is at this point that I find the greatest divergence between my own view and that of Moltmann. Moltmann considers the crucial Pauline text that has guided our discussion here — "God was in Christ . . ." (2 Cor 5:19) — and correctly draws from it the clear implication of God-in-Christ suffering and dying "for us" on the cross: "Logically this means that God (himself) suffered in Jesus, God himself died in Jesus for us. God is on the cross of Jesus 'for us.'"[51] While I quite agree with Moltmann on this point, I find nonetheless that he tends to-

47. Cf. Ware, *Orthodox Way*, p. 80.
48. Cf. Fiddes, *Past Event and Present Salvation*, pp. 51-58, 108-10, 192-95. Fiddes writes (p. 109): "the idea of the participation of God in human alienation avoids the danger of separating the persons of the Godhead, while no less recognising their distinction."
49. Moltmann, *Crucified God*, p. 246.
50. Moltmann, *Crucified God*, p. 152.
51. Moltmann, *Crucified God*, p. 192. Curiously, however, I find not a single citation of this crucial Pauline text ("God was in Christ") in Moltmann's decisive chapter, "The 'Crucified God,'" including his discussion of the Trinitarian theology of the cross (pp. 235-49).

ward a "transactional" account of the cross: "what happened on the cross was an event between God and God"; "The suffering and dying of Jesus, understood as the suffering and dying of the Son of God . . . are works of God toward himself. . . ."[52] Moltmann's view effectively reduces the cross to an event internal to God, an intra-Trinitarian transaction between the first and second persons of the Godhead: the cross is God's action toward God-self. What is true of the cross is then also true of the resurrection, which is also God's action toward God-self, the action of the Father to reconcile with the Son he has abandoned at the cross. But if the cross is only "between God and God," then we have lost sight of the *other-directed* purpose of the cross, that the cross of Christ is God's action *for us* and *for our salvation.* And if the cross is essentially the action of "God toward himself," then we have obscured the *world-ward* stance of the cross, that Christ's cross demonstrates God's love *toward us* (Rom 5:8; 1 John 4:10), that God-in-Christ reaches through the cross *to the world* in order to reconcile the world to God. The cross of Christ reveals not "God against God" but *God against evil* (Rom 8:31-39) and *God for the world* (John 3:16-17).

Through the cross, God-in-Christ enters into the deepest wound of a broken world — a wound opened by sin, generating corruption, and leading unto death — and so comes to know by personal experience real humiliation and weakness, pain and loss, all in order to heal that wound. When we depict the cross as that which "separates the Son from the Father" or "divides God against God,"[53] we risk emptying the message of the cross of what is perhaps its most scandalous word. The cross of Christ takes humiliation and weakness, brokenness and pain, death and loss into the personal life of God precisely because "God was in Christ" on the cross.[54] The cross of Christ reveals God on a cross; the crucified Christ belongs to the very identity of God. Again, Bauckham:

> . . . we must consider Jesus as the revelation of God. The profoundest points of New Testament Christology occur when the inclusion of the exalted Christ in the divine identity entails the inclusion of the crucified Christ in the divine identity, and when the christological pattern of humiliation and exaltation is recognized as revelatory of God, indeed as the definitive revelation of who God is.[55]

52. Moltmann, *Crucified God,* pp. 244, 193; cf. pp. 149-52, 192.
53. Moltmann, *Crucified God,* pp. 151, 152: "The abandonment on the cross which separates the Son from the Father is something which takes place within God himself; it is *stasis* within God — 'God against God'"; "The cross of the Son divides God from God to the utmost degree of enmity and distinction." Elsewhere, Moltmann speaks of a "'bifurcation' in God" (p. 246). Cf. Fiddes, *Past Event and Present Salvation,* pp. 192-93.
54. This suggests developing a "theology of weakness." See Marva J. Dawn, *Powers, Weakness, and the Tabernacling of God* (Grand Rapids, MI: Eerdmans Publishing, 2001).
55. Bauckham, *God Crucified,* p. 46.

As Orthodox bishop Kallistos Ware puts it, "Looking upon Christ crucified, I see not only a suffering man but *suffering God*."[56]

Finally, the cross as viewed by Stott and Moltmann — the event that "divides God from God," where "God abandons God" — confronts the believer with a crisis of hope. If the Father separates himself from the Son in death, if God abandons his own Son at the very moment he surrenders his life, then how can Jesus' death as "one of us" grant us assurance that God is "with us" and "for us"? That was precisely Paul's threefold message of hope: that God is "for us" no matter who or what might be "against us" (Rom 8:31); that God "did not withhold his own Son, but gave him up for all of us" and so will also "give us everything else" (v. 32); that God is "for us" in the face of all powers of evil that threaten to "separate us from the love of God in Christ Jesus our Lord" (vv. 33-39). But if, in reality, the cross reveals that God left his own Son derelict as he faced the powers of darkness and death, what assurance do we have that God will not abandon us to "peril" and "sword"?

---

56. Ware, *Orthodox Way*, p. 80, emphasis original. Cf. Marshall, *Aspects of the Atonement*, pp. 57-58, Baillie, *God Was in Christ*, pp. 198-99.

CHAPTER 17

"Crucified with Christ":
Substitution, Participation, and Imitation

I have been crucified with Christ.

GALATIANS 2:19

Christ also suffered for you,
leaving you an example,
so that you should follow in his steps.

1 PETER 2:21

17.1. "Baptized into His Death"

The penal substitution model, by making Jesus God's propitiatory victim and humanity's penal substitute, struggles also to make sense of Paul's teaching concerning the relation of the baptism of the believer to the cross and resurrection of Jesus. If Jesus' death "for us" means that Jesus died "in our place," as penal substitution says, then it is hard to see what sense we are to make of Paul speaking of our "dying with Christ."

17.1.1. What Paul Says

Paul expresses this intimacy of "dying with Christ" in very personal terms:

> For through the law I died to the law, so that I might live to God. *I have been crucified with Christ;* and it is no longer I who live, but it is Christ who lives in

me. And the life I now live in the flesh I live by faith in the Son of God, who
loved me and gave himself for me. (Gal 2:19-20)

Paul depicts Jesus' death "for me," not as something that has happened "in
place of" and so outside of himself (per penal substitution), but as something
that has happened *to* himself personally: "*I* have been crucified with Christ."
And that the death of Jesus is something that has happened *to* himself rather
than "in place of" himself makes all the difference: "it is no longer I who live,
but it is Christ who lives in me." In Romans, Paul connects this transformative
"exchange" between dying "with Christ" and Christ living "in me" to the believer's dying and rising "with Christ" through baptism. Indeed, Paul speaks of
such an intimate relationship between Jesus' death and the believer's baptism
that some commentators interpret Paul to mean that the believer not only
symbolically identifies with Jesus' death but really participates in death "with
Christ."

Paul tells us that baptism incorporates us into the death of Jesus: "Do
you not know that all of us who were baptized into Christ Jesus were *baptized into his death?* Therefore, we have been buried with him *by baptism into
death*" (Rom 6:3-4a). By baptism, we have died with Christ, so that Jesus'
death to sin becomes our own death to sin and, hence, our own freedom
from sin: "We know that our old self was *crucified with him* so that the body
of sin might be destroyed, and we might no longer be enslaved to sin. For
whoever has died is freed from sin. . . . The death he died, he died to sin,
once for all. . . . So you also must consider yourselves dead to sin . . ." (vv. 6-
7, 10-11). And having died with Christ, not only are we freed from sin, but
also we will be raised to new life with him: "For if we have been *united with
him in a death like his,* we will certainly be united with him in a resurrection
like his. . . . But if we have *died with Christ,* we believe that we will also live
with him" (vv. 5, 8).

Notice, first, that Paul's language is *corporate,* not individual — "all of us"
were baptized into Christ, "we" have died with him. Baptism, therefore, concerns the relationship of the entire community of faith to Christ: as "the body
of Christ," the believing community identifies with Christ's death and resurrection through the ritual of baptism. Notice, second, that Paul's language is *participatory.* He speaks of us being baptized "into Christ Jesus" *(eis Christon
Iēsoun)* and so being buried "with him" *(synetaphēmen autō)* into death. By
baptism we have been crucified "with him" *(synestaurōthē)* and so have died
"with Christ" *(syn Christō);* in this way, we are "united with him" *(symphytoi)* in
death and resurrection.[1] Paul thus speaks of baptism as a corporate event that is

---

1. Concerning Paul's language of "participation" in Christ, see James D. G. Dunn, *The Theology of Paul the Apostle* (Grand Rapids, MI: Eerdmans Publishing, 1998), pp. 390-412.

both symbolic and participatory: by baptism, the community of faith identifies and participates with Jesus in his death and resurrection.[2]

From Paul's language concerning baptism, Charles Cousar draws the inference: "Romans 6:1-11 expresses the meaning of Jesus' death not as a vicarious substitution (Jesus in place of us) but as a participatory event (we were crucified with Christ)."[3] Even while recognizing the limited adequacy of the terminology of "representation" and "participation," James Dunn draws a similar conclusion:

> . . . Paul's teaching is *not* that Christ dies "in the place of" others so that they *escape* death (as the logic of "substitution" implies). It is rather that Christ's sharing *their* death makes it possible for them to share *his* death. "Representation" is not an adequate single-word description, nor particularly "participation" or "participatory-event." But at least they help convey the sense of a continuing identification with Christ in, through, and beyond his death. . . .[4]

David Brondos is skeptical of a "participatory" reading of Paul's language of dying and rising "with Christ" in baptism, arguing that such a view depends on later Platonist-metaphysical interpretations of Christian doctrine foreign to Paul's thinking.[5] We disagree. Brondos argues that neither Romans 6 nor any other Pauline text

> provides any firm evidence for the claim that Paul understood the relationship between Christ and believers in terms of some type of "mystical participation" or "ontological union." In order to interpret them in such a manner, such an idea must be read back into the texts, and metaphorical language must be taken literally.[6]

We do not propose here any "theory of participation" that attempts to explain in mystical terms or ontological categories how it is that we partake of the death

---

2. Cf. Luke Timothy Johnson's "realistic" interpretation of Paul at Romans 6 (*Reading Romans: A Literary and Theological Commentary* [Macon, GA: Smyth and Helwys Publishing, 2001], pp. 103-4, emphasis original): "Whatever its roots, Paul's understanding of baptism is startlingly realistic; he does not think of ritual in terms of an arbitrary set of signs, but rather as a *symbol* that participates in that which it signifies. . . . Paul regards the ritual of baptism as a such a symbol, an event that activates within the community the experience of Jesus' death and resurrection. . . . This realistic apprehension of baptism is pertinent to Paul's main point here, which is that the gift of God in Christ is not remote from them. It has happened to and in them, with their baptism."

3. Charles B. Cousar, *A Theology of the Cross: The Death of Jesus in the Pauline Letters* (Minneapolis, MN: Fortress Press, 1990), p. 74.

4. Dunn, *Theology of Paul the Apostle*, p. 223, emphasis original.

5. David A. Brondos, *Paul on the Cross: Reconstructing the Apostle's Story of Redemption* (Minneapolis, MN: Fortress Press, 2006), pp. 151-89.

6. Brondos, *Paul on the Cross*, p. 189.

and resurrection of Christ in baptism. Whatever sense we make of our being baptized into the death and resurrection of Christ, Brondos is correct that Paul's language of our dying and rising "with Christ" cannot be read strictly literally; for it is obvious that none of us here now literally died on Christ's cross or rose from Christ's tomb with him.

Nonetheless, we diverge from Brondos's interpretation of Paul's sense of the reality of Jesus' death. According to Brondos, Paul viewed Jesus' death as a historical event without any transcendent meaning, not necessarily having greater significance for the course of history than any other event: "Certainly that event changed the course of human history in many ways, but other events have also changed the course of history. In fact, *every* event alters the course of history in some way, making the world a different place."[7] In Brondos's view, Jesus' death is only one historical event among others. Because Jesus' death is a merely historical event with no trans-historical meaning, there is no sense in which anyone can in any way "partake of" or be "joined to" Jesus' death in the present. Jesus' death remains entirely in the past, and all we can do is remember it: "What is true of Christ concretely with regard to his passion, death, resurrection, and exaltation is *not* true of anyone else. These events cannot be brought out of the past into the present except by recalling them, just like any other past event."[8] While we do agree, of course, that Jesus' death "once for all" is an unrepeatable event, we do not agree with Brondos that it thus follows that Jesus' death is "just like any other past event."

To make sense of Paul's language of being baptized "into" the death and resurrection of Christ and of being "in" Christ, in the present tense, I think that we need to acknowledge that Paul's sense of reality is larger than merely literal, historical reality. As Brondos acknowledges, Paul understands Jesus' death as in some sense both a past event and an ongoing happening, speaking of it using a perfect tense, rather than aorist tense, participle: "Christ having-been-crucified" (1 Cor 1:23; 2:2). Christ's death is a past accomplishment with present reality.[9] I do not think we need to turn Paul into a Neoplatonist philosopher in order to say that he thinks of Jesus' death as *both* a past event that is unrepeatable ("once for all") and a present reality in which we might partake, any more than to say that he thinks of God's salvation as a past, present, and future reality. To say that we either read Paul as regarding Jesus' death as a merely historical event like any

7. Brondos, *Paul on the Cross*, pp. 191-92, emphasis original.
8. Brondos, *Paul on the Cross*, p. 194, emphasis original.
9. Cf. Paul S. Fiddes, *Past Event and Present Salvation: The Christian Idea of Atonement* (Louisville: Westminster/John Knox, 1989), and D. M. Baillie, *God Was in Christ: An Essay on Incarnation and Atonement* (New York: Scribner's, 1948), pp. 190-97, 199-200. That present reality, we would say, is made possible by Christ's resurrection and ascension. The risen and ascended Christ continues to mediate to us the reconciliation of the cross on earth through his priestly intercession from heaven. See Chapter 18 below.

other or impose a Platonist metaphysics onto Paul's theology, as Brondos would have us think, seems a false dilemma.

17.1.2. The Penal Substitution View

It seems to us that the penal substitution model fails to adequately capture Paul's depiction of Jesus' death as something into which we are incorporated by baptism. If Jesus died "in our stead," then what sense are we to make of Paul saying that "we have died with Christ" by baptism? If Jesus "takes our place" in bearing the divine penalty of sin upon the cross, then why would we ever speak of ourselves as being "crucified with him" by baptism? And if Jesus' substitutionary death was divinely designed precisely to bear God's wrath and so spare the believer a similar fate, then what would be the point of having the believer be "united with him in a death like his" by baptism? We may sum up the question: How can we be brought "into" the death of one who dies "in our place"?

John Stott's interpretation of Rom 6:1-11 illustrates the awkward exegetical task this text creates for the penal substitution model. He draws the same implication from these verses as do Cousar and Dunn: "So then baptism visibly dramatizes our participation in the death and resurrection of Jesus."[10] But if Jesus on the cross is our literal substitute, taking our place in a death imposed by God as payment of penalty for our sins, then the possibility of our participating in Jesus' death is categorically excluded: our lives cannot both be forfeited in death "with Christ" as payment of penalty for our sins and be spared from paying that penalty by Christ's death. Our actual participation in Jesus' death would thwart the substitutionary purpose and efficacy of the cross, for in dying "with Christ" we also would in effect be dying to pay the penalty for our sins, which would undercut the penal substitution logic of the cross. As Brondos points out, including Paul's language of participation within the logic of substitution either entails a contradiction or requires equivocating on the meaning of "dying":

> The problem, however, in combining the ideas of substitution and participation is that according to the first, believers *do not* die because Christ dies in their stead, but according to the second, believers *do* die together with Christ by sharing in his death. It is hard to see how these two ideas are not mutually exclusive, unless "dying" is understood in two different senses.[11]

Rom 6:1-11 is an anomalous text for the penal substitution model, therefore, failing to fit the model's explanation of the cross.

---

10. John R. W. Stott, *The Cross of Christ* (Downers Grove, IL: InterVarsity Press, 1986), p. 277.
11. Brondos, *Paul on the Cross,* p. 159.

17.1.3. An Attempt at Reforming Penal Substitution

Stott, recognizing that Paul's depiction of Jesus' death as a participatory event cannot be comprehended strictly within the terms of penal substitution, accommodates this anomaly by expanding the model to include the category of representation.

> It is in this respect that the death of Jesus must rightly be called "representative" as well as "substitutionary." A "substitute" is one who acts in place of another in such a way as to render the other's action unnecessary. A "representative" is one who acts on behalf of another, in such a way as to involve the other in his action. . . . Just so, as our substitute Christ did for us what we could never do for ourselves: he bore our sin and judgment. But as our representative he did what we by being united to him have also done: we have died and risen with him.[12]

What, then, is the sense of our participation in the death of Christ our representative?

> Having paid sin's wage (or borne its penalty) by dying, he has risen to a new life. We too have died to sin, not in the sense that we have personally paid its penalty (Christ has done that in our place, instead of us), but in the sense that we have shared in the benefit of his death. Since the penalty of sin has been borne, and its debt paid, we are free from the awful burden of guilt and condemnation. And we have risen with Christ to a new life, with the sin question finished behind us.[13]

Stott's interpretation of our dying and rising "with Christ" falls short, however. He does not make substantive use of the category "representative" that he introduces for the purpose.[14] He thus fails to account adequately for Paul's language of participation.

---

12. Stott, *Cross of Christ*, p. 276. By introducing the category of representation and distinguishing it from substitution, Stott diverges from Packer, who regards the distinction as "a distinction without a difference" (J. I. Packer, "What Did the Cross Achieve? The Logic of Penal Substitution," in J. I. Packer, *Celebrating the Saving Work of God: The Collected Shorter Writings of J. I. Packer* [Carlisle, UK: Paternoster Press, 1998], I, pp. 85-123, here p. 98). Stott's definition of "substitute" is compatible with the definition we developed in Chapter 15, but it lacks the crucial element that distinguishes it from "representative," viz., a substitute's action *excludes* the participation of the other.

13. Stott, *Cross of Christ*, p. 277.

14. Stott's introduction of the category of representation into the penal substitution model seems ad hoc. It appears late in his study of the cross (276 pages into a 350-page work) and seems intended only to deal with what would otherwise be an anomalous text and an awkward exegetical task. As far as I can tell, this is the only use he makes of the category of representation. Therefore, it seems to be only an "epicycle" on his penal substitution model.

Stott reconciles the penal substitution model with Romans 6 by downplaying the realistic sense of Paul's language of participation, thus minimizing our personal involvement in Jesus' death. On Stott's account, we do *not really* participate in Jesus' death by baptism: we have only "shared in the benefit" of Jesus' death but have not shared in Jesus' death itself. Although Stott's own category of "representative" would imply active involvement of the believer in Jesus' representative death, his view reduces the baptized believer from active participant *in* Jesus' death to passive beneficiary *of* Jesus' death.

Stott's view is effectively that Jesus is our "representative substitute" (see Chapter 15 above): Jesus dies in our place (to pay the penalty for our sin) and for our benefit (we are freed from the penalty of sin); we do not participate actively in Jesus' death itself ("Christ has done that in our place, instead of us") but only benefit passively from it ("the sin question [is] finished behind us"). In Stott's view, then, Jesus' death *qua penalty for sin* is exclusive of us, and Jesus' death *qua benefit of forgiveness* is inclusive of us. And that solution to the question at hand is coherent on the penal substitution model's own terms. But such a solution is inadequate to account for Paul's language of participation precisely because it reduces the involvement of the believer in Jesus' death from active participant to passive beneficiary — and so falls short of Paul's language concerning the believer's baptismal participation in Christ's death. Paul does use the passive voice in saying that we were "crucified with *(synestaurōthē)* him" (Rom 6:6) and "buried with *(synetaphēmen)* him" (v. 4) through baptism. That is the natural expression: both crucifixion and burial are done *to* a person by another. In expressing the believer's relationship to Christ's death itself, however, Paul uses the *active* voice: "we died *(apethanomen)* with him" (v. 8). As Paul sees it, the believer's relationship through baptism to Christ's death itself is one of active participation, not only passive benefit. It is this active participation by the believer in Christ's death itself, and not only passive receipt of any benefit that might accrue to the believer on account of it, that is most striking in Paul's language but which Stott's account downplays to neglect.

17.2. "Carrying the Death of Jesus"

17.2.1. What Paul Says

The "syndetic" aspect of baptism — that it joins the life of the community of believers to Christ in his death and resurrection — carries a practical implication: it prefigures the community of believers suffering as Jesus did, for Jesus' sake, in witness to Jesus as Lord. Baptism "into Christ," and so being "united with him" in death and resurrection, is baptism into the way of the cross, a way of suffering service. Just as participating by baptism in the death, burial, and resurrection of Christ is essential to identifying with Christ and belonging to the community of believers, so also is bearing suffering with and for one another part and parcel of the life of the community of believers (Col 3:12-13). Baptism marks the church and the Christian life with the sign of the cross: as Jesus suffered and died for our sake, so also the baptized community continues participating in the death of Jesus through its suffering with and for others.

Paul thus writes in his second letter to the church of Corinth:

> For we do not proclaim ourselves; we proclaim Jesus Christ as Lord and ourselves as your slaves for Jesus' sake. . . . We are afflicted in every way, but not crushed; perplexed, but not driven to despair; persecuted, but not forsaken; struck down, but not destroyed; always carrying *(periphero) in the body* the death of Jesus, so that the life of Jesus may also be made visible *in our bodies.* For while we live, we are always being given up to death for Jesus' sake, so that the life of Jesus may be made visible *in our mortal flesh.* (2 Cor 4:5, 8-11)

In three parallel phrases, Paul speaks of us carrying the death of Jesus "in the body," suffering affliction and being handed over to death for Jesus' sake, and making visible the resurrection life of Jesus "in our bodies . . . in our mortal flesh." Charles Cousar aptly comments: "Identification with [Jesus] results in carrying in one's body his dying. . . . Jesus' way is the way of the cross, and identifying with him means that afflictions are simply part and parcel of the apostolic existence."[15] We thus see here the practical definition of both the baptismal life of the believer and the apostolic character of the church: the apostolic church is to exist bearing the death of Jesus in its corporate body, thereby making visible through the afflictions of its member believers the resurrection life of Christ, which sustains church and believer in suffering witness to the gospel. Hebrews puts the point similarly. Because Jesus suffered self-sacrificially to make his people holy, identification with Jesus means that we also are to bear the suffering that Jesus himself endured: "Therefore Jesus also suffered outside the city gate in order to sanctify the people by his own blood. Let us then go to him outside the camp and bear *(phero)* the abuse he endured" (Heb 13:12-13). By suffering with and for sake of others, the church and its members bear the sufferings of Christ and so continue identifying with and participating in the death and resurrection of Jesus.

17.2.2. The Penal Substitution View

It seems to us that the penal substitution model falls short in making sense of Paul speaking of the church corporately bearing "the death of Jesus." If the

15. Cousar, *Theology of the Cross,* p. 152.

death of Jesus substitutes for the death of believers, if Jesus died "in our place" so we might be spared the death that Jesus died "for us," then why does Paul say that "we are . . . always carrying in the body the death of Jesus"?

Stott deals with 2 Cor 4:10-11 by effectively avoiding it. Distinguishing "the death of Jesus" referred to here from Jesus' death "for us," Stott does not interpret "the death of Jesus" in this text in connection with the atonement. He takes "the death of Jesus" here as "referring to the infirmity and mortality of our human bodies," which Jesus shared with us through his human nature.[16] As he sees it, "the death of Jesus" which we are "always carrying in the body" refers to the frailties of mortality that afflict us now, that Jesus knew as a human being, and that will be remedied through resurrection.

The difficulty with Stott's interpretation is that it fails to capture the association Paul intends to make here between Jesus' sufferings for us and our sufferings for others. By speaking of us as "always being given up to death for Jesus' sake" (v. 11), Paul seems to be alluding to Jesus himself being given up to death for our sake (cf. Rom 4:25). That is, Paul places our self-sacrificial suffering and dying for the sake of others ("ourselves as your slaves for Jesus' sake," v. 5) in implied parallel with Jesus' self-sacrificial suffering and death "for our sake" ("for your sakes he became poor," 2 Cor 8:9). Indeed, if "the death of Jesus" refers to the frailties of mortality in which Jesus shared, as Stott says, then Paul's reference here to "the death *of Jesus*" is superfluous. For we have no need to be "always carrying in the body the death *of Jesus*" to be reminded of the frailties of mortality; we are carrying more than enough of our own frailties "in our mortal flesh" to remind us daily of death.

I conclude that Paul intends to say that, through our afflictions for sake of Christ and others, we both bear Jesus' death "for us" and bear witness to Jesus' resurrection life "in our bodies." Paul's portrayal of the suffering of the church in its members as related intimately to the cross and resurrection of Jesus thus underscores his understanding of the atoning death of Jesus as a participatory, rather than substitutionary, event of salvation.

17.3. Dying for One Another

We encounter similar questions when considering how other New Testament writers describe the relation of the life of the believer to the death of Jesus. The earliest traditions of the church present the death of Jesus as establishing a pattern that his followers are called to imitate in their own lives (and deaths).

This could be made no clearer than by the story of Stephen (Acts 7). The first martyr of the church, Stephen dies an unjust death at the hands of the

---

16. Stott, *Cross of Christ*, p. 245, cf. pp. 279-80.

same religious authorities who handed Jesus over to death at the hands of Pilate. At his trial, Stephen brings a sentence of condemnation upon his head by making the same "blasphemous" pronouncement as Jesus did at his trial (Acts 7:54-57; Luke 22:66-71). And at his execution, Stephen utters the same words of trust in God and forgiveness of his executioners that Jesus had uttered from the cross (Acts 7:59-60; Luke 23:34, 46). Jesus, by his righteous suffering and unjust death, has shown those who serve God in his name how they are to live (and die): witnessing to truth, trusting in God, loving their enemies.

This same theme appears again in Hebrews, whose composition likely precedes the passion narratives of the Gospel accounts. After reviewing the great figures of the faith tradition and appealing to this "great cloud of witnesses" to exhort the reader to "run with perseverance the race that is set before us," the writer turns our attention to "Jesus, the pioneer and perfecter of our faith" (Heb 12:1-2). Jesus' faithful suffering is both example and encouragement to his followers who are also suffering for the faith:

> for the sake of the joy that was set before him [he] endured the cross, disregarding its shame, and has taken his seat at the right hand of the throne of God. Consider him who endured such hostility against himself from sinners, so that you may not grow weary or lose heart. In your struggle against sin you have not yet resisted to the point of shedding your blood. (Heb 12:2-4)

Paul appeals to what many commentators regard as a pre-Pauline hymn in exhorting believers in the church to pursue a life of self-less humility and mutual concern in imitation of the *kenosis* and death of Jesus:

> Let the same mind be in you that was in Christ Jesus, who, though he was in the form of God, did not regard equality with God as something to be exploited, but emptied himself, taking the form of a slave, being born in human likeness. And being found in human form, he humbled himself and became obedient to the point of death — even death on a cross. (Phil 2:5-8)

And one chapter later Paul connects together the themes of participation and imitation in personal terms: "For his sake I have suffered the loss of all things. . . . I want to know Christ and the power of his resurrection and the sharing of his sufferings by becoming like him in his death, if somehow I might attain the resurrection of the dead" (3:8, 10-11). For Paul, then, a personal relationship with Christ ("knowing Christ") means nothing less than participating ("sharing") in Christ's suffering and imitating ("becoming like") Christ in his death, in the hope of resurrection in Christ.

Just as we have found the Pauline idea of participation in Christ's suffering to be foreign to the penal substitution model, so also we think the common New Testament theme of imitation of Christ's death to be at odds with the notion of Christ dying "in our place." Here we will consider the teaching of the Apostles Peter and John, who also affirm that Jesus' death is exemplary for the community of believers. While Peter emphasizes the behavior of believers toward enemy outsiders and John emphasizes the love of Christians for "one another" within the covenant community, both point to Jesus' suffering and death as the definitive pattern for Christian conduct.[17]

17.3.1. Peter: "Follow in His Steps"

Peter writes that Jesus' death provides an example for the faithful who are enduring persecution and suffering injustice:

> For it is a credit to you if, being aware of God, you endure pain while suffering unjustly. If you endure when you are beaten for doing wrong, what credit is that? But if you endure when you do right and suffer for it, you have God's approval. For to this you have been called, because Christ also suffered for you *(hyper hymōn)*, leaving you an example, so that you should follow in his steps. "He committed no sin, and no deceit was found in his mouth." When he was abused, he did not return abuse; when he suffered, he did not threaten; but he entrusted himself to the one who judges justly. He himself bore our sins in his body on the cross, so that, free from sins, we might live for righteousness; by his wounds you have been healed. (1 Pet 2:19-24)

This text, acutely aware of the passion narrative and drawing from the Song of the Suffering Servant (Isaiah 53), proclaims two things: Jesus' suffering and death "for us" is an example that we are to follow; and he is our example to follow *because,* in suffering and dying thus, Jesus practiced what he preached. We are to follow in the way that Jesus taught us, which Jesus himself exemplified for us in his suffering and death.

Jesus taught his disciples not to retaliate against enemies, those who abuse or persecute, but to pray for their good (Matt 5:38-48; Luke 6:27-36). And in his own arrest, trial, torture, and execution he did not return the threats and abuse he received, but prayed to God for his abusers and persecutors (Luke 23:34). Jesus taught his disciples to not fear those having the power to put them on trial and put them to death, but to speak their words by the Holy Spirit and entrust their lives to God (12:4-12). And in his own trial and execution, Jesus spoke the truth fearlessly and committed his life into God's

---

17. See Mary H. Schertz, "Nonretaliation and the Haustafeln in 1 Peter," and David Rensberger, "Love for One Another and Love of Enemies in the Gospel of John," in Willard M. Swartley, ed., *The Love of Enemies and Nonretaliation in the New Testament* (Louisville, KY: Westminster John Knox Press, 1992), pp. 258-86 and 297-313.

hand (John 18:19–19:12; Luke 23:46). When we endure human injustice and bodily suffering in the cause of truth and justice and for the sake of the gospel while trusting God for our vindication, we imitate our Lord and Savior, Jesus Christ, who also endured human injustice and suffered bodily for our sake (cf. 1 Pet 3:13-18; 4:12-19).

Now if, as penal substitution says, Jesus dies "in our place" as our substitute, it is not clear how such a death would be exemplary "for us." According to Stott, "A 'substitute' is one who acts in place of another in such a way as to render the other's action unnecessary." But a *substitute* in this sense cannot be our *exemplar* because, by his taking our place in the action performed, our performance of such action is rendered unnecessary. Once the substitute has acted "for us" there is no need for us to follow him in likewise action. And it does not really make sense to exhort that we "*should* follow" in action one whose very action has rendered our acting unnecessary. What, one may reasonably ask, would be the point? To imitate in action one whose action "for us" has rendered our acting unnecessary would seem to render our acting likewise superfluous.

When we consider a "substitute" as one whose action "for us" *excludes* our involvement (see Chapter 15 above), moreover, the problem becomes acute. Jesus' death as our substitute not only renders unnecessary our imitation of him in death, but his dying excludes us from following him in like action. Should we follow Jesus "in his steps," we would be attempting to do what he has done "in our place" — and so to retake "our place." To imitate Jesus in death, according to the logic of substitution, would effectively be to displace Jesus from the cross, contrary to the very idea of penal substitution. An exemplar, by contrast, far from excluding our action, shows us the way to act precisely so that we might act in that way. It is thus difficult to see how penal substitution is to make sense of Jesus' death as exemplary "for us." The call to "follow in his steps" makes better sense if we think of Jesus' death "for us" as participatory rather than substitutionary, as inviting rather than excluding our involvement.

17.3.2. John: "As I Have Loved You"

Consider further 1 John 3:16 and John 15:12-13. These texts typify the Johannine emphasis on love, depicting the voluntary death of Jesus ("he laid down his life") as the demonstration of God's love for us and thus the model and mandate, the example and command, of Christian love for one another. 1 John 3:16 reads:

> We know love by this,
> that he laid down his life for us —
> and we ought to lay down our lives for one another.

Using a standard poetic form (A-B-C-D//A′-B′-C′-D′) in the latter two lines, John deliberately places our voluntary dying "for *(hyper)* one another" in parallel with Jesus' voluntary dying "for us *(hyper hēmōn)*."[18] This parallelism implies that the imperative to die voluntarily "for one another" is to be a reflection (mimesis) of Jesus' voluntary dying "for us," so that the disciples' obedience is conformed to the master's example. John thus depicts a symmetry between Jesus' death "for us" and our deaths "for one another." The immediate application of this teaching is mutual aid in the believing community, sharing "the world's goods" with brothers and sisters in need (v. 17).

John's exhortation echoes Jesus' own commandment in his farewell address to his disciples: "This is my commandment, that you love one another as I have loved you. No one has greater love than this, to lay down one's life for *(hyper)* one's friends" (John 15:12-13). Here Jesus draws out the implications of the "new commandment" that "Just as I have loved you, you also should love one another" (13:34). Jean Vanier comments: "In the Law of Moses, the Hebrews were called to love God with all their soul, heart, mind and strength and to love their neighbours as themselves. Here Jesus is calling his disciples not only to love others as they love themselves but to love as he — Jesus — loves them. That is what is new."[19] Jesus' new command, that the love of the disciples should be a reflection (mimesis) of the love of the master, recalls his earlier demonstration of love by washing their feet: "For I have set an example, that you also should do as I have done to you" (13:15). Jesus' new commandment, based on his own living example, implies an analogy: as Jesus has done for us, so we are to do for one another; as Jesus has loved us, so we are to love one another. And the supreme measure of Jesus' love for us is his voluntary dying for us; hence, as he lays down his life in love for us, so we are to lay down our lives in love for one another. Again, John depicts a symmetry between Jesus' love for us and our love for one another.

Despite the deliberate parallelism in 1 John 3:16 and the implied parallelism in John 15:12-13, reading these texts in penal substitution terms requires us to ignore the symmetries and assert an asymmetry between Jesus' laying down his life "for us" and our laying down our lives "for one another." If Jesus dies "for us" in the sense that he "takes our place" under divine wrath and punishment, then we certainly cannot do "for one another" as Christ has done "for us" —

---

18. The Greek text of 1 John 3:16 reads: *en toutō egnōkamen tēn agapēn, hoti ekeinos hyper hēmōn tēn psychēn autou ethēken — kai hēmeis opheilomen hyper tōn adelphōn tas psychas thenai.* We might translate literally, preserving the Greek word order: "in this we have known love, that he for us his life laid down — and we ought for the brothers the lives to lay down." The more fluid NRSV translation thus reverses the order of the Greek while preserving intact the original parallelism.

19. Jean Vanier, *Drawn into the Mystery of Jesus though the Gospel of John* (Ottawa: Novalis, 2004), p. 251.

otherwise, the penal substitution logic of the cross would be undermined. This asymmetry implies that Jesus' dying "for us" and our dying "for one another" are incomparable; there is no analogy between Jesus' death "for us" and the death of his disciples "for one another," such that "dying for" must be understood in distinct senses in the two cases. Our dying "for one another" cannot mean anything like Jesus' dying "in our place" on the cross; for it surely cannot mean that, like Christ "for us," we are to undergo divine wrath and punishment "in place of" others.[20]

This asymmetry and incomparability together generate, further, a practical problem. If Jesus' love-demonstrating death "for us" is the model and mandate for Christians to demonstrate love by dying "for one another," but there is no analogy between Jesus' death "for us" and our dying "for one another," then it is not at all clear how we would actually practice what is commanded here and, moreover, what would be our reason for doing so. If Jesus laid down his life on the cross "for us" as our penal substitute, yet none of us can serve as another's penal substitute, then how and why are we to lay down our lives "for one another"? If Christ demonstrates love for us by bearing divine wrath and punishment "in our place," then how can we demonstrate Christlike love for one another, since, unlike Christ, we cannot act the part of a penal substitute? We thus could not look to Jesus' death as that of a master whose example his disciples' actions might reflect; for in dying as our penal substitute, Jesus has done "for us" precisely what none of us can possibly do "for one another," much less imitate. Yet, John seems quite clearly to intend that we should look to Jesus' voluntary death as the supreme practical example of love that we ought and can mirror in our life together in the body of Christ (1 John 3:11-24; 4:7-21).

Morna Hooker, studying the relationship between the cross and discipleship in the Gospel of Mark, arrives at the same conclusion:

> If the first thing we learn about Jesus' death was that it is now understood to have been inevitable, then the second is that it must be shared by others. Those who wish to be his disciples must live as he lived — and that means they must be prepared to die as he died They must be willing to share his pain, his shame, his weakness, his death. His death is not seen as a substitute for theirs, but rather as a pattern.[21]

---

20. Packer, "What Did the Cross Achieve?" embraces such asymmetry and incomparability as the virtue, not weakness, of the penal substitution view (cf. p. 113). But insisting on this as he does requires a reading of 1 John 3:16 that must either ignore the obvious poetic-parallel form of the Greek text, or at least dismiss the semantic and theological implications of such textual forms. And neither option seems reasonable to me.

21. Morna D. Hooker, *Not Ashamed of the Gospel: New Testament Interpretations of the Death of Christ* (Grand Rapids, MI: Eerdmans Publishing, 1994), p. 53.

We thus conclude that the exemplary character of Jesus' death — as the demonstration of divine love and, hence, the model and mandate for Christian love — cannot be comprehended within the penal substitution model. Instead, 1 John 3:16 and John 15:12-13 are better read to say: as Jesus died "on our behalf" to demonstrate God's love toward us, so we ought also to demonstrate love toward one another by dying on behalf of our brothers and sisters; as Jesus voluntarily took our part, laying down his life "for our sake," so we ought also to voluntarily take one another's part, laying down our lives for the sake of our brothers and sisters.[22]

22. There is, of course, something singular about Jesus' life and death that marks them out from all other human lives and deaths: his is the life and death of God incarnate. But this must not be explained in such a way that makes Jesus' life and death *utterly other* than all other human lives and deaths; for that would obscure a crucial orthodox doctrine, that his life and death were also a very human life and a very human death, in every way like the lives we live and the deaths we face, except only that Jesus was "without sin" (Heb 2:14; 4:15). It is precisely for this reason that Jesus' life and death is a life and death with which all humanity can identify, in which all humanity can participate by means of baptism and discipleship, and because of which and in imitation of which all humanity can walk in obedience to God and love for one another.

PART II

SECTION C

Antiphon

CHAPTER 18

Jesus: God "for Us and for Our Salvation"

If God is for us, who is against us?
He who did not withhold his own Son,
but gave him up for all of us,
will he not with him also give us everything else?

ROMANS 8:31-32

For our sake and for our salvation
he came down from heaven. . . .
For our sake he was crucified under Pontius Pilate. . . .

THE NICENE CREED

18.1. Convergence and Divergence with Penal Substitution

Throughout Part II, we have considered a varied body of scriptural evidence from the Law, Prophets, Psalms, Gospels, and Epistles. No doubt, if one already believes that penal substitution is "the biblical view," one can then "search the Scriptures" to find evidence to support that view.[1] While one might read Scripture through a penal substitution lens, I have found such an interpretation to be not only unwarranted by, and at best a forced fit of, the scriptural evidence,

---

1. Steve Jeffery, Michael Ovey, and Andrew Sach, *Pierced for Our Transgressions: Rediscovering the Glory of Penal Substitution* (Wheaton, IL: Crossway Books, 2008), is a good example of how, having presupposed that penal substitution is the true theory of atonement, one can find penal substitution almost wherever one looks in the Bible.

but also premised upon extrabiblical presuppositions that are questionable on biblical grounds.

Nonetheless, this does not mean that I am in complete disagreement with the penal substitution viewpoint. I affirm the seven "basic truths" that I. Howard Marshall considers "essential to a New Testament theology of salvation" (see Chapter 6 above).[2] And I affirm what Peter Schmiechen identifies as the four "positive assumptions" in the penal substitution model: (1) "sin offends God and disrupts all human relations," (2) "the problem cannot be resolved by simply ignoring or forgetting it," (3) "from our perspective as sinners, Jesus dies the death of a sinner and in this way does in fact *take our place*," and (4) "from the standpoint of the history of Israel and faith in the risen Christ, there is a certain kind of necessity involved in the death of Jesus."[3] How we interpret these elements makes a crucial difference, however. In particular, I diverge from the penal substation view at points (3) and (4), concerning the vicarious character and necessity of Jesus' death.[4]

18.1.1. *The Vicarious Character of Jesus' Death*

Concerning the vicarious ("for us") character of Jesus' death, penal substitution apologists are correct to emphasize that Christ's priestly and prophetic ministry through the cross has a "substitutionary" aspect. The sacrificial, liberating, and reconciling aspects of Jesus' death do imply that, in a sense, God-in-Christ "takes our place."[5] Through the cross, God-in-Christ has done "for us" something necessary for our salvation of which we were incapable by ourselves: we could not, of our own initiative and by our own doing, remove our sins from us, take away the judgment upon our sins, free ourselves from captivity to the power of sin, and reconcile ourselves to God. For all that we needed God's own initiative, and God has done all that "for us" through the life, death, and resurrection of Christ. We thus affirm that atonement through the cross of Christ, if it is to deal adequately with the problem of sin, must be

2. I. Howard Marshall, *Aspects of the Atonement: Cross and Resurrection in the Reconciling of God and Humanity* (London: Paternoster, 2007), pp. 9-10. Thus, we agree with much of Jeffery et al., *Pierced for Our Transgressions*, in their overview of Christian theology (pp. 100-148), even if we are not convinced of their view that penal substitution is the lynchpin that holds Christian theology together.

3. Peter Schmiechen, *Saving Power: Theories of Atonement and Forms of the Church* (Grand Rapids, MI: Eerdmans Publishing, 2005), p. 118, emphasis original.

4. We have, of course, found numerous flaws with the penal substitution model, but focus here on only these two points.

5. Cf. Thomas R. Schreiner, "Penal Substitution View," in James Beilby and Paul R. Eddy, eds., *The Nature of the Atonement: Four Views* (Downers Grove, IL: InterVarsity Press, 2006), pp. 67-98, here pp. 68-70; Marshall, *Aspects of the Atonement*, pp. 38-52.

understood to this extent as "objective" — an action done on our behalf "from God's side."

Such "doing for" another what the other cannot do for or by himself, however, need not entail that one's action excludes the other's involvement or participation. There is a crucial distinction to be observed, between exclusive place-taking (substitution, strictly speaking) and inclusive place-taking (representation). God's atoning work in Christ "for us" thus need not be conceived as "substitutionary" in the sense of penal substitution — an action done "in place of" us. Our study has shown that the atoning work of God-in-Christ "for us" is not of the character supposed by penal substitution — a death "in our place" that propitiates God by satisfying retribution. For neither the priestly nor the prophetic ministries in God's covenant relationship with Israel, which Jesus fulfills, are understood properly in terms of propitiation and retribution (see Chapters 10 and 12 above); and Christ's death "for all" is an "all"-*inclusive*, not exclusive, event (see Chapter 15 above).

I do not want to overstate my divergence from penal substitution. God-in-Christ has done "for us" what is necessary for our salvation but we were powerless to do for ourselves (Rom 5:6-11), by dealing with our sin and its consequence of death (Rom 8:1-3; Col 2:13-14; 1 Pet 2:24) and doing so "once for all" (Rom 6:10; Heb 7:27; 9:26; 10:10). In doing so, God has both condemned (or judged) sin (Rom 8:3) and cleansed (or expiated) our sin from us (Rom 3:25; Heb 9:26; 10:10; 1 John 1:7, 9), no longer counting our transgressions against us (2 Cor 5:19) but instead removing our transgressions from us and nailing them to the cross (Col 2:13-14). Insofar as by all this is meant a "substitutionary" or "objective" atonement, I agree.

But I do dissent from the penal substitution view that God's wrath against sinners necessarily requires penal satisfaction in order that God might forgive sin in accord with divine justice, and hence that Christ satisfies God's wrath by substituting himself for sinners under God's retribution, suffering God's penalty of death for sin in our place. As I have shown, the two chief elements of this account are irredeemably problematic: that God's wrath necessarily requires penal satisfaction is biblically unfounded (see Chapter 12 above); and that God punishes Jesus and Jesus appeases God is theologically offensive to the Trinitarian orthodoxy of the Nicene Creed (see Chapter 16).

Yet, even if the biblically unfounded and theologically offensive notions central to the standard account of penal substitution were removed and the model were revised,[6] the penal substitution model of the action of God-in-Christ "for us" would still be inadequate. For it is difficult to see how the vicarious character and the participatory aspect of Christ's death can cohere on the terms of the penal substitution model. According to penal substitution, Christ

---

6. Cf. Marshall, *Aspects of the Atonement.*

"takes our place" such that Christ's death is an event that happens outside of, apart from, and instead of us — and thus without any involvement by us. We are only passive beneficiaries of what Christ's death has accomplished "in our place." This point is crucial to the logic of penal substitution: Christ's death "for us" is an event involving Christ *exclusively* of ourselves; for the grace of the cross is precisely that Christ *instead of us* pays the penalty of death for sin.

If, however, as Paul says, Christ's death "for all" implies the death of all — "one has died for all, therefore all have died" (2 Cor 5:14) — then it must be that Christ's death, rather than being exclusive, is an inclusive event of salvation, including all those for whom he died. Christ himself is thus not the universal substitute, acting "in place of" each human individually, but rather the corporate representative of humanity, acting "on behalf of" all at once (see Chapter 15 above). And if, as Paul testifies personally, "I have been crucified with Christ" and by this event my present existence has been mysteriously changed such that "it is no longer I who live, but it is Christ who lives in me" (Gal 2:19-20), then it must be that Christ's death itself, and not only its beneficial outcome, is an event that happens *to* and *in* me also — and, hence, is an event that involves me, my very person, in a real way (see Chapter 17). N. T. Wright comments: "The spectacular, unique events at the heart of the Christian story *happen to us,* not just at the end of our own lives and beyond . . . but while we are continuing to live in the present time."[7] It thus does not seem possible both to take Paul for what he actually says — "one died for all, therefore all died," and "I have been crucified with Christ" — and to maintain that Christ died "in our place" or "instead of me." The place-taking in Jesus' death is evidently *not* an *exclusive* place-taking (substitution) but rather an *inclusive* place-taking (representation).

In one respect, Jesus' death (and resurrection) does "for us" that which we cannot do for ourselves. By the power of God, the cross of Christ cleanses us of sin, removes our guilt, and frees us both from the weight and chain of sin and the ultimate end of sin in death. That is the "objective" aspect of atonement, and in that sense we may speak of a "substitutionary" atonement of God-in-Christ "for us." In another respect, however, Jesus' death (and resurrection) does "for us" that which it renders us capable of doing likewise. It gives us the example to follow, showing us both what is the true sacrifice we are to make (not the offer of a substitute victim in our name on an altar but rather the offer of our very own lives in the name of Jesus in devotion to God) and how we are to love our neighbor and overcome evil with self-sacrificial love. In both respects, the death (and resurrection) of Jesus is an event of salvation that we ourselves enter by baptism "into Christ." In both respects, therefore, Jesus' death and resurrection *involves us* — it is "for us" but not "instead of us" (see Chapters 14 and 17).

7. N. T. Wright, *Simply Christian: Why Christianity Makes Sense* (New York: HarperOne, 2006), p. 214, emphasis original.

18.1.2. The Necessity of the Cross

When thinking about the "certain kind of necessity involved in the death of Jesus," Schmiechen's comment is apt to be kept in mind:

> To find some principle established by human experience or reason that requires the death of Jesus is a precarious enterprise. If there is a reason for Christ's death, it lies in the faithfulness to God's purpose. We may even go so far as to say that it is ultimately bound up with the righteousness of God as such finds expression in justice and love. But such a statement is quite different from any claim to necessity based on distributive justice.[8]

We concur with Schmiechen that the necessity of the cross "lies in the faithfulness to God's purpose." Understanding the necessity of the cross in this way both cautions us against certain ways of thinking and points us toward an alternative way of thinking.

We should not think of the necessity of the cross as a logical or moral or metaphysical necessity that constrains God's action by external principle or directs God's action toward some higher end. God need not act this way or that way in working salvation (punish Jesus instead of humanity) in order to satisfy some higher principle (retribution). Nor is the necessity of the cross a metaphysical limit on God's power or options. God did not concede the cross because God could not do otherwise in the face of cosmic powers or because cosmic circumstances left God no other choice. There are no principles or powers — whether logical, moral, cosmic, or metaphysical — that subject God's freedom to prior conditions and so bind God's action, for there are no principles or powers prior to God. To think of God as acting under the universal necessity of a prior condition (a necessity that God punish Jesus because it is impossible that sins be forgiven without a satisfaction to justice) would not only restrict God's freedom but also undercut the voluntary, self-giving character of Jesus' suffering and death.

Rather than any logical principle or moral requirement or causal mechanism or metaphysical limit, it is God's own purpose and promise only, to which God is characteristically faithful, that determines what is necessary for God to do to bring about salvation. The "certain kind of necessity" involved in the life, death, and resurrection of Christ is thus none other than *divine integrity*. In other terms, we might say that the necessity of God's action involves a *teleological* or *final* causality ("in order to") rather than a mechanical or efficient causality ("as a result of"): God acts ultimately only on account of and for the sake of self-chosen ends, never as the mere result of external reasons.[9]

---

8. Schmiechen, *Saving Power*, p. 118.

9. Another way to put this point is that God transcends the Principle of Sufficient Reason: there are no causes "prior" to God, for God-self is prior to all causation.

The testimony of Scripture to God's work of redemption bears this out. Consider the exodus. Having heard the cries and pleas of the Israelites in Egypt, God resolves to bring about their deliverance from slavery, not simply because of the misery of the Israelites but ultimately on account of God's own prior promises to the patriarchs (Exod 2:24). God acts with righteousness and justice for Israel's redemption according to his own promise, out of faithfulness to his own covenant. Echoing the exodus story, Zechariah and Mary sing of the Messiah's coming as God's covenant faithfulness in fulfillment of God's promise of redemption (Luke 1:46-48, 54-55, 68-70, 72).

In his first sermon, Paul directly connects the purpose of the death and resurrection of Jesus Christ to the prior promise of God: "And we bring you the good news that what God promised to our ancestors he has fulfilled for us, their children, by raising Jesus" (Acts 13:32-33). Paul's gospel thus proclaims the message of the integrity of divine purpose and promise in the life, death, and resurrection of Jesus Christ — that God has acted faithfully in Jesus Christ, despite humanity's unfaithfulness, to complete God's own purpose of redemption in fulfillment of God's own promise. Insofar as God has revealed his promise through Scripture, therefore, Paul attests that Christ died and was raised "in accordance with the Scriptures" (1 Cor 15:3-4).[10]

In this regard, I quite agree with Anselm's nuanced thinking in *Cur Deus Homo* concerning the necessity of the Incarnation.[11] Anselm writes that "all necessity, and all impossibility, is subject to [God's] will. For nothing is necessary or impossible for any reason other than he himself so wills it."[12] Accordingly, Anselm distinguishes between "antecedent" and "consequent" causality and maintains that God acts necessarily only in the sense of antecedent causality (according to freely-willed, self-chosen ends), not in the sense of consequent causality (under constraint of external conditions), for there are no causes antecedent to God's will of which God's action is the consequent. To put it another way: God acts necessarily, not under compulsion, but only on account of self-consistency.[13] For Anselm, the rationale for the Incarnation of the Son and the redemption of creation lies within God and not in any external reason. Where we speak of the necessity involved in God's action as the integrity of divine purpose, Anselm speaks of the "unchangeability of divine will" or the "immutability of divine honor."[14]

---

10. Cf. David A. Brondos, *Paul on the Cross: Reconstructing the Apostle's Story of Redemption* (Minneapolis, MN: Fortress Press, 2006), pp. 46-48, 67-77.

11. Cf. Schmiechen, *Saving Power*, pp. 208-9.

12. Anselm, *Cur Deus Homo* II.17, in Brian Davies and G. R. Evans, eds., *Anselm of Canterbury: The Major Works* (Oxford: Oxford University Press, 1998), p. 343.

13. *Cur Deus Homo* II.5.

14. *Cur Deus Homo*, II.17 and 5, respectively. Recalling the discussion in Chapter 3 concern-

What, though, does Anselm understand God's ultimate will in saving humanity to be? The standard account of Anselm's theory in *Cur Deus Homo* goes along these lines: it was necessary for God to become human and suffer death because God's honor required satisfaction on account of human disobedience, a satisfaction that humans owed but which only God-as-human could make. That is correct as far as it goes, but it prompts the question: what was God's purpose in making atonement on behalf of humanity by means of the Incarnation — simply to fulfill the requirement of retribution? In Anselm's theory, the requirement of retribution regulates the *means* of God's act of atonement — sin cannot be forgiven unless satisfaction for sin is made by compensation to God or else punishment must be imposed upon the sinner — but does not determine the *end* for which God acts. The ultimate cause of God's action lies elsewhere — in God's constant will to restore his fallen creation and so bring his own purpose to completion.[15]

In taking this view, Anselm reflects the thinking of Irenaeus and Athanasius: what God seeks to accomplish through the Incarnation is the completion of God's original purpose in creation. As promised through Prophets (Isa 65:17-25), affirmed by Apostles (Acts 3:12-26; Romans 8; 2 Cor 5:17; Eph 1:8-10; Col 1:15-20), and confirmed by Seers (Rev 21:1-6), God's constant purpose throughout the ages is the renewal of all creation. The life, death, and resurrection of Christ both demonstrates God's faithfulness to this purpose and effectively brings God's "plan for the fullness of time" (Eph 1:10) toward its ultimate completion in "universal restoration" (Acts 3:21), "a new heaven and a new earth" (Rev 21:1).

What we need to avoid is abstracting the cross from the biblical narrative of God's purpose and promise and placing it into a logical scheme that converts the cross into the necessary and sufficient, but previously missing, causal linkage between humanity's situation and God's salvation. Neither Jesus himself nor the Apostles present the point of Jesus' death in such a manner (see Chap-

---

ing Anselm's two different notions of divine honor, Anselm is invoking here the second of those notions, divine honor as personal (covenant) faithfulness.

15. Here, again, we see the contrast between Anselm's satisfaction theory and Calvin's penal substitution theory: while in both theories divine justice is understood according to the retributive principle, in Calvin's view divine justice serves a punitive function, whereas in Anselm's view divine justice serves a restorative purpose. Anselm thinks the divine purpose for the Incarnation so important he devotes four chapters to it: God acts to save humanity from sin and death in order to fill the places in heaven left vacant by the fall of angels; Christ substitutes for sinful humans on earth in order that humans might substitute for fallen angels in heaven (*Cur Deus Homo* I.16-19). The reason this is ignored by most commentators, I suspect, is that Anselm's reasoning belongs to a thought-world foreign to the modern mind. Schmiechen, *Saving Power*, comments: "While the relevance of this discussion may elude us, what is particularly important is that the issue driving Anselm's consideration of it is the necessity of God's purpose" (pp. 202-3).

ters 7, 8, and 9 above). Paul proclaims that the Incarnation of the Son brings to fruition God's purpose of salvation by fulfilling God's promise of redemption: "But when the fullness of time had come, God sent his Son, born of a woman, born under the law, in order to redeem those who were under the law, so that we might receive adoption as children" (Gal 4:4-5). And John testifies that the moving cause of God's action in Christ lies ultimately in God-self, in God's personal passion for the salvation of the world: "For God so loved the world that he gave his only Son . . . in order that the world might be saved through him" (John 3:16-17). The Nicene Creed thus appropriately identifies the Father's purpose of bringing about salvation as the moving cause of the Son's life and death: "For the sake of us humans and for the sake of our salvation, he came down from heaven. . . . For our sake he was crucified under Pontius Pilate. . . ." Or, as the seventeenth-century hymn puts it:

> Love caused thine incarnation;
>   Love brought thee down to me.
> Thy thirst for my salvation
>   procured my liberty.[16]

18.1.3. An Alternative to Penal Substitution?

Therefore, I am moved to seek an alternative understanding of the "substitution" of Christ "for us" in which Christ "takes our place" in an inclusive way and in which the necessity of Christ's death is derived from God's own purpose of redemption as revealed in the Scriptures. Colin Gunton: "there is required a concept of substitution, albeit one controlled not by the necessity of punishment so much as by the gracious initiative of God in re-creation."[17] In developing an alternative account to penal substitution, further, we need an account that not only avoids the theological problems I have laid out but also understands Jesus' life-ministry, death, and resurrection (a) as an integral whole and (b) as integral to and fulfilling God's purpose of redemption.[18]

16. Paul Gerhardt, "O, How Shall I Receive Thee" (1653), translated by Arthur T. Russell (1851).

17. Colin E. Gunton, *The Actuality of Atonement: A Study of Metaphor, Rationality and the Christian Tradition* (Grand Rapids, MI: Eerdmans Publishing, 1989), pp. 164-65.

18. This search for an alternative to penal substitution, I came to learn at a late stage in the writing of this book, shares something in common with the view put forth by the Scottish evangelical theologian P. T. Forsyth in *The Work of Christ*, (London: Hodder & Stoughton, 1910), chapter V, "The Cross: The Great Confession." Forsyth's work was brought to my attention in Marshall, *Aspects of Atonement*, pp. 34-37. Where Forsyth speaks of "solidary reparation" to summarize Christ's work of atonement, we (following Christopher Marshall) will speak of Christ's "redemptive solidarity."

18.2. Redemptive Solidarity by Divine-Human Interchange "in Christ"

My chief aim here is to understand the "substitution" of Christ "for us" in a way that is true to the biblical witness and apostolic faith. Christopher Marshall's assessment of Paul's theology of the cross is helpful in pointing toward a more adequate understanding. I concur with Marshall that Paul's gospel of Jesus' death "for us" is understood better in terms of redemptive solidarity than penal substitution:

> . . . Paul himself does not understand the atonement as a matter of penal substitution as *conventionally understood*. He does not view Christ's sacrificial death as an act of vicarious punishment that appeases God's punitive wrath. . . .
>
> It is true . . . that Paul sees a *substitutionary dimension* to Christ's death. But it is substitutionary not in the sense of one person *replacing* another . . . but in the sense of one person *representing* all others, who are thereby made present in the person and experience of their representative. Christ died not so much instead of sinners as on behalf of sinners, as their corporate representative. . . . If anything, the substitutionary aspect of Christ's death applies not to his role as an innocent third party substituting for humankind in the face of God's punishment but to the activity of God (in Christ) substituting himself for humankind in the face of sin. . . . Christ suffers the penalty for sin not because God transfers our punishment onto him as substitute victim but because Christ fully and freely identifies himself with the plight and destiny of sinful humanity under the reign of death and pays the price for doing so. The thought is not one of legal imputation of guilt to Christ but of Christ's costly solidarity with humanity in its shameful and culpable situation.[19]

18.2.1. The Apostolic Witness

Paul writes at several places of "Christ's costly solidarity with humanity" in our situation of sin and death. At one place, Paul depicts this redemptive solidarity from Jesus' perspective: he "emptied himself, taking the form of a slave, being born in human likeness" (Phil 2:7a). Jesus voluntarily set aside the privileges of deity and took the part of humanity; he became one of us, for our sake, at cost to himself. By condescending from the position of deity to the position of hu-

---

19. Christopher Marshall, *Beyond Retribution: A New Testament Vision for Justice, Crime, and Punishment* (Grand Rapids, MI: Eerdmans Publishing., 2001), pp. 61-62, emphasis original. Cf. Hans Boersma, *Violence, Hospitality, and the Cross: Reappropriating the Atonement Tradition* (Grand Rapids, MI: Baker Academic, 2004), pp. 170-79, who cites Marshall in presenting "a model of penal representative atonement."

manity enslaved to sin, Jesus took fully upon himself the burden of human sin
and submitted himself to the end of all those enslaved to sin: "And being found
in human form, he humbled himself and became obedient to the point of death
— even death on a cross" (vv. 7b-8). Because of his suffering solidarity with humanity and his costly obedience to God, God exalts Jesus to the position of universal honor and cosmic lordship (vv. 9-11).

At another place, Paul depicts this redemptive solidarity from God's perspective: God sent "his own Son in the likeness of sinful flesh, and to deal with
sin, he condemned sin in the flesh" (Rom 8:3). God sends the Son "in the likeness of sinful flesh" on a mission "to deal with sin." In order to deal decisively
with sin itself, which the law had failed to do, God personally "takes on sin,"
confronting sin "in the flesh" through the Incarnation of the Son, passing judgment and pronouncing a death sentence upon sin. And God's purpose in doing
so was to redeem us who, "weakened by the flesh," are enslaved to sin and disobedient to God. God has thus "set [us] free from the law of sin and death . . . so
that the just requirements of the law might be fulfilled in us" (Rom 8:2, 4), so
that we might live in faithful obedience to God (cf. 1:5; 16:26).

Paul summarizes this thought of redemptive solidarity in various compact
formulas. In one place, he summarizes from Christ's perspective: "Christ redeemed us from the curse of the law by becoming a curse for us *(hyper hēmōn)*"
(Gal 3:13). In another place, he summarizes from God's perspective: "For our
sake *(hyper hēmōn)* he made him to be sin who knew no sin, so that in him we
might become the righteousness of God" (2 Cor 5:21). Peter parallels Paul's
thought: "He himself bore our sins in his body on the cross, so that, free from
sins, we might live for righteousness" (1 Pet 2:24). And again: "For Christ also
suffered for *(peri)* sins once for all, the righteous for *(hyper)* the unrighteous, in
order to bring you to God" (1 Pet 3:18).

There is more going on in these formulations of Christ's death "for us"
than costly solidarity with humanity, we should notice. Consider the latter
Petrine formula: Christ suffered once concerning sins so that the unrighteous
might be brought to God by the righteous action of Christ on their behalf. The
redemptive action here comprises three elements: (a) Christ suffered concerning the sins of humanity,[20] (b) the righteous one has acted on behalf of the unrighteous many, and (c) sinners are reconciled to God in Christ. In the midst of
Christ's suffering solidarity with humanity in its sinful situation, and human-

20. Some commentators see in the phrase *peri harmartiōn* ("for sins") in 1 Pet 3:18 an implicit reference to atoning sacrifice, inasmuch as *peri harmartias* is a formula used in the Septuagint in reference to the sin offering. If that is implied here, then Christ's suffering is being portrayed as sacrificial: Christ offers himself in death as an atoning sacrifice to expiate sins. But
even if so, this does not alter the character of Christ's action "for us" in this text. For, as we have
demonstrated (Chapters 10 and 11), atoning sacrifice for sin in the Levitical cult is not understood as a simple exchange or substitution.

ity's reconciliation to God through solidarity with Christ, there is an "exchange" between Christ and sinners: "the righteous for *(hyper)* the unrighteous." This action is not two parties "trading places" or one party "replacing" another; for both parties, the righteous one and the unrighteous many, end up in the same place — with God. We thus have here, not a simple exchange or substitution, but rather what Morna Hooker has called "interchange."[21] Even this term "interchange," as Hooker recognizes, is not entirely adequate. For the action here is not mutual or reciprocal between Christ and sinners. Sinners are included in Christ's action on their behalf; we are reconciled to God "in Christ." But the action begins at Christ's initiative, and it is through the action of Christ that we are brought to God.[22] We may, nonetheless, observe this pattern: solidarity/interchange/reconciliation. At the heart of Christ's redemptive solidarity for the sake of humanity's reconciliation, then, is a divine-human interchange "in Christ."

Hooker is thus right to identify in Paul's formulas of redemptive solidarity an interchange between Christ and humanity:

> Paul has now given us three statements that the death of Christ took place in order that something might happen to us; three sets of opposites — *death leads to life, curse leads to blessing, sin leads to righteousness.* Christ shared our condition of sin and alienation and death in order that we might share his victory. . . . These bold sentences express Paul's conviction that Christ shares fully in the human situation in order that, *in him,* we may share in his.[23]

In another concise formulation, Paul depicts redemptive solidarity — Christ's solidarity with humanity, and humanity's redemption in Christ — as an interchange of riches for poverty (Christ) and poverty for riches (humanity): "For you know the generous act of our Lord Jesus Christ, that though he was rich, yet for your sakes he became poor, so that by his poverty you might become rich" (2 Cor 8:9). As in the Petrine formula examined above, the redemptive action here comprises three elements: (a) Christ has taken up the "poverty" of the human condition, (b) the "rich" one has acted on behalf of the "poor" many, and (c) the "poor" many receive the "riches" of God in Christ. We thus have here the same pattern: solidarity/interchange/redemption. Again, this is not a simple exchange or substitution, one party "in place of" another; for both parties, the "rich" one who becomes "poor" and the "poor" many who become

---

21. Morna D. Hooker, *From Adam to Christ: Essays on Paul* (Cambridge: Cambridge University Press, 1990), pp. 13-71.

22. Cf. Hooker, *From Adam to Christ,* pp. 26-27.

23. Morna D. Hooker, *Not Ashamed of the Gospel: New Testament Interpretations of the Death of Christ* (Grand Rapids, MI: Eerdmans Publishing, 1994), p. 35, emphasis original, citing 1 Thess 5:10; Gal 3:13; and 2 Cor 5:21.

"rich," ultimately share in the "riches" of God (cf. Eph 1:7, 18; 2:7; 3:8). And, again, the action is not mutual or reciprocal: the action begins at Christ's initiative, and it is through Christ's action on our behalf, in taking our "poverty" on himself, that we are able to gain God's "riches."

Both redemptive solidarity and divine-human interchange are integral, essential aspects of God-in-Christ's action "for us and for our salvation."[24] For Christ not only shares in the conditions of human existence (solidarity) but also assumes the liabilities of human action (interchange) — so that we might be delivered from *both* captivity to sin *and* the consequence of sin to become righteous (or "rich") "in Christ." Christ has taken on himself not only the frailties of our nature but also the responsibility for our sin. Jesus has thus identified himself with us not only *qua* mortals, but also *qua* sinners: "For our sake [God] made him to be sin who knew no sin . . ." (2 Cor 5:21); "He himself bore our sins in his body on the cross . . ." (1 Pet 2:24).

Theologian A. James Reimer is thus quite right to argue that Christ's solidarity "with us" in life and death is by itself insufficient for our redemption from sin and death. There is needed also "vicarious, representative suffering" as "a way of taking seriously sin and the fallenness of the world as well as redemptive transformation and the struggle for social justice."[25] Reimer recalls Bonhoeffer's notion of "deputyship," according to which one takes responsibility for others, to supply the needed "for us" of representation in addition to the "with us" of solidarity:

> Jesus . . . lived in deputyship for us as the incarnate Son of God, and that is why through Him all human life is in essence a life of deputyship. Jesus was not the individual, desiring to achieve a perfection of his own, but He lived only as the one who has taken up into Himself and who bears within Himself the selves of all men. All His living, His action, and His dying was deputyship.[26]

Jesus is thus not only "with us" but also "for us" in his life, ministry, and death. But, again, this "for us" is inclusive, not exclusive, of us. Jesus is not the universal substitute, replacing each of us individually, but rather the representative human, whose living and acting and dying includes us all. Jesus is "the one who has taken up into Himself and who bears within Himself the selves of all men." This inclusive aspect of Jesus' "deputyship" is crucial for Bonhoeffer's ethics, in which

24. Cf. Hooker, *From Adam to Christ*, p. 27.

25. A. James Reimer, "Jesus Christ, the Man for Others: The Suffering God in the Thought of Paul Tillich and Dietrich Bonhoeffer," *Laval théologique et philosophique* 62 (October 2006), 499-509, here p. 500.

26. Dietrich Bonhoeffer, *Ethics* (New York: Touchstone, 1995), p. 222. In the newest edition of *Ethics* (Minneapolis: Fortress, 2005), p. 258, *Stellvertretung*, "deputyship," is rendered "vicarious representation," "vicarious representative action."

Jesus as "the man for others" provides the supreme example of a responsible human life: "In Him there is fulfilled what the living, the action and the suffering of men ought to be. In this real deputyship which constitutes His human existence He is the responsible person *par excellence*."[27] It is precisely because Jesus lived, suffered, and died both "with us" and "for us" that he becomes the ethical example we are called to imitate in our own living, suffering, and dying: Jesus exemplifies perfectly what we "ought to be" — responsible for others.

One final observation. We must be careful to avoid the kenotic Christology that was popular in the nineteenth century, according to which Christ divested himself of all the distinctive attributes of deity he shares with God the Father and became fully but only human. That view runs contrary to orthodox doctrine, according to which the incarnate Christ is both fully human and fully God (Chalcedon). The divine-human interchange is *not* that Christ exchanges divinity for humanity, but rather that the incarnate Christ — in both his humanity and his deity — takes up the part of humanity in its "poverty" so that humanity may take part in the "riches" of God "in Christ."[28] There is a contemporary version of kenotic Christology, based on Phil 2:6-11 and Heb 2:14-18 (and other texts), that is compatible with orthodoxy and with which I am sympathetic. The Son, while nonetheless remaining one in substance (so equally God) with the Father and the Spirit, did voluntarily and temporarily deprive his person of certain powers and prerogatives of deity (still retained fully by the Father and the Spirit); and the Son did so in order that he might accept the limitations of human form, thus becoming vulnerable to suffering and death, and take upon himself the liabilities of human sin. That is, the co-Creator freely chose creaturely limits for the sake of redeeming creation. Such a notion of kenosis, I think, is essential to the idea of substitution by solidarity and interchange.[29]

18.2.2. What Happens to Sin? The "Objective" Aspect of Atonement

I. Howard Marshall has expressed dissatisfaction with such readings of Paul: "Some scholars see here simply an exchange: he became what we are in order that we might become what he is. But this leaves unexplained what actually happens. To put it plainly, what happens to the sin that is taken by Christ?"[30] Marshall's

27. Bonhoeffer, *Ethics*, p. 222.

28. For a critique of nineteenth-century "kenotic Christology," see D. M. Baillie, *God Was in Christ: An Essay on Incarnation and Atonement* (New York: Scribner's, 1948), pp. 94-98.

29. Concerning an orthodox version of kenotic Christology, see the essay by John G. Stackhouse, Jr., "A Christ We Can Follow," *Books & Culture*, 17/1 (January-February 2011), 16-19.

30. Marshall, *Aspects of the Atonement*, p. 48. Hooker, by the way, makes it quite clear that what takes place "in Christ" for our salvation is "not a matter of a simple exchange," contrary to what Marshall asserts here. See Hooker, *From Adam to Christ*, pp. 17-18.

question concerns the "objective" aspect of atonement, God's action in Christ "from the outside" to deal with sin. And, yes, we do leave unexplained "what actually happens" — if by that one desires a theory of how God's action in Christ "works" to deal with sin. As we have observed (Chapter 10), the Bible nowhere offers a "mechanics" of *how* atoning sacrifice "works" to take away sin, but offers only the assurance that it *does* so. Likewise, as Marshall points out, "The rationale is not explained" concerning exactly *how* it is that Christ's death reconciles us to God.[31] Paul simply proclaims the good news that it *does* so. The implication is that we are to put our trust in this good news — and thus in the God who has dealt with our sins in Christ — without need for a theoretical accounting.

Even so, Marshall's question is not entirely out of order. God has dealt "once for all" with sin through the cross, bearing our sin within himself in Christ's death — that is the gospel.[32] As Peter puts it, Christ "bore our sin in his body on the cross" in such a way that we become "free from sins" (1 Pet 2:24). What, then, "actually happens" to the sin that God-in-Christ takes upon himself? And how does this set us free from sin? Insofar as an answer to that question is sought, I suggest we let Paul's account suffice. At three places, Paul addresses what God-in-Christ does concerning sin.

In Rom 8:1-3, Paul writes that God acting in Christ has both "set [us] free from the law of sin and of death" and "condemned sin."[33] According to Paul here, we are no longer under the "condemnation" *(katakrima)* of law (v. 1) because we have been liberated from the condemnation of law by the Spirit in Christ (v. 2). And God has liberated us from condemnation under law by doing "what the law could not do": he "sent his own Son in the likeness of sinful flesh" and "to deal with sin" *(peri hamartias)* he "condemned sin *(katekrinen tēn hamartian)* in the flesh" (v. 3).[34]

31. Marshall, *Aspects of the Atonement*, p. 48.

32. Cf. Baillie, *God Was in Christ*, p. 201: "The Christian message tells us that God was incarnate in Jesus, and that His sin-bearing was incarnate in the Passion of Jesus."

33. This "law of sin and of death," as we interpret it here, is the law that condemns us on account of our sin (cf. Rom 8:1). One might also interpret this as the law that death is the end result *(telos)* of sin, the final consequence of life lived "according to the flesh" (cf. 6:16, 21; 7:5; 8:5-6). On the latter, see Dunn, *Theology of Paul*, pp. 124-26. In a sense, of course, these are two sides of the same coin.

34. There is much scholarly debate, of course, over the phrase *peri hamartias* in Rom 8:3. In the Septuagint, this is a common formula for "sin offering." Is that what Paul intends here? Possibly — see N. T. Wright, *The Climax of the Covenant* (London: T&T Clark, 1991), pp. 220-25, for an argument in favor. If so, however, some such translations, which read that God sent his Son "in the likeness of sinful humanity *to be* [or *as*] a sin offering" (cf. NIV, NJB, NRSV text note), run roughshod over the Greek syntax. Such translations ignore the "and" *(kai)* between "likeness of sinful humanity" and "sin offering" in the Greek text, which indicates two grammatically independent clauses. Being mindful of the Greek, and reading *peri hamartias* as "sin offering," Paul would be saying that God has set humanity free from "the law of sin and of death" by doing *two* things that the law could not do (Rom 8:2): he sent his Son "in the likeness of sinful flesh"

Notice the disparity between what Paul says here and the penal substitution account: we are released from the condemnation under law on account of sin, *not* because God has condemned Christ in our place, but rather because God in Christ has condemned sin itself; condemnation has been passed, *not* from us to Christ, but from us to sin itself. Paul does not explain here the internal connection between these two divine acts — the Incarnation of the Son and the condemnation of sin — but only assures us that, by means of the Incarnation ("in the likeness of sinful flesh"/"in the flesh"), God has dealt decisively with sin and its death-generating power such that sin itself has been "condemned" to death and humanity has been freed from sin and death.

In Col 2:13-14, Paul makes a similar statement: "And when you were dead in trespasses and the uncircumcision of your flesh, God made you alive together with him, when he forgave us all our trespasses, erasing the record that stood against us with its legal demands. He set this aside, nailing it to the cross." God has forgiven our sins, expunging any record against us; he has removed from us both our sins and the record of sin that condemns us, nailing them both to the cross of Christ.

Notice again the disparity between what Paul says here and the penal substitution account. Paul does not say that God has canceled the "record" of sin or "certificate" of debt *(cheirographon)* charged against us because Christ has paid our debt to God in his blood by his death on the cross.[35] Rather, Paul says, God has "obliterated" or "expunged" or "wiped away" *(exaleiphō)* our account of sin from the heavenly book of record. What Paul says God does at the cross on our behalf is precisely what David petitioned God to do on his behalf: "according to your abundant mercy, blot out (LXX *exaleipson*) my transgressions" (Ps 51:1; cf. v. 9). It is also what the prophet Isaiah testified that God does on behalf of Israel: "I, I am He, who blots out (LXX *exaleiphōn*) your transgressions for my own sake" (Isa 43:25). And it is what Peter proclaims that God will do in the name of the risen Jesus on behalf of all who repent: "Repent therefore, and turn to God so that your sins may be wiped out *(exaleiphthēnai)*" (Acts 3:19). What we thus have here is not debt cancellation by an intra-Trinitarian transaction

---

and "as [or "by"] a sin offering" he "condemned sin in the flesh" (v. 3). If "sin offering" is the correct reading, then insofar as the sin offering served an expiatory purpose (see Chapters 10 and 14 above) we might interpret: God sent his Son "in the flesh" and, in order to remove sin from humanity, condemned sin "in the flesh." We might infer here that God "condemns" and so "removes" sin specifically by means of the death of the Son, but Paul does not say as much and the text does not imply that. We might infer instead that God removes sin by means of the entire Incarnation, the Son's full ministry "in the flesh," including both his life and his death.

35. This erroneous view is found in, e.g., F. F. Bruce, *The Epistles to the Colossians, to Philemon, and to the Ephesians* (Grand Rapids, MI: Eerdmans Publishing, 1984), p. 109, and C. F. D. Moule, *The Epistles of Paul the Apostle to the Colossians and to Philemon: An Introduction and Commentary* (Cambridge: Cambridge University Press, 1968), p. 98.

between God and Christ (God transfers our sin-debt to Christ, and Christ pays our sin-debt to God), but rather debt cancellation by a sovereign act of divine forgiveness: God blots out our sin for his own sake according to his abundant mercy.[36]

Nor does Paul say that God has forgiven us our transgressions because, no longer reckoning our sins against us (cf. 2 Cor 5:19), he has reckoned them against Christ instead. Rather, Paul says, God has taken away our transgressions and nailed them to the cross. Nor does Paul say that God spares us from the death penalty by putting Jesus to death in our place as penalty for our sins. Rather, Paul says, what God puts to death at the cross is our sin and the law that demands (or the judgment that decrees) death as the penalty (or sentence) for sin.[37] Marianne Meye Thompson comments:

> It is striking that this verse [v. 14] does not say that Christ was nailed to the cross, but rather that the "bond of indebtedness" was put to death. . . . Similarly, there is here no explicit reference to a penalty due to sin that Christ bore for sinful humanity on the cross. Rather, in an unusual and fresh image, Paul speaks of the accusing record itself being destroyed on the cross.[38]

According to Paul, therefore, through the Incarnation of Christ, God has put sin on trial, pronouncing a sentence of death upon sin itself (Rom 8:3); and through the cross of Christ, God has crucified sin, putting it to death (Col 2:14). In this way, God-in-Christ has acted through the Incarnation and cross to nullify sin — to "kill" sin, as Irenaeus put it — and so to deprive sin of its "life," its power to produce death in us.[39]

Paul himself uses this very metaphor of divine violence against sin employed later by Irenaeus. Through the cross, Paul writes, Christ has broken

---

36. I thus disagree with Ben Witherington III, *The Letters to Philemon, the Colossians, and the Ephesians: A Socio-rhetorical Commentary on the Captivity Epistles* (Grand Rapids, MI: Eerdmans Publishing, 2007), who reads Paul as saying here that God has cancelled our "certificate of debt" because "Jesus paid it all" (p. 158). His interpretation must read "payment" into the text; for Paul does not use any language of payment here, only forgiveness *(charizomai)* and cancellation *(exaleiphō)*.

37. Scholars diverge on how to interpret these *dogmata* that attach to the "record" or "certificate" *(cheirographon)*. Some see here "legal demands" in reference to the law of Moses (so NRSV; cf. Eph 2:15); others see here an "official decree" or "judicial order" (cf. Jerry L. Sumney, *Colossians: A Commentary* [Louisville: Westminster John Knox Press, 2008], pp. 144-45).

38. Marianne Meye Thompson, *Colossians and Philemon: A Two Horizons Commentary* (Grand Rapids, MI: Eerdmans Publishing, 2005), p. 58.

39. Of course, to say that God "condemns" and "crucifies" or "kills" sin is to speak metaphorically — sin is no concretely existing "thing" that can be literally destroyed. Metaphorical language does not deprive divine action of its objective reality, but rather expresses that reality in concrete terms appropriate to human experience and, thus, conducive to human understanding.

down the wall of hostility that divides humanity into warring factions and alienates humanity from God's covenant (Eph 2:11-14). By breaking down this wall, Christ acts to reconcile the warring factions, thus creating "one new humanity," and to reconcile formerly warring humanity "in one body to God through the cross" (vv. 15-16 NET). Now, by what means has Christ done this? And what has happened to the human enmity *(echthra)* that caused the war and alienation? Christ does all of this "in his flesh" *(en tē sarki autou)* or "in himself" *(en autō)*. And Christ acts to brings about reconciliation — humanity with humanity, and humanity to God — by absorbing human enmity into his own body through the cross and "killing *(apokteinas)* the enmity in himself" (v. 16, my translation). Through the Incarnation and cross, Paul says, God-in-Christ takes into himself the war-causing, alienation-producing sin of enmity and puts that sin to death.

18.2.3. The Early Church Testimony

The Pauline idea of divine-human interchange in Christ resonates throughout the writings of the early church. In his late first-century letter to the Corinthians, Clement, bishop of Rome, writes: "our Lord Jesus Christ, at the will of God, gave His blood for us *(hyper hēmōn)* — His flesh for *(hyper)* our flesh, His life for *(hyper)* our lives" (1 *Clement* 49:6).[40] In one of his early second-century letters, Ignatius, Bishop of Antioch, writes of "Jesus Christ, who died for us *(di' hēmas)* in order that by believing in his death you might escape death" (*Trallians* 2:1).[41] This idea is elaborated in the second-century *Epistle to Diognetus,* which proclaims the good news of God's expectation-exceeding, retribution-transcending work of redemption by mysterious interchange in Christ:

> Accordingly, when our iniquity had come to its full height, and it was clear beyond all mistaking that retribution in the form of punishment and death must be looked for, the hour arrived in which God had determined to make known from then onwards His loving-kindness and His power. How surpassing is the love and tenderness of God! In that hour, instead of hating us and rejecting us and remembering our wickednesses against us, He showed how long-suffering He is. He bore with us, and in pity He took our sins upon Himself and gave His own Son as a ransom for us *(hyper hēmōn)* — the Holy for *(hyper)* the wicked, the Sinless for *(hyper)* sinners, the Just for *(hyper)* the unjust, the Incorrupt for *(hyper)* the corrupt, the Immortal for *(hyper)* the

---

40. M. Staniforth and A. Louth, trans., *Early Christian Writings* (London: Penguin, 1987), p. 43.

41. Michael W. Holmes, ed., *The Apostolic Fathers: Greek Texts and English Translations,* rev. ed. (Grand Rapids, MI: Baker Books, 1999), p. 161.

mortal. For was there, indeed, anything except His righteousness that could have availed to cover our sins? In whom could we, in our lawlessness and ungodliness, have been made holy, but in the Son of God alone? O sweet exchange! O unsearchable working! O benefits unhoped for! — that the wickedness of multitudes should thus be hidden in the One holy, and the holiness of One should sanctify the countless wicked! (9:2-5)[42]

Colin Gunton's comment, that this ancient text exclaims a "sense of the sheer goodness of God's gift of himself in Jesus," sounds the right note: "Not here some grim balancing of accounts, but rejoicing in a liberation. The Son of God has given himself to be where we are so that we might be where he is, participants in the life of God."[43]

Gunton here implicitly paraphrases, and Hooker directly quotes, Irenaeus, bishop of Lyon (second century), to summarize the Pauline idea of divine-human interchange in Christ: "He became what we are in order that we might become what he is" (*Against Heresies*, V, preface).[44] Irenaeus elaborates:

For it behoved Him who was to destroy sin, and redeem man under the power of death, that He should Himself be made that very same thing which he was, that is, man; who had been drawn by sin into bondage, but was held by death, so that sin should be destroyed by man, and man should go forth from death. . . . God recapitulated in Himself the ancient formation of man, that He might kill sin, deprive death of its power, and vivify man. (*Against Heresies*, III.18.7)[45]

This idea was elaborated further by Athanasius, Bishop of Alexandria (fourth century):

For this purpose, then, the incorporeal and incorruptible and immaterial Word of God entered our world. . . . Thus, taking a body like our own, because all our bodies were liable to the corruption of death, He surrendered His body to death in place of all, and offered it to the Father. This He did out of sheer love for us, so that in His death all might die, and the law of death thereby be abolished because, having fulfilled in His body that for which it was appointed, it was thereafter voided of its power for men. This He did that He might turn again to incorruption men who had turned back to corruption, and make them alive through death by the appropriation of His body and by the grace of His resurrection. Thus He would

---

42. *Early Christian Writings*, pp. 147-48.

43. Gunton, *Actuality of Atonement*, p. 140.

44. Hooker, *Not Ashamed of the Gospel*, p. 35.

45. Ireneaus, *Against Heresies*, in Philip Schaff, *Ante-Nicene Fathers*, Vol. I (Grand Rapids, MI: Christian Classics Ethereal Library), p. 745.

make death to disappear from them as utterly as straw from fire. (*On the Incarnation*, II.8)[46]

Athanasius writes that Jesus died "in place of all" as an offering to God. His death was no substitutionary sacrifice, however, for Jesus gave his life "so that in His death all might die." This is not the death of a universal substitute (exclusive place-taking) but that of a corporate representative (inclusive place-taking): one died for all, therefore all died (cf. 2 Cor 5:14).

Irenaeus and Athanasius do thus employ a notion of "exchange" or "substitution" in their theology of salvation through the Incarnation, but with the sense of redemptive solidarity and divine-human interchange: God the Son becomes incarnate so to take the part of humanity under sin and death and thus suffer the death of sinners "one on behalf of all," thereby to redeem humanity from tyranny under sin and death and thus to restore humanity to communion with God. Again, Athanasius:

> For this reason, therefore, He assumed a body capable of death, in order that it, through belonging to the Word Who is above all, might become in dying a sufficient exchange for all, and, itself remaining incorruptible through His indwelling, might thereafter put an end to corruption for all others as well, by the grace of the resurrection. It was by surrendering to death the body which He had taken, as an offering and sacrifice free from every stain, that He forthwith abolished death for His human brethren by the offering of an equivalent. For naturally, since the Word of God was above all, when He offered his own temple and bodily instrument as a substitute for the life of all, He fulfilled in death all that was required. Naturally also, through this union of the immortal Son of God with our human nature, all men were clothed with incorruption in the promise of the resurrection. For the solidarity of mankind is such that, by virtue of the Word's indwelling in a single human body, the corruption which goes with death has lost its power over all. (*On the Incarnation*, II.9)

None of this has anything to do with satisfaction of God's honor (per Anselm) or appeasement of God's wrath (per Calvin). The notion of Christ satisfying or appeasing God by his death is almost absent from the soteriology of both Irenaeus and Athanasius.[47] Nor is this the later idea of the Cappadocian

46. Citations from Athanasius, *On the Incarnation of the Word of God* (Grand Rapids, MI: Christian Classics Ethereal Library).

47. Only twice in his great work *Against Heresies* (as far as I can find) does Irenaeus speak of Christ "propitiating" God by his death (IV.8.2; V.17.1), but the idea is not at all developed such that propitiating divine wrath becomes the central purpose of the cross as it is in the penal substitution view. In any case, Irenaeus quite thoroughly rejects the idea that God needed sacrifice from humans to appease his wrath and, hence, that the Old Testament sacrifices were intended

Fathers of "paying a ransom to the devil."[48] The idea here is that the Incarnation of the immortal Word of God, through death and resurrection, overcomes death and reverses the corruption caused in creation by sin, thereby renewing creation and restoring human nature to its divine likeness and end. Christ became "one of us," sharing our corruptible nature and our mortality, in order to redeem all of us from sin, corruption, and death through his life, death, and resurrection so that we might share in his incorruptible nature and immortality.[49]

18.2.4. The Eastern Orthodox Tradition

As evident from the title of Athanasius's great work, it is of course by the Incarnation that Christ voluntarily shares in the conditions of human existence and assumes the liabilities of human sin (viz., corruption and death) — and, hence, by the Incarnation that God acts to bear the consequences of sin and bring about the redemption of creation from corruption and death. The Incarnation as the central act of God in the history of redemption has remained the teaching of Eastern Orthodox Christianity since Irenaeus and Athanasius.[50]

Orthodox bishop Kallistos Ware presents the Eastern view:

> The Christian message of salvation can best be summed up in terms of *sharing*, of solidarity and identification. . . . The Incarnation . . . is a doctrine of sharing or participation. Christ shares to the full in what we are, and so he makes it possible for us to share in what he is, in his divine life and glory. He became what we are, so as to make us what he is.
> . . . Christ . . . saves us by becoming what we are; he heals us by taking our broken humanity into himself, by "assuming" it as his own, by entering

---

to propitiate God (IV.17.1). Sacrifice, Irenaeus says, is only one of a number of "those things by which sinners imagined they could propitiate God." For his view, Irenaeus appeals to the prophets, who rejected a system of religion that would allow one to commit injustice against one's neighbor, thus provoking God's wrath, but then offer sacrifice to propitiate God's wrath. Regarding Athanasius, the idea of Christ propitiating God by his death is nowhere to be found in his chief work, *On the Incarnation*.

48. Cf. Jaroslav Pelikan, *The Christian Tradition: A History of the Development of Doctrine*, Vol. 1: *The Emergence of the Catholic Tradition (100-600)* (Chicago: University of Chicago Press, 1989), p. 148.

49. For an exposition of the ideas of Irenaeus and Athanasius, see J. N. D. Kelly, *Early Christian Doctrines*, 5th ed. (New York: Continuum International Publishing, 2000), pp. 171-74, 377-80; Gustaf Aulén, *Christus Victor: An Historical Study of the Three Main Types of the Idea of Atonement* (New York: Macmillan Publishing, 1969), pp. 16-60, and Schmiechen, *Saving Power*, pp. 123-30, 169-85.

50. See Kharalambos Anstall, "Juridical Justification Theology and a Statement of the Orthodox Teaching," in B. Jersak and M. Hardin, *Stricken by God?* (Grand Rapids: Eerdmans, 2007), pp. 482-502.

into our human experience and by knowing it *from the inside,* as being himself one of us.[51]

The cross of Christ is the extreme demonstration of God's incarnational identification and redemptive solidarity with humanity:

> The Cross signifies, in the most stark and uncompromising manner, that this act of sharing is carried to the utmost limits. God incarnate enters into *all* our experience. Jesus Christ our companion shares not only in the fullness of human life but also in the fullness of human death. . . . "The unassumed is the unhealed": but Christ our healer has assumed into himself everything, even death.[52]

This healing of humanity by the assumption of sin and death into God's own life — and so the nullification of sin and death in God — through the Incarnation, cross, and resurrection of Christ is thus the objective means by which God works salvation "for us":

> Christ's suffering and death have, then, an objective value: he has done for us something we should be altogether incapable of doing without him. At the same time, we should not say that Christ has suffered "instead of us," but rather that he has suffered *on our behalf.* The Son of God suffered "unto death," not that we might be exempt from suffering, but that our suffering might be like his. Christ offers us, not a way *round* suffering, but a way *through* it; not substitution, but saving companionship.[53]

18.3. The Incarnation: Christ's Sevenfold Redemptive Solidarity

In the sense of redemptive solidarity by divine-human interchange in Christ through the Incarnation, then, we may speak appropriately of the "substitution" of God-in-Christ "for us and for our salvation."[54] The New Testament accounts depict Jesus Christ, for the sake of our redemption, voluntarily binding himself to, identifying himself with, and sharing in solidarity with humanity under sin and death in a sevenfold way: descent/birth, baptism/temptation, ministry, agony, death, descent, and resurrection/ascension. Although I will not emphasize here the unity of Christ with God in the work of salvation, as I have in accordance with orthodox Trinitarian theology (in Chapter 16), still we must

51. K. Ware, *The Orthodox Way* (Crestwood: St. Vladimir's Seminary Press), pp. 73-75.

52. Ware, *Orthodox Way,* pp. 78-79.

53. Ware, *Orthodox Way,* p. 82, emphasis original.

54. Brad Jersak, "Nonviolent Identification and the Victory of Christ," in Jersak and Hardin, *Stricken by God?* pp. 32-53, has elaborated similarly the idea of Christ's "nonviolent identification," which includes the elements of solidarity, union, and exchange.

keep in mind that, in becoming one with humanity so that humanity might become one with God, Christ is and remains one with God.

18.3.1. Descent/Birth

First, by being born in human flesh, born of a woman, and born "under the law," Jesus, the eternal Son of God, condescends to identify himself as "one of us" (John 1:14; Luke 2:7; Gal 4:4; Phil 2:6-7). Luke's genealogy of Jesus emphasizes Jesus' unity with the whole human race: Jesus is both "son of Adam" and "son of God." Although the Son of God, Jesus refers to himself as "the Son of Humanity" *(ho huios tou anthrōpou),* thus emphasizing his full identification with humanity and his full sharing in the lot of mortals (cf. Ps 8:4). As Johnson observes, Jesus intentionally correlates his self-reference as "Son of Humanity" with his suffering, death, and resurrection (cf. Mark 8:31; 9:31; 10:33).[55] Hebrews also closely connects Jesus' full humanity with his atoning death. Incarnation — becoming "one of us" and sharing our lot in all respects — is necessary in order that Jesus might make atonement for sins, defeat the power of death and the devil, and liberate us from fear of death (Heb 2:5-18).[56] Hooker comments:

> Throughout this section the author [of Hebrews] insists very firmly on Christ's full humanity: it is only someone who is "one of us" who can be our high priest. It was necessary for Christ to share human suffering in order to bring men and women to glory, necessary for him to share our flesh and blood in order to set us free from the fear of death, necessary for him to experience testing or temptation in order to offer expiation for sins. The assumptions here are very similar to those significant statements of Paul's in which he declares that Christ became what we are, in order that we might become what he is.[57]

18.3.2. Baptism/Temptation

Second, by voluntarily undergoing the baptism of John, Jesus, though himself without sin, identified with humanity's situation in sin and, hence, with our

---

55. Luke Timothy Johnson, *Living Jesus: Learning the Heart of the Gospel* (San Francisco: HarperSanFrancisco, 1999), p. 138.

56. The Greek text expresses the necessity of Jesus' identification and solidarity with humanity through the Incarnation in Heb 2:17, using the imperfect indicative *ōpheilen* with the aorist passive infinitive *homoiōthēnai* — "he *had to become like* his brothers and sisters in every respect."

57. Hooker, *Not Ashamed of the Gospel,* pp. 113-14. Concerning the importance of incarnation for the theology of sacrificial atonement in Hebrews, see Stephen Finlan, *Options on Atonement in Christian Thought* (Collegeville, MN: Liturgical Press, 2007), pp. 48-53.

need of repentance, cleansing, and release from sin.[58] God had ordained John to proclaim and perform "a baptism of repentance for the forgiveness of sins" (Mark 1:4; Luke 3:3; cf. Luke 1:76-77; Matt 3:6). That Jesus' baptism inaugurated his messianic vocation signals that his life-mission, undertaken in solidarity with humanity, is to redeem humanity from sin (John 1:29-34). Jesus would ritualize this divine purpose at the Last Supper, blessing bread and wine as symbols of his body and blood, which are given "for many for the forgiveness of sins" (Matt 26:26-28). He binds himself by baptism to humanity in sin so that he might offer his sinless life, body and blood, in solidarity with sinners — on their behalf and for the sake of their redemption from sin.

Jesus' solidarity with sinners is realized immediately and dramatically through the trial and testing that ensues from his baptism. Having identified with sinners and their need of redemption, and having been identified by God as his beloved Son, Jesus undergoes the temptation of sinners (Mark 1:12-13; Matt 4:1-11; Luke 4:1-13). Satan tempts Jesus with promises of earthly life, glory, and power, all for the price of obedience: if only Jesus will place himself in Satan's service, all will be his. In effect, Jesus is faced with the temptation put to Adam and Eve. Having been offered a share in God's life (Gen 2:9, 16-17), they receive a counter-offer from the serpent. The serpent promises them the knowledge of the gods all for the price of obeying the serpent; if only they will listen to the serpent, god-like status will be theirs (3:1-5). Whereas Adam and Eve fell to temptation and thereby alienated themselves from God and lost the promise of life with God (vv. 6-25), Jesus does not fall to temptation, but stays true to God. Having identified with sinners suffering under temptation and yet having resisted sin is the essential premise for Jesus to serve as God's "faithful and merciful high priest" who ministers to us in our "time of need" (Heb 2:18; 4:14-16).

18.3.3. Ministry

Third, Jesus ministers directly to the human situation corrupted by sin and ruled by death, taking upon himself all the sin-generated ills of the human condition (Matt 8:16-17). He acts with divine power and authority to reverse the corruption of sin and the rule of death among humanity, dispensing freely the "benefits" of God's grace — releasing the sinners from sin, restoring the sick to health, and raising the dead to life (Matt 4:23-25; Luke 7:22; cf. Ps 103:2-4). Jesus even acts to liberate those in bondage to and oppressed by the devil (Luke 13:10-17; Acts 10:38). At the same time, Jesus calls sinners to repentance, teaching the way of God's kingdom of righteousness that leads to life rather

---

58. M. Winter, *The Atonement* (Collegeville: Liturgical, 1995), p. 102; Wright, *Simply Christian*, p. 213.

than death (Mark 1:14-15; Matt 5-7; cf. Deut 30:15-20). Jesus makes his invitation to repentance from sin, conversion of life, and reconciliation with God precisely by identifying with sinners, by sharing with them in a communion of grace rather than by shunning or condemning them (Mark 2:15-17; Luke 19:1-10; John 8:2-11).

18.3.4. Agony

Fourth, by submitting to God in the midst of agonizing over his fate, Jesus resists the temptation to forsake identifying fully with humanity under sin and death (Mark 14:32-36). At this point, Jesus not only yields himself to God's purpose — "not what I want, but what you want" (v. 36) — but also shares fully in the lot of suffering and sorrow that attends the human condition — "I am deeply grieved, even to death" (v. 34). And in the midst of his submitting to God and sharing with humanity, Jesus knows personally the very weakness of human will that gives way to sin, for before he submits to God's will he asks his Father, "remove this cup from me" (v. 36). In this moment, as Johnson observes, "what is true of his followers who sleep is also true of him: the spirit is willing but the flesh is weak (14:38)."[59] Overcoming weakness, Jesus seals his identification with sinners by willingly surrendering himself rather than resisting arrest (Matt 26:47-56; Luke 22:35-38, 47-53). By submitting in obedience to God and suffering in solidarity with humanity, Jesus himself becomes the way of salvation:

> In the days of his flesh, Jesus offered up prayers and supplications, with loud cries and tears, to the one who was able to save him from death, and he was heard because of his reverent submission. Although he was a Son, he learned obedience through what he suffered; and having been made perfect, he became the source of eternal salvation for all who obey him. (Heb 5:7-9)

Den Heyer comments: "Jesus knows about human existence from his own experience. He knows what it is to be human. This 'solidarity' is the source of our salvation."[60]

18.3.5. Death

Fifth, condemned under law and hung between criminals (Matt 27:38; Mark 15:27-28; Luke 22:37; 23:32-33; John 19:17-18), Jesus, although innocent, identifies fully with both humanity's alienation under sin and God's judgment of death

---

59. Johnson, *Living Jesus*, p. 139.
60. C. J. den Heyer, *Jesus and the Doctrine of the Atonement* (Harrisburg: Trinity, 1998), p. 115.

for sin (Genesis 3; Rom 5:12-21).[61] Richard Nelson comments, with reference to Hebrews:

> His death is first and foremost a matter of solidarity with those sisters and brothers for whom he serves as priest (2:10-11, 17-18; 4:15). In sharing the fate of death with them, he was able to destroy the power of death and free those enslaved to the fear of death (2:14-15). . . . Christ thus partakes in the same sequence of "first death and then judgment" common to all humanity.[62]

Identification with sinners in death, however, does not entail penal substitution, that God punishes Jesus on the cross in place of sinners to "pay the penalty" for sin. Fiddes comments: "To say that Jesus dies under the judgement of God does not mean, therefore, that God directly *inflicts* some kind of penalty upon him. It is to speak of his complete identification with humankind, and so his experience of the consequences of human sinfulness."[63] Indeed, we simply cannot see God punishing Jesus at the cross, as if God stands apart from and acts over against Jesus; for "God was in Christ" on the cross suffering for our salvation (2 Cor 5:19). In Christ's death, it is God who identifies with sinners and bears the evil of their sin. Thus I. Howard Marshall:

> the death [of Christ] is the death of God himself, since the Son is one with the Father, and we are correct to see God dying on the cross. . . . The death [of Christ] is God identifying with humanity in its need, and this is important in showing how God in Christ absorbs the suffering that evil and sinners inflicted upon humanity.[64]

As Paul depicts the cross, Christ's death "for us" both implicates and incorporates all humanity. First, Christ's death implicates humanity because he died on account of our sins (Rom 4:25). It was on account of human sins that we were in need of redemption from death by God in Christ through the Incarnation in the first place, and it was because of human sins that he was put to death on the cross.[65] Second, Christ's death incorporates us because in his death

---

61. Cf. Raymund Schwager, *Jesus in the Drama of Salvation: Toward a Biblical Doctrine of Redemption*, trans. James G. Williams and Paul Haddon (New York: Crossroad Publishing, 1999), pp. 169-72; and Fiddes, *Past Event and Present Salvation*, pp. 90-96.

62. R. D. Nelson, "He Offered Himself," *Interpretation* 57 (2003) 251-65, here p. 254.

63. Fiddes, *Past Event and Present Salvation*, p. 91, emphasis original.

64. Marshall, *Aspects of the Atonement*, p. 62.

65. The idea of the corporate responsibility of humanity for Jesus' death is thus the correlate of Jesus' corporate representation of humanity in his death: Christ was crucified on account of *our* sins — past and present. These correlated ideas of corporate representation and corporate responsibility require further the idea of the corporate reality and identity of humanity: that "one died for all, therefore all have died" implies that the "all" exists (in some real sense) as well as the "one." In the modern mindset, founded upon the assumptions of only individual

Christ has identified with us. Paul: "we are convinced that one has died for all; therefore all have died" (2 Cor 5:14). One of us, Christ, has identified with and died on behalf of all of us, so that all of us are incorporated into the death of this one. Again, this text does *not* speak of substitution per penal substitution, Jesus dying "in our place" — an event of *exclusive* place-taking. Had Paul been thinking such, he would have written, "one has died for all, therefore all are exempted from death." Paul, however, says exactly the opposite. Jesus' death is an event of *inclusive* place-taking (see Chapter 15). This is *not penal substitution,* therefore, but *representative-redemptive solidarity.* By suffering and dying, as "one of us" and "for us," Jesus has "tasted death on behalf of all" and has thus become "the pioneer of [our] salvation" (Heb 2:9-10). As "pioneer" *(archēgos),* Jesus is not a substitute that takes our place in the salvation event, but the one who "goes first," who goes ahead of us in death and resurrection as the originator and founder of the way of our salvation.

In dying the death of a sinner on behalf of sinners, moreover, Jesus' sinless death redeems sinners from death and rights them with God (cf. 2 Cor 5:21; 1 Pet 2:24; 3:18). Together, Paul and the Gospels depict God-in-Christ's act of redemption and reconciliation through the cross in a three-part drama:

"while we were still weak, at the right time, Christ died for the ungodly" (Rom 5:6-7) — Jesus' unjust sentence and innocent death during the Passover festival redeems from captivity and death the murderous rebel Barabbas (Matt 27:15-23, 26; Mark 15:6-15; Luke 23:18-25; John 18:39-40);[66]

"while we were still sinners Christ died for us" (Rom 5:8-9) — Jesus' merciful intercession from the cross demonstrates God's love and channels God's forgiveness to those with his blood on their hands, thus "justifying" these sinners "by his blood" and securing their release from divine judgment (Luke 23:34);

"while we were enemies, we were reconciled to God through the death of his son" (Rom 5:10-11) — Jesus' gracious word reconciles the repentant to God and promises life to the condemned (Luke 23:39-43).[67]

(atomic) reality, identity, and responsibility, this does not make sense. And, yet, that is what Paul's message of the cross implies, it seems to me: Christ bears representatively the human responsibility for sin, because corporate humanity bears responsibility for sin and Christ is the corporate human representative (see Chapter 15 above).

66. According to the consistent witness of the Gospel accounts, Barabbas is the one (and only one) "in place of" whom Jesus dies, strictly speaking.

67. We thus see no incompatibility between the "objective" and "subjective" aspects of atonement, between God's action "for us" and the effective realization of God's action "in us." Cf. Baillie, *God Was in Christ,* pp. 197-202. Baillie writes (p. 200): "the love of God dealing with the sin of the world and overcoming it as only love can do . . . is the 'objective' work of atonement."

18.3.6. Descent into Hell

Sixth, by descending into the realm of the dead, Jesus dramatically completes his solidarity with humanity under sin and death (1 Pet 3:18-20; 4:6; Eph 4:8-10). Jesus' descent demonstrates that his death is no mere appearance, but that in human flesh he has shared fully in the life and lot of mortals dwelling under sin. By this, moreover, Jesus not only demonstrates solidarity with humanity in death, but also opens a way of redemption for humanity from death. For in dying, descending, and being raised, Jesus proclaims the gospel to the dead (1 Pet 3:19; 4:6), breaks the dominion of death (Acts 2:24; Rom 6:9), takes hold of the keys of death and hell (Rev 1:17-18), and liberates from captivity those imprisoned by death (Eph 4:8-9).[68] His victory over death and hell in solidarity with humanity thus sets humanity free from the fear of death:

> Since, therefore, the children share flesh and blood, he himself likewise shared the same things, so that through death he might destroy the one who has the power of death, that is, the devil, and free those who all their lives were held in slavery by the fear of death. (Heb 2:14-15)

18.3.7. Resurrection/Ascension

Seventh, having been raised by God in victory over death and corruption (Acts 2:24-31), Jesus' redemptive solidarity with humanity continues unbroken beyond his death. That unbroken solidarity with humanity is demonstrated to the world by Jesus' resurrection body, which although transformed and glorified by God not only remains human "flesh and bones" but still bears the marks of his suffering on our behalf (Luke 24:36-43; John 20:19-23).[69] The risen Christ is "God with us" for all time (Matt 1:23; 28:20). Christ not only dies "for us" but he is also "raised for [us]" (2 Cor 5:15) — indeed, Christ has been "raised for our justification" (Rom 4:25).

By his ascension, moreover, Jesus' redemptive solidarity is extended beyond his earthly ministry through his heavenly intercession.[70] Marshall remarks:

---

68. The early church called this "the Harrowing of Hell." Two early, extra-canonical witnesses to this are the early second-century letter of Ignatius, bishop of Antioch, to the *Magnesians* (9:2) and the third-century *Apostolic Tradition* of Hippolytus of Rome (4.8).

69. That Christ continues eternally in his humanity, as well as his deity, beyond death and resurrection is essential to the orthodox doctrine of the Incarnation — cf. Baillie, *God Was in Christ,* pp. 151-52.

70. Regarding how to think about the ascension, see N. T. Wright, *Surprised by Hope: Rethinking Heaven, the Resurrection, and the Mission of the Church* (New York: HarperCollins, 2008), pp. 109-16.

"Christ continues to be the agent of salvation in his heavenly activity."[71] Baillie elaborates:

> [T]he atoning work of Christ . . . is not confined to His passion on earth and did not end with His death on the Cross. That work on Calvary was indeed a finished work, a perfect sacrifice made once for all on earth. Yet it was the beginning of a priesthood which goes on for ever in the unseen realm, in heaven, in the Holy Place beyond the Veil, into which our High Priest entered through death, and where he "ever liveth to make intercession for us," being continually "touched with feeling of our infirmities."[72]

In his exalted position at the right hand of God and in company with the Spirit, which has been poured out on us, Jesus forever makes intercession — on our behalf and for the sake of our salvation — "according to the will of God" (Rom 8:26-34; Heb 7:23-28; 9:24).[73] Jesus' priestly ministry thus manifests a continuity between death and resurrection/ascension, suffering and exaltation. So Nelson (with reference to Hebrews):

> His willing death was the first phase of a complex priestly action that continued in his ascension through the heavenly realms and entrance with blood into the heavenly sanctuary. It concluded with a decisive act of purification and being seated beside God's throne, where Christ can continually intercede for his followers. The cross was no mere prologue to, or presupposition for, Christ's priestly work in heaven, but an essential first element in his multi-stage act of sacrificial offering. Suffering, entrance, offering, and sacrifice are firmly bracketed together in 9:25-26. The inherited hymnic creed likewise underscores the continuity between Christ's suffering and his exaltation in the story of salvation. (5:7-10)[74]

As Hebrews emphasizes, the essential premise of this continuity is precisely Jesus' solidarity and interchange with humanity.[75] Having identified with us as

71. Marshall, *Aspects of the Atonement*, p. 77.
72. Baillie, *God Was in Christ*, pp. 190-97, citing Hebrews.
73. Winter, *Atonement*, p. 195.
74. Nelson, "He Offered Himself," p. 255.
75. Hooker, *Not Ashamed of the Gospel*, comments regarding Hebrews: "for our author *what* Christ *does* depends very clearly on *who* he *is*. He is Son of God . . . But equally important is his identity with humanity and his obedience to God. Both emphases are necessary for his argument" (p. 122, emphasis original). Similarly, J. Carroll and J. Green, *The Death of Jesus in Early Christianity* (Peabody: Hendrickson, 1995): "The Christology of Hebrews is simultaneously 'high' and 'low': Jesus is the eternal Son of God . . . yet . . . he fully entered the human condition, with its challenges, its sufferings, and its finitude. The author [of Hebrews] sharply accents the humanity of Jesus, for . . . only as one who stands in solidarity with humankind can he exercise his priestly function. And at the heart of that experience of the human condition lies suffering" (pp. 137-38).

sinners, undergone temptation like us, and shared in our suffering, Jesus is able to be a merciful high priest who ministers God's grace to us in our weakness (Heb 2:17-18; 4:14-16).

By his suffering, death, resurrection, and ascension as both Son of God and Son of Humanity, Jesus has become the perfect mediator of a new covenant between God and humanity (Luke 22:20; 1 Cor 11:25; Heb 2:10; 5:8; 8:6; 9:15). The redemptive work of his life and death is multiplied "for many" after his resurrection and ascension through the outpouring of covenant benefits — repentance and forgiveness, healing and the Holy Spirit — upon all humanity "in the name of Jesus Christ" (Mark 10:45; 14:24; Luke 24:47; Acts 2:32-33, 38-39; 10:43-48). Indeed, a new relationship between God and the whole cosmic reality is being made "in Christ" (2 Cor 5:17; Eph 1:7-10; Col 1:15-20). Paul writes of creation groaning in hope of being "set free from its bondage to decay" and of the faithful waiting in hope for "the redemption of our bodies" (Rom 8:18-25); and John envisions the renewal of all creation, "a new heaven and a new earth," a marriage of heaven and earth in which the immortal God makes his eternal home among mortals (Revelation 21). The ultimate benefit to us is the promise of participating in God's victory in Christ over death and corruption. For "in Christ" we are promised incorruptible bodies by the transformation of our corruptible bodies through resurrection by God (1 Cor 15:20-22, 50-57; 2 Cor 5:1-5; Phil 3:21; 2 Tim 1:9-10; 2 Pet 1:4).[76] Hooker comments (with reference to Hebrews): "In dying, he was identified with men and women — he 'tasted death for all' (2.9); in his resurrection/ascension, they are identified with him, for he is their forerunner (6.20; cf. 2.10)."[77]

18.4. Jesus: God "with Us" and "for Us"

The incarnate ministry of Christ — birth and ministry, death and resurrection — is God's action "with us" to bring about salvation "for us." That the entire Incarnation is the locus and vehicle of God's work of salvation is reflected in the Nicene Creed, which joins Jesus' descent from heaven, birth by Mary, death by crucifixion, resurrection by God, and ascent to glory together into a single (Greek) sentence under the one heading, "For us humans and for our salvation." Recognizing the saving work of God "for us" throughout Christ's ministry "with us" points us to the answer to that perennial question:

> The gospels make clear from beginning to end that Jesus was one of us, identified with us, and took part in our life . . . If he was the chosen one of God,

---

76. The renewal of all creation and the redemption of our bodies through resurrection "in Christ" is the great hope of Christian faith — see Wright, *Surprised by Hope*.

77. Hooker, *Not Ashamed of the Gospel*, p. 123.

the Word incarnate, why did he suffer and die? That question appears in the New Testament and throughout early Christian literature. The answer, given without qualification, is that he chose to be for us by being with us.[78]

The upshot here, as Karl Barth observed, is that because of the Incarnation, because God-in-Christ has taken our part in a concrete way by becoming "one of us," God's history "with us" in Christ is our history of salvation:

> And in Jesus Christ God becomes and is human, the fellow-human being of all people. . . . The human speaking and acting and suffering and triumphing of this one person directly concerns us all, and his history is our history of salvation which changes the whole human situation, just because God himself is its human subject in his Son, just because God himself has assumed and made his own our human nature and kind in his Son, just because God himself came into this world in his Son, and as one of us "a guest this world of ours he trod."[79]

Acting as the agent of God's redemption, reconciliation, and re-creation, Jesus the righteous one faithfully advances God's just cause against the reality and power of evil in all its forms — "against all injustice and impiety" among humanity (Rom 1:18), against the dominion of sin and death in the cosmos (5:12–6:23), against the rulers and authorities of this present world-age (8:38-39). Jesus does so "with us" by becoming "one of us" in order to take our part in the struggle against sin and for righteousness, and he does so "for us" so that we might not only benefit from but also participate in God's victory over evil and death.

God-in-Christ's action "for us" does not sideline us in the divine struggle against sin and death and for righteousness and life. Christ is God "for us" — but "with us" rather than "without us," "on our behalf" rather than "in our place," inclusive of us rather than exclusive of us. Rather than displacing us from action and rendering us passive and unnecessary, God's initiative and action "for us" in Christ renders us capable of actively participating in God's own victory over evil so that we, too, might be "more than conquerors" through Christ. We might thus say that Jesus is our *partisan*, commissioned by God into the world to take up as his own the cause of our liberation from sin and death for the sake of righting and reuniting us with God. Again, Barth:

> "God with us" . . . means that *God* has become *human* in order as such, but in divine sovereignty, to take up our case . . . He, the Creator, does not scorn to become a creature, human like us, in order that as such he may bear and do what must be borne and done for our salvation . . . The human being in

78. Schmiechen, *Saving Power*, p. 348.

79. Karl Barth, *Church Dogmatics* IV/2, excerpted in Clifford Green, ed., *Karl Barth: Theologian of Freedom* (Minneapolis: Fortress Press, 1991), pp. 200-201.

whom God himself intervenes for us, suffers and acts for us, closes the gap between himself and us as our representative, in our name and on our behalf, this One is not merely the confirmation and guarantee of our salvation, but because he is God he is salvation, our salvation . . . God has made himself human with us, to make our cause his own, and as his own to save it from disaster and to carry it through to success.[80]

Jesus himself is God's loving initiative in history for the salvation of the world (John 3:16-17). Jesus' life, death, and resurrection is God's faithful and righteous action to take our part in the struggle against evil and for justice, to conquer sin and death, to make us righteous and to give us life. Jesus — his whole living and dying and rising — is God's personal presence and power by which *God* is "with us" and "for us" no matter who or what powers of evil may be against us, by which we know "that God is on our side to deliver us from our sins and their consequences."[81] Jesus is God's concrete answer to the very human plea for justice, deliverance, and life: "Who rises up for me against the wicked? Who stands up for me against evildoers? If the LORD had not been my help, my soul would soon have lived in the land of silence. When I thought, 'My foot is slipping,' your steadfast love, O LORD, held me up" (Ps 94:16-18). God's gift "for us all" in the life, death, and resurrection of the Son is thus the unshakeable assurance that, yes, God is "for us" and Christ Jesus intercedes "for us" in our present situation under sin, that despite suffering all things even now we may participate through Christ in God's victory over evil and death, and that ultimately nothing at all "will be able to separate us from the love of God in Christ Jesus our Lord" (Rom 8:31-39). Thanks be to God!

---

80. Karl Barth, *Church Dogmatics* IV/1, excerpted in *Karl Barth: Theologian of Freedom,* pp. 213-16, emphasis original.

81. Marshall, *Aspects of the Atonement,* p. 58.

CODA

Athanasius, *On the Incarnation:* Penal Substitution?

In our exposition of an alternative view of "substitutionary" atonement in terms of redemptive solidarity and divine-human interchange rather than penal substitution, we have deliberately appropriated the ancient thinking of Irenaeus and Athanasius, orthodox theologians of the Eastern-Greek tradition. Jeffery et al., writing from a Calvinist perspective, have attempted to force-fit the thinking of Athanasius, in particular, into the framework of penal substitution.[1] Nowhere in his theology of salvation through the Incarnation, however, does Athanasius put forward the notion of penal substitution, that God punished Jesus with death in place of humans to pay the penalty for sin.[2]

Athanasius does speak of Jesus' death being required because "there was a debt owing which must needs be paid." This "debt," however, is not the debt for sin as understood by Anselm or Calvin, a debt owed to God and so requiring that "satisfaction" be made to God by Christ through compensation (Anselm) or punishment (Calvin). Rather, the "debt" of which Athanasius writes is due, not to God, but to death: "all men were due *to die.*" Jesus thus "pays" our "due," not to God, but to death itself. Athanasius writes:

> Here, then, is the second reason why the Word dwelt among us, namely that having proved His Godhead by His works, He might offer the sacrifice on be-

---

1. Steve Jeffery, Michael Ovey, and Andrew Sach, *Pierced for Our Transgressions: Rediscovering the Glory of Penal Substitution* (Wheaton, IL: Crossway Books, 2008), pp. 169-73.

2. Nor did Irenaeus. See Andrew P. Klager, "Retaining and Reclaiming the Divine: Identification and the Recapitulation of Peace in St. Irenaeus of Lyons' Atonement Narrative," in Brad Jersak and Michael Hardin, *Stricken by God? Nonviolent Identification and the Victory of Christ* (Grand Rapids, MI: Eerdmans Publishing, 2007), pp. 422-80, who argues against Boersma's penal substitution reading of Irenaeus. Klager concludes: "Irenaeus . . . understands the atonement for humanity's apostasy to consist of restoration rather than penal retribution" (p. 480).

362

half of all, surrendering His own temple *to death* in place of all, to settle man's account *with death* and free him from the primal transgression.

On account of Adam's "primal transgression," all who sow sin reap death as their "due." Redemption of humanity from sin and death, therefore, requires that one "pay death its due" on behalf of all who have sinned: "Death there had to be, and death for all, so that the due of all might be paid" (*On the Incarnation* IV.20, emphasis added).

Now, when read through a Western-Latin lens, it is easy to see here the notion of penal substitution, Jesus paying God his due for our sin by his death in our place. In Calvinist thinking, especially, death is understood as necessarily an external punishment imposed by God upon humanity as retribution for sin. Thus Jeffery et al. write: "The very fact of our mortality . . . is a penalty for sin. . . . It is impossible to escape the conclusion that death is God's punishment for sin."[3] This view leads directly to the equation of sacrifice (which requires the death of the animal offered) with punishment, an equation which we have demonstrated to be a deficient understanding of atoning sacrifice in the biblical tradition (Chapters 11 and 12 above). This equation of death with punishment is evident in how Jeffery et al. interpret Athanasius.[4] In any case, this view does not represent how Athanasius himself thinks about the relationship between sin and death. Contrary to the Calvinist view, moreover, the Eastern tradition, following Athanasius, does not interpret human mortality in penal terms.[5]

In Athanasius's thinking, death as the "due" of sin is not understood as divine retribution for sin in the sense of an external punishment imposed by God's intervention in the created order. Athanasius depicts death in terms of *corruption* brought on by sin and leading to *non-existence.* God did not create humans as immortal beings; humans were created "essentially impermanent" — mortal and corruptible — as all of God's other earthly creatures. God created human beings in such a way ("from the dust of the ground") that death is the future of humans apart from God ("you are dust, and to dust you shall return," Gen 3:19). Even so, God created humans in such a way ("in the image of God") that humans were capable of receiving immortality as a gift of God's grace.[6] But this gift was conditional upon human choice: continue in obedience

---

3. Jeffery et al., *Pierced for Our Transgressions,* pp. 122-23.

4. Cf. Jeffery et al., *Pierced for Our Transgressions,* p. 172.

5. See Kallistos Ware, *The Orthodox Way,* rev. ed. (Crestwood, NY: St. Vladimir's Seminary Press, 1995), p. 60.

6. That God created humans mortal and intended immortality as something to be received by grace was the common understanding among the church Fathers, including Irenaeus (*Against Heresies* IV.38), Athanasius (*On the Incarnation* I.3), and Augustine (*City of God* XII.22; XIII.1). See further J. N. D. Kelly, *Early Christian Doctrines,* 5th ed. (New York: Continuum International Publishing, 2000), pp. 171, 346-47, 362.

to God and receive eternal life, or turn away from God and face inevitable death. When humans take their freedom and turn from God (choose sin), they "come under the natural law of death" that applies to all earthly created reality (I.3).

If we turn away from God the source of our existence, then we will inevitably go the way of all earthly creatures: we suffer the corruption that is the natural course for earth-creatures and so fall inevitably into non-existence. Death, then, is the natural outworking of sin in the natural order of things that God has ordained in creation.

> But men, having turned from the contemplation of God to evil of their own devising, had come inevitably under the law of death. Instead of remaining in the state in which God had created them, they were in process of becoming corrupted entirely, and death had them completely under its dominion. For the transgression of the commandment was making them turn back again according to their nature; and as they had at the beginning come into being out of non-existence, so were they now on the way to returning, through corruption, to non-existence again. (I.4)

Death as the natural consequence of sin, Athanasius says, is the "penalty of which God had forewarned them for transgressing the commandment." But the death that follows from sin as its consequence is a penalty that human beings impose upon themselves by their own choice, not an external punishment imposed directly by God's action:

> This, then, was the plight of men. God had not only made them out of nothing, but had also graciously bestowed on them His own life by the grace of the Word. Then, turning from eternal things to things corruptible, . . . they had become the cause of their own corruption in death. (I.5)

Athanasius thus views the penalty of death due to sin as coming to humanity, not by primary causation though the direct action of God, but as a result of their sin by secondary causation, through the mediation of the created order ("the natural law of death"): human beings themselves are "the cause of their own corruption in death." J. N. D. Kelly summarizes Athanasius's view:

> . . . the first human beings, Adam and Eve . . . turned away . . . from Him Who alone is being in the true sense to things which have no real being of their own. So they fell . . . they were reduced to the corruption which, after all, was their nature . . . It was through the fault committed by their free volition that the disintegrating forces in any case latent in our nature were released.[7]

7. Kelly, *Early Christian Doctrines*, p. 347.

Athanasius's account, we observe, parallels the biblical narrative. God creates Adam "a living being" *(nepheš ḥayyāh)* (Gen 2:7), the same as all of God's other creatures (cf. 1:20, 24, 30; 2:19), such that Adam is vulnerable to corruption and death by nature. Having been created mortal, Adam can avoid death only by eating of the tree of life that God has provided in the garden. Adam is exposed to death by his exile from the garden, by which he is cut off from the source that would sustain his life forever (3:22-24). While done on account of Adam's sin, God's sentence of exile suspends indefinitely God's prior sentence of death (2:17), such that Adam will die, not immediately by God's hand, but eventually by natural causes (3:19). In effect, by choosing to withdraw the threatened retribution, God consents to let the consequences of Adam's choice take their course in the order of creation, with the inevitable end of death. God's choice here has a profound implication — Adam's death is not the first. The first death in the biblical narrative is that of Abel, who is murdered by Cain (4:8). Death enters the world, not by divine agency as an imposed penalty for sin, but by human agency as the actual consequence of sin.[8] It is thus human sin, not divine punishment, that brings death into the world (cf. Wis 1:12-13). Paul's statement briefly summarizes the Genesis account: "sin entered the world through one man and death through sin" (Rom 5:12 NET).[9] Sin and death enter the world in the same way, therefore, by means of human agency — sin by Adam, death by Cain.[10] Athanasius's account also fits with the patristic understanding of the nature of evil: sin and death are neither independent powers, existing apart from the cosmos and arrayed over against God, nor original creations, the direct effects of God's personal power; rather, the power of sin to produce death is parasitic on the God-created capacities of the natural order, which have been perverted to evil ends (death) by human disobedience (sin).

8. Because human agency is a causal capacity within the created order, death originates from sin by natural causes; that is, death results from sin by secondary causation rather than divine intervention. This reading of the Genesis narrative thus coheres with the understanding of divine wrath at Romans 1 that I developed in Chapter 12: God responds to sin by "giving up" humans to the consequences of their disobedience.

9. The key word here is the twice-used preposition *dia* ("through"), which in the genitive case takes an instrumental sense: "by means of," "by agency of," or "because of." Nothing in Paul's text states or implies the involvement of divine agency here. And the parallel phrasing "sin . . . through *(dia)* one man" and "death through *(dia)* sin" suggests that the agency in both is human.

10. This parallel reading of Genesis 1–4 and Rom 5:12 provides the basis for an alternative account to Augustine's doctrine of "original sin" (which, as is well-known, is premised on the mistranslation of Rom 5:12 in the Latin Vulgate): we are liable to death as the consequence of sin (in Athanasius's terms, we are "debtors to death"), not because we are biological descendents of a "first sinner," whose sin and its penalty have been transmitted down the generations by procreation, but rather because, having inherited a world already warped by the sins of our forebears, in which God has chosen to let us go our own way and suffer the consequences, we, too, have made Adam's choice and are thus are liable to its consequence.

In Athanasius's view, then, it is this situation of corruption-generating, death-begetting sin in the created order that the Incarnation is designed to remedy. Jesus "pays death its due" on our behalf in the sense that his death and resurrection reverses the corruption and death brought by sin, which we could in no way accomplish by our own will.[11] Jesus' death on behalf of all has reversed "the natural law of death" as the "due" of sin: "Now that the common Savior of all has died on our behalf, we who believe in Christ no longer die, as men did aforetime, in fulfillment of the threat of the law. That condemnation has come to an end" (IV.21). The cross of Christ, Athanasius thus says, is not payment to God but victory over death: "He it is Who has destroyed death and freely graced us all with incorruption through the promise of the resurrection, having raised His own body as its first-fruits, and displayed it by the sign of the cross as the monument to His victory over death and its corruption" (V.32).

11. Jeffery et al., *Pierced for Our Transgressions*, state concerning Athanasius's account of salvation that "Jesus' *death* was the purpose of the incarnation" (p. 172, emphasis original). This is a serious distortion of Athanasius's view, completely ignoring *On the Incarnation* V, "The Resurrection." Moreover, in IV ("The Death of Christ") Athanasius says explicitly: "The supreme object of his coming was to bring about the resurrection of the body" (IV.22).

"Christ Is Our Peace"

The Cross, Justice, and Peace

•   •

The Cross and Justice

Redemption beyond Retribution

CHAPTER 19

The Pauline Vision: The Justice of God
through the Faithfulness of Jesus Christ

For I am not ashamed of the gospel;
it is the power of God for salvation to everyone who believes,
to the Jew first and also to the Greek.
For in it the justice of God is revealed
from faithfulness to faithfulness;
as it is written, "The one who is just by faithfulness will live."

ROMANS 1:16-17A

But now, apart from law,
the justice of God has been disclosed,
and is attested by the law and the prophets,
the justice of God through the faithfulness of Jesus Christ
to all having faith.

ROMANS 3:21-22

19.1. The Justice of God

Paul envisions the cross of Jesus Christ as both the faithful completion of God's covenant righteousness to Israel and the faithful demonstration of God's justice to all the nations. Paul announces this theme — God's justice-doing through faithfulness — three times in Romans. This would thus seem to be his major thesis in the letter.[1]

---

1. Concerning "the righteousness of God" as the dominant theme of Romans, see Richard B. Hays, *Echoes of Scripture in the Letters of Paul* (New Haven, CT: Yale University Press,

For in it [the gospel] the justice of God *(dikaiosynē theou)* is revealed from faithfulness to faithfulness *(ek pisteōs eis pistin)*. (Rom 1:17a)[2]

But now, apart from law, the justice of God *(dikaiosynē theou)* has been disclosed, and is attested by the law and the prophets, the justice of God *(dikaiosynē theou)* through the faithfulness of Jesus Christ *(dia pisteōs Iēsou Christou)* to all having faith *(eis pantas tous pisteuontas)*. (3:21-22)[3]

Therefore, because we have been justified *(dikaiōthentes)* out of faithfulness *(ek pisteōs)*, we have peace with God through our Lord Jesus Christ. (5:1)

If we paraphrase the latter verse in the active voice, we not only hear it more in tune with Paul's previous gospel announcements, but also hear in it echoes of the first Servant Song in Isaiah 42: Because God has done justice for us (or put us right) out of faithfulness (the faithfulness of Jesus Christ), we have peace with God through our Lord Jesus Christ.[4]

God has been faithful and done justice, Paul announces, on behalf of both his covenant people and also all those of the nations who put their trust in the God whose gospel he is announcing. And God has done justice for all through the saving power of the gospel (Rom 1:16), "apart from law" (3:21). The means through which God has chosen to demonstrate justice to all is the life and death of Jesus Christ, and Jesus Christ demonstrate God's justice through faithfulness, most fully through the cross. Jesus is thus the righteous servant of God, the one who brings forth justice, out of faithfulness, to the nations:

1989), pp. 34-83; Christopher D. Marshall, *Beyond Retribution: A New Testament Vision for Justice, Crime, and Punishment* (Grand Rapids, MI: Eerdmans Publishing, 2001), pp. 38-40; and A. Katherine Grieb, *The Story of Romans: A Narrative Defense of God's Righteousness* (Louisville, KY: Westminster John Knox Press, 2002).

2. These three translations are my variations of the NRSV.

3. We follow Richard Hays and Luke Timothy Johnson, reading Paul's crucial phrase, *pisteōs Iēsou Christou*, as a subjective genitive — "faith(fullness) of Jesus Christ." That is, Jesus Christ is not the *object* of faith (per the traditional translation, "faith *in* Jesus Christ") but the *subject* of faith. The grammatical form of the phrase does not determine which meaning is intended. Regarding scholarly debate on the translation, see Daniel B. Wallace, *Greek Grammar beyond the Basics: An Exegetical Syntax of the New Testament* (Grand Rapids, MI: Zondervan, 1996), pp. 114-16. Luke Timothy Johnson, *Reading Romans: A Literary and Theological Commentary* (Macon, GA: Smyth & Helwys, 2001), pp. 59-62, makes the case that Paul intends that Jesus is the subject, not object, of faith — so, "through the faith(fullness) of Jesus Christ." Johnson writes (p. 61): "It is Jesus' faith that reveals God's way of making humans righteous before God. The 'faith of Christ' therefore lies at the heart also of Paul's theological argument in Romans." James D. G. Dunn, *The Theology of Paul the Apostle* (Grand Rapids, MI: Eerdmans Publishing, 1998), pp. 379-85, argues for the traditional objective genitive reading, "faith in Christ."

4. This theme, that God's justice is demonstrated by his faithfulness in putting sinners right, is stated also by John: "If we confess our sins, he is faithful *(pistos)* and just *(dikaios)*, so that he might forgive us our sins and purify us from every injustice *(adikias)*" (1 John 1:9, my translation).

Here is my servant, whom I uphold, my chosen, in whom my soul delights; I have put my spirit upon him; *he will bring forth justice to the nations . . . he will faithfully bring forth justice.* He will not grow faint or be crushed until he has established justice in the earth; and the coastlands wait for his teaching." (Isa 42:1-4)

Jesus Christ is thus the *telos* of the covenant (Rom 10:4), the one through whom God's teaching *(torah)* is fulfilled and God's saving justice (covenant righteousness) is revealed, as the demonstration of God's faithfulness, for Israel and the nations.

The very purpose of God's justice-doing through the faithfulness of Jesus Christ is to "establish justice in the earth" through the faithfulness of humanity to God's law (Isa 42:4) — or, as Paul puts it, "to bring about the obedience of faith" (Rom 1:5; 16:26) — among not only God's covenant people but all the nations. This, I think, is the significance of Paul's economic phrase, "from faith(fulness) to faith(fulness)" *(ek pisteōs eis pistin)*. I see a direct parallel between this compact formula in Rom 1:17 and the longer formulation in 3:21-22:

the justice of God *(dikaiosynē theou)* is revealed
   from faithfulness *(ek pisteōs)* to faithfulness *(eis pistin)* (1:17)
the justice of God *(dikaiosynē theou)* has been disclosed . . .
   through the faithfulness of Jesus Christ *(dia pisteōs Jēsou Christou)* to
   all having faith *(eis pantas tous pisteuontas).* (3:21-22)

The gospel is "the power of God for salvation" (1:16) because it reveals "the justice of God from faith(fulness) to faith(fulness)" (1:17), "the justice of God through the faithfulness of Jesus Christ to all having faith" (3:22). That is, the justice of God is demonstrated *from* (i.e., out of, through, or by means of) the faithfulness of Jesus Christ *to* (i.e., toward, leading into, or for bringing about) "the obedience of faith" (1:5; 16:26), human faithfulness to God's way of righteousness.[5]

As we have seen in discussing Rom 3:21-26 (Chapter 8), Paul depicts the cross of Christ as framed by the justice of God and places grace and redemption at the center of God's justice demonstrated through the faithfulness of Jesus. The Pauline vision, therefore, is that the justice of God is demonstrated, not through satisfaction of law, but through faithfulness to covenant, by means of grace, for the sake of redemption. Katherine Grieb retells Paul's story of God's

---

5. Michael J. Gorman, *Cruciformity: Paul's Narrative Spirituality of the Cross* (Grand Rapids, MI: Eerdmans Publishing, 2001), pp. 117-18, confirms this reading: "Preserving the sense of the Greek prepositions, which indicate the origin and goal of faith, we may paraphrase Rom 1:17a as follows: The gospel proclaims that God's righteousness both *originates* in fidelity — God's fidelity, revealed in Christ's fidelity — and *engenders* fidelity — ours" (emphasis original).

faithful, redemptive justice "apart from law" revealed through Jesus Christ along similar lines:

> But now apart from the law, though the law and prophets testify to it (3:21), God has acted in covenant faithfulness, answering the plea of the psalmist (Ps. 143:11) that in spite of the fact that no one living is righteous before God, God will nevertheless save the psalmist, Israel, and the world from danger. God has acted in covenant fidelity to the covenant people Israel quite apart from their own righteousness. Even though everyone has been a liar, God has nevertheless been true (3:4). God has done for the world what Israel could not do for the world, or even for itself, by providing the one true Israelite who would act in covenant faithfulness to do and be what Israel should have done and been. That one true Israelite is Jesus Christ. He is Israel's representative, as the Israelite who keeps covenant with God. He is also God's representative, since the righteousness of God is enacted through his own faithfulness, his obedience unto death on the cross. . . . The faithful obedient death of Jesus Christ on the cross was simultaneously God's own action of covenant fidelity to Israel and to all humanity.[6]

This key Pauline gospel thesis — that "apart from law" God demonstrates justice through faithfulness to the covenant, by means of grace, for the purpose of redeeming humanity — should guide our thinking when interpreting how the cross of Christ reveals and fulfills the justice of God. This means that our interpretation of the cross, as depicted by Paul, must hold together God's justice with God's faithfulness, such that the faithfulness and justice of God work together in the cross toward the redemption of humanity.

Before we examine the justice of God as revealed through the cross of Christ, we need to attend briefly to this little phrase that is so important: "apart from law." In Chapter 12, we saw that the biblical narrative from the beginning depicts God doing covenant justice "apart from law" — dealing righteously with sin outside the prescriptions of the sacrificial system. There, we read "apart from law" as meaning, roughly, "apart from the requirements of sacrificial atonement." One might read "apart from law" *(choris nomou)* also as "irrespective of law" (cf. Anglicized NRSV). This moves nearer to the nuance of Paul's thesis that we consider in the present discussion: God's saving justice is demonstrated through the faithfulness of Jesus Christ "irrespective of law" — irrespective of legal requirements, outside the bounds of "the rule of law."

6. Grieb, *The Story of Romans*, pp. 36-37.

19.2. The Justice of God through the Cross of Christ

To see how God does justice "apart from law" yet in covenant faithfulness through Jesus Christ, let us view the cross through the lens of criminal justice. The canonical accounts of the death of Jesus reveal the cross as a crime scene: human authorities commit gross injustice — the judicial murder of an innocent person (Matt 27:4; Luke 23:47). All four Gospels attest to this injustice: Jesus is tried on false charges (Matt 27:18; Mark 15:10; Luke 23:2-5; John 18:30), accused by false witnesses (Matt 26:59-60; Mark 14:55-59), convicted on insufficient evidence (Matt 27:23; Mark 15:14; Luke 23:13-24; John 18:38; 19:4, 6), and executed without due process (Matt 27:26; Mark 15:15; Luke 23:25; John 19:13-16).[7] At the cross, humanity commits the ultimate crime: we kill the Son of God (Mark 15:39)!

If any sin necessitates atonement, if any wrong must be put right, then surely it is this crime of cosmic proportion and incalculable magnitude. Not only is God's life in the person of Jesus taken unlawfully, but this crime strikes at the very authority of law. For human authority has presumed to judge and execute the official representative of the Author of Law. The crucifixion of Jesus is, in effect, the murder of Justice personified, the murder of the One who is truly righteous (Luke 23:47).

We may put the question of the cross thus: God sends his Son to put the world aright, only to have his Son murdered by the very ones he came to save — What, then, is God to do? In framing the cross by this question, we echo Athanasius, who asked (*On the Incarnation* II.6): "As, then, the creatures whom He had created reasonable . . . were in fact perishing, and such noble works were on the road to ruin, what then was God, being Good, to do?" Athanasius argued that it would be "unfitting and unworthy" of God to allow his work of creation to succumb completely to the power of sin and death, for then God would have abandoned his own purpose and proved false to himself. He thus sought to understand the Incarnation as God's initiative to bring to completion God's own purpose in creation. Likewise, we seek to understand the cross of Christ as God's gracious initiative to deal justly with guilty humanity in faithfulness to God's own redemptive purpose begun in Christ. We thus ask: How is God to right this wrong beyond measure? How is God to redeem humanity through the cross?

The retributive paradigm, which seeks justice according to "the rule of law," demands that the offender receive punishment "equal to the crime" to "balance the scales" (cf. Chapter 3 above). This view is expressed no more clearly than by the greatest of Enlightenment philosophers, Immanuel Kant:

7. Concerning the legal details of Jesus' execution, see Gardner C. Hanks, *Capital Punishment and the Bible* (Scottdale, PA: Herald Press, 2002), pp. 161-73.

But whoever has committed murder must *die*. There is, in this case, no juridical substitute or surrogate, that can be given or taken for the satisfaction of
justice. There is no *likeness* or proportion between life, however painful, and
death; and therefore there is no equality between the crime of murder and
the retaliation of it but what is judicially accomplished by the execution of
the criminal.[8]

Anything less than strict retribution fails to vindicate both the dignity of the
victim and the integrity of the law that protects the innocent.

Now, however, what punishment inflicted upon humanity could equal the
crime of murdering God incarnate? If under the law of Moses the sin of murdering a human being could not be expiated by animal blood but only by shedding the blood of the murderer himself, how could the sin of murdering God's
Son be expiated by the shedding of merely human blood? What life could be
taken from humanity as just retribution for taking the life of God's Son, what
amount of human blood could be shed as expiation for shedding God's blood?
These questions parallel the question asked by Peter Abelard: "And if that sin of
Adam was so great that it could be expiated only by the death of Christ, what
expiation will avail for that act of murder committed against Christ?"[9]

Such questions expose the logical incompleteness of penal substitution,
which models atonement within the retributive paradigm. Justice, this model
claims, demands satisfaction for sins according to the law of retribution, which
requires a death to atone for sins; and satisfaction for sins is achieved through
the death of Jesus upon the cross. This satisfaction of justice, however, is
achieved by a most unjust act — the condemnation of Innocence incarnate, the
murder of Justice personified. The killing of Jesus is itself a grave sin, for which
justice demands satisfaction according to "the rule of law." How, though, is satisfaction for *this* sin to be achieved? Not by Jesus' death; for it is precisely on account of his murder that justice is *not* satisfied — and, hence, that satisfaction
for sin is yet required. The law of retribution requires satisfaction for murder by
death; another death is thus needed. But, now, whose death could atone for the
ultimate of sins? Whose death could cancel the death of God's Son? The satisfaction of justice for sin by the unjust death of Jesus, therefore, generates further sin requiring satisfaction, but for which justice according to the law of retribution can never be satisfied. Seeing this, I think, helps us make sense of why

8. Immanuel Kant, *The Philosophy of Law,* excerpted in *Philosophical Perspectives on Punishment,* ed. Gertrude Ezorsky (Albany: State University of New York Press, 1972), p. 105, emphasis original. For an extended treatment of Kant's retributivism, see Lloyd Steffen, *Executing
Justice: The Moral Meaning of the Death Penalty* (Cleveland, OH: Pilgrim Press, 1998), pp. 69-87.
    9. Quoted by Joel B. Green and Mark D. Baker, *Recovering the Scandal of the Cross: Atone-
ment in New Testament and Contemporary Contexts* (Downers Grove, IL: InterVarsity Press,
2000), p. 137.

Paul proclaims that God has done justice through the cross "apart from law" —
apart from the law of retribution and its demands for satisfaction.

We can see our way to this same inadequacy of penal substitution by following another line of questioning. Penal substitution, as Charles Hodge wrote,
affirms that Jesus' suffering and death on the cross "were designed . . . for the
satisfaction of justice" (see Chapter 5 above). Now, if God willed and designed
the death of Jesus as a just punishment for sin, then the judicial killing of Jesus
must itself be a righteous act, an execution of God's will, a satisfaction of God's
justice. Thus, it would seem that those who participate in this righteous death
would also be doing a righteous deed, a deed in conformity with God's holy
will. If God willed Jesus' death, then those who hand Jesus over to death and
those who execute him are doing only what is for God's satisfaction.

The Gospel narratives, however, present the killing of Jesus as a most unrighteous, unholy thing — a sin. Judas, who hands Jesus over to the Jewish authority, repents of his treacherous deed and confesses truly: "I have sinned by
betraying innocent blood" (Matt 27:3-4). And before Pilate, Jesus testifies: "You
would have no authority over me unless it have been given you from above; the
one who handed me over to you is guilty of a greater sin" (John 19:11). This implies two things: Pilate sins by exercising his authority to condemn Jesus rather
than to release him; and those who have handed Jesus over to Pilate have committed an even greater sin. Further, Jesus prays from the cross that God forgive
his accusers and executioners (Luke 23:34), which evidently implies that they
have sinned against him.

If the killing of Jesus were a righteous act, pleasing God's holy will by executing God's just punishment for sin, per penal substitution, then why would
the execution of that just punishment be a sin needing forgiveness? If the executors of God's just penalty for sin upon Jesus are only doing God's will, satisfying the divine law, then why would their participation in the divine design need
forgiveness? But Judas's confession and Jesus' prayer imply that they *are* in need
of forgiveness. The canonical accounts of Jesus' death thus seem to run contrary to the implications of penal substitution.

Penal substitution is inadequate on this point, I think, because it presupposes that Jesus' death itself is the necessary and sufficient answer to the question of how God's justice deals with humanity's crimes against God's law. Given
this assumption, despite the clear implications of the canonical accounts to the
contrary, penal substitution can see the cross only under the category of punishment, not crime. Thus, Hans Boersma:

> The gospel accounts inform us that Jesus died at the hands of Jewish and Ro-
> man authorities. This brings us into the realm of punishment rather than the
> realm of crime. Theologically speaking, penal substitution *assumes* that Je-
> sus' crucifixion was not only a human punishment but also a divine punish-

ment. Either way, whether considered from the historical or the theological perspective, the cross is a form of punishment enacted by an authority in a legal position to execute it. Penal substitution, therefore, takes us into the realm of punishment, not into the realm of crime.[10]

The penal substitution model thus hides from view, and hence neglects to give an accounting for, what the canonical accounts actually show, that the trial and execution of Jesus is *itself* a crime against both God's servant and God's law (see Chapter 7 above). The crucifixion of Jesus is not justice done, but justice murdered.

Here we are reminded of our analysis of the Song of the Suffering Servant (in Chapter 13 above). From the perspective of "we" the people, the suffering of the Servant bears the punishment of God — his death is God's judgment: "We accounted him . . . struck down by God" (Isa 53:4). The prophet confesses, to the contrary, that the people were mistaken in their judgment of the Servant — the Servant dies, not by the just punishment of God, but from the unjust deeds of the people: "He was wounded from our transgressions, crushed from our iniquities" (v. 5a, my translation). The parallel between the Servant and Jesus is striking: just as "we" the people put the Servant on trial and sentenced him to death, to give his unjust death the divine stamp of a "just punishment" (vv. 7-9), so the religious and political leaders put Jesus on trial and sentenced him to death, to give his unjust death the divine stamp of a "just punishment." The penal substitution view, which insists on seeing Jesus' death as a just punishment, is thus analogous to the "we" view in the Song of the Suffering Servant. Just as the people were, because of their assumptions concerning God's justice, unable to see the suffering of the Servant as the result of human injustice, so the penal substitution view is unable, because of its assumptions concerning God's justice, to see the cross of Christ as the doing of human injustice.[11] Just as the prophet's confession challenges the popular perception of the Servant, therefore, so the gospel proclamation challenges the popular theology of the cross. The cross of Christ, as much as the suffering of the Servant, is a crime committed in the guise of punishment: *The cross of Christ is crime by punishment.*

10. Hans Boersma, "Eschatalogical Justice and the Cross: Violence and Penal Substitution," *Theology Today*, July 2003, retrieved from http://findarticles.com/p/articles/mi_qa3664/is_200307/ai_n9251886/pg_1, emphasis added.

11. As we discussed in Chapter 7, from the fact that the cross of Christ was comprehended within "the definite plan and foreknowledge of God" (Acts 2:23; cf. 4:28) it does not follow that the death of Jesus was the doing of God. In fact, as we observed there, the apostolic accounts are consistent in attributing responsibility for Jesus' death to human agents while attributing Jesus' resurrection to divine action. The apostolic accounts of Jesus' death, that is, recognize both human freedom and divine providence.

We have demonstrated that the cross of Christ cannot be understood as the satisfaction of justice according to the law of retribution. Instead of answering the question of justice, the unjust death of Jesus presses that question upon us with all the more emphasis. We are forced to ask: Can there be atonement for the sin of murdering Jesus within the limits of justice as prescribed by the law of retribution? For many Christians, this question will make no sense. "Of course," many will want to say, "Jesus' death on the cross satisfies legal justice perfectly. Jesus suffered the divinely required penalty to pay for humanity's sins." Yet, this is precisely the question put to us by the cross. We should not simply assume, as does penal substitution, that God's justice must necessarily follow the law of retribution.

We have seen already (Chapter 10) that, if we assume (mistakenly) that the Levitical sacrifices operated on the retributive principle, then the particulars of the sin offering make no sense; instead, if we look to see what the particulars of the sin offering reveal to us, we see in atoning sacrifice, not the principle of retribution, but the grace of God. The same is true regarding the cross of Jesus: if we make the prior assumption that the cross is the ultimate satisfaction of retributive justice, then we will fail to see the grace at the heart of the justice that God reveals to us through the cross. Instead, as Paul's gospel tells us, we must allow the cross to reveal to us the justice of God irrespective of the rule of law: "But now, apart from law, the justice of God has been disclosed . . . through faithfulness . . . by his *grace* as a gift . . ." (Rom 3:21-24). As Colin Gunton writes, "the death of Jesus under the law reveals the way in which God puts right the lawlessness of the universe, not punitively but transformatively, by sheer grace."[12]

The cross of Christ reveals to us, not a God that seeks to satisfy the law of retribution by the death of Jesus, but a God who seeks redemption beyond retribution through the death of Jesus. For this crime of immeasurable wrong — the murder of God's Son — the only practical outcome of the legal logic of retributive justice would be penal bloodshed for human sin to the fullest measure. If "the rule of law" were followed in response to humanity's crime committed against God at the cross in the murder of Jesus, God's justice would be vindicated in one narrow sense — God's sovereign prerogative of retribution would be satisfied when sinful humanity receives its "just deserts" — but only at the cost of the destruction of humanity. That, however, would defeat God's cause of redemption in Christ, so bringing God's purpose to naught. That is, had God followed strictly the rule of law, justice would have been served in the narrow sense of retribution, but the result would be utterly *un*redemptive, contrary to God's own purpose to save humanity from sin and death. In Pauline terms, had God prosecuted justice against humanity "to the fullest extent of the

<hr />

12. Colin E. Gunton, *The Actuality of Atonement: A Study of Metaphor, Rationality and the Christian Tradition* (Grand Rapids, MI: Eerdmans Publishing, 1989), p. 138.

law" in response to the criminal crucifixion of Jesus, then God's initiative in Christ would have failed utterly "to bring about the obedience of faith," which is the very purpose of "the gospel of God" (Rom 1:1-6; 16:25-26). In order to fulfill God's own redemptive purpose in Christ, God's saving work through the cross holds together justice with faithfulness by means of grace.

The justice that God demonstrates through the cross of Christ and exercises by means of grace is *covenant justice* — justice that fulfills God's promise and so manifests God's faithfulness, justice that redeems humanity from sin and restores humanity to righteousness. In order that God might redeem humanity according to his own purpose in Christ, God's justice must transcend retribution through the cross. In order that God's covenant faithfulness and God's redemptive purpose might converge in the cross, God's justice graciously breaks "the rule of law" and annuls the requirements of retribution (Rom 8:1-3; Col 2:13-14). God's redemptive justice is not defined, measured, or "ruled" by law and its requirements but rather is exercised by grace through God's own faithfulness to his covenant as demonstrated in the cross of Jesus Christ (Rom 1:16-17; 3:21-26). God's redemption of humanity from sin through the faithful cross of Christ demonstrates God's saving justice, which graciously transcends "the rule of law," outstrips the limits of legal justice, and escapes the logic of retribution.[13]

19.3. The Justice of God, the Rule of Law, and the Reign of Sin and Death

Let us consider a further way in which retributive justice according to the "rule of law" fails to comprehend God's redemptive justice through the cross of

13. To the above discussions, we might add the following argument: If we agree with Paul that the justice of God is revealed through the cross of Christ but insist on viewing the justice of God according to the law of retribution, then, insofar as the law of retribution requires reward of good for righteousness and punishment of evil for sins, we have two logical possibilities for interpreting the cross, either as God's reward of good for righteousness or as God's punishment of evil for sins. On the first possibility, Jesus would suffer death as God's reward for his (or others') righteousness, but that would invert retribution (righteousness deserves the good of life, not the evil of death) such that God's justice would be unjust (i.e., contrary to the law of retribution). On the second possibility, Jesus would suffer death as God's punishment for his sins, but that would contradict orthodoxy, for Jesus, as God's Son, is sinless. If we are to interpret the cross according to the law of retribution and yet save the appearances of orthodoxy, therefore, we must make a further assumption: the cross must be God's punishment, not for Jesus' sins, but for others' sins. This assumption, the central idea of penal substitution, is seriously problematic for many reasons, however, as we have demonstrated in Part II. We are thus left with a dilemma: either embrace one of the untenable implications (God is unjust or Jesus is sinful) or reject one of the initial premises. Maintaining the Pauline premise that the justice of God is revealed through the cross of Christ leads us to reject the other premise, that the justice of God is to be viewed according to the law of retribution.

Christ. A rule-of-law-prescribed response to the murder of Jesus would fail to deal decisively with sin and instead would only multiply the results of sin — death — to the maximum. As Paul writes, the "end" or "wages" of sin is death (Rom 6:21, 23). This "law of sin and of death" (8:2) works in two ways: death is both the fruit of the power of sin working within us and "just retribution" for sin imposed upon us by the law.

First, sin corrupts and weakens us, and the power of sin "exercises dominion" over us by producing death, bodily and spiritually, in and through us (Rom 5:12–6:23). Subject to the dominion of sin, the very members of our bodies become "weapons of wickedness" (6:13) in the service of the forces of death. It is this oppression by the overwhelming and indwelling power of sin that Paul speaks of as being "sold into slavery under sin" (7:14-24). Giving us over to the power of sin already working within us ("the lust of their hearts"), God reveals his wrath against sin by letting us fall into slavery to death-producing sin (1:18-32).[14] In this sense, "the law of sin and of death" concerns the death produced in and through us as we surrender to the reign of sin in both personal and social arenas of existence. This slavery to the power of sin and the death it produces are revealed from humanity's beginning through cycles of bloodshed, violence, and vengeance, from Cain and Lamech onward, until "the earth was corrupt in God's sight, and the earth was filled with violence" (Gen 6:11; cf. 4:8, 14, 23-24; 9:6). Second, the law condemns us to death and thereby "pays back in kind" to us the "wages" of our sin. In this sense, "the law of sin and of death" is simply the logical conclusion of the *lex talionis*, which measures out retribution to the offender.

Now, in order that the cross might deal decisively with sin and its deadly results, it must liberate humanity from "the law of sin and of death" in *both* senses — both sin as a death-producing power to which humanity is enslaved and death as law-prescribed punishment for sin. But retributive justice according to "the rule of law" is incapable of redeeming from captivity to the dominion of sin and death. Retributive justice entails punishment that "equals the crime" and thus demands death as the penalty for murder. Hence, bloodshed necessitates bloodshed, and consequently death by murder begets death by punishment — which does not deal decisively with sin but only brings sin to fruition by multiplying death. Retributive justice, therefore, cannot save, cannot liberate from the dominion of sin and death, but can only strengthen "the law of sin and of death" that enslaves humanity. Retributive justice is thus powerless to accomplish God's redemptive justice, for it cannot deal decisively with sin but can only multiply its deathly results.

Retributive justice addresses sin only in the narrow, legal sense — and,

---

14. For a full discussion of "sin and death" in Paul's thought, see Dunn, *Theology of Paul,* pp. 91-127.

even so, can deal with sin only by dealing out death according to "the rule of law." In this way, retributive justice effectively manifests and reinforces the reign of death — and thus is incapable of addressing sin in its ontological depth and cosmic scope, sin as a power that exercises dominion in death (Rom 5:12-21). For, again, sin is not merely the transgression of divine law. It is that, to be sure. But the law is given for the sake of life: to choose God's way is to "choose life," and to reject God's way is to choose death (Deut 30:15-20; Luke 10:25-28). To choose a life of sin is thus to surrender to the dominion of death. The objective reality of sin — sin as a power contrary to God's will that dominates the cosmos and humanity — is all that oppresses life and produces death in us and in creation, from which we need redemption by God (Romans 8).

How, then, does God deal with death-producing sin in its full reality, as both transgression of law and oppression of life, through the cross of Jesus Christ? Regarding sin as transgression of law: God deals justly with sin, not by satisfying the law of retribution for sin, but rather by forgiving our transgressions, cancelling our record of wrongs, and nailing the death-demanding law of retribution to the cross — thus nullifying the power of sin to produce death through the law (Rom 8:1-3; Col 2:13-14).[15] Regarding sin as oppression of life: God deals decisively with sin by dealing death a final defeat through the life, death, and resurrection of Jesus Christ — thereby making a way for us to participate in God's victory over death and enabling us to participate in God's immortal life through resurrection and new creation in Christ (Rom 6:5-11; 1 Cor 15:20-28, 50-57; 2 Cor 5:17). It is thus God's own law-nullifying retribution-transcending, life-redeeming, creation-restoring work of faithfulness through the cross that discloses and demonstrates the justice of God.

15. See the extended discussions of this question and these texts in Chapters 18 and 25.

CHAPTER 20

The Foolish Cross, the Upside-Down Kingdom, and the Math of Grace

I choose to give to this last the same as I gave to you.
Am I not allowed to do what I choose with what belongs to me?
Or are you envious because I am generous?

· MATTHEW 20:14-15

20.1. The Cross of Christ and the Kingdom of God

Seeing the cross of Jesus Christ as the revelation of the retribution-transcending, redemption-favoring justice of God requires nothing less than a reversal of perspective:

> from seeing the cross as "resolving" the "problem of divine wrath" to seeing it as multiplying the *need* for God's mercy and forgiveness,
>
> from seeing the cross as the "answer" to the "question of human guilt" to seeing it as posing the *question* of how God is to deal with humanity's crime against God in the person of Jesus, and
>
> from seeing the cross as the perfect "satisfaction" of retribution, the fulfillment of justice according to "the rule of law," to seeing the work of God-in-Christ through the cross as *outstripping* the bounds of legal justice.

Such a reversal of perspective is difficult to make, however, for it requires us to see the cross in a way that inverts the "normal" orientation of our perception. Here we recall our first guiding rule (Chapter 2 above) — that the cross of Christ, as much as the teaching of Jesus, is the distinctive revelation of God's upside-down kingdom. It thus will be helpful to revisit the teachings of Jesus concerning the kingdom of God in order to enable us to reorient our view of the cross.

In Chapter 3, we considered Jesus' renunciation of retaliation in the Sermon on the Mount: "You have heard that it was said, 'An eye for an eye and a tooth for a tooth.' But I say to you . . ." (Matt 5:38-48). There we showed how Jesus' teaching reverses both the philosophical principle and the popular practice of retribution. Here we consider two parables — the lost son (Luke 15:11-32) and the laborers in the vineyard (Matt 20:1-16) — through which we can see the retribution-inverting, redemption-favoring "constitutional principles" of God's "upside-down" kingdom.[1] Jesus' parables about God's kingdom address both domains of justice in the classical theory — commutative justice and distributive justice — and in so doing provoke a gestalt shift in our seeing and thinking about the aim and substance of justice. As Richard Hays notes, "To "understand" these parables is to be changed by them, to have our vision of the world reshaped by them."[2] And as Christopher Marshall observes, these two parables in particular demonstrate that "The ultimate counter-theme [to retribution] is the Christian gospel, where the whole notion of just deserts and repayment in kind is turned on its head."[3]

20.1.1. Kingdom Justice: The Parable of the Lost Son

The parable of the "lost son" (Luke 15:11-32) presents us with a son that has left and returned to a father, a father that has compassion on the repentant son, and another son that is angered at both the brother's behavior and the father's response.[4] It is also a story of justice, but not of justice denied because punishment is not meted out as retribution for wrong done. Instead, this is a story of justice done through a father's steadfast love and faithfulness toward both of his sons, the bad and the good alike, a father's constant will to redeem his lost son and to restore both of his sons to right relationship. In this, the father models

1. The upside-down principles of God's kingdom of justice and peace as revealed by Jesus in the Gospels are explored in Donald B. Kraybill, *The Upside-Down Kingdom,* 25th Anniversary Edition (Scottdale, PA: Herald Press, 2003).

2. Richard B. Hays, *The Moral Vision of the New Testament: A Contemporary Introduction to New Testament Ethics* (San Francisco: HarperCollins Publishers, 1996), p. 301.

3. Christopher D. Marshall, *Beyond Retribution: A New Testament Vision for Justice, Crime, and Punishment* (Grand Rapids, MI: Eerdmans Publishing, 2001), p. 127.

4. In no way can I do justice to this story here. See the excellent treatments in Henri J. M. Nouwen, *The Return of the Prodigal Son: A Story of Homecoming* (New York: Doubleday, 1992), and Miroslav Volf, *Exclusion and Embrace: A Theological Exploration of Identity, Otherness, and Reconciliation* (Nashville, TN: Abingdon Press, 1996), pp. 156-65. My discussion here is indebted especially to Volf.

for us the retribution-transcending justice of God revealed through the sinner-redeeming, enemy-embracing cross of Jesus Christ.

The wrong done here is not that the younger son takes what does not belong to him: he receives his due share of the father's property.[5] Rather, the son does wrong by breaking relationship with his family. By asking for his "fair share" of the inheritance while his father is still living, he effectively wishes his father dead; and by taking his share and leaving home, he not only divides the family property but breaks the family solidarity. As Miroslav Volf puts it, by taking "what is his own" and striking out "on his own," he declares himself to be "his own," a "non-son," breaking the traditional rules of household solidarity and severing himself from the familial relationships that give him his identity and define his obligations. After "coming to himself" and returning, the son confesses the wrong he has done and acknowledges the reality of the wrong created by his actions: "Father, I have sinned against heaven and before you; I am no longer worthy to be called your son" (vv. 18-19, 21). Having squandered the family property (v. 13), the son has already formulated in his mind what he thinks are just terms for repaying the debt he owes; he deserves to lose his status as son — "treat me like one of your hired hands" (v. 19). The father, however, does not give the lost-and-returned son "what he deserves." Before the son can offer terms of restitution, the father, "filled with compassion," embraces the one that has wronged the family, restoring him to right relationship and naming him by his true identity, "this son of mine" (vv. 20-24).

When the elder son hears of this, he becomes angry and refuses to come into the house to celebrate his brother's return. Just as he had gone out to meet the younger son, the father now goes out to plead with the elder son. The elder son charges the father with injustice; for he has not received from the father what he (thinks he) deserves: "Listen! For all these years I have been working like a slave for you, and I have never disobeyed your command; yet you have never given me even a young goat so that I might celebrate with my friends" (v. 29). He also refuses to receive the younger son back into right relationship, referring to him as "this son of yours" rather than "this brother of mine." In doing so, the elder son reminds the father of the wrong done to him and the family — "this son of yours . . . has devoured your property" (v. 30). But the father assures the elder son that no wrong has been done to him; his status as elder son and his due inheritance are secure: "Son, you are always with me, and all that is mine is yours" (v. 31).[6]

In the classical theory of justice, this story addresses commutative justice,

5. By ancient custom, the eldest son was due to receive twice the inheritance received by the other sons (a "double portion" — cf. Deut 21:15-17). Because the father in the story has two sons, the elder son is due two-thirds of the father's property and the younger son is due one-third.

6. If the younger son has already taken and squandered his share of the father's property, then all that remains belongs by right to the elder son.

concerning "what is due" within interpersonal relationships, what each of us owes to others to whom we stand in social, legal, or contractual relationship. Essentially, commutative justice concerns relationships of obligation: to be in familial or legal or contractual relationship is to have obligations to those to whom one is so related; to fail one's obligation is to break right relationship. As conceived within the retributive paradigm under the principle of retribution, such failure creates the obligation to render "due" to the offended party by making compensation or restitution or else to suffer punishment.[7]

In the traditional household of the ancient world, each position — "father," "husband," "master," "mother," "wife," "son," "daughter," and "servant/slave" — carried its own obligations within the social structure of domestic relationships.[8] The father, as head of household, is obligated to provide for and protect the household, to steward the family property inherited from previous generations, to safeguard the family honor, and to teach his sons to act wisely and uprightly in society. A son's chief obligation is to obey and learn from his father (cf. Proverbs 1–7). Hence, a father's obligation is to reprimand and correct his sons for disobedient actions that harm the household security or dishonor the family name. That is, "sparing the rod" not only "spoils the child" but threatens to unravel the social fabric of the family structure.[9]

7. It is this idea of commutative justice that governs Anselm's theory of the death of Jesus as "satisfaction" to God for the sins of humanity, in which Anselm portrays the God-human relationship as that between lord and servant (or creator and creature). The driving logic of Anselm's theory runs as follows: the human obligation to God is to obey God's will; but humans have failed to render God the obedience that is God's due, dishonoring God; humans thus owe a moral debt to God's honor that requires satisfaction, such that humans must make compensation to repay God's honor or else suffer punishment from God; humanity, however, finds itself in a position of not being able to make proper satisfaction to God and so faces punishment for its sins; but Jesus, through his life and death, renders the obedience humans owe to God on behalf of humanity, so sparing humanity divine punishment. In Jesus' parable of the lost son, the father does *not* require satisfaction from his wayward son to repay the honor stolen from the family, but remits the son's sin and restores him to familial relationship by a gracious act of forgiveness and reconciliation. Insofar as this parable pictures God's relationship with humanity as transcending the retributive paradigm, therefore, Anselm's satisfaction theory of atonement falls short in representing Christ's work of atonement.

8. See Aristotle, *Politics* I for the classic discussion of the traditional household. As we observed in Chapter 3, this traditional understanding of household order is evident in Augustine's thinking (see *City of God*, XIX.14, 16). The traditional household code is characterized by a hierarchical order based on serial subordination — husband over wife, parent over child, master over slave. In the Greco-Roman worldview, as Aristotle made explicit, such serial subordination was justified by the supposed natural order of things: men are suited by nature to command and women are suited by nature to obey, masters are born for ruling and slaves are born for subjection (Aristotle, *Politics* I.2-5, 12-13).

9. Such household codes are reflected in Paul's letters (Eph 5:21–6:9; Col 3:18–4:1). Significantly, Paul does not accept the "natural order of things" as taught in Greco-Roman philosophy and affirmed by Augustine. Instead, Paul transforms the traditional household order by premis-

In our story, the younger son — by dividing the family estate and squandering his share, and by his shameful way of life — has broken the traditional rules of the household and dishonored his family. Having made himself "an enemy of the domestic peace," he is subject to retribution at the father's hand and thus is to be "reproved by a word, or by a blow, or any other kind of punishment that is just and legitimate."[10] And his thinking and actions show that he himself expects retribution from the father. The older son explicitly points out that, by contrast, he has fulfilled his obligation to the father: "I have never disobeyed your command." And by his anger at his brother's reception, the elder son shows that he, too, expects to see retribution done and the household rules upheld. This father does not rule his household by a rigid retributive justice, however. The father does fulfill his familial obligation to the elder son, assuring him that the younger son's share of the inheritance is not to be restored ("all that is mine is yours"). Yet, by embracing the younger son as a son and not as a servant, the father is moved by compassion to transcend retribution in favor of redemption, restoring the lost son to right relationship. Moved by this same compassion, the father leaves the celebration and goes out to embrace his elder son, assuring him of his rightful place and inheritance and inviting him to be reconciled to his redeemed brother. Volf comments:

> Far from completely discarding the order of the "household," the father continues to uphold it. What the father did was to "re-order" the order! . . . What is so profoundly different about the "new order" of the father is that it is not built around the alternatives as defined by the older brother: either strict adherence to the rules or disorder and disintegration; either you are "in" or you

---

ing all family relationships — between husbands and wives, parents and children, even masters and slaves — on *mutual* or reciprocal subordination *in Christ:* "Place yourselves under one another in reverence of Christ" (Eph 5:21, my translation; cf. Thomas R. Yoder Neufeld, *Ephesians* [Believers Church Bible Commentary; Scottdale, PA: Herald Press, 2002], pp. 243-45, and John Templeton Bristow, *What Paul Really Said about Women: An Apostle's Liberating Views on Equality in Marriage, Leadership, and Love* [San Francisco: HarperSanFrancisco, 1988], pp. 38-41). It is true, of course, that Paul does not call for slaves to be liberated, much less for slavery to be abolished. We wonder, however, what remains of the status "slave" and the institution of slavery within a Christian household where masters and slaves, being mutually subordinate to one another out of reverence for Christ and both being servants of Christ, are thus made equals in Christ. It is not without warrant that John Howard Yoder characterized Paul's domestic ethic as "revolutionary subordination" (*The Politics of Jesus: Vicit Agnus Noster* [Grand Rapids, MI: Eerdmans Publishing, 1972], pp. 163-92). The revolutionary implication of Paul's ethic is evident in how Paul deals with the runaway slave Onesimus. Paul does send Onesimus back to his master Philemon, according to law and custom, but not for punishment. Instead, Paul appeals to Philemon "on the basis of love" to receive Onesimus back into his household voluntarily, "no longer as a slave but more than a slave, a beloved brother . . . both in the flesh and in the Lord" (Phlm 8-10, 16). Paul thus exhorts Philemon to receive Onesimus back as an *equal.*

10. Augustine, *City of God*, XIX.16 (London: Penguin Books, 2003), p. 876.

are "out," depending on whether or not you have broken a rule. He rejected this alternative because his behavior was governed by the one fundamental "rule": relationship has priority over rules. . . . The father's most basic commitment is not to rules and given identities but to his sons. . . .[11]

By embracing equally both sons, the father reorders his household so that the family solidarity is maintained, not by the rigid rules of retribution, but by the steadfast love and faithfulness of the father. The father thus does justice for both sons. But the father's justice is retribution-transcending, redemption-favoring justice, the justice that redeems the lost to life, reconciles the alienated to relationship, and restores the repentant to righteousness — the very justice of God disclosed through the cross of Christ.

20.1.2. Kingdom Justice: The Parable of the Laborers in the Vineyard

Jesus' teaching that the justice of God's kingdom transcends retribution is evident further in the parable of the laborers in the vineyard (Matt 20:1-16). The kingdom of God, Jesus tells us, is like this: A landlord goes out "early in the morning to hire laborers for the vineyard . . . agreeing with the laborers for the usual daily wage" (vv. 1-2). Later in the day he hires more laborers, promising, "I will pay you whatever is right" (v. 4). He does the same three more times, the last time just one hour before quitting time. When it comes time to pay the laborers, he orders his manager to pay them "beginning with the last and then going to the first" (v. 8). Although hired at various times during the day, he pays each worker the same amount — "the usual daily wage" (v. 9). The "usual daily wage" was the *denarius* — the basic subsistence wage for day laborers, the minimum needed to sustain oneself from day to day, to secure one's "daily bread." This equal distribution of wages angers the laborers hired first, who charge that the landowner has wronged them by acting unfairly. The landowner replies that, indeed, he has done no wrong to anyone but has paid each of them according to what has been agreed.

In the classical theory of justice, this story addresses distributive justice, concerning "what is due" to each person as a member of society, how the total good society produces is to be divided among its members, the just distribution of benefits and burdens.[12] As conceived within the retributive paradigm, distributive justice prescribes that each person is due to receive benefit of reward

---

11. Volf, *Exclusion and Embrace*, pp. 164-65.

12. Aristotle's classic discussion of distributive justice, concerning "honour or money or the other things that fall to be divided among those who have a share in the constitution," is found in *Nicomachean Ethics* V.3. The quotation is from the W. D. Ross translation in Richard McKeon, ed., *The Basic Works of Aristotle* (New York: Random House, 1941).

in proportion to the burden of labor he or she has carried. Giving "to each what is due," distributing "just deserts," requires proportionality between burden borne (hours labored) and reward received (wages paid).

The laborers' complaint is not that the landowner has failed to fulfill his contractual obligation — the complaint is not made on grounds of commutative justice. Indeed, by paying each worker one denarius the landowner fulfills all his contractual obligations. Rather, the complaint is made on grounds of distributive justice — the first-hired and the last-hired have borne *unequal burdens* in the vineyard, but they are *rewarded equally:* "These last have worked only one hour, and you have *made them equal* to us who have borne the burden of the day and the scorching heat" (v. 12). Seeing the last-hired laborers paid "the usual daily wage," the first-hired "thought they would receive more" than the usual daily wage that they had been promised (vv. 9-10). This expectation of the first-hired was not based on the stated terms of their contract, which promised "the usual daily wage" for a full day's work (v. 2). Rather, their expectation was based on the unstated assumption that their contract subsumed the principle of retribution, which would require that "just due" for their labor be proportional to the wages paid the other laborers: "if they were paid a *denarius* for *one* hour's labor, then for *twelve* hour's labor we deserve. . . ." The charge of injustice levied against the landowner thus rests upon the inference from the principle of retribution that it is wrong to distribute benefits equally under the condition that not all those receiving equal benefits have borne equally the burden of labor being rewarded.[13]

The story illustrates that "what is just *(dikaion)*" (v. 4) in the upside-down economy of God's kingdom is not measured by the principle of retribution. The key to the parable lies in noticing that, while the landlord promises the first-hired "the usual daily wage," he promises the later-hired "what is just." Like the first-hired laborers, we are inclined to think that the landlord's promise of "what is just" to the later-hired laborers is to be reckoned by the principle of retribution — and, hence, that each will be paid his "just due" according to hours labored. When the landlord pays each the same wage, we thus think that an injustice has transpired — the landlord fails to distribute "just deserts." And so we miss the point: the landlord has made the *same* promise to all the labor-

---

13. The laborer's implicit thinking here accords precisely with Aristotle's theory that distributive justice satisfies a proportionality or equality of ratios. Aristotle's discussion reads almost as a commentary on this parable: "The just, therefore, involves at least four terms; for the persons for whom it is just are two, and the things in which it [the just] is manifested, the objects distributed, are two. And the same equality will exist between the persons and between the things concerned; for as the latter — the things concerned — are related, so are the former; *if they are not equal, they will not have what is equal, but this is the origin of quarrels and complaints — when either equals have and are awarded unequal shares, or unequals equal shares*" (*Nicomachean Ethics* V.3.1131a18-25, emphasis added).

ers. In God's kingdom, "what is just" is accomplished, not by distribution of "just deserts," but rather by satisfaction of human needs: God's justice is satisfied when the production of the vineyard is divided in such a way that satisfies the needs of all the laborers. To dispense "the usual daily wage" regardless of hours labored *is* "what is due" in God's kingdom; for God's will "on earth as in heaven" is to "give us this day our daily bread" (Matt 6:10-11).

God's justice thus turns retribution on its head; for God's reward is distributed, *not* over what has been *earned* by hours labored, but rather over what is *needed* to sustain life: although unequal as measured by labor, the laborers are equal as measured by need. According to the life-giving purpose of God's justice, each laborer receives his "daily bread." The economy of God's kingdom, therefore, is not an economy of exchange, underwritten by retribution, but rather an economy of grace, funded by God's generosity. We can thus see a parallel between kingdom parable and sacrificial cult: whether one brings a sheep or a goat or turtledoves or grain as a sin offering, God grants forgiveness to sinners, not according to the means of the sinner and the value of his offering, but rather according to God's mercy and the sinner's need (see Chapter 11 above).

Yet there is more. What matters chiefly in the vineyard of God's kingdom is the landowner's — God's — prerogative to dispense the goods of the vineyard as he sees fit; and God's vision of what is "fitting" does not fit the human expectation of retribution. God sees fit to dispense the goods of the vineyard in the same way on those that have labored little as on those that have labored long, just as God sees fit to bless the wicked and the righteous alike with the sun and the rain (Matt 5:45). By charging the landowner with injustice, the laborers presume to bring to account the landowner's right over what belongs to him. The landowner thus replies (vv. 14-15): "Take what belongs to you and go; I choose to give to this last the same as I give to you. Am I not allowed to do what I choose with what belongs to me? Or are you envious because I am generous?"

This parable asks us to consider: What belongs to God? To God belongs not only the vineyard, but justice itself, and God's prerogative to do justice as God wills is not to be held accountable to the principle of retribution. God's justice, the parable reveals, is not rooted in retribution, contrary to human expectation. Justice belongs to God, and God's just will is expressed in generosity. Jesus thus overturns the economy of exchange by undercutting the retributive principle underwriting it: "So the last will be first, and the first will be last" (v. 16). Faced with God's generous justice, or God's just generosity, the parable puts the question to us: Do we have a problem with that?!

By these two parables — the lost son and the vineyard laborers — Jesus radically reorients the aim of justice and wholly transforms the substance of justice, breaking both commutative justice and distributive justice out of the retributive paradigm and investing them with the priorities and objectives of God's kingdom.

☙ 20.2. The Justice of God and the Scandal of the Cross

Seen from the reversal of perspective induced by the upside-down "constitutional principles" of the kingdom of God, which turn retribution on its head, the foolishness of the cross becomes evident. We, humanity, have perpetrated the most heinous crime imaginable — we have murdered Jesus, the Son of God, God-in-the-flesh. Retributive justice according to "the rule of law" requires the offender be "paid back" a punishment proportionate to the crime: death by crime requires death by punishment to "balance the scales." Yet the victim of this crime, Jesus himself, who might have petitioned heaven's "just retribution" against humanity, has instead taken the part of the offender, interceding on our behalf and pleading God's mercy. Jesus has asked God to forgive humanity this crime of cosmic magnitude, and God has graciously accepted Jesus' plea of mercy and offered forgiveness to all humanity in the name of Jesus. Retributive justice according to "the rule of law" is *not satisfied;* the scales of crime and punishment are *not balanced.*

Yet, the center holds, the cosmic order is not upset, the world does not come unhinged. The cross of Christ, consistent with Jesus' own teaching (Matt 5:38-48), demonstrates that the God-created cosmos, at its divine origin and deepest center, is not ordered rationally on human terms. The cosmic order is sustained and conserved, not by "the rule of law," but by God's gracious generosity. The cross is foolishness in that it reveals the divine wisdom and power, by which the cosmos was created and ultimately hangs together, as transcending retribution — such that the message of the cross confounds human wisdom and rationality. The cross demonstrates precisely what the prophet testified, that divine justice transcends human logic (Isa 55:6-9). Thus Paul, citing Isaiah, declares that the revelation of the wisdom and power of God through the cross of Christ is an affront to human thinking (1 Cor 1:18-25).

This is the real scandal — the stumbling block — of the cross for most Christians: our thinking about God's justice has not been transformed by the cross but remains "conformed to this world," shaped by the scheme of this age (Rom 12:2). We thus expect to see in the cross the confirmation of our all-too-human assumptions about justice; we expect divine justice to be the perfect instantiation of the retributive paradigm. And so we miss the point: the cross presents us with a reversal and thus challenges us to shift our perspective, to re-vision and rethink the justice of God in the shape of the cross.

The theological and psychological stumbling blocks to achieving such a reversal of perspective or "gestalt shift" are evident in Phillip Yancey's book, *What's So Amazing about Grace?* At one place, Yancey has made the gestalt shift we are trying to achieve here. In a chapter on revenge titled "Getting Even," he draws out the meaning of the cross in a passage pregnant with implication for the question of capital punishment:

Kangaroo courts of Judea found a way to inflict a sentence of capital punishment on the only perfect man who ever lived. From the cross, Jesus pronounced his own countersentence, *striking an eternal blow against the law of unforgiveness*. Notably, he forgave those who had not repented: "For they do not know what they are doing."

The Roman soldiers, Pilate, Herod, and members of the Sanhedrin were "just doing their jobs"—the limp excuse later used to explain Auschwitz, My Lai, and the Gulag — but Jesus stripped away that institutional veneer and spoke to the human heart. It was forgiveness they needed more than anything else. We know, those of us who believe in the atonement, that Jesus had more than his executioners in mind when he spoke those final words. He had us in mind. *In the cross, and only in the cross, he put an end to the law of eternal consequences.*[14]

Upon the cross Jesus pronounces a "counter-sentence" of forgiveness upon those who have wrongly executed him, who are guilty of murder and thus deserving of death according to "the rule of law." Absorbing human violence into his own body and yet not seeking divine vengeance against his murderers, Jesus "put an end to the law of eternal consequences." Yancey here uses two parallel expressions to name that which Jesus puts to an end through the cross — "the law of unforgiveness" and "the law of eternal consequences." Elsewhere, he uses several other expressions to name the same thing: "the law of nature," "the law of retribution," "the logic of unforgiveness," "the law of revenge," and "the chain of ungrace." All of these expressions, I think, are variations of Paul's phrase "the law of sin and of death" — the law that condemns, the law demanding death as the punishment or "consequence" or "wages" for sin.

The saving significance of the cross, then, is that through the cross God-in-Christ decisively transcends retribution, breaking and overcoming the "Newtonian law" that "For every atrocity there must be an equal and opposite atrocity."[15] And all for the sake of redeeming humanity from the (literally) dead-end consequence of condemnation for sin (Rom 8:1-2). By pronouncing his divinely ordained, retribution-transcending, redemption-favoring "counter-sentence" of forgiveness, Jesus strips away the veneer of legitimacy from legally sanctioned retributive violence (capital punishment) that receives the official stamp of "justice." Elsewhere, Yancey writes perceptively:

The pale figure nailed to a crossbeam revealed the ruling powers of the world as false gods who broke their own promises of piety and justice. Religion, not irreligion, accused Jesus; the law, not lawlessness, had him executed. By their

---

14. Philip Yancey, *What's So Amazing about Grace?* (Grand Rapids, MI: Zondervan Publishing House, 1997), pp. 119-20, emphasis added.

15. Yancey, *What's So Amazing about Grace?* p. 114.

rigged trials, their scourgings, their violent opposition to Jesus, the political and religious authorities of that day exposed themselves for what they were: upholders of the status quo, defenders of their own power only. Each assault on Jesus laid bare their illegitimacy.[16]

The implications of such a perspective-reversing reading of the cross are profound — and scandalizing. What God puts to death at the cross is not Jesus himself but the law of retribution — "the law of eternal consequences" — which demands that humanity be punished with death to pay for the crime of murdering Jesus (Col 2:13-14).[17] That is, *God does not sacrifice Christ through the cross for the sake of satisfying the law of retribution, but rather God sacrifices the law of retribution through the cross of Christ for the sake of redeeming humanity.*[18]

Making this shift in perspective is difficult precisely because it requires overcoming an ingrained instinct rooted deeply in the human psyche warped by sin. The retributive instinct originates with the Fall. The instinctive desire for, and fear of, vengeance is immediately evident following the first sins — Cain fears vengeance for killing Abel, and Lamech desires vengeance against his enemy (Gen 4:14-15, 23-24). It is rooted so deeply in the human psyche that we will not let ourselves believe that we have been saved by God unless we are assured that retribution has been satisfied. What the cross of Christ scandalously reveals, however, is that retribution is not near the heart of God. Recognizing this can produce double-mindedness: we might think that the cross reveals grace *and* satisfies retribution at the same time — for, the voice from deep within our psyche says, the law of retribution simply *must* be satisfied, after all.

This ambivalence is evident in Yancey's book. In a chapter on "The New Math of Grace," he discusses the parables of the "upside-down" kingdom (examined above) and then considers Hosea, the prophet of God's mercy. Referring to Hosea, Yancey writes: "God reserves the right to alter the rules of retribution. Although Israel has finally earned his rebuff, they will not get what they deserve."[19] Instead, God will persist faithfully in showing mercy to unfaithful Israel. Yancey is correct here. The exclusive divine prerogative of retribution (Deut 32:35) subsumes the inherent divine right to "alter the rules of retribution." This is illustrated by the story of David's murder of Uriah to cover up his adultery with Bathsheba (2 Samuel 11). After being confronted with his sin by the prophet Nathan, David confesses, "I have sinned against the LORD." Nathan then says to him: "Now the LORD has put away your sin; you shall not die. Nevertheless, because by this deed you have utterly scorned the LORD, the child

16. Philip Yancey, *The Jesus I Never Knew* (Grand Rapids, MI: Zondervan Publishing House, 1995), p. 203.

17. See the discussion of this text in Chapter 18.

18. We will develop this theme further in Chapter 25.

19. Yancey, *What's So Amazing about Grace?* p. 65.

that is born to you shall die." And then, "The LORD struck the child that Uriah's wife bore to David" (2 Sam 12:13-15). Effectively, the innocent child dies as the consequence of David's guilt, which directly contravenes a specific statute that explicitly prohibits such substitutionary punishment: "Parents shall not be put to death for their children, nor shall children be put to death for their parents; only for their own crimes may persons be put to death" (Deut 24:16). By taking the life of the child for the sin of the father, God has superseded the Torah's own rules restricting retribution.

Still, noting that "God reserves the right to alter the rules of retribution" does not get to the heart of the scandal of the cross, for it keeps our thinking "conformed to this world." It is precisely the power of the parables of the "upside-down" kingdom to break our thinking about God's justice out of the retributive paradigm. Despite these parables, Yancey's God of "amazing grace" is free only to "alter the rules of retribution" but is not free to put an end to retribution. This God, shared by many Christians, can change the rules regarding who pays the penalty for which sin — God can put to death an innocent substitute victim as vicarious punishment for another's sin — but cannot abrogate the law of retribution: the penalty for sin must nonetheless be paid. This God, who sees to it that "the law of sin and of death" is satisfied by Jesus' death for humanity's sins, can transfer legal condemnation from one to another but is unable to annul the law of condemnation. Ultimately, this God is not sovereign over all but subservient to the law of retribution: before forgiving sin, this God must pay retribution its due.

That Yancey's thinking about the cross, like that of many Christians, remains confined within the retributive paradigm is evident when Yancey offers his interpretation of Paul's message of the cross:

> Aware of the apparent scandal of grace, Paul took pains to explain how God made peace with human beings. Grace baffles us because it goes against the intuition everyone has that, in the face of injustice, some price must be paid. A murderer cannot simply go free. . . . Anticipating these objections, Paul stressed that a price has been paid — by God himself. God gave up his own Son rather than give up on humanity. . . . "There is only one real law — the law of the universe," said Dorothy Sayers. "It may be fulfilled either by way of judgment or by the way of grace, but it *must* be fulfilled one way or another." By accepting the judgment in his own body, Jesus fulfilled that law, and God found a way to forgive.[20]

The quotation from Dorothy Sayers makes clear that, viewing the cross through the retributive paradigm, grace is subordinate to retribution, for grace satisfies a law higher than itself, "the law of the universe." One way or another, the law of

20. Yancey, *What's So Amazing about Grace?* p. 67, emphasis original.

retribution — the "only real law" — *must* be fulfilled; it is the ultimate law of the cosmos to which, it would seem, even God's own mercy is subject. Whether God punishes humanity ("judgment") or punishes Jesus in place of humanity ("grace"), someone *must* die for sins, retribution *must* be satisfied. Regarding such a view of the cross framed by the law of retribution, Paul Fiddes comments, with reference to the parable of the lost son in Luke 15:

> As the elder brother wants to set a principle of retribution and compensation over the mercy of the father, so theories of legal satisfaction set a law above the character of God. The theory runs that God cannot forgive us until the punishment demanded by justice is exacted. This conceives justice as law with ultimate authority; even when the law is said to be God's own law, the theory still requires God to act in a way which is confined by legal restraints. Law has ceased to be a useful guideline to the purpose of God for his creatures, and has become a supreme principle.[21]

20.3. Kingdom and Cross: The "Math of Grace" v. the Logic of Retribution

The scandal of the cross — that grace is not a substitute for justice, for God's justice is rooted in grace (Rom 3:21-26) — is still very real, so much so that we feel the need to explain away the scandal so that retribution is satisfied in the end. Yancey points us to "the new math of grace" in the parables of the kingdom, but when interpreting the cross he upholds the old math of retribution. In Yancey's view of the cross, the equation of sin and death must still be balanced — sin on one side of the equal sign and death on the other side — only now Jesus' death is substituted into the equation in place of humanity's death in order to balance things out. God may be free to make a substitution into the equation, but God is not free to transcend the equation: God *must* see to it that the equation is satisfied, one way or the other. In this view, there is no fundamental change in "mathematics," because the underlying logic of retribution, expressed in the equation of sin and death, remains unaltered. Despite Yancey's best intentions, there is nothing new here, only an epicycle on the same old logic of retribution.

Yancey does well in looking to Gospel stories — the parable of the lost son and the parable of the laborers in the vineyard — to illustrate the point that the divine economy of God's kingdom is not founded upon the retributive principle. And he draws the appropriate lesson: "God dispenses gifts, not wages."[22]

21. Paul S. Fiddes, *Past Event and Present Salvation: The Christian Idea of Atonement* (Louisville: Westminster/John Knox, 1989), p. 101.

22. Yancey, *What's So Amazing about Grace?* p. 62.

But when interpreting the cross, he (perhaps unconsciously) falls back upon the exchange economy of the retributive paradigm: God dispenses our "wages," the just deserts for our sinful deeds, upon Jesus in order to dispense to us the gift of salvation. God may forgive our sins, but only because Jesus has "paid our penalty" — Jesus' death for our death — such that God's kingdom remains an exchange economy founded upon the retributive principle.

In making this point, we do not suggest that somehow salvation through the cross of Jesus Christ is not costly to God. God's exercise of divine freedom to transcend retribution *is* costly to God, precisely because doing so costs the life of the Son. In order for God-in-Christ to transcend divine retribution for the sake of humanity's redemption, Christ willingly suffered in his own body the death generated by humanity's death-deserving sin. God chooses to bear in Christ's flesh the violent, murderous sin of humanity and yet also chooses not to exercise the divine prerogative of retribution, which would only produce more death from humanity's sin. Such divine redemption — forgoing retribution and forgiving humanity — *is* a costly venture.

Yet, framing the cross by the requirement of retribution removes the scandal. The scandal of the cross is that it reveals a God who is free to remain faithful and true and just — should all others prove false, should all else go wrong, even if the very "law of the universe" goes unsatisfied. The scandal of the cross is that it reveals a God who, despite suffering all cruelty and hate at the hands of humanity, despite even suffering the shameful death of the cross, is free to reconcile the very ones that have put him upon the cross. The scandal of the cross is thus the scandal of divine freedom and integrity, that God is who God is and will be who God will be — faithful and true and just — irrespective of human failings, rational formulas, and legal requirements. A retribution-framed vision of the cross thus fails to recognize that only a God who is *already free* — free *from* "the law of the universe" and thus free *to* transcend retribution — can do "what the law could not do" and "set [us] free from the law of sin and of death" (Rom 8:1-3).[23]

Having come so close to seeing the cross as liberation from retribution and yet still needing to see the cross as the satisfaction of retribution, Yancey's book illustrates how strongly ingrained and deeply rooted in the human psyche is the need for retribution, how primitively the retributive paradigm has shaped human thinking.[24] I suggest that the law of retribution — "the law of the universe" (Sayers) — belongs to the *stoicheia*, the elemental principles and fundamental laws of the cosmos, that hold sway over a humanity dominated by sin and death and to which human thinking and doing have been enslaved through

---

23. See the discussion of this text in Chapter 18.

24. Concerning how deep-seated retribution is in the human psyche, see Margaret Atwood, *Payback: Debt and the Shadow Side of Wealth* (Toronto: House of Anansi Press, 2008).

the desires of the flesh since Cain and Lamech. Paul warns us to not allow such "rudiments of the world," which are "according to human tradition" and "not according to Christ," to rule over our thinking and doing (Col 2:8). As Walter Wink puts Paul's point, "Christ alone is the first principle of the universe."[25]

The "foolish" wisdom and "upside-down" justice of God are revealed not only through the cross of Christ and the parables of the kingdom, but are evident elsewhere in Scripture. In the next two chapters, we will re-read Scripture and re-vision the cosmos within a cruciform paradigm, looking for God's grace-rooted, retribution-transcending, redemption-favoring justice revealed in both the covenant and wisdom literature of the Bible. We will be guided by this question: Do the canon of Scripture and the order of the world reveal retribution at the heart of divine character and at the center of cosmic reality? We thus pose two questions for testing in light of the evidence: Do the Torah, Prophets, and Psalms manifest an essentially wrathful, retributive God? Does reason discover retribution to be the natural law of justice?

---

25. Walter Wink, *Naming the Powers: The Language of Power in the New Testament* (Philadelphia: Fortress Press, 1984), p. 74. Wink comments: "Thus *stocheia* here seems to refer to the basic principles or constituent elements of reality, to which some people . . . are apparently granting an ultimacy that threatens the sole sufficiency of Christ."

CHAPTER 21

Divine Character and Covenant Justice: Forgiving from the First, Redeeming to the Last

*I will be gracious to whom I will be gracious
and will show mercy to whom I will show mercy.*

EXODUS 33:19

The cross of Christ and the teachings of Jesus reveal to us the justice of God that transcends retribution for the sake of redemption. Insofar as the life, death, and resurrection of Jesus Christ fulfill God's purpose "according to the Scriptures," the Old Testament as well as the New Testament should reveal God's retribution-transcending redemption. We will thus re-read Scripture to see how God's redemptive justice beyond retribution is evident in God's self-disclosure of divine character and in God's expression of covenant loyalty to Israel. We will do this in four stages. In the first stage, we reflect on God's self-disclosure of the divine character to Moses on Mount Sinai and how that self-disclosure is evident in the Prophets and Psalms. In the second stage, we look at the overall "story" of the Torah as it concerns retribution. In the third stage, we consider how God deals with Israel's disobedience to the covenant, how God's justice and loyalty operate in a tension that seeks ultimately, not retribution for sin, but redemption of Israel. And in the fourth stage, we examine how the prophets depict the surprising ways of divine retribution and the implications of that for thinking about God's final judgment.

We preface this chapter with an important point to be kept in mind. As we have stated before and will argue again below, God holds the prerogative of judgment, the right of retribution: "Vengeance is mine" (Deut 32:35); "it is God who executes judgment" (Ps 75:7). That to God belongs the prerogative of retribution does not tell us anything about God's character, however, only about God's status — YHWH is Sovereign Lord. What reveals God's character is how

God chooses to exercise, or refrain from exercising, that prerogative of retribution. We saw this sovereign freedom in the parables of the kingdom: "I choose to give to this last the same as I give to you. Am I not allowed to do what I choose with what belongs to me?" The right of retribution belongs to God, and God can do as God chooses with what belongs to him: retribution is the right, not a necessity, of God. According to Jesus, "what is just" in God's kingdom is revealed by God's choice to give us what we need rather than what we deserve (Matt 20:1-16). According to Paul, God dispenses justice and rights sinners through the cross, not according to what we deserve, but "by his grace as a gift" (Rom 3:21-26). The question before us is whether God's choice of generosity over desert, for redemption beyond retribution, proclaimed by Jesus and manifest in the cross, is characteristic of God, as revealed in the Old Testament and as regards the final judgment.

21.1. The Divine Character

21.1.1. YHWH's Self-Disclosure: Mercy Surpassing Anger

Evangelical Old Testament scholar John Goldingay has recently commented: "What of Yhwh's characteristic traits? Everyone knows that the Old Testament God is a God of wrath; the New Testament God a God of love. Oh no they don't."[1] That the thinking Goldingay rebukes is off the mark can been seen by considering God's self-disclosure to his prophet Moses on the holy mountain Sinai.

God's first self-disclosure to Moses on Sinai was by means of the "burning bush," when God announced his plan to redeem Israel from slavery in Egypt, called Moses to be his chosen liberator, and revealed God's own mysterious name, "I am who I am" or "I will be who I will be" (Exodus 3–4). Having liberated the Israelites from Egypt and brought the people to Sinai as promised, YHWH discloses himself to Moses again on Sinai, this time at Moses' request, which YHWH grants: "I will make all my goodness pass before you, and will proclaim before you the name, 'YHWH'; and I will be gracious to whom I will be gracious and will show mercy to whom I will show mercy" (Exod 33:19). YHWH invites Moses to ascend Sinai to receive this second self-disclosure:

> The LORD, the LORD, a God merciful and gracious, slow to anger, and abounding in steadfast love *(ḥesed)* and faithfulness *('ĕmeth)*, keeping steadfast love for the thousandth generation, forgiving iniquity and transgression

---

1. John Goldingay, *Old Testament Theology,* vol. II: *Israel's Faith* (Downers Grove, IL: Inter-Varsity Press, 2006), p. 108.

and sin, yet by no means clearing the guilty, but visiting the iniquity of the
parents upon the children and the children's children, to the third and the
fourth generation. (Exod 34:6-7)

Notice two things about this self-disclosure of God's character. First, God's
anger is expressed but hedged — on the one side, by mercy and grace, on the
other side, by steadfast love and faithfulness. Anger is neither the first nor the
last of God's character. God's character first and last is mercy and grace, steadfast love and faithfulness, expressed in forgiveness of "iniquity and transgression and sin." God is "slow to anger" — anger is not God's characteristic first or
last response to iniquity and injustice; God is "longsuffering" (KJV) with humanity in its sinful situation. Goldingay thus observes: "The popular impression that the First Testament God is a God of wrath reflects the impression that
wrath has priority over mercy, but at this key point when the First Testament
directly speaks to that question, it affirms the opposite."[2]

Second, although God does become angry in the face of iniquity and does
pour out wrath and retribution upon injustice, God's wrath is far surpassed by
God's steadfast love (ḥesed), and God's retribution is far outlasted by God's
faithfulness ('ĕmeth). God's anger is "slow," but God's steadfast love is "abounding." God's retribution for sin is only "to the third and the fourth generation,"
but God's steadfast love is to "the thousandth generation." To see the latter
comparison, consider the social setting. A traditional household in the ancient
world comprised three or four generations at any given time: grandparents,
parents, and (grand-)children, plus possibly great-grandparents and great-
grandchildren, all living together. God's wrath and retribution upon iniquity
and injustice "to the third and the fourth generation" is thus limited to the *present.* God's steadfast love, by contrast, extends "for the thousandth generation,"
from now until a near-unimaginably far-off future — or, practically speaking,
forever.

21.1.2. Witness of the Prophets: The Tension between Anger and Mercy

The prophets confirm God's self-disclosure of anger-surpassing mercy and
retribution-transcending steadfast love and faithfulness. Consider, first, Isaiah
64–65. In Isaiah 64, the prophet confesses sin on behalf of Israel in exile, acknowledges God's judgment on Israel, and pleads for God's mercy: "We have all
become like one who is unclean, and all our righteous deeds are like a filthy
cloth. . . . Do not be exceedingly angry, O LORD, and do not remember iniquity
forever" (Isa 64:6, 9). In Isaiah 65, God responds to the prophet's prayer. God la-

---

2. Goldingay, *Israel's Faith,* p. 160.

ments that, though he has held himself out to Israel in love, Israel has not responded with loyalty (65:1-2). Instead, Israel has provoked God to anger with its iniquity (vv. 3-5), so that God considers executing retribution upon the nation: "I will measure into their laps full payment for their actions" (vv. 6-7). But God reconsiders and pulls back from retribution "to the full," pledging to "not destroy them all" and proclaiming mercy "for my servants' sake . . . for my people who have sought me" (vv. 8-10). Yet, God does pronounce a judgment of death upon those who have forsaken God and pursued evil (vv. 11-16). But, even then, God's judgment of death is not the end; retribution for sin does not bring God's justice to victory. For God promises a glorious redemption for Jerusalem, a "new creation" that brings *shalom* — prosperity and security, reconciliation and peace (vv. 17-25). Isaiah thus depicts a dialectical tension between God's anger and God's mercy in which mercy supersedes anger, making possible God's redemption beyond retribution in the end.

The prophet Hosea depicts this dialectical tension between God's anger against and God's compassion upon Israel in terms of an ever-faithful husband persistently seeking the return of his unfaithful wife (Hosea 9–14). The prophet pronounces God's accusation of Israel's infidelity to the covenant and warns of God's judgment to come (Hos 9:1-17). Exile and captivity are imminent (v. 3) as God's punishment for sin: "The days of punishment have come, the days of recompense have come . . . he will remember their iniquity, he will punish their sins" (vv. 7-9). God brought Israel out of Egypt and led them through the wilderness in love (11:1-4), but Israel has "plowed wickedness" and "reaped injustice" (10:13). Although God sentences Israel to exile and captivity (11:5-7), God's mercy and compassion restrain his wrath and retribution: "How can I hand you over, O Israel? . . . My heart recoils within me; my compassion grows warm and tender. I will not execute my fierce anger . . ." (vv. 8-9). Yet, despite God's mercy, Israel still refuses to be faithful to God; violence and falsehood flourish in the land (11:12–12:1). God again makes an indictment against Israel and pledges punishment and retribution (12:2), but also once again calls Israel to return to covenant loyalty: "But as for you, return to your God, hold fast to love and justice" (v. 6). God sends his prophets to woo Israel back into covenant relationship, but Israel persists in its infidelity (12:10–13:3). Yet once more God remembers his redemption of Israel from Egypt and his care for Israel in the wilderness (13:4-6). But in the face of Israel's repeated infidelity, God pronounces a judgment of death upon Israel (vv. 9-14). Amazingly, God's judgment of death for sin is not the last word! For, after all that has been said and done, God's compassion and loyalty still surpass God's wrath and retribution. God thus persists to the end to call Israel back, inviting repentance, offering forgiveness: "Return O Israel, to the LORD your God. . . . Take words with you and return to the LORD. . . . I will heal their disloyalty; I will love them freely, for my anger has turned from them" (14:1-2, 4).

The God of "steadfast love and faithfulness" is witnessed elsewhere by the prophets. The prophet Joel announces to Israel a coming plague of locusts that will devour the land like an advancing army and a sweeping fire. This devastation, he declares, is the judgment of the Almighty (Joel 1:2–2:11). But then, in the very midst of the destroying host still swarming over the land, Joel calls the people to repentance. And the premise of both the prophet's call and the people's repentance is the character of God disclosed at Sinai: "Return to the LORD, your God, for he is gracious and merciful, slow to anger, and abounding in steadfast love, and *relents from punishing*" (2:13).

The faith of Israel in the "gracious and merciful" God who "relents from punishing" because he is "slow to anger, abounding in steadfast love," creates irony in the ministry of Jonah. Jonah is reluctant to go and preach to Nineveh, the capital city of Israel's enemy, and call its people to repentance, as YHWH commands, precisely because he knows that YHWH is gracious and merciful beyond bounds and thus desires the redemption of Nineveh more than retribution upon it. When Nineveh repents and God characteristically shows mercy, Jonah testifies to his displeasure with the God who revealed himself at Sinai: "O LORD! Is not this what I said while I was still in my own country? That is why I fled to Tarshish at the beginning; for I knew that you are a gracious God and merciful, slow to anger, and abounding in steadfast love *(ḥesed)*, and *ready to relent from punishing*" (4:1-2).

God's self-disclosure of the divine character at Sinai is not only the abiding faith of the prophets but also the deep well from which springs Israel's prayer and praise.[3] When Israel recites the story of redemption from Egyptian captivity and settlement in the promised land, the repeated refrain is, "O give thanks to the LORD, for his steadfast love *(ḥesed)* endures forever" (Psalms 106 and 136). After God had returned the exiles from Babylonian captivity, the priest Ezra read the Torah in the hearing of all the people gathered in Jerusalem (Nehemiah 8). Ezra then led the people in a prayer of confession, remembering God's wondrous acts of creation and redemption and recounting Israel's disobedience and rebellion (Nehemiah 9). In his prayer, Ezra testifies to the God who remains faithful despite Israel's infidelity, echoing God's self-revelation at Sinai: "But you are a God *ready to forgive*, gracious and merciful, slow to anger and abounding in steadfast love *(ḥesed)*, and you did not forsake them" (Neh 9:17).

Thus Israel's prophets and priests amplified YHWH's self-disclosure, adding "ready to forgive" (Ezra) or "ready to relent from punishing" (Joel and Jo-

---

3. Goldingay, *Israel's Faith*, p. 160, concerning Exod 34:6-7: "The location of that statement and the recurrence of its phrases elsewhere in the First Testament suggest that this self-description stands at the heart of First Testament theology." On the many varied recitations of this text in Israel's testimony to YHWH, see Walter Brueggemann, *Theology of the Old Testament: Testimony, Dispute, Advocacy* (Minneapolis: Augsburg Fortress Press, 1997), pp. 215-24.

nah) to the text. By its covenantal relationship and historical experience with YHWH, Israel had come to understand God to be merciful before and beyond punitive. A God who is "gracious and merciful" is a God who is "ready to forgive." A God who is "abounding in steadfast love" is one who is "ready to relent from punishing." And a God who is "ready to forgive" and "ready to relent from punishing" is one who is willing to forgive from the first and seeking to redeem until the last.

In God's self-disclosure, therefore, forgiveness flows readily from God's abounding steadfast love and faithfulness. This is reflected in Psalm 103, which summons us to "Bless the LORD" and remember "all his benefits." The first of God's "benefits" reflects God's steadfast love: "who forgives all your iniquity, who heals all your diseases, who redeems your life from the Pit, who crowns you with steadfast love *(ḥesed)* and mercy" (vv. 3-4). Forgiveness, healing, and redemption — these flow first from the heart of God. As God disclosed at Sinai, so the psalmist testifies — anger is hedged by grace and mercy (vv. 8-9), so that retribution is circumscribed and surpassed by love and compassion (vv. 10-14). Praise of the God who is "merciful and gracious, slow to anger and abounding in steadfast love," echoes elsewhere in Israel's prayer book (Pss 86:15; 145:8).

The prophets thus teach us that God's steadfast love and covenant faithfulness are the characteristic frame within which God's wrath is to be understood. God's wrath expresses his personal displeasure toward his people's sins; it is the sad, grief-laden displeasure of a committed lover whose spouse has turned away to infidelity, or that of a loving parent whose child has turned from instruction to disobedience.[4] Indeed, it is precisely because God is characteristically loving and faithful toward his covenant people that Israel's sins provoke God's wrath; and it is thus toward Israel's return to faithfulness and obedience in covenant with God, not Israel's destruction, that God's wrath is directed. John Driver has aptly described God's wrath as "wounded covenant love":

> In the Old Testament divine wrath is viewed as a personal activity of the covenant-establishing God. It is the form which God's wounded covenant love takes. . . . The wrath of God toward Israel is the reverse side of his covenant love. . . . It was the personal response of the covenant-making God to the faithlessness of his people. Its aim was not so much the destruction of his rebellious people as it was their restoration. It was a way of taking the sin of his people seriously while remaining steadfast in his love for Israel. It was a jealous anger whose last word was the mercy of covenant love.[5]

---

4. Concerning God's relationship with Israel as loving parent and committed lover, see Goldingay, *Israel's Faith*, pp. 108-13, 121-22, 130-34.

5. John Driver, *Understanding the Atonement for the Mission of the Church* (Scottdale, PA: Herald Press, 1986), pp. 158-59.

21.1.3. Israel's Prayer Book: YHWH Is Not an "Angry God"

This God praised by Israel and preached by the prophets — a God "merciful and gracious, slow to anger, abounding in steadfast love and faithfulness," a God "ready to forgive" and "ready to relent from punishing" — is perhaps a foreign God to many Christians in contemporary America. The Baylor Religion Survey (2006) found that beliefs among American Christians concerning God's character and behavior vary widely. From the data, the researchers drew the conclusion that Americans in general believe in four different Gods — some in an Authoritarian God (31.4%), some in a Benevolent God (23%), some in a Critical God (16%), some in a Distant God (24.4%). The most popular God in America is the Authoritarian God, who is not only "responsible for global events," but "is quite angry and is capable of meting out punishment to those who are unfaithful or ungodly." A majority of folks who attend church weekly (50.9%), who pray several times a day (54.8%), and who read the Bible literally (60.8%), as well as a majority of Evangelical Protestant Christians (52.3%), believe in the Authoritarian God.[6] The main God of evangelical Christians, then, is an "angry God."

The image of an "angry God" immediately evokes the memory of Jonathan Edwards, the renowned preacher, theologian, and leader of the Great Awakening in eighteenth-century America. The title of Edward's most famous sermon, "Sinners in the Hands of an Angry God" (1741), sums up the divine-human relationship as a majority of evangelical Christians believe it to be.[7] Yet there is no "angry God" to be found in the Bible. Many readers will no doubt be incredulous at what I have just written. It is quite literally true, nonetheless. No English translation of the Bible, not even the Geneva Bible or the King James Version, ever speaks of an "angry God," as far as I know.[8] Certainly, as we have consid-

---

6. Baylor Institute for Studies of Religion, "American Piety in the 21st Century: New Insights to the Depth and Complexity of Religion in the US," September 2006, http://www.baylor.edu/content/services/document.php/33304.pdf, pp. 26-30. The category "Evangelical Protestant" in the Baylor Study covers a broad spectrum: "Anabaptist, Assemblies of God, Bible Church, Brethren, Christian Church, Christian and Missionary Alliance, Christian Reformed, Church of Christ, Church of God, Church of the Nazarene, Free Methodist, Lutheran Church Missouri Synod, Mennonite, Pentecostal, Presbyterian Church in America, Seventh-day Adventist, and Southern Baptist" (p. 9).

7. And as some erstwhile evangelical Christians believe it to be — cf. Bart D. Ehrman, *God's Problem: How the Bible Fails to Answer Our Most Important Question — Why We Suffer* (New York: HarperOne, 2008), chapter 2.

8. A computer search of twenty different English translations — Geneva Bible, King James Version, New King James Version, New American Standard Bible, New English Translation, New Jerusalem Bible, New International Version, New Revised Standard Version, English Standard Version, Contemporary English Version, Holman Christian Standard Bible, American Standard Version, Young's Literal Translation, Darby Translation, Douay-Rheims 1899 American Edition, New Living Translation, Amplified Bible, New Century Version, New American Bible, and Jewish Publication Society — returned zero references for "angry God."

ered (Chapter 12), there are numerous texts in nearly every book of the Old Testament that speak of God becoming angry in the face of iniquity or expressing wrath upon injustice. But there is no text in all of Scripture, as far as I am aware, that characterizes God as *being* an "angry God." We need to distinguish here between a God who *becomes* angry or *expresses* wrath and a God who simply *is* angry or wrathful.[9] Edwards preaches a God that not only expresses anger but is eternally angry. Near the end of his sermon, Edwards states concerning God's wrath, "It is *everlasting* wrath" (Edwards's emphasis). Taking Edwards literally, God's wrath is co-eternal with God-self. If God is *eternally* angry or wrathful, then God is *essentially* angry or wrathful — if God is *always* angry or wrathful and so never otherwise, then anger or wrath is not only a possible mode of God's character, but is the necessary state of God's being.

There is no God to be found in the Bible who is essentially angry or eternally wrathful, however. Indeed, the Psalms testify time and again to a God who is anything but eternally angry or essentially wrathful, giving thanks and praise to a God who is "slow to anger" (Pss 86:15; 103:8; 145:8). Although the psalmist warns the kings of earth to obey God, "for his wrath is quickly kindled" (2:11), even this warning affirms that God's wrath is not an eternal fire but rather is "kindled." And when God's anger is aroused on account of iniquity, it is, relatively speaking, momentary: "For his anger is but for a moment; his favor for a lifetime" (30:5). God, though roused to anger by sin, does not hold sinners in anger forever: "He will not always accuse, nor will he keep his anger forever" (103:9). As we have seen, moreover, God's wrath upon iniquity is turned away not only by the one who "stood in the breach" (106:23), but also by God on account of his own mercy or for the sake of his name (78:38; 85:1-3; 106:45).

Far from God's anger or wrath being everlasting, the Psalms bears manifold witness that God's steadfast love *(ḥesed)* and faithfulness *('ĕmeth)* are everlasting *('ôlām)*. At one point the psalmist asks God, "Will you be angry with us forever? Will you prolong your anger to all generations?" (85:5), but then petitions God in the faith that God's anger is surpassed by steadfast love: "Show us your steadfast love, O LORD, and grant us your salvation" (v. 7). It is thus the refrain, "his [your] steadfast love endures forever," that resounds again and again and again in the Psalms (106:1; 107:1; 118, 5x; 136, 26x; 138:8). The psalmist even declares that God's steadfast love is co-eternal with God: "the steadfast love of the LORD is from everlasting to everlasting" (103:17).

The Psalms make parallel comparisons of God's steadfast love and faithful-

9. Cf. Goldingay, *Israel's Faith*, p. 135, emphasis original: "No, Israel's God is not simply a God of wrath. But Yhwh *is* a God of wrath. God gets fed up with the way we turn away, withdraws in response, lets anger find expression, and does so in ruthless fashion." Goldingay's emphasis on "is," I take it, is intended to warn us against playing a God of love against a God of wrath — an emphasis with which I would agree.

ness. The psalmist uses a cosmic scale to measure God's steadfast love and faith-fulness: "Your steadfast love, O LORD, extends to the heavens, your faithfulness to the clouds" (36:5; 57:10). At another place, the psalmist uses the duration of history to measure God's steadfast love and faithfulness: "his steadfast love endures forever, and his faithfulness to all generations" (100:5; cf. 117:2). And still elsewhere, the psalmist declares that God's steadfast love and faithfulness are as sure as God's creation: "I declare that your steadfast love is established forever; your faithfulness is as firm as the heavens" (89:2; cf. 146:6). It is precisely because of this faith that God's love and faithfulness are everlasting that the faithful can pray in a time of need: "Do not, O LORD, withhold your mercy from me; let your steadfast love and faithfulness keep me safe forever" (40:11).

Even Psalm 90, which laments the lot of mortals living under the wrath of God (vv. 7, 9, 11), can continue to hope in and pray for God's steadfast love (vv. 13-14). Similarly with Psalm 89: while acknowledging God's wrath upon a corrupted monarchy, expressed through military defeat (vv. 38-48), the psalmist can continue to affirm in faith that the way of God's rule over the cosmos and the foundation of God's relationship with the covenant community are God's steadfast love and faithfulness (vv. 1, 14, 24, 28, 33). This testimony of the Psalms is confirmed by the prophets.[10] Jeremiah, who speaks of God's anger as a fire that is kindled and will "burn forever" (Jer 15:14; 17:4), also proclaims God's promise of mercy surpassing anger: "I will not look on you in anger, for I am merciful, says the LORD; I will not be angry forever" (Jer 3:12).[11]

The overwhelming testimony of the Psalms is that God's steadfast love and faithfulness, not God's anger or wrath, is everlasting. It is thus evident that steadfast love *(ḥesed)* and faithfulness *('ĕmeth)* belong to God's character in an essential way that anger or wrath does not; anger or wrath is not the dominant side or controlling element of God's character, but love and mercy.[12] As Goldingay has observed: "Anger is not a divine attribute in the same sense as love is; the instinct to love emerges from God without any outside stimulus, but

10. It is also confirmed at the end of the biblical canon. In Revelation 15 and 16, which depict the outpouring of seven plagues of God's wrath in judgment upon the worshipers of the beast, we find that "with them the wrath of God is ended" (Rev 15:1). The text goes on to speak of the "seven golden bowls full of the wrath of God, who lives forever and ever" (v. 7). If "the wrath of God is ended" while God "lives forever and ever," then wrath cannot be essential to God's being God.

11. For testimony elsewhere in the Prophets to God's anger-surpassing steadfast love and faithfulness see Isa 54:7-8; 57:16; 60:10; Hos 2:19-20; Mic 7:18.

12. Here we must be careful to distinguish two different ideas: that anger/wrath is an essential element of God's character, and that anger/wrath is an integral dimension of God's response to injustice. It is only the former we deny, not the latter. Indeed, the Psalms and the Prophets give ample testimony to the latter. We thus concur with Willard M. Swartley, *Covenant of Peace: The Missing Peace in New Testament Theology* (Grand Rapids, MI: Eerdmans Publishing, 2006), p. 396.

God gets angry only as a reaction to outside stimulus."[13] Or, concisely and poetically: YHWH is "wrathful, but not from the heart."[14]

21.2. The "Story" of Vengeance in the Torah

Not only does God's steadfast love and faithfulness characteristically transcend wrath and retribution, but God teaches his covenant people to do likewise. This, we aim to show, is evident in the overall narrative pattern of the Torah as concerns vengeance.[15]

Before proceeding, we must address briefly a matter of language. Some readers may want to make a mental distinction between "vengeance" and "retribution." The Hebrew text of the Bible, however, draws no sharp distinction between them in reference to God's judgment, which is our concern here. The Hebrew word *nāqām*, usually translated "vengeance," is used in parallel with various words that are translated variously as "render," "repay," "requite," "recompense" or "retribution" (e.g., Isa 34:8; 35:4; 59:17-18; Jer 50:28-29; 51:6). Perhaps most significantly, *nāqām* is used in parallel with *šillēm* and *šalam* — translated variously "retribution" or "repay" or "recompense" — at Deut 32:35 and 32:41, respectively, where YHWH asserts sovereign prerogative over vengeance.

21.2.1. *The Mark of Cain and the Boast of Lamech*

We begin at the beginning, with the first murder (Genesis 4). Cain has slain Abel, and Abel's blood cries out for God to vindicate Abel against Cain (vv. 8-10). God hears the plea of Abel's blood and pronounces that Cain is now "cursed from the ground" (v. 11). God sentences Cain to wander the earth as a fugitive (v. 12), and Cain pleads with God for mercy: "My punishment is more than I can bear! . . . I shall be hidden from your face . . . and anyone who meets me may kill me" (vv. 13-14). Cain fears both the absence of God and the vengeance of humanity: without divine protection, he is vulnerable to the avenger of blood. Just as God heard and answered the plea of Abel's blood, so God hears and answers the plea of Cain's fear: "Not so! Whoever kills Cain will suffer a seven-fold vengeance" (v. 15a). Not only does God not punish Cain with death

---

13. Goldingay, *Israel's Faith*, p. 141.

14. Goldingay, *Israel's Faith*, p. 165.

15. See also Millard C. Lind, *Yahweh Is a Warrior: The Theology of Warfare in Ancient Israel* (Scottdale, PA: Herald Press, 1980); Vernard Eller, *War and Peace from Genesis to Revelation* (Scottdale, PA: Herald Press, 1981; Eugene, OR: Wipf & Stock, 2003); and Patricia M. McDonald, *God and Violence: Biblical Resources for Living in a Small World* (Scottdale, PA: Herald Press, 2004).

for murdering Abel, but God protects Cain's life from the avenger of blood: "And the LORD put a mark on Cain, so that no one who came upon him would kill him" (v. 15b). By marking out Cain's life for divine protection, God warns humanity not to take vengeance upon even those guilty of bloodshed; and God backs up that warning with a pledge of vengeance upon the avenger of blood. From the beginning, then, God prohibits human-executed vengeance and asserts exclusive right to retribution: retribution is a divine prerogative. See the striking contrast: God's judgment upon bloodshed is exile, not death; but God's judgment upon human retribution is divine vengeance! The "mark of Cain" thus expresses God's intent to stop the cycle of violence and vengeance from ever starting.

Lamech, however, hears of God's pledge to protect Cain's life with divine vengeance and in his pride boasts that he will not only outdo his fellows in vengeance but also outdo God. Cain feared that his fellows would take vengeance on him for murder; Lamech boasts that he has taken blood vengeance for only an injury: "I have killed a man for wounding me" (Gen 4:23). Having outdone his fellows, Lamech boasts that he will outdo God: "If Cain is avenged sevenfold, truly Lamech seventy-sevenfold" (v. 24). By taking blood vengeance for a mere injury and boasting of it, Lamech puts his fellows in fear. But by taking retribution into his own hand, Lamech usurps the divine prerogative; and by promising to surpass God in vengeance, Lamech exalts himself above God. To take vengeance into human hands and execute retribution upon another is thus to make oneself a god, a rival of YHWH.

Lamech's boast of self-exalting, God-surpassing vengeance is a signpost in human history pointing the way of things to come: violence and vengeance without end will be the path chosen by humanity in every generation. Because of the human penchant for usurping the divine prerogative, bloodshed-for-bloodshed escalates down the generations until, in the days of Noah, "the earth was filled violence *(ḥāmās)*" (Gen 6:11). Even God's own violent act to reverse creation and destroy evildoers, to cleanse the earth of violence and bloodshed (v. 13), does not reverse this human inclination toward evil (cf. 6:5; 8:21). The post-deluge covenant with Noah thus recognizes the fact that violence and vengeance, bloodshed for bloodshed, will continue to be the way of humanity (9:6).

The subsequent narrative of the family of Abraham bears witness to this reality. Although God has promised blessing to all humankind through Abraham and his offspring (Gen 12:1-3), and despite the generally peaceable character of the patriarchs (cf. chs. 13, 26, 32, and 33),[16] Abraham's family nonetheless continues the pattern of violence and vengeance from the days of Noah. After Dinah is raped by Shechem, two of Jacob's sons, Simeon and Levi, avenge their sister's honor — "Should our sister be treated like a whore?" (34:31) — by visit-

---

16. See McDonald, *God and Violence*, pp. 59-72.

ing vengeance upon the clan of Hamor. They "took their swords" and murdered all the men of the clan, including Hamor and Schechem, "with the sword" (vv. 25-26). The other sons of Jacob then join in, plundering the clan's wealth and enslaving the women and children. When he comes to die, with his sons gathered around him, Jacob censures Simeon and Levi for their violence and curses the vengeance they sought by the sword:

> Simeon and Levi are brothers; weapons of violence *(ḥāmās)* are their swords. May I never come into their council; may I not be joined to their company — for in their anger they killed men, and at their whim they hamstrung oxen. Cursed be their anger, for it is fierce, and their wrath, for it is cruel! I will divide them in Jacob, and scatter them in Israel. (49:5-7)

Here, then, is the narrative trajectory of the Torah concerning vengeance so far: Cain murders Abel; God prohibits human vengeance-taking; Lamech seizes vengeance for himself; the human generations from Lamech to Noah propagate vengeance until the earth is filled with violence; vengeance is now a fact of human history, reflected in the covenant with Noah and continued in the family of Abraham. The human practice of retributive violence thus reflects the sinful situation engendered by humanity's self-exaltation, not God's original will for humanity. Insofar as retribution appears to be the "natural law" of moral order, it is so due to the pattern of violence and vengeance that has been propagated by humanity, not God's will from the beginning, which prohibited human-executed retribution. Human vengeance-taking thus signifies the extent to which humanity has overstepped the bounds set by God and usurped the divine prerogative over life, thus bringing chaos into the cosmos and undoing the order of creation.

21.2.2. *Legal Limitation and Proscription of Vengeance*

God's covenant with Israel introduces legal limits on the human practice of retribution. These covenant statutes concerning retribution seek to constrain the already existing reality of blood vengeance, as evident in the story of Dinah.[17] Chief among these constraints on vengeance, introduced in the Covenant Code, is the *lex talionis:* "life for life, eye for eye, tooth for tooth . . ." (Exod 21:23-25; cf. Lev 24:19-20). As the Latin name for this law suggests, the *lex talionis* places strict limits on retribution. Limiting "payback" to an "equality of repayment," the *lex talionis* thus prohibits the very vengeance of which Lamech boasted (Gen 4:23). By permitting only measured retribution, the *lex talionis*

---

17. We will examine these more carefully and thoroughly in Chapters 24 and 25.

seeks to prevent the escalation of violence through vengeance that can lead from insult to murder to war — as, for example, in the stories of Dinah (noted above) and of Samson and the Philistines (Judges 13–16). As such, therefore, the *lex talionis* does not so much sanction as constrain an already existing practice of retribution.

That even measured vengeance, retribution limited by the *lex talionis,* does not express the full justice of God's will is evident further on in the Torah. In the Holiness Code, we find the familiar law of love of neighbor that the rabbis, including Jesus, will cite as the heart of the Torah. What we usually do not see is that the Torah's command to love one's neighbor is put in parallel with a prohibition against taking vengeance upon one's neighbor. In fact, the text gives us parallel sets of contrasting parallels:

> (A) You shall not hate in your heart anyone of your kin;
>> (B) you shall reprove your neighbor, or you will incur guilt yourself.
> (A′) You shall not take vengeance or bear a grudge against any of your people,
>> (B′) but you shall love your neighbor as yourself: I am the LORD.
>>> (Lev 19:17-18)

Taking these separately, we see the contrasts: in the first set, hating a neighbor in one's heart (A) contrasts with reproving one's neighbor (B); in the second set, taking vengeance upon a neighbor (A′) contrasts with loving one's neighbor (B′). Taking these together, we see the parallels: hating one's neighbor (A) is parallel with taking vengeance upon one's neighbor (A′) — and both are prohibited; likewise, reproving one's neighbor (B) is parallel with loving one's neighbor (B′) — and both are commanded. Repaying harm for harm and injury for injury in due measure, while following the rule of the law *(lex talionis),* does not fulfill God's intent for his covenant people. Not retribution but reproof fulfills the righteousness that God wills; not hate but love is the holiness that God desires. As we have seen (Chapter 3), this is precisely Paul's message: Christians ought to renounce retribution for the sake of fulfilling the law of love (Rom 12:9–13:10).

21.2.3. Vengeance Belongs to God

At the end of the Torah, God returns to the beginning, as it were. Through his prophet Moses, after delivering the law and pronouncing blesses and curses upon Israel, God reasserts (with threefold emphasis) exclusive divine prerogative over vengeance and retribution — and in so doing reaffirms God's sovereign dominion over life:

Is not this laid up in store with me, sealed in my treasuries? Vengeance is mine, and recompense, for the time when their foot shall slip; because the day of their calamity is at hand, their doom comes swiftly.... See now that I, even I, am he; there is no God besides me. I kill and I make alive; I wound and I heal; and no one can deliver from my hand.... I will take vengeance on my adversaries, and will repay those who hate me.... Praise, O heavens, his people, worship him, all you gods! For he will avenge the blood of his children, and take vengeance on his adversaries; he will repay those who hate him, and cleanse the land for his people. (Deut 32:34-35, 39, 41b, 43)

Vengeance rests in God's hand; retribution is reserved to God's doing. Moses thus admonishes Israel that they are *not* to take vengeance for bloodshed or execute retribution against enemies; for it is God alone who will avenge blood and execute retribution on behalf of Israel. Here, God's prerogative and providence go hand-in-hand: God's providence is demonstrated by God's exercise of vengeance on Israel's behalf. Likewise, Israel's patience and faith go hand-in-hand: to defer vengeance is to trust God. For Israel to take vengeance into its own hands is thus not only to infringe on God's dominion but also to fail to trust in God's providence (cf. Psalms 37 and 94).

Concerning vengeance/retribution, therefore, the Torah shows us an overall narrative pattern, which can be represented by this chiastic ("X") structure:

A   God reserves retribution to himself (Gen 3:15).
    B   Humans seize retribution from God (4:23-24).
        C   In human hands, the cycle of violence and vengeance spirals without limit (6:11; 9:6).
            D   In the family of Abraham, the cycle of violence and vengeance continues (ch. 34).
            D′   The patriarch of Israel censures the violence and curses the vengeance of the sons of Israel (ch. 49).
        C′   God limits human vengeance-taking by covenant law (Exod 21:23-25).
    B′   God prohibits vengeance-taking for the covenant community (Lev 19:18).
A′   God reserves retribution to himself (Deut 32:35).

This narrative pattern teaches us two correlated truths: God holds and exercises exclusive prerogative over vengeance and retribution, and, from the beginning, it was never God's intent for his people to take vengeance into their own hands and execute retribution upon either one another or their enemies. The human practice of retributive violence thus neither reflects God's original intent nor fulfills God's covenant will, but rather usurps God's prerogative, infringes God's dominion, and distrusts God's providence.

21.3. Covenant Loyalty and Covenant Justice

Having seen that retribution is a divine prerogative, we now consider how God deals with the disobedience of his covenant people. We have already witnessed a dialectical tension within God's character between anger and mercy, with mercy both preceding and surpassing anger. Here we examine the parallel tension between God's covenant justice and God's covenant loyalty, by which God holds Israel to account but never breaks faith with Israel.[18] God, as covenant-maker, may and sometimes does elect to execute punishment upon Israel for sin — but with a view toward Israel's redemption. Redemption is God's first act of covenant loyalty to Israel, a fulfillment of promises to the patriarchs (Exod 2:23-25); redemption is thus both prologue and epilogue of God's covenant with Israel (Exod 20:2; Deut 5:6; 6:20-25) as well as the substance of Israel's trusting faith in God (Deut 26:5-10). And just as redemption is God's first act for Israel, so redemption remains God's final promise to Israel — and God is true to that word to the end. God thus acts both "for" and "against" Israel, delivering and defending Israel *and* bringing Israel under judgment, but God's action "against" Israel derives its motivation and function entirely from God's action "for" Israel: God judges Israel ultimately for the sake of Israel's redemption.[19] There is, we might say, a "redemptive tension" between God's covenant justice and God's covenant loyalty.[20]

Before proceeding, let us expand briefly on God's covenant loyalty as an expression of the divine character. God's covenant loyalty is depicted in the very terms of God's self-disclosure to Moses on Mount Sinai: ḥesed ("steadfast love," NRSV; "loving kindness," KJV) and 'ĕmeth ("faithfulness," NRSV; "truth," KJV). As such, God's covenant with Israel is rooted in God's character as well as in God's work of redemption: God's covenant with Israel is everlasting because God is characterized by ḥesed and 'ĕmeth. Ḥesed names the reliability of God in covenant relationship: in dealing with his people, God shows himself as the

18. The "tension" I have in mind here is analogous to the physics of a spring: as one end of a spring is pulled away from the other, a force internal to the spring pulls back, increasing proportionally to the distance that the end is displaced from its normal position. So also in God's covenant with Israel: God's justice and loyalty are like respective ends of a spring — as God's justice pulls toward judgment, God's loyalty pulls back with an equal and opposite "force" toward restoration of right ("normal") relationships.

19. Concerning this "two-sidedness" of God's character and action, see Goldingay, *Israel's Faith*, pp. 156-70.

20. Cf. Brueggemann, *Theology of the Old Testament*, p. 283 (emphasis original): "Here I will suggest that the largest thematization concerning Yahweh, as testified to by Israel, is that *Yahweh is at the same time sovereign and faithful*, severely preoccupied with self-regard and passionately committed to life with the [covenant] partner. Finally I shall suggest that these two themes, in considerable tension with each other, have their proximate — but no more than proximate — resolution in Yahweh's *righteousness*."

ever-reliable, always-trustworthy one. *Ḥesed* expresses God's unfaltering and undying love for the people that God has chosen for his own and called by his name; it is embodied in God's unwavering will to redeem until the end those whom he has redeemed from the beginning (cf. Isa 43:1-7). *'Ĕmeth* names the quality of God's covenant commitment: in dealing with his people, God shows himself as the ever-true, always-faithful one. *'Ĕmeth* characterizes the loyal God who is true to his word and faithful to his promise, from beginning to end.[21]

21.3.1. The Tension between Judgment and Redemption

As does the book of Deuteronomy, the Holiness Code (Leviticus 17–26) concludes with a set of promises and warnings to Israel. YHWH promises Israel: if you give faithful obedience to my covenant, then I will grant you *shalom,* prosperity and security, and my holy presence will dwell with you to enable you to walk in the way of justice (Lev 26:3-13). But YHWH warns Israel: if you disobey me and break my covenant, then I "will bring terror on you" and "set my face against you," resulting in devastating punishment, conquest by foreign powers, and exile (vv. 14-39). Yet, even if this comes to pass, there is still hope for Israel; for YHWH makes a further promise: "But if they confess their iniquity and the iniquity of their ancestors . . . if then their uncircumcised heart is humbled and they make amends for their iniquity, then will I remember my covenant . . ." (vv. 40-41). That is, YHWH promises to remain loyal to his covenant and so open to relationship despite Israel's disloyalty and injustice. And this promise of covenant loyalty means that YHWH's covenant justice, the purpose of which is to discipline Israel in order to bring about contrition and repentance and so to restore Israel to covenant loyalty, extends through exile and aims at Israel's redemption. YHWH thus pledges *never* to abandon or bring final destruction upon Israel:

> Yet for all that, when they are in the land of their enemies, I will not spurn them, or abhor them so as to destroy them utterly and break my covenant with them; for I am the LORD their God; but I will remember in their favor the covenant with their ancestors whom I brought out of the land of Egypt in the sight of the nations to be their God: I am the LORD. (vv. 44-45)

For YHWH to utterly "spurn" or "abhor" or "destroy" Israel, even as punishment for their sins, would be for YHWH to "break covenant" — to prove *dis*loyal and thus *un*just.

The redemptive tension between God's justice and God's loyalty is found

---

21. As Brueggemann, *Theology of the Old Testament,* observes, although Israel's "testimony" is to YHWH's reliability, there is occasional "dispute" of this theme in the biblical text. Our argument here is, of course, premised on Israel's testimony.

also in the prophet Jeremiah. YHWH commissions Jeremiah to call Israel to repent from idolatry, injustice, and violence and to return to covenant loyalty, or else face the dire consequences of national calamity. Three times does YHWH warn the people of divine punishment and retribution (Jer 5:9, 29; 9:9): "Shall I not punish them for these things? says the LORD; and shall I not bring retribution on a nation such as this?" Even so, three times does YHWH assure the people that all is not lost, that though retribution come and exile result, redemption remains God's will: "But even in those days, says the LORD, I will not make a full end of you" (5:18; cf. 4:27; 5:10).[22] YHWH may "make an end of all the nations" of Israel's exile but pledges to Israel, "of you I will not make an end" (30:11; cf. 46:28). Were YHWH to mete out retribution for sin "to the full" and so "make an end" of Israel, then God's very purpose in redeeming Israel in the first place — for YHWH "to be their God" and for Israel "to be my people" (30:22; 31:33) — would come to nothing. YHWH's covenant justice, in order to accomplish its redemptive purpose, is held in dialectical tension with covenant loyalty. YHWH's punishment of his people's sins, therefore, is not determined by any fixed principle of retributive justice. Rather, the "just measure" with which YHWH punishes his people (30:11) is circumscribed by his own steadfast love and covenant loyalty (31:3), which seeks to redeem his people — forgiving their sins, restoring them to health, and renewing them in loyalty (chs. 30 and 31).

The Psalms also witness to the tension between covenant loyalty and justice — that the integrity of YHWH's promise and purpose, rather than any law of retribution, sets the limit of YHWH's punishment. Psalm 89 begins by praising YHWH's covenant loyalty and steadfast love (vv. 1-4), but ends by appealing to YHWH to show loyalty and fulfill his promise to David in a time of national crisis (vv. 38-51). The psalmist's appeal is premised on YHWH's self-declaration that his loyalty to his covenant stands firm forever and so limits his punishment of Israel's disobedience:

> Forever will I keep my steadfast love for [David], and my covenant with him will stand firm. . . . If his children forsake my law and do not walk according to my ordinances, if they violate my statutes and do not keep my command-

---

22. In Jer 4:27b this phrase, "yet I will not make a full end," follows a description of divine punishment in terms of the reversal of creation (vv. 23-26), which is summed up: "For thus says the LORD: the whole land shall be a desolation" (v. 27a). Walter Brueggemann, *A Commentary on Jeremiah: Exile and Homecoming* (Grand Rapids: Eerdmans Publishing, 1998), p. 60: "This expression, "not a full end," is a serious counterpoint to its context, either for Jeremiah or for Yahweh. Thus we may best take it as an expression of uncertainty on Yahweh's part, wrought out of Yahweh's yearning not to destroy. Yahweh has been provoked to a harsh resolve from which Yahweh momentarily draws back. . . . [I]t is this reluctance on Yahweh's part that becomes the ground for hope in the midst of exile, for the yearning on God's part persists, even in the face of the relentless devastation in this poetry."

ments, then I will punish their transgression with the rod and their iniquity with scourges; but I will not remove from him my steadfast love, or be false to my faithfulness. I will not violate my covenant, or alter the word that went forth from my lips. (vv. 28-34)

YHWH's justice in dealing with Israel's sin thus stands in tension with YHWH's loyalty to his covenant promise: YHWH's promise of redemption circumscribes YHWH's exercise of retribution. Were YHWH to exercise retribution "to the full" and put an end to Israel, YHWH would "be false to my truth (*'ĕmûnâh*)."

21.3.2. Covenant Loyalty beyond Retribution for Redemption

The dialectical tension between justice and loyalty — witnessed by the Torah, Prophets, and Psalms — implies that God's justice in administering his covenant is not governed strictly by the law of retribution, but is exercised ultimately through God's steadfast love and fulfilled by redemption of his people according to his promise. In covenant relationship, therefore, God's judgment upon Israel's disobedience does not necessarily follow an absolute "rule of law." God does at times exercise the divine prerogative of retribution concerning Israel — not for the sake of satisfying retribution, but rather for the sake of redeeming Israel from injustice and restoring Israel to covenant loyalty. As YHWH says to Israel: ". . . my judgment goes forth as the light. For I desire steadfast love . . ." (Hos 6:5-6). It is thus God's loyalty to his promises and his purpose in his covenant, not the law of retribution, that define the purpose and set the limit of punishment.[23] God's covenant with Israel is thus not a rigid system of retributive justice. Even though the covenant holds out calamity and exile as punishment for disobedience (Deuteronomy 27–30), therefore, punitive measures are not the first, nor the last, much less the necessary, way in which God deals with disobedient Israel. When Israel falls into disobedience, God raises up judges and rulers to restore the ways of right worship of God and right living according to God's law. When idolatry and injustice overtake the temple and palace, God sends prophets to warn the nation concerning its sins and call it to repentance. As Boersma observes, exile is God's punishment of last resort:

---

23. We have thus developed here an Old Testament basis for the idea of "restorative justice" or "redemptive punishment" (in contrast with retributive justice/punishment) that has been presented from a New Testament perspective in Christopher D. Marshall, *Beyond Retribution: A New Testament Vision for Justice, Crime, and Punishment* (Grand Rapids, MI: Eerdmans Publishing, 2001).

Significantly, exile is God's last option. He resorts to this climactic punishment only when it becomes clear that Israel as a whole has consistently refused to repent and so to obtain forgiveness and a restoration of the relationship with Yahweh. God does not delight in punishment but keeps the violence of penal force at bay as much as possible.[24]

After many centuries of patient dealing with his covenant people, when God does punish the nation for their accumulated sins (2 Kgs 23:24-27; 24:1-4, 18-20; 2 Chron 36:15-16), God imposes upon Israel, not the ultimate sanction of national death, but a limited sentence of foreign exile. And God sends Israel into exile with a view to ransom from captivity and restoration as God's people (Jeremiah 29). Even this punitive measure of last resort is intended by God to reestablish Israel as a people devoted to right worship of God and righteous living according to God's law (Ezekiel 20). This point is summed up in one of Ezekiel's allegories:

> You must bear the penalty of your lewdness and your abominations, says the LORD. Yes, thus says the Lord GOD: I will deal with you as you have done, you who have despised the oath, breaking the covenant; *yet* I will remember my covenant with you in the days of your youth, and I will establish with you an everlasting covenant. (Ezek 16:58-60)

God's justice and faithfulness are balanced upon this "yet," the promise and hope of covenant renewal. God does deal with Israel's sins and will punish sin as a last resort, but not as an end in itself. God, loyal to his covenant, deals justly with Israel's sin with a view toward Israel's redemption and for the sake of Israel's renewal as his covenant people. Indeed, it is precisely by God's redemption beyond retribution in dealing with sins that Israel knows that God is the Lord (Ezek 20:44). God's dealing with Israel as a nation parallels his dealing with Adam and Cain. God does not punish them with death for their sins, not even for Cain's shedding of innocent blood; rather, God sentences them to exile and, even so, extends his merciful care to them in exile (clothing for Adam and Eve, protection for Cain). Even in dealing with the worst offenders, God's justice seeks, not retribution per se, but repentance from sin, return to righteousness, and restoration of life (33:11): "As I live, says the Lord GOD, I have no pleasure in the death of the wicked, but that the wicked turn from their ways and live; turn back, turn back from your evil ways; for why will you die, O house of Israel?"[25]

24. Hans Boersma, *Violence, Hospitality, and the Cross: Reappropriating the Atonement Tradition* (Grand Rapids, MI: Baker Academic, 2004), p. 175.
25. We will witness such redemptive justice in dealing with sin by Jesus himself in the episode of "the woman caught in adultery" (John 8) in Chapter 24 below.

21.4. Divine Retribution

21.4.1. Prerogative, Not Imperative

Divine retribution is not necessitated by either cosmic law or human sin, but is a divine prerogative, subject to God's sovereign choice: God is free to execute retribution, free to transcend retribution. Because retribution is God's *prerogative*, we cannot know beforehand either when or how God's justice must appear: we must wait and see what God will reveal. Whether and how God exercises the prerogative of retribution in executing justice is not determined by any prior principle but is God's alone to determine: God's justice will be God's justice. Thus, as Walter Brueggemann has observed, we must remain open to the possibility that God might reveal judgment in a surprising way that confounds rather than confirms human expectations and frustrates rather than satisfies human desires:

> In my judgment, this is the true data of Yahweh's character: the capacity of Yahweh (and Israel's testimony) to surprise us by intervention that may move destructively or rehabilitatively on any given occasion. Thus our thematization of Yahweh must be inherently open and relatively unstable, for we cannot know ahead of time at which extreme Yahweh may be disclosed.[26]

We might restate the point this way: that retribution is a divine prerogative does *not* entail that retribution is a divine *imperative;* from the truth that vengeance belongs to God it does not follow that God *must* execute vengeance upon sinners or else fail to be God. Retribution belongs to God alone, but we cannot say that it is necessary that God exercise a divine prerogative. For if it were necessary that God execute retribution, then retribution would not be God's prerogative but God's obligation. God would thus be obliged to the law of retribution such that God's will would be "overruled." We must be very cautious in making claims that God must be this or do that or else not be God. Not only can we not assume *that* God must execute retribution, moreover, we also cannot suppose that we know in advance *how* God's judgment must appear in history. God's sovereign freedom means that we must wait and see what God will reveal to us regarding what belongs to God alone. Hence, we cannot have any *a priori* knowledge of God's judgment, but can know God's judgment only *a posteriori* by way of God's word and works. We thus need to listen to the word of God's prophet and look to the work of God's servant to know God's judgment and to see God's retribution.

---

26. Brueggemann, *Theology of the Old Testament*, p. 281.

21.4.2. Divine Retribution Revealed in the Prophets

The Scriptures testify that God may elect to execute retribution upon, or act with redemption for, the nations. God does at times choose to execute retribution upon the nations for their sins. The prophet Jeremiah testifies to God's purpose to carry out vengeance against Babylon, for its desecration of YHWH's Temple and for the violence and bloodshed it has dealt to Israel and to the nations (Jeremiah 50–51). Foreign invaders will bring on the land of Babylon the destruction and death that Babylon has brought on other lands. The prophet of YHWH thus gives the command to the armies of the surrounding nations to lay siege to Babylon: "Repay her according to her deeds; just as she has done, do to her — for she has arrogantly defied the Lord, the Holy One of Israel" (Jer 50:29). God ordains destruction and death for Babylon as "payback" for her crimes against humanity.[27] But God also chooses at times to act with redemption for the nations of the earth. That is the heart of the message of Jonah: God sends his reluctant prophet to Nineveh for the sake of the repentance and salvation of Israel's enemy. The second Servant Song in Isaiah, moreover, declares that God redeems Israel from exile in Babylon for the salvation of the nations, in order that he might give Israel "as a light to the nations, that my salvation may reach to the end of the earth" (Isa 49:1-6).

Not only may God act for redemption or execute retribution as God wills, but God's vengeance, the prophet tells us, may well look very different from human expectation. In Isaiah 59 and 63, we see God's vengeance depicted as we expect. In Isaiah 59, God is the divine warrior who, in absence of someone to intervene to do justice, takes matters into his own hand to bring justice to victory (59:15b-16). Here, God's justice comes full of wrath and payback for the evil deeds of his enemies:

> He put on righteousness like a breastplate, and a helmet of salvation on his head; he put on garments of vengeance *(nāqām)* for clothing, and wrapped himself in fury as in a mantle. According to their deeds, so will he repay; wrath to his adversaries, requital to his enemies; to the coastlands he will render requital. (vv. 17-18)

In Isaiah 63, God is depicted as treading "the grapes of wrath" in the divine winepress (63:3). And again, God's justice exercises vengeance with wrath and violence upon the wicked of the earth: "For the day of vengeance *(yôm nāqām)* was in my heart, and the year of my redeeming work had come. . . . I trampled

---

27. This image of God rendering "payback to Babylon" is reflected in the pronouncement of divine judgment on Rome ("Babylon the great") for her evildoing to others: "Render to her as she herself has rendered, and repay her double for her deeds; mix a double draught for her in the cup she mixed" (Rev 18:6).

down peoples in my anger, I crushed them in my wrath, and I poured out their lifeblood on the earth" (vv. 4, 6). In both texts, God's salvation and redemption are put in parallel with divine vengeance *(nāqām)* — and thus are portrayed as being worked through vengeance that is exercised with wrath and retribution (59:17; 63:4). This confirms our human expectation of divine redemption by a violent vengeance.

Yet this is not the prophet's only depiction of divine vengeance. In chs. 35 and 61, we find a strikingly different portrayal of God's salvation worked through vengeance. In Isaiah 35, God's vengeance, rather than dealing payback to the wicked, brings healing and hope to the weak and fearful:

> Strengthen the weak hands, and make firm the feeble knees. Say to those who are of a fearful heart, "Be strong, do not fear! Here is your God. He will come with vengeance *(nāqām)*, with terrible recompense. He will come and save you." Then the eyes of the blind shall be opened, and the ears of the deaf unstopped; then the lame shall leap like a deer, and the tongue of the speechless sing for joy. For waters shall break forth in the wilderness, and streams in the desert. . . . (Isa 35:3-6)

God's salvation comes with "vengeance," but in a surprising way that confounds our human expectations: God's "terrible recompense" restores sight to the blind, hearing to the deaf, agility to the lame, voice to the speechless, and life to the desert (cf. vv. 1-2, 7).

In Isaiah 61, we again see God's "day of vengeance" *(yôm nāqām)* but portrayed in a way that contrasts sharply with Isaiah 63. Here, rather than being the work of God alone and expressing God's wrath (63:5), God's "day of vengeance" is the work of God's anointed Servant and expresses God's grace ("favor"). And rather than bringing destruction and death on God's enemies, God's "day of vengeance" brings justice and peace, liberation and provision for the poor and oppressed:

> The spirit of the Lord GOD is upon me, because the LORD has anointed me; he has sent me to bring good news to the oppressed, to bind up the brokenhearted, to proclaim liberty to the captives, and release to the prisoners; to proclaim the year of the LORD's favor, and the day of vengeance *(yôm nāqām)* of our God; to comfort all who mourn; to provide for those who mourn in Zion — to give them a garland instead of ashes, the oil of gladness instead of mourning, the mantle of praise instead of a faint spirit. They will be called oaks of righteousness, the planting of the LORD, to display his glory. They shall build up the ancient ruins, they shall raise up the former devastations; they shall repair the ruined cities, the devastations of many generations. (61:1-4)

Again, God's salvation ("favor") is exercised through vengeance, but in a most surprising way beyond all expectation. Instead of the enemies of God having their heads trampled and blood spilled, those who mourn are comforted with joy, those whose cities were destroyed rebuild their homes and repair their streets.

In these prophetic pictures of God's "day of vengeance," God's justice is manifest, not in retribution against evildoers, but in the reversal of evil. Divine vengeance is *divine reversal* — God overturns the wickedness of the wicked, the injustice of the unjust, the violence of the violent, and the oppression of the oppressors (cf. Luke 1:46-55). What the wicked, the unjust, the violent, and the oppressors have done is undone by God — and in the place of wickedness and injustice, violence and oppression, God works righteousness and justice, salvation and redemption. In these oracles, God brings redemption on his "day of vengeance" through acts of release, restoration, and renewal: the sick are restored to health, the poor are freed from their debts, the victims of injustice are vindicated, the mourners of the victims are renewed in joy, the refugees of war are returned to their homes, the prisoners of conscience are released from their cells, the captives of slavery are liberated from their chains, the deserted places are restored to life, and the abandoned places are rebuilt for living. Instead of wrathful retribution, these prophetic texts envision God's "day of vengeance" bringing "good news" — and thus induce a reversal of perception, a reorientation of thinking.

The divine reversal imagined by the prophet is (to be) fulfilled in the word and work of Jesus Christ. In his inaugural sermon (Luke 4:16-30), Jesus cites Isa 61:1-2 as the pretext of his ministry. Jesus thus reveals himself to be "the one" anointed by the Spirit to proclaim "the year of the Lord's favor," to bring "the day of vengeance of our God" — the time of divine judgment of evildoers and divine vindication of the oppressed, for which God's people have waited.[28] Now, some may want to downplay the theme of divine retribution in Jesus' sermon in Luke 4, pointing out that Jesus reads Isaiah 61 only to "the year of the LORD's favor," stopping short of "the day of vengeance of our God." That would be a mistake, for two reasons. First, it would ignore the obvious poetic parallel between "the year of the LORD's favor" and "the day of vengeance of our God" in the original text (Isa 61:2) — to invoke one phrase is to evoke the other (cf. 63:4). Second, it would rob Jesus' sermon of the prophetic power to reorient our vision of divine retribution. By citing Isaiah 61 and saying, "Today this scripture has been fulfilled in your hearing" (Luke 4:21), Jesus announces himself as the

28. As argued by N. T. Wright, *Surprised by Hope: Rethinking Heaven, the Resurrection, and the Mission of the Church* (New York: HarperCollins, 2008), two key messianic texts, Isaiah 11 and Psalm 2, explicitly depict the Lord's anointed as exercising the divine prerogative of judgment in the service of establishing the reign of God and the peace of heaven on earth. "So the early Christians, who had concluded from Easter that Jesus was indeed the Messiah, naturally identified him as the one through whom God would put the world to rights" (p. 139).

God-appointed executor of "the day of vengeance." We need to remember, however, that the prophecy that Jesus cites as the mandate of his mission depicts a vision of divine retribution that inverts the human expectation of redemptive violence.

Just as the prophet's oracle confounds our expectations, so also Jesus' sermon confounds the expectations of his hearers, revealing the "good news" of the surprising ways of divine justice. The people are expecting God to send to them "the one" who will execute wrathful retribution upon their enemies, the foreign nations that have been oppressing them. Instead, Jesus proclaims God's mercy for those who do not deserve it, citing stories of God's prophets being channels of grace — provision for foreigners (Elijah and the widow at Zarephath) and healing for enemies (Elisha and Naaman the Syrian). In his ministry, furthermore, Jesus brings forth God's justice as imagined by the prophet — healing of the blind, restoration of the lame, resurrection of the dead, and good new for the poor (Luke 7:18-23). The justice of God that Jesus proclaims and enacts overturns the human expectation of redemptive violence; it is a redemptive justice that is merciful to foreigners and enemies and to the poor and ailing alike. That the people do not wish to have their desire for divine vengeance frustrated and their thinking about divine grace reoriented is evident in their response to Jesus' sermon: they attempt to kill him.

21.5. Final Judgment

The prophets (including Jesus) teach us the same lesson as the Torah: retribution is a divine prerogative, but not a divine imperative. God is free to exercise retribution in judgment, free also to transcend retribution for sake of redemption. What, though, we are bound to wonder, about "the end"? Will not God exercise divine vengeance with wrath and retribution "in the end" in order to bring all wrongdoing to account and all evildoers to justice? It simply *must* be so, we are wont to think. This question has generated much discussion recently among theologians about God's moral character and violence.[29]

21.5.1. Revelation: Divine Retribution by Redemptive Violence?

Evangelical theologian Miroslav Volf maintains that God's final judgment upon and redemption of the world *must* be violent in order to deal satisfactorily with injustice and deal fairly with the victims. While the cross of Christ is God's

---

29. For a review and assessment of this discussion, see Swartley, *Covenant of Peace*, pp. 377-98.

merciful "embrace" of sinful humanity, Volf argues, in the end there must be a "final exclusion" of those who refuse God's cruciform embrace. Referring to the rider on the white horse in Revelation 19, who makes war and wields a sword, cutting down the enemies of heaven, Volf writes:

> The violence of the Rider on the white horse, I suggest, is the *symbolic portrayal of the final exclusion of everything that refuses to be redeemed by God's suffering love.* For the sake of the peace of God's good creation, we can and must affirm *this* divine anger and *this* divine violence, while at the same time holding on to the hope that in the end, even the flag bearer will desert the army that desires to make war against the Lamb.
>
> Should not a loving God be patient and keep luring the perpetrator into goodness? This is exactly what God does: God suffers the evildoers through history as God has suffered them on the cross. But how patient should God be? The day of reckoning must come, not because God is too eager to pull the trigger, but because every day of patience in a world of violence means more violence and every postponement of vindication means letting insult accompany injury.[30]

While God's original act of creation and God's work of redemption through the cross of Christ are peaceful, Volf continues, God's final work of salvation must be violent in order to deal with those who reject the cross and to restore the peace of creation:

> The creation of the world involved no violence. . . . The chaos sets in as a distortion of the peaceful creation. Redemption cannot, therefore, be an act of pure positing but entails negation and struggle, even violence. First God suffers violence on the cross for the salvation of the world. Then, after God's patience with chaotic powers who refuse to be redeemed by the cross has come to an end, God inflicts violence against the stubbornly violent to restore creation's original peace.[31]

With Volf, I believe that God has promised ultimate vindication and that God, ever faithful and true, will perform on that promise of justice, for the sake of God's name and for the salvation of the victims.[32] Volf assumes, however, that final vindication of the victims of violence *necessitates* a violent vanquishing of the perpetrators of violence. There is no other way, ultimately, to deal

---

30. Miroslav Volf, *Exclusion and Embrace: A Theological Exploration of Identity, Otherness, and Reconciliation* (Nashville, TN: Abingdon Press, 1996), p. 299, emphasis original.

31. Volf, *Exclusion and Embrace*, p. 300.

32. I thus agree also with N. T. Wright that final judgment, in which God "puts the world to rights," is an essential element of biblical faith and Christian hope — see *Surprised by Hope*, pp. 137-45, 178-79.

with evil, to right injustice, and restore peace, not even for God, than to deal out punitive payback to evildoers. That is simply how it *must* be, Volf argues, or else God will have failed the victims and made himself an accomplice to evil. What, though, is the source and force of this "must"? Volf's point that God created the cosmos in peace and suffered violence upon the cross in peace, prompts the very question we are pressing: If it was not necessary that God deal with chaos by violence in the beginning,[33] if it was not necessary that God deal with injustice by violence at the cross, then why should it be *necessary* that God deal with evil by violence in the end?

I concede that, given the magnitude of evildoing in the world, we, as human beings, can imagine no other way that God's final righting of wrong and restoration of peace might be accomplished than by a violent judgment.[34] We then assume that the apocalyptic vision fulfills the human desire for divine vengeance executed by means of retributive violence. And so we interpret the rider on the white horse in Revelation 19 to fit our human imagination and expectation. As people of faith, however, we have inherited the inspired imagination of the prophets, to whom the Spirit gave an alternative vision of divine vengeance. The oracles of Isaiah have shown us that we cannot simply assume how "the day of God's vengeance" *must* appear. Volf's "must," I thus suggest, has its source in the depths of human desire and derives its force from the limits of human thinking. The stories of Cain and Lamech reveal how deeply vengeance is rooted in the sin-warped psyche and how forcefully the retributive paradigm has shaped human being and thinking since the Fall. From beginning to end, however, God's vengeance belongs to God alone — and no depth of human desire or limit of human thinking can place any necessity whatsoever on what belongs to God, whose thoughts and ways transcend our thoughts and ways (Isa 55:6-9).

21.5.2. *Jesus, Executor of Divine Judgment*

We are correct to see Jesus Christ as the rider whose name is "Faithful and True" (Rev 19:11). And we are correct to see him as the God-appointed executor of

---

33. The "deep" *(tᵉhôm)* and the "sea" *(yam)* in Gen 1:2 represent the primordial chaos that God's creative work brings into order through the peaceful work of God's "wind" *(rûaḥ,* "Spirit" or "breath")* and word. On creation as God's work of peace to overcome chaos, see Ben C. Ollenburger, "Peace and God's Action against Chaos in the Old Testament," in Marlin E. Miller and Barbara Nelson Gingerich, eds., *The Church's Peace Witness* (Grand Rapids, MI: Eerdmans Publishing, 1994), pp. 70-88.

34. Cf. Wright, *Surprised by Hope,* p. 180 (emphasis original): "I find it quite impossible, reading the New Testament on the one hand and the newspaper on the other, to suppose that there will be no ultimate condemnation, no final loss, no human beings to whom, as C. S. Lewis put it, God will eventually say, '*Thy* will be done.'"

"the day of vengeance" — that, we have argued, is implied in Jesus' inaugural sermon in Luke 4 (citing Isaiah 61). Paul, moreover, depicts Jesus as the apocalyptic executor of divine vengeance (2 Thess 1:5-10).

But, we need to ask, who is the Jesus Christ who comes on "the day of God's vengeance" in Revelation 19? The same Jesus Christ who proclaims "the year of the Lord's favor" in Luke 4? The same Jesus Christ who fulfills the Suffering Servant of Isaiah 53, bearing our sorrows and sins out of love "for us"? "Jesus Christ is the same yesterday and today and forever" (Heb 13:8). The Jesus Christ who preached and healed in Galilee and died on the cross (yesterday) is the same Jesus Christ who is risen and intercedes mercifully for us (today) is the same Jesus Christ who will come again to execute God's judgment (forever).[35] Just as we have emphasized coherence between the life and death of Jesus in understanding God's revelation of justice through the cross, so now we emphasize coherence between Incarnation and Judgment in understanding God's revelation of vengeance "in the end." That Incarnation and Judgment are one ministry of the same Christ is implied in the Nicene Creed: "he came down from heaven," "he became incarnate," "he was crucified . . . he suffered death and was buried," "he rose again," "he ascended into heaven," and "he will come again in glory to judge the living and the dead" are *all* conjoined in a single (Greek) sentence beginning with the phrase, "For us humans and for our salvation." Jesus' apocalyptic execution of divine judgment is the final phase of his one mission "for us and for our salvation" worked throughout his life, death, resurrection, and ascension.[36]

At the beginning of his ministry, Jesus proclaimed that the time of divine redemption and vengeance is fulfilled in himself. The prophetic vision of divine redemption and vengeance that Jesus claims as the mandate of his mission is one which confounds rather than confirms the human expectation of redemption by violence against God's enemies (Luke 4; Isaiah 61). Furthermore, Jesus' ministry of teaching and healing, suffering and death, was understood by the New Testament writers as fulfilling the Suffering Servant (Isaiah 53). As we showed earlier (Chapter 13), the Suffering Servant does God's justice in a situation of transgression and iniquity, bringing peace and healing, but without violence. And both the teaching and the cross of Jesus reveal the justice of God transcending retribution for the sake of redemption (Chapters 19 and 20 above).

35. Cf. Wright, *Surprised by Hope*, p. 141: "the future judgment is highlighted basically as good news, not bad. Why so? It is good news, first, because the one through whom God's justice will finally sweep the world is not a hard-hearted, arrogant, or vengeful tyrant but rather the Man of Sorrows, who was acquainted with grief; the Jesus who loved sinners and died for them; the Messiah who took the world's judgment upon himself on the cross."
36. Cf. Luke Timothy Johnson, *The Creed: What Christians Believe and Why It Matters* (New York: Doubleday, 2003), pp. 192ff.

This point is made with striking clarity in the death and resurrection of Jesus. The cross of Christ *does* reveal the vengeance of God, but in a way that shatters human expectation and transcends human logic. Humanity has murdered God's own Son — there is no greater evil to be done than this crime against divinity. What justice shall the victim, Jesus, demand from the Judge for this evil? And how shall the Judge, God, vindicate the victim of evil with justice? Jesus, for his part, does not simply "write off" this greatest of all evils. Jesus seeks justice in God's court under the laws of God's kingdom, filing a petition with the Judge for mercy upon his murderers while entrusting himself to the Judge for vindication of his innocence (Luke 6:27-36; 23:34, 46; 1 Pet 2:21-25). God, for his part, does not simply "pass over" this greatest of all evils, either. God does vindicate the victim, by raising him to life and exalting him to authority (Acts 2:22-36). And God does visit the blood of the victim upon the heads of the perpetrators — but in an unexpected way that completely confounds the legal logic of retributive justice: not by punishing the perpetrators with death (bloodshed for bloodshed), but by calling them to repentance of life and offering them forgiveness of sin "in the name of Jesus Christ," the very one whose innocent blood they had unjustly shed (Acts 2:37-38; 3:19; 5:31; 10:43; 13:38-39).

God's retribution ("payback") to humanity for the death of Jesus is to open the way of repentance of life and forgiveness of sin to all in the name of Jesus. In this way, God "brings justice to victory" through the death and resurrection of his Son and Servant (Matt 12:17-21; Isa 42:1-4). *The resurrection-vindication of the crucified one and the repentance-justification of the crucifiers is the vengeance of God!*[37] According to merely human thinking, this is an "upside-down" divine vengeance, to be sure, but such is the perspective-reversing, values-inverting revelatory surprise of the cross. Through the cross of Christ, God vindicates the victim of violence but without executing violent retribution against the perpetrators.[38] Now, if God can vindicate the ultimate victim in cosmic history without retributive violence through the cross, why cannot God vindicate all other victims without retributive violence in the end?

37. Here I have adapted an idea from Ronald Roper.

38. Peter W. Martens, "The Quest for an Anabaptist Atonement: Violence and Nonviolence in J. Denny Weaver's *The Nonviolent Atonement*," *Mennonite Quarterly Review* 82 (April 2008), 281-311, argues that, unless it be granted that God rights the wrong of Jesus' murder by dealing out retributive punishment upon Jesus' executioners, then atonement theology will have failed to take seriously the evil of Jesus' death. While I do not defend Weaver's "nonviolent atonement," to which Martens's argument is addressed, Martens needs to explain why "the absence of retributive justice" in atonement theology "fails to take the evil of Jesus' killers seriously" (p. 306). His argument begs the very question we are pressing here. It is Jesus himself, the victim in this case, after all, who does not demand divine retribution but petitions divine mercy. Evidently, retribution was not essential to Jesus' own understanding of how God rights wrong and deals with evil. Martens's argument would imply that it is Jesus himself who fails to take seriously the evil of his own death!

21.5.3. Re-Reading Revelation

All this is sufficient, I think, to give us serious pause before insisting upon reading Revelation 19 as the fulfillment of divine vengeance by redemptive violence. If Jesus Christ is the One who "judges and makes war" by means of "righteousness *(dikaiosynē)*" (Rev 19:11), then it is by the very justice of God that Jesus himself revealed through his life and death, his teaching and his cross — justice that redeems by grace (Rom 3:21-26). This, then, warrants considering an alternative reading of the text.

First, what is the *weapon* wielded by the rider whose name is "The Word of God" (Rev 19:13)? John writes, "From his mouth comes a sharp sword with which to strike down the nations" (v. 15). Christ "makes war" with the "sword" of his mouth (cf. v. 21). What is this "sword"? At the beginning of Revelation, John sees "one like the Son of Man . . . and from his mouth came a sharp, two-edged sword" (1:13, 16). This image of a "two-edged sword" *(romphaia distomos)* appears elsewhere in Scripture. In the Old Testament, the psalmist envisions Israel executing God's judgment:

> Let the faithful exult in glory; let them sing for joy on their couches. Let the high praises of God be in their throats and two-edged swords (LXX *romphaiai distomai*) in their hands, to execute vengeance on the nations and punishment on the peoples, to bind their kings with fetters and their nobles with chains of iron, to execute on them the judgment decreed. This is glory for all his faithful ones. (Ps 149:5-9)

In the New Testament, the writer uses this image to depict judgment by the divine word: "Indeed, the word of God is living and active, sharper than any two-edged sword *(machairan distomos)* . . . it is able to judge the thoughts and intentions of the heart" (Heb 4:12). The "weapon" by which Jesus "makes war" is thus the "two-edged sword" of God's judgment. That Jesus wields this "sword" signifies that he himself exercises divine authority to execute judgment upon the nations: his judgment is God's vengeance. And Jesus executes "the judgment decreed" according to the word of God — judgment that binds the rebellious powers and so constrains the evildoing of the nations, judgment that penetrates the thoughts and frustrates the plans of the rulers that have rebelled against God (cf. Psalm 2). Jesus thus "will rule [the nations] with a rod of iron" (Rev 19:15; cf. Ps 2:9), exercising kingship and lordship over the kings and lords of the nations, executing divine wrath on those who refuse to submit to God's rule.

The "sword" image here is also reminiscent of God's message through the prophets. Isaiah uses the "sword" image in the second Servant Song: "He made my mouth like a sharp sword *(machairan oxeian),* in the shadow of his hand he hid me; he made me a polished arrow; in his quiver he hid me away" (Isa 49:2). Effectively, the Servant is God's weapon, whom God will wield for his glory. As suggested by the other Servant Songs (cf. 42:4; 50:4), the "sword" of the Servant is his teaching or word, by which he will establish justice and sustain hope. Elsewhere, Isaiah writes of the "branch" of Jesse, whom tradition interpreted as the Messiah and whom the New Testament writers identified with Jesus, using a related image: "He shall not judge by what his eyes see, or decide by what his ears hear; but with righteousness he shall judge the poor, and decide with equity for the meek of the earth; he shall strike the earth with the rod of his mouth, and with the breath of his lips he shall kill the wicked" (11:3b-4). The Messiah will judge the earth on behalf of the poor and oppressed; and he will do so with "the rod of his mouth . . . the breath of his lips." The "weapon" by which the Messiah will "kill the wicked" is thus, again, the word of God's judgment. Similarly, Hosea, of YHWH: "Therefore I have hewn them by the prophets, I have killed them by the words of my mouth, and my judgment goes forth as the light" (Hos 6:5). God has "hewn" and "killed" Israel "by the words of my mouth" spoken "by the prophets."

The "sword" image also recalls the divine warfare against evil depicted by Paul, in which the faithful are enabled to participate by God's power and weaponry, including "the sword of the Spirit *(pneumatos),* which is the word of God" (Eph 6:17). That the "sword" of the rider comes "from his mouth" recalls another text where Paul speaks of God's battle with evil through Christ: "And then the lawless one will be revealed, whom the Lord Jesus will destroy with the breath *(pneumati)* of his mouth" (2 Thess 2:8). Given the close connection between "Spirit" and "breath" (same Greek word, *pneuma*), and given the background of the prophets, this suggests that the "sword" by which the rider "makes war" and executes judgment is none other than the word of God: Christ the incarnate Word of God conquers the enemies of God's kingdom by spiritual warfare and judges the peoples of the nations by the word of God.

Second, who is the *enemy* against whom the rider "makes war"? John writes, "Then I saw the beast and the kings of the earth with their armies gathered to make war against the rider on the horse and against his army" (Rev 19:19). John describes no physical battle, reporting only that "the beast was captured, and with it the false prophet," and that "the rest were killed by the sword of the rider on the horse, the sword that came from his mouth" (vv. 20-21). Now, if the "sword" here is not a literal weapon of carnal warfare, then it is plausible to wonder whether "the kings of the earth" who are "killed by the sword" might not be literal human beings. If Christ "makes war" against God's enemies by spiritual warfare, then "the beast" and "the kings of the earth," one might think, are symbolic of spiritual realities in rebellion against God's will.

The "beast" is a servant of the "dragon." Having fought and lost a war in heaven with the archangel Michael and his angels, the dragon and his angels are consequently thrown down to earth (Rev 12:7-8). John identifies the dragon as "the Devil and Satan" (v. 9). Now upon earth, the dragon sets about persecuting the faithful servants of God. To this end, the dragon gives "his power and his throne and great authority" to the "beast," a many-horned, many-headed being that has risen out of the sea (13:1-2). This beast holds in thrall "the whole earth," and "all the inhabitants of the earth" follow the beast and worship it, proclaiming its praise: "Who is like the beast, and who can fight against it?" (vv. 4, 8). The beast then goes about blaspheming God and making war upon the saints (vv. 5-7).

As the war in heaven of Michael against the dragon and his angels was a spiritual war, so we suggest the war on earth of Christ against the beast and his servants — the "false prophet," who exercises authority on behalf of the beast and enforces the worship of the beast (13:11-15), and the rulers of the nations, over whom the beast has been given authority (v. 7) — is also a spiritual war. Again, we are reminded of Paul's depiction of the spiritual struggle of the faithful as a participation in the divine warfare against evil, in which the real enemies are not human beings: "For our struggle is not against enemies of flesh and blood, but against the rulers, against the authorities, against the cosmic powers of the present darkness, against the spiritual forces of evil in the heavenly places" (Eph 6:12). Given the absence of any physical battle, it would appear that the war in Revelation 19 is spiritual, not carnal: Christ "makes war" by the "sword" of the word of God against the "rulers" and "authorities," the "cosmic powers" and "spiritual forces" that have rebelled against God's kingdom. In this final battle, Jesus binds and defeats these enemies, nullifying their power to do evil, and thereby brings all the enemies of God into subjection under God's rule (cf. 1 Cor 15:24-25).[39]

Recognizing the symbolic dimensions of the biblical text opens up the possibility for, and lends plausibility to, alternative interpretations of the violent imagery of the apocalyptic vision of divine judgment in Revelation 19.[40] At the very least we can say that it is surely not *necessary* to read the final battle and judgment by Christ as depicting literal divine violence against literal human enemies. The symbolism can be interpreted in other ways that are consistent with both the scriptural witness and the orthodox faith.

---

39. Lest the reader misunderstand, I do not intend a Platonist-Gnostic reading of the text that would downplay or ignore material reality in favor of spiritual reality. Rather, I am warning the reader against the all-too-materialistic orientation of a literalist reading. In particular I am concerned that we are in danger of abandoning the biblical worldview, within which evil is *not* identified with material reality (as it is in the Platonist and Gnostic worldviews), when we identify God's enemies with material beings.

40. See, e.g., Swartley, *Covenant of Peace*, pp. 324-55, and McDonald, *God and Violence*, pp. 245-77.

21.5.4. A Nonviolent God?

Nonetheless, we do not presume a "nonviolent God" as some contemporary theologians have done.[41] To the contrary, we have maintained with the biblical witness that vengeance is God's prerogative, and God may exercise that prerogative as God chooses, including by means of violence. God may forgo violence — and, as the Scriptures testify, actually *does* so through the cross of Christ, suffering for the sake of humanity. Yet that is the sovereign *choice* of God acting in Christ for our salvation, not something necessitated by divine nature or cosmic law. Yes, Jesus himself is the "icon" and "character" of God; and, yes, the cross of Christ reveals the justice and wisdom and power of God (Col 1:15; Heb 1:3; Rom 3:21-26; 1 Cor 1:18-25). Jesus Christ, his life and his cross, is the "focal lens" through which we see God and know God's justice; and together these reveal God transcending retribution for the sake of redemption. Nevertheless, the cross is not the *eschaton* and Christology does not exhaust Theology. We must be careful not to reduce the essential being *(ousia)* of God to one person *(hypostasis)* of the Godhead and so undermine a key distinction for Trinitarian orthodoxy. All claims to knowledge of God must conform to the revelation of Christ, but it does not follow that God is reducible to that revelation. God reveals himself as transcending all dichotomous categories of human logic: "I am who I am, I will be who I will be." God is thus neither essentially violent nor essentially nonviolent. God, as Barth rightly reminded us, *is* free.[42]

On the side of a "nonviolent God," there are only two texts as far as I know, found among the Fathers of the early church. In the *Epistle to Diognetus,* we read: ". . . for violence *(bias)* does not belong to God" (7:4, my translation). The context concerns the Incarnation, how God worked through Christ to save humanity by persuasion rather than by compulsion. This same idea is elaborated by Irenaeus:

> And since the apostasy tyrannized over us unjustly, and, though we were by nature the property of the omnipotent God, alienated us contrary to nature, rendering us its own disciples, the Word of God, powerful in all things, and not defective with regard to His own justice, did righteously turn against that apostasy, and redeem from it His own property, not by violent means, as the

---

41. On this, see Swartley, *Covenant of Peace,* pp. 387-91, and Michael Hardin, "Out of the Fog: New Horizons for Atonement Theory," in Brad Jersak and Michael Hardin, eds., *Stricken by God? Nonviolent Identification and the Victory of Christ* (Grand Rapids, MI: Eerdmans Publishing, 2007), pp. 54-76. For a careful critique of the argument for a "nonviolent God" see my essay "Nonviolent God: Critical Analysis of a Contemporary Argument," *Conrad Grebel Review* 29 (2011), 49-70.

42. Karl Barth, *Epistle to the Romans,* trans. Edwyn C. Hoskyns (London: Oxford University Press, 1933), p. 92. Cf. Brueggemann, *Theology of the Old Testament,* pp. 227-28.

[apostasy] had obtained dominion over us at the beginning, when it insatiably snatched away what was not its own, but by means of persuasion, as became a God of counsel, who does not use violent means to obtain what He desires; so that neither should justice be infringed upon, nor the ancient handiwork of God go to destruction. (*Against Heresies* V.1.1)

The idea here is that God voluntarily renounces violence as the means of redemption through the Incarnation out of respect for both the integrity of creation and the freedom of humanity: God does not achieve salvation by divine force. Given that creation and humanity have become subject to an unjust and violent tyranny under the dominion of sin and death, God renounces the means of tyranny — injustice and violence — as inconsistent with accomplishing the redemption of creation and humanity. In Irenaean soteriology, nonviolence is an integral aspect of the Incarnation by which God works redemption.[43] I would argue likewise that God-in-Christ's renunciation of vengeance and violence through the Incarnation is an integral aspect of Christ's *kenosis* for the sake of our redemption by solidarity and interchange: God is "with us" and "for us" — and so not "against us" — in Christ (see Chapter 18 above).

It is more than a simple inference from this idea, however, to the conclusion that the divine nature is essentially nonviolent. From the fact that nonviolence is integral to the Incarnation, therefore, it does not follow that nonviolence is essential to God, that God lacks the capacity for or right to violence. Nor does it follow from the fact that God willed to renounce violence in and through Jesus' life, death, and resurrection for the sake of accomplishing redemption by just means, that God has willed to renounce violence in all things.[44]

I agree with Volf and Swartley, therefore, that the Christian practice of non-retaliation and renunciation of vengeance, far from presupposing faith in a nonviolent God, is premised upon and impossible apart from both recognition of God's prerogative of vengeance and trust in God's providence in exercising that prerogative.[45] "The certainty of God's just judgment at the end of his-

43. Cf. Andrew P. Klager, "Retaining and Reclaiming the Divine: Identification and the Recapitulation of Peace in St. Irenaeus of Lyons' Atonement Narrative," in Jersak and Hardin, *Stricken by God?* pp. 422-80, here pp. 452-69.

44. Thus, Klager, "Retaining and Reclaiming the Divine," concerning Irenaeus: "Where Irenaeus makes an important contribution is with respect to the Incarnate Christ's nonviolence and its implications for the Father's capacity for violence *at the time of the atonement*" (p. 479, emphasis original). This leaves open the Father's capacity for, right to, and will concerning violence "in the end." Indeed, in his "rule of faith," Irenaeus himself expressly expects Jesus to return to execute divine vengeance in final judgment by dispensing the punishment of "everlasting fire" upon "the ungodly, and unrighteous, and wicked" (*Against Heresies* 1.10.1).

45. Volf, *Exclusion and Embrace*, pp. 301-4; Swartley, *Covenant of Peace*, pp. 393-98. This essential connection between the human renunciation of retribution and the divine prerogative for retribution is evident in Paul's argument in Romans 12–13: Christians ought to *both* re-

tory," Volf writes, "is the presupposition for the renunciation of violence in the middle of it."[46] Swartley echoes: "the rationale for constraint in the human role to combat evil is based in God's right to vengeance and judgment."[47] I would add that, insofar as the Christian ethic is patterned after Christ, such Christian renunciation finds its mandate and model in Christ's own renunciation of vengeance in both life and death.[48] In his teaching, Jesus' renunciation of retribution is premised upon faith that God is sovereign over both the righteous and the wicked (Matt 5:38-48). At the cross, Jesus' renunciation of retribution is premised upon faith that God's judgment will vindicate his Servant (Luke 23:46; 1 Pet 2:23). Christian renunciation of retribution thus cannot proceed on a "presumption of nonviolence" any more than did Christ's own renunciation of retribution. The necessary correlate of living faithfully in the face of evil, waiting patiently on God's judgment (Psalm 37), is trust in the God who says, "Vengeance is mine" (Deut 32:35).

21.5.6. Final Judgment: God's Prerogative

Will God execute judgment with retributive violence in the end? John envisions such a final judgment: "And I saw the dead, great and small, standing before the throne, and books were opened. . . . And the dead were judged according to their works, as recorded in the books . . . all were judged according to what they had done" (Rev 20:12-13). Sinners of various sorts, those not found in "the book of life," will be shut out of the city of God and destroyed in "the lake of fire" (20:14-15; 21:8, 27; 22:15). The judgment of Christ, John envisions, effects a violent "final exclusion."

Paul also anticipates a final judgment of retribution: "the day of wrath when God's righteous judgment will be revealed. For he will repay according to each one's deeds. . . . There will be anguish and distress for everyone who does evil . . . but glory and honor and peace for everyone who does good" (Rom 2:5-10). And he envisions Christ himself as executor of God's judgment: "For all of us must appear before the judgment seat of Christ, so that each may receive recompense for what has been done in the body, whether good or evil" (2 Cor

---

nounce retribution and subordinate themselves to "the powers that be," which function as God's servant to execute retribution upon evildoers. Regarding Romans 13, see John Howard Yoder, *The Politics of Jesus: Vicit Agnus Noster* (Grand Rapids, MI: Eerdmans Publishing, 1972), pp. 193-214, and Walter E. Pilgrim, *Uneasy Neighbors: Church and State in the New Testament* (Minneapolis, MN: Fortress Press, 1999), pp. 8-12, 27-35.

46. Volf, *Exclusion and Embrace*, p. 302.

47. Swartley, *Covenant of Peace*, p. 377.

48. Cf. Richard B. Hays, *The Moral Vision of the New Testament: A Contemporary Introduction to New Testament Ethics* (San Francisco: HarperCollins Publishers, 1996), pp. 317-44.

5:10). Indeed, Paul sees the "apocalypse" of Jesus as the dispensing of God's judgment, with Jesus coming "from heaven with his mighty angels" and "inflicting vengeance on those who do not know God and on those who do not obey the gospel of our Lord Jesus" (2 Thess 1:6-8).

Jesus, too, talks of final judgment. In John's Gospel, Jesus identifies himself as the authorized executor of divine retribution:

> The Father judges no one but has given all judgment to the Son. . . . For just as the Father has life in himself, so he has granted the Son also to have life in himself; and he has given him authority to execute judgment, because he is the Son of Man. Do not be astonished at this; for the hour is coming when all who are in their graves will hear his voice and will come out — those who have done good, to the resurrection of life, and those who have done evil, to the resurrection of condemnation. (John 5:22, 26-29)

And in the parable of the sheep and goats Jesus depicts himself ("the Son of Man") as the one sitting on the throne of God's kingdom and judging "all the nations." This parable envisions final judgment as a separation of the peoples, some to reward and some to punishment, according to what they have done, whether they have acted with mercy and justice for "the least of these" or not (Matt 25:31-46).

Yet, as we have seen, Scripture presents us with diverse, contrasting images of divine judgment. Jesus' own parable of the laborers in the vineyard offers a counter-picture of divine judgment that contrasts with that in the parable of sheep and goats, a picture that inverts human thinking framed by the retributive paradigm (Matt 20:1-16). Dispensing wages for work, the central issue of the parable, is a common biblical metaphor for executing judgment: giving recompense to each according to his deeds. The landowner dispenses wages for work, not according to the law of retribution, but according to his own will, which treats all the laborers equally and gives to each, not what he deserves, but what he needs. Jesus concludes this parable by emphasizing divine prerogative, which appears to us as injustice: "'I choose to give to this last the same as I gave to you. Am I not allowed to do what I choose with what belongs to me? Or are you envious because I am generous?' So the last will be first, and the first will be last" (vv. 14-16). Judgment belongs to God, to execute as God chooses, and divine judgment reverses human expectation: those least deserving by human measure ("last") will receive the full "wages" of the kingdom ("first"). Regardless of human expectation and legal calculation of "just deserts," God remains free from beginning to end to be generous and give to all what no one deserves (cf. Ps 103:8-13 and Ezek 20:44).

Paul also does not present a single picture of "the end." Indeed, he presents a counter-picture that contrasts with both John's vision and his own. Instead of the books of heaven being opened and all people being judged by the record of their sins, with the righteous being rewarded and the wicked being punished, as John sees (Rev 20:11-15) and Paul predicts (Rom 2:5-10), Paul also depicts the record of sin in the book of heaven as having been wiped clean, expunged, through the cross of Christ, so that sinners receive life rather than death (Col 2:13-14). Elsewhere, in contrast to John's vision of a "final exclusion," Paul envisions that God's "plan for the fullness of time" is "to gather up all things [in Christ], things in heaven and things on earth (Eph 1:9-10). The key event in God's plan "for the fullness of time," Paul is convinced, has happened already in the cross of Christ: "through [Christ] God was pleased to reconcile to himself all things, whether on earth or in heaven, by making peace through the blood of his cross" (Col 1:20). Rather than a final exclusion executed through the judgment of Christ, Paul here envisions a final gathering of "all things" made possible by the cross of Christ. Rather than the cosmos being put right by the execution of divine violence, Paul here envisions the cosmos being made whole by the very means through which God-in-Christ has suffered violence: the cross.

The orthodox faith confessed by the apostolic church is that Christ "will come again to judge the living and the dead." Will God's coming judgment through Christ be executed with retributive violence? We do not know; the testimony of Scripture gives no single answer to that question. Retributive violence is only one among several depictions of divine judgment in both Old and New Testaments. Both Paul and Jesus present us with contrasting pictures of divine judgment. As we have distinguished between the creedal affirmation that Christ died "for our sake" and the various theories of atonement, so also we distinguish between the definitive creedal affirmation and the various biblical visions of divine judgment. Luke Timothy Johnson comments helpfully in this regard:

> This central and critical conviction can and must be distinguished from the several scenarios offered by the New Testament writings that imagine *how* that future coming and judging will occur. . . . The mystery of God's working in the world remains a mystery, as Paul reminds us, even when it is disclosed (Rom 16:25; 1 Cor 15:51) . . . the variety of scenarios presented by the New Testament itself argues against choosing any one of them as definitive.[49]

When and how God might exercise divine prerogative in final judgment is neither open to human scrutiny nor subject to human determination but is left

---

49. Johnson, *Creed,* pp. 196-97, emphasis original. Johnson, pp. 197-206, surveys several such scenarios and the implications of this plurality of biblical visions for the contemporary church. Even though Johnson appropriately warns us not to make any assumptions about what God's judgment "in the end" must look like, he himself asserts that God's judgment must "balance the scales of this-worldly iniquity and suffering" (p. 206), thus assuming implicitly that divine justice is necessarily and ultimately retributive.

only to God's sovereign choice. Even the Son of God disavowed having knowledge of the day of judgment; that, too, belongs to God the Father alone: "But about that day or hour no one knows, neither the angels in heaven, nor the Son, but only the Father" (Mark 13:32).

Volf, however, is certain that "God's just judgment at the end of history" must necessarily be accomplished by divine violence. Will there be a "final exclusion"? Possibly. If so, will it be violent? Possibly.[50] How John's "final exclusion" in the end fits with Paul's "all things reconciled" in "the fullness of time," however, Volf does not explain. So, again, we ask: if God's first two great acts in cosmic history — creation in the beginning, and redemption through Christ — were nonviolent, why then *must* God's final act in cosmic history — judgment that "puts the world to rights" — be violent?

Knowledge of how and when God might exercise divine prerogative "to repay according to everyone's work" (Rev 22:12b) belongs to the transcendent one alone. To know the recompense of God, we must await what the judgment of Christ reveals in the end: "See I am coming soon; and my reward is with me" (v. 12a). If God *must* execute judgment with retributive violence in the end, then it turns out that not God but the law of retribution is the first and final cause of the cosmos. It is not the law of retribution that is the ultimate reality, however, but God-in-Christ who is "the Alpha and the Omega, the first and the last, the beginning and the end" (v. 13). If it was not necessary for God-the-Alpha to create the world by violence "in the beginning," then it is not necessary for God-the-Omega to redeem the world by violence "in the end" either. Nonetheless, the exercise of violence in the execution of vengeance remains God's prerogative. *Both* the presumption of violence (Volf) and the presumption of nonviolence (Weaver) presume upon God.[51]

What we do know, that which the creed of the church affirms and to which the canon of Scripture witnesses consistently, is that judgment belongs to God: "At the set time that I appoint I will judge with equity . . . it is God who executes judgment, putting down one and lifting up another" (Ps 75:2, 7). Who, and by

---

50. Wright, *Surprised by Hope*, pp. 180-83, imagines a "final exclusion" of recalcitrant sinners that is brought about, not by divine violence, but by human choice. The scenario of "final exclusion," then, need not entail divine violence. That noted, one wonders how even such a nonviolent "final exclusion" as Wright imagines would fit with God's ultimate purpose to redeem and renew "all of creation," which he (correctly) insists is the biblical vision of salvation.

51. The presumption of violence also would seem to limit God's power by foreclosing certain (nonviolent) options to God's will. Volf's view does, I think, come close to compromising the orthodox doctrine of divine omnipotence: in a world beset by violence and lies, God seems to have no option but to exercise violence to do justice, for not even God appears powerful enough to redeem the vicious beasts and false prophets (*Exclusion and Embrace*, pp. 297-300). Again, I agree with Volf that the redemption of the recalcitrant seems beyond imagination, but the necessity of divine violence in final judgment does not follow, for the power of God's justice to save is not limited to the possibilities of human imagination.

what means, will God "put down" and "lift up" in the final judgment? The psalmist is confident that God's judgment will put down the wicked and lift up the righteous (v. 10). Yet he also imagines that God's judgment will redeem both the violent and the oppressed: when judgment is announced from heaven, the weapons of war are destroyed, the armies of the nations are rendered impotent, the oppressed of the earth are saved, and the wrath of humanity is turned to the praise of God (76:3-10). Regarding "the end," therefore, I suggest that we return to "the beginning," to God's self-disclosure at Sinai — "I will be gracious to whom I will be gracious, and will show mercy on whom I will show mercy" (Exod 33:19b) — and pray accordingly, for both ourselves and our enemies, for both victims and perpetrators, that God will be gracious and judge mercifully.[52]

---

52. Consider Paul: "all, both Jews and Greeks, are under the power of sin" (Rom 3:9); "For God has imprisoned all in disobedience so that he may be merciful to all" (11:32). Cf. Wright, *Surprised by Hope*, pp. 183-85.

CHAPTER 22

<hr>

Cosmic Order and Retributive Justice:
The Problem of Evil and the "Law of Nature"

For he makes his sun rise on the evil and on the good,
and sends rain on the righteous and on the unrighteous.

MATTHEW 5:45

22.1. The Common Wisdom

We have seen how the principle of retribution fails to comprehend the grace-rooted, redemption-seeking justice of God revealed through biblical narrative of salvation and the faithful life and death of Jesus Christ. And I have argued that retribution neither essentially characterizes God nor necessarily governs God's relationship with humanity, as witnessed by Scripture. We might still wonder: Is there not a difference between the grace of God and the "law of nature"? God may redeem by grace, but justice is retributive by nature, we are inclined to insist. So, is not retribution the justice discovered by human reason when it reflects objectively on the natural order open to sense observation?

As we have observed, the common human understanding is that justice is based on the law of retribution: each person ought to receive his "just deserts," such that good deserves to be rewarded with good and evil deserves to be punished with evil. In doing justice, therefore, we ought to "pay back in kind," rendering good for good and evil for evil. This common view is buttressed, often unconsciously, by the ancient belief that, because God is both creator and judge of the world, the cosmic order is necessarily a moral order, such that all things are ordered ultimately according to the law of retribution. By God's design, therefore, a universal law of retributive justice is woven into the cause-effect pattern of the cosmic fabric from beginning to end. And this divine design is

434

manifest to human observation and reason whenever the righteous succeed and the wicked fall, or whenever evil deeds return upon the evildoers. The common wisdom is thus that retribution is the "law of nature" — the causal structure of the created order supports the effective functioning of the law of retribution in the course of events.

This retributive worldview is well represented in the book of Proverbs, which maintains the common wisdom that retributive justice is the created order. Thus, the prosperity of the righteous and the suffering of the wicked simply follow the natural ordering of things: "Whoever is steadfast in righteousness will live, but whoever pursues evil will die" (Prov 11:19); "No harm happens to the righteous, but the wicked are filled with trouble" (12:21); "Misfortune pursues sinners, but prosperity rewards the righteous" (13:21). The Bible does not speak with a single voice on this matter, however. As we have observed (Chapter 12), the Psalter affirms that the judgment of God is revealed when evildoing generates its own punishment: "The LORD has made himself known, he has executed judgment; the wicked are snared in the work of their own hands" (Ps 9:16). Yet, the Psalter also acknowledges the universal problem with the common wisdom: "I saw the prosperity of the wicked" (73:3). The psalmist knew well what we know: empirical observation confounds the common wisdom.

We do not, of course, question whether creation has either a causal structure or a moral ordering. The question before us, rather, is whether the God-created natural order is a retributive system.[1] Our aim here is to challenge the common wisdom that retribution is the "natural law" of justice. We will do so in two stages. We consider, first, whether the cosmos exhibits a retributive order in light of the "problem of evil" as presented by the biblical wisdom literature — Job, Ecclesiastes, and the Sermon on the Mount.[2] We will look for how they teach us not only to question the common wisdom of the retributive worldview but also to see the cosmos as confirming the wisdom of the cross — the retribution-transcending justice of God revealed through the cross of Christ. We consider, second, whether human-executed retribution accords with the God-created nature of things. We will examine this from the perspectives of

---

1. We thus affirm the basic premise of natural law ethics, which has sufficient biblical support (cf. Rom 2:14-15). The question here concerns the content of such an ethic.

2. My reading of Job and Ecclesiastes has been helpfully informed by Peter Kreeft, *Three Philosophies of Life* (San Francisco: Ignatius Press, 1989), and Bart D. Ehrman, *God's Problem: How the Bible Fails to Answer Our Most Important Question — Why We Suffer* (New York: HarperOne, 2008), pp. 162-96. Although I do not share Ehrman's personal skepticism and agnosticism, his treatment of the question of suffering in Job and Ecclesiastes does well to bring out the assumptions and implications of these texts. In particular, I share his view that these books function in the biblical canon as a critique of the common wisdom: "like the poetic dialogues of Job, Ecclesiastes is a kind of 'anti-Wisdom' book, in the sense that the insights it gives run contrary to the traditional views of a book like Proverbs, which insists that life is basically meaningful and good, that evil is punished and right behavior rewarded" (p. 189).

two ancient philosophers, Socrates and Lactantius, each of whom argued, contrary to the common view, that retribution does not accord with the nature of things. And we will look for confirmation of this counter-cultural wisdom in empirical evidence from contemporary experience.

22.2. Cosmic Order and the Problem of Evil

22.2.1. *The Perennial Problem*

The retributive worldview sets the stage for the story of Job and all subsequent discussion of the question at hand. The default paradigm for the ancient teller and hearer of this wisdom story is the belief and expectation that God has so ordered the natural course of things that the righteous will prosper for their good deeds and the wicked will suffer for their bad deeds. The observation that, in fact, the righteous are suffering and the wicked are prospering, and thus that the natural order does not appear to favor the righteous over the wicked, therefore, confounds this expectation and gives rise to the perennial questions, "Why do the righteous suffer? Why do the wicked prosper?"

These questions, which define the "problem of evil," generate a double crisis for faith. First, there is an ethical crisis: If the righteous suffer and the wicked prosper, why not join the wicked? If I am not to be rewarded with prosperity for my righteousness, but instead suffer for it, then why should I persevere in righteousness? That is Asaph's crisis: "I was envious of the arrogant; I saw the prosperity of the wicked. . . . All in vain I have kept my heart clean and washed my hands in innocence" (Ps 73:3, 13). And it is to this crisis that David offers the counsel of patience and hope in the just providence of God: "Be still before the LORD, and wait patiently for him; do not fret over those who prosper in their way, over those who carry out evil devices. . . . For the wicked shall be cut off, but those who wait for the LORD shall inherit the land" (37:7-9). The implication is profound: these psalms recognize that the God-created natural order does not necessarily deal out retribution for sin; the faithful are not to rely on nature but rather to wait on God to see the judgment of sinners and the vindication of the righteous.

Second, there is a theological crisis for the faithful. For these questions are effectively complaints against God, accusations that God has failed to be just, that God has failed to uphold the cosmic moral order that he himself ordained in creation — that, in a sense, God has failed to be God. If God has ordained the workings of the world to reward the righteous and punish the wicked, then only God can be to blame when the cosmic moral order goes awry. To ask "Why do the righteous suffer?" or "Why do the wicked prosper?" is thus to question the paradigm that sees the world as governed providentially by a just God according to the law of retribution — and, implicitly, to petition God to vindicate human faith in a retributive order of things.[3]

22.2.2. *Job: God's Ways Are Unjust*

As some readers will be aware, the story of Job is actually two stories preserved in one book. The familiar story of Job, taught in Sunday School and oft-retold in sermons, is found in the "bookends" of the canonical book. In this folk story, Job is a man who stands righteous — "blameless and upright" — before God, who fears God and rejects evil. Job is also very wealthy — "the greatest of all the men of the east" (Job 1:1-3). One day he is accused before God in the court of heaven: he fears God, the Accuser ("Satan") charges, only because God rewards him with wealth; let him suffer and Job will curse God. To test the accusation, God agrees to hand Job over to suffering (vv. 6-12). In the midst of his suffering, Job's friends come to comfort him and sit with him in silence (2:11-13). Despite losing all his property, family, and health at the Accuser's hand, he passes the test of suffering, refusing to curse God. God thus rewards Job's steadfastness, giving back all he has lost, times two. Job then lives a long life and dies a happy man (42:10-17). In this story, Job's suffering has a known cause and a divine purpose: God allows Job to suffer as a test of faith. What is more, and of importance here, Job does not question God's justice on account of his suffering: "In all this Job did not sin or charge God with wrongdoing" (1:22).[4]

It is the "other" story of Job that concerns us, for here both the justice of God and the piety of Job are called into question. This less familiar story is a lengthy poetic dialogue between Job and his friends (ch. 3 through 42:6). Job does not accept suffering with equanimity; in the opening speech of the dialogue he curses the day he was born (ch. 3). And Job's friends do not sit with

---

3. The classic problem of evil is thus quite different from the modern problem of evil. Whereas the latter *questions* belief in the existence of God, the former *assumes* belief in the existence of God; that is, whereas the classic problem presupposes a position of faith, the modern problem presupposes a position of skepticism. Ehrman, *God's Problem*, p. 121, comments (emphasis original): "In modern discourse, the question of theodicy is, How can we possibly believe that an all-powerful and all-loving God exists given the state of the world? In ancient discourse . . . that was never a question. Ancient Jews and Christians never questioned *whether* God existed. They knew he existed. What they wanted to know was how to *understand* God and how to *relate* to him, given the state of the world. The question of whether suffering impedes belief in the existence of God is completely modern, a product of the Enlightenment." This book, like Ehrman's, addresses only the classic problem.

4. Although the folk tale itself does not call God's justice into question, the reader might do so (Ehrman, *God's Problem*, pp. 167-68). Ironically, the Job of the folk story does not question God because, it would seem, he believes in the very God that Ehrman himself derides (cf. Job 1:21; 2:10).

him in silence; they offer him no comfort in his suffering but instead counsel him, "If I were you . . ." (cf. chs. 4–5). Here, the cause of Job's suffering is unknown and its purpose is inscrutable. Such ambiguity opens Job's suffering to interpretation: Who is at fault, Job or God? Job and his friends thus hold court in search of a proper judgment of the matter.

Job and his friends present conflicting cases. The friends question not God's justice but Job's innocence. They accuse him of having sinned and thus judge him as deserving of his suffering; it is not God who is to blame, but Job himself. They assume that he is receiving only his "just deserts" for his sin and thus declare that he must confess his guilt and repent of his ways to put things right and so find favor with God.[5]

Job persists throughout the dialogue in protesting his innocence before both his friends and God and thus maintains his complaint against what he sees as God's injustice: "It is all one; therefore I say, he destroys both the blameless and the wicked. When disaster brings sudden death, he mocks at the calamity of the innocent. The earth is given into the hand of the wicked; he covers the eyes of its judges — if it is not he, who then is it?" (9:22-24). God is unjust, Job complains, because the order of things treats the innocent and the wicked, not according to their deeds, but in the same way. The cosmic order appears indifferent to innocence and guilt, and God alone is responsible for the order of things: "if not he, then who?" Further on in the dialogue, Job strengthens his case by appealing to the strength of the wicked as evidence of the injustice of God: "Why do the wicked live on, reach old age, and grow mighty in power? . . . Their houses are safe from fear, and no rod of God is upon them. . . . They spend their days in prosperity, and in peace they go down to Sheol" (21:7, 9, 13). If God's ordering of things permits the wicked to prosper in life and then die in peace, without fear of punishment from God, then what is the purpose of serving God, Job asks (v. 15). Again he points to the crux of the issue: the natural order that God has created and supervises compounds injustice with injustice, not only allowing the wicked to prosper but also treating the wicked and righteous alike in the end: "One dies in full prosperity, being wholly at ease and secure. . . . Another dies in bitterness of soul, never having tasted of good. They lie down alike in the dust, and the worms cover them" (vv. 23-26).

What Job and his friends share, which none of them questions, is the retributive paradigm, evident in both Job's complaint and his friend's arguments. They presume a divinely created cosmic moral order that rewards good and punishes evil. Thus, Eliphaz: "Think now, who that was innocent ever perished? Or where were the upright ever cut off? As I have seen, those who plow iniquity and sow trouble reap the same" (4:7-8). Job and his friends differ only on the

---

5. Cf. Job 8:5-7; 11:6; 22:4-5. This summary statement, of course, overlooks many nuances in the various speeches.

question of *which party* has contravened the retributive order of things, God (Job's claim) or Job (his friend's claim). Surprisingly, although God rebukes Job for presuming the right to challenge the justice of the creator (chs. 38–41), and although Job falls prostrate before God in humble repentance in response to this rebuke (42:1-6), in the end God vindicates Job and rebukes his friends. YHWH says to Eliphaz, "My wrath is kindled against you and against your two friends; for you have not spoken of me what is right, as my servant Job has" (v. 7).[6]

Notice how remarkable is this outcome: it is Job that has spoken rightly, not his friends; God thus rebukes Job's friends for their speeches in *defense* of God! Their defense of God and judgment of Job was premised upon the assumption that the cosmic order God has created and governs is a retributive system. According to this paradigm, Job's suffering entails one of two possibilities: *either* Job has sinned, in which case Job deserves his suffering and God's justice is vindicated, *or* Job is innocent, in which case Job does not deserve his suffering and God is proven unjust. We thus expect God to affirm one or the other of these alternatives. God's ultimate response, however, affirms *neither* alternative: Job is innocent, as he has insisted, such that he does not deserve his suffering, and yet God's justice is vindicated. Job's friends have *both* judged wrongly of Job *and* spoken wrongly of God. The inference to be drawn here is that the fault lies, neither with Job nor with God, but with the default paradigm within which we understand the ways of God and so frame the problem of evil. The conclusion here thus upsets the retributive paradigm of human thinking about God, the cosmos, and justice: the cosmic order ordained by God is not necessarily a retributive system.

This conclusion carries a profound implication: God's just governance of the cosmos allows innocent human suffering; the story of Job, that is, *affirms* the reality of undeserved (innocent) suffering in the God-created cosmic moral order. Such a conclusion, of course, leaves us without any explanation for Job's

---

6. Whether Job 42:7-9 belongs to the folk story or to the poetic dialogue is uncertain. The view of many commentators is that it belongs to the folk story: it is prose, after all, not poetry. This view generates an anomaly: God rebukes Job's friends because they have spoken wrongly of God (42:7), but in the folk story they weep aloud at Job's plight but do not speak at all (2:11-13). For what misguided speech, then, does God rebuke them? To maintain this view requires postulating, without any supporting evidence and contrary to what the extant text actually says, an unknown, long lost section of the folk story in which the friends have made speeches offensive to God. If we restrict ourselves to the available evidence of the extant text, one might come to a different view. Looking at YHWH's speech in 42:7-8, one sees that it has the discernible poetic form ABB'A': you have spoken wrongly/you will sacrifice/Job will pray/you have spoken wrongly. One also notices that, in calling on Job's friends to offer sacrifice, it echoes the folk story (cf. 1:5). One might thus see 42:7-9 as an editorial splice, joining the end of the poetic dialogue with the continuation of the folk story. In this view, while Job sounds the first word of the poetic dialogue, it is YHWH who gets the last word, which seems appropriate to the outcome.

suffering: the meaning of innocent suffering remains as mysterious as the God who speaks from the whirlwind. Nonetheless, this conclusion does reveal that God's ordering of the cosmos and dealing with humanity transcends human standards of what is reasonable and right and, hence, that God's justice does not necessarily accord with the law of retribution.

In the poetic story of Job, God both rebukes the human presumption of making ultimate judgments *and* overturns the retributive paradigm according to which human wisdom understands the cosmic order. Following Elihu's lengthy speech (chs. 32–37) — in which Elihu charges that Job is deservedly punished for his sin, asserting that Job "opens his mouth in empty talk" and "multiplies words without knowledge" (35:16), YHWH answers from the whirlwind (38:2): "Who is this that darkens counsel by words without knowledge?"[7] It is the retributive paradigm framing Elihu's speech that "darkens counsel by words without knowledge." The retributive paradigm does not reveal the God who is both creator and judge of the cosmos; instead, the retributive paradigm obscures the ways of God's wisdom and justice.

22.2.3. Ecclesiastes: God's Ways Are Unknown

Qoheleth's ruminations on the meaning of human existence are collected in the book of Ecclesiastes.[8] He draws this same conclusion — that the ways of God, as evident to reason through the workings of the world, do not conform to the retributive paradigm — from his observations of what actually happens "under the sun." After musing that nature follows a regular order — "For everything there is a season, and a time for every purpose under heaven . . ." (Eccl 3:1-8) — he makes an observation that confounds this sense that everything is in its proper place: "Moreover I saw under the sun that in the place of justice, wickedness was there, and in the place of righteousness, wickedness was there as well" (v. 16). Not everything is in order: wickedness has displaced justice. Still, despite the evidence, Qoheleth affirms his faith in the retributive paradigm, that God has so ordered things that, though there be a time of injustice, there is a time for judgment: "I said in my heart, God will judge the righteous and the wicked, for he has appointed a time for every matter, and for every work" (v. 17).

Later on, we find Qoheleth going through the same thought process again.

---

7. Some commentators argue that Elihu's speech does not belong to the original dialogue. He is not mentioned in the folk story at least. Nonetheless, his speech shares the same perspective as that of Eliphaz, Bildad, and Zophar.

8. "Qoheleth" is a transliteration of the Hebrew, meaning "speaker." The book begins, "The words of the speaker (*qôheleth*). . . ." The identity of the "speaker" is never revealed. Because he is called "son of David," tradition assigns his identity to Solomon.

He makes further anomalous observations that fail to fit the pattern predicted by the retributive paradigm. This shakes his confidence that retribution is the way of God woven into the workings of things, but he then reaffirms his faith in a retributive cosmic order. At first, he sees in the death of the wicked what might be taken as God's law of retribution at work (8:10a-b). But, as before, there is counter-evidence: "This also is vanity. Because sentence against an evil deed is not executed speedily, the human heart is set to do evil" (vv. 10c-11). Nonetheless, despite the evident delay of just retribution, he remains confident that retribution will prevail because he believes that the cosmos is so designed that it will go well with those who fear God but not with those who do not (vv. 12-13).

Yet a third time Qoheleth observes that the way of things "under the sun" confounds human expectation: "There is a vanity that takes place on earth, that there are righteous people who are treated according to the conduct of the wicked, and there are wicked people who are treated according to the conduct of the righteous. I said that this also is vanity" (8:14). Here we have the complete inversion of retributive justice: the reward due to the righteous is given instead to the wicked, and the punishment due to the wicked is given instead to the righteous. Not only has wickedness displaced righteousness, but the wicked themselves have displaced the righteous in the reckoning of justice. This is the ultimate folly: justice and injustice have exchanged places.[9] At this point, Qoheleth can no longer reasonably accommodate the accumulating anomalies within his retributive paradigm without wondering whether its basic premise might be wrong. Rather than offering reassurance that retribution will prevail, he now counsels us simply to enjoy life during the days God has afforded us "under the sun" (v. 15).

Qoheleth then draws two conclusions from his analysis of the evidence. First, because the workings of the world do not conform to the retributive paradigm, God's ways remain a mystery to human reason:

> When I applied my mind to know wisdom, and to see the business that is done on earth, how one's eyes see sleep neither day nor night, then I saw all the work of God, that no one can find out what is happening under the sun. However much they toil in seeking, they will not find it out; even though those who are wise claim to know, they cannot find it out. (8:16-17)

Qoheleth recognizes the implications of this conclusion: we cannot make sense of God's ways from the workings of the world within the default paradigm of human reason. God's ways, as evident in the created order, are anomalous, fail-

---

9. In Greek philosophy, this scenario of the complete inversion of retribution presents the ultimate test for the philosopher's conviction that, despite all, justice is still the best path of life. See Glaucon's challenge to Socrates in Plato, *Republic* II.

ing to conform to the human expectations of a retributive order of things. Having only the retributive paradigm with which to make sense of how God's ways are evident in the workings of the world, human reason thus inevitably falls into skepticism about the character of God:

> All this I laid to heart, examining it all, how the righteous and the wise and their deeds are in the hand of God; whether it is love or hate one does not know. Everything that confronts them is vanity, since the same fate comes to all, to the righteous and the wicked, to the good and the evil. . . . As are the good, so are the sinners. . . . This is an evil in all that happens under the sun, that the same fate comes to everyone. (9:1-3a)

Second, Qoheleth infers that nature distributes good and evil, reward and punishment, not according to the law of retribution but according to the laws of chance:

> Again I saw that under the sun the race is not to the swift, nor the battle to the strong, nor bread to the wise, nor riches to the intelligent, nor favor to the skillful; but time and chance happen to them all. For no one can anticipate the time of disaster. Like a fish taken in a cruel net, and like birds caught in a snare, so mortals are snared at a time of calamity, when it suddenly falls upon them. (9:11-12)

Qoheleth thus concludes that the cosmos deals alike with the righteous and the wicked, the good and the evil: "time and chance happen to them all." This conclusion reinforces the first, because it undermines the common wisdom that there is a retributive ordering of things ordained and upheld by a just creator. In the face of ambiguous, anomalous evidence, and lacking an alternative to the retributive paradigm, even the wisest person does not know "whether [the hand of God] is love or hate" and the world appears meaningless (1:2; 12:8). Qoheleth, we should observe, does not reject belief in God's existence any more than does Job — indeed, faith in God is the presupposition of the problem! Qoheleth rejects only the beliefs that the ways of God are knowable and, thus, that the world God has created is meaningful.

I think Qoheleth draws the correct conclusion: given that the empirical evidence shows that retribution is *not* the necessary order of things, we cannot maintain faith in a retributive order upheld by a just God. Reconciling faith and reason in the face of the evidence requires logically that we reject at least one of our initial assumptions concerning God and justice. Something here has to give: either God is not just or else God does not order the cosmos by the law of retribution — or, if one thinks that a just God simply *must* order things retributively, then all faith must be abandoned.

Bart Ehrman has chosen the latter option: faced with the facts of suffering in the world, intellectual honesty and personal integrity are incompatible with maintaining faith:

> But what else could I do? What can *you,* or anyone else, do when you're confronted with facts . . . that contradict your faith? I suppose you could discount the facts, say they don't exist, or do your best to ignore them. But what if you are absolutely committed to being true to yourself and to your understanding of the truth? What if you want to approach your belief with intellectual honesty and to act with personal integrity?[10]

I agree with Ehrman that faith must confront the facts. What, though, if we choose to maintain faith along with Job and Qoheleth? Rejecting faith is not the only alternative in facing the facts: one might just as well reject the *human assumption* that frames the problem — that God's just ways and cosmic governance are necessarily retributive. Insofar as our thinking remains conformed to the retributive paradigm — insofar as we maintain the false dichotomy that either the law of retribution is the cosmic law or else God and the world make no sense at all — such a worldview will only continue to obscure the wisdom and ways of God. We need not, however, resign ourselves to either Qoheleth's skepticism about God's ways or Ehrman's agnosticism concerning God's existence. We need, rather, to shift perspective to a retribution-transcending paradigm from which to comprehend God, the cosmos, and human existence.

22.2.4. *Jesus: God's Ways Are Loving and Just to All*

Jesus' teaching takes the anomalous evidence that confounds the retributive paradigm and transforms it into a new paradigm that transcends the common view that God's cosmic governance necessarily follows a retributive pattern. In the Sermon on the Mount, Jesus teaches that the cosmic order confirms what the cross reveals, that God does *not* rule by the law of retribution (Matt 5:38-48). Unlike Qoheleth, however, Jesus does not draw the skeptical conclusion that we cannot know anything about the ways of God. Instead, Jesus teaches us to see the workings of the cosmos as confirming the grace-rooted, enemy-loving, redemption-seeking justice of God that is revealed through the cross. The "hand of God," Jesus teaches, is both loving and just to all — but seeing that it is so requires us to see God's justice as transcending retribution.

Two of the original gifts of God to his creatures are the sun and the rain, and God has bestowed these natural gifts, necessary to life, on all creatures equally. As anyone can readily observe, patterns of sunshine and rainfall do not vary with the righteousness or wickedness of the recipients. True, sunshine and

10. Ehrman, *God's Problem,* p. 126.

rainfall are not distributed equally across the globe; but in any one location the sun shines and the rain falls on everyone the same. And sunshine and rainfall, especially in a subsistence agrarian economy such as that of Jesus' Galilee, are essential elements of human well-being and prosperity. Now, sunshine and rainfall here symbolize all the God-provided necessities of life that the natural order distributes on an equal-opportunity basis regardless of moral qualification. Thus, through the created order of nature, observation tells us, God providentially bestows the goods necessary for human flourishing on everyone the same, making no distinction between who is righteous and who is wicked. We can then draw the inference: if God ruled the cosmos strictly by the law of retribution, then we would reasonably expect the righteous to enjoy an abundance of sunshine and rainfall and the wicked to suffer deprivation of sunshine and rainfall; but that is not what is observed; therefore, God does not rule strictly by the law of retribution. The evidence of the cosmos, therefore, leads us to conclude that God's providential governance transcends retribution; for a strictly retributive cosmic order would lead us to expect to see all (and only) the righteous being rewarded with sun- and rain-generated prosperity and all (and only) the wicked being punished with sun- and rain-deprived suffering, which is not what is observed to happen. Retribution, observation and reason tell us, is not the necessary law of nature.

We hasten to note here, as Qoheleth observed, that the natural order in general does not discriminate between the righteous and the wicked. Nature distributes from its storehouse good and bad to all alike. Floods, earthquakes, hurricanes, tornados, and tsunamis sweep away the righteous along with the unrighteous, despite the pleas of the righteous for rescue from God (Psalm 26). We must add here that the disastrous effects of natural disasters are often aided and abetted by human choices. It is not by the sheer whim of nature alone that the primary victims of Hurricane Katrina in New Orleans in 2005 were black and poor: long before the Lower Ninth Ward was overwhelmed by flood waters, the people living there were victims of racism and neglect, and the levee system that was supposed to protect them was victim of incompetence and indifference.[11] Yet, the human suffering caused by natural disasters cannot be completely accounted for by human sin. Concerning both good and evil, then, biblical wisdom discerns that the natural order is not a strictly retributive system: the order of things that God has ordained in creation does not necessarily recompense us according to our deeds.

---

11. Concerning the human contribution to and responsibility for the evil done by the forces of nature, see Don Howard, "Physics as Theodicy," in Nancey Murphy, Robert Russell, and William Stoeger, S.J., eds., *Physics and Cosmology: Scientific Perspectives on the Problem of Natural Evil* (Vatican City: Vatican Observatory, 2007), pp. 323-32.

22.2.5. The Problem of Suffering and the Ways of God

What, then, are we to conclude? Logically, we have three options: either deny that anyone who suffers is truly righteous, or deny that the natural order has any moral ordering (discernible to human reason, at least), or affirm that God has ordained a natural order that does not conform to the law of retribution.

The first option is that of Job's friends, defended in the patristic period by Augustine: human suffering is divine punishment deserved for sin.[12] That suffering marks the wicked and spares the righteous is the message of Father Paneloux in Albert Camus's novel, *The Plague:* "The just man need have no fear, but the evil doer has good cause to tremble. For plague is the flail of God." The rational difficulty with Augustinian theodicy is obvious: even the newborn baby that suffers and dies from a congenital defect justly deserves its suffering and death — there are no true innocents.[13] As Camus's novel implies, Augustinian theodicy invites us to identify naturally occurring events as divinely appointed agents of judgment upon evildoing. Surely, that is a very human thing to do — as happened after both the tsunami of 2004 and Hurricane Katrina in 2005.[14] Considered in themselves, however, disease and other natural events that cause pain and suffering are indiscriminate, having no correlation with the moral qualifications of their victims. If anything, as noted above, such strike the poor with greater consequence because they lack available protections from the forces of nature due to patterns of injustice and practices of oppression. Unless we are to regress to the view that the poor deserve their poverty and the ills that go with it, Augustinian theodicy is impossible to maintain. The identification of divine judgment in natural events is thus fraught with the danger of self-righteousness, the presumption that "they" deserve their suffering while "we" deserve our comfort.[15]

12. See Augustine, *City of God* XI and XII. For a critique of Augustine's theodicy, see David Ray Griffin, "Augustine and the Denial of Genuine Evil," in Michael L. Peterson, ed., *The Problem of Evil: Selected Readings* (Notre Dame, IN: University of Notre Dame Press, 1992), pp. 197-214.

13. The baby deserves its suffering, Augustine would explain, because it has inherited "original sin" from Adam through its parents: because Adam sinned, all humanity for all time has become a "mass of damnation" (*City of God* XIII.3; *On the Grace of Christ and on Original Sin* II.34). For a summary of Augustine's theory of original sin, see J. N. D. Kelly, *Early Christian Doctrines*, 5th ed. (London: Continuum International Publishing, 2000), pp. 361-66. For a critique of and alternative to Augustine's theory of original sin, see James McClendon, Jr., *Doctrine: Systematic Theology*, vol. 2 (Nashville: Abingdon, 1994), pp. 125-35.

14. Alan Cooperman, "Where Most See a Weather System, Some See Divine Retribution," *Washington Post*, September 4, 2005.

15. I thus share Fiddes's concern with identifying divine punishment in natural events. Cf. Paul S. Fiddes, *Past Event and Present Salvation: The Christian Idea of Atonement* (Louisville: Westminster/John Knox, 1989), p. 93.

The second option is that of Qoheleth: the natural order — and, by inference, the author of that order — is indifferent to suffering and justice, as far as human reason can discern. Qoheleth's skepticism found a modern defender in David Hume. In his *Dialogues Concerning Natural Religion,* the character Philo argues that, given the evidence of nature, skepticism is the most probable — and thus reasonable — position:

> The true conclusion is that the original source of all things is entirely indifferent to all these principles, and has no more regard to good above ill than to heat above cold, or to drought above moisture, or to light above heavy.
>
> There may *four* hypotheses be framed concerning the first causes of the universe: that they are endowed with perfect goodness; that they have perfect malice; that they are opposite and have both goodness and malice; that they have neither goodness nor malice. Mixed phenomena can never prove the two former unmixed principles; and the uniformity and steadiness of general laws seem to oppose the third. The fourth, therefore, seems by far the most probable.[16]

A rational analysis of the evidence, Hume argues, leads to the conclusion that we inhabit a morally indifferent cosmos having its source in a morally indifferent "first cause." It is thus no more reasonable to believe that the sun and the rain are signs of God's love than to believe that pain and suffering are signs of God's punishment.

The third option is that of Jesus, which rejects both the view of Qoheleth and Hume, on the one hand, and the view of Job's friends and Augustine, on the other: God's justice distributes good and evil in nature, neither according to the law of retribution (Job's friends and Augustine), nor according to laws of chance (Qoheleth and Hume), but according to the "law of love" (Matt 5:43-48). Thus, yes, sun and rain are gifts of God's love, dispensed equally upon the righteous and the wicked, but, no, pain and suffering are not necessarily the punishment of God dispensed upon the wicked.[17]

The latter point deserves some discussion. In Jesus' view, human suffering does not necessarily bear divine judgment and, hence, does not necessarily wit-

16. David Hume, *Dialogues Concerning Natural Religion,* ed. Nelson Pike (Indianapolis: Bobbs-Merrill, 1970), Part XI, p. 104, emphasis original.

17. It is important to note here that Jesus does *not* reject the *possibility* that human suffering might bear divine judgment. In Luke 13:1-5, he evidently shares the view that God's judgment upon sin might be dispensed through either human actions or events of nature. But the thrust of his teaching is against self-righteousness: do not suppose that because they died and you were spared that "they were worse sinners" than you. In John 9:1-3, moreover, Jesus *does* explicitly reject the view, held by his disciples, that *all* suffering is divine punishment for sin: the man was born blind, not because of any sin (whether his own or his parents'), but to allow God's glory to be made manifest in his healing.

ness to the sin of the sufferer. To the contrary, suffering may become the blessed way having divine approval — when it results from the faithfulness of the sufferer to God's will in the face of the injustice of the world. In revealing the way of divine wisdom, Jesus teaches that those who endure persecution on earth for the sake of righteousness or on account of loyalty to himself are blessed in the kingdom of heaven (Matt 5:10-11). Peter teaches likewise: far from being the sign of God's judgment, to endure suffering "for doing what is right" or for loyalty to "the name of Christ" receives divine approval (1 Pet 2:20; 3:14; 4:14). Indeed, Jesus says, those who suffer on his account are to "rejoice and be glad, for [their] reward is great in heaven" (Matt 5:12; cf. Jas 1:12; 5:10-11). And, Peter adds, such suffering in the way of righteousness and faithfulness is both an imitation of and a participation in the sufferings of Christ (1 Pet 2:21; 4:13).[18]

The true conclusion is not, as Hume supposes, that the cosmos is morally indifferent, nor, as Augustine supposes, that suffering is divine punishment, but rather that the moral order of the creation is not strictly retributive — and that by design of its creator. The moral order of the creation, according to the personal character of its creator, transcends the law of retribution: God loves both the righteous and the wicked.[19]

---

18. A caveat is in order here: neither Jesus nor Peter says that any and all suffering that Christians endure entails God's blessing and approval. Both are quite specific: suffering *for the sake of righteousness* or *on account of faithfulness* is God-blessed. Such suffering implies both the wholehearted intention to do God's will and the free choice to accept and endure any consequence, however costly, that might ensue from persevering in God's will. That, of course, is how Jesus faced his own suffering and death (Luke 22:42) and how Peter counseled the early Christians to face their own suffering in imitation of Christ (1 Pet 2:19-23; 3:17; 4:19). The suffering that finds God's blessing and approval results from the deliberate decision to "take up one's cross and follow Jesus." When the poor and weak suffer simply because of their external condition of poverty or weakness, therefore, telling them to "rejoice and be glad for great is your reward in heaven" does *not* proclaim a true gospel. To the contrary, to tell the poor and weak that God "blesses" their suffering is blasphemy, for it implies that God approves of the injustice and oppression that causes their suffering.

19. What, then, of those who suffer, not as a result of faithfully pursuing righteousness in the face of injustice, but simply for lack of some good (e.g., food, clothing, housing, or medicine)? If God dispenses good in the world according to the law of love, then does God *not* love them? Ehrman (*God's Problem*, pp. 128-31) quite appropriately raises this question. As he notes (pp. 125-26), this question presupposes that God intervenes in the world to determine the distribution of good and evil. Why, though, should we suppose that the distribution of good and evil in the world is only God's direct doing and is determined solely by God's will? We would argue that God can and does at times intervene in the world to work his will. But God, as sovereign, does not *have* to do so — God is free to allow events to take their course in his creation, and his creatures are free to choose contrary to God's will. The inequitable distribution of food that exists in the world today, for example, letting some feast while leaving others to starve, is an evident evil. But it is due to human sin rather than divine will: there is no natural crisis of land productivity or global shortage of food supply, only a human-designed inequity of food distribution. Of course, as Ehrman points out (pp. 11-13), this response generates another perennial

Here our observation of and reasoning about the cosmos need to be interpreted in light of the revelation of the cross. Such a conclusion, that nature's
workings do not conform to a retributive pattern, makes no sense to human
reason apart from faith in the God who is both creator and redeemer, who
demonstrates through the cross the justice that redeems the cosmos. For when
the "natural" mind looks at the empirical evidence, it sees, not a sign of God's
generous grace to all but an unjust distribution of rewards and punishments,
not a sign of divine justice transcending retribution but the failure of God to be
just. Qoheleth, lacking the light of the cross, could thus make no sense of the
evidence he observed. Insofar as human vision and reason are limited to seeing
and thinking "under the sun," we can get no further than Qoheleth's skepticism
about the ways of God and the meaning of life. Our perception and thinking
need to be reoriented within a cruciform paradigm: contrary to human expectation and moral calculation according to the law of retribution, the cross of
Christ reveals the justice of God by dispensing divine good (righteousness, justification) in exchange for human evil (sin, transgression) (Rom 3:21-26). Indeed, the cross reveals God's justice precisely through Christ's costly demonstration of divine love for "the ungodly" and "sinners" and "enemies" (5:6-10).
Having our perception and thinking reoriented by the cross, then, we can make
sense of what Jesus teaches us to see, that the cosmos confirms God's
retribution-transcending justice, demonstrated through indiscriminate love.[20]

All this makes sense from a broader biblical-theological perspective as well.
For God is both creator and redeemer, such that one should not expect the cosmos and the cross, the orders of "nature" and "grace," to be fundamentally at
odds.[21] Rather, if God's just ways (albeit "higher" than human ways) are consis-

---

question: Why doesn't God intervene to counteract the evil consequences of human choices?
Isn't that what divine love would do? In fact, we believe, God *has* intervened in history, directly
and personally, to confront the evil ways of humanity and counteract the evil forces in the cosmos, by means of the life, death, and resurrection of Jesus Christ, as a demonstration of God's
own love for the world. The historical outcome of this divine intervention may not be to human
satisfaction: all evil has not (yet) been brought to an end. Ehrman takes this "not yet" to be a refutation of faith: not yet, not ever. One might instead take the "not yet" to imply that faith in
God's salvation is impossible without hope, as does Paul (Rom 8:18-25). If we lose hope in the
promise of God to put all things to right, then in the face of the evil of this world the loss of faith
is near at hand.

20. These few comments do not, and are not meant to, resolve the classic problem of evil.
Observing that God's created order is not necessarily retributive does lead us to reject certain
theological interpretations of suffering — e.g., the view that pain and suffering are necessarily
divine punishment for sin. But this still leaves us with the question of the meaning of suffering
in light of the cross. On that see Marilyn M. Adams, "Redemptive Suffering: A Christian Solution to the Problem of Evil," and Kenneth Surin, "Taking Suffering Seriously," in Peterson, *The
Problem of Evil*, pp. 169-87 and 339-49; and Fiddes, *Past Event and Present Salvation*, pp. 207-20.

21. The view here is that because God-in-Christ is both creator and redeemer of the cosmos, what we know of God's ways through the cross can be confirmed by observation of the

tent, one would expect the cosmos to confirm what the cross reveals concerning the justice of God. Because God is consistently both creator and redeemer, therefore, we should expect God's retribution-transcending way of redemption revealed through the cross of Christ to be consistent with the God-created order of nature as viewed through a cruciform lens.[22]

22.3. Human Retribution and Natural Order

We now take up our second question concerning retribution and the "natural law" of justice — whether *human*-executed retribution accords with the God-created nature of things. Once we have recognized that the cosmic order is not governed strictly by the law of retribution, such that retribution is not executed in human affairs as a matter of course, we might nonetheless maintain that justice requires retribution and so regard it as the obligation of human authority to execute retribution where nature "fails" to guarantee "right order." We do what is both right and good, we are wont to think, when we "pay back" evildoing to evildoers; and giving "payback" is right and good, we think further, because that is what accords with "the nature of things." Is that so? Two ancient philosophers, one Greek and pagan (Socrates), the other Roman and Christian (Lactantius), thought it far less than obviously the case precisely for natural law reasons.

---

cosmos through a cruciform lens. We thus maintain that the way of the cross runs with, not against, "the grain of the universe"; cf. Stanley Hauerwas, *With the Grain of the Universe: The Church's Witness and Natural Theology* (Grand Rapids, MI: Brazos Press, 2001). This idea has an ancient precedent: that cross and creation are consistent, not contradictory, is the premise underwriting Athanasius's understanding of redemption by means of the Incarnation (*On the Incarnation* I.1). On the unity of creation and redemption in the Bible, see Fiddes, *Past Event and Present Salvation*, pp. 17-22. Concerning the relation between creation, redemption, and Christology, see Alister E. McGrath, *A Scientific Theology*, vol. 1: *Nature* (Grand Rapids, MI: Eerdmans Publishing 2001), pp. 185-91.

22. Now, in holding that creation and cross are consistent, not contradictory, because both creation and redemption are the work of the same Christ, we neither suppose nor suggest that non retaliatory love, manifest through the cross, can be derived from a scientific study of creation. Indeed, in the fallen state of things, in which violence and injustice appear the norm, it is not possible to infer the gospel ethic inductively from empirical evidence. It is thus only when creation is studied theologically, when it is viewed from the cross, that the consistency of cross and creation becomes evident: what we know of God's ways through the cross can be confirmed by observation of the cosmos through a cruciform lens. How can this be despite the fall? As the patristic theologians maintained, evil is not primordial but parasitic, a corruption of creation; the original good of the created order has not been destroyed by evil but awaits redemption from decay and death (Rom 8:18-25). Thus, although at present the way of the cross conflicts with the fallen powers of the cosmos, we expect an eschatological convergence of cross and cosmos in Christ, through whom and for whom all things were created (Col 1:15-20), a convergence we can glimpse even now from the vantage point of the cross.

22.3.1. Socrates: Retribution Harms the Human Soul

In Athens around 400 BC, Socrates made a natural law argument against taking retribution upon one's enemies. Essentially, Socrates argues that retribution harms the soul, and whatever is harmful to the soul is contrary to both nature and justice. His argument is found in Plato's *Republic* and *Crito*.

In the opening book of the *Republic*, Socrates is engaged in a dialogue on the nature of justice, and the first to put a definition of justice to the test is Polemarchus.[23] He claims that to do justice is to "pay one's debts," a variation on the classic formula that justice is "giving each his due." After some questioning by Socrates to clarify what he means, Polemarchus restates his definition in line with the popular version of retribution: justice means doing good to friends and harm to enemies. After further critical questioning, Polemarchus refines his formulation of retribution: "it is just to benefit the friend if he is good and harm the enemy if he is bad."

Socrates then brings the conversation to the crucial issue, which is not a matter of definition but concerns the substance of justice: "Is it then the part of a good man to harm anybody whatsoever?" Socrates here calls into question the unexamined assumption that retribution, returning harm for harm, belongs to justice in the first place. Polemarchus unhesitatingly defends the common view: "Certainly it is. A man ought to harm those who are bad and his enemies."[24] What follows is a page or so of typically Socratic, analogical argument, the basis of which is the notion that justice by nature serves the human good or promotes human flourishing, and hence that whatever is to be called justice must improve the condition of the human soul *(psychē)*. The gist of the argument, then, is that being injured — even if "deserved," in return for injury done — makes worse the condition of the soul of the one to whom retribution is done. Therefore, Socrates concludes, because retribution is contrary to what is good for the soul, making the offender worse as a human being, it is contrary to justice.

> If, then, anyone affirms that it is just to render to each his due and he means by this that injury and harm is what is due to enemies from the just man and benefits to his friends, he was no truly wise man who said it. For what he meant is not true. For it has been made clear to us that *in no case is it just to harm anyone.*[25]

Socrates makes a parallel argument in his dialogue with long-time friend Crito concerning whether Socrates ought to escape from prison to avoid his

23. Socrates' dialogue with Polemarchus on justice is found in book I of the *Republic*, 331d-36a.

24. *Republic* 335a-b, Paul Shorey's translation in Edith Hamilton and Huntington Cairns, eds., *The Collected Dialogues of Plato* (Princeton, NJ: Princeton University Press, 1961).

25. *Republic* 335e, emphasis added.

impending execution. In the course of the conversation, he gets Crito to agree that they should stick to the (unpopular) principle they have always followed — that "in no circumstance must one do wrong . . . one must not even return injustice when one is wronged, which most people regard as the natural course." After further exchange, he restates his conviction, contrary to the common notion that retribution is the natural law of justice: "So one ought not to return an injustice or an injury to any person, whatever the provocation. . . . I know that there are and always will be few people who think like this. . . ."[27] With his own life in the balance, Socrates remains convinced that retribution is wrong. Again, he gives a natural law argument: justice serves the natural good of the soul, "which is impaired by unjust actions and benefited by just ones." Life with a soul ruined by unjust deeds is not worth living, for "the really important thing is not to live, but to live well."[28] Acting with retribution is thus harmful to one's own soul, ruinous of even the one who returns harm for harm in order to right a wrong. Justice improves the condition of the soul, making the justice-doer better as a human being; but by returning injury for injury, you bring ruin to your own soul. Socrates thus affirms categorically: "it is never right to commit injustice or return injustice or defend one's self against injury by retaliation."[29]

Putting the arguments from *Republic* and *Crito* together, we have Socrates' full view. Justice, rendering "what is due," as a cardinal virtue of the human soul, accords with human nature and thus serves the human good: both the one doing justice and the one to whom justice is done are made thereby better as human beings. Retribution — repaying harm for harm or returning injury for injury — harms the souls of *both* the executor and recipient of retribution, however. Retribution thus only multiplies the original injury, making both parties worse as human beings. So, retribution is unjust, because it is contrary to nature — contrary to what improves the human soul and so what promotes human flourishing. Retribution, therefore, is not the natural law of justice. Socrates thus did not reject outright the formula that justice is to "give each his due," but he did critique and reject the conventional understanding of that formula that sanctioned returning harm for harm. Nonetheless, we should note, this view of Socrates does allow for the possibility that just punishment, exclusive of retribution, could serve the improvement of the soul.[30] We will return to that idea when considering positive alternatives to retributive justice.

27. Plato, *Crito* 49b-d, Hugh Tredennick and Harold Tarrant's translation in *The Last Days of Socrates* (New York: Penguin, 1993).

28. *Crito* 47d, 48b. Similarly, before the jury which had just sentenced him to death, Socrates said (*Apology*, 39a): "the difficulty is not so much to escape death; the real difficulty is to escape from wickedness [i.e., wrongdoing, injustice], which is far more fleet of foot."

29. *Crito* 49d.

30. In Plato's *Gorgias,* one finds Socrates presenting an argument that retribution, when

22.4.2. Lactantius: Retribution against Humans
Fails to Render Due to God

Lactantius was a Roman philosopher who converted to Christianity around AD
300. In his *Divine Institutes*, he developed, from a theological perspective, a natural law argument against retributive violence, including capital punishment
and war. As did Socrates, Lactantius works from the classical formula that justice is to "render what is due," but interprets it from the perspective of biblical
revelation. He also shares with Socrates the natural law view that actions appropriate to human nature do no injury to anyone. The basis of Lactantius's argument is the biblical understanding of human nature: because humankind is
created in the image of God, the "due" one renders to other human beings is
also rendered to God; whatever one does to God's image, one does also to God.
So, "the first office of justice is to be united with God, the second with man."
What we owe to others, therefore, must comport with what we owe to God,

---

imposed justly upon the wrongdoer as punishment for his wrongdoing, improves the soul by
removing the badness from it (476-80). That argument would seem at odds with the preceding
argument of the same dialogue, however. For Socrates has just argued, on the premise that the
evil of wrongdoing (injustice) consists in the pain or harm that is inflicted upon the soul
(along lines parallel to that of *Republic* and *Crito*), that not only is the one who suffers wrong
(injustice) worse off for it, but the one who does wrong (injustice) suffers the greater evil (474-
75). Yet Socrates goes on to argue that retributive punishment can improve the soul of the
wrongdoer. Socrates must thus argue either that retribution does not involve inflicting pain, or
that the pain of just punishment is not harmful to the soul. The former being contrary to the
truth, Socrates argues the latter by way of an analogy between justice and medicine, the judge
and the physician: as the physician applies the cure of medicine to the body, so the judge applies the cure of punishment to the soul: "to be punished is to be cured of the worst of all ail-
ments, wickedness. . . . Because justice is a moral physician" (478). The analogy fails, however,
precisely at the point it is supposed to support the claim that the pain of punishment cures
wickedness in the soul: while medical cures do (sometimes) cause pain, it is not the pain itself
that cures but the medicine; unlike the pain of retributive punishment, which is intended as
payback to the wrongdoer, the pain of medicine is an unintended and undesirable side effect
of the intended and desired cure. Hence the argument that retributive punishment restores the
health of the soul is suspect. I thus take the previous argument in *Gorgias*, which squares with
the arguments from *Republic* and *Crito*, as the trustworthy presentation of Socrates' view. And
those arguments, taken together, would allow that just punishment could serve the improvement of the soul, provided that it does not involve retribution, repaying harm for harm. (Why
does Plato put a bad argument into the mouth of Socrates? Irony, I think. The theme of
Gorgias is "On Oratory," and Socrates uses the above arguments to best the professional orator
Polus. That Polus is convinced by such a poor analogy confirms, ironically, that oratory without reasoning is of dubious value. As Socrates says to Polus at the beginning of the argument,
"while I thought you admirably well-trained in oratory you seemed to me to have neglected
the art of reasoning" [471]. Indeed, by his neglect of reasoning, Polus is convinced by Socrates'
oratory.) Citations from Plato, *Gorgias*, trans. Walter Hamilton (London: Penguin Books,
1960).

which is worship: we ought not to act toward others in any way contrary to our duty of worship toward God.[31]

It follows that doing justice, rendering "what is due" to others, can*not* be *in*compatible with offering worship to God. The implication is evident: it is unjust (i.e., we ought not) to injure or destroy our fellow human beings by any means or for any reason, for to do so is to harm or destroy the image of the God to whom we owe worship. Retributive violence — rendering "due" by returning injury for injury — thus violates our duty to worship the God in whose image human beings are created. Because such retribution is contrary to nature, Lactantius holds that the true natural law, "the principle of common life," is not retribution but "mercy or kindness." Lactantius thus sums up the natural law as known from the theological perspective of biblical revelation: "On account of this relationship of brotherhood, God teaches us never to do evil, but always good. And he also prescribes in what this doing good consists: in affording aid to those who are oppressed and in difficulty, and in bestowing food on those who are destitute." He thus concludes: "Therefore, if it is contrary to nature to injure a man, it must be in accordance with nature to benefit a man; and he who does not do this deprives himself of the title of a man, because it is the duty of humanity to succour the necessity and peril of man."[32] The natural law is not retribution, to repay evil with evil, but beneficence, to do good to all.

For millennia it has been taken as evident by the majority of philosophers, ethicists, theologians, and scientists that human reason, reflecting objectively on empirical evidence, discovers in nature a moral order that accords with the law of retribution. From Aristotle to Aquinas and until today, this "natural law" tradition has maintained that retribution defines justice as evident in the nature of things; retributive justice, therefore, because it accords with nature, promotes human well-being and civil peace. The majority Christian tradition since Augustine has appealed to the Greco-Roman (Aristotelian-Ciceronian) natural law of retributive justice to underwrite practices of retributive violence, namely, just war and capital punishment. And this same tradition has assumed that God is the ultimate guarantor of this natural law of retributive justice.

Now, however, our inquiry into ancient wisdom — from Job to Qoheleth to Jesus and from Socrates to Lactantius — calls into question the majority tradition that retribution is the law of nature. Is retribution woven into the cosmic fabric? Drawing from personal experience and empirical observation, and aided by a "whirlwind" theophany, Job and Qoheleth each answer No. Jesus affirms this view but goes beyond skepticism about the nature of things and the

31. Similarly, Jas 3:9-10 argues that our speech toward fellow humans should comport with our worship of God, in whose image humans are made.

32. Lactantius, *The Divine Institutes*, book VI ("Of True Worship"), chapters X–XI, in Philip Schaff, *The Ante-Nicene Fathers*, vol. 7: *Fathers of the Third and Fourth Centuries* (Grand Rapids, MI: Christian Classics Ethereal Library, 2004), pp. 282-87.

ways of God, teaching us by light of the cross to see at work in the created order of the cosmos the retribution-transcending justice of God. Does retribution accord with what promotes human flourishing? Socrates answers No because paying back in kind, harm for harm, harms the souls of both the one giving and the one receiving retribution. Retribution only multiplies the original injury. Lactantius takes the argument further, arguing that retribution fails to accord with the nature of things, and so does not promote human flourishing, precisely because it is contrary to our creaturely nature. We cannot duly worship God our creator and deal out retribution against our neighbor who also is created in the image of the God whom we worship.

22.3.3. Empirical Confirmation of Ancient Wisdom

The philosophical view of Socrates that retribution is contrary to nature because it is counter to human flourishing is open to empirical confirmation. Not only is it not obvious that retribution is the natural law, but we can find evidence — in social relations and human psychology — that retribution does not accord with the created nature of things.[33] Let us consider Socrates' view in the context of criminal punishment. His point seems to have been that, instead of nurturing what is best in human beings (rationality), retribution tends to bring out the worst (the "passions").[34] When we are injured, even if in return for an injury, we tend to respond, not rationally, but instead "from the gut": the instinctive response to an inflicted injury is to become angry and desire to give back the pain. This view, that retribution does not serve human psychological health well, is corroborated by the evidence of our contemporary penal system.[35]

Consider the offender. Receiving retribution for a crime committed, even if "justified" or "deserved," does not tend to bring an offender to his senses such

33. Nancey Murphy and George F. R. Ellis, *On the Moral Nature of the Universe: Theology, Cosmology, and Ethics* (Minneapolis, MN: Fortress Press, 1996), argue that the physical sciences of cosmology and physics confirm a non-retributive, nonviolent natural order compatible with the cross.

34. Socrates' argument thus implicitly assumes that rationality is the better part of human nature and that the "passions" are the basest part of human nature. This assumption, shared by all the major schools of Greek philosophy — Platonism, Aristotelianism, Stoicism, and Epicureanism — and by the majority of philosophical schools of thought through the centuries, might be challenged in the contemporary context. However, this is an assumption common to all natural law philosophical perspectives and thus would not be questioned by any philosopher arguing that retribution is the natural law of justice. So Socrates' argument does not beg the question here.

35. Cf. Howard Zehr, *Changing Lenses: A New Focus for Crime and Justice*, 3rd ed. (Scottdale, PA: Herald Press, 2005), pp. 19-59; and T. Richard Snyder, *The Protestant Ethic and the Spirit of Punishment* (Grand Rapids, MI: Eerdmans Publishing, 2001), pp. 126-57.

that he recognizes his wrong and realizes his guilt; much less does retribution call the offender to repentance and change of life. Instead, experiencing retribution tends to nurture a sense of having been injured on the part of the offender — and, hence, hostility toward society and its norms. This sense of victimization is often multiplied by the brutality the offender experiences at the hands of guards or other inmates. Retribution thus tends to perpetuate harm. Those who are "paid back" their crime and thus "pay back" their "debt to society" by serving prison sentences are rarely made thereby better persons, much less more responsible citizens:

> The entire prison setting is structured to dehumanize. The prisoners are given numbers, standardized clothing, and little or no personal space. They are denied almost all possibilities for personal decision and power. Indeed, the focus of the entire setting is on obedience, on learning to take orders. In that situation, a person has few choices. He or she can learn to obey, to be submissive. This is the response the prison system encourages, yet it is the response least likely to encourage a successful transition to free society. Our offender got into trouble because of his inability to be self-governing, to take charge of his own life in a legitimate way. Prison will further deprive him of that ability. Thus it should not be surprising that those who conform to prison rules best are *not* those who make the most successful transition in the community after prison.[36]

Moreover, many incarcerated for nonviolent offenses learn the ways of violence from their imprisonment and go on to commit further crimes that are even more costly to society. Imprisoned offenders "learn that conflict is normal, that violence is the great problem solver, that one must be violent in order to survive. That is, after all, normal in the distorted world of the prison."[37] Some ex-offenders even commit further crimes in order to go back to prison because they cannot adjust to survival "on the outside."

Consider also the situation of the victim. A victim's desire to seek retribution against an offender tends to feed from, and thus may in turn nurture, the "passions" — anger, hatred, fear, humiliation, shame, bitterness, etc. — aroused by the original injury. Human psychology tells us that a victim who out of anger has desired retribution against an offender cannot automatically release that anger once the offender is sentenced and imprisoned. By sustaining a desire for retribution, the victim might also become imprisoned by the crime, chained to the "passions" it has aroused. A victim whose offender does suffer retribution from the penal system may nonetheless remain afraid of that person and may even project that fear into other relationships and situations.

36. Zehr, *Changing Lenses,* p. 37.
37. Zehr, *Changing Lenses,* p. 35.

Moreover, many victims continue to carry the humiliating and inhibiting stigma of victimization long after the offense is committed and the offender is imprisoned:

> Many victims of crime find themselves as isolated as the prisoners. The bars behind which they live are invisible but just as strong as those holding the criminals, making escape difficult or impossible. Often feelings of shame accompany the trauma of victimization, especially for sexual crimes. Guilt, fear, and rage are common experiences for the victimized. Victims find it difficult and sometimes impossible, in their day-to-day relationships, to deal with their feelings openly and in ways that could contribute to release and healing.[38]

Inflicting pain on the offender does nothing to help heal such wounds suffered by the victim, much less restore the victim to psychological health. In his article telling of experiences of members of the support group Parents of Murdered Children, journalist Eric Schlosser finds that the retribution-based criminal justice system does not serve well those on behalf of whom punishment is executed:

> After a natural death the family of the deceased can begin the process of mourning. After a murder the criminal-justice system usually delays and disrupts the grieving of the victim's loved ones. If the murderer is never found, the death lacks a sense of closure; if the murderer is apprehended, the victim's family may face years of legal proceedings and a resolution that is disappointing. Insufficient evidence may lead the prosecution to drop the charges or to reduce them from murder to manslaughter. Co-defendants may be given a lesser punishment, despite a role in the murder, in order to obtain their cooperation. Each new hearing may stir up feelings that were seemingly laid to rest. "You never bury a loved one who's been murdered," one survivor has explained, "because the justice system keeps digging them up." The sense of powerlessness the murder inspires in a victim's family is frequently reinforced by the courts. When the victim's family is barred from the courtroom during a trial (while the murderer's family is allowed to attend, looking somber and well dressed), it seems that the murderer still has the upper hand, still exerts more power. Even when a trial ends in a verdict of guilty and a sentence that seems appropriate, the family of a murder victim may be left with a hollow feeling. They may realize for the first time that no amount of punishment given to the murderer can relieve their sorrow or bring the victim back to life.[39]

---

38. Snyder, *Protestant Ethic*, p. 133.

39. Eric Schlosser, "A Grief Like No Other," *The Atlantic Monthly*, September 1997, pp. 37-76, here p. 52.

It is often argued that capital punishment, the only just retribution (i.e., penal equivalent) for murder, provides essential goods that families of murder victims need and deserve — satisfaction of the desire for vengeance, release from fear of the one who murdered their loved one, relief from the ongoing trial through which they are put by the court system, and closure on the pain and grief of their loss. Rachel King, who teaches at Howard Law School, reports from her decade of research that the families of *both* murder victims and defendants are adversely affected by the death penalty:

> There are many ways in which the death penalty harms families. For the murder victims' family members, the death penalty establishes a hierarchy of victims where some lives are valued more than others. It turns family members against each other. It creates a class of "good" victims and "bad" victims. The families of the condemned are traumatized by the process and feel ostracized and alienated as they watch their government systematically prepare to kill their loved one. They feel as if their entire community has turned against them.[40]

As for the claim that murder victims' families need the execution of their loved one's murderer in order to heal, King's research finds no supporting evidence:

> One of the primary justifications for capital punishment is that the victims need it to heal. Executions are held out as a talisman that will provide the victim with closure. This belief serves, in large part, as the rationale for state-sanctioned killing. However, this belief is completely unsubstantiated. There is no data or research that suggests that executions help people heal. There is significant anecdotal evidence that the opposite may be true. Until research establishes that executions have some healing property, let's not pretend that we are killing people on behalf of the victims. Some victims support the death penalty; many do not.[41]

The experience of one murder victim's family member, Jeanne Bishop, a Cook County, Illinois public defender who opposes the death penalty, corroborates King's research:

> "Closure," a neatly wrapped-up end to the horror and grief of murder, simply doesn't exist — nor perhaps should it. The most blatant perpetrators of this lie are death penalty proponents who promise executions that bring psychological resolution, even peace, to family members on a specific date. It doesn't happen this way. Grief, the culmination of sweet memories and the bitter loss of possibilities, lives on — and it should. The grief I felt after my

40. Rachel King, "The Impact of Capital Punishment on Families of Defendants and Murder Victims' Family Members," *Judicature* 89/5 (March-April 2006), 292-96, here p. 292.

41. King, "Impact of Capital Punishment," p. 296.

sister's murder is not closed. It lives in me today, but differently. At first it was a grief that numbed, that paralyzed. Now it is a grief that energizes me to love more passionately, to share more generously, to live more fearlessly, to work to prevent the violence which could inflict on another family the suffering mine has endured. . . . The memories of Nancy's life and death, painful as they are, also bring tremendous joy. Why would I "close" that, even if I could? The notion that killing another human being, no matter how despicable his act, could somehow honor this grief, even heal it, is a lie.[42]

This evidence confirms Socrates' view that, at least in contemporary penal practice, retribution neither improves the condition of the human soul nor promotes human flourishing, either for those to whom retribution is done or for those on behalf of whom retribution is done.[43] Not only do these retributive practices not improve human well-being, but active participants in retributive violence are often themselves harmed psychologically. Those who perpetrate killing in wars or executions often suffer post-traumatic stress disorder, the same as or worse than the passive victims of wars, crimes, and disasters.[44] The one who executes retributive violence — even legally justified, state-sanctioned

42. Jeanne Bishop, "Grief, Closure, and Forgiveness," available online at http://features.pewforum.org/death-penalty/reader/27.html. The personal perspectives of murder victims' family members opposed to the death penalty are collected in Susannah Sheffer, ed., *Not in Our Name: Murder Victims' Families Speak Out Against the Death Penalty*, 4th ed. (Cambridge, MA: Murder Victims' Families for Reconciliation, 2003). See also Rachel King, *Don't Kill in Our Names: Families of Murder Victims Speak Out against the Death Penalty* (New Brunswick, NJ: Rutgers University Press, 2003). Robert Renny Cushing and Susannah Sheffer, *Dignity Denied: The Experience of Murder Victims' Family Members Who Oppose the Death Penalty* (Cambridge, MA: Murder Victims' Families for Reconciliation, 2002), describes how a criminal justice system bent on executing murderers is systematically biased against murder victims' family members who oppose the death penalty.

43. I am not denying the possibility of redemptive suffering, that one might learn or be transformed through one's suffering. After all, Jesus himself was "made perfect" through suffering (Heb 2:10). But the coercive suffering imposed on offenders by the penal system does not fit the pattern of redemptive suffering as displayed, for example, in the life and writing of Martin Luther King, Jr., suffering that is inevitably incurred in pursuit of the just end that one wills, suffering that is willingly endured out of love for one's enemy. Even such suffering we do not wish for others nor pray to receive. Iris Murdoch: "The kind of suffering which brings wisdom cannot be named and cannot without blasphemy be prayed for" (quoted in Timothy Gorringe, *God's Just Vengeance: Crime, Violence and the Rhetoric of Salvation* [Cambridge: Cambridge University Press, 1996], p. 241). It is of such suffering that Robert F. Kennedy spoke in personal terms on the night King was assassinated, quoting the Greek dramatist Aeschylus: "God, whose law it is that he who learns must suffer. And even in our sleep pain that cannot forget falls drop by drop upon the heart, and in our own despair, against our will, comes wisdom to us by the awful grace of God" (Maxwell Taylor Kennedy, *Make Gentle the Life of This World: The Vision of Robert F. Kennedy* [New York: Broadway Books, 1998], p. 147).

44. Rachel M. MacNair, *Perpetration-Induced Traumatic Stress: The Psychological Consequences of Killing* (Santa Barbara, CA: Praeger Publishers, 2002).

retribution — against others does harm thereby to the health of his own psyche. This evidence thus confounds rather than confirms the common view that retribution is the "natural law" of justice.[45]

In addition to such negative evidence, one can also look to community-based, retribution-transcending approaches to criminal justice for positive evidence that retribution is not necessary to a well-functioning criminal justice system — and, hence, that retribution is not essential to a rational, empirically confirmed conception of the nature of things. Recognizing, as noted above, that Socrates' argument allows that just punishment (excluding retribution) could serve the improvement of the soul, one might then consider the possibilities for "restorative punishment."[46] "Restorative justice" alternatives — for example, the Victim-Offender Reconciliation Program pioneered in the 1970s by Mennonite Central Committee in Kitchener, Ontario, and Elkhart, Indiana — seek to serve the needs of both victims and offenders in ways that the penal system systematically fails to do (as noted above).[47] The success of these programs thus shows that society can go beyond retribution and still deal seriously and effectively with crime in ways that hold offenders accountable and promote the psychological health of victims and offenders as well as peaceable relations among victims, offenders, and community.[48]

45. The negative relationship between vengeance or vengefulness and psychological health has also been studied scientifically in various contexts. See Renate Ysseldyk, Kimberly Matheson, and Hymie Anisman, "Rumination: Bridging a Gap between Forgivingness, Vengefulness, and Psychological Health," *Personality and Individual Differences* 42/8 (June 2007), 1573-84; Ryan P. Brown, "Vengeance Is Mine: Narcissism, Vengeance, and the Tendency to Forgive," *Journal of Research in Personality* 38 (2004) 576-84; Alean Al-Krenawi, Vered Slonim-Nevo, Yaniv Maymon, and Salem Al-Krenawi, "Psychological Responses to Blood Vengeance among Arab Adolescents," *Child Abuse and Neglect* 25/4 (April 2001), 457-72; Jennifer Sommers and Stephen J. Vodanovich, "Vengeance Scores among College Students: Examining the Role of Jealousy and Forgiveness," *Education,* Fall 2000. These scientific studies were located online by a Google search using "vengeance + psychological health."

46. Christopher D. Marshall, *Beyond Retribution: A New Testament Vision for Justice, Crime, and Punishment* (Grand Rapids, MI: Eerdmans Publishing, 2001), pp. 131-40.

47. Zehr, *Changing Lenses,* pp. 158-74, describes the early experiments with Victim-Offender Reconciliation Programs in Canada and the U.S. See also Howard Zehr, *Justice: The Restorative Justice Vision* (Akron, PA: Mennonite Central Committee U.S. Office of Criminal Justice, 1989); idem, *Mediating the Victim/Offender Conflict: The Victim-Offender Reconciliation Program* (Akron, PA: Mennonite Central Committee U.S., 1990). Snyder, *Protestant Ethic,* pp. 74-100, and Gorringe, *God's Just Vengeance,* pp. 251-65, survey various community-based justice alternatives in theory and practice.

48. In addition to evidence from the criminal justice arena, the positive relationship between forgiveness and psychological health has also been studied scientifically. See G. Bono, M. E. Mccullough, and L. M. Root, "Forgiveness, Feeling Connected to Others, and Well-Being: Two Longitudinal Studies," *Personality and Social Psychology Bulletin* 34/2 (2008), 182-95; Kathleen Lawler, Jarred Younger, Rachel Piferi, Rebecca Jobe, Kimberley Edmondson, and Warren Jones, "The Unique Effects of Forgiveness on Health: An Exploration of Pathways," *Journal*

What all these arguments and evidence show, I think, is that whether human reason determines retribution to be the law of nature or not turns crucially upon our prior perception of nature. This suggests to me that, instead of discovering retribution in nature by objective observation and rational reflection, we have read our retributive way of thinking and acting into the nature of things. That is, our observations of nature regarding justice are "theory-laden": reason has "discovered" the "natural law" of retribution because retribution is what we have expected to see in nature. Seeing the cosmos instead through a cruciform lens enables us both to resolve anomalies generated by the retributive paradigm and to see new things in the world that our old paradigm obscured from view.[49] A cruciform paradigm also enables us to develop a coherent Christian worldview in which cosmos and cross reflect consistently a God who is consistently both creator and redeemer. A cruciform paradigm, moreover, enables us to envision and implement retribution-transcending practical alternatives for doing justice that hold out potential for remedying failures in the contemporary penal system.

of Behavioral Medicine 28/2 (April 2005), 157-67; John Maltby, Liza Day, and Louise Barber, "Forgiveness and Mental Health Variables: Interpreting the Relationship Using an Adaptational-Continuum Model of Personality and Coping," Personality and Individual Differences 37/8 (December 2004), 1629-41; C. V. O. Witvliet, T. E. Ludwig, and K. L. Vander Laan, "Granting Forgiveness or Harboring Grudges: Implications for Emotion, Physiology, and Health," Psychological Science 12 (2001), 117-23; M. E. McCullough, "Forgiveness as Human Strength: Theory, Measurement, and Links to Well-Being," Journal of Social and Clinical Psychology 19 (2000), 43-55; M. E. McCullough, K. Rachal, S. J. Sandage, E. L. Worthington, S. W. Brown, and T. L. Hight, "Interpersonal Forgiving in Close Relationships II: Theoretical Elaboration and Measurement," Journal of Personality and Social Psychology 75 (1998), 1586-1603. These scientific studies were located online by a Google search using "forgiveness + psychological health."

49. Although, as we argued above, discovering the consistency of the cross and the cosmos requires viewing the cosmos through a cruciform lens, nonetheless it is possible to discover, as did Socrates, the negative conclusion that retribution is not the natural law of the created order from within the default paradigm of human thinking.

• •

Redemptive Justice-Doing

Solidarity with the Poor, Release for the Captives

CHAPTER 23

Covenant Justice in the Life of Israel and the Ministry of Jesus: Keeping Faith by Defending the Poor

23.1. Covenant Justice: Keeping Faith by Defending the Poor

In Chapter 21, we saw how covenant law is framed by God's redemptive work and is rooted in God's gracious character, his steadfast love and mercy. The justice of this gracious and merciful God is characterized by a special concern — a "preferential option" — for "the poor and needy."[1] The Torah reveals that the God above all gods is a God of justice for the poor and needy: "For the LORD your God is God of gods and Lord of lords, the great God, mighty and awesome, who is not partial and takes no bribe, who executes justice for the orphan and the widow, and who loves the stranger, providing them with food and clothing" (Deut 10:17-18). The psalmist thus confesses that faith is knowledge of God's justice for the poor and needy: "I know that the LORD maintains the cause of the needy, and executes justice for the poor" (Ps 140:12).

This biblical faith in the God of justice is set forth no more clearly than in Psalm 146. The God who created heaven and earth is the same God who makes covenant with humanity, the same God who provides for the poor and needy. YHWH "keeps faith forever" (Ps 146:6) by doing justice for the poor and protecting the weak:

who executes justice for the oppressed; who gives food to the hungry. The LORD sets the prisoners free; the LORD opens the eyes of the blind. The LORD lifts up those who are bowed down; the LORD loves the righteous. The LORD

1. For development of the biblical basis for the "preferential option" in Catholic Social Teaching, see U.S. Catholic Bishops, *Economic Justice for All: Pastoral Letter on Catholic Social Teaching and the U.S. Economy* (Washington, D.C.: National Conference of Catholic Bishops, 1986), pp. 15-63; Peter J. Henriot, S.J., *Opting for the Poor: A Challenge for North Americans* (Washington, D.C.: Center for Concern, 1990).

watches over the strangers; he upholds the orphan and widow, but the way of the wicked he brings to ruin. (vv. 7-9)

The prophet Jeremiah, speaking to a corrupt king concerning his righteous father, proclaims that to do justice for the poor and needy is to "know" this God: "He [viz., Josiah] judged the cause of the poor and needy; then it was well. Is not this to know me? says the LORD" (Jer 22:16). Likewise, the prophet Isaiah exposes the fact that, though the people seek after God, they do not practice justice for the poor but instead oppress the weak: "Yet day after day they seek me and delight to know my ways, as if they were a nation that practiced righteousness and did not forsake the ordinance of their God" (Isa 58:2). Jeremiah's expression, "the knowledge of me *(hadda'ath 'ōthî),*" parallels Isaiah's expression, "knowledge of my way *(da'ath dᵉrāchay)*" — and both link knowledge of God and God's way to justice for the poor and needy. To do justice for the poor and needy, and to "know" the Lord of heaven and earth, are the same thing (cf. Jer 9:23-24). Chris Marshall summarizes this point well:

> Justice is the objective foundation of all reality. This justice is known, not primarily through philosophical speculation, but through observing God's *actions* to liberate the oppressed, and through heeding God's *word* in the Law and the Prophets to protect and care for the weak.
>
> This means that our knowledge of justice springs ultimately from our knowledge of God, and that there can be no true knowledge of God without an appreciation of God's own unfailing dedication to justice.[2]

There is not space here, nor is it my purpose, to make a comprehensive survey of God's justice for the poor and needy as revealed in Scripture.[3] We seek only to emphasize a few salient features of God's "preferential option" that bear directly on our study.[4] Let us begin by drawing two implications from Psalm 146.

First, all those marked out by God's justice for special concern share a common situation. God's justice renders preferential treatment to those who are disadvantaged in securing, and thus easily deprived of, basic needs (food, cloth-

---

2. Chris Marshall, *The Little Book of Biblical Justice: A Fresh Approach to the Bible's Teaching on Justice* (Intercourse, PA: Good Books, 2005), p. 25, emphasis original.

3. For shorter, more accessible expositions of justice in the Old Testament, see Perry B. Yoder, *Shalom: The Bible's Word for Salvation, Justice, and Peace* (Nappanee, IN: Evangel Publishing, 1987), and Bruce V. Malchow, *Social Justice in the Hebrew Bible: What Is New and What Is Old* (Collegeville, MN: Liturgical Press, 1996). For longer, more scholarly expositions of biblical justice, see Moshe Weinfeld, *Social Justice in Ancient Israel and in the Ancient Near East* (Jerusalem: Magnes Press, 1995), and Enrique Nardoni, *Rise Up, O Judge: A Study of Justice in the Biblical World,* trans. Seán Charles Martin (Peabody, MA: Hendrickson Publishers, 2004).

4. Cf. Marshall, *Little Book of Biblical Justice,* pp. 38-44, and Ronald J. Sider, *Rich Christians in an Age of Hunger: A Biblical Study* (Downers Grove, IL: InterVarsity Press, 1977), pp. 59-112.

ing, shelter, rest), those whose rights are especially vulnerable to exploitation and, hence, whose dignity is vulnerable to degradation, and those whose cause is helpless because they have no one to advocate on their behalf. Each of those mentioned in Psalm 146 satisfies one or more of these criteria: people who are oppressed, hungry, imprisoned, enslaved, blind, or otherwise disabled, physically or mentally, bowed down by the burden of hard labor or heavy debt, honest and loyal and not breaking promises or contracts to serve their own interests, widowed and orphaned, and strangers in the land, foreign nationals and immigrants. God's justice acts on behalf of such as these to provide their needs and protect their rights.

Second, God's preferential treatment of the poor and needy is not in any way a fulfillment of the law of retribution, but rather transcends the narrow limits of retributive justice. God does not show favor to the poor and needy on account of "moral merit" or "just desert," nor do the poor and needy receive God's help because they have "earned" it by their self-righteousness. God shows favor to the poor and needy, not because God is retributive, rewarding good for good and evil for evil, but because God is *faithful* and *just* (Ps 146:6-7); and the poor receive God's help, not because they deserve it, but because they *need* it. Indeed, God's justice acts preferentially in favor of the poor and needy precisely where human rulers and authorities — the "princes . . . in whom there is no help" (v. 3) — have failed to do so. The psalmist thus declares: "'Because the poor are despoiled, because the needy groan, I will now rise up,' says the LORD; 'I will place them in the safety for which they long'" (Ps 12:5). God's faithful and just action to sustain and defend the poor and needy is thus rooted in God's *grace.*

The Psalms testify throughout to the "preferential option" of God's justice for the poor, needy, and oppressed.[5] We witness this "preferential option" in Scripture also through the story of redemption, the statutes of covenant, and the critique of prophets. The liberation of Israel from slavery, and the establishment of Israel as a nation freed from bondage to serve God, demonstrates God's "preferential option" for the oppressed.[6] As the exodus story tells us, God acts on behalf of Israel and calls Moses as his servant of liberation for two reasons: because God has remembered his covenant promises to the patriarchs, and because God has heard the groans and cries of the people and has looked upon them and seen their misery (Exod 2:23-25; 3:7-10). God's redemption of Israel from slavery was nothing less than God's faithful action to liberate the oppressed. After Israel has been liberated but before it has entered the promised land, Moses reminds the people of the reason for God's favor. It was not be-

---

5. God's special concern for the poor is reflected in nearly one-fifth of the psalter: Psalms 9, 10, 12, 14, 15, 22, 40, 41, 68, 69, 70, 72, 76, 82, 86, 94, 102, 103, 109, 113, 119, 123, 140, and 146. See Malchow, *Social Justice in the Hebrew Bible,* pp. 50-57; Nardoni, *Rise Up, O Judge,* pp. 122-32.

6. Nardoni, *Rise Up, O Judge,* pp. 42-67.

cause of Israel's greatness or righteousness that God acted on their behalf to redeem them from oppression; rather it was because of God's covenant loyalty
and steadfast love (Deut 7:7-8; 9:4-5).

God's "preferential option" for the poor and oppressed continues in the
covenant law, which is shaped significantly by the story of redemption: statute
(halakhah) is framed by story (haggadah), such that the law was intended to
continue the benefits of God's redemption among the covenant community.[7]
The Decalogue of basic law is thus prefaced by the declaration that the God
who legislates for Israel is the God who redeemed Israel from slavery (Exod
20:2; Deut 5:6). Israel's covenant law, then, reflects the special concern of the
God who provides for the poor and liberates the oppressed; and Israel is motivated to walk in the way of justice by remembrance of God's act of redemption
on its behalf. God's gracious redemption of Israel demonstrated to Israel that
"the LORD your God is God" and that Israel's God is "the faithful God who
maintains covenant loyalty (ḥesed)" (Deut 7:9). Remembrance of God's steadfast love manifest in redeeming Israel, in turn, was to be the basis of Israel's covenant loyalty in keeping God's commandments, which were intended by God to
protect both the freedom of Israel and the poor within Israel. Israel is thus exhorted again and again to remember God's grace on their behalf: "take care that
you do not forget the LORD, who brought you out of the land of Egypt, out of
the house of slavery" (6:20; cf. 8:1-3, 11-20; 10:12–11:21). Accordingly, as the law of
the Lord was handed down to each generation, Israel was to explain its meaning
by reciting the story of God's gracious redemption by which Israel was liberated
from slavery and granted the land promised to the ancestors — the story of
God's covenant loyalty, steadfast love, and concern for the oppressed (6:20-25).

This special concern for the poor and oppressed and motivation for covenant loyalty is evident in several statutes of covenant law.

> There was to be no oppression or abuse of any alien, widow, or orphan, for
> Israel had been a nation of oppressed aliens in Egypt (Exod 22:21-24;
> 23:9).
> There was to be one law for the alien, the convert, and the native Israelite,
> for, again, the Israelites were once an oppressed people in a foreign
> land (Exod 23:9; Lev 19:33-34; Deut 10:19).
> Each Sabbath day, not only were adult freepersons to rest, but also children,
> slaves, animals, and aliens, in recognition that they were not merely
> beasts of burden, but were created for the praise of God and intended
> to participate in the grace of God's redemption (Exod 20:8-11; Deut
> 5:12-15).

7. Malchow, Social Justice in the Hebrew Bible, pp. 20-30; Nardoni, Rise Up, O Judge, pp. 68-
94; Yoder, Shalom, pp. 71-84.

There was to be no perpetual servitude, indebtedness, or acquisition, because Israel's freedom was purchased by God's redemption and Israel's land is the gift of God's promise. Thus, slaves were to go free and debts were to be forgiven every seventh (Sabbath) year; and all land was to be returned to the dispossessed every fiftieth (Jubilee) year (Leviticus 25; Deuteronomy 15).[8]

Lenders were not to charge interest on loans to the poor for the purpose of securing basic goods, in order to avoid indebtedness that could lead to servitude and dispossession (Exod 22:25-27; Lev 25:35-39).

Each harvest, the field hands were to make only one pass over the field or vineyard or olive grove and leave the edges of the field untouched, so that the poor, widow, orphan, and alien could glean and gather what they needed for their daily provision (Lev 19:9-10; 23:22; Deut 24:19-22).

Every third year, one-tenth of the harvest was to be put in storage to provide for the needs of the Levites, aliens, orphans, and widows. (Deut 14:28-29)

Every seventh (Sabbath) year, landowners were to let their fields, groves, orchards, and vineyards lie fallow, allowing the land to rest and the poor to gather food for their needs from what nature provided (Exod 23:10-11).

Within the covenant community established by God's grace, therefore, the measure of justice is how well the most vulnerable are faring — whether the poor, widow, orphan, and alien receive equal protection under law, are granted adequate access to basic goods (food, clothing, shelter, rest), and are allowed full participation in society.[9]

The "preferential option" of God's justice is expressed further in God's prophetic judgment upon the rulers of the people.[10] The leaders of the covenant community — kings, judges, and elders — were specially charged by God with the responsibility of providing the needs and securing the rights of the poor and needy (Ps 72:1-4).[11] When the "princes" of the people failed their responsibility to act on behalf of the poor and needy, God pronounced judgment upon them from his heavenly position in the divine council (Psalm 82). God also sent prophets to Israel to advocate on behalf of the poor and needy by confronting the powerful and wealthy, charging them with injustice, and calling them back to their responsibility (or else face God's judgment). Thus, Isaiah:

8. Weinfeld, *Social Justice in Ancient Israel,* pp. 152-78.
9. Cf. Ronald J. Sider, *The Scandal of Evangelical Politics: Why Are Christians Missing the Opportunity to Really Change the World?* (Grand Rapids, MI: Baker Books, 2008), pp. 117-25.
10. Malchow, *Social Justice in the Hebrew Bible,* pp. 31-49; Nardoni, *Rise Up, O Judge,* pp. 95-121.
11. Weinfeld, *Social Justice in Ancient Israel,* pp. 45-56.

> The LORD rises to argue his case; he stands to judge the peoples. The LORD enters into judgment with the elders and princes of his people: It is you who have devoured the vineyard; the spoil of the poor is in your houses. What do you mean by crushing my people, by grinding the face of the poor? says the Lord GOD of hosts. (Isa 3:13-15)

> Ah, you who make iniquitous decrees, who write oppressive statutes, to turn aside the needy from justice and to rob the poor of my people of their right, that widows may be your spoil, and that you may make the orphans your prey! (10:1-2)

God sent Jeremiah into the royal house to speak to the king and his government:

> Hear the word of the LORD, O King of Judah sitting on the throne of David — you, and your servants, and your people who enter these gates: Thus says the LORD: Act with justice and righteousness, and deliver from the hand of the oppressor anyone who has been robbed. And do no wrong or violence to the alien, the orphan, and the widow, or shed innocent blood in this place. (Jer 22:2-3)

In all these ways — redemption story, covenant law, prophetic critique — the "preferential option" of God's justice reveals God's solidarity with the poor and oppressed. This solidarity is made especially evident at two crucial moments in Israel's early history — deliverance at the sea and founding of the cult. With Israel pinned between the sea before them and Pharaoh's army behind them, God intervened in the pillar of cloud to stand between Israel and their pursuers. God then opened the sea for Israel to pass through but closed the sea back upon their pursuers (Exodus 14). God is not a neutral judge here, but a partisan deliverer; God has sided in favor of the oppressed against the oppressor: "Moses said to the people, 'Do not be afraid, stand firm, and see the deliverance that the LORD will accomplish *for you* today; for the Egyptians whom you see today you shall never see again. The LORD will fight *for you,* and you have only to keep still'" (Exod 14:13-14). Having liberated Israel (Exodus 14), having revealed his covenant law at Sinai (chs. 20–23), and having sealed this covenant by sacrifice (ch. 24), God instructs Moses to initiate a cult of worship. Moses and the people are to build a tabernacle, where God will dwell among Israel on their journey (chs. 25–26). The Hebrew word "tabernacle" *(miškān)* literally means "dwelling" or "tent," and is derived from the verbal root, "dwell" or "set up (tent)" *(šākan)*. We should not miss the imagery here: God has pitched his tent in the midst of the camp of the migrant workers and the war refugees. God delivers the oppressed and dwells with the poor.

23.2. The Life and Death of Jesus:
God's Solidarity with the Poor and Oppressed

In Chapter 18, we elaborated the idea of the Incarnation of Jesus Christ — including his life, death, and resurrection — as God's personal commitment of "redemptive solidarity" with humanity: Jesus is God "with us" and "for us," "for our salvation." Through the Incarnation, we also see the "preferential option" of God's justice for the poor and needy reach its culmination. Jesus is the definitive demonstration, displayed openly to the world, of God's personal solidarity with the poor and oppressed.

This solidarity is announced from "the beginning" in the Gospel of John, which depicts the mystery of Incarnation in terms that make deliberate allusion to the exodus story: "And the Word was made flesh, and dwelt among us" (John 1:14 KJV). The Greek verb "dwell" or "take up residence" *(skēnoō)* means literally "pitch tent" and is related to the noun "tent" *(skēnē),* which is used in the Septuagint to translate the Hebrew *miškān* and is used to speak of the "tabernacle," the tent in which God's presence dwelled with Israel in the wilderness (Heb 8:5; 9:2, 21). As with the tabernacle in the wilderness, God has "pitched tent" and "taken up residence" among humanity in Jesus Christ.

Where does Jesus begin his life among humanity? Among the homeless and the refugees. In Luke, we find Mary giving birth to her firstborn son and Jesus drawing first breath, in a place for keeping and feeding animals, "because there was no place for them in the inn" (Luke 2:6-7). In Matthew, in another deliberate allusion to the exodus story, we find Joseph, Mary, and Jesus about two years later, vacating their house in the middle of the night and taking to the road. They must flee for their lives and seek asylum in Egypt in order to escape the political violence of a paranoid ruler: "Get up, take the child and his mother, and flee to Egypt, and remain there until I tell you; for Herod is about to search for the child, to destroy him" (Matt 2:13-15). In Jesus, therefore, God "pitches tent" with humanity, taking up residence first among the homeless, second among the refugees — among those who lack shelter and security, and whose defenseless lives are threatened by injustice and violence. The very conditions of the Incarnation thus demonstrate God's solidarity with and concern for the poor and oppressed.

Jesus' life-ministry demonstrates further a "preferential option" for the poor and oppressed. Jesus is not only born among the poor and oppressed, but he himself *chooses* a life *with* the poor and oppressed.[12]

> At his inaugural sermon, Jesus declares that "the Spirit of the Lord" has
> anointed him "to bring good news to the poor," "to proclaim release to

---

12. Nardoni, *Rise Up, O Judge,* pp. 173-200.

the captives," and "to let the oppressed go free." Jesus is God's servant
to the poor and oppressed, whose messianic vocation is essentially one
of solidarity and liberation (Luke 4:18-19).

Although a skilled artisan *(tektōn)* possessing a respectable socio-
economic position, Jesus enters a life of voluntary poverty and homeless wandering among the rural peasantry and urban poor of Galilee
(Matt 8:20; 13:55; Mark 6:3; Luke 9:58).

Jesus ministers to the poor and oppressed, the sick and weak; he teaches
and heals for the sake of both those that have been maltreated by
power and authority and those who have maltreated others with their
power and authority (Luke 5:12-26; 6:20-25; 7:18-23; 10:25-37; 14:1-24;
15:3-32; 22:47-53).

In his ministry of healing, Jesus makes solidarity with the people's suffering for the sake of their salvation. Citing a prophecy fulfilled in Jesus,
"He took our infirmities and bore our diseases" (Matt 8:17, quoting Isa
53:4a), Matthew portrays Jesus as entering personally and physically
into the suffering of the people in order to release them from their suffering by the power of his touch and his word.

Jesus interprets and practices covenant law, especially the Sabbath, to show
special concern for the welfare of the poor and oppressed (Luke 6:1-11;
13:10-17).

During the course of his ministry, Jesus socializes intimately with the outcast and downtrodden and offers forgiveness freely to sinners and
wrongdoers, so much so that religious elites criticize him for welcoming "tax collectors and sinners" (Luke 5:29-32; 7:36-50; 15:1-2; 19:1-10;
23:39-43).

As he enters Jerusalem, Jesus goes straight into the temple and disrupts
business as usual, making a demonstration of God's desire that justice
be done for the poor and needy (Matt 21:12-17; Mark 11:15-17; Luke
19:45-46).

In the final week of his life, Jesus teaches that he is present among the poor
and needy, the least and lowest — the hungry needing food, the thirsty
needing drink, the stranger needing shelter, the naked needing clothing, the sick needing care, and the imprisoned needing companion-
ship. Whatever we do or do not do "to one of the least of these," we do,
or fail to do, to Jesus himself (Matt 25:31-46).

In his death, Jesus provides freedom for the condemned prisoner Barabbas.
If there is anyone of whom we might say that Jesus died "in his place,"
it is surely Barabbas: Jesus is crucified instead of the condemned
Barabbas; and Barabbas is acquitted instead of the innocent Jesus.
Now, Barabbas was a rebel *(stasiastēs)* and guerilla *(lēstēs)* who fought
against Roman occupation and who had fomented revolution and in-

surrection in the capital city. Quite literally, therefore, Jesus dies for the poor and oppressed, and his faithfulness to God as far as death brings "release to the captive" (Matt 27:15-26; Mark 15:6-15; Luke 23:18-25; John 18:39-40).

Jesus is crucified between two "bandits" *(lēstai),* "with the criminals" *(kakourgoi).* Jesus not only dies the death of the rebel and criminal, but dies in suffering solidarity with condemned sinners (Matt 27:38; Mark 15:27; Luke 23:33).

Paul's letters also testify to the Incarnation as God's solidarity with the poor and oppressed, fulfilled through the "interchange" of Christ with humanity in its situation of poverty and slavery (see Chapter 18 above).[13] At one place, Paul writes: "For you know the generous act [*tēn charin,* "the grace"] of our Lord Jesus Christ, that though he was rich, yet for your sakes he became poor, so that by his poverty you might become rich" (2 Cor 8:9). Exhorting believers to voluntary generosity for the sake of their brothers and sisters in need (8:1–9:15), Paul reminds his readers of the example of Jesus' own voluntary poverty for the sake of humanity in its need. Jesus takes the part of the poor, choosing a life of poverty lived among the poor, in order that the even the poorest of humanity might know the generosity of God.

Elsewhere, Paul cites an early Christian hymn to depict Jesus' solidarity through the Incarnation with the lowest and least of humanity:

> who, though he was in the form of God, did not regard equality with God as something to be exploited, but emptied himself, taking the form of a slave, being born in human likeness. And being found in human form, he humbled himself and became obedient to the point of death — even death on a cross. (Phil 2:6-8)

Jesus' Incarnation expresses a twofold solidarity with humanity, in his life and in his death. In his life, Jesus "empties" *(kenoō)* himself of the prerogatives of divinity and fills the human position of slave *(doulos),* the lowest of all in the social order. Paul introduces this Christological hymn with this exhortation to the church: "Let each of you look not to your own interests, but to the interests of others. Let the same mind be in you that was in Christ Jesus" (Phil 2:4-5). Elsewhere, Paul exhorts the followers of Jesus, "do not be haughty, but associate with the lowly" or "give yourselves to humble tasks" (Rom 12:16). Paul thus commends Christian conduct in conformity with the *kenosis* of Christ, by which he lowered himself into the least position and gave his life to the humble

13. Cf. Morna D. Hooker, *Not Ashamed of the Gospel: New Testament Interpretations of the Death of Christ* (Grand Rapids, MI: Eerdmans Publishing, 1994), p. 35; James D. G. Dunn, *The Theology of Paul the Apostle* (Grand Rapids, MI: Eerdmans Publishing, 1998), p. 291.

task of serving for the benefit of others (Mark 10:42-45). In contrast to Roman society, which ordered itself politically and economically toward the prerogatives of power and wealth, the Christian community was to orient its life toward the interests of the weak and poor, as Christ himself had done in both life and death.[14]

Metaphorically, by taking the form of a slave, Jesus signifies his identity with humanity in its situation of slavery to sin. In his death on the cross, he "humbles" himself in obedience to God. Having taken the part of a slave, Jesus dies the death of a slave in order to redeem humanity from its slavery to sin.[15] The cross is both Christ's supreme act of obedience and God's supreme act of generosity, Christ's demonstration of undying loyalty to God's will and God's demonstration of suffering solidarity with the lowest and least. Jesus lives the life of the least and dies the death of the lowest, so that all might receive the abundance of God's grace. Charles Cousar:

> The cross, then, as a self-sacrificing act of obedience to God, becomes the paradigm for the life and ethics of the believing community. In this context, it is striking that the letters include no references to features of Jesus' life and ministry that otherwise might be taken as mandates — no healing of the sick, no exorcism of demons, no concern for the poor. The symbol of the cross for Paul is sufficient.[16]

That Jesus voluntarily undertakes his divine commission in the position of a *slave* (Phil 2:6-8) and exercises his authority through *servitude* (Mark 10:42-45; Luke 22:24-27); that he begins his life among the *homeless and refugees* (Luke 2:6-7; Matt 2:13-15) and lives out his life in *voluntary poverty* (Matt 8:20; 2 Cor 8:9); that he defines his mission as being "the Lord's favor" to the *poor and oppressed* (Luke 4:18-19); that from the beginning of his ministry he identified with the *despised and rejected*, the "sinners and tax collectors," and suffered persecution for it (Mark 2:15-17); that at the end of his ministry he was "counted among the *lawless*" (Luke 22:37) and died "with the *criminals*" (23:33) — all this shows us that through the Incarnation God demonstrates a "preferential option" for the last and least, the outcast and downtrodden, the poor and oppressed, the despised and rejected, the tortured and condemned. It should thus be no surprise that the early Christians would tell the story of Jesus using the

---

14. Cf. Louise Schottroff, "'Give to Caesar What Belongs to Caesar and to God What Belongs to God': A Theological Response of the Early Church to Its Social and Political Environment," in *Love of Enemy and Nonretaliation*, ed. Willard Swartley (Louisville: Westminster John Knox Press, 1992), pp. 223-57, here p. 249.

15. Crucifixion was a means of execution reserved for slaves and rebels.

16. Charles B. Cousar, "Paul and the Death of Jesus," *Interpretation* 52/1 (1998) 38-52, here pp. 46-47.

Song of the Suffering Servant (Isaiah 52–53), which depicts God's faithful servant being disfigured by cruel tortures (52:14), being despised and rejected (53:3), suffering oppression in silence (v. 7), and being unjustly condemned and executed (vv. 8-9).

The collective testimony of Torah, Psalms, and Prophets, of Gospels and Epistles, testifies consistently that God's justice — worked through exodus, continued through covenant, proclaimed by prophets, fulfilled by Jesus, and confirmed by Apostles — is oriented by a "preferential option" that provides for the poor and needy and that liberates the weak and oppressed.

CHAPTER 24

Covenant Justice, Capital Punishment, and the Teaching of Jesus: A Death Penalty Moratorium

With my mouth I will give great thanks to the LORD;
I will praise him in the midst of the throng.
For he stands at the right hand of the needy,
to save them from those who would condemn them to death.

PSALM 109:30-31

In Chapters 24 and 25, we address the very question that prompted the inquiry that led to the writing of this book: What ought Christians think about the death penalty *on account of the Gospel?* We thus seek to develop here a distinctively Christian view of capital punishment. A distinctively Christian view will be shaped primarily by the teaching and cross of Jesus Christ. Accordingly, we develop our argument here along two lines: that Jesus' teaching amounts effectively to a permanent moratorium on capital punishment in fulfillment of covenant law, and that Paul's gospel announces that God has put a final end to the death penalty through the cross of Christ.

In the Gospel of John we find the only instance where Jesus addresses directly the question of the death penalty — "the woman caught in adultery" (John 8:2-11).[1] This story depicts Jesus acting to fulfill God's covenant justice —

---

1. As this story is quite familiar to most readers, I do not cite the full text. Verse citations in this chapter refer to this text.

This chapter comprises a revised version of my article, "Capital Punishment, Covenant Justice, and the Cross of Christ: The Death Penalty in the Life and Death of Jesus," *Mennonite Quarterly Review* 83 (2009), 375-402. My thanks to the editor of *Mennonite Quarterly Review* for permission to reuse this material.

justice that brings good news for the poor, justice that transcends retribution for the sake of redemption.

24.1. Preliminary Objections

Before we examine this text, we need to address a few potential preliminary objections that might be made to the arguments that follow. First, some may want to object that the authority or veracity of this text is questionable because it is not found in the earliest manuscripts of the New Testament and is found at various places in later manuscripts.[2] Leading textual scholar Bruce Metzger argued that, such variations notwithstanding, this story "has all the earmarks of historical veracity."[3] In any case, that this text has been handed down as part of the accepted canon of Holy Scripture, and has been commented on as Holy Scripture since the patristic period,[4] is sufficient, in my view, to establish its authority for the church. Second, some may want to object that that the story concerns, not capital punishment, but lynching — Jesus intervenes to stop an illegal procedure, to thwart mob justice. The details of the story, however, appear consistent both with the Torah and with the legal custom of rabbinic Judaism of the time. Gardener Hanks has argued, persuasively, that the evidence shows that "Jesus' intervention stopped a legal execution fully sanctioned by the Jewish authorities."[5]

Third, some may want to object that this case is presented to Jesus as a trap. Because Jesus' reply is intended to avoid the horns of a dilemma, the objection goes, we cannot read any "moral" from the story because, again, capital punishment is not the issue. Thus argues H. Wayne House: "The real issue placed be-

2. Cf. Lloyd R. Bailey, *Capital Punishment: What the Bible Says* (Nashville, TN: Abingdon Press, 1987), p. 69.

3. Bruce M. Metzger, *A Textual Commentary on the Greek New Testament*, 2nd ed. (Stuttgart: German Bible Society, 1994), p. 188.

4. See Joel C. Elowsky, *John 1–10* (Ancient Christian Commentary on Scripture: New Testament IVA; Downers Grove, IL: InterVarsity Press, 2006), pp. 272-78.

5. Gardner C. Hanks, *Capital Punishment and the Bible* (Scottdale, PA: Herald Press, 2002), p. 154., cf. p. 148. J. Duncan M. Derrett, *Law in the New Testament* (London: Darton, Longman & Todd, 1970), pp. 166-68, takes the view that this was to be a lynching. His view is premised on the assumption that, because around AD 30 the Roman provincial authority stripped Jewish courts of jurisdiction in capital crimes, there was no Jewish court to try her case. Whether that edict was already in effect at the time of this incident is debatable, and it appears that after it was in effect the Roman authority was willing to look the other way while Jewish courts tried capital cases and carried out public executions, as in the case of Stephen (Acts 7). In the case of Jesus himself, moreover, at which time the edict seems to have been in effect, it is the Jewish leaders, not the Roman governor, that insist on this capital case being handled in a Roman court. Pilate expressly wanted the Jewish council to judge Jesus according to Jewish law and evidently would not have objected had they executed him themselves (John 18:31).

fore Jesus was not a guilty woman but a baited trap. . . . Capital punishment never became an issue for Jesus."[6] It does not follow from the fact that Jesus' answer is aimed at avoiding a dilemma, however, that it is therefore lacking authority concerning ethical practice. Recall the question of the imperial tax, also presented to him in the temple as a trap (Matt 22:15-22; Mark 12:13-17; Luke 20:20-26). Jesus does not answer directly the question put to him, whether he and his fellow Jews are obligated to pay the tax or not. Nonetheless, his reply — "Render unto Caesar what is Caesar's, and render unto God what is God's" — teaches three central principles of covenant faithfulness even as it avoids the trap laid for him: that the agenda of God's kingdom is to be distinguished from the imperial agenda (for Caesar does not represent the will of God), that the agenda of God's kingdom stands in judgment over the imperial agenda (for everything in heaven and on earth, including "what belongs to Caesar," ultimately belongs to God the Creator), and, therefore, that one should pledge allegiance to God's kingdom above Caesar's empire and always choose the former whenever the two conflict (which in certain circumstances might require tax resistance). The question of loyalty goes deeper, Jesus teaches us, than the alternatives supposed by his inquisitors.[7] Likewise with our present story.

Fourth, some may want to object that the inference of ethical principles from biblical narratives is dubious and inappropriate. Whether a trap or not, we should not read any "moral" from this story precisely because it is a story. Thus argues Lloyd Bailey: "One should not deduce *halakah* (ethical guidelines) from *haggadah* (scriptural narrative). Rather, ethical guidelines are to be sought in formal teachings, whose purpose is instruction in ethical behavior."[8] There is a reasonable caution to observe here. To read the "moral" from a story assumes whose words and deeds in the story are meant to be exemplary, and, even if we agree on the exemplar, the applicability of that "moral" may be ambiguous. In this story, the exemplar is indisputably Jesus. Regarding applicability, we propose to read this story in a way that inverts the question. Instead of "What ethical principle are we to infer from Jesus' teaching?" we ask "How does Jesus' teaching fulfill covenant?" Rather than reading this story as promulgating a new teaching, we read it as fulfilling "the law and the prophets." This story

6. H. Wayne House, "In Favor of the Death Penalty," in H. Wayne House and John Howard Yoder, *The Death Penalty Debate* (Dallas: Word Publishing, 1991), pp. 63-65.

7. I interpret Jesus' reply regarding the imperial tax as an instance of his stance of "critical distance" from the powers that be; cf. Walter E. Pilgrim, *Uneasy Neighbors: Church and State in the New Testament* (Minneapolis: Fortress Press, 1999), pp. 64-72. Of course, many readers may not agree with such a reading of the text. Even so, the traditional reading of Jesus' saying "render unto Caesar" has served to legitimate the "two kingdom" model in Protestant ethics, such that the point here remains the same: simply because Jesus is replying to a trap, it does not follow that his reply is lacking ethical instruction.

8. Bailey, *Capital Punishment*, p. 70.

shows us a living parable of covenant justice. Now, although Jesus puts covenant justice into practice here, it does not follow that his ruling in this case teaches us nothing new concerning the law. This story has the same triadic structure as the "antitheses" in the Sermon on the Mount:

> STATEMENT: You have heard that it is written, "An adulterer shall be put to death."
>
> PROHIBITION: But I say to you, "Only one without sin may execute the death penalty."
>
> IMPERATIVE: Go and sin no more.[9]

Jesus' ruling points beyond the letter to the true meaning of the law, just as do his teachings in the Sermon on the Mount.

24.2. Examining the Text

Let us, then, proceed to examine the text by drawing out various aspects of the story. It would seem that the case is being brought to Jesus on appeal. The woman has evidently already been tried and convicted in a council of elders. Certain scribes and Pharisees, apparently members of the council that has tried her case, bring the case and the woman before Jesus for his interpretation and ruling concerning her sentence (vv. 3-5). The council has likely already sentenced her to death, and they want to see if he will uphold the council's sentence of death according to the law of Moses. Their appeal to Jesus thus concerns whether this case meets the legal requirement for a death sentence.[10] Although done with an ulterior motive, their action might have been following a legal course. The Torah and rabbinical tradition provided precedents and procedures for appeals to a recognized judicial authority in difficult or questionable cases (cf. Exod 18:13-26; Deut 1:17; 17:8-13).[11] By taking this case to Jesus, the scribes and Pharisees effectively recognize Jesus as having juridical authority to decide such cases, whether in fact he had such authority *ex officio* or

---

9. See Glen H. Stassen, *Just Peacemaking: Transforming Initiatives for Justice and Peace* (Louisville: Westminster/John Knox, 1992), pp. 33-51.

10. Because the question is framed by "in the law Moses commanded us to stone . . . ," some commentators have suggested that the question concerned, not whether she should be executed, but only the *manner* of execution, whether by stoning or some other method, which would depend legally on whether she was married or not. Derrett, *Law in the New Testament*, pp. 168-69, is convinced that the appropriate manner of execution was not in doubt in this case, and Jesus' reply supports that view.

11. Regarding legal process in rabbinical tradition, see Hanks, *Capital Punishment and the Bible*, pp. 78ff.

not.[12] Should Jesus rule against them but they ignore him and stone her anyway, their actions would expose their evil intentions and so convict themselves as lawbreakers instead of Jesus.

There is one basic statute that guides the judges of Israel: "You shall not render an unjust judgment; you shall not be partial to the poor or defer to the great: with justice you shall judge your neighbor" (Lev 19:15; cf. Deut 16:18-20). Jesus' chief responsibility as a judge of Israel is to render judgment that treats the parties equally. And, as we will see, that is precisely what he does in this case.

Yet, in his situational role as appellate judge, Jesus does not so much as even review the woman's case. He does not challenge her conviction or question her sentence on evidential, procedural, or substantive grounds — and thus looks past the issues that dominate the contemporary debate on the death penalty. Concerning evidential matters, Jesus does not rule on whether the facts are sufficient to prove guilt "beyond a reasonable doubt" or whether new exculpatory evidence might be discovered. Indeed, Jesus does not express any interest in the evidence — and thus effectively stipulates the truth of the prosecution's case, that she "was caught in the very act of committing adultery" (v. 4).

Concerning procedural issues, Jesus' ruling does not address whether irregularities have occurred in the prosecution. He does not rule on whether she has received a fair trial, or whether her legal rights have been respected, or whether she has received "due process of law" or "equal protection under law." There were legal provisions for making such a challenge.

Regarding due process, the law required the testimony of at least two eyewitnesses for a death sentence (Num 35:30; Deut 17:6; 19:15), but Jesus does not even ask who the witnesses were, much less cross-examine them. Had he done so and found their testimony inconsistent, exposing them as false witnesses, they themselves would have been subject to a death sentence (Deut 19:16-19).[13] The law required further that "The hands of the witnesses shall be the first raised against the person to execute the death penalty . . ." (17:7). Elmer Martens thus argues that Jesus releases the woman because the two required witnesses, who must "cast the first stone," were not present, so that the execution could not proceed legally.[14]

---

12. Concerning this question of Jesus' authority, see Derrett, *Law in the New Testament*, pp. 158-60. Whatever Jesus' actual authority for the actors in the story, regarding Jesus' authority for *us,* Derrett comments aptly: "Christians . . . will see him in a guise of more than a *iurisprudens:* for them he acted not merely as a referee, but as a legislator" (p. 160).

13. An example is found in the story of Susanna, ch. 13 of the Greek version of Daniel. After Susanna has been falsely accused, wrongly convicted, and condemned to death, Daniel intervenes to expose the false witnesses, who are themselves then put to death. Andrew T. Lincoln, *The Gospel According to Saint John* (London: Continuum, 2005), pp. 534-36, offers an interesting comparative analysis of the two stories.

14. Elmer A. Martens, "Capital Punishment and the Christian," in *On Capital Punishment* (Winnipeg, MB: Kindred Press, 1987), p. 23.

This seems implausible for two reasons. First, it would imply that the scribes and Pharisees, while attempting to trip up Jesus on one point of law, were themselves carelessly tripping over another point of law. We would then conclude that the scribes and Pharisees, rather than being experts in the law, were actually mere bunglers, which seems unlikely. Second, it would leave us with more questions than when we started: if Jesus' ground for dismissing the case were that obvious, then why such a cryptic response (writing in the dirt), and why speak to the sins of the accusers rather than the number of witnesses?

Regarding equal protection, the law charges both man and woman with the same crime and sentences them to the same death (Lev 20:10; Deut 22:22). That only the woman has been charged, tried, convicted, and sentenced for adultery indicates that the law is not being applied equally. Jesus might have justified releasing her on the ground of inequitable treatment under law, but he did not do so.

Concerning substantive grounds, Jesus' ruling does not address whether a death sentence would be an appropriate outcome for this case, whether death is a disproportionate (or "cruel and unusual") punishment for the crime. As the scribes and Pharisees point out (v. 5), the law prescribes a penalty of death for adultery (Lev 20:10; Deut 22:22-24), and Jesus raises no question about whether that penalty is appropriate for this sin. Nor does Jesus rule that due to "mitigating factors" the court should show mercy and commute her sentence. This was a legal option at Jesus' disposal. The prophet Ezekiel had amended the law: those who show repentance by their actions, even if the law prescribe a death sentence for their crimes, should have their lives spared (Ezek 18:21-32; 33:14-15). In the end Jesus does warn the woman to repent (v. 11), but he releases her from judgment *before* she has done anything to show repentance. Jesus' ruling is not based on the mitigating factor of the sinner's repentance.

Jesus' ruling on the question put to him, "Should she be executed or not?" suggests, therefore, that he agrees that legal justice has indeed been satisfied in this woman's case — and would be satisfied if she were put to death. A ruling challenging her conviction or sentence on strictly legal grounds would have been the obvious way for Jesus to avoid the trap laid for him. But he does not pursue that safer option. We thus concur with Chris Marshall that "it is with full cognizance of the legal justifiability of capital punishment in this specific case that Jesus refuses to condone the woman's execution."[15] Jesus agrees that the woman is guilty as charged and deserving of death under law. But it is precisely this "under law" that is the key to understanding the "moral" of Jesus' ruling. For Jesus, the real question concerning the justice of the death penalty lies deeper than "the rule of law." The justice of God, which Jesus represents, is irreducible to legal correctness, to satisfaction of law (cf. Matt 5:20; 23:23).

---

15. Christopher D. Marshall, *Beyond Retribution: A New Testament Vision for Justice, Crime, and Punishment* (Grand Rapids, MI: Eerdmans Publishing, 2001), p. 232.

24.3. Interpreting Jesus' Ruling

With this in mind, let us interpret Jesus' ruling: "Let anyone among you who is without sin be the first to throw a stone at her" (v. 7). Jesus is invoking the legal requirement that the witnesses against the accused be the ones to initiate an execution (Deut 17:7). Unless the witnesses cast the first stone, the execution cannot proceed legally. Jesus rules that only one without sin may execute a death sentence.

Now, who is "the one without sin"? Jesus himself is "without sin" (2 Cor 5:21; Heb 4:15). So, a possible interpretation of "the one without sin" is that Jesus refers to himself. Jesus would thus be saying that, among those present, only he has authority to initiate the execution of a death sentence — which he elects not to do, refusing to endorse a legal death sentence.[16] While it is plausible, I am not convinced of this view. First, had the audience understood Jesus to be claiming sinless perfection for himself and in that way claiming equality with God, one would expect *that* to have become the central point of controversy, as it did on other occasions in John's Gospel (e.g., John 5:17-18; 8:58-59; 10:30-31, 38-39). Indeed, had Jesus been claiming equality with God, he would have handed the scribes and Pharisees grounds for a charge of blasphemy and so given cause for stoning him instead of her. Second, casting the first stone was the exclusive legal privilege and duty of the eyewitnesses, and Jesus himself was not a witness to the adulterous act. According to the law, while Jesus could have participated in the stoning with the assembly once the first stones had been thrown by the witnesses, he could not claim the right to throw the first stone. Had he claimed that right, he would have been showing himself to be a lawbreaker and again fallen into the trap set for him. So, self-reference seems unlikely here.

We suggest looking elsewhere in the Gospels to find a clue for how we might interpret this saying. Nowhere in the Gospels do we find Jesus claiming sinless perfection for himself, at least not directly.[17] But on another occasion, we do find Jesus pointing explicitly to God alone as having moral perfection (Mark 10:17-18). While this does not undermine the orthodox doctrine that Jesus was both God incarnate and in fact sinless, it does suggest that Jesus' audience likely did not understand him to be saying as much in this circumstance. I thus think the audience in our present story hears this saying of Jesus in the same way, as reminding them of the twin affirmations of their shared faith tradition: that all humans, even members of the covenant community, are sinners

16. Cf. John H. Redekop, "An Analysis of Capital Punishment," in *On Capital Punishment*, pp. 6-7; Marshall, *Beyond Retribution*, p. 233; Lincoln, *The Gospel According to Saint John*, p. 533.

17. Marshall, *Beyond Retribution*, p. 233, cites John 8:21, 24, and 46 in support of interpreting Jesus' saying in v. 7 as a claim to be perfectly sinless, but these texts do not say as much, although one might read such an interpretation into them.

(Pss 14:3; 53:3; Isa 64:6) and hence that there is only one without sin — God, as Job's friends rightly (if self-righteously) reminded him (Job 4:17; 25:4).

Jesus' ruling thus effectively raises the legal standard for executing a death penalty to a humanly impossible level: legally justified killing demands complete blamelessness or sinless perfection, which belongs to God alone. Prior to executing a legal judgment of death on the life of another, one's own life must first withstand God's absolute judgment, which no mortal's life can do. Jesus' ruling recalls the psalmist: "If you, O LORD, should mark iniquities, Lord, who could stand?" (Ps 130:3); "Do not enter into judgment against your servant, for no one living is righteous before you" (Ps 143:2). Jesus' ruling implies that only God may execute a death sentence, reminding those who would take life, even with legal justification, that sovereignty over life belongs exclusively to God. Jesus' ruling thus effectively shifts the question from the case at hand to one that applies in every capital case: not whether the woman *should* be executed (whether her actions deserve condemnation), but whether she *can* be executed (whether mere mortals qualify to condemn).

Thus interpreted, Jesus' ruling both culminates the canonical development of biblical law as well as exceeds its prophetic and rabbinical interpretation. The biblical law assesses the death penalty for some twenty-five crimes.[18] At the same time, it implements several measures restricting execution of the death penalty in order to protect the lives of the innocent: those who cause death unintentionally can flee to cities of refuge (Num 35:9-15; Deut 19:1-13); children cannot be put to death for their parents' sins, and vice versa (Deut 24:16); no one can be put to death on the testimony of a single witness (Num 35:30; Deut 17:6; 19:15); giving false witness in a capital trial incurs a penalty of death (Deut 19:16-19); and only witnesses can initiate an execution (Deut 17:7). The prophets amend the law so that repentant sinners are spared the death penalty (Ezekiel 18 and 33). In the Mishnah, the Jewish rabbinical authorities sought to balance the Torah's profound respect for the value of human life and the Torah's clear instruction that certain crimes were to be punished by death.[19] They did so by retaining the death penalty in principle but restricting it in practice even further than the Torah, establishing stringent criteria and instituting elaborate procedures that erected barriers to the legal execution of a death penalty. Gardner Hanks summarizes the rabbinical position:

> The process is clearly stacked in favor of an acquittal. Those who can be witnesses are severely limited. Further evidence of innocence is allowed after the witnesses are heard, but no additional evidence of guilt is accepted. Judges

---

18. For a listing and discussion, see Hanks, *Capital Punishment and the Bible*, pp. 53-65.

19. On the value of human life in biblical law, see Moshe Greenberg, "Some Postulates of Biblical Criminal Law" (1960), in *Studies in the Bible and Law* (Philadelphia: Jewish Publication Society, 1995), pp. 25-41.

are not permitted to change from an innocent vote to one for conviction. . . .
The Mishnah did not outlaw the death penalty. . . . However, the comprehensive restrictions placed on the witnesses and judges in capital trials would
have made it extremely difficult to impose death sentences if the restrictions
were strictly applied.[20]

The death penalty is never abolished in Jewish law, but rather is so qualified "as
to make execution a virtual impossibility," as Gerald Blidstein comments: "Jewish law abolished capital punishment in fact not by denying its conceptual
moral validity but rather by allowing it only this conceptual validity."[21]

Likewise, Jesus' ruling does not abolish the death penalty outright. He
nonetheless puts the death penalty unconditionally beyond human reach.
While retaining the death penalty in principle, Jesus' ruling extends the legal requirement that no execution can proceed unless initiated by the witnesses, imposing a condition — sinless perfection — that no witness can satisfy in practice. Jesus' ruling effectively reduces the number of legally permissible
executions to exactly zero and thus constitutes a *permanent moratorium* on the
human practice of capital punishment.

24.4. Objections to This Interpretation

Now, some might want to object that our interpretation has taken Jesus' ruling
in this case too far. We consider three such possible objections here. One might
argue that Jesus did not intend to make execution of a death sentence legally
impossible, but rather to ensure only that all wickedness is excluded from the
prosecution of capital cases.[22] Jesus' ruling should be interpreted more narrowly to mean that anyone who is guilty of a capital crime, or that anyone who
is guilty of the specific capital crime being tried, is henceforth excluded from
giving testimony, rendering a verdict, or pronouncing sentence in a capital case.
Such a narrowly tailored ruling would thus require greater care in selecting witnesses, jurors, and judges, but not a moratorium on death sentences. This objection, it seems to me, reads too much into what Jesus actually says. He does
not say, "Let the one who has committed no sin deserving of death cast the first
stone," or "Let the one who has never committed this sin cast the first stone," or
"Let the one who has committed no sin in this case cast the first stone." He says,

---

20. Hanks, *Capital Punishment and the Bible*, pp. 82-83, cf. pp. 78-85; David Novak, *Jewish
Social Ethics* (New York: Oxford University Press, 1992), pp. 163ff.

21. Gerald L. Blidstein, "Capital Punishment: The Classic Jewish Discussion," in Glen H.
Stassen, ed., *Capital Punishment: A Reader* (Cleveland, OH: Pilgrim Press, 1998), pp. 107-18,
p. 113. Cf. Novak, *Jewish Social Ethics*, pp. 174ff.

22. Cf. Derrett, *Law in the New Testament*, pp. 175ff.

"Let the one who is without sin cast the first stone." The Greek expression *ho anamartētos* means, literally, "the one not having sinned." "Without sin" — period. To narrow the interpretation of Jesus' ruling, we must *add* to Jesus' words to make them say *less* than what he actually says.

Some might argue that Jesus' ruling applies only to cases of adultery and perhaps other offenses against sexual morals. He meant only to rule that adultery is not deserving of death, and thus his ruling does not necessarily apply to other kinds of capital crimes. Judge Jesus may grant mercy in an adultery case, but it by no means follows that he would even entertain a mercy plea in a murder case.[23] Such an objection, it seems to me, misses the point that Jesus' ruling concerns neither the gravity of the crime nor the proportionality of the punishment. Jesus does not ask whether a penalty of death is fitting for the sin of adultery, but rather only whether mortals/sinners are fit to execute a death sentence. As such, Jesus' ruling applies to *all* crimes we might judge deserving of death.

And some might argue that if our interpretation of Jesus' ruling were accepted, it would mean a moratorium on not only executions, but any punishment whatsoever. There could be no guilty verdicts, much less any prison sentences, fines, reparations, or even requirements of community service. Thus, Bailey: "What would be the consequence if, in every case, the jurors were told, 'Let him [or her] who is without sin . . .'? . . . The result would be that no one could condemn anyone for anything! Thus the argument, when pursued to its logical conclusion, leads to an absurdity."[24] By assuming that there is no relevant distinction between the kind of case considered here and all other kinds of cases, this argument falls prey to the classic "slippery slope" fallacy. The way Bailey has framed the argument illustrates the point: he elides the latter part of Jesus' ruling, which concerns specifically the execution of a death sentence. Ignoring the distinction between capital and non-capital cases, the argument slides over the distinction between lethal and non-lethal punishment, between judgment that *kills* and judgment that does not. This distinction matters dearly to covenant law. For covenant law reflects the special value of human life especially in how it handles capital cases. Jesus' ruling places a moratorium only on judgment that kills, leaving us free and responsible to judge wrongdoing in a way that redeems offenders and restores community (Matt 18:15-20; Gal 6:1).[25] Jesus himself practices such redemptive-restorative justice in this case. He judges the woman's actions as sin, but releases her with a judicial warning to turn from sin that leads to death and walk in the way of righteousness that leads to life, according to the law (Deut 30:15-20) and the prophets (Ezek 18:21-23, 30-32).

23. Cf. Bailey, *Capital Punishment*, pp. 71-72.

24. Bailey, *Capital Punishment*, p. 73.

25. Marshall, *Beyond Retribution*, pp. 131-40, considers the potential for "restorative punishment" in a communal approach to criminal justice. See also Howard Zehr, *Changing Lenses: A New Focus for Crime and Justice*, 3rd ed. (Scottdale, PA: Herald Press, 2005).

24.5. The Basis of Jesus' Ruling in Covenant Law

As important as it is to see *that* Jesus makes a judicial ruling with far-reaching implications for the human institution of legal justice, it is at least as important that we understand *why* he does so in this concrete situation. As we have seen, Torah, prophets, and rabbis took great care to protect the innocent from wrongful conviction and execution and to preserve the life of guilty ones who repented of their sins. But here Jesus raises the legal standard for the death penalty to a humanly impossible threshold neither for the sake of the innocent nor on behalf of the repentant. Why, then, does he do it? The covenant provides the answer: Jesus intervenes to save the life of one who is created "in the image of God," who is "poor and needy," who is weak and vulnerable, who stands defenseless and helpless before the rulers and authorities. In doing so, he acts on behalf of the God "who made heaven and earth, the sea, and all that is in them; who keeps faith forever; who executes justice for the oppressed" (Ps 146:6b-7a).

Clearly, this woman is being exploited, and those who accuse her and would condemn her are abusing their authority.[26] It takes two to commit adultery — if *she* has been caught in the act, then so has *he*. And, as observed above, the law subjects both to penalty of death. In fact, the law puts the emphasis on the man's actions before the woman's: "If a man is caught lying with the wife of another man, both of them shall die, the man who lay with the woman as well as the woman" (Deut 22:22; cf. Lev 20:10). But the scribes and Pharisees bring only the woman for judgment. His life is not on the line, only hers. Evidently, the scribes and Pharisees have seized her case as an opportunity to pursue their plan to trap Jesus into convicting himself of lawlessness or blasphemy. Or, perhaps, they have conspired to catch her committing adultery for that same end.[27] Either way, she is an expendable pawn in their evil ploy. In their eyes, her life has no more value than the success or failure of their scheme. Indeed, their scheme is premised upon the willingness to trade her life in exchange for "the goods" on Jesus. Thus, William Barclay: "They were not looking on this woman as a person at all; they were looking on her only as a thing, an instrument whereby they could formulate a charge against Jesus. They were using her, as a man might use a tool for their own purposes."[28]

---

26. I thus think this story better titled "The Elders Caught Abusing Power"!

27. Derrett, *Law in the New Testament*, pp. 160-63, points out that it is unlikely that the adulterous act was discovered by chance by random passersby: adultery is usually committed out of public view, in close quarters, behind secured doors. Rules of testimony would have required the witnesses to have seen the act itself in progress and to have agreed on the details. That the woman was seen "in the very act of committing adultery" thus suggests that the witnesses might have been "lying in wait," which would suggest further a conspiracy, perhaps initiated by her suspicious husband.

28. William Barclay, *The Gospel of John*, vol. 2 (Philadelphia: Westminster Press, 1975), p. 5.

The very notion that a human life should be reducible to an instrumental value, to a means of exchange, is repugnant to the Torah. As Jewish Bible scholar Moshe Greenberg observes, "the bedrock of the biblical evaluation" of humankind is that the human being "is no tool, no instrument, no means."[29] And that the human being cannot be measured by any utilitarian standard, Chris Marshall writes, is rooted in creation: "As the height of God's creative activity, human beings ought never to be considered mere instruments for some "higher" end. Each person is an end in himself or herself. And the reason for this lies in the *manner* of human creation, for humans alone are created in the image of God."[30] Exploiting one created in God's image as a mere means to an end is the penultimate sin against God's law, following only the sin of failing to acknowledge and worship God alone as God. Indeed, the one sin is akin to the other: if we refuse to reverence God as God, we will not respect the life of one created in God's image; and if we refuse to respect the life of one created in God's image, we will not reverence the one in whose image she is created.[31]

It is, of course, the poorest and weakest members of the community who are most vulnerable to exploitation by the selfish schemes of others and the unjust structures of society. Now as then, the legal system of capital punishment seizes upon the poorest and weakest members of the community for the death penalty; hence the saying, "those without the capital get the punishment."[32] Hence also

29. Moshe Greenberg, "The Biblical Grounding of Human Value," in *The Samuel Friedland Lectures, 1960-1966* (New York: Jewish Theological Society of America, 1966), pp. 39-52, here p. 47. Greenberg shows how the value of human life underlies biblical law and is reflected in the creation story.

30. Christopher D. Marshall, *Crowned with Honor and Glory: Human Rights in the Biblical Tradition* (Telford, PA: Pandora Press U.S., 2001), p. 55, emphasis original. Cf. Greenberg, "Biblical Grounding of Human Value," and Aharon W. Zoera, *In the Image of God: A Christian Response to Capital Punishment* (Lanham, MD: University Press of America, 2000), pp. 13-15. I would add this qualification: God alone exists as an "end in himself," strictly speaking, for God alone is uncreated and *is* good in a final sense (Mark 10:18). As creatures of the creator, we are created not for the sake of ourselves, but ultimately for the glory of the creator. Nonetheless, that humans alone among all creatures are created "in the image" of the creator invests the individual human being with an incomparable value relative to all other created things.

31. This, I think, is why Jesus paired "Love God" and "Love your neighbor as yourself" (i.e., as one also created in God's image) as the two commandments on which hang all the law and the prophets (Matt 22:36-40). Ethics thus reflects worship: proper fear of the one in whose image the other is created is reflected in proper respect for the other created in God's image, such that right worship toward God is reflected in right action toward others. Here we recall the view of the early fourth-century Christian writer Lactantius (*Divine Institutes* VI.10-11).

32. In the U.S., the death sentence is given disproportionately to the poor (those unable to hire a lawyer), the under-educated, the mentally disabled, and African American defendants convicted of killing white victims. See Hugo Adam Bedau, *The Death Penalty in America: Current Controversies* (New York: Oxford University Press, 1997), pp. 249-309; Gardner C. Hanks, *Against the Death Penalty: Christian and Secular Arguments against Capital Punishment* (Scottdale, PA: Herald Press, 1997), pp. 95-110.

the many statutes in covenant law to protect the rights and provide for the needs of widows, orphans, debtors, and immigrants in the community. The scribes and Pharisees, who are experts in the law and bring this case to Jesus with the ostensible purpose of upholding the law, are in fact violating the law at its very heart. For them to succeed in their scheme would be to deface God's image, dishonor God, and so bring down the whole edifice of "the law and the prophets." Jesus thus acts in this concrete situation in order to uphold the creation-rooted biblical principle that underlies covenant justice: because humankind is created in God's image, not the poorest or weakest or even most sinful member of the human community is to be made a mere instrument for human ends.[33]

She is a woman, moreover. This obvious fact frames the legal charge and moral stance of the scribes and Pharisees — ". . . *this woman* was caught in the very act of committing adultery. Now in the law Moses commanded us to stone *such women . . .*" (vv. 4-5) — and thus, in a way, frames the whole situation. According to legal custom, her testimony carries no weight. She cannot even speak for herself, much less protest her innocence. Only a man — her husband, say, or a brother or a son of legal age — has the right to act in her defense; but no man has come forth on her behalf. She stands alone before judgment without defense. Jesus stands in as her defense, advocating on her behalf before humans and God, defending the accused and shaming the accusers, in order to save the life of the defenseless from condemnation. Jesus thus upholds the tradition of "the law and the prophets" that measures the overall justice of the covenant community by the welfare of its least — poorest and weakest — members. By his advocacy, Jesus effectively speaks God's answer to the prayer of the accused on behalf of this woman:

> But you, O LORD my Lord, act on my behalf for your name's sake. . . . For I am poor and needy, and my heart is pierced within me. . . . I am an object of scorn to my accusers. . . . Help me, O LORD my God! . . . My accusers will be clothed with dishonor; may they be wrapped in their own shame as a mantle. With my mouth I will give great thanks to the LORD; I will praise him in the midst of the throng. For he stands at the right hand of the needy, to save them from those who would condemn them to death. (Ps 109:21-31)

Jesus pursues the covenant justice that defends the dignity and saves the life of the weak and vulnerable, regardless of moral merit, irrespective of legal rights. Jesus advocates on behalf of the life of the woman before him, not because she qualifies as "innocent," nor because she "deserves" it, but solely because she *needs* it — because, no less than any other person created in the image of God,

---

33. Such thinking might well be extended to the question of abortion. See Richard B. Hays, *The Moral Vision of the New Testament: Community, Cross, New Creation; A Contemporary Introduction to New Testament Ethics* (San Francisco: HarperSanFrancisco, 1996), pp. 444-61.

she is a sinner who needs saving help.[34] Jesus' verdict does God's justice; for, as Perry Yoder observes, "God's action for justice is not based on the merit of individuals, but on their need."[35] Jesus' advocacy is thus simply an act of divine grace. The grace of Jesus releases her from judgment under law, thus opening the way for her repentance from a life of sin: "Neither do I condemn you. Go your way, and from now on do not sin again" (v. 11). She is restored to the covenant community in order to live the way of righteousness that God desires.

Jesus' ruling makes possible not only her repentance, but also the repentance of her accusers and would-be executioners. Jesus has reminded them that they are no less blameworthy under God's judgment than she; they, too, need to repent from their evil deeds. But after exposing them to public shame as they have exposed her, Jesus again stoops down to write on the ground, giving them the same opportunity as her, to "go and sin no more." And, wisely, they take Jesus' offer of grace: "When they heard it, they went away, one by one, beginning

34. The ethic of Jesus is thus more radical than the "consistent ethic of life" or "completely pro-life stance" promoted by both Catholic and Evangelical Christians (see Joseph Cardinal Bernardin, *Consistent Ethic of Life* [Kansas City, MO: Sheed & Ward, 1988]; Ronald J. Sider, *Completely Pro-Life: Building a Consistent Stance on Abortion, the Family, Nuclear Weapons, the Poor* [Downers Grove, IL: InterVarsity Press, 1987]; Evangelicals and Catholics Together, "That They May Have Life: A Statement of Evangelicals and Catholics Together," *First Things* 166 [2006], 18-27). I certainly agree that Christians should maintain a consistent stance concerning life-ethical issues (see Darrin W. Snyder Belousek, "Toward a Consistent Ethic of Life in the Peace Tradition Perspective: A Critical-Constructive Response to the MC USA Statement on Abortion," *Mennonite Quarterly Review* 79 [2005] 439-80). Yet the Catholic-Evangelical ethic, premised on the principle that *innocent* life *only* is inviolable, hedges the value of human life and so permits capital punishment (and just war) as much as it prohibits abortion. Bernardin himself emphasized this point: "The principle which protects *innocent* life distinguishes the unborn child from the convicted murderer" (*Consistent Ethic*, p. 16, emphasis original). This distinction is inconsistent with the ethic of Jesus, which adds no moral qualification to the value of human life created in the image of God and thus consistently defends all human life, even the lives of those who fail the "innocence" test. Bernardin did address the question of the death penalty, but on grounds other than the principle that prohibits taking innocent life, namely, God's demonstration of love to us, Jesus' ethic of forgiveness, the gospel call to reconciliation, and the social cycle of violence. Similarly, Sider, in his more recent writing, has included opposition to capital punishment within "a consistently pro-life agenda": "Abortion . . . and capital punishment . . . destroy persons created in the image of God" (Ronald J. Sider, *The Scandal of Evangelical Politics: Why Are Christians Missing the Opportunity to Really Change the World?* [Grand Rapids, MI: Baker Books, 2008], p. 155). But, tellingly, the central reason Sider gives for placing capital punishment on a par with abortion is the teaching and ministry of Jesus in John 8 and Matthew 5, not the principle that prohibits taking innocent life, which Sider still cites as the "starting point" of a consistent ethic of life (p. 147). This suggests that both Bernardin and Sider recognize that this principle is an insufficient basis for a consistent ethic of life completely compatible with the gospel of Jesus Christ. A "consistent ethic of life" founded on the principle of the inviolability of *innocent* life *only* turns out to be less than "completely pro-life" after all.

35. Perry B. Yoder, *Shalom: The Bible's Word for Salvation, Justice, and Peace* (Nappanee, IN: Evangel Publishing, 1987), p. 34.

with the elders" (vv. 8-9).[36] Jesus' advocacy on behalf of the defendant, therefore, does not in the least compromise his impartiality as judge, for he judges
equally the sins of the defendant and the sins of her accusers.

Jesus' gracious action on behalf of this woman and those who would condemn her fulfills the covenant justice that God desires, as attested by the prophets. God's justice desires for the sinner, not death by retribution, but rather life
by repentance that restores the sinner to righteous living (Ezek 18:23): "Have I
any pleasure in the death of the wicked, says the Lord GOD, and not rather that
they should turn from their ways and live?" The justice of God is neither satisfied by the death of the wicked nor compromised by mercy upon the guilty. For
it is precisely God's desire for turning from sin to righteousness, leading from
death to life, that expresses the heart of God's covenant law:

> Therefore I will judge you, O house of Israel, all of you according to your
> ways, says the Lord GOD. Repent and turn from all your transgressions; oth-
> erwise iniquity will be your ruin. . . . Why will you die, O house of Israel? For
> I have no pleasure in the death of anyone, says the Lord GOD. Turn, then, and
> live. (Ezek 18:30-32)

"Turn, then, and live." Or, Jesus says, "Go and sin no more." As God judges Israel, so Jesus judges this woman. By his words and deeds, Jesus points the way
of repentance and offers the hope of redemption, thus fulfilling the intention of
God's covenant justice.

Jesus' ruling on behalf of this woman does covenant justice in three ways:
by upholding the value of human life created in the image of God, which underlies covenant law; by advocating for one who is "poor and needy," who
stands defenseless and needing protection; and by opening the way for repentance from sin, redemption of sinners, and restoration of community. Insofar
as Jesus judges on God's behalf in this case, his words and deeds present us with
a model of God's own justice-doing, which is not a punitive justice that seeks
retribution to satisfy the demands of law. Indeed, in this case, law's demand is
not fulfilled, retribution is *not* satisfied, punishment is *not* executed — and yet
God's covenant justice is done. God's covenant justice, executed here by Jesus,
does not necessarily — and thus does not essentially — have to do with legal
demands and retributive punishment, but rather is *saving-redemptive* justice.
From the biblical principle of *imitatio Dei* (Lev 19:2; Matt 5:45), therefore, we
can argue that human-executed justice, including punishment, ought to serve a
redemptive purpose: as God judges Israel, so Jesus judges this woman, and so
ought we judge one another.

36. Gail R. O'Day, *The Gospel of John,* in *The New Interpreter's Bible* (Nashville: Abingdon
Press, 1995), 9:630.

CHAPTER 25

Covenant Justice, Capital Punishment, and the Cross of Christ: The Death Penalty Crucified

And when you were dead
in trespasses and the uncircumcision of your flesh,
God made you alive together with him,
when he forgave us all our trespasses,
erasing the record that stood against us
with its legal demands.
He set this aside, nailing it to the cross.

COLOSSIANS 2:13-14

There is an intimate relationship between Jesus' death on the cross and the death penalty, witnessed by the Nicene Creed: "For our sake he was crucified under Pontius Pilate." Jesus died "for us" by the legal execution of a death sentence under Roman authority. But what are the implications? What does Jesus' death by execution entail for the death penalty itself? Surprisingly, this question seems not to have been much asked by Christian theologians during most of the church's two millennia, perhaps not at all until the twentieth century. In his survey of the history of Christian thinking concerning the death penalty, James Megivern cites only one major theologian, Karl Barth, dealing with the question of the cross and capital punishment.[1]

---

1. James J. Megivern, *The Death Penalty: An Historical and Theological Survey* (Mahwah, NJ: Paulist Press, 1997), pp. 275-77.

This chapter comprises a revised version of my article, "Capital Punishment, Covenant Justice, and the Cross of Christ: The Death Penalty in the Life and Death of Jesus," *Mennonite Quarterly Review* 83 (2009), 375-402. My thanks to the editor of *Mennonite Quarterly Review* for permission to reuse this material.

The teaching of Jesus, we have argued, leads to a twofold conclusion: a permanent moratorium on capital punishment, because no human being is worthy to execute the death penalty — such privilege belongs solely to divine prerogative. This prompts the questions: Does God continue to uphold the death penalty? And does the gospel have anything more to say on the matter? We will present the view here that God has brought the death penalty to a final end through the cross of Christ — indeed, that God has put the death penalty itself to death on the cross. Through the cross of Christ, the death penalty has lost divine sanction because it has lost its very life by the action of God. We will develop this view in two parts, each addressing a particular rationale for the death penalty: expiation and retribution. The cross of Christ, we will argue, nullifies the death penalty on both counts.

25.1. The Expiatory Rationale: Jesus' Death Removes Sin "Once for All"

25.1.1. The Expiatory Rationale for the Death Penalty

One rationale for capital punishment down the centuries has been that the death penalty serves as an expiation of the murderer's sin. The expiatory rationale continues to some extent in Jewish, Lutheran, and Catholic thought.[2] Within Catholic tradition, Pius XII stated (1952), "It is reserved to the public power to deprive the condemned of the good of life in expiation of his crime after he has already disposed himself of the right to life."[3] John Paul II argued in *The Gospel of Life* (1995) for a severe limitation of the death penalty: it can be justified only "in cases of absolute necessity . . . when it would not be possible otherwise to defend society" (ch. III, ¶56). The *Catechism of the Catholic Church* nonetheless maintains expiation as a secondary rationale for the death penalty:

> Legitimate public authority has the right and duty to inflict punishment proportionate to the gravity of the offense. Punishment has the primary aim of redressing the disorder introduced by the offense. When it is willingly accepted by the guilty party, it assumes the value of expiation. (3.1.2.3.1, ¶2666)

Within covenant law, as evident in the Torah, capital punishment did serve an expiatory function — as a cleansing, purging, or "wiping away" of sin and its consequences. This expiatory rationale is found at the end of Numbers and throughout Deuteronomy. In Numbers, the idea is that bloodshed pollutes the land and destroys its fertility (cf. Gen 4:10-12), such that maintenance of the

---

2. Megivern, *The Death Penalty,* pp. 272, 280, 283, and 430; David Novak, *Jewish Social Ethics* (New York: Oxford University Press, 1992), pp. 174-78.

3. Quoted in Megivern, *The Death Penalty,* p. 280.

holy land requires removal of the murder-induced pollution. The only means of making expiation for the land to cleanse it from blood-pollution was the death of the murderer:

> Moreover you shall accept no ransom for the life of a murderer who is subject to the death penalty; a murderer must be put to death. . . . You shall not pollute the land in which you live; for blood pollutes the land, and no expiation *(kipper)* can be made for the land, for the blood that is shed in it, except by the blood of the one who shed it. (Num 35:31, 33)

The use of cultic language *(kipper)* suggests that executing the death penalty upon a murderer was intended as a ritual expiation. In Deuteronomy, the idea is that evildoing sows contamination among the people, such that maintenance of covenantal integrity requires purging the evildoer from the community. Repeatedly, the law appends the following motivation to a command to execute the death penalty: "So you shall purge the evil from your midst" (Deut 13:1-11; 17:2-7, 12; 19:11-13, 18-19; 21:1-9, 18-21). The Hebrew word translated "purge" *(bā'ar,* piel) signifies something burned or consumed by fire; although not specifically cultic language, the connotation of expiation can be seen here. A biblical rationale for capital punishment, therefore, would be to expiate the sin of bloodshed or other serious evildoing for the sake of protecting the integrity of the covenant community and the fertility of the holy land.[4]

25.1.2. *Jesus' Death Removes the Expiatory Rationale "Once for All"*

The argument can thus be made that the atoning death of Jesus removes the expiatory rationale for the death penalty. The New Testament depicts his death as vicarious ("for us") and sacrificial in manifold ways, including as sin offering (Heb 7:27; 9:23-26; 10:3-18) and as atoning sacrifice for sins (Rom 3:25; Heb 2:17; 1 John 2:2; 4:10).[5] The writer of Hebrews testifies that Jesus' death is the final sacrifice and ultimate expiation for sin: Jesus has come in the flesh "to make a sacrifice of atonement *(hilaskesthai)* for the sins of the people" (Heb 2:17); "he has appeared once for all at the end of the age to remove sin by the sacrifice of himself" (9:26); "Christ . . . offered for all time a single sacrifice for sins" (10:12). And John witnesses that Jesus' death atones for the sins of all humanity: "he is the atoning sacrifice *(hilasmos)* . . . for the sins of the whole world" (1 John

---

4. Cf. J. Greenberg, "Crimes and Punishments," in *The Interpreter's Dictionary of the Bible* (New York: Abingdon Press, 1962), 1:733-44; Raymond Westbrook, "Punishments and Crimes," in *The Anchor Bible Dictionary* (New York: Doubleday, 1992), 5:546-56.

5. John Driver, *Understanding the Atonement for the Mission of the Church* (Scottdale, PA: Herald Press, 1986), pp. 129-62.

2:2).[6] Since the cross of Christ serves as an all-sufficient ("once for all") sacrificial expiation of sin that is of cosmic scope ("for the whole world"), his vicarious death removes expiation as a rationale for capital punishment for all crimes and "for all time."

Barth put forth this argument in the form of a rhetorical question: "Now that Jesus Christ has been nailed to the cross for the sins of the world, how can we still use the thought of *expiation* to establish the death penalty?"[7] Yoder elaborates:

> It is the clear witness of the New Testament, especially the Epistle to the Hebrews, that the ceremonial requirements of the Old Testament find their fulfillment and their end in the high-priestly sacrifice of Christ. "Once for all" is the triumphant claim of the Epistle. Henceforth no more bloodshed is needed to testify to the sacredness of life, and no more sacrifices are called for to expiate a man's usurping of the power to kill. With the cross of Christ the moral and ceremonial basis of capital punishment is wiped away.[8]

Marshall summarizes this argument, drawing out the theological implications concerning the expiatory rationale for capital punishment after the cross:

> The atoning value of all Old Testament practices is thus fulfilled and superseded by the death of Christ. This means that the language of atonement cannot be used to defend capital punishment in the Christian era. By doing so, [one] ends up in a theological quagmire in which God requires dual atonement for murderers, once by their own death and once by Christ's. . . . [A]rguments which construe the offender's death as expiating his or her objective guilt before God must be rejected as inconsistent with New Testament teaching on atonement.[9]

As Marshall himself concedes, this argument is limited in scope: it does not undermine punishment per se, nor does it address all biblical rationale for capital punishment.

---

6. The Greek verb *hilaskomai* ("make atonement" or "expiate"), from which the related noun *hilasmos* ("atoning sacrifice") is derived, is used (in the form *exhilaskomai*) in the Septuagint to translate Hebrew *kipper* and thus is explicitly cultic language.

7. Karl Barth, *Church Dogmatics* III/4, quoted in Megivern, *The Death Penalty*, p. 276, emphasis original.

8. John Howard Yoder, *The Christian and Capital Punishment* (Newton, KS: Faith and Life Press, 1961), pp. 8-9.

9. Christopher D. Marshall, *Beyond Retribution: A New Testament Vision for Justice, Crime, and Punishment* (Grand Rapids, MI: Eerdmans Publishing, 2001), p. 222.

25.2. The Retributive Rationale:
God's Justice Nails Retribution to the Cross

25.2.1. The Penalty of Death as the Satisfaction of Law

The above argument does not undermine entirely the biblical case for capital punishment because the need for expiation is not the only biblical rationale for the death penalty. Although atoning sacrifice "wiped away" the pollution of sin, one might think that law itself still needs to be satisfied, that justice must be "paid its due" for sin by the death of the sinner. This is the retributive rationale for capital punishment.

In the modern era, the retributive rationale has found no greater exponent than the Enlightenment philosopher and German Pietist, Immanuel Kant:

> But whoever has committed murder must *die*. There is, in this case, no jurid-ical substitute or surrogate, that can be given or taken for the satisfaction of justice. There is no *likeness* or proportion between life, however painful, and death; and therefore there is no equality between the crime of murder and the retaliation of it but what is judicially accomplished by the execution of the criminal.[10]

In order to right a wrong, from the retributivist perspective, justice requires "retaliation," a proportionate punishment that "pays back" the wrong done to the wrongdoer. In the case of murder, as Kant argues, the only judicial sentence that achieves an adequate "retaliation" or due proportion between crime and punishment is the death penalty — life for life (or death for death). Anything less would fail to satisfy the law of justice.

Kant's logic of retribution is premised on the *lex talionis*, the ancient law that justice is satisfied by a "likeness" between crime and punishment: justice pays back "like for like." Such a retributive rationale premised upon the *lex talionis* is found within two major sections of biblical law, the Covenant Code (Exodus 20–23) and the Holiness Code (Leviticus 17–26). In Exod 21:12-32, one finds a subsection of laws concerning homicide and other potentially capital crimes. This legislation distinguishes cases for the sake of assigning degrees of culpability and assessing a fitting penalty. In cases of intentionally caused in-jury and death, the penalty is assessed according to the *lex talionis* (vv. 23-25). This section of the Covenant Code thus provides a retributive rationale for the

---

10. Immanuel Kant, *The Philosophy of Law*, excerpted in *Philosophical Perspectives on Punishment*, ed. Gertrude Ezorsky (Albany: State University of New York Press, 1972), p. 105, emphasis original. For an extended treatment of Kant's retributivism, see Lloyd Steffen, *Exe-cuting Justice: The Moral Meaning of the Death Penalty* (Cleveland, OH: Pilgrim Press, 1998), pp. 69-87.

death penalty. This retributive rationale is repeated in the Holiness Code, where the *lex talionis* assigns appropriate penalties in cases of murder or injury:

> Anyone who kills a human being shall be put to death. Anyone who kills an animal shall make restitution for it, life for life. Anyone who maims another shall suffer the same injury in return: fracture for fracture, eye for eye, tooth for tooth; the injury inflicted is the injury to be suffered. One who kills an animal shall make restitution for it; but one who kills a human being shall be put to death. (Lev 24:17-21)

There is nothing obviously cultic about this legislation; the rationale behind the death penalty here is evidently legal, an equality or proportionality between transgression and penalty: life for life. This same legal principle appears again in Deut 19:15-21, a section of laws concerning trial procedure in which the *lex talionis* sanctions penalties against witnesses. Those who falsely accuse another of wrongdoing in a court trial are to be punished with the penalty that the accused would have received if convicted. The false witness is treated as an evildoer attempting to inflict an unjust punishment upon the accused, which punishment is then inflicted back in kind *(hon tropon)* upon the evildoer (v. 19). The *lex talionis* measures out the appropriate retribution: "life for life, eye for eye, tooth for tooth . . ." (v. 21). In a capital case, the punishment would be death, of course; in effect, therefore, the *lex talionis* sanctions the death penalty as retribution against false witnesses in a capital trial.

Biblical law thus sanctions a retributive rationale for capital punishment, which remains the primary reason for popular support of the death penalty in contemporary America.[11] A comprehensive Christian view concerning the death penalty must thus address directly the retributive rationale for capital punishment. And we shall present here an argument that the cross of Christ not only removes any expiatory rationale for the death penalty, but also nullifies any retributive rationale.[12]

---

11. See Phoebe C. Ellsworth and Samuel R. Gross, "Hardening of the Attitudes: Americans' Views on the Death Penalty," in Bedau, *The Death Penalty in America*, pp. 90-115.

12. The reader might wonder concerning deterrence as a rationale for the death penalty. One does find a deterrent aspect to the biblical rationale for capital punishment in Deuteronomy: "Then all Israel shall hear and be afraid, and never again do any such wickedness" (13:11; cf. 17:13; 19:20; 21:21). Two comments: First, the deterrent rationale appears always paired with and following, and so evidently subordinate to, the expiatory rationale ("purge the evil"). Second, the biblical grounding of covenant law in the value of human life created in the image of God would seem to entail that deterrence cannot be a *sufficient* (i.e., stand-alone) reason for capital punishment, since to take the life of one person who has committed a crime *solely* to deter another from committing a crime would be to give human life an instrumental value, a mere means to an end, which is repugnant to the Torah.

25.2.2. *The Biblical Trajectory of the* Lex Talionis

To prepare the way for this argument, we will review the biblical trajectory of the *lex talionis*. My path of thinking here follows that of Millard Lind.[13] Lind traces the practice of retribution as it is introduced and reassessed within covenant law, from Moses in receiving the law at Mount Sinai (Torah) to Elijah in his theophany at Mount Horeb (prophets) to Jesus in his Sermon on the Mount (gospel). Overall, this journey "across three mountaintops" manifests a shift from law as retribution to law as covenant love. We extend Lind's path of thinking to the fourth mountaintop, the hill of the cross.

We begin with Lamech, who boasts, "I have killed a man for wounding me," and pledges seventy-sevenfold vengeance against anyone else who would do him injury (Gen 4:23-24). Lamech's way of excessive retribution and escalating violence becomes the way of fallen humanity, exemplified in the stories of Dinah, Samson, and David (Genesis 34, Judges 13–16, and 1 Samuel 25).[14] Against this cycle of violence and vengeance and amidst a clan culture of blood feuds, the *lex talionis* in biblical law functions to *limit* the retaliatory violence characteristic of human relations (Exod 21:23-24). As such, it does not represent God's perfect intention for the covenant community, but rather reflects the sinful reality of the human situation.[15]

As evidence of the limiting function of the *lex talionis* in the Covenant Code, consider the section of statutes in which it is introduced (Exod 21:12-32), which concerns injuries done to human beings. Strict retaliation is implemented only for crimes that willfully take or maliciously jeopardize life (murder, kidnapping, cursing — vv. 12-17). Losses due to injury are remedied not by retaliation but by financial compensation (vv. 18-32). Within the Covenant Code, therefore, strict retribution was the limit case. In effect, the *lex talionis* places a twofold limit on judicial life-taking: first, life can be taken in exchange for only *life*, never for personal injury or property damage; second, only *one* life can be taken for a life. The *lex talionis* functions in covenant law, not to sanction retribution as an absolute principle, but to restrain the entrenched practices of human vengeance.

The Torah and prophets limit retribution further by qualifying the death penalty as a punishment sanctioned by the *lex talionis*.

---

13. Millard Lind, *Sound of Sheer Silence and the Killing State: The Death Penalty and the Bible* (Telford, PA: Cascadia Publishing, 2004).

14. Concerning the Samson story, see my essay "Tragic Zeal: The Spiral of Violence, Vengeance, and Death," *The Mennonite*, September 7, 2004, pp. 16-17.

15. On the historical and cultural background of biblical law and the function of the *lex talionis*, see Gardner C. Hanks, *Capital Punishment and the Bible* (Scottdale, PA: Herald Press, 2002), pp. 25-85, and Marshall, *Beyond Retribution*, pp. 215ff.

The Torah limits the *lex talionis* from the beginning to only cases of intentional murder (Exod 21:12-14), and subsequent legislation established
"cities of refuge" to which those who cause death without intent may
flee to escape the "avenger of blood" (Num 35:9-15; Deut 19:1-7).

Moses, the first prophet of Israel, qualifies the *lex talionis* further with the
requirement of individual responsibility: "only for their own crimes
may persons be put to death" (Deut 24:16).

Moses adds a further qualification, requiring at least two eyewitnesses in
order for the *lex talionis* to be imposed: "no one shall be put to death
on the testimony of a single witness" (Num 35:30; cf. Deut 17:6; 19:15).

The prophet Ezekiel qualifies the *lex talionis* even further with the proviso
that, if the criminal repents of his crimes and amends his ways, then
his life should be spared (Ezek 18:21-24; cf. 33:10-11).

So, not only can life be taken only for life, and only one life for a life, but only
the life of the guilty party, and then only if the guilty party killed with intent,
and then only if there were at least two witnesses, but even then only if the
guilty party is unrepentant. The Torah and prophets thus deliberately and repeatedly hedge the *lex talionis* with qualifications that limit retribution and
leave room for redemption.

Jesus, the final prophet and authoritative teacher of the law, completes this
trajectory and so fulfills the intent of "the law and the prophets" (Matt 5:17). He
rejects outright the *lex talionis* as specifying the right response of the covenant
community to an evildoer in its midst: "You have heard that it was said, 'An eye
for an eye and a tooth for a tooth.' But I say to you, 'Do not resist an evildoer *(tō
ponērō)*. . .'" (vv. 38-42). As Dorothy Jean Weaver has argued, the Old Testament
background for Jesus' citation of the *lex talionis* is Deut 19:15-21, where it underwrites the community's religious and moral obligation to "purge the evildoer
(ton ponēron)" from its midst.[16] This canonical context carries two relevant implications: first, Jesus' rejection of the *lex talionis* refers to the legal practice of
the covenant community; and, second, that context links the talionic formula
directly to sanction of capital punishment (as we observed above). The upshot
is that Jesus rejects the *lex talionis* precisely insofar as it sanctions the death
penalty as the necessary and justified means of dealing with evildoers by the
covenant community. Thus, Weaver:

The impact of this negative command can hardly be overestimated. With the
words "do not resist," Jesus disallows both the principle of *hon tropon*, "pun-

---

16. Dorothy Jean Weaver, "Transforming Nonresistance: From *Lex Talionis* to 'Do Not Resist the Evil One,'" in Willard M. Swartley, ed., *The Love of Enemy and Nonretalition in the New
Testament* (Louisville, KY: Westminster John Knox Press, 1992), 32-71.

ishment in kind," and the *lex talionis,* the "law of retaliation" which embodies that principle. In so doing, he invalidates the most ancient and fundamental standard that individuals and societies have for dealing with "the one who is evil."[17]

25.2.3. *The* Lex Talionis *Ends at the Cross of Christ*

At the cross of Christ we see the consummation of this development: the transcendence of God's covenant justice beyond the law of retribution and yet the vindication of God's covenant justice in the redemption of sinners. Paul's message of the cross proclaims this good news in astonishing terms at Col 2:13-15, a text whose significance concerning the death penalty has been hitherto underappreciated.[18] Ernest Martin's analysis and layout of this text helps us see its features in relief:

> 13 a. When *you* were dead in your transgressions and the uncircumcision
>   of your flesh,
>   b. HE MADE *YOU* ALIVE TOGETHER WITH HIM,
>   c. having forgiven *us* all our transgressions,
> 14 a. having cancelled out *the certificate of debt* consisting of decrees against us and which was hostile to us,
>   b. HE HAS TAKEN *IT* OUT OF THE WAY,
>   c. having nailed *it* to the cross.
> 15 a. When he had disarmed *the rulers and authorities,*
>   b. HE MADE A PUBLIC DISPLAY OF *THEM*,
>   c. having triumphed over *them* through him.[19]

Notice carefully what Paul has written here. First, the subject of the verbs here would seem to be God (at least in vv. 13-14, perhaps Christ in v. 15). God has acted with a threefold redemption: to deal graciously *(charizomai)* with us concerning our transgressions and to give us life; to obliterate or expunge *(exaleiphō)* our sin record (or cancel our legal debt) and remove *(airō)* the legal decree against us; and to defeat, disarm, and humiliate "the rulers and authori-

---

17. Weaver, "Transforming Nonresistance," p. 54.

18. Our analysis and interpretation of this text does not attempt to consider it in relation to the epistle as a whole. To some extent, as is unavoidable in such discussions, we take this text "out of context."

19. Ernest D. Martin, *Colossians, Philemon* (Believers Church Bible Commentary; Scottdale, PA: Herald Press, 1993), p. 113, emphasis original. Martin follows the NASB. Verse citations in this section refer to this text unless otherwise evident.

ties" that crucified Christ. Second, the recipient of God's redeeming activity is
"us," who were "dead in our transgressions" but who now have received God's
grace. God acts to forgive our transgressions, save us from death, and raise us to
life "with Christ." Third, God acts to redeem us by means of Christ and the
cross. The phrase *en autō* in v. 15c can be translated either "through him
[Christ]" (NASB) or "in it [the cross]" (NRSV). Both make sense: God acts for
our redemption through Christ in the cross. But Paul nowhere says that God
acts in any way *upon* or *against* Jesus: God acts *through* Christ *in* the cross.

Fourth, the pronoun "it" in both v. 14b ("this" NRSV) and v. 14c refers
back to the entire preceding phrase in v. 14a, "the record that stood against us
with its legal demands" (NRSV) or "the certificate of debt consisting of decrees against us" (NASB). This "certificate" *(cheirographon)* is the legal record
of our transgressions (or the accounting sheet of our debts) that is kept in the
heavenly books (cf. Dan 7:10; Rev 20:12).[20] The "legal demands" *(dogmata)*
that attach to this record, one may plausibly interpret, refer to the decrees of
the commandments in the law of Moses. In Ephesians, Paul uses the same
term to refer to "the law of commandments in decrees" *(ton nomon tōn entolōn
en dogmasin)* that is abolished or nullified in Christ through the cross (Eph
2:15-16 NET).[21] There, the "law" *(nomos)* divides Gentiles from Jews (v. 14) —
and, hence, the *dogmata* would seem to concern the law of Moses. One might
thus infer that the *dogmata* in Col 2:14 also concern the law of Moses. In
Colossians, then, these *dogmata* can be interpreted as representing the con-
demnatory decrees of the law — the law insofar as it sanctions penalties for
transgressions (levied according to the *lex talionis*). In this sense, we would be
"dead in our transgressions" because we stood condemned under law on account of the legal record against us (cf. Rev 20:11-15). Jerry Sumney gives another interpretation: *dogma* represents here, not a legal demand, but an official
decree of condemnation or a judicial order of execution — a death sentence.[22]
Both interpretations, however, come to the same point: God has acted *both* to
render of no account our record of sin *and* to render null and void our condemnation on account of sin (whether by legal penalty or judicial order), having expunged our sin record, taking it away with the sentence of death at-
tached to it and nailing *both* to the cross. We are thus released from both sin
and condemnation.

Fifth, let us attend also to what Paul does *not* say in Col 2:13-15.[23] Paul does

20. Jerry L. Sumney, *Colossians: A Commentary* (Louisville: Westminster John Knox Press,
2008), p. 144. The only other (deutero-)canonical uses of this Greek word are in Tobit (5:3; 9:5),
where it refers to a bond of financial obligation.

21. On the possible relation between these two texts, see Thomas R. Yoder Neufeld, *Ephesians* (Believers Church Bible Commentary; Scottdale, PA: Herald Press, 2002), pp. 117-18.

22. Cf. Sumney, *Colossians,* pp. 144-45.

23. See the discussion of this text in Chapter 18 above.

not say that God has canceled the "certificate of debt" charged against our account because Christ has paid our debt to God in his blood by his death on the cross. Rather, Paul says, God has "obliterated" or "expunged" *(exaleiphō)* our account of sin from the heavenly book of record. Nor does Paul say that God has forgiven our transgressions because, having removed our transgressions from us, he has reckoned them against Christ instead. Rather, Paul says, God has taken away our transgressions and nailed them to the cross. Nor does Paul say that God spares us from the death penalty by putting Jesus to death in our place as penalty for our sins. Rather, Paul says, what God puts to death at the cross is our sin itself and the law that demands (or the judgment that decrees) death as the penalty (or sentence) for sin. Paul's argument is not that of penal substitution.

Paul's language in Col 2:13-15, therefore, does not say, explicitly or implicitly, that God has satisfied the requirement of retribution, that God has fulfilled the legal demand of death for sin. In fact, Paul writes here, quite the opposite is the case. God has acted through Christ in the cross to do away with legal records and to nullify such legal requirements. The legal demand of death against us has *not* been fulfilled, but removed; the requirement of retribution for sin has *not* been satisfied, but crucified.

And yet, as he emphasizes elsewhere, Paul is convinced that God, in redeeming humanity from sin through the atoning death of Christ, has done justice in faithfulness to the covenant (Rom 3:21-26). How, though, can God *both* redeem humanity from sin *and* do justice in faithfulness to the covenant if retribution is not satisfied? This is possible, Paul says there, because the covenant justice of God that redeems sinners is the expression of God's own grace — sinners are put right ("justified") by God through the cross of Christ, not according to the law of retribution ("just deserts"), but rather as a divine gift (v. 24).[24] While the cross fulfills the purpose of "the law" in that it manifests the covenant righteousness (justice) of God through the faithfulness of Christ (vv. 21-22), it nonetheless does so in a way that transcends the law of retribution — and, indeed, brings the law of retribution to an end.

Through the cross of Christ, we see *the death penalty crucified* — and, yet, God's justice vindicated in covenant faithfulness. We thus observe a remarkable consistency between the teaching of Jesus and the cross of Christ: as did the judgment of Jesus, so does the cross of Christ reveal the covenant justice of God beyond retribution for the sake of redemption. Whereas Jesus' teaching puts the death penalty out of practice (see Chapter 24 above), God's redemption nails the death penalty to the cross. God nails to the cross *both* the legal record of our sins *and* the legal demand (or judicial order) that condemns us to death on ac-

---

24. Charles B. Cousar, *A Theology of the Cross: The Death of Jesus in the Pauline Letters* (Minneapolis, MN: Fortress Press, 1990), p. 46.

count of our sins. Instead of satisfying the legal demand (or judicial order) of retributive justice, God works redemption by nailing the law of retribution (or judicial order) itself to the cross. Whereas "the rulers and authorities" had crucified Jesus, *God crucifies the death penalty,* "nailing it to the cross." At the cross, God does execute the death penalty — not upon Christ, but upon the death penalty itself! By God's faithful action of saving justice through the cross of Christ, the death penalty is finally dead, once and for all.

25.3. The End of the Argument?

Is that the end of the argument concerning capital punishment from a Christian perspective? Not quite. The universal implications in the arguments above concerning the expiatory and retributive rationales for capital punishment are conditional upon the universal significance of the cross of Christ. One could thus avoid the above conclusions simply by denying that the cross of Christ is of universal significance. And there are two ways that one might do so with respect to the argument presented here.

First, concerning the expiatory rationale, one might argue that Christ's death effects a "limited atonement." Marshall states that using an expiatory rationale for the death penalty after the cross would lead us into "a theological quagmire in which God requires dual atonement for murderers, once by their own death and once by Christ's."[25] This assumes, however, that the cross of Christ concerns the sins of all humanity — a theological view which we share and which we infer from John's testimony: Jesus' death atones "for the sins of the whole world" (1 John 2:2; cf. John 1:29; 3:16). One might thus challenge the argument by rejecting this assumption, taking instead the Calvinist view that Jesus' vicarious death does not benefit all humanity: Jesus died "for us" but not for everyone, "the people" for whom he has made "a sacrifice of atonement" being restricted to "the elect" predestined by God for salvation. From the Calvinist perspective of a "limited atonement," one could continue to maintain the validity of the expiatory rationale for the death penalty: Jesus' death makes expiation for the sins of "the elect," but others still need to make expiation for their sins by their own deaths.

Second, concerning the retributive rationale, one might argue that the legal import of Christ's death is covenant bound. At the cross, God does away with only the "legal demands" derived from the law of the covenant with Moses. The covenant with Noah still stands, however, and that covenant sanctions and requires the death penalty: "Whoever sheds the blood of a human, by a human shall that person's blood be shed; for in his own image God made humankind"

---

25. Marshall, *Beyond Retribution,* p. 222.

(Gen 9:6).[26] The covenant with Noah is inclusive of all humankind (indeed, all creatures), and its terms last as long as the earth itself (vv. 8-17). The legal demands of the Noachide law must thus be satisfied, such that capital punishment remains necessary and justified. As one could resort to a Calvinist view to avoid the universal implication of the atoning value of Jesus' death, so also one could resort to a "dispensationalist" view to avoid the universal implication of the legal import of the cross. From a dispensationalist view, therefore, one might argue for the continuing legitimacy of capital punishment.[27]

26. Is Gen 9:6 actually intended to sanction the death penalty, to command the shedding of blood for blood shed? Three comments. First, the grammatical form of the key verb ("shall be shed"), in both Hebrew and Greek, does allow for an imperatival interpretation ("let his blood be shed"), but does not necessarily require it. In both cases, the indicative interpretation ("his blood will be shed") is possible, and, given the poetic form of the text, an indicative interpretation (as, say, a proverb rather than a command) might seem more natural: one who sheds blood will have his blood shed by another. Second, if this text were read as sanctioning the shedding of blood for blood shed, then the final clause, "for in his own image God made humankind," would serve as *both* the rationale for *not* shedding blood *and* the justification *for* shedding blood. This appears contradictory. If God prohibits shedding human blood precisely because humankind is created in God's image, then it would seem that the same notion would prohibit all the more shedding blood for blood shed. Third, to interpret Gen 9:6 as sanctioning the shedding of blood for bloodshed creates a tension with the *inclusio* that frames the text: "Be fruitful and multiply" (vv. 1 and 7). The purpose of the Noachide law is to promote the flourishing of life, and, it would seem, *both* taking life and taking life for life stand in tension with that purpose. See also Perry B. Yoder, "The Noachide Covenant and Christian Mission," in *Beautiful upon the Mountains: Biblical Essays on Mission, Peace, and the Reign of God*, ed. Mary H. Schertz and Ivan Friesen (Elkhart, IN: Institute for Mennonite Studies, 2003), pp. 3-16.

27. Marshall (*Beyond Retribution*, pp. 216-17) has argued, however, that the covenant with Noah does come under the cross of Christ and hence that it needs to be interpreted in light of New Testament teaching.

•   •

The Cross and Peace

Reconciliation beyond Hostility

CHAPTER 26

―――――――

"The Things That Make for Peace": A Story

And a harvest of justice is sown in peace
by those who make peace.

JAMES 3:18

Michael Chacour, a Christian from the Palestinian village of Biram in Galilee, taught his twelve-year-old son Elias, who was soon to begin the long preparation for the priesthood, to follow in the way of Jesus the man of Galilee, the way of peace: "If you become a true man of God — you will know how to reconcile enemies — how to turn hatred into peace. Only a true servant of God can do that."[1] Years later, in the summer of 1965, Elias was now Abuna Chacour, a Melkite priest in his first parish assignment in the Palestinian village of Ibillin in Galilee. The multiplying years of conflict in Galilee — between Jewish and Arab Israelis, between Christian and Muslim Arabs, between Melkite (Eastern Rite Catholic) and Orthodox Palestinian Christians — had created walls that divided families, neighbors, and parishes. Village life was choked by weeds of hostility, its fruit withered and bitter. There was no peace in Ibillin.

After his initial attempts to break down walls and quench hostility went without success, Abuna Chacour found his own heart hardening — against the village, against his neighbors, against his own parishioners. One night, meditating on his bed, he realized that, despite his best intentions to imitate the man of Galilee, seeds of hostility had sprouted in his own heart — and that the only way to deal with the hostility was to tear it out by the roots, to murder hostility in himself with forgiveness, as the man of Galilee had taught and done:

―――――

1. Elias Chacour, *Blood Brothers: The Unforgettable Story of a Palestinian Christian Working for Peace in Israel,* expanded edition (Grand Rapids: Chosen Books, 2003), p. 83.

Silent, still, I lay there, aware for the first time that I was capable of vicious, killing hatred. Aware that all men everywhere — despite the thin veneer of society — are capable of hideous violence against other men. Not just the Nazis, or the Zionists, or the Palestinian Commandos — but me. I had covered my hurts with Christian responses, but inside the anger had gnawed. With this sudden, startling view of myself, a familiar inner voice spoke firmly, without compromise: *If you hate your brother you are guilty of murder.* Now I understood.

I was aware of other words being spoken. A Man was dying a hideous death at the hands of his captors — a Man of Peace, who suffered unjustly — hung on a cross. *Father, forgive them,* I repeated. *And forgive me, too.*

In that moment, forgiveness closed the long-open gap of anger and bitterness inside me. From the time I had been beaten as a small boy [by Israeli soldiers], I had denied the violence inside me. Now . . . the taming hand that taught me compassion on the border of West Germany had finally stilled me enough to see the deep hatred in my own soul.[2]

Imitating Jesus at the cross, having murdered hostility in himself through the sacrifice of forgiveness, Abuna Chacour was now ready to break down the walls of division and mediate reconciliation among the people of Ibillin.

It was Palm Sunday 1966, and the Melkite church in Ibillin was full beyond seating capacity. As he prepared to celebrate the liturgy, Abuna Chacour knew that there was something not right about his divided parish community sharing the Eucharist, partaking of the body and blood of Christ, God's sign of grace and peace to us. At the end of the liturgy, he made his decision and took action quickly — rushing down the center aisle to the back of the church, he shut and locked the church doors, taking his own parishioners hostage! He returned to the front of the church, faced the people, and said:

I want you to know how beloved you all are to me and how saddened I am to find you hating and decrying one another. I have tried so often in the six months I have been here to help you reconcile with each other, but I have been unable to do so. . . .

This morning while I celebrated the liturgy, I found someone who is able to help you. In fact, he is the only one who can work the miracle of reconciliation in this village. This person who can reconcile you is Jesus Christ, and he is here with us. . . .

So on Christ's behalf, I say this to you: The doors of the church are locked. Either you will kill each other right here in your hatred and then I will celebrate your funerals gratis, or you use this opportunity to be reconciled together before I open the doors of the church. If that reconciliation

2. *Blood Brothers,* p. 175, emphasis original.

happens, Christ will truly become our Lord, and I will know that I am becoming your pastor and your priest. That decision is now yours.[3]

Silence hung over the assembly. Abuna Chacour looked out over the people,
and the people looked around — but not at each other. The silence continued
for ten minutes . . . until one man stood up. It was Abu Muhib, the one person
nearly all of Ibillin despised in common; he had come to church wearing his Israeli police uniform. He stretched out his arms to the people and then looked at
Abuna Chacour, saying: "Abuna, I ask forgiveness of everybody here and I forgive everybody. And I ask God to forgive me my sins."[4] The two men embraced,
beginning a feast of reconciliation:

> In an instant the church was a chaos of embracing and repentance. Cousins
> who had not spoken to each other in years wept together openly. Women
> asked forgiveness for malicious gossip. Men confessed to passing damaging
> lies about each other. People who had ignored the sisters and me in the
> streets now begged us to come into their homes. . . . This second church ser-
> vice — a liturgy of love and reconciliation — went on for nearly a full
> hour. . . .
>
> Even then it did not end. The momentum carried us out of the church
> and into the streets where true Christianity belongs. For the rest of the day
> and far into the evening, I joined groups of believers as they went from house
> to house throughout Ibillin. At every door, someone had to ask forgiveness
> for a certain wrong. Never was forgiveness withheld. Now I knew that inner
> peace could be passed from man to man and woman to woman.
>
> As I watched, I recalled . . . an image that had come to me as a young boy
> in Haifa. Before my eyes, I was seeing a ruined church rebuilt at last — not
> with mortar and rock, but with living stones.[5]

In several ways, this story illustrates "the things that make for peace" (Luke
19:42) revealed by the cross of Jesus Christ and demonstrates how "a harvest of
justice is sown in peace by those who make peace" (Jas 3:18). Throughout Section C, we will integrate this story into our reflection on Paul's depiction of the
peacemaking cross in Ephesians 2 within the context of interpersonal and inter-
ethnic/inter-religious hostility and conflict; and we will develop a "cruciform"
perspective on peacemaking based on our exegetical analysis of the text. In the
course of our reflection, we will link this text to other Pauline texts concerning
the meaning of the death of Jesus as well as to the Torah, the Psalms, the proph-

---

3. Elias Chacour, *We Belong to the Land: The Story of a Palestinian Israeli Who Lives for
Peace and Reconciliation* (San Francisco: HarperSanFrancisco, 1990), pp. 30-31.
4. *We Belong to the Land,* p. 32.
5. *Blood Brothers,* pp. 178-79.

ets Isaiah and Jeremiah, and the Gospels of Matthew and Luke. Then, in Section D, we will use this lens of cruciform peacemaking to interpret Luke's narrative of Jesus' life-ministry. We will also draw out implications for the church in its preaching and practice of the gospel of peace and apply this cruciform perspective to the analysis of human conflict, both political and ecclesial.

CHAPTER 27

The Pauline Vision:
God Saves by Making Peace through Jesus Christ

So he came and proclaimed
peace to you who were far off
and peace to those who were near.

EPHESIANS 2:17

27.1. Paul's Good News: God's Universal Peace in Christ

The Pauline vision of the good news of salvation and peace is articulated magnificently in Eph 2:11-22, which falls into three sections, marked by the phrases "at one time," "but now," and "no longer":[1]

> So, then, remember that *at one time* you Gentiles by birth, called "the uncircumcision" by those who are called "the circumcision" — a physical circumcision made in the flesh by human hands — remember that you were at that time without Christ, being aliens from the commonwealth of Israel, and strangers to the covenants of promise, having no hope and without God in the world.

---

1. Regarding the structure of this passage, see Thomas R. Yoder Neufeld, *Ephesians* (Believers Church Bible Commentary; Scottdale, PA: Herald Press, 2002), pp. 107-8; idem, "'For He Is Our Peace': Ephesians 2:11-22," in Mary H. Schertz and Ivan Friesen, eds., *Beautiful upon the Mountains: Biblical Essays on Mission, Peace, and the Reign of God* (Elkhart, IN: Institute of Mennonite Studies, 2003), pp. 216-18.

Both "through it (the cross)" and "in himself," are grammatically possible translations of *en autō* in v. 16b. I have chosen the latter because I see it in parallel with three preceding prepositional phrases: "in his flesh" (*en tē sarki autou*, v. 14), "in himself" (*en autō*, v. 15), and "in one body" (*en heni sōmati*, v. 16a).

> *But now* in Christ Jesus you who once were far off have been brought near by the blood of Christ. For he is our peace; in his flesh he has made both groups into one and has broken down the dividing wall, that is, the hostility between us. He has abolished the law with its commandments and ordinances, that he might create in himself one new humanity in place of the two, *thus making peace,* and might reconcile both groups to God in one body through the cross, thus putting to death that hostility in himself. So he came and proclaimed peace to you who were far off and peace to those who were near; for through him both of us have access in one Spirit to the Father.
>
> So then you are *no longer* strangers and aliens, but you are citizens with the saints and also members of the household of God, built upon the foundation of the apostles and prophets, with Christ Jesus himself as the corner-stone. In him the whole structure is joined together and grows into a holy temple in the Lord; in whom you also are built together spiritually into a dwelling place for God.

At the heart of this passage, Paul points us to the very purpose of God's mission of salvation through Jesus: "thus making peace." God saves by making peace through Jesus Christ. God's saving, peacemaking purpose in Jesus is twofold: that "he [Jesus] might create in himself one new humanity in place of the two [Jew and Gentile]"; and that he "might reconcile both groups to God in one body through the cross" (vv. 15-16). In order to initiate this salvation purpose, "[Jesus] came and proclaimed peace to you who were far off [Gentiles] and peace to those who were near [Jews]" (v. 17). The Apostle thus imagines Jesus as bringing to fullness the prophet's vision of God's messenger of peace: "Peace, peace, to the far and the near, says the LORD" (Isa 57:19a).

The Pauline vision helps us see both the unity and universality of the gospel. The unity of the gospel is evident in that the message of salvation and the good news of peace are *one gospel* proclaimed by and fulfilled in Jesus. Paul's gospel cannot imagine divorcing salvation from peacemaking, or peacemaking from salvation; for God's salvation in Jesus *is* peace — indeed, Jesus himself "is our peace" (v. 14). And the universality of the gospel is evident in that there is one message of salvation and peace for the peoples of all nations: the message of Jesus proclaimed to Jews ("the near") is the same as proclaimed to Gentiles ("the far") — peace. Through Christ, Paul envisions, the peoples of all nations are to be made citizens of God's city and thereby enjoy the salvation of God's peaceable reign (vv. 19-22).

This Pauline vision of the unity and universality of the gospel fulfilled in Jesus — *one* message of salvation and peace under God's reign for *all* peoples — both parallels the preaching of Peter (Acts 10:34-43) and echoes the oracle of the prophet:

How beautiful upon the mountains are the feet of the messenger who announces peace, who brings good news, who announces salvation, who says to Zion, "Your God reigns." . . . The LORD has bared his holy arm before the eyes of all the nations; and all the ends of the earth shall see the salvation of our God. (Isa 52:7, 10)

The prophet places four phrases — "announces peace," "brings good news," "announces salvation," and "Your God reigns" — in poetic parallel, thus emphasizing that each phrase expresses an essential dimension of a single message: peace/good news/salvation/reign of God. To excise any one of these — whether peace or salvation or the reign of God — would leave less than the full gospel message. The implication is clear: salvation and peace are inseparable aspects of evangelism in God's kingdom. Moreover, the prophet proclaims, as does Paul, this good news — peace/salvation/reign of God — is universal, intended for "all the nations" and to be revealed "to the ends of the earth." In the Pauline vision, the prophetic oracle of good news of salvation and peace at the advent of the reign of God is fulfilled through the preaching and cross of Jesus Christ.[2]

27.2. God's Peace in Christ is Both Spiritual and Social

In this and the next two chapters, we will consider carefully the multi-dimensionality of the Pauline message of God's saving, peacemaking initiative through the preaching and cross of Jesus Christ. First, this salvation and peace have earthly, social significance: the peacemaking work of Jesus through the cross entails and effects, not only the personal salvation of souls for eternity in heaven, but also the social reconciliation of peoples on earth in history.

As with the message from the prophets and poets of ancient Israel, the Pauline message proclaims that God's mission of salvation and peace in Jesus encompasses both the "horizontal" and the "vertical" — that is, the peace of Jews and Gentiles *both* with each other *and* with God. By emphasizing the inseparability of the "vertical" and the "horizontal" in God's salvation and peace revealed in Jesus Christ, Paul recalls the ancient poet's depiction of God's reign of salvation and peace.

In Psalm 85, we hear the poet proclaim a single message of peace and salvation and then imagine God's reign on earth bringing a harvest of social justice and prosperity:

---

2. Concerning the significance of Isa 52:7 for the Gospel presentations of Jesus and his mission of peace and the kingdom of God, see Willard M. Swartley, *Covenant of Peace: The Missing Peace in New Testament Theology and Ethics* (Grand Rapids, MI: Eerdmans Publishing, 2006), pp. 15-23.

Let me hear what God the LORD will speak, for he will speak peace to his people, to his faithful, to those who turn to him in their hearts. Surely his salvation is at hand for those who fear him, that his glory may dwell in our land. Steadfast love and faithfulness will meet, righteousness and peace will kiss each other. Faithfulness will spring up from the ground, and righteousness will look down from the sky. The LORD will give what is good, and our land will yield its increase. Righteousness will go before him, and will make a path for his steps. (Ps 85:8-13)

We cannot do justice to the rich imagery here, but will draw our attention to three aspects. First, the source of peace for the people is God's word: YHWH will "speak peace." In New Testament theology, Christ himself is God's word; and God's word in Christ to us is none other than "peace": God was "preaching peace by Jesus Christ" (Acts 10:36). Likewise, Paul says, Christ himself "is our peace," the one who "came and proclaimed peace to you who were far off and peace to those who were near" (Eph 2:14, 17). Peace on earth is thus peace from God in Christ (Luke 2:10, 14).

Second, Psalm 85 shows that God's saving peace proceeds from God's own steadfast love (ḥesed), which God persists in extending to us despite our unfaithfulness (vv. 7, 10; cf. vv. 1-3). God's peace is not dependent on our prior doing, but rather is the expression of God's own character: we do not "make peace" with God; rather, peace is God's gift to us. But God's peace does not leave us in our unfaithfulness; for it is *saving* peace, peace that proceeds from God's steadfast love and brings us back into covenant loyalty ('ĕmeth). God's salvation, which demonstrates steadfast love, speaks peace to us and invites our return to true relationship with God (v. 8). Salvation is thus consummated where God's steadfast love (ḥesed) and covenant righteousness (ṣedeq) meets our faithful response ('ĕmeth) and embraces repentant sinners in peace (šālôm, v. 10). This is the spiritual dimension of God's peace, which, Paul proclaims, we receive through Christ by being justified through faith (Rom 5:1).

Yet, third, the effect of this saving peace is social. When we hear the Hebrew prophet or poet depict God "speaking peace" to us, we should hear *shalom*. *Shalom* is not merely "spiritual tranquility" or "mental repose" — an "interior peace" possessed "in the soul."[3] Such is the peace that was sought by the Stoic

---

3. Joseph Grassi, *Peace on Earth: Roots and Practices from Luke's Gospel* (Collegeville, MN: Liturgical Press, 2004), unfortunately characterizes the peace that Jesus came to establish as "an inner peace" (pp. 1-13). Grassi's point is to contrast the peace of God in Christ with the peace of Rome in Caesar, which is appropriate, but he does so by withdrawing the heavenly peace on earth, brought by Jesus, from the world into the heart. The opposition between *pax Christi* and *pax Romana* is not, as Grassi depicts, between an "inner" peace and an "external" peace; both claim to encompass the whole of life, but the former is a peace in accord with God's kingdom while the latter is a peace premised on human power.

philosophers. For the prophets and poets of Israel, *shalom* is outwardly visible in its manifestation and concrete in its particulars; it is embodied in both personal and social realities. The Hebrew *shalom,* moreover, signifies far more than simply the cessation of hostility or absence of violence (cf. *pax* in Latin). *Shalom* implies the comprehensive well-being of both individual and society — spiritual, physical, social, economic, and environmental. *Shalom* denotes a fundamentally "all right" situation in which everything has its proper place and function; it implies right-relationship — each person with him- or herself and with one another, humans with the earth, and humans with God. *Shalom* is thus a situation of harmony and wholeness in which God's original intention in creation is realized. This is the "peace" that the poet in Psalm 85 envisions God "speaking" to his people — a peace that effects and embodies a situation of multilateral right relationship. Earth's people bring forth the fruit of covenant loyalty as heaven rains down God's blessing of covenant righteousness (v. 11). And this marriage of God's righteousness and human faithfulness generates justice and peace, righteousness and prosperity, in abundance (vv. 12-13).

Similarly, in the Pauline vision of Ephesians 2, salvation "by grace through faith" creates "one new humanity" — a social peace among humans, a peace realized among former enemies now reconciled together in Christ. We have seen this harvest of social righteousness and peace, brought about by reconciliation, come alive in the story of Abuna Chacour in the Galilean village of Ibillin. Having witnessed real reconciliation among the villagers, Chacour testified: "Now I knew that inner peace could be passed from man to man and woman to woman."

27.3. Peace with God Is Peace with Others

27.3.1. Human-to-Human Reconciliation, Then Human-to-God Reconciliation

Paul's vision of peace with God through Christ in Ephesians 2 implicitly premises the "vertical" upon the "horizontal." Both groups, Jew and Gentile, can be reconciled to God "in one body" *only if* they are reconciled to one another in Christ to make "one new humanity." Perry Yoder thus comments on Eph 2:14-17:

> The death of Christ was meant to bring about a reconciliation between enemies — here between Jews and Gentiles. This reconciliation was to be primary. Following this reconciliation, people in their new relationship were reconciled *together* to God. Note well the order of this passage. Reconciliation between peoples comes before reconciliation to God. We usually reverse this order. . . . Here we see that reconciliation to God comes after old enemies

have made peace, becoming one, so that they together might be reconciled [to God].[4]

The spiritual peace between humans and God that is the "vertical" effect of salvation is not independent of the social peace among humans that is the "horizontal" effect. There can be no "separate peace" with God, therefore — no standing justified before, or in right relationship with, God independent of reconciliation and right relationship with one's neighbors. Thus, Leon Morris: "Reconciliation with God means also reconciliation with man. . . . It is impossible to enter into the reconciliation that Christ died to accomplish and at the same time hold grudges against other people. The two reconciliations are closely connected."[5] We have seen this, also, in the story of reconciliation in Ibillin. Abuna Chacour realized that he could not make a "separate peace" for himself with God apart from the peace of his village. He thus recognized that true peace with God, symbolized by participation in the Eucharist, required the righting of relationships among the people: there could be no peace with God apart from peacemaking in Ibillin.

The Pauline message of salvation through the peacemaking cross thus implicitly reaffirms a key principle of atonement-making in the Levitical code (Lev 5:14–6:7; cf. Num 5:5-10). When guilty of wrongdoing against a neighbor (e.g., robbery or fraud), the Levitical code instructs that, prior to bringing a guilt offering to the priest to make atonement before God, one must first rectify matters with the neighbor. There are four steps that an offender must follow: (1) recognize guilt and feel remorse, (2) confess the wrongdoing, (3) make restitution to the victim, and (4) offer sacrifice to repair the offense against God.[6] The Levitical code thus premises being righted with God upon doing right by the neighbor one has wronged — restitution to the neighbor *precedes* the offering to God. So, Jacob Milgrom: "And the texts on the reparation offering make it absolutely clear that in matters of expiation man takes precedence over God; only after rectification has been made with man can it be sought with God."[7] The precedence of inter-human reconciliation over God-human reconciliation is also manifest in the story from Ibillin: Abu Muhib first petitions forgiveness from and seeks reconciliation with his fellow villagers and only then asks God's forgiveness.

The Levitical principle that reconciliation to God is preceded by and inseparable from righting wrong done to one's neighbor, and the Levitical process

4. Perry B. Yoder, *Shalom: The Bible's Word for Salvation, Justice, and Peace* (Napanee, IN: Evangel Publishing House, 1987), pp. 67-68.

5. Leon Morris, *The Atonement: Its Meaning and Significance* (Downers Grove, IL: InterVarsity Press 1983), p. 143.

6. John H. Hayes, "Atonement in the Book of Leviticus," *Interpretation* 52 (1998), 5-15.

7. Jacob Milgrom, *Leviticus 1–16* (Anchor Bible; New York: Doubleday, 1991), p. 51.

for "making right," are enacted in the story of Zacchaeus (Luke 19:1-10).[8] Hearing the grumbling of the crowd, Zacchaeus is confronted with his wrongdoing. He realizes that, if he is to accept Jesus' invitation to fellowship and receive Jesus into his home in truth and honesty, he must first make right the injustices he has committed as chief tax collector. He must repent of his crimes of extortion, robbery, and oppression and be reconciled to the neighbors he has wronged (cf. 3:12-13). He thus recognizes that entering a covenant of peace with God by welcoming God's prophet in friendship requires making peace by being reconciled with one's neighbors. As the terms of reconciliation with his neighbors, Zacchaeus pledges half his possessions to the poor and promises fourfold restitution to anyone he has defrauded.[9] Jesus then proclaims that Zacchaeus, who by acts of mercy and justice has borne "fruits worthy of repentance," is now a redeemed child of the covenant whose deeds fulfill the spirit of Torah (3:8). By means of right-making and peacemaking, therefore, the salvation of God has been realized among his people: "Today salvation has come to this house, because he too is a son of Abraham" (19:10).

The order of this story — as with the Levitical code for the guilt offering and Paul's depiction of the peacemaking cross — emphasizes human-to-human reconciliation as the precedent of human-to-God reconciliation: Jesus pronounces salvation only once Zacchaeus has made right with his neighbors. This Gospel story thus illustrates the central message of the Pauline vision: Jesus brings about reconciliation of humanity with God by bringing about reconciliation of human beings one with another. Here again, as in the story of Abuna Chacour in Ibillin, we see how "a harvest of justice is sown in peace by those who make peace" (Jas 3:18).

The same Levitical principle and process of reconciliation are also taught by Jesus in the Sermon on the Mount. If you are bringing a gift to the altar and remember that you have acted unjustly toward a neighbor ("your brother or sister has something against you"), Jesus says, then you must leave your gift at the altar and first go and be reconciled to the neighbor before making your offering to God (Matt 5:23-24). This teaching was carried over into the early church in its practice of worship. The *Didache*, a late first-century manual of catechesis and church order, summarizes the teaching of Jesus as handed down to the Apostles. Concerning Sunday worship, the *Didache* instructs the church to celebrate the Eucharist at each Lord's Day assembly, adding this caveat: "but

8. Regarding the story of Zacchaeus as a model example of repentance and just generosity, see Richard J. Cassidy, *Jesus, Politics, and Society: A Study of Luke's Gospel* (Maryknoll, NY: Orbis Books, 1978), p. 31, and Grassi, *Peace on Earth*, p. 45.

9. Rather than Lev 6:1-7, which requires the wrongdoer in cases of fraud or robbery to restore the loss plus one-fifth to the victim, Zacchaeus might be invoking Exod 22:1-4, which requires fourfold or fivefold restitution in cases of stolen livestock that has been sold or slaughtered.

first make confession of your faults, so that your sacrifice may be a pure one. Anyone who has a difference with his fellow is not to take part with you until they have been reconciled, so as to avoid any profanation of your sacrifice" (14:1-2).[10] Prior to partaking in offering the sacrifice of thanksgiving to God (Eucharist), therefore, the baptized members of the church are to confess their sins to, and seek reconciliation with, one another.

Glen Stassen's exegesis of the heart of the Sermon on the Mount shows that Jesus' exhortations in Matthew 5 follow a triadic pattern of (1) statement ("You have heard it said: Do not murder"), (2) prohibition ("But I say to you: Do not even be angry"), and (3) imperative ("Go and be reconciled"). Jesus' teaching thus puts the emphasis on taking positive peacemaking action, what Stassen calls a "transforming initiative." The command to "go and be reconciled" is the first of fourteen "transforming initiatives" that Jesus teaches to help us break cycles of violence and mechanisms of bondage and thereby to promote "just peacemaking."[11] The entire presentation here of the Pauline vision of salvation and peace in Ephesians 2 might be stated thus: the cross of Jesus Christ is God's "transforming initiative" to break humanity's bondage to hostility and thereby reconcile human beings to one another and to God.

27.3.2. God Forgives Us as We Forgive Others

Jesus again emphasizes this point — the priority of inter-human reconciliation — in his teaching on prayer (Matt 6:9-13). Jesus instructs us to pray boldly, to command God in prayer to do what God has promised through the covenant: provide for our needs ("give us this day our daily bread") and protect us from harm ("rescue us from the evil one").

Jesus' teaching regarding forgiveness ("forgive us our debts") is different, however. Like the other petitions, we are to command God in prayer to do what God has promised through the covenant — forgive his people when they confess and repent (*aphes*, "forgive," is in the imperative mood here). Unlike the petitions for provision and protection, the petition for forgiveness is conditional — our petition that God act to forgive us is conditioned upon our *prior* action to forgive others: "And forgive us our debts *as we also did forgive* our debtors" (Matt 6:12, my translation). We thus ask God to forgive us according to our own past record of forgiveness ("forgive," *aphēkamen*, is in the aorist indicative here). He immediately emphasizes the point: "For if you forgive others

10. Maxwell Staniforth and Andrew Louth, trans., *Early Christian Writings* (London: Penguin Books, 1987), p. 197.
11. Glen H. Stassen, *Just Peacemaking: Transforming Initiatives for Justice and Peace* (Louisville, KY: Westminster/John Knox, 1992), pp. 33-51.

their trespasses, your heavenly Father will also forgive you; but if you do not forgive others, neither will your Father forgive your trespasses" (vv. 14-15).

As an underscore of this point, when Peter asks "how often should I forgive?" (Matt 18:21), Jesus tells a parable that is a companion piece to the Lord's Prayer. The parable of the unmerciful servant illustrates that mercy and forgiveness in God's realm is inseparable from mercy and forgiveness in human relations (vv. 23-35). After having forgiven his slave's debt in response to the slave's petition for mercy, the king withdraws his offer of forgiveness on hearing that this same slave has refused to have mercy and forgive his fellow slave's debt. Jesus sums up the parable in words that parallel his teaching in the Sermon on the Mount: "So my heavenly Father will also do to every one of you [refuse forgiveness], if you do not forgive your brother or sister from your heart" (v. 35).

Jesus thus teaches two things regarding forgiveness and reconciliation: if you have wronged another, seek reconciliation with the one you have wronged before seeking reconciliation with God (Matt 5:23-24); if you have been wronged by another, forgive the one who has wronged you before asking God to forgive you the wrong you have done (6:12, 14-15; 18:21-35). In each case, forgiveness by and reconciliation with God are inseparable from forgiveness of and reconciliation with others.[12]

27.3.3. Forgiveness in Action: The Amish of Nickel Mines

There is perhaps no other Christian faith community that takes this teaching of Jesus more to heart than the Amish. The tragic school shooting near Nickel Mines, Pennsylvania, in October 2006 brought to light for the whole world how Amish Christians seek to practice forgiveness as Jesus taught us to do.[13] On the very same day that ten Amish schoolgirls were shot, five of whom would die, within hours of the girls' shooting and the killer's subsequent suicide, members of the Amish community visited the killer's family in their home, expressing forgiveness and offering condolences, extending gestures of friendship and comfort. By their actions, the Amish community made clear that there would be no call for revenge, no holding of a grudge, no breach of relationship. In days to come, members of the Amish community, including family members of the victims, would attend the killer's funeral, and the elders of the Amish commu-

12. Reconciliation and forgiveness are not the same but related: forgiveness is constitutive of reconciliation, such that there can be forgiveness without reconciliation (a victim can forgive an unrepentant offender), but not reconciliation without forgiveness (righting a relationship depends on the giving and receiving of grace).

13. The story of the Nickel Mines tragedy is told in clear and compelling terms by Donald B. Kraybill, Steven M. Nolt, and David L. Weaver-Zercher in *Amish Grace: How Forgiveness Transcended Tragedy* (San Francisco: Jossey-Bass, 2007).

nity would designate a portion of the (unsolicited) funds donated from around the world to the killer's wife and children. A stunned world quickly shifted its attention from a tragic story of violence to a surprising story of forgiveness. In disbelief and suspicion, the media asked, Why? Had there been a meeting to decide whether and how to forgive? No, the Amish do not have a standing "Forgiveness Committee" that plans forgiveness in such events!

Over a five-hundred-year history, the Amish have cultivated forgiveness as a way of life by weaving Jesus' teaching into the warp and woof of their community: by praying the Lord's Prayer several times daily, by hearing Matthew 18 read and preached twice yearly, by practicing intra-communal reconciliation before partaking of the Lord's Supper, by remembering the stories of Jesus' forgiveness of his killers and of the Anabaptist martyrs who forgave their killers as Jesus had forgiven his, and by following a communal rule of humility toward others and submission to God. Forgiveness is a habitual communal ethic among Amish Christians rooted in the Sermon on the Mount. When asked why they had chosen forgiveness in the face of violence, an Amish bishop explained that refusing forgiveness "is not an option. It's just a normal part of our living. Forgiveness was a decided issue. It's just what we do as nonresistant people. It was spontaneous. It was automatic. It was not a new kind of thing." Another Amish man said, "Why is everybody surprised? It's just standard Christian forgiveness. . . ."[14]

Nearly everyone, however, Christians included, was surprised. There are two main reasons for this, I think. The first is that, as I laid out in Part I, the dominant tradition in Western Christianity has departed from the teaching of Jesus and followed instead a retributive paradigm for addressing matters of justice and peace. When faced with injustice and violence, the native instinct of mainstream Christianity is retribution. Forgiveness may be *standard* for Christianity, but it is not *normal* among Christians.

Second, Protestant theology in particular tends to understand the relationship between divine and human forgiveness in terms just the opposite of what Jesus taught and the Amish practice. Regarding why the Amish chose forgiveness, an Amish woman said simply, "We have to forgive. We have to forgive him in order for God to forgive us."[15] An Amish writer points to the Lord's Prayer as the basis for such a statement: "When we pray the Lord's Prayer, we ask the Father to forgive us as we FORGIVE others. Forgiving and being forgiven are inseparable."[16] Kraybill, Nolt, and Weaver-Zercher elaborate on the Amish understanding of forgiveness:

14. Kraybill et al., *Amish Grace*, p. 49.
15. Kraybill et al., *Amish Grace*, p. 45.
16. Kraybill et al., *Amish Grace*, p. 96, emphasis original.

The Amish believe if they don't forgive, they won't be forgiven. This forms the core of Amish spirituality and the core of their understanding of salvation: forgiveness from God hinges on a willingness to forgive others. The crucial phrase, repeated frequently by the Amish in conversations, sermons, and essays, is this: *to be forgiven, we must forgive.*[17]

This view contrasts with conventional Protestant theology concerning the relationship between divine and human forgiveness:

The Amish formula of forgiveness is unfamiliar to many Christians. In fact, Amish assumptions about forgiveness flip the standard Protestant doctrine upside down. The more common understanding asserts that because God has forgiven sinners, they should forgive those who have wronged them. In the Amish view, however, people receive forgiveness from God *only if* they extend forgiveness to others. To those who are surprised that Amish forgiveness differs from other Christians' views, the Amish response is simple: look at the Scriptures and see what they say. As Sadie [an Amish woman] told us, "It's pretty plain, don't you think?"[18]

Some Protestant writers have agreed with the Amish reading of Jesus' teaching on forgiveness. Søren Kierkegaard, the nineteenth-century Lutheran philosopher:

Jesus says, "Forgive, and you will also be forgiven" (Mt. 6:14). That is to say, forgiveness *is* forgiveness. Your forgiveness of another is your own forgiveness; the forgiveness you give is the forgiveness you receive. . . . God forgives you neither more nor less than *as* you forgive your trespassers.[19]

Likewise, William Barclay, a twentieth-century Presbyterian biblical scholar:

Of all petitions of the Lord's Prayer this is the most frightening. "Forgive us our debts as we forgive our debtors." The literal meaning is: "Forgive us our

---

17. Kraybill et al., *Amish Grace*, p. 95, emphasis original. The authors helpfully distinguish between forgiveness (the victim relinquishing the right of vengeance), pardon (releasing the offender from consequences of wrongdoing), and reconciliation (restoring victim and offender to right relationship). Forgiveness, they emphasize, is possible apart from both pardon and reconciliation. In this case, neither pardon nor reconciliation was possible, strictly speaking, because the offender had taken his own life. But the Amish bishops and elders made clear to the offender's family, in word and deed, that there would be no grudges held or consequences imposed and that there was a genuine desire for healing of relationship from the breach in the community caused by the offender's actions.

18. Kraybill et al., *Amish Grace*, p. 96, emphasis original.

19. Charles E. Moore, ed., *Provocations: Spiritual Writings of Kierkegaard* (Farmington, PA: Plough Publishing, 1999), p. 116.

sins *in proportion as* we forgive those who have sinned against us." Matthew
goes on in verses 14 and 15 to make that quite clear by showing us that Jesus
says in the plainest possible language that if we forgive others, God will forgive us; but if we refuse to forgive others, God will refuse to forgive us. It is,
therefore, quite clear that, if we pray this petition with an unhealed breach,
an unsettled quarrel in our lives, we are asking God *not* to forgive us. . . . No
one is fit to pray the Lord's Prayer so long as the unforgiving spirit holds
sway within his heart. If a man has not put things right with his fellow-men,
he cannot put things right with God.[20]

Not only is the Amish reading of Jesus teaching on forgiveness not lost on all
Protestants, but it has not been lost in the Catholic tradition, either. The prayer
of St. Francis, "Lord, make me an instrument of your peace," reads in its penultimate line, "for it is in pardoning that we are pardoned."

Some readers may be concerned that, with the emphasis on the inseparability of divine and human forgiveness, the priority of God's grace has been
lost: God's saving initiative in Christ is prior to anything that we might do to
put things right. Here, the parable of the unmerciful servant in Matthew 18 is
helpful in clarifying the relationship between divine initiative and human response. Kraybill et al. comment from an Amish perspective on the "cross-stitch
between divine and human forgiveness" in this text:

> In the parable, the king's forgiveness, representing divine forgiveness, comes
> *first,* before the servant's actions. But although the king's graciousness does
> not *initially* depend on the servant's actions, the *continuation* of his gracious-
> ness does. . . . This story clarifies the Amish view that God's continuing for-
> giveness depends on their willingness to forgive.[21]

Richard Gardner echoes this view, commenting on Matt 6:14-15:

> . . . Jesus correlates God's forgiveness and human forgiveness in precise terms
> . . . the point made is not that we have to earn or prove ourselves worthy of
> God's forgiveness. Matthew agrees with the view expressed elsewhere in the
> NT that God's forgiveness precedes and underlies our forgiveness of one an-
> other [citing Matthew 18]. The point of Jesus' saying is that there has to be a
> reciprocity between the way we respond to the misdeeds of others and the way
> God responds to our own. If we refuse to practice forgiveness in our relation-
> ships with others, then we void God's forgiveness in our own lives as well.[22]

20. William Barclay, *The Gospel of Matthew,* vol. 1, 2nd ed. (Edinburgh: Saint Andrews
Press, 1958), pp. 223-24, emphasis original.
21. Kraybill et al., *Amish Grace,* p. 98.
22. Richard B. Gardner, *Matthew* (Believers Church Bible Commentary; Scottdale, PA:
Herald Press, 1991), pp. 120-21.

He comments later on the "reciprocity" between divine and human forgiveness concerning the parable of the unmerciful servant in Matthew 18:

> God as a gracious sovereign forgives the debt of all our unmet obligations. Freed and shaped by that gift, we in turn will forgive the shortcomings of fellow servants in the church. If instead we act contrary to the mercy we have received, denying forgiveness to our brothers and sisters, then we place ourselves outside the orbit of mercy as well.[23]

The relationship between the "vertical" and the "horizontal" dimensions of reconciliation — as emphasized in the Pauline vision of the cross and the teachings of Jesus on forgiveness and as evident in the stories of Zacchaeus in Jericho, Abuna Chacour in Ibillin, and the Amish in Nickel Mines — implies that salvation is essentially a *corporate-social,* as well as individual-personal, reality.[24] The implication is profound: right spiritual ("vertical") relationship with God is inseparable from right social ("horizontal") relationship with one's neighbor; there is no personal salvation from God apart from peaceable dealings with one's neighbor. Effectively, personal salvation is embedded within a matrix of corporate peace: reconciliation with God and reconciliation with the neighbor are inseparable dimensions of one salvation, a single atonement. Salvation may be by God's grace alone, but we are not saved "alone," in isolation from others. Our salvation through peace with God in Christ is thus personal, but not private.

27.4. Peace from God Is Peace on Earth

Paul tells us that God's mission of salvation in Jesus is no "pie-in-the-sky" or "sweet bye-and-bye" dream of a peace to be realized only in another world or another time. Jesus' peacemaking mission through the cross is addressed precisely to this historical world of hostility and conflict, violence and injustice. Indeed, we see in Ephesians 2 that God makes peace through the cross of Jesus in the midst of this very world broken by division, hatred, oppression, and war. Ulrich Mauser describes the real world of Jewish-Gentile animosity in the first-century Hellenistic-Roman context:

> The "dividing wall of hostility" (Eph. 2:14, RSV) erected by the law (2:15) between Jews and non-Jews is a stark and concrete reality at the time of the writing of Ephesians. Jewish awareness of a special place on the scene of world his-

---

23. Gardner, *Matthew,* p. 284.

24. In fact, the grammatical object (i.e., recipient) of salvation throughout Ephesians 2 is consistently plural — "we," "us," "you Gentiles," etc. — not singular. Cf. the consistently plural language of Rom 5:1-11: it is *we* who "have peace with God through Jesus Christ" (v. 1), *we* who "were reconciled to God through the death of his Son" and *we* who "will be saved by his life" (v. 10).

tory, often resulting in suspicion, fear, and even hatred of the vastly more numerous pagan population, is as real as the pagan resentment of Jews, which expresses itself on a scale of feelings and acts ranging from bafflement, credulity of fantastic rumors, to contempt and organized massacres. The declaration of peace in Ephesians 2:14-18 is to be understood against this background as offering a new reality of peace in which the old enmity is effectively removed.[25]

The world-reality of suspicion, fear, and hatred that Mauser describes is the same world of Zacchaeus in first-century Jericho, the same world of Abuna Chacour in twentieth-century Ibillin, the same world of the Amish in twenty-first-century America. God's peace, made through the cross of Jesus, speaks a new world-reality into all of these situations.[26]

Ephesians 2 thus reveals that God's mission of salvation, God's "transforming initiative" through the peacemaking cross of Jesus Christ, is a real-world transforming event, changing a situation of actual social division, hostility, conflict, alienation, and despair — the former situation "without Christ" — into a reality of unity, peace, friendship, and hope — the new reality "in Christ." This dramatic transformation through the cross is evident in the threefold structure of Eph 2:11-22: vv. 11-12 describe the situation prior to the cross of Jesus Christ, vv. 13-18 depict Jesus' peacemaking work in the world through the cross, and vv. 19-22 announce the new reality created by the peacemaking cross of Christ. *Before* "you were without Christ, aliens from the commonwealth of Israel, and strangers to the covenants of promise, having no hope and without God in the world" (v. 12). The effect of God's saving, peacemaking work in Jesus — which creates "one new humanity" in Christ, and reconciles this "one body" to God through the cross (vv. 15-16) — is peace "through the cross" and relationship to God "in one Spirit." God's peacemaking initiative in Jesus through the cross transforms the "before" situation of exclusion into the "after" reality of inclusion: "you are no longer strangers and aliens, but you are citizens with the saints and also members of the household of God" (v. 19).

Thus, the social ("horizontal") effect of the cross, on earth in history, is precisely the church — the unified body of Christ (cf. Eph 1:22-23), through which both Jews and Gentiles are together reconciled to God, a body which is growing "into a holy temple in the Lord" and being "built together in the Spirit into a dwelling place for God" (2:16, 21-22). The salvation and peace of Jesus thus creates

---

25. Ulrich Mauser, *The Gospel of Peace: A Scriptural Message for Today's World* (Louisville, KY: Westminster/John Knox Press, 1992), pp. 159-60.

26. It is also the world-reality of a North American church divided for many generations by interracial hostility. Spencer Perkins and Chris Rice, *More Than Equals: Racial Healing for the Sake of the Gospel,* revised and expanded ed. (Downers Grove, IL: InterVarsity Press, 2000), pp. 151-63, set Ephesians 2 and the stories of inter-ethnic reconciliation in Acts in the context of racial reconciliation in the church today.

through the cross a visible, concrete, spiritual-political entity, a living people consecrated to God's service on earth, who are to carry on God's mission of peace inaugurated in Jesus (cf. 2 Cor 5:17-20). We are saved by God's grace through Christ into the church; salvation through the cross of Christ incorporates us — we who were formerly "near" and "far" — into God's covenant people of peace. This building-up of the church in the Spirit to be the place of God's presence, which is the first fruit of reconciliation in Christ, is precisely what Abuna Chacour witnessed happening that Palm Sunday in Ibillin, which is why he declared: "Brothers and sisters, this is not Palm Sunday any longer. This is our resurrection! We are a community that has risen from the dead, and we have new life."[27]

27.5. Christ's Peace is God's Gift

The origin of God's peace in Christ is nothing other than *grace:* "For by grace you have been saved . . . it is the gift of God" (Eph 2:8). God's peace initiative is extended to us through Christ; and we may partake of that peace only because we "who were once far off have been brought near" (v. 13). This "bringing near" is the gracious invitation of God to us that we might know peace by entering the peaceable kingdom; it is the act of heavenly hospitality welcoming us to the feast of salvation that has been prepared for us by God, "who is rich in mercy" (v. 4). The peace of God's salvation is not achieved at the negotiating table, where opposing powers and competing interests seek an "equilibrium" or "status quo" that balances the forces of both sides. Indeed, we are in no position to "bargain with God" for our salvation. Rather, the biblical writers all imagine that God's peace is realized at *the banquet table* (Psalm 23, Isaiah 55, and Luke 14). We may enter the salvation of God's peaceable kingdom only according to God's favor (Luke 2:14). We cannot buy, earn, or negotiate a place for ourselves at the table of God's grace, but can only take the place God prepares and offers.

Further, we can be "brought near" to God through Christ only because God has already come near to us in Christ. We may heed the word of the prophet to "seek the Lord while he may be found" precisely because God has already taken initiative and come "near" to us (Isa 55:6). Those "who were far off" and those "who were near" can be brought near one another "in one body" and brought near God by "access in one Spirit" only because God has already come near to both of us, because Jesus came and preached peace to both the near and the far. The peace of God's salvation is possible for us because, and only because, God has first made the initiative toward us through Jesus.[28]

27. Elias Chacour, *We Belong to the Land: The Story of a Palestinian Israeli Who Lives for Peace and Reconciliation* (San Francisco: HarperSanFrancisco, 1990), p. 32.

28. Paul repeatedly emphasizes this theme — the gracious peace initiative of God in Christ — in Rom 5:1-11.

CHAPTER 28

God Makes Peace in Christ through the Cross

As he came near and saw the city,
he wept over it, saying,
"If you, even you, had only recognized on this day
the things that make for peace!
But now they are hidden from your eyes."

LUKE 19:41-42

God's gracious salvation and peace initiative through Jesus is inseparable from the *cross:* God's saving peace in Christ is essentially *cruciform.* Tom Yoder Neufeld observes: "The cross is the shape of God's risky embrace of hostile humanity."[1] The peace between Jew and Gentile is made in Christ's body, and the reconciliation of "both groups to God in one body" is accomplished "through the cross."

28.1. The Peace of the Cross is a Prophetic Word

That God makes peace through the cross of Christ was, and still is, a major scandal to the world. Jews viewed the cross as God's curse on the crucified (Deut 21:22-23); Romans used the cross as brutal humiliation of the conquered. By requesting his crucifixion, the Jewish authorities wanted to discredit Jesus as a false Messiah; by imposing his crucifixion, the Roman authorities sought to intimidate all would-be messiahs. The cross was not merely a means of executing criminals. Rome put down resistance and rebellion in the province of Judea

---

1. Thomas R. Yoder Neufeld, "'For He Is Our Peace': Ephesians 2:11-22," in Mary H. Schertz and Ivan Friesen, eds., *Beautiful upon the Mountains: Biblical Essays on Mission, Peace, and the Reign of God* (Elkhart, IN: Institute of Mennonite Studies, 2003), p. 227.

by nailing Jews to crosses by the thousands and lining the main roads with the crucified to send a clear message to the subjugated that no challenge to imperial rule would be tolerated. Rome handily crucified both the fiery Zealots, who resisted oppression of the peasants with violent insurrection, and the pious Pharisees, who resisted desecration of the Temple with nonviolent protest.

For those subjugated to Roman rule, the cross was not only a cruel instrument of death but a threatening symbol of state terror. But by the power and wisdom of God in Christ (1 Cor 1:24-25), the cross becomes for us an instrument of grace and a sign of peace. Through the cross, in his own blood, Jesus makes peace, not by beating and bloodying human enemies into submission, but by beating Rome's sword into God's plowshare, Rome's spear into God's pruning hook. Through his own crucifixion, Jesus hammers the emperor-exalting, death-dealing instrument of cruel torture and imperial domination into the gospel-proclaiming, life-giving implement of God's reign of peace. God's dramatic reversal of — and, hence, judgment upon — imperial hubris through the cross of Christ thus recalls the ancient prophet's glorious vision of God's kingdom, in which the warring and domineering ways of the nations are transformed into the peaceable and just ways of the Lord (Isa 2:2-4; Mic 4:1-4).

The cross of Christ, which inverts the imperial means of "securing the peace," thus becomes a prophetic word for our own time: God's cruciform peacemaking through Christ is a judgment upon the violent ways in which the strong among the nations "secure the peace" by dominating the weak. Indeed, the cross of Christ inverts and judges every state-sanctioned intention and instrument of violent torture wielded in the name of "peace and security." In this time, when appalling images and reports from Abu Ghraib, Guantanamo, and Bagram of bodies brutalized and dignity degraded still haunt the memory, it is especially sobering to recall that the cross was Rome's way of torturing and dehumanizing those it considered "unlawful enemy combatants." The cross was Rome's way of dealing with the "terrorists" and "insurgents" of its day.

This intimate connection between cross and torture may be lost on our modern consciousness. In an extensive article on torture in the War on Terror, moral philosopher David Gushee identifies five reasons why Christians should allow no exceptions to the "no torture" rule: torture violates the dignity of the human being; torture mistreats the vulnerable and violates the demands of justice; authorizing torture trusts government too much; torture dehumanizes the torturer; and torture erodes the character of the nation that tortures.[2] While all solid reasons for abhorring torture, the obvious Christian reason escapes his attention: because Jesus, in suffering for all, was himself a victim of state torture on the cross, in every victim of torture we ought to see the face of Christ. Each

---

2. David P. Gushee, "5 Reasons Torture is Always Wrong," *Christianity Today* 50/2 (February 2006).

and every body-brutalizing, dignity-degrading act of torture — whether ratio-
nalized in the name of "security" or "freedom" — comes under the divine judgment of the cross of Christ.[3]

God's peacemaking through Christ is a costly, very costly, initiative, for
Christ "our peace" bears "in his flesh" the cost of making peace through the
cross (Eph 2:14). Unlike the warring ways of the nations which secure peace at
the expense of the blood of the enemy, God does not make peace through
Christ at the expense of the blood of his enemies, but at the expense of his own
blood. The cost of God's peace is God's own life graciously given for our sake
through Christ, and the measure of God's outpoured grace is the cross. Yoder
Neufeld comments: "Peace is costly even more because it costs the life of the
peacemaker. In contrast to the 'peace of this world' (John 14:27) or the Pax
Romana, which purchased peace through the death of the enemy, Christ kills
enmity with his own blood (v. 13) on the cross (v. 16)."[4]

Paul elsewhere emphasizes this essential connection between cross and
peace. He writes that "through [Christ] God was pleased to reconcile to himself
all things, whether on earth or in heaven, by making peace through the blood of
his cross" (Col 1:20). Although God does not make peace by shedding the blood
of his enemies, that God-in-Christ makes peace "through the blood of his
cross" means nonetheless that God's peace does not come cheap. There is no
"bloodless peace": our covenant of peace with God is sealed with Jesus' blood
(Luke 22:20).

28.2. The Peace of the Cross and Cruciform Peacemaking

28.2.1. Cruciform Peacemaking Confronts the Powers

That God's peacemaking through Christ is essentially cruciform carries practical implications for Christian peacemaking. In this real world of sin, in which
evil still holds sway over the cosmos and humanity, cruciform peacemaking
must *confront* the real-world "rulers and authorities" that wield powers of violence. Such confrontation will inevitably provoke *conflict* with those who resist
the coming of God's kingdom and thus will be *costly* to the peacemaker who
seeks God's kingdom.

Cruciform peacemaking, as did the life-ministry and cross of Jesus, *confronts* the powers. The peacemaking cross of Christ (Col 1:20) is God's open
confrontation with the powers, a confrontation that divests them of their abil-

---

3. This point is not lost in the Catholic tradition. See Stephen M. Colecchi, "No Excuses for
Torture," *America: The National Catholic Weekly,* January 18, 2010.

4. Yoder Neufeld, "For He Is Our Peace," p. 221. Verse citations refer to Ephesians 2.

ity to dominate and thus exposes their weakness. Through the cross of Christ, Paul writes, God "disarmed the rulers and authorities and made a public example of them, triumphing over them" (2:15). The cross of Christ is thus God's victory over those who put Jesus to death, not only the human agents of political rule and religious authority that conspired to have Jesus crucified, the "rulers of this age" (1 Cor 2:8), but also the powers of law and religion working through them. The cross of Christ is God's confrontation with and victory over the "legitimate authorities" that "justify" violence in the name of "peace and security" or "God" — who deem it "necessary" that some, even the innocent, should die to "save" the nation (John 11:50).

These "powers" are as real now as then. In addition to "rulers and authorities" ("principalities and powers," KJV), Paul speaks of spiritual forces ("pneumatics") and world-ruling powers ("cosmocrats") that are manifest visibly in organized forms through religious, educational, political, legal, economic, and media institutions and systems (Eph 6:12).[5] We may think of the patriotic fervor of the nation and the impersonal power of bureaucracy as concrete realizations of "pneumatics" and "cosmocrats." Such "powers" are not primitive forms of evil. Indeed, within a biblical worldview, primitive evil does not exist because all things were created from nothing by God and thus are good by nature. All evil, rather, is a perversion of what God has created for good. These "powers" that do evil are thus themselves creations of God that have turned away from God ("fallen"). Working through what God has created or ordained, these "pneumatics" and "cosmocrats" can warp what has been intended by God for good toward evil ends.

Such institutions and systems of power, wearing the mask of "legitimate authority," tend to justify violence against the weak and vulnerable in the name of "God" or "peace and security." As they did in the crucifixion of Jesus, these powers often reinforce one another and "conspire together" against the rule of God (Psalm 2; Acts 4:26-27). The religious authorities invoke "God" to bless the military campaign commissioned by the political authorities to preserve the "peace and security" of the state.[6] The violence of legitimate authority is fil-

---

5. The classic discussions are G. B. Caird, *Principalities and Powers: A Study in Pauline Theology* (Oxford: Clarendon Press, 1956), and Hendrikus Berkhof, *Christ and the Powers*, trans. J. H. Yoder (Scottdale, PA: Herald Press, 1962). My renditions "pneumatics" and "cosmocrats" are simply transliterations of the Greek terms Paul uses.

6. In the United States, the President functions as both Commander in Chief and Chief Priest. During the service for the national day of prayer and remembrance on September, 14 2001 at Washington National Cathedral, President George W. Bush launched the War on Terror with these remarks that proclaimed sovereign control of the U.S. over the course of history: "Just three days removed from these events, Americans do not yet have the distance of history. But our responsibility to history is already clear: to answer these attacks and rid the world of evil. War has been waged against us by stealth and deceit and murder. This nation is peaceful, but fierce when stirred to anger. This conflict was begun on the timing and terms of others. It

tered for public viewing by a technical management of official "truth" that
dares not question the legitimacy of the powers that kill.[7] If the legitimate authorities do publicly acknowledge the human victims of their violence, their
deaths are obscured from moral scrutiny by means of official language that
makes them other than human and less than victims.[8] The faces of thousands
detained, tortured, and killed are covered from conscience by the masks "enemy
combatant," "terrorist," "extremist," "militant," "insurgent," "Iraqi," "collateral
damage."[9]

The cross of Christ unmasks these powers, exposing them for what they
truly are, which allows us to see and name the victims of legitimate authority
for who they truly are. Walter Wink makes this point well (with reference to Col
2:14-15):

> What killed Jesus was not irreligion, but religion itself; not lawlessness, but
> precisely the law, not anarchy, but the upholders of order. . . . And because he
> was not only innocent, but the embodiment of true religion, true law, and
> true order, this victim exposed their violence for what it was: not the defense
> of society but an attack against God. . . . The Law by which he was judged is
> itself judged, set aside, and nailed to the cross. The authorities that publicly
> shamed him, stripping him naked, have been stripped of their protective
> covering and exposed as agents of death. The very Powers that led him out to
> Golgotha are now led in God's triumphal procession, vanquished by the
> cross. . . . The cross marks the failure, not of God, but of violence.[10]

Jesus himself was a victim of the powers — tried, tortured, and crucified as a
rebel insurgent by the legitimate authorities of temple and throne. These powers conspired together to do away with Jesus for a "just cause": Caiaphas argued

will end in a way, and at an hour, of our choosing." Near the close of his remarks, he presumed
God's blessing on the war: "On this national day of prayer and remembrance, we ask almighty
God to watch over our nation, and grant us patience and resolve in all that is to come."

7. See Frank Rich, *The Greatest Story Ever Sold: The Decline and Fall of Truth from 9/11 to
Katrina* (New York: Penguin Press, 2006).

8. William Brennan, *Dehumanizing the Vulnerable: When Word Games Take Lives* (Chicago,
IL: Loyola University Press, 1995), exhibits "the semantics of oppression" that has been used to
dehumanize a variety of enemies and social undesirables, including Native Americans, African
Americans, Soviet enemies, European Jews, women, the unwanted unborn, and disabled persons.

9. In the Iraq war, even "Iraqi" became a mask behind which to hide the victims of war, the
death of an "Iraqi" being "justified" as "collateral damage." An investigative report by Chris
Hedges and Laila Al-Arian, "The Other War: Iraq Vets Bear Witness," *The Nation*, July 30, 2007,
revealed that indiscriminate killing of Iraqi civilians by U.S. troops was commonplace. One
young soldier interviewed said, "I guess while I was there, the general attitude was, A dead Iraqi
is just another dead Iraqi."

10. Walter Wink, *Engaging the Powers: Discernment and Resistance in a World of Domination* (Minneapolis, MN: Fortress Press, 1992), pp. 139-40.

that it would be good to let Jesus be killed to preserve the nation (John 11:45-53), and Pilate sentenced Jesus to death to defend his honor as governor of Judea and friend of Caesar (19:12-16). Preserving the state and defending its honor, we will recall, were precisely what Cicero named as just causes for war (Chapter 3 above). The cross of Christ thus challenges the human tradition that sanctions violence by "legitimate authority" for the sake of a "just cause." The cross exposes and judges every attempt by "legitimate authority" to "justify" the torture and death of war's victims and shows us what *true* legitimate authority is: *it exposes the violence that makes victims and mourns them, and it denounces the justification of their deaths.*[11]

28.2.2. Cruciform Peacemaking Provokes Conflict

Confronting the powers inevitably provokes resistance from, and hence *conflict* with, the entrenched "rulers and authorities" whose interests are threatened by an honest and just accounting of their deeds. Jeremiah exposed the false peace of Jerusalem by publicly denouncing the crimes of both temple and crown, the policies of oppression and practices of bloodshed by which the powerful exercised power to their own advantage. Thus was Jeremiah arrested and tried for treason by the legitimate authorities of temple and palace, whom he had confronted with their injustice and violence (Jeremiah 22, 26, 37-38). John, like Jeremiah, also publicly exposed the crimes of the crown, rebuking King Herod for "all the evil things that Herod had done" (Luke 3:19). As "the powers that be" are wont to do, Herod used the repressive tactics of state domination to silence the troublesome critic of a corrupt regime, "shutting up John in prison" (3:20) — indefinite detention without charge or trial, a routine procedure in the War on Terror.

As it was with his prophetic predecessors, Jeremiah and John, so it would be with Jesus. Jesus, too, publicly exposed the oppression and violence of Jerusalem, "the city that kills the prophets" (Luke 13:34). What is typically called the "triumphal entry," which culminates Jesus' journey to Jerusalem and points to the cross awaiting him there (9:51; 13:33-35), was really the first act by which Je-

---

11. The just war tradition invests the right to wage war in "legitimate authority," but offers no prophetic criterion by which to judge the legitimacy of authority. According to the cross, any authority that creates victims delegitimizes itself. Not only do even "good" wars that ostensibly satisfy the just war criteria inevitably create victims by the multitudes (47 million of the 72 million people killed in World War II, about two-thirds, were civilians), but war inevitably makes victims of the poor, the weak, and the vulnerable, if only by robbing them of their "daily bread" to fund the killing of the enemy. For an excellent critical examination of the traditional criteria of just war, see John Howard Yoder, *When War Is Unjust: Being Honest in Just War Thinking*, rev. ed. (Maryknoll, NY: Orbis Books, 1996).

sus "made a public spectacle" of "the rulers and authorities" (Col 2:15 TNIV). When Jesus comes in sight of Jerusalem, shouts of "peace in heaven" still echoing down the valley, he laments the failure of the "City of Peace" to recognize "the things that make for peace . . . the time of your visitation from God" (Luke 19:38, 41-44). Coming into Jerusalem, Jesus directly confronts the powers; he promptly "entered the temple and began to drive out" the workers of injustice and oppression, quoting the prophets: "It is written, 'My house shall be a house of prayer'; but you have made it a den of robbers" (Luke 19:45-46; cf. Isa 56:7; Jer 7:11). The "rulers and authorities," their oppression and bloodshed having been publicly exposed, predictably plot the demise of the prophet (Luke 19:47).

28.2.3. Cruciform Peacemaking Is Costly Sacrifice

The twentieth century was marked by prophets who decried the "peace" that is no peace, exposed the "legitimate authorities" for their crimes of injustice and violence, and willingly bore the cost of cruciform peacemaking with their own blood: Dietrich Bonhoeffer, Martin Luther King, Jr., and Oscar Romero. The examples of the prophets confirm that there can be no "bloodless peace," no peace "on the cheap," no peacemaking without the willingness to make sacrifice and accept suffering, to bear the cost of making peace. That the peace of Christ is cruciform entails that Christian peacemaking is *costly* to the peacemaker. Because cruciform peacemaking confronts, and hence provokes conflict with, the powers, the Christian peacemaker must be prepared for the real possibility of persecution. Thus, in his kingdom manifesto, Jesus juxtaposes "Blessed are the peacemakers" with "Blessed are those who are persecuted for the sake of justice" and "Blessed are you when people revile you and persecute you and utter all kinds of evil against you falsely on my account" (Matt 5:9-11).

Cruciform peacemaking not only is potentially costly in body and blood, but also is costly to the self — both the personal self and the national self. As Jesus voluntarily "emptied himself" for the sake of his cruciform mission (Phil 2:6-8), so Christian peacemaking requires "self-emptying" — renouncing exploitation of position and abuse of power, yielding selfish ambition for the sake of the common good, living in solidarity with and serving the needs of the least and lowest (Mark 10:35-45). Such "kenotic" peacemaking is possible by entrusting oneself to God's vindication, even in the face of humiliation, persecution, and death, following the example of Jesus (1 Pet 2:21-23).

In this real world of sin, in which hatred corrupts both the human heart and the national spirit, real peacemaking requires unilateral disarmament of both heart and hands. Unless we root out the sins of personal and national ego, we will make "peace" that is only a brief intermission between acts of exclusion and violence in the tragic drama of humanity at war with itself and against

God. A century ago, Leo Tolstoy observed the connection between patriotism (the collective egotism of the nation) and war: "And so, in order not to have any war, it is not necessary to preach and pray to God about peace. . . . All that is necessary is to destroy what produces war. But that which produces war is the desire for an exclusive good for one's own nation, and is called patriotism."[12] Accordingly, a young Jordanian prophet in our own time has observed, "To make peace you have to go to war against yourself"[13] — that is, there is no way of making true peace except by willingness to sacrifice the ever-justifiable cause of "one's own," of even one's own nation if necessary.[14]

28.3. The Peace of the Cross and the War on Terror

One of the most obvious disparities between the War on Terror and the way of the cross is the unexamined American assumption that God favors "our own." In his sermon at Washington National Cathedral on 14 September 2001, with the nation still deep in shock and mourning, President Bush pledged to wage a war "to answer these attacks and rid the world of evil." His concluding prayer expressed the presumption that God's blessing would favor America in the war to come:

> As we have been assured, neither death nor life, nor angels nor principalities nor powers, nor things present nor things to come, nor height nor depth, can separate us from God's love. May He bless the souls of the departed. May He comfort *our own*. And may He always guide *our country*. God bless America.[15]

In citing Rom 8:38-39, the President conveniently omits the last phrase — "nothing can separate us from the love of God *in Christ Jesus our Lord*." The official rhetoric of the War President has made a subtle confusion here of the Apostle Paul's use of the pronouns "us" and "our." When the Apostle Paul

---

12. Letter from Leo Tolstoy, "Patriotism or Peace" (1896).

13. Quoted from "The War Inside," *Newsweek*, October 3, 2005, p. 9, paraphrasing Jennifer Miller, *Inheriting the Holy Land: An American's Search for Hope in the Middle East* (New York: Ballentine Books, 2005).

14. There is a love of "one's own" that originates in natural affinity and serves the common good of human flourishing in one's self, one's family, and one's community. We are concerned here with an exclusive love that denies that the good of "the other" is also the good of "one's own," that denies the right of "the other" to "his own," that elevates "one's own" to the supreme good, and thus that justifies destruction of other selves, families, and communities in the name of "one's own." As Augustine observed, such is the love that constitutes the "City of Man" and that wars against the kingdom of God.

15. George W. Bush, "President's Remarks at National Day of Prayer and Remembrance," September 14, 2001, emphasis added.

speaks of God's love for "us," he means God's love for all those who are secured "in Christ Jesus our Lord," the very Lord who loved his enemies by dying for them and commands his followers to do the same. When the War President speaks of God's love for "us," he means a special love for "our own" and "our country," a love that excludes America's enemies, a love that blesses America in killing its enemies. The War President has read the Bible through the lens of the U.S. Constitution, so that the biblical "we" becomes "We the people of the United States."

President Bush employed this same hermeneutic in his speech to the nation on the anniversary of the 9/11 attacks. Standing in view of the Statue of Liberty, the War President cited John 1:5 to proclaim the good news that America itself is the darkness-overcoming light of the world that gives hope to all humanity:

> Tomorrow is September the 12th. A milestone is passed, and a mission goes on. Be confident. Our country is strong. And our cause is even larger than our country. Ours is the cause of human dignity: freedom guided by conscience and guarded by peace. This ideal of America is the hope of all mankind. That hope drew millions to this harbor. That hope still lights our way. And the light shines in the darkness. And the darkness will not overcome it. May God bless America.[16]

The War President has made a subtle substitution here of America in place of Christ in God's plan of salvation: America is now God's Messiah. Stephen Chapman's comment on President Bush's nationalistic theology is right on target:

> Bush's use of John 1:5 involves an analogy in which the referent of the language undergoes crucial shift. In John, the light of the world is Christ; in Bush's speech that same light is now America. . . . [B]y using John 1:5 Bush has applied unmistakably christological language to the United States of America, now investing the nation with *messianic* meaning. In other words, George Bush used the occasion of his September 11th anniversary speech to describe the U.S. with the same language that the New Testament reserves for Christ alone. As the president stood in front of the dazzling "light" of the Statue of Liberty, his symbolic substitution could not have been any more plain — or idolatrous.[17]

16. George W. Bush, "President's Remarks to the Nation," September 11, 2002.

17. Stephen B. Chapman, "Imperial Exegesis: When Caesar Interprets Scripture," in Wes Avram, ed., *Anxious about Empire: Theological Essays on the New Global Realities* (Grand Rapids, MI: Brazos Press, 2004), p. 95, emphasis original. See also Jim Wallis's critique of President Bush's theology: "Dangerous Religion: George W. Bush's Theology of Empire," *Sojourners Magazine,* September-October 2003, online at http://www.sojo.net/index.cfm?action=magazine .article&issue=sojo309&article=030910; idem "The Theology of Torture: Fallible Creatures Are

Absent the blasphemous abuse of Holy Scripture, the theme of "our own" is manifest also in the National Security Strategy of 2002. In the opening section, it declares, "We must defeat these threats to *our* Nation, allies, and friends." This emphasis returns in the third section, which sets forth the "Bush Doctrine" of preemptive war: "we will not hesitate to act alone, if necessary, to exercise our right of self-defense by acting preemptively against such terrorists, to prevent them from doing harm against *our* people and *our* country." And as if to emphasize the point, the National Security Strategy defines the War on Terror: "In the war against global terrorism, we will never forget that we are ultimately fighting for *our* democratic values and way of life." Because "we" are fighting for the ever-justifiable cause of "our own" — "our democratic values and way of life" — the National Security Strategy assures America of its righteousness: "The reasons for our actions will be clear, the force measured, and the cause just."[18]

Allen Hilton has perceptively observed that both President Bush's rationale for the War on Terror and the "Bush Doctrine" of preemptive war are shaped by an essentially self-serving American narrative. The national narrative, implicit in the U.S. Constitution, privileges America and pledges the President to "preserve, protect and defend" this one nation over all others. Hilton keenly points out also the stark contrast between this national narrative that shapes the identity of America as essentially a community "for our own" and the Christian narrative that shapes the identity of the church as essentially a community "for others." While America is in truth a nation "like other nations" (1 Sam 8:5), constituted for itself, "[t]he Christian community is constituted . . . not primarily for its own sake but for the sake of others" precisely because "[t]he character in whom Christianity finds its identity [viz., Christ] is eminently oriented to the well-being of others."[19] And it is the cruciform story of Christ's self-giving, peacemaking death "for us" that essentially defines the church's being "for others."

Many U.S. Christians share President Bush's view that America is *not* "like other nations," that America is special to God. According to the Baylor Religion Survey (2006), 26% of evangelical Protestants, 20% of Catholics, and 17% of mainline Protestants believe that God favors America. The conviction that God favors America against its enemies not only speaks through official war rhetoric, but also buttresses popular belief that America wages war for righteous

---

Not to Be Trusted with Empire," *Sojourners Magazine,* August 2004, online at http://www.sojo.net/index.cfm?action=magazine.article&issue=sojo408&article=040851.

18. George W. Bush, "The National Security Strategy of the United States of America," reprinted as an appendix in Avram, *Anxious about Empire,* pp. 187-215. See also the reflection by Wes Avram, "On Getting Past the Preamble: One Reading of the *Strategy,*" in *Anxious about Empire,* pp. 27-41.

19. Allen R. Hilton, "Who Are We? Being Christian in an Age of Americanism," in Avram, *Anxious about Empire,* pp. 153-54.

causes. The survey found evidence of a very strong correlation between beliefs whether or not the Iraq War is justified and beliefs whether or not God favors America. The survey found that 45% of Americans at the time believed that the Iraq War was justified. Of those surveyed who believe that God favors America, 79.2% believed the Iraq War was justified, while only 37.3% of those surveyed who do not believe that God favors America believed that the Iraq War was justified.[20] Thus, believing that God favors America not only increased belief in the justification of the Iraq War by 76% over the national average, but believing so more than doubled the likelihood of believing that the Iraq War is justified over not believing that God favors America.

The U.S. Constitution is not the only, and perhaps not even the primary, source of this belief in American "exceptionalism." A significant source of the belief among American Christians that God favors America is a peculiar understanding of church history that depicts America as the "new Israel" — or, per President Bush, as the "new Christ." Stephen Webb is an evangelical theologian who agrees with President Bush's theology that America is now God's Messiah among the nations. He subscribes to a popular version of church history that draws a "straight and narrow line . . . from Constantine, through the Reformation, to America. . . ."[21] Adapting Eusebius's fourth-century account of church history, which saw Constantine's victory and Rome's success as the working of divine providence to promote Christianity, Webb effectively substitutes Bush for Constantine and America for Rome. In this account, God's intention for the salvation of humanity is being worked through America's global success:

> I still value the account of church history taught to me by the evangelical church of my youth. It involved three basic stages. The early Christians were persecuted, but God chose Constantine to save the church and conquer paganism. The Reformation purified the medieval church in order to set free the Word of God for a renewed mission of proclamation. Finally, America, for all her faults and limitations, has been chosen by God to spread Protestantism across the globe, thus fulfilling the Great Commission.[22]

In Webb's theology, "Protestantism" has replaced Jesus Christ as the content of evangelism — and not just any Protestantism, but a distinctively American Protestantism that "is inseparable from the American cultural landscape."[23]

---

20. Baylor Institute for Studies of Religion, "American Piety in the 21st Century: New Insights to the Depth and Complexity of Religion in the US," September 2006, http://www.baylor.edu/content/services/document.php/33304.pdf, p. 37.

21. Stephen H. Webb, "On the True Globalism and the False, or Why Christians Should Not Worry So Much about American Imperialism," in Avram, *Anxious about Empire*, pp. 124-25.

22. Webb, "On the True Globalism and the False," p. 124.

23. Webb, "On the True Globalism and the False," p. 124.

Webb's account of church history dovetails neatly with President Bush's theology that the "ideal of America is the hope of all mankind." This gospel of America, with its self-justifying account of church history, has immediate implications for the War on Terror. Because God's providence is manifest through America's success, it must be that God's face is against America's enemies: the enemies of America, therefore, are the enemies of God; whoever is against "us" is against God, who is on "our" side. Because God's providence favors America's success, therefore, "God bless America" implies "and not America's enemies."

Such self-assurance of national righteousness, such presumption of divine blessing for "our own" and "our country," not only denies God's mercy upon America's enemies, but fails to recognize the realistic possibility that a war "to rid the world of evil" might entail ridding "us" of evil. If Americans were to recognize the truth that the line between good and evil does not run between "us" and "them" but through all of us, and hence acknowledge the realistic possibility that evil must be uprooted from America itself as well as from America's enemies, then Americans might also realize the wisdom of the cross — that a war "to rid the world of evil" can never succeed by ridding the world of enemies. That is why when Martin Luther King, Jr. "broke silence" and "declared independence" from the Vietnam War on April 4, 1967, one year to the day before he was martyred, he not only protested the violence and bloodshed of war and spoke out for the victims of war (which are always overwhelmingly the poor), but also called his own nation to repent from the "triple evils" of racism, materialism, and militarism.[24]

28.4. The Peace of the Cross and the Love of Enemies

The terrorist attacks of September 11 might have prompted the United States to self-examination, perhaps even repentance, but instead "the powers that be" manipulated the nation's mourning to "justify" a war in the name of "God" and "our own." Yet, the ensuing War on Terror will never bring peace to the world because the wisdom of the Crucified teaches us that there is no way to make real peace — except by first dealing with one's own sins before dealing with one's opponent (Matt 7:1-5), except by examining prejudices and renouncing privileges that exalt and benefit oneself and one's own but oppress and exclude the neighbor and stranger, except by repenting of injustice and violence, both personal and social, and seeking forgiveness from neighbors near and far, ex-

24. Martin Luther King, Jr., "A Time to Break Silence," in James M. Washington, ed., *A Testament of Hope: The Essential Writings and Speeches of Martin Luther King, Jr.* (New York: HarperCollins, 1986), pp. 231-44. See also "Where Do We Go from Here?" in *Testament of Hope*, pp. 245-52.

cept by uprooting the noxious weed of hostility from one's own heart and from the heart of one's nation and tending those places where one's own words and deeds have sown seeds of hostility in the hearts of others, and except by beating one's own sword into a plowshare and tilling the soil of the heart so that seeds of mercy and justice might be planted, take root, and "bear fruits worthy of repentance" (Luke 3:8).

Cruciform peacemaking thus calls the Christian peacemaker to a costly discipline of spiritual warfare, a war to "disarm the heart" as well as the hands.[25] Even for the monk who seeks peace in solitude, as desert father Abba Antony of Egypt said, "There is only one war left in which to fight, and that is the battle for your own heart."[26] Jean Vanier, the founder of the L'Arche communities for people with disabilities, quotes Patriarch Athenagoras of Constantinople speaking of this "waging war against oneself," the struggle to disarm one's own heart in order to make peace with others: "I have waged this war against myself for many years. It was terrible. But now I am disarmed. I am no longer frightened of anything because love banishes fear. I am disarmed of the need to be right and to justify myself by disqualifying others."[27] As prophet and martyr Oscar Romero preached, this "war against oneself" is waged, not with the violence of human weapons, but with "the violence of love" as demonstrated through the cross of Christ:

> We have never preached violence, except the violence of love, which left Christ nailed on a cross, the violence that we must each do to ourselves to overcome our selfishness and such cruel inequalities among us. The violence we preach is not the violence of the sword, the violence of hatred. It is the violence of love, of brotherhood, the violence that wills to beat weapons into sickles for work.[28]

25. John Dear, *Disarming the Heart: Toward a Vow of Nonviolence* (Scottdale, PA: Herald Press, 1993).

26. As commonly cited from the sayings of the desert fathers.

27. Jean Vanier, *Drawn into the Mystery of Jesus through the Gospel of John* (Ottawa, Canada: Novalis, 2004), p. 301. Patriarch Athenagoras's testimony reminds us of Abuna Elias Chacour's struggle toward forgiveness among his community in Ibillin (see Chapter 26 above).

28. Oscar Romero, homily of November 27, 1977, quoted from *The Violence of Love*, compiled and translated by James R. Brockman, S.J. (Farmington, PA: Plough Publishing, 1998), p. 12. Such language as "waging war against oneself" and "violence of love" can be misunderstood and perverted to purposes contrary to God's peace in Christ. The call to "love our enemies" can be used to justify the evil that others do when the weak and vulnerable among us are counseled to "love" an abuser or oppressor by submitting quietly and passively enduring violence. So we must add here a cautionary note: the cross of Jesus — which, as much as Jesus' life-ministry, demonstrates God's personal, undying solidarity with all victims of abuse, oppression, persecution, and torture — must never be used to justify or excuse violence against women, children, the elderly, immigrants, prisoners, those with mental illness or developmental disability, or anyone else in a position of weakness or vulnerability. Concerning the cross and suffer-

Cruciform peacemaking by "the violence of love" is no less than obedience to Jesus' command that we love our enemies as God loves us (Matt 5:43-48). Paul tells us explicitly that the cross of Christ is nothing other than a practical demonstration of God's own love for his enemies: "But God proves his love for us in that while we still were sinners Christ died for us . . . while we were enemies, we were reconciled to God through the death of his Son" (Rom 5:8, 10). Loving enemies is thus integral to God's salvation and peace through the cross of Christ: the peace of the cross *is* the love of enemies. We who have been reconciled to God through the enemy-loving cross of Christ, therefore, cannot but do the same — to love our enemies as God has loved us in Christ. Salvation and peace through the cross without love of enemies is the "cheap grace" against which Bonhoeffer protested.[29] Because the cross of Christ is God's demonstration of love for enemies, we cannot with integrity proclaim salvation through the cross but divorce our peace with God from loving our enemies as Christ.

Salvation through the cross of Christ thus calls us to costly peacemaking that voluntarily lays down one's life rather than even regretfully killing the enemy. The enemy-loving cross forbids us to make either retaliatory strikes against those who transgress against us (Matt 5:38-42; Luke 6:29-31; 9:52-56) or even preemptory strikes against those who threaten us (Matt 26:51-52; Luke 22:49-51). The cross of Christ thus voids all "just cause" for war — whether retaliation or preemption — among the followers of Christ. At the same time, the enemy-loving cross commands us to "do good to those who hate us" — to feed our enemies and heal their wounds, not to starve them out by embargoes and sanctions (Luke 6:27-28; Rom 12:14-21). If we say "peace, peace" through the cross of Christ, who died for us while we were God's enemies, but wield the sword against our own enemy, for whom also Christ died, then we lie.

Augustine, who adopted Cicero's "just war" idea and adapted it to Christian use, tried to reconcile loving enemies with waging war. Earlier we observed Augustine's ambivalence toward Jesus' teaching that his disciples renounce retribution (Chapter 3). Here we observe Augustine's ambivalence toward Jesus' command that his disciples love their enemies. The first book of his treatise on biblical interpretation, *On Christian Teaching*, is a minor catechism of Christian faith.[30] After outlining the basic doctrines of the creed — God/Trinity, Incarnation, the church, forgiveness of sins, resurrection of the body, judgment,

---

ing, especially pertaining to women and discipleship, see Mary H. Schertz, "God's Cross and Women's Questions: A Biblical Perspective on the Atonement," *Mennonite Quarterly Review* 68 (1994), 194-208. Concerning the way atonement theology can be abused to justify the suffering of women, see Rita Nakashima Brock and Rebecca Ann Parker, *Proverbs of Ashes: Violence, Redemptive Suffering, and the Search for What Saves Us* (Boston: Beacon Press, 2001).

29. Dietrich Bonhoeffer, *The Cost of Discipleship* (New York: Macmillan, 1959).

30. Augustine, *On Christian Teaching*, trans. R. P. H. Green (Oxford: Oxford University Press, 1999). Augustine wrote the first part of this work between 395 and 397.

and eternal life — Augustine proceeds to a discussion of the dual commandment to love God and love neighbor.

Augustine argues first that loving God is a whole-life obligation: "And
when it says, 'all your heart, all your soul, all your mind,' it leaves no part of our
life free from this obligation." He argues that in loving our neighbor we ought
to relate ourselves to God, the ultimate object of love, and so love the neighbor
on account of God, such that proper love of neighbor is also for the whole life:
"So a person who loves his neighbor properly should . . . aim to love God with
all his heart, all his soul, and all his mind."[31] He then argues that this whole-life
love of neighbor is to be inclusive and impartial: "every human being, *qua* human being, should be loved on God's account. . . . All people should be loved
equally."[32] This inclusive and impartial love of neighbor, he emphasizes, excludes no one: "That the commandment to love our neighbor excludes no human being is made clear by our Lord himself in the gospel and by the apostle
Paul."[33] Citing the parable of the good Samaritan and the Sermon on the
Mount, Augustine argues that Jesus teaches that the neighbor we are to love is
anyone who needs our compassion without exception, including our enemies:
"Who can fail to see that there is no exception to this, nobody to whom compassion is not due? The commandment extends even to our enemies; in the
words of our Lord once again, 'Love your enemies, do good to those who hate
you.'"[34] And citing Rom 13:9-10, Augustine argues that Paul teaches that love of
neighbor is all-inclusive and forbids doing evil to anyone without exception:

> Anyone who thinks that the apostle was not here giving commandments that
> embraced all people is compelled to admit something totally absurd and to-
> tally wicked: that Paul thought it not sin to violate the wife of a non-
> Christian or an enemy, or to kill him or covet his property. If this conclusion
> is absurd, it is clear that all people must be reckoned as neighbors, because
> evil must not be done to anyone.[35]

Augustine thus interprets the commandment to love the neighbor to categorically include loving the enemy and so to unequivocally exclude killing the
enemy.[36]

---

31. Augustine, *On Christian Teaching*, 1.42-43.
32. Augustine, *On Christian Teaching*, 1.60-61.
33. Augustine, *On Christian Teaching*, 1.67.
34. Augustine, *On Christian Teaching*, 1.69.
35. Augustine, *On Christian Teaching*, 1.70.
36. Paul states in Rom 13:9-10 that "love your neighbor" sums up the various commandments of the Decalogue concerning relations to fellow humans, including "you shall not kill."
Thus, because Augustine has argued (based on Jesus' teaching) that love of neighbor subsumes
love of enemy, he concludes (based on Paul's teaching) that "love your enemy" subsumes the
commandment against killing.

Nonetheless, a few years later, Augustine would substantially qualify this teaching, making it possible to both love the enemy and kill the enemy. Whereas he had argued previously that love of neighbor, as love of God, is a whole-life obligation excluding no part of the self, he argues later that love of neighbor — hence, love of enemy — obligates less than the whole self. He does this by interpreting Jesus' command of non-resistance (Matt 5:38-42) so that loving enemies shrinks from a deed of the hand to a disposition of the heart:

> If it is supposed that God could not enjoin warfare, because in after times it was said by the Lord Jesus Christ, "I say unto you, That ye resist not evil: but if any one strike thee on the right cheek, turn to him the left also," the answer is, that what is here required is not a bodily action, but an inward disposition.[37]

The precepts of Jesus, which enjoin us to forsake retaliation against enemies, Augustine comments on the Sermon on the Mount, are to be properly understood "with regard to the preparation of the heart, and not with regard to the visible performance of the deed."[38] This qualified interpretation effectively denies what Jesus explicitly taught, that the love of enemies is to be not only an inward intention but an outward action: "Love your enemies, *do good* to those who hate you. . . . *Do* to others as you would have them do to you" (Luke 6:27, 31). Such qualification of Christ's teaching makes it possible for the Christian to love the enemy in the heart, in obedience to Christ, and to conquer the enemy with the hands, in obedience to Caesar — and so avoid a conflict of loyalties. Augustine thus writes, several years later, with all sincerity:

> [W]ar is waged in order that peace may be obtained. Therefore, even in waging war, cherish the spirit of a peacemaker, that by conquering those whom you attack, you may lead them back to the advantages of peace; for our Lord says: "Blessed are the peacemakers; for they shall be called the children of God."[39]

Augustine reconciles peacemaking and war-waging by divorcing hands from heart: one can war against the enemy with the hands while being an enemy-

---

37. Augustine, *Reply to Faustus the Manichaean* XXII.76, in Philip Schaff, ed., *The Nicene and Post-Nicene Fathers*, series I, vol. IV (Grand Rapids, MI: Christian Classics Ethereal Library), p. 415. Augustine wrote his refutation of the Manichaean teacher Faustus in 400.

38. Augustine, *Our Lord's Sermon on the Mount, According to St. Matthew*, I.XIX.59, quoted in Lisa Sowle Cahill, *Love Your Enemies: Discipleship, Pacifism, and Just War Theory* (Minneapolis, MN: Fortress Press, 1994), p. 71; cf. pp. 72-74.

39. Augustine, *Letter* 189; in Arthur F. Holmes, ed., *War and Christian Ethics: Classic Readings on the Morality of Warfare* (Grand Rapids, MI: Baker Books, 1975), p. 63. Augustine wrote this letter in 418 or 419 to Count Boniface, who was defender of the city of Carthage against the barbarian invasions.

loving peacemaker at heart. This is a dualistic ethic that dissolves the integrity of the "inner" and "outer" person, dividing loyalty between two lords: the heart for Christ, the hands for Caesar.[40]

Desiring peace in one's heart while wielding the sword with one's hands, as Augustine allows, is not truly Christian peacemaking precisely because it refuses to bear in one's own body the cost of making peace and instead forces the enemy to pay the price of peace with his blood. That is quite contrary to the peacemaking of our Lord Jesus Christ, who voluntarily bore the cost of making peace with God's enemies through the cross — in his own body, with his own blood. To reconcile sword and cross — killing enemies and loving enemies — is thus, in truth, to reject the cross. Ron Sider:

> Jesus' cross, where He practiced what He preached about love for one's enemies, becomes the Christian norm for every area of life. Only if one holds biblical authority so irrelevant that one can ignore explicit, regularly repeated scriptural teaching; only if one so disregards Christ's atonement that one rejects God's way of dealing with enemies; only then can one forsake the cross for the sword.[41]

Any atonement theology that would accommodate the cross to the sword, therefore, is a counter-cross theology. Again, Sider: "Because Jesus commanded his followers to love their enemies and then died as the incarnate Son to demonstrate that God reconciles his enemies by suffering love, any rejection of the nonviolent way in human relations involves a heretical doctrine of the atonement."[42] Indeed, as John Howard Yoder pointed out, insofar as "the Christian sees the world and its wars from the viewpoint of the cross," and thus sees any and all enemies from the perspective of God's cause of salvation in Christ, the Christian will no longer have "just cause" to take up the sword because he will no longer see a world of enemies, but rather a world that God loves and seeks to save:

> No one created in God's image and for whom Christ died can be for me an enemy, whose life I am willing to take, unless I am more devoted to some-

---

40. Augustine's dualism of heart/intention and hands/action parallels the dualism of spirit and matter in the Platonist worldview that so influenced his thinking. Both James and John condemned a dualistic ethic that separates hands from heart, deeds from faith (Jas 1:22–2:26; 1 John 3:11-24): love must be enacted, not only intended — "Let us love, not in word or speech, but in truth and action." On the theme of integrity of heart and hands in relation to participation in war, see my reflection, "Is Jesus Lord?" in Donald B. Kraybill and Linda G. Peachey, eds., *Where Was God on September 11? Seeds of Faith and Hope* (Scottdale, PA: Herald Press, 2002), pp. 57-59.

41. Ronald J. Sider, *Christ and Violence* (Scottdale, PA: Herald Press, 1979), p. 38.

42. Sider, *Christ and Violence*, p. 34.

thing else — to a political theory, to a nation, to the defense of certain privileges, or to my own personal welfare — than I am to God's cause: his loving invasion of this world in his prophets, his Son, and his church.[43]

Loving our enemies, with both hands and hearts, is the costly sacrifice of the peacemaking cross of Christ, who died for us, God's enemies. Yoder thus continues: "The Christian has no choice: If this was God's pattern, if his strategy for dealing with his enemies was to love them and give himself for them, it must be ours as well."[44]

---

43. John Howard Yoder, "The Way of Peace in a World at War," in *He Came Preaching Peace* (Scottdale, PA: Herald Press, 1998), pp. 20-21.

44. Yoder, *He Came Preaching Peace*, p. 21. What Yoder argued is a matter of faithfulness, King argued is a practical strategy of converting enemies into friends by destroying hate through love. See Martin Luther King, Jr., "Loving Your Enemies," *Sermon Dexter Ave. Baptist Church Christmas 1957* (Essay Series 1; New York: A. J. Muste Memorial Institute, 1968).

CHAPTER 29

The Peace of Christ:
Destroying Division, Murdering Hostility

For he is our peace;
in his flesh he has made both groups into one
and has broken down the dividing wall,
that is, the hostility between us.
He has abolished the law with its commandments and ordinances,
that he might create one new humanity in place of the two,
> *thus making peace,*
and might reconcile both groups to God
in one body through the cross,
> *thus putting to death that hostility in himself.*

EPHESIANS 2:14-16

We now consider *how* it is that God-in-Christ makes peace through the cross. Notice that at the heart of Ephesians 2 the phrase "thus making peace" is parallel to "thus putting to death that hostility in himself." Jesus makes peace through the cross by breaking down "the dividing wall, that is the hostility between us" (v. 14). Through the cross, in his flesh, Jesus *puts to death* — literally, murders! — the "hostility" that not only divides Jew from Gentile (v. 16) but disrupts relationship with God (vv. 16, 18). Thus, Jesus makes peace by "murdering hostility." To understand what Paul might mean by this astonishing word — that through the cross Jesus has abolished division and murdered hostility, thereby making peace — recall the twofold Pauline vision of God's salvation: Christ "creates in himself one new humanity" out of former enemies (Jew and Gentile), and "reconciles both groups to God in one body through the cross" (vv. 15-16).

As we observed in previous chapters, this re-creative, reconciling, peacemaking work of salvation in Christ through the cross is necessary in history because there exists real division and hostility — war! — among human enemies and of humanity against God. In order to heal humanity of its war wounds and to make a peaceable relationship with God, it is necessary that this war of humanity with itself and against God be brought to an end. Humanity, in its position of weakness, enslaved to sin and under the dominion of death (the real enemy), is incapable of such a task; indeed, fallen humanity has been conscripted into the service of the forces of death that war against God's reign (Romans 5-6). Dealing decisively with this persistent conflict requires a unilateral peace initiative from God. Jesus is the gracious peace initiative of God that brings salvation from war, the peace with one another and with God that we cannot make by our own efforts.

How, then, does God make peace in Christ through the cross? By *making war*, but *not* against humanity. Even though humanity has put itself at enmity with God by its rebellion against God's rule (Rom 5:10; Col 1:21), human beings are not the real enemy. The real struggle in this war "is not against enemies of flesh and blood" (Eph 6:12). Instead, the *real enemy* that must be dealt with decisively is the dominion of *sin* that works *death* through the war of humanity with itself and against God (Romans 5–6; 1 Corinthians 15). God makes war in Christ through the cross on the very sinful conditions that have engendered the state of war — division and hostility. To see all this more clearly, notice that Paul describes actual peacemaking work of Christ in the cross using five verbs: *break down, abolish, murder, create, reconcile* (Eph 2:14-17).[1] What is the **object** of each of these verbs? And who is their subject?

29.1. The Peace of Christ Destroys Division

First, Jesus *breaks down* the **dividing wall** between Jew and Gentile by *abolishing* the **law** that separates them into two unequal classes before God (vv. 14-15a).[2] The "dividing wall" was the barrier erected by the law (and its oral interpretation) between clean and unclean, pure and impure, that had separated Jews and Gentiles into two distinct social groups. The Jew-Gentile distinction was symbolized in the body (for males) by circumcision. This mark of distinction, which had been instituted with Abraham as a sign of membership in God's covenant community (Genesis 17), had been used to erect a fence partitioning humanity into the "circumcised" and the "uncircumcised" (cf. Eph 2:11). What had been given by God as a means of separating the covenant com-

---

1. Here, for the sake of this analysis, I treat all of these as finite verbs in the indicative mood; in the Greek, some are participles and some are in the subjunctive mood.

2. Concerning the meaning of the dividing wall or "fence," see Thomas R. Yoder Neufeld, *Ephesians* (Believers Church Bible Commentary; Scottdale, PA: Herald Press, 2002), pp. 115-19. On the role of "works of the law" in separating Jews from Gentiles, see James D. G. Dunn, *The Theology of Paul the Apostle* (Grand Rapids, MI: Eerdmans Publishing, 1998), pp. 354-59.

munity *unto* God had been perverted into a means of separating the nations *from* God — so that circumcision obstructed Gentile access to God's grace and alienated Gentiles from God and the blessings of the covenant.

Such alienating obstruction was made concretely visible by means of an actual dividing wall in the Temple at Jerusalem during Jesus' day. This wall separated the "Court of Gentiles" from the "Court of Israel," a literal barrier keeping the "uncircumcised nations" from participating in the worship of God around the altar; any Gentile daring to transgress that barrier risked a penalty of death.[3] Not only could "Jew" and "Gentile" not worship God together, but they also could not be "one people" in fellowship — by, say, common meals or common prayer in the home — because of the strict Pharisaic prohibitions against Jews associating freely and intimately with Gentiles (cf. Acts 10:28). The rabbis justified such oral prohibitions separating "clean" from "unclean" on the basis of the Holiness Code (Leviticus 17–26) so that, again, what God had intended to separate the covenant community *from the surrounding nations* (20:22-26) had been interpreted to separate the nations *from God.*

The use of Israelite distinctiveness to separate the nations from God ran counter to both the Torah and the Prophets.[4] God's covenant with Abraham, sealed by circumcision, was intended from the beginning to bring blessing, not only to the family of Abraham, but also to the family of nations (Gen 12:1-3). That such barriers did indeed pervert the intent of the law, moreover, is evident from the Holiness Code itself. Far from prohibiting the *gērîm* (non-Israelite "sojourners" or "alien residents" in Israel) from participating in cultic worship, the Holiness Code gives specific instructions concerning those *gērîm* desiring to approach the altar and offer a free-will sacrifice (Lev 17:8-9; 22:17-25). The Holiness Code, that is, explicitly sanctions Gentile participation in the cultic worship of Israel. Solomon's prayer of dedication for the Temple, furthermore, petitions YHWH to receive the prayers of the *nokrîm* (foreigners from distant lands), who, having heard of the great name and mighty acts of YHWH, have come to the Temple to worship (1 Kgs 8:41-42; 2 Chron 6:32-33). The prophets recovered this original intent of the Torah, that God's vision for peace in Israel includes Gentiles, both "near" and "far." Isaiah envisioned the nations, rather than being separated from God by the law, being drawn by the light of Torah to worship at the mountain of YHWH, so that all peoples would be brought into the peace of God's reign. Under this peaceable reign of God, the hostility and conflict between nations is extinguished through God's justice (Isa 2:2-4). God's vision for Israel was thus inclusive, not exclusive, of "the nations" (42:1-9; 49:1-6; 56:3-8; 66:18-23).

---

3. There was also a wall separating the "Court of Women" from the "Court of Israel," keeping women from equal membership and full participation in the covenant community.

4. Cf. Dunn, *Theology of Paul*, p. 535.

Paul's message of the cross in Ephesians 2 is that all this is to be realized through Jesus and the cross, by whom and through which the true intent of God's covenant is fulfilled. This entails that the law of separation — and with it the theological significance of circumcision as a distinctive mark in the flesh that separates some *for* God and all others *from* God — is nullified in Christ's body on the cross. In the body of Christ, Paul thus writes, the Jew-Gentile distinction, marked in the flesh by circumcision, is no longer of any account in God's covenant community (Gal 3:26-29; 5:6; 6:15).[5] Peter, in his speech to the Gentile household of Cornelius (Acts 10:35-36), proclaims this same good news, the gospel of peace "preached by Jesus Christ," namely, that Jew and Gentile, in Christ, have the same means of access to God, are acceptable to God on the same terms, and enjoy the same benefits of belonging to the people of God.

29.2. The Peace of Christ Murders Hostility

Second, Jesus *murders* the inter-human **hostility** — Jew against Gentile, Gentile against Jew — that is engendered by this division and justified by the law of separation (vv. 14, 16). As Paul indicates, the distinctive sign of circumcision not only divides and separates Jew from Gentile, but comes to define both groups: Jews are the "circumcision," Gentiles are the "uncircumcision" (Eph 2:11). Inter-ethnic/inter-religious hostility and conflict are inevitable whenever the "people of God," defined and divided over against all other peoples by the law of separation (circumcision), claim a special role in history and a superior place among the nations that justifies them before God and grants them right of judgment in God's name. Having denied other nations right standing before God, such presumed self-righteousness and superiority justifies the actual execution of "God's wrath" in history upon the "unrighteous nations" (cf. Psalm 149).

The law of separation, which engendered a self-righteous sense of spiritual superiority within Israel, also caused mutual hostility between Jews and Gentiles.[6] It is this "hostility between us" that Jesus "puts to death . . . in himself" through the cross (Eph 2:14b, 16b). Jesus' death extinguishes the mutual hostility by abolishing the law of separation that divides Jew and Gentile — Jew for God, Gentile from God. Because, in Christ, Jew and Gentile stand before God on the same ground of grace (vv. 8-9), there is no longer any ground for

5. This is the counterpart to Paul's argument that circumcision does not distinguish law-keepers from law-breakers and thus does not confer any value on the circumcised apart from the really important thing, keeping the law, which is a matter of the heart rather than a mark in the flesh (Rom 2:25-29).

6. Cf. Ulrich Mauser, *The Gospel of Peace: A Scriptural Message for Today's World* (Louisville, KY: Westminster/John Knox Press, 1992), pp. 157-60.

hostility. The field of war has been transformed into a plain of peace through the cross, such that "he [Jesus] is our peace" (v. 14a).

Paul himself undercuts this claim of self-righteousness and ethnic superiority in Romans 2 and 3 by invoking the Torah, which might be seen as the source of Israel's superiority (cf. Ps 147:19-20), as the judge of Israel's shortcoming. Although Israel identifies itself as "a people apart" by the mark of circumcision, it is not really distinguished concerning the basic human situation: "both Jews and Greeks are under the power of sin" (Rom 3:9). Although Israel has received the Torah through the prophet of God, it enjoys no special status before God: "For there is no distinction, since all have sinned and fall short of the glory of God" (v. 23). Circumcision and Torah notwithstanding, therefore, "there is no distinction" among humanity — "all have sinned"; and because "there is no distinction" with respect to the law, there can be no distinction regarding membership in God's covenant: Jews and Gentiles alike must be "justified by grace" (v. 24; cf. Eph 2:8-9). And the grace of God that justifies sinners is available to all through the enmity-murdering, enemy-reconciling cross of Jesus Christ.[7]

29.3. The Peace of Christ Re-Creates Humanity and Reconciles to God

Now that the dividing wall between Jew and Gentile is broken down through the abolition of the law of separation, so that the sinful cause of the inter-human hostility is destroyed, the hostile parties can be reconciled and the war ended. Because "in his flesh" Jesus has abolished the law of separation and has broken down the dividing wall (v. 14), and thereby has "murdered in himself" that hostility (v. 16b), Jesus can "*create* in himself **one new humanity** in place of the two, thus making peace" (v. 15b). Finally, having created "one new humanity" in himself, Jesus can "*reconcile* **both groups to God** in one body through the cross" and thereby put a final end to the war (v. 16).

We can summarize the Pauline story in Ephesians 2 of God's peacemaking work of salvation accomplished in Christ through the cross as follows:

Agent	Action	Means	Object/Result of Action
Jesus	destroys	in his flesh	dividing wall (Jew v. Gentile, v. 14b)
Jesus	abolishes	in his flesh	law of separation (circumcision, v. 15a)
Jesus	murders	in himself	hostility (Jew v. Gentile, vv. 14b, 16b)
Jesus	creates	in himself	one new humanity (Jew and Gentile, v. 15b)
Jesus	reconciles	in one body, through the cross	both groups to God (v. 16a)

7. We will return to the peacemaking implications of justification by faith in Christ in Chapter 33.

We thus see that the peacemaking work of salvation is entirely the work of God-in-Christ-through-the-cross. It is not we who make peace with God by our act of good faith; rather, God makes peace with us by his own initiative. Indeed, our part in the cross is anything but an act of good faith — we murdered Jesus! Humanity is saved, therefore, not by the hostile murderous act we commit against God-in-Christ at the cross, but by what God-in-Christ freely and faithfully does for us through the cross to nullify human division and mortify human hostility. As Paul summarizes: "For by grace you have been saved through faith, and this is not your own doing; it is the gift of God" (Eph 2:8).

29.4. The Peace of Christ: A Gestalt Shift

Our reading of the Pauline vision of God's salvation through the peacemaking cross clarifies that, while we are "brought near by the blood of Christ" (Eph 2:13), it is *not* the human-executed violence committed against Jesus that saves us. Rather, it is Jesus' own non-retaliatory, reconciliatory response to the body-breaking, blood-shedding violence committed against himself that makes peace.

Here is where the Pauline vision induces a gestalt shift in our perception of the cross. Paul helps us to see that, in effect, there are *two murders* that occur at the cross — the hostile murder *of* Jesus by humanity, and the murder of human hostility *by* Jesus. And it is the latter which is effective unto God's salvation and peace through Christ. It is not we who effect salvation and peace with God by means of the bloodletting act of killing Jesus. Instead, it is Jesus himself who accomplishes God's salvation and peace by his law-abolishing, division-destroying, hostility-murdering, new-creating, humanity-reconciling work. To see the cross as Paul sees it, we must shift the focus from humanity's murder of Jesus to Jesus' murder of hostility. As Paul depicts the saving, peacemaking cross, Jesus is *not* the *object* but the *subject* of murder. The object of the murder that effects salvation and makes peace through the cross is the hostility engendered by the division of humanity over against itself. By his own blood, in his own flesh, through the cross, Jesus effectively "puts to death in himself" the human hostility that alienates us from one another and from God.

The killing of Jesus does not in and of itself accomplish salvation by making peace but only escalates the war of humanity with itself and with God. The situation God addresses in Christ at the cross is that we, humanity, are not only engaged in hostilities one against another (Ephesians 2), but are also in active rebellion against God's kingdom (Rom 1:16-32; 5:1-11; Col 1:21). As seen through Luke's Gospel, we enact this rebellion by oppressing the poor and weak and idolizing wealth and power, by murdering God's prophets and plundering God's vineyard — ultimately conspiring to murder the master of the vineyard, the Lord of the kingdom, Jesus, God's own Son (Luke 11:37-54, 20:9-19). Indeed, by murdering Christ, the one whom God sends preaching peace to all near and far (Eph 2:17; Acts 10:36), humanity magnifies the war to the limit: we kill God's anointed ambassador of peace! Were there ever a "just cause" for war, response to humanity's murder of Jesus would be it. If God were to defend his kingdom by responding in kind to this escalation, retaliating against humanity for the violent bloodshed it has committed against God's own peace emissary, however, then humanity would surely be finished.

Salvation from this end-state of the war is possible only because Jesus does *not* beg for God's vengeance and God does *not* retaliate against humanity. Instead, Jesus mercifully petitions God to forgive humanity for the sin of murdering him (Luke 23:34); and God accepts Jesus' faithful donation of his own blood to be the seal of a new God-made covenant of peace with humanity (Luke 22:20; Col 1:20). Rather than making total war on humanity because we crucified Jesus, God-in-Christ faithfully persists in making peace with humanity — not despite the cross, but indeed "through the cross," by putting war-begetting hostility to death in himself at the cost of his own life, at the price of his own blood being shed. Rather than being provoked by the crucifixion of Jesus to carry the war to its ultimate consummation (the destruction of all humanity), God instead graciously transforms the cross into a new-life-giving sign of grace, freely making a costly covenant of peace sealed with "the blood of Christ," by which we who were once in rebellion against God ("far off") may now be in fellowship ("brought near") with God through faith (Eph 2:13-17). John Howard Yoder thus comments:

> The gospel does not only *imply* an ethic of peacemaking or being set at peace, nor does it merely *lead to* a nonviolent lifestyle. It *proclaims* a reconciled view of the world. . . . That is the gospel — not that *war is sin*. That also is true, but alone it would not be the gospel. The gospel is that *the war is over.*[8]

The persistent message of the gospel is that we are saved, not by retributive violence, but rather through God's "transforming initiative" in Christ to freely give his own life rather than take the lives of even his enemies, for the sake of love of humanity. Jesus does not make peace by waging violent conflict against human enemies estranged from and rebellious against God. Jesus "murders hostility" through "the violence of love" — not by defeating and destroying human enemies, but by defeating the sinful conditions that impede and destroy peace, by destroying division that engenders hostility ofone group over against another in the first place, by nullifying criteria and marks of identity and difference that exclude and oppress in offense against God's mercy. Jesus "murders hostility" through "the violence of love" — not by returning violence for vio-

---

8. John Howard Yoder, "What Are You Doing More Than They?" in *He Came Preaching Peace* (Scottdale, PA: Herald Press, 1998), pp. 54-55, emphasis original.

lence or shedding blood for blood shed, but by returning forgiveness for injustice, love for hate, blessing for cursing. And this Jesus does supremely through the cross.

Here, then, we see how God makes peace and does justice, how God heals brokenness and rights wrong, how God reconciles humanity through the cross of Jesus Christ — restoring both wholeness to humanity and right relationship with God: *Shalom!* The re-creative and reconciling cross of Jesus Christ is the atoning (right-making, one-making) work of God, the authentic peacemaking that truly saves.

•   •

SECTION D

Cruciform Peacemaking

Extinguishing Hostility, Transforming Conflict

CHAPTER 30

Peacemaking by "Murdering Hostility": The Life-Ministry of Jesus

Whatever house you enter, first say,
"Peace to this house!"
And if anyone is there who shares in peace,
your peace will rest on that person;
but if not, it will return to you.

LUKE 10:5-6

30.1. Jesus' Ministry as a Peacemaking Campaign of "Murdering Hostility"

Our exegesis of the Pauline vision of God's salvation through the peacemaking cross, as depicted in Ephesians 2 (Part III, Section C), fits well with Luke's narrative of the life-ministry, passion, and resurrection of Jesus the Messiah. We may thus use this cruciform paradigm of God's peacemaking derived from Paul's depiction of the cross as a lens through which to interpret Luke's narrative of Jesus' life-ministry.[1] While the cross of Christ epitomizes most dramatically the "murder of hostility" pivotal to God's peacemaking work of salvation, if we read the story of Jesus from the view of the cross, we will find that Jesus commits "murder" many times along the way to reveal God's salvation and peace, both before his death and after his resurrection.

First, Jesus calls and names both tax collectors and zealots — mortal enemies — to be fellow disciples and apostles (Luke 5:27-28; 6:12-16).

---

1. By reading Luke through the lens of Paul, we effectively extend the significance of Paul's phrase "in his flesh" (Eph 2:14) to include the entire Incarnation: Jesus "is our peace" and makes peace "in his flesh" through his life and his death.

Through his discipleship community, Jesus breaks down enmity so
that former enemies might be reconciled together for the sake of the
mission of God's kingdom.

Jesus welcomes and openly shares table fellowship with "sinners" and tax
collectors and other outcast and "unclean" folk (Luke 5:27-32; 14:1-24;
15:1-2; 19:1-10) — those whom the Pharisees and scribes judged to be
transgressors. Jesus' ministry of hospitality, a sign of God's kingdom,
thus destroys the dividing wall created by the human criteria that defined "inside" and "outside" among God's covenant people. The Apostle Peter, inhibited by his own orthodoxy and piety, is prompted by the
Spirit of Jesus to cross these same Pharisaic boundaries and break
down these same legal barriers by dwelling with Simon the tanner (an
"unclean" trade) and welcoming Gentiles, also sent by the Spirit. This
act of hospitality in the Spirit of Jesus opens the way for full inclusion
of Gentile believers into the church (Acts 10–11).

Jesus forgives the outcast sinner and heals the unclean sufferer simply on
account of their faith, bringing wholeness and peace to lives marked
by exclusion and overshadowed by shame (Luke 7:36-50; 8:43-48; 17:11-
19). By his ministry of mercy and healing, Jesus breaks down barriers
and "murders" hostility between those "inside" and "outside" (according to human criteria) the covenant people of God's grace. The Apostles Peter and John, empowered by Jesus' resurrection Spirit and acting
in the name of Jesus, continue this ministry by healing the man lame
from birth at the Temple gate (Acts 3), thus granting him access to the
Temple courts to which the physically deformed were denied entry.

As Jesus and his disciples enter Samaria en route to Jerusalem, the disciples
encounter hostility and rejection from Samaritans who are suspicious
of Jesus' intentions. The disciples want God's judgment and wrath to
be poured out on those who rejected God's prophet: "Lord, do you
want us to command fire to come down from heaven and consume
them?" But Jesus rebukes his disciples, thus renouncing retribution in
favor of the saving, peacemaking way of God's kingdom (Luke 9:51-
56). Before he can commission his disciples to be emissaries of the gospel in Samaria ("enemy territory"), Jesus must first extinguish his own
disciples' hostility toward Samaritans, "murdering" that hostility by
his word: "The Son of Man has not come to destroy the lives of human
beings but to save them."

Jesus then sends his disciples into Samaria on mission in vulnerability
("like lambs in the midst of wolves"), dependent on the gracious hospitality of strangers and even potential enemies, in order to share the
healing peace brought by the good news of the kingdom of God (Luke
10:1-12). The first word they are to say when coming to a Samaritan

house is, "Peace to this house!" By sending the disciples with words of peace and works of healing for the people of Samaria, the kingdom mission of Jesus seeks to extinguish the historical enmity between Samaritans and Jews and break down the dividing wall that separates into hostile factions those who worship the same God. Contrasting Jesus' peacemaking mission in Samaria in Luke 9-10 with Joshua's violent conquest of Canaan by ethnic cleansing, Willard Swartley observes: "Rather than eradicating the enemy, as was the goal of Joshua's conquest narrative in the earlier story — in a similar location — the new strategy eliminates enmity."[2]

Jesus reconciles to God and God's covenant people the repentant tax collector who does mercy and justice by giving his wealth to the poor and making restitution for his crimes (Luke 19:1-10; more about this story below).

In Gethsemane, after struggling in prayer with the destiny that lay before him and having "entrusted himself to the one who judges justly" (1 Pet 2:23), Jesus once more resists the temptation to employ violence either in defense of himself or to advance the mission of God's kingdom (Luke 22:47-53). When the arresting party arrives, the disciples ask, "Lord, should we strike with the sword?" Jesus rebukes the disciple who attacks with the sword — "No more of this!" — and heals the wound inflicted by the sword, showing that the peace of God heals even its enemies, even while they remain hostile to God's kingdom. And by healing the wounds of his enemies, inflicted by his own disciple, Jesus acts to "murder the hostility" between his disciples and the authorities that would soon kill him and later persecute them.

In teaching and practice, Jesus renounces hostility-nurturing retribution, instead showing love for his enemies, doing good to those who hate him, blessing those who curse him, and praying for those who abuse him (Luke 6:27-28) — even, and especially, through the cross, by petitioning God's mercy upon all those who have conspired in and contributed to his murder instead of invoking God's vengeance upon them: "Father, forgive them; for they do not know what they are doing" (Luke 23:32-38). Even while being murdered by hostility, Jesus "murders in himself" the very hostility that is putting him to death and offers his murderers reconciliation with God.

On the cross, Jesus welcomes the condemned, yet contrite and repentant, sinner into the kingdom of God (Luke 23:39-43). Although the man crucified beside him passes judgment on himself, affirming the justice

---

2. Willard Swartley, *Covenant of Peace: The Missing Peace in New Testament Theology and Ethics* (Grand Rapids, MI: Eerdmans, 2006), p. 144.

of Rome's sentence, Jesus announces that even this one is invited to the banquet of God's grace. Jesus thus rejects the justice of the Roman court and despises the shame of the Roman cross as the final word on the fate of the sinner, thereby "murdering in himself" the imperial hostility toward God's kingdom.

In resurrection, Jesus returns to reconcile his failed and fallen disciples to himself, greeting those who deserted and denied him, "Peace be with you" (Luke 24:36-43).

By his resurrection Spirit, in the context of gracious hospitality toward the sinner, Jesus reconciles former enemies — Saul, feared persecutor of the church, and Ananias, devoted disciple of Jesus — as brothers in the fellowship of faith (Acts 9:1-31). Through this, Jesus "murders the hostility" of Saul toward the church, transforming that hostility into passion for preaching and practicing the gospel of peace.

By giving the Holy Spirit to Samaritan and Roman (Gentile) believers the same as to Jewish believers (Acts 8:14-17; 10:34–11:18; 15:6-11), Jesus continues to destroy division and extinguish hostility between church "insiders" and their "enemies."

In all these ways, Jesus reveals and fulfills "the things that make for peace" (Luke 19:42). In all these ways, God was "preaching peace by Jesus Christ" (Acts 10:36). In all these ways, "God was in Christ reconciling the world to himself" (2 Cor 5:19).

30.2. Peacemaking by "Murdering Hostility": The Story of Zacchaeus

With a little imagination, we can see Jesus "murdering hostility in himself" and so enacting "the things that make for peace" in the story of Zacchaeus (Luke 19:1-10).[3] Stating that Zacchaeus "was a chief tax collector and was rich" not only reports his status and finances, but also exhibits the popular sentiment (Luke 19:2). The popular judgment upon tax collectors is evident from the Pharisee in the Temple, whose prayer places tax collectors alongside "thieves, rogues, adulterers" — with the lawless and unfaithful, those who exploit and betray others (Luke 18:11). As chief tax collector who had amassed wealth by extortion and robbery under protection of imperial law and armed escorts, Zacchaeus is not well liked by the people of Jericho. We can imagine the hostil-

---

3. Regarding how the "quest" story of Zacchaeus fits into the literary patterns and themes of Luke's narrative, see Robert C. Tannehill, *The Narrative Unity of Luke-Acts: A Literary Interpretation,* vol 1: *The Gospel according to Luke* (Philadelphia: Fortress Press, 1986), pp. 122-25. My retelling of the story here draws in part from Tannehill's analysis.

ity of the people for this man: they regard him as a thief for taking their money by force, a traitor for collaborating with the Romans, a sinner for his daily dealings with unclean pagans, and an oppressor for his profiting from the poverty of others. We can thus imagine plotting and scheming in the houses of Jericho and around the campfires of the Zealot rebels in the countryside: "Let us send a message to all would-be collaborators by making an example of Zacchaeus." "How shall we do away with this evildoer?"

Zacchaeus is not only hated by the crowds for these reasons, but on account of his injustice is also lost from God and alienated from his own people — and, perhaps, even ashamed of himself. It might be that climbing a tree in order to see Jesus reveals that lostness, alienation, and shame (Luke 19:3-4). It might also reveal the crowd's hostility toward him — perhaps he must climb the tree because the crowd refuses to grant him space to get a clear view. Up a tree, Zacchaeus is exposed as one of the "lost sheep" looking for a way back, who needs to repent of injustice and return to the fold of God's flock under the hand of God's shepherd (Luke 15:3-7). Up a tree, displaced from his compatriots in the street, he is like the tax collector in the temple, "standing far off" and praying for mercy (Luke 18:9-14).

Now Jesus, who is hailed by the people as the prophet of God (Luke 7:16) and the messianic Son of David (Luke 18:38-39), is entering Jericho, having just blessed the children, healed the blind, and promised God's reward in this life and the next to those who leave all and follow him for the sake of the kingdom (Luke 18:15-17, 28-30, 35-43). Expectations were surely running high among the people of Jericho: "What will God's prophet do for us?" But there would be no blessings for the children, no works of healing, and no promises of reward. Instead, Jesus seeks out the hated Zacchaeus, inviting himself home to dinner, and Zacchaeus readily and joyously welcomes Jesus (Luke 19:5-6). The hostility of the people thus turns quickly from Zacchaeus toward Jesus: "All who saw it began to grumble and said, 'He has gone to be the guest of one who is a sinner'" (Luke 19:7). In grumbling so, they implicitly question whether Jesus is truly God's prophet, just as Simon the Pharisee had once questioned whether Jesus was truly a prophet when Jesus allowed "a woman in the city, who was a sinner" to wash and anoint his feet (Luke 7:36-39). We can thus imagine some Pharisees in the crowd stoking the flames of righteous indignation (cf. Luke 5:30; 15:1-2): "We've seen this fellow welcoming sinners and eating with tax collectors in other cities also." The grumbling of the people then grows: "He must be a false prophet." "Yes, and he spoke as if he were already friends with Zacchaeus, calling him by name." "A friend of thieves is a thief himself." "Maybe he's a collaborator, too." "I'll bet he gets a cut of Zacchaeus's profits." The crowd's mood is shifting quickly from acclaiming Jesus as prophet to accusing Jesus — "Sinner! Robber! Traitor!" This seething crowd is on the verge of rioting; Zacchaeus and Jesus both are in danger of losing their lives: "Stone them both!"

And then salvation appears! Zacchaeus acknowledges his sin, repents of his injustice, and offers terms of restitution: mercy to the poor and justice for those he has wronged (cf. Chapter 27 above). Notice here what makes possible this hostility-extinguishing, violence-averting, life-saving, justice-doing reconciliation between Zacchaeus and the people of Jericho. Jesus intercedes, interposing himself into danger, placing his own body between the hostile crowd and the hated Zacchaeus, taking upon himself the hostility of the crowd at the risk of his own blood being shed by their hands. Jesus offers his life to save this one lost sheep (Luke 19:10), offers forgiveness to the wayward, despised sinner; and through Jesus' self-sacrificing initiative, covenant righteousness is fulfilled: mercy and justice is done for the poor and oppressed. What Paul Fiddes writes of one who forgives another applies here to Jesus as intercessor in a situation of hostility:

> The forgiver must absorb the hostility of the other, to bear it and receive it into himself. By offering the word of forgiveness he has taken the first step across the gulf which separates the two who are apart, and so he has exposed himself to attack. He has made himself vulnerable, laying himself open to aggressive actions. . . . He has acted to bring the matter out into the open in the first place; now he must neutralize the hostility by submissively bearing with the other in love.[4]

By his intercessory, transforming, peacemaking initiative, Jesus willingly "murders that hostility in himself" — the hostility dividing Zacchaeus from the people and preventing their communion in God's peace — thus making possible reconciliation both of Zacchaeus with the people of Jericho and of Zacchaeus and the people with God. This is the peacemaking way of the cross — the way of God's atoning (right-making, one-making) salvation in Christ: "Today salvation has come to this house" (Luke 19:9)!

Remarkably, Jesus' peacemaking initiative and Zacchaeus's justice-doing response together illustrate three of the ten practices of "just peacemaking" identified by Glen Stassen and Duane Friesen: support nonviolent direct action, take independent initiatives to reduce threat, and acknowledge responsibility for conflict and injustice and seek repentance and forgiveness.[5] Jesus acts directly and creatively to right wrong and liberate the oppressed in Jericho by redemptive, nonviolent means. He confronts the oppressor directly but lovingly, calling forth hospitality and generosity (by inviting himself to dinner!), which Zacchaeus readily displays with joy. Zacchaeus's joyous acceptance of Je-

---

4. Paul S. Fiddes, *Past Event and Present Salvation: The Christian Idea of Atonement* (Louisville, KY: Westminster/John Knox Press, 1989), p. 174.
5. Glen Stassen, ed., *Just Peacemaking: Ten Practices for Abolishing War* (Cleveland, OH: Pilgrim Press, 1998).

sus' invitation stirs hostility in the crowd, and the crowd's response faces the oppressor with his wrongdoing toward those in the crowd whom he has previously excluded from hospitality and denied generosity. Yet this awkward situation gives the oppressor an opportunity for public repentance. Zacchaeus thus takes independent initiative with a unilateral offer of alms-giving and restitution-making, which reduces the gathering threat from the hostile crowd. And by giving alms and making restitution, Zacchaeus acknowledges implicitly his responsibility for the injustice that has created the conflict at hand and asks forgiveness from those he has wronged.

One can readily see the parallels between the stories of peacemaking by Abuna Elias Chacour in the Galilean village of Ibillin (Chapter 26 above) and by Jesus in Jericho. In Ibillin, by prayer and action, Abuna Chacour intercedes in the hostility dividing his village and congregation against themselves and from God, provoking repentance by the despised Abu Muhib, which precipitates reconciliation among all the people. In Jericho, by his gracious welcome of sinners, Jesus intercedes in the hostility dividing the people against themselves and from God, provoking repentance by the despised Zacchaeus, which precipitates Zacchaeus's acts of mercy and justice as the fruits of repentance and the terms of reconciliation with the people of Jericho.[6]

6. For a further contemporary story of cruciform peacemaking following the pattern of Ephesians 2 in an African context, see David W. Shenk, *Justice, Reconciliation and Peace in Africa*, rev. ed. (Nairobi: Uzima, 1997), pp. 165-66.

CHAPTER 31

Cruciform Realism, Spirituality, and Community

May we all so love each other and all selfish claims deny,
so that each one for the other will not hesitate to die.
Even so our Lord has loved us, for our lives he gave his life.
Still he grieves and still he suffers, for our selfishness and strife.

"Heart with loving heart united"
Nicolaus L. von Zinzendorf, 1723[1]

31.1. Christian Realism:
Imagining Reality through the Cross and Resurrection

Jesus' lament reminds us that when "the things that make for peace" are "hidden" from view (Luke 19:41-44), cruciform peacemaking in a world divided by hostility will not only provoke conflict, but may also result in tragedy. Jesus' peacemaking in Jericho does not lead straightway to a "peaceful transition of power" in Jerusalem. Because of the real possibility of tragedy, cruciform peacemaking must yield control of history to God just as Jesus yielded his life to God in the garden and on the cross. Cruciform peacemaking places trust and hope, not in the calculation of means-to-ends by the law of cause-and-effect, but in the divine promise that the end of history has been secured already through the cross and resurrection of Jesus Christ. Thus, John Howard Yoder:

---

1. "Herz und Herz vereint zusammen" (1723), translated by Walter Klassen (1983), "Heart with Loving Heart United," in *Hymnal: A Worship Book* (Scottdale, PA: Mennonite Publishing House, 1992), no. 420, verse 2.

[O]ur effort to perceive, and to manipulate a causal link between our obedience and the results we hope for must be broken. . . . If our faithfulness is to be guided by the kind of man Jesus was, it must cease to be guided by the quest to have dominion over the course of events. We cannot sight down the line of our obedience to the attainment of the ends we seek. . . . Why then is it reasonable that we should continue to obey in a world which we do not control? *Because that is the shape of the work of Christ.* The relation between our obedience and the achievement of God's purpose stands in analogy to the hidden lordship of Him who was crucified and raised.[2]

Nonetheless, yielding control of history to God while acknowledging the real possibility of tragedy need not mean yielding imagination concerning what is possible in history to what the many call "reality." And we need not do so precisely on account of the cross and resurrection of Jesus, which demonstrate that history and nature are not a closed causal system but are the arena of God's free and faithful action.[3] We thus need not limit our imagination to what is possible according to the empirical law of cause-and-effect, therefore, but are free to imagine possibilities and take action according to the transcendent pattern of cross-and-resurrection. Not only is cross-and-resurrection the pattern enacted by God through Christ in history to fulfill the divine purpose (Acts 2:23-24; 13:26-33), but through Jesus' living, dying, and rising God has surpassed the law of cause-and-effect and thereby created new possibilities for humanity and history.

Cruciform peacemaking is thus free to relinquish control of history in the face of tragedy precisely because it reckons reality and imagines possibilities according to the cross and resurrection of Jesus Christ. In other words, cruciform peacemaking trusts God that Jesus' prayer — "Your kingdom come, your will be done, on earth as in heaven" — is no mere slogan of idealism but a platform for faithful action. It has been said that "History changed on 9/11." From a secular perspective, that may be true; but from a Christian perspective, it is false. The cross and resurrection of Jesus signal "a new world-age" already coming to be in the midst of "the present evil world-age" that is passing away (Gal 1:4; 1 Cor 7:31b; 1 John 2:17); and by this new beginning are created new possibilities that can be known and realized "in Christ" (Romans 6; Gal 6:14-16; 2 Cor 5:16-17). The divine triumph of the cross and resurrection, by which Christ has "conquered the world" (John 16:33), entails that no subsequent historical development (not even 9/11) can foreclose those new possibilities. What is "already" in Christ cannot be undone or outdone by the "not yet" of the present world-

2. John Howard Yoder, *The Original Revolution: Essays on Christian Pacifism* (Scottdale, PA: Herald Press, 1971), pp. 159-60, emphasis original.

3. Concerning the resurrection and reality, see N. T. Wright, *Surprised by Hope: Rethinking Heaven, the Resurrection, and the Mission of the Church* (New York: HarperCollins, 2008).

age. These new possibilities thus always remain imaginable and actionable for those who are "in Christ."

This reveals what is fundamentally inadequate about the so-called realist ethic of Reinhold Niebuhr, which treats the teaching and example of Christ, not as a realistic path for Christian faithfulness, but as an "impossible ethical ideal." Niebuhr writes:

> The religion of Jesus is prophetic religion in which the moral ideal of love and vicarious suffering . . . achieves such a purity that the possibility of its realization in history becomes remote. His Kingdom of God is always a possibility in history, because its heights of pure love are organically related to the experience of love in all human life, but it is also an impossibility in history and always beyond every historical achievement. Men living in nature and in the body will never be capable of the sublimation of egoism and the attainment of the sacrificial passion, the complete disinterestedness which the ethic of Jesus demands.[4]

While affirming that the gospel ethic, including Jesus' command to love enemies, is the ultimate norm of human behavior that exposes and judges all social systems as falling short of the kingdom ideal, Niebuhr argues that it is irrelevant and inapplicable for doing justice and making peace in a sinful world. On the one hand, "Christ defines the actual possibilities of human existence." On the other hand, the reality of sin entails that these possibilities for humanity are impossible in history, where love must be compromised to attain relative justice and approximate peace. In Niebuhr's interpretation of Christian ethics, loyalty to Christ and his teaching "does not actually mean the full realization of the measure of Christ" but requires only realizing love in one's intention.[5]

Niebuhr's "Christian realism" is neither truly Christian nor truly realistic.[6] Niebuhr reckons reality on the assumptions and possibilities of the present world-age — as if the cross and resurrection had not actually happened, as if God had not reversed history by raising Jesus, as if the restoration of creation in Christ were not already underway. This contrasts with what Yoder Neufeld calls "Christic realism," which reckons on

---

4. Reinhold Niebuhr, *An Interpretation of Christian Ethics* (New York: Median Books, 1956), pp. 36-37.

5. Reinhold Niebuhr, "Why the Christian Church Is Not Pacifist," in Arthur F. Holmes, ed., *War and Christian Ethics: Classic Readings on the Morality of Warfare* (Grand Rapids, MI: Baker Books, 1975), pp. 301-13. Niebuhr's view, by narrowing Christian faithfulness from action to intention, parallels that of Augustine (see Chapter 28 above).

6. For helpful critiques of Niebuhr's ethics, see Richard B. Hays, *The Moral Vision of the New Testament: A Contemporary Introduction to New Testament Ethics* (New York: HarperCollins Publishers, 1996), pp. 215-25, and John Howard Yoder, *Reinhold Niebuhr and Christian Pacifism* (Scottdale, PA: Concern Pamphlet, 1961).

both Easter *and* the brokenness of present reality. . . . Realism is usually thought of as the opposite of idealism; it commonly refers to the adjustments one makes morally and spiritually to sin and brokenness, whether individual or corporate — compromises with the way things are. But Paul and his students were realistic about this still-broken world and also especially about life in Christ. It is a betrayal of God's act in Christ to allow this world-age to define the limits of what is possible for those who are *together with Christ.* Christic realism takes seriously the *not yet* but especially also the *already* of what it means to confess Jesus as Lord.[7]

"Christic realism" fits with "inaugurated eschatology." N. T. Wright:

[T]he new life of the Spirit, in obedience to the lordship of Jesus Christ, should produce radical transformation of behavior in the present life, *anticipating* the life to come even though we know we shall never be complete and whole until then . . . a radical transformation of the way we [viz., the church] behave as a worldwide community, *anticipating* the eventual time when God will be all in all even though we all agree that things won't be complete until then.[8]

Imagining new possibilities realized by God through the death and resurrection of Jesus and anticipating God's future being realized in our present through the ascension and lordship of Christ, the church is called to act on such possibilities in hope of that future.[9]

The "revolution of the candles" in East Germany in 1989 enlarged my own imagination of reality in a powerful way.[10] The fall of the Berlin Wall demonstrated that there are possibilities in history that the law of cause-and-effect

7. Thomas R. Yoder Neufeld, *Ephesians* (Believers Church Bible Commentary; Scottdale, PA: Herald Press, 2002), p. 97, emphasis original.

8. N. T. Wright, *Surprised by Hope,* pp. 221-22, emphasis original. Inaugurated eschatology is thus to be clearly distinguished from both the "realized eschatology" of liberalism (the kingdom is fulfilled from within history) and the "deferred eschatology" of fundamentalism (the kingdom is to be fulfilled only beyond history).

9. One might call this an "eschatological ethic": the church is called to act even now in accordance with the kingdom that is coming from God's future into our present, as inaugurated and demonstrated through the life and death, resurrection and ascension of Jesus Christ. Cf. Wright, *Surprised by Hope,* pp. 284-86: "The resurrection was the full bursting in to this world of the life of God's new creation; Christian ethics is the lifestyle that celebrates and embodies that new creation. Living out a life of Christian holiness makes sense, perfect sense, *within God's new world,* the world into which we are brought at baptism. . . . Paul is urging that *we should live in the present as people who are to be made complete in the future*" (emphasis original).

10. Concerning the role of the East German Protestant Church in the 1989 revolution, see Jörg Swoboda, *The Revolution of the Candles: Christians in the Revolution in the German Democratic Republic* (Macon, GA: Mercer University Press, 1996). For a firsthand account of the fall of the Berlin Wall, see Timothy Garton Ash, *The Magic Lantern: The Revolution of '89 Witnessed in Warsaw, Budapest, Berlin and Prague* (New York: Vintage Books, 1999), pp. 61-77.

cannot predict, possibilities that God is free to realize through the faithful action of God's people. Being a twenty-year-old college student at the time, I had grown up in world that presupposed the Cold War and the East-West division. For my generation, it was as if the "iron curtain" were a necessary fixture of the world: it had always existed and was not an historical accident that might simply be undone. Not only the map, but the world itself seemed so divided: this was how things appeared to be because that is how things really were and how they could reasonably be expected to continue. I could literally imagine no other realistic possibility of any other ordering of things in the world coming to be within my lifetime; this was solid reality to which all hope for peace had to yield. (Soon enough the same may be true also for those who will have grown up with the War on Terror — they will see the world, and be able to imagine possibilities for their world, only within the limited horizon of "either you are with us or you are with the terrorists.")

The Berlin Wall stood as a solid, enduring symbol of the division and hostility between East and West. And as judged from a "realist" perspective according to the law of cause-and-effect, it would be staying put. On both sides of that wall were positioned millions of soldiers. Flanking those soldiers were armored divisions of tanks. Protecting the soldiers and armor on each side were large air forces prepared to drop massive quantities of bombs on the opposing side's cities. And backing the air forces on both sides were arrays of nuclear missiles, each ready to annihilate the other side at the touch of a button. In this "equilibrium" situation of balancing forces, the Wall was not going anywhere.[11] The opposing forces encompassing the Berlin Wall constituted a closed causal system such that the "realistic" possibilities were limited to decisions by the governing authorities who controlled the forces on either side. According to this "realist" calculation by the law of cause-and-effect, the outcome of any independent initiative to break down the dividing wall and end the enmity was a foregone conclusion: failure.

Yet, thankfully, a few Christians in East Germany were not "realists." They imagined possibilities — a new beginning! — outstripping any "realist" reckoning of history. Since the beginning of the 1980s, the Nikolai Church in Leipzig had hosted weekly prayers for peace. These Monday gatherings opened a space for independent thinking and, eventually, independent action. In September to November 1989, prayers of faith and hope became the seeds of action and change, as the peace prayers grew into peace marches and the gatherings grew from hundreds to thousands to ten-thousands to hundred-thousands of people over the course of several weeks. For several consecutive Mondays, the

---

11. That the public in the West understood the situation in such terms was evident by the regular reporting in the mainstream press concerning troop, tank, bomber, and missile "strengths" lined up on either side of the "iron curtain," as if the outcome of the East-West confrontation in Europe would be decided by the relative sizes of the opposing military forces.

people of faith prayed and marched. And then the "unrealistic" and "impossible" — the miraculous! — happened before the eyes of a watching world: in the face of marchers armed only with prayers and candles, without the massive bloodshed expected by all, the Berlin Wall was opened and then dismantled.[12]

None of this would have happened had not a small group of Christians, trusting that God would answer their prayers, hoping that God could act once again to remake history, acted in faith and hope on possibilities made imaginable by the cross and resurrection of Jesus, possibilities realized in history by the God who raised our Lord Jesus from the dead. Raphaela Russ, then 19 and a participant in the Monday marches, wrote about the miraculous events: "When I look back over the past months I thank God. The bloodless events on the ninth of October rang in a new era. Who would have believed it could have happened that way? Who hindered the intervention by the security forces? For me, God wrote history here."[13] She then cited Mary's Song: "He has shown strength with his arm; he has scattered the proud in the thoughts of their hearts. He has brought down the powerful from their thrones, and lifted up the lowly" (Luke 1:51-52).

31.2. Cruciform Spirituality: Surrender, Patience, Hope

Conforming imagination and action to God's history-reversing, world-renewing pattern of cross-and-resurrection, cruciform peacemaking sacrifices the all-too-human desire to rule the world by force so to control the end of history. The immediate practical necessity of yielding control of history is yielding one's own life to God. One cannot forgo trusting in means-to-ends calculation according to the law of cause-and-effect — one cannot step out of the church into the street armed only with prayer and a candle to face the heavily armed, notoriously brutal state security forces — unless one sacrifices self-preservation as the highest goal of personal existence. Cruciform peacemaking in a world at war, therefore, must begin with *surrender* — surrendering to God control over the end of one's own life: "not my will but yours be done."

Yet, because cruciform peacemaking trusts in God's pattern of cross-and-resurrection, surrendering to God by sacrificing self-preservation is a realistic possibility. Following in the steps of Jesus, we can entrust our lives "to the one who judges justly" (1 Pet 2:21-23). We can offer our lives for God's mission, because we now reckon reality according to the cross and resurrection of Jesus. Jim Amstutz thus observes that to be threatened with death, for the Christian, is really to be threatened with resurrection:

---

12. On the crucial role of the Monday gatherings, see Andrew Curry, "Before the Fall," *Wilson Quarterly*, Autumn 2009.

13. Swoboda, *Revolution of the Candles*, p. 131.

The keystone to this approach is the resurrection. Without the resurrection those who put Jesus to death win. The forces of evil prevail. Injustice and "might makes right" are vindicated. But on the third day Jesus rose from the dead. Not only does that fact save us from sin and eternal death at the end of our life, it also sets the stage for overcoming evil with good while we're alive, and when we are face-to-face with death. So those times when we are threatened with death, we are really threatened with resurrection.[14]

We can overcome fear of death and make the necessary sacrifice of self-preservation by staking our hope in God's power of resurrection demonstrated in Jesus:

> When we say YES to Jesus and confess him as Lord and Savior we also claim is resurrection hope. . . . [R]esurrection hope can empower us to overcome that fear [of death] and guide us in our discernment of faithful discipleship. . . . Our faith calls us to challenge the assumption of choosing self-preservation at all costs and instead claim the power of God as we follow Christ in life and death and resurrection.[15]

Having overcome fear of death through trust in God, we are free to recognize that in fact it is those who threaten with death that are overcome by fear. Ingrid Ebert, a journalist and participant in the "revolution of the candles," wrote in her diary entry of October 7, 1989, two days before the Monday march of October 9 in Leipzig:

> Fear is in the air. But there is no fear among those Christian activists who have been interrogated hour after hour during the last weeks, no fear among those who were subject to high fines, no fear among those who were spied upon while taking part in peace activities. No! Rather, fear is manifested by those who are exerting the pressure, who are spying, who are interrogating.[16]

The prisoners may be captive to their jailers, but it is those that spy, detain, interrogate, and torture that are truly captive to fear. Recall the story of Paul and

14. Jim S. Amstutz, *Threatened with Resurrection: Self-Preservation and Christ's Way of Peace* (Scottdale, PA: Herald Press, 2002), p. 18. Amstutz's book belongs to a lineage of books through the twentieth century on Christian discipleship, including Dietrich Bonhoeffer, *The Cost of Discipleship* (New York: Macmillan Publishing, 1963), Eberhard Arnold, *Salt and Light: Living the Sermon on the Mount*, 4th ed. (Farmington, PA: Plough Publishing, 1998), and J. Heinrich Arnold, *Discipleship: Living for Christ in the Daily Grind* (Farmington, PA: Plough Publishing, 1994).

15. Amstutz, *Threatened with Resurrection*, p. 19. John Howard Yoder draws out the implications of the resurrection for addressing the personal ethical dilemma of a violent person threatening oneself or a loved one in *What Would You Do? A Serious Answer to a Standard Question*, expanded ed. (Scottdale, PA: Herald Press, 1992).

16. Swoboda, *Revolution of the Candles*, p. 112.

Silas in the jail at Philippi: their jailer holds them captive out of fear for his own life at the hands of his superiors (Acts 16). So also with the War on Terror — the detention and torture of prisoners in Guantanamo Bay, Abu Ghraib, and Bagram could never overcome terrorism because such actions, born of fear, are merely iterations of terror under another name.

The story of Christians in the former East Germany illustrates also that the practice of cruciform peacemaking, because it resists the temptation to control and sacrifices self-preservation, is not possible apart from a spirituality of patience and hope. Patience and hope, in turn, are possible precisely because we yield control and sacrifice self-preservation in the trust that God's resurrection power has secured our future just as much as it has raised Jesus from the dead. Christian Wolf, reflecting in the wake of the "revolution of the candles," wrote about Christian patience and hope:

> Patience in the biblical sense is not a passive waiting for something to happen, but rather it is actively bearing up under one's load. . . . Christians need not be incapacitated by the pressure of time. Their actions can be objective and patient since their future stands under the sign of grace. . . . In the Bible "future" has two meanings. On the one hand is the "grammatical future," that which proceeds from the present through human planning and organizing. The other is the Advent of God, which will take place not as a result of our planning. We do not have any control over it, but we can open ourselves to it in active anticipation.
>
> The end has come more quickly than we thought. It came upon us as a harbinger of God's gracious future. . . . We can begin with patience, because God's graciousness long ago provided for our future.[17]

Still, Christian patience and hope in the service of cruciform peacemaking acknowledges the possibility of tragedy: the Christians in Leipzig went to the streets expecting to be attacked by the state security forces. Only by God's intervention, this did not happen in Leipzig during the crucial October 9 march. The spirituality of cruciform peacemaking must embrace tragedy as a real possibility, therefore, because the powers that be have not yet discarded the illusion that security is created and maintained through violence.

Stanley Hauerwas comments perceptively on the relationship between peaceableness, tragedy, and spirituality:

> . . . tragedy resides in the fact that the peace to which we Christians witness may well make the world more dangerous, since we do not give up our violent illusions without a struggle.
>
> Thus Christians must acquire a spirituality which will make them capa-

---

17. Swoboda, *Revolution of the Candles,* pp. 183-84.

ble of being faithful in the face of the inexorable tragedies their convictions entail. A spirituality that acknowledges the tragic is one that is schooled in patience. . . . For Christians hope not in "the process of history," but in the God whom we believe has already determined the end of history in the cross and resurrection of Jesus Christ.[18]

Such hopeful patience, in the face of tragedy in a world still clinging to the illusion of violence, becomes the source of joy for those whose hope for peace is staked on God's world-transforming, cruciform peacemaking in Christ. Again, Hauerwas: "Joy thus becomes the disposition born of a hope based on our sense that it cannot be our task to transform the violence of this world into God's peace, for in fact that has been done through the cross and resurrection of Jesus."[19]

31.3. Cruciform Community: Absorbing Tragedy, Witnessing to Hope[20]

As the "revolution of the candles" illustrates, cruciform peacemaking is the calling and work of a faith community. Yielding control, sacrificing self-preservation, and hopeful patience, all of which are necessary to sustain cruciform peacemaking, are not possible apart from a community of faith conformed to the pattern of cross-and-resurrection, a community that cultivates such peaceable habits of character in its daily practice.[21] These peaceable habits are cultivated in a community whose members pledge their lives for one another according to the pattern of Jesus, who gave his life for us (1 John 3:16). Paul expressly emphasizes the communal context where we learn and practice compassion and patience, bear each other's burdens and forgive each other as Christ has forgiven us, and "let the peace of Christ rule in [our] hearts" (Col 3:12-17; cf. Eph 4:1-6; Romans 12).[22] It should thus not surprise that the two

18. Stanley Hauerwas, *The Peaceable Kingdom: A Primer in Christian Ethics* (Notre Dame, IN: University of Notre Dame Press, 1983), p. 145.

19. Hauerwas, *Peaceable Kingdom*, p. 147.

20. This section adapts material from my article "Toward a Consistent Ethic of Life in the Peace Tradition Perspective: A Critical-Constructive Response to the MC USA Statement on Abortion," *Mennonite Quarterly Review* 79 (2005), 439-80. My thanks to the editor of the journal for permission to reuse this material.

21. For an insightful development of the argument that sustaining Christian witness requires a stable faith community, see Gerald W. Schlabach, *Unlearning Protestantism: Sustaining Christian Community in an Unstable Age* (Grand Rapids, MI: Brazos Press, 2010).

22. Richard B. Hays, *The Moral Vision of the New Testament: A Contemporary Introduction to New Testament Ethics* (New Yorker: HarperSanFrancisco, 1996), rightly identifies community, alongside cross and new creation, as one of the "focal images" of the moral vision of the New

guides to Christian discipleship that have stood the test of time were written as rules for community life: *The Rule* of St. Benedict and Thomas à Kempis's *The Imitation of Christ*.[23]

Faith community is thus an essential dimension of cruciform peacemaking. Recognizing that the "foolishness of the cross" can result in tragedy in a world still under the illusion of violence, cruciform peacemaking requires a community willing to absorb tragedy as the cost integral to being a people conformed to the cross. So Hauerwas:

> Yet such a life cannot be sustained apart from a community that has so been formed by God that our constant tendency to self-deception and violence can constantly be checked. For growth in peaceableness requires . . . a community capable of absorbing the necessary tragedies that result without making others pay for those tragedies.[24]

And because a cruciform community will not forgo faithful action to avoid painful (even potentially deadly) consequences, cruciform peacemaking must prepare for the eventuality that tragedy will produce harmful results. A community capable of absorbing tragedy into its own body, as Jesus did into his body, therefore, must also be ready and willing to care for the victims that might result from such tragedies. Again, Hauerwas:

> Yet there is another requirement such a peace places on us. For if it is an unsettling peace, it is also a caring peace. If Christians are required to speak the truth about our world, to challenge the powers that offer us some order, they must also be a people capable of caring for the injured that result from such a challenge. We are not a people who cause turmoil and then stand by as if we bear no responsibility for the results. No, if we are a people capable of speaking the truth, we are such only because we are also a people who refuse to abandon those whose lives have been disrupted by that truth.[25]

Testament. Alan Kreider, Eleanor Kreider, and Paulus Widjaja, *A Culture of Peace: God's Vision for the Church* (Intercourse, PA: Good Books, 2005), depict the church as a community of faith in which the habits of peacemaking are learned and practiced. Philip D. Kenneson, *Life on the Vine: Cultivating the Fruit of the Spirit in Christian Community* (Downers Grove, IL: InterVarsity Press, 1999), also emphasizes the communal context of the cultivation of peaceableness.

23. See Joan Chittister, O.S.B., *The Rule of Benedict: Insights for the Ages* (New York: Crossroad Publishing, 1992), and William C. Creasy, *The Imitation of Christ: A Timeless Classic for Contemporary Readers* (Notre Dame, IN: Ave Maria Press, 1989). For two twentieth-century guides to discipleship in Christian community, see Dietrich Bohhoeffer, *Life Together* (San Francisco: Harper & Row, 1954), and Eberhard Arnold, *Why We Live in Community*, 3rd ed. (Farmington, PA: Plough Publishing, 1995).

24. Hauerwas, *Peaceable Kingdom*, p. 145.

25. Hauerwas, *Peaceable Kingdom*, pp. 145-46.

A community that would absorb tragedy and care for victims as the cost of cruciformity, therefore, must also cultivate compassion for the weak and hospitality to the stranger.[26]

That a faith community — characterized by yielding control, sacrifice of self-preservation, hopeful patience, compassion, and hospitality — is essential to cruciform peacemaking in potentially tragic circumstances is made evident by a contrast of two twentieth-century films. Consider first the tragic situation of the heroine Amy Fowler in the classic Western film *High Noon*. She and her husband, Sheriff Will Kane, having just been married and about to embark on their honeymoon, are abandoned by the townspeople in the face of the approaching threat of the Miller Gang. Will's commitment to defend the town from outlaws leaves Amy with the agonizing "choice" between remaining loyal to her husband and keeping true to her Quaker pacifist conviction. The town's Protestant congregation lacks strong leadership and fragments under pressure; and there is no local Friends meeting she can summon to her aid. The town's moral resolve having melted away in the heat of the moment, and lacking the support of a faith community committed to her pacifist convictions, one can hardly blame Amy in the end for "choosing" to pick up a gun and shoot one of the "bad guys" to defend the life of her husband. The absence of a supportive community standing in solidarity with her in the face of possible suffering and death leaves her existentially incapable of consistently practicing her faith convictions without sacrificing marital fidelity. She can see no "third way" between "fight or flight" precisely because the faith community in which peaceable alternatives might be envisioned and enacted has scattered in fear. Violence ensues and tragedy unfolds, not because of a flaw in character, but because of the failure of community.

The more recent film *Witness* provides an illuminating contrast, showing us the kind of community that makes cruciform peacemaking possible. The "hero" is not the police detective, John Book, who dominates the promotional poster, but rather the Amish community where Book is convalescing.[27] An Amish boy, Samuel Lapp, traveling with his mother, Rachel, has witnessed a murder committed by a corrupt police officer, and Book, investigating the case,

---

26. On compassion and community, see Henri J. M. Nouwen, Donald P. McNiell, and Douglas A. Morrison, *Compassion: A Reflection on the Christian Life* (New York: Doubleday, 1982); on hospitality, see Michele Hershberger, *A Christian View of Hospitality: Expecting Surprises* (Scottdale, PA: Herald Press, 1999).

27. Ironically, the synopsis of the film on the video box misses completely the phenomena of faith community, socially shared conviction, and mutual commitment that so powerfully permeate the entire story (e.g., the barn-raising scene) and figure crucially in the resolution of the climactic conflict. It reads: "When a young Amish woman and her son get caught up in the murder of an undercover narcotics agent, their savior turns out to be hardened Philadelphia detective John Book." Not so!

has been wounded. The three flee to the Lapps' farm, where Book is given sanctuary. The Lapp family extends hospitality to this stranger even though doing so puts them in danger: if the corrupt cops find Book, they find Samuel, too. While Book heals under the care of Rachel and the Amish doctor, Samuel becomes fascinated with Book's revolver, necessitating a lesson from his grandfather, Eli. The Lapps belong to a faith community long shaped by an ethic of nonresistance and a spirituality that yields control to God and does not esteem self-preservation above all else.[28] In a poignant scene, the elder hands down this tradition to the younger:

> This gun of the hand is for the taking of human life. We believe that taking life is only for God. Many times wars have come and people have said to us, "You must fight. You must kill. It is the only way to preserve the good." But, Samuel, there is never only one way — remember that.

As the story reaches its climax, the community's faith is put into practice. Threatened by the corrupt police officers who have tracked down Book, the Lapps rely for their defense, not on Book's gun but on a prepared signal — a ringing bell — that summons neighbors in times of need. Although Eli, Rachel, and Samuel are held at gunpoint, the gathered community, standing in solidarity with those whose lives are threatened, disarms the threat without loss of life. The "other way" to "preserve the good" is imagined and realized through the habitual practices of the discipleship community. In vulnerable solidarity, the gathered community shares the risk of faithfulness by being willing to absorb suffering and loss into its corporate body rather than use violence to defend its members. In doing so, the community witnesses to a shared resurrection hope.

In a sense, *High Noon* is the "negative image" of *Witness*. In the former, the absence of a coherent faith community renders our lone heroine incapable of practicing the pacifism to which she is committed; indeed, she is unable to resist the temptation to use evil means to good ends because alone she is unable to imagine and enact alternative possibilities. In the latter, the presence of a gathered community of faith, ready and willing to absorb tragic loss of life into its own body as the cost of faithfulness, makes possible the peaceable resolution of a conflict situation full of potential for violence. What both films illustrate is that a faith community shaped by the cross, trusting in resurrection, and thus united by mutual commitment to solidarity in suffering, is essential if human

28. The Amish-Mennonite tradition of discipleship *(Nachfolge)*, with its twinned ethic of nonresistance and spirituality of "yieldedness" *(Gelassenheit)* and self-sacrifice, which is demonstrated in this story, grows out of the Anabaptist movement in the "radical" wing of the Reformation. For an excellent introduction to the ethic and spirituality of the Anabaptists, see C. Arnold Snyder, *Following in the Footsteps of Christ: The Anabaptist Tradition* (Maryknoll, NY: Orbis Books, 2004).

beings are to live out the practicable, peaceable alternatives to violence in the face of evil, alternatives made possible by the cross and resurrection of Jesus Christ.[29]

Here, then, we see that Niebuhr's "Christian realism" is deficient, not only by neglect of the cross and resurrection in its consideration of the possible, but also by the absence of the church in its understanding of ethics. Ironically, in his essay on why the Christian *church* is not pacifist, Niebuhr does not discuss the church as such — a unique corporate reality, constituted in faith, identified with the cross, existing by the Spirit. Indeed, insofar as he grants legitimacy to Christian pacifism in its medieval-monastic and Protestant-sectarian forms, he characterizes these social movements as "the effort to achieve a standard of perfect love in *individual* life."[30] Niebuhr seems to suppose that Christian ethics is solely a matter of individual action. Yet Jesus' command is addressed, not to isolated individuals, but to individuals incorporated into a discipleship community. Indeed, the medieval-monastic and Protestant-sectarian movements that Niebuhr cites were self-consciously *communal* expressions of Christian faith. It might be that Christians acting individually cannot fulfill the law of love. It might nonetheless be possible — and has been demonstrated historically — that Christians acting as the body of Christ can fulfill the law of love. For the power of the Holy Spirit can render "we" the church capable of doing corporately what no one of us is able to do individually.

---

29. The real-life tragedy played out in October 2006 in the Amish community of Nickel Mines, Pennsylvania, provides an actual example of this kind of cruciform peacemaking by a faith community that yields control, sacrifices self-preservation, exhibits hopeful patience, welcomes the stranger, and cares for not only the victims of violence but also those who perpetrate violence. See Donald B. Kraybill, Steven M. Nolt, and David L. Weaver-Zercher, in *Amish Grace: How Forgiveness Transcended Tragedy* (San Francisco: Jossey-Bass, 2007).

30. Niebuhr, "Why the Christian Church Is Not Pacifist," p. 303, emphasis added.

CHAPTER 32

The Cross of Christ and Inter-Ethnic/Inter-Religious Conflict

So, then, remember that at one time you Gentiles by birth,
called "the uncircumcision" by those who are called "the
*   circumcision" . . .*
remember that you were at that time without Christ,
being aliens from the commonwealth of Israel,
strangers to the covenants of promise,
having no hope and without God in the world.

EPHESIANS 2:11-12

32.1. The "Wall of Hostility": Alienation by Exclusion

At the heart of God's peacemaking through the cross, Jesus destroys the wall of division and abolishes the law of separation, thus "murdering the hostility" that generates conflict between Jews and Gentiles and opening equal access for all humanity to the grace of God. As we have seen (Chapter 29), God's intention was to overcome a self-justifying identity that exalted one nation before God and excluded all other nations from God's grace. The distinctiveness of being the "circumcised of God" justified waging violent conflict against the "uncircumcised," who are the presumed enemies of God that can be extinguished or "cleansed" from the "holy land." A clear instance in the biblical narrative of the use of the distinctiveness of circumcision to name inter-ethnic/inter-religious conflict and justify violence is found in 1 Samuel 14, where Jonathan the son of Saul leads the Israelites in battle against the Philistines. In this story, Jonathan distinguishes the "Hebrews" (Semitic peoples practicing circumcision) from the "uncircumcised" (non-Semitic peoples), and the narrative assumption is that God will favor the "Hebrews" in their battle with the "uncircumcised."[1]

Centuries later, after various empires (Assyrian, Babylonian, Persian, Greek, and Roman) had in succession conquered the land of Israel and the people of Israel had become dispersed throughout the cities of the Middle East and the Mediterranean basin, the emergence of an other-exclusive, self-justifying Jewish identity became not only the cause that justified fighting for national independence (the Maccabean revolt against Syrian overlords) but also a cause of mutual hostility between Jews and Gentiles. James Dunn comments on how Jewish national identity in the Hellenistic period (second century B.C.) was defined over against Greek identity and, hence, how that identity might generate enmity toward, even "zealous" violence against, "the nations":

> For it [viz., the term "Judaism"] first appears in 2 Maccabees, and in each case it denotes the national religion of Judea, "Judaism," presented as a rallying cry for resistance to the Syrians and for maintenance of national identity as the covenant people of the Lord. Alternatively expressed, "Judaism" was coined as a title to express opposition to "Hellenism" (2 Macc. 4.13).
>
> In other words, the term "Judaism" seems to have been coined as a means of giving focus to the determination of the Maccabean patriots to defend the distinctive national identity given them by their ancestral religion. It was not simply a neutral description of "the religion of the Jews," as we wish to use it today. From its earliest usage it carried overtones of a religious identity shaped and hardened in the fires of persecution, of a religion which identified itself by its determination to maintain its distinctiveness and to remain free from corruption of other religions and peoples. . . . An important point emerges from this: "Judaism" defined itself over against the wider Hellenism, including Hellenizing Jews.[2]

Concerning the other side of this conflict, Ulrich Mauser writes of how Jewish national identity, defined over against "the nations" and protected by the Torah, generated a reciprocal Gentile hostility toward Diaspora Jews in the Hellenistic and Roman empires:

> The law of Moses was often likened, in Jewish thought, to the erection of a fence around Israel which was to safeguard its purity of life and guarantee the necessary separation from pagan life-styles and customs whenever a Jewish community lived together with non-Jewish populations. . . . Jewish sepa-

1. This distinction reappears in the song commissioned by David in honor of the deaths of Saul and Jonathan at the hands of the Philistines (2 Sam 1:20).

2. James D. G. Dunn, *The Theology of Paul the Apostle* (Grand Rapids, MI: Eerdmans Publishing, 1998), pp. 347-48; cf. pp. 350-52.

rateness, enforced and guarded by the Mosaic law, became constantly a source of irritation, and often the cause of downright hatred, among the pagan population, who ridiculed, resented, and oppressed the Jewish inhabitants of their cities. When Eph 2:14 speaks of the Mosaic law as "the dividing wall of hostility," the word "hostility" must be taken in the full and literal sense. There is plenty of evidence that the law brought about both an attitude of hostility on the part of Jews against their pagan neighbors and intense enmity on the part of pagans against Jews.[3]

We can thus see clearly the taproot of the Jew-Gentile conflict addressed at the cross: identity, not a neutral identity, but identity defined over against the Other, identity that defines "who we are" by "who we are *not*" — "we" are "not them."

32.2. Identity Conflict: Purging the "Other"

Identity-generated conflict is a universal phenomenon that connects the ancient world known by the cross to the contemporary world known by us. The peacemaking cross of Jesus Christ reveals that at the heart of the inter-ethnic/inter-religious conflict raging throughout history is hostility rooted in identity. Self-justifying, other-exclusive self-definition was the common cause underlying inter-ethnic/inter-religious hostility and conflict the world over during the twentieth century: Bosnian Muslim v. Serbian Orthodox, Serbian Orthodox v. Croatian Catholic, Croatian Catholic v. Bosnian Muslim, Tutsi Catholic v. Hutu Catholic, Israeli Jew v. Palestinian Arab, Sunni Muslim v. Shi'ite Muslim, Indian Hindu v. Indian Muslim, Irish Protestant v. Irish Catholic, etc. In some of these conflicts, ethnic identity is the primary dividing factor that drives conflict (e.g., Hutu Catholic v. Tutsi Catholic), in others religious identity is the primary divisive, conflict generating element (e.g., Hindu Indian v. Muslim Indian). Some such conflicts are messy entanglements of ethnic and religious identity (e.g., Bosnian Muslim v. Serbian Orthodox v. Croatian Catholic). And the dynamics of many inter ethnic/inter religious conflicts have been exploited in the past by, and continue to be exacerbated by the legacies of, colonial and imperial powers (e.g., Irish Protestant v. Irish Catholic, Tutsi Catholic v. Hutu Catholic, and Arab Sunni Muslim v. Arab Shi'ite Muslim in Iraq). Yet, given the variations, a common thread runs through all these conflicts: self-justifying, other-exclusive self-definition — identity purged of the Other.[4]

---

3. Ulrich Mauser, *The Gospel of Peace: A Scriptural Message for Today's World* (Louisville, KY: Westminster/John Knox Press, 1992), pp. 157-58.

4. As Daniel J. Goldhagen, *Worse than War: Genocide, Eliminationism, and the Ongoing Assault on Humanity* (New York: Perseus Books, 2009), argues, while "eliminationist" beliefs that

Inter-ethnic/inter-religious conflict is one of what I understand to be three major veins of violent conflict coursing through human history: reactionary conflict, revolutionary conflict, and identity conflict. Reactionary conflict is violence among self-interested actors, both individual and national, competing for scarce resources, both tangible (land, food, water, oil, etc.) and intangible (honor, power, status, etc.). Such violence has a "conservative" aim — to possess and protect what is deemed necessary for self-preservation or self-satisfaction — and is justified in the name of what is "ours" or to claim what belongs to others as "our own."[5] This is the violence of both defensive wars to protect "the homeland" and aggressive wars to control foreign resources and maintain vested interests (land routes, waterways, banana plantations, oil fields, etc.).[6] Thomas Hobbes, the seventeenth-century philosopher, described a "war of every one against every one" as the "natural state" of both interpersonal and international relations in *The Leviathan* (1651). A domestic example of Hobbesian conflict is found on the streets of America's inner cities, where individuals and groups compete for "respect" as much as "turf."[7] Hobbes's analysis of human conflict has been extended to social behavior and economic activity, explained in terms of "competing interests."

Revolutionary conflict is violence for the sake of "the cause" or "the vision," intended to create "a new society" or "a new world." Such violence has a "progressive" aim — to promote and produce a new and better situation through destruction of the old — and is justified in the name of "the ideal" (whether "justice" or "equality" or "liberty" or "peace"). This is the violence of both Communist revolution (e.g., Russia in 1917) and Islamic revolution (e.g., Iran in 1979), both the "killing fields" of Cambodia and the bloodied jungles of Colombia. Karl Marx, the nineteenth-century sociologist and economist, ana-

---

justify exclusion of the "other" are a *necessary* component of such conflicts, those beliefs are *not sufficient* to explain such conflicts. Regarding why those beliefs are implemented in action, Goldhagen points to political conditions and objectives, with special emphasis on the role of political leaders: eliminationist beliefs are transformed into action when elimination of the "other" becomes state policy. It may thus be that, in practice, identity conflict is always entangled with reactionary (interest) conflict or revolutionary (ideology) conflict (discussed below).

5. Cicero, we recall from Chapter 3, held that preserving the life of the state and defending the honor of the emperor were "just cause" for war.

6. In *Republic* 372-74 Plato identifies the origin of war, not in competing desires for what is necessary, but rather in unrestrained desire *(pleonexia)* "exceeding the bounds of what is necessary." War is thus initiated, not to defend what we need, but to acquire what we want. We find essentially the same diagnosis of interpersonal conflict — vice leading to violence — in Jas 4:1-2. I put wars of acquisition and of defense in the same category because both serve self-interested desire, whether that desire be necessary or excessive, between which we often find it difficult to distinguish.

7. Elijah Anderson, *Code of the Street: Decency, Violence, and the Moral Life of the Inner City* (New York: Norton, 1999).

lyzed human relations in terms of class structures and, in the opening line of the *Manifesto of the Communist Party* (1848), declared "class conflict" to be the dominant factor explaining the course of history: "The history of all hitherto existing society is the history of class struggles." Envisioning an egalitarian society created out of the shell of the capitalist class structure, the *Manifesto* concludes by issuing a call to revolution: "Let the ruling classes tremble at a Communist revolution. The proletarians have nothing to lose but their chains. They have a world to win. Working men of all countries, unite!"

Most contemporary analyses of human relations recognize these two veins of conflict, reactionary and revolutionary, conflicts of interests and conflicts of ideologies. But such modern secular perspectives on human conflict fail to recognize the reality of the third major vein of conflict coursing through human history, conflict of identities, which is significantly different from the other two. Identity conflict is overlooked by Hobbesian and Marxist analysis alike, each of which assumes that consciousness, and hence identity, is reducible to either interest or class, to biology or economics, respectively. Identity is distinct from interest: where interest always promotes self-preservation, identity sometimes motivates self-sacrifice. Identity is distinct from class, also; whereas Marx hoped class-consciousness would unite the working poor across national boundaries, identity cuts across class lines (witness, for example, the mass of white-clothed Muslim pilgrims on the annual Hajj to Mecca).

Identity conflict is thus aimed neither at securing resources for self-preservation, nor at creating a new world order. This is ethnicity- and religion-based conflict, the "righteous" or "holy" struggle to "purify" "us" and "the land" of "contamination" by "them," a cause that justifies "us" expelling, even annihilating, "them." It is conflict defined by neither self-interests nor class structures, but by group identity — "*who* we are" and, mostly, "who we are *not*." Such conflict generates the violence of genocide and ethnic cleansing.[8] The Nazi genocide of Eastern European Jews was based on the delusion of "Aryan identity" and justified in the name of "purifying" "the blood" and "the Fatherland" of "Jewish contamination" in the service of creating "the pure race."[9]

---

8. The use of the term "ethnic cleansing" is not without controversy. Goldhagen, *Worse than War*, pp. 16-17, calls it an "unfortunate term," a "euphemism" for the perpetrator's cause. Yet, in conflicts such as those in the former Yugoslavia, where the overt objective of the Serbs was to eliminate and so purge Bosnian Muslims (by various strategies) from their political territory and ethnic identity, the term seems entirely apt and need not diminish the evil involved, as long as we recognize the evil in all campaigns of elimination.

9. We should not fail to mention here a fourth source of conflict and violence brought to light by René Girard: mimetic desire. See Girard, *Things Hidden Since the Foundation of the World* (Stanford: Stanford University Press, 1987). This type of conflict is distinct from each of the other three: mimetic rivalry neither requires a scarcity of goods, nor aims at producing a new world, nor seeks to eliminate the Other on account of his otherness, but rather seeks to consummate the desire to replace the other whom one admires. The root of this violence is not

32.3. Identity Conflict: The Absent Analysis

What modern analyses of human relations have often overlooked, imperial and colonial powers throughout history have known all too well. Recognizing the indissolubility of ethnic-religious identity and hence the potential for ethnic-religious identity to generate rebellion and strife, imperial and colonial authorities have devised various policies and strategies intended to either mitigate or exploit the power of identity. Here are some examples: mass deportation and forced migration by the Assyrians and Babylonians to separate ethnic-religious groups from their homelands; exploitation of ethnic-minority groups to subdue ethnic-majority groups in European-colonized Africa;[10] the Chinese government policy of resettling ethnic-majority Han Chinese in western provinces to dilute and suppress the language, culture, and religion of indigenous ethnic-minority Tibetan (Buddhist) and Uighur (Muslim) populations; the Russification of non-Slavic republics within the Soviet Union — importation of Slavic, Russian-speaking populations into the Baltic region to dilute and suppress the language and culture of Lithuanians, Latvians, and Estonians; and promotion of intermarriage among Jews, Christians, and Muslims in Tito's Yugoslavia to dilute religious identity and loyalty.[11] The dramatic failure of the latter two strategies in the 1990s — as evident from the resilience of national identity in the Baltics that sustained successful (nonviolent) independence

---

interest, ideology, or identity, but imitation. That such mimetic desire and rivalry as described here is found in children of all cultures implies that imitation may be as deeply rooted in the human psyche as identity and interest. Girard's contribution is the theory that such mimetic desire and the violent rivalry it generates lie at the foundation of religion and culture by way of the scapegoat mechanism, a "hidden" truth revealed through the gospel, especially at the cross. If Girard's theory is in fact true, then mimesis would be the fundamental source of conflict and violence in human relations, underwriting the other three types of violent conflict outlined above. As yet, I am not convinced that there is a single fundamental factor to explain the entire range of violent conflict in human relations, much less that mimesis is that single factor. Just as I am critical of Hobbesian and Marxist analysis for reducing identity to psychology or economics respectively, I remain hesitant to reduce interest and identity to imitation. I thus regard mimesis as a factor among others. For exploration and examination of Girard's theory, see Gil Bailie, *Violence Unveiled: Humanity at the Crossroads* (New York: Crossroad Publishing, 1995), and Willard M. Swartley, ed., *Violence Renounced: René Girard, Biblical Studies, and Peacemaking* (Scottdale, PA: Herald Press, 2000).

10. On the exploitation of inter-ethnic enmity in the European colonization of Africa, see Thomas Pakenham, *The Scramble for Africa: White Man's Conquest of the Dark Continent from 1876 to 1912* (New York: Avon Books, 1991), and Gerald Caplan, "The Conspiracy against Africa," *The Walrus* 3/9 (November 2006).

11. Goldhagen, *Worse than War*, observes five "eliminationist" strategies used by various governments throughout history: transformation, repression, expulsion, prevention of reproduction, and extermination. As Goldhagen's comprehensive survey observes, "eliminationism" cuts across all three kinds of conflict dealt with here — reactionary, revolutionary, and identity.

movements and from the resilience of ethnic-religious identity in the Balkans that gave way to "successful" ethnic cleansing campaigns — demonstrates the indissolubility of ethnic and religious identity into class consciousness. "Class conflict" has also been used as a cover for identity violence — eliminating the ethnic or religious "Other" in the name of "saving the revolution." For example: the deportation of non-Russian ethnic groups to Siberia in the Soviet Union under Stalin, the "disappearance" of indigenous Mayans by Spanish descendants in the Guatemalan civil war, and the slaughter of Vietnamese, Chinese, and other ethnic minorities in Pol Pot's Cambodia.

Recognizing identity conflict as a source of violence distinct from both reactionary and revolutionary conflicts is thus not merely a theoretical matter, but has practical implications for understanding and addressing contemporary conflict situations. Failure to recognize identity-driven conflict can lead to inadequate analysis of a conflict situation, and inadequate analysis can result in policy failure. Some complex conflict situations comprise reactionary, revolutionary, and identity conflicts all together. The ongoing Israeli-Palestinian conflict, for example, comprises competing interests (land, water, etc.), revolutionary ideologies (both Zionism and Palestinian nationalism), and religious-ethnic identities (Israeli Jewish, Israeli Arab, Palestinian Arab Muslim, and Palestinian Arab Christian). As David Smock, director of the Religion and Peacemaking program of the U.S. Institute of Peace, has observed, standard methods of conflict resolution are insufficient for such complex conflict situations, because identity conflicts are not merely matters of competing interests or clashing ideologies.[12] Standard methods of conflict resolution, as typically employed by both state diplomats and non-governmental organizations engaged in negotiating peace agreements, are inadequate to resolve identity conflicts precisely because ethnic-religious identities are *not negotiable.*

A good example of a complex conflict in which inadequate analysis led to policy failure that exacerbated the conflict is the situation in Iraq after the U.S. invasion in 2003 (ongoing as of 2011). For the first three years of this war, most U.S. government officials and media commentators had analyzed the conflict as an "insurgency" against the American military occupation and Iraqi national (Shi'ite) government. This insurgency comprised diverse parties representing both reactionary and revolutionary motivation: secularized Sunni Ba'athists loyal to Saddam Hussein and fighting to regain the dominant political position they had lost (reactionary violence), and religious terrorists fighting to establish an Islamic state and permanent base for al-Qaeda (revolutionary violence). What most commentators were missing or refusing to acknowledge — despite

---

12. David Smock, "When Religion Makes Peace Not War," John Howard Yoder Dialogues on Nonviolence, Religion and Peace, Joan B. Kroc Institute for International Peace Studies, University of Notre Dame, September 28, 2007.

the historical record, and even as the empirical evidence mounted — was the wide and deep current of inter-ethnic/inter-religious violence cutting across the entire conflict.

For example, George Will is a political commentator who analyzes conflicts in Hobbesian terms.[13] Will commented in April 2004 on the threat posed by the rise of Moqtada al Sadr, a Shi'ite leader in command of a sizable militia in southern Iraq:

> In the war against the militias, every door American troops crash through, every civilian bystander shot — there will be many — will make matters worse, for a while. Nevertheless, the first task of the occupation remains the first task of government: to establish a monopoly on violence. . . . Regime change, occupation, nation-building — in a word, empire — are a bloody business. Now Americans must steel themselves for administering the violence necessary to disarm or defeat Iraq's urban militias, which replicate the problem of modern terrorism — violence that has slipped the leash of states.[14]

Writing two years later, Will repeated the same basic analysis:

> Almost three years after the invasion, it is still not certain whether, or in what sense, Iraq is a nation. And after two elections and a referendum on its constitution, Iraq barely has a government. A defining attribute of a government is that it has a monopoly on the legitimate exercise of violence. That attribute is incompatible with the existence of private militias of the sort that maraud in Iraq.[15]

Will's prescription for what ailed post-invasion, conflict-torn Iraq was typically Hobbesian: peace and stability will come once there has been established a central government that holds a "monopoly on violence" and can keep all sub-state actors (Ba'athists and terrorists) in fear. The necessary task to restoring civil order, therefore, is for the U.S. military, and the U.S.-backed Iraqi government, to "administer the violence necessary to disarm or defeat Iraq's urban militias." Such was the thinking behind the U.S. "troop surge" policy — suppress violence through violent force to a degree sufficient to allow Iraqis to form a government that can control the conflict on its own.

What is remarkable about Will's analysis of the conflict in Iraq is the system-

13. See, for example, George F. Will, "July 10, 1941, in Jedwabne" *Newsweek*, July 9, 2001, p. 68, an analysis of one incident during the Holocaust. Will's Hobbesian analysis of the killing of the Jews of Jedwabne by their Polish neighbors is blind to the obvious datum: only Polish Catholics were killing only Ashkenazi Jews. Rather than a case of reactionary violence, as Will claims, this was evidently a case of identity violence.

14. George F. Will, "A War President's Job," *The Washington Post*, April 7, 2004, p. A31.

15. George F. Will, "Rhetoric of Unreality," *The Washington Post*, March 2, 2006, p. A21.

atic lack of attention to the role of ethnic-religious factions. The empirical data showed that the vast majority of the casualties of violence in Iraq were being generated by the ongoing Iraqi-against-Iraqi conflict, not attacks directly upon American troops or even the Iraqi government. And underlying the Iraqi-against-Iraqi conflict is a complex mixture of inter-ethnic/inter-religious hostility — between Sunni and Shi'ite Muslims (and, to a lesser degree, Kurdish Muslims and Arab Muslims) — and tribal loyalties. Yet, even three years into the conflict, Will's Hobbesian perspective could see armed groups only as "*urban militias*" or "*private* militias," not as Sunni or Shi'ite. Such a perspective is blind to the ethnic-religious identity and tribal loyalty of the various actors and so misunderstands the motivations behind the internal struggle being waged for control of Iraq. After yet another year of sectarian violence killing thousands of Iraqis every month, most commentators and analysts had come to recognize by 2007 that ethnic-religious identity and tribal loyalty comprise the basic reality of the Iraq conflict. And once one had recognized the "civil war" as essentially a sectarian conflict, the manifold evidence came into focus: sectarian expulsions from Baghdad neighborhoods, sectarian divisions in the Iraqi security forces, sectarian taunts at Saddam Hussein's execution, sectarian murders by the dozens daily, etc. This recognition has given way to the realization that political reconciliation among Iraq's ethnic-religious parties and tribal leaders is the essential priority if there is to be a peaceable future for Iraq.[16] As shown by the example of Bosnia, again on the verge of violent fragmentation, a post-conflict political arrangement to balance interests among competing factions is insufficient to establish civic peace and sustain national unity — ethnic-religious reconciliation is necessary.[17]

16. For a secular analysis that describes the Iraq conflict in fundamentally sectarian terms and points to political reconciliation as the top priority, see Anthony H. Cordesman, "Looking beyond a Surge: The Tests a New US Strategy in Iraq Must Meet," Center for Strategic and International Studies (Washington, D.C.), January 4, 2007, formerly online at http://www.csis.org/index.php?option=com_csis_pubs&task=view&id=3659. Concerning the role of ethnic-religious identity in the previous (failed) British attempt to impose order on Iraq by force, see David Fromkin, *A Peace to End All Peace: The Fall of the Ottoman Empire and the Creation of the Modern Middle East* (New York: Henry Holt and Company, 1989), pp. 449-54.

17. Patrice C. McMahon and Jon Western, "The Death of Dayton: How to Stop Bosnia from Falling Apart," *Foreign Affairs*, September-October 2009. McMahon and Western observe: "Although Bosnia professes to seek the creation of a unified multiethnic state, its political institutions support ethnic partition at every level of government. . . . Reversing these centrifugal trends will require a renewed focus on Bosnia to address core issues: rising ethnic nationalist pressure, weak central governance, and endemic corruption. . . . It is tempting to assert that it is now time — nearly 14 years after Dayton — for Bosnians to take charge. But this is impossible within an institutional structure based on ethnicity that rewards those who appeal to fear and ethnic chauvinism. If the international community does not reverse these trends, the result may well be the redivision of Bosnia and a return to war." The exception is the Brčko District, which has achieved a relatively stable local peace and where Croatian Catholics, Serbian Orthodox, and Bosnian Muslims have demonstrated a degree of reconciliation.

32.4. Identity Conflict: Confirmation of the Cross

The peacemaking cross of Jesus Christ addresses all three major veins of human conflict, but has a special relevance concerning identity conflict, precisely where modern secular analyses of human relations and methods of conflict resolution are inadequate. Better than either a Hobbesian or a Marxist perspective, a cruciform paradigm helps us see the world and humanity for how they really are, in a way that is practically relevant for addressing conflict situations. The cross teaches us that ethnic-religious identity is a stubborn fact of the human situation, as real as the psychological drive for self-preservation out of fear of death. Unless we recognize this reality, we cannot make any sense of either the patient suffering of the faithful servant or the perverse violence of the suicide bomber. Viewing reality through the lens of the cross reveals the worldly truth of identity conflict — hostility and violence rooted in identity purged of the Other. And what the cross reveals has been confirmed repeatedly by those whose life-experience and profession have placed them in situations of inter-ethnic/inter-religious conflict.

Drawing from extensive international experience in the practice of conflict transformation, John Paul Lederach analyzes the process by which "enemies are created":

> Lay aside all the other factors, from social conditioning to real physical threat. In the end, an enemy is rooted and constructed in our hearts and minds and takes on social significance as others share in the social construction. . . . *First,* to construct an image of the enemy, I must *separate* myself from another. . . . Who I am is defined by who I am not. The origin of enmity lies in a self-definition built upon a negative projection about another. . . . A *second* phenomenon goes hand in hand with separation. I see myself as *superior.* . . . Though I am in the form of a common person, the same as others, I raise myself above them and take the position of God. To construct an enemy, we must both lose sight of our sameness and create a sense that we are superior. *Third,* separation and superiority lead to *dehumanizing* the other person(s). . . . I rob them of being created in the image of God. I lose the sight of God in their faces.[18]

Having separated ourselves from the "other" via a self-definition granting "us" a superior position over "them" (e.g., via circumcision), and so having raised ourselves into a position of divinely appointed judgment over the Other (i.e., self-justification), "we" may proceed directly to dehumanize and destroy "them." Here, then, lies exposed the persistent taproot of sin that feeds enmity

---

18. John Paul Lederach, *The Journey toward Reconciliation* (Scottdale, PA: Herald Press, 1999), pp. 47-48, emphasis original.

and produces the evil fruit manifest in inter-ethnic/inter-religious conflict. Lederach names this sin as robbing the Other of being created in the image of God, or losing sight of God in the face of the Other.

Self-justifying self-definition is the taproot of hostility generating inter-ethnic/inter-religious conflict. In the mind of Croatian theologian Miroslav Volf, writing out of experience of war in the Balkans, the pursuit of such false, self-created purity characterizes the sin that drives the dynamics of differentiation, exclusion, and judgment:

> [T]he *pursuit of false purity* emerges as a central aspect of sin — the enforced purity of a person or a community that sets itself apart from the defiled world in a hypocritical sinlessness and excludes the boundary breaking other from its heart and its world. Sin is here the kind of purity that wants the world cleansed of the other rather than the heart cleansed of the evil that drives people out by calling those who are clean "unclean" and refusing to help make clean those who are unclean. . . . Consider the deadly logic of the "politics of purity." The blood must be pure: German blood alone should run through German veins, free from all nonAryan contamination. The territory must be pure: Serbian soil must belong to Serbs alone, cleansed of all nonSerbian intruders. . . . In extreme cases we kill and drive out. To ensure that the vengeance of the dead will not be visited upon us in their progeny, we destroy their habitations and their cultural monuments. . . . This is exclusion by *elimination,* most recently at work with such shameless brutality in places like Bosnia and Rwanda. . . . Alternatively, we are satisfied to assign "others" the status of inferior beings. We make sure that they cannot live in our neighborhoods, get certain kinds of jobs, receive equal pay or honor; they must stay in their proper place, which is to say the place we have assigned for them. . . . We subjugate them so we can exploit them in order to increase our wealth or simply inflate our egos. This is exclusion by *domination,* spread all over the globe in more or less diffuse forms, but most glaring in the caste system in India and former apartheid policies in South Africa.[19]

Journalist Chris Hedges, drawing from his experience reporting from war zones around the world, reflects on "the myth of war" that justifies violence. He describes how self-justifying self-definition generated hostility and violence in the Balkan conflict:

> Nationalist and ethnic conflicts are fratricides that turn on absurdities. They can only be sustained by myth. The arguments and bloody disputes take place over tiny, almost imperceptible nuances within the society — what Sigmund Freud calls the "narcissism of minor differences." In the Balkans,

19. Miroslav Volf, *Exclusion and Embrace: A Theological Exploration of Identity, Otherness, and Reconciliation* (Nashville: Abingdon Press, 1996), pp. 74-75, emphasis original.

for example, there were heated debates over the origin of gingerbread hearts — cookies in the shape of hearts. The Croats insisted the cookies were Croatian. The Serbs angrily countered that the cookies were Serbian. The suggestion to one ethnic group that gingerbread hearts were invented by the other ethnic group could start a fight. To those of us on the outside it had a Gilbert and Sullivan lunacy to it, but to the participants it was deadly serious. It had to be. For the nationalist myths stand on such miniscule differences. These myths give neighbors the justification to kill those they had gone to school and grown up with. The Serbs, Muslims, and Croats struggled, like ants on a small hill, to carve out separate, antagonistic identities. But it was all negative space. One defined oneself mostly by what the other was not.[20]

Italian diplomat Roberto Toscana, drawing from Lithuanian philosopher Emmanuel Levinas's ethical theory of "otherness," confirms the field observations and theological insights of Lederach, Volf, and Hedges. Identity and difference per se do not generate conflict; rather, says Toscana, conflict originates in "narcissistic identity," a constructed group-identity that makes every difference definitive of good and evil:

> Not all identity is conflict generating. . . . What is conflict generating is not identity per se, it is what can be called "narcissistic identity," the kind of identity whose affirmation, pursuit, and defense form an integral part of the essence of nationalism (and of its lesser but not less murderous counterparts ethnicism and tribalism). Why is this so? In the first place, because at the root of group identity lies . . . a lie, or — put in less blunt terms — a cultural artifact, an intellectual construct. . . . It is commonly believed . . . that in order to maintain the cohesion of a group it is not enough to define its identity in objective terms: all those born on the same territory, all those sharing the same religion, all those speaking the same language. For this reason, there must be what has been called "the invention of tradition," there must be the creation of "imagined communities," there has to be a "founding myth." . . . The point is that such an artificial, ideological path to identity is inherently conflict-generating . . . most of all, because narcissistic group identity, by making one's own group's value incomparably higher, qualitatively incommensurable with that of any other group, ends up denying the ethical relevance of the Other, i.e., expels the other from the scope of applicability of moral rules.[21]

20. Chris Hedges, *War Is a Force That Gives Us Meaning* (New York: Public Affairs, 2002), p. 32.

21. Roberto Toscano, "The Face of the Other: Ethics and Intergroup Conflict," in Eugene Weiner, ed., *The Handbook of Interethnic Coexistence* (New York: Continuum, 1998), pp. 65-66. E.g., in the Rwandan conflict, Tutsis and Hutus are not differentiated on the basis of origins, language, or religion. The "difference" between them is a matter of culture and tradition.

Having defined "one's own" in terms that are "incommensurable" with the Other, and thereby having elevated "one's own" in value far above the Other, one denies the Other standing in the moral community. The ancient command "You shall not kill" thus need not apply in dealing with the Other. Should "one's own" be threatened, the Other can be eliminated without any further justification. Indeed, self-identity — which defines "one's own" as intrinsically good and the Other as intrinsically evil — is justification enough for wholly eliminating the Other via "ethnic cleansing" or outright genocide.

All these observations and analyses confirm what the cross reveals. What, then, does the cross teach concerning "the things that make for peace" in identity conflict? If inter-ethnic/inter-religious conflict is rooted in identity purged of the Other, how does the cross address the sin-root of the problem? Reconciliation among ethnic-religious parties entrenched in mutual hostility requires a mutual reconfiguration of identity — from identity purged of the Other to identity embracing the Other, from identity exclusive of the Other to identity *in*clusive of *both* oneself and the Other. Within the church, the atoning cross reconfigures all identities "in Christ" — the body of Christ comprises both Jew and Greek (see Chapter 33 below). Volf, retelling the Parable of the Lost Son (Luke 15:11-32), comments that the father's gracious initiative to reconcile his lost son to himself requires a reconfiguration of their respective identities: "identities need to be reconstituted if broken relationships are to be restored."[22] Lederach's observation in the field confirms this cruciform lesson: "Here is another paradox of reconciliation. We must learn how to develop a positive identity of self and group that is not based on criticizing or feeling superior to another person or group."[23]

As a concrete example of such reconfiguration of identities in the transformation of conflict, consider Northern Ireland. "The Troubles" has not been primarily a conflict of interests, but of identities. The Irish novelist Colm Tóibín, has recently observed a subtle impact of the peace process in Northern Ireland on Irish self-consciousness.

> The battle in Ireland over the past 40 years has not been a struggle over territory. No one has wanted to take land away from others and claim it for themselves. It has, instead, been a struggle over identity: a long effort to find agreement over language and symbols, the terms of competing and complex definitions of what it means to be Irish . . . it is often easier, if you come from

22. Volf, *Exclusion and Embrace*, p. 156.

23. Lederach, *Journey toward Reconciliation*, p. 49. Lederach has used the imagery of Psalm 85 — "Truth and mercy have met together, justice and peace have kissed" — as the basis for a process of reconciliation that brings together the four "voices" (truth and mercy, justice and peace) needed to transform conflict and build a sustainable peace through a reconfiguration of identities (pp. 51-80).

Ireland in any of its guises or aspects, to state what you are not than what you are. What works wonders now in Ireland is not the bomb or bullet, but two humble and ancient objects: the hyphen and the word "and."[24]

In Tóibín's view, hopeful progress toward a sustainable peace has been made, not by an integration of identities into a singular Irish identity, but by the mutual agreement to embrace complex, compound identities (e.g., "Northern Irish and British") that both allow for difference and make room for the Other.

24. Colm Tóibín, "What Does It Mean to Be Irish?" Newsweek, March 30, 2009, p. 39.

CHAPTER 33

Cruciform Peacemaking within the Church:
Justification and Ecumenism

I therefore . . . beg you to lead
a life worthy of the calling to which you have been called . . .
making every effort to maintain
the unity of the Spirit in the bond of peace.

EPHESIANS 4:1, 3

33.1. Identity Conflict and "Faith in Christ":
Justification as Peacemaking

Essentially, the cross makes peace amidst hostility precisely by means of a reconfiguration of identities "in Christ." In light of the cross, we thus see that justification and reconciliation are dual aspects of a single salvation through the cross. Let's reexamine Paul's message of the cross in Ephesians and Galatians to draw out the peacemaking implications of his doctrine of justification concerning identity conflict.

Through the cross, Jesus breaks down the "dividing wall" between "us" and "them" by abolishing the legal criterion defining "us" separate from and over-against "them," the legal criterion that exalts "us" and so justifies "us" expelling "them." And he has done so in order to create a "we" in which "us" and "them" may belong on equal terms to God's people. The intended result is that, even while ethnic-religious particularities remain, there is no longer any ultimate distinction between "us" and "them" because *both groups* belong together equally in a newly created people of God.

As Paul depicts the cross in Eph 2:11-22 (see Chapter 29 above), Jesus takes two peacemaking initiatives, one destructive and one creative: he uproots inter-ethnic hostility by *nullifying the old demarcations of identity* that have divided humanity into mutually exclusive, mutually hostile parties (the "circumcised" and the "uncircumcised"); and he makes inter-ethnic peace by *creating in himself a new identity* through which those who were at enmity might be reconciled "in one body" as members of "one new humanity." Through the cross, Jesus embraces the mutually exclusive, mutually hostile parties, Jew and Gentile, reconciling *both* into the "one body" of the "new humanity," giving *both* equal access to God "in one Spirit," and including *both* as equal members in "the household of God." The identity of this "one body" of the "new humanity" is marked out by, and membership in "the household of God" is based upon, nothing other than the crucified One, Jesus. Paul can thus write that now, on the basis of the peacemaking cross of Christ, where there once had been inter-ethnic division and hostility, "There is one body and one Spirit, . . . one hope . . . , one Lord, one faith, one baptism, one God and Father of all, who is above all and through all and in all" (Eph 4:4-6).

Seen against this background of inter-ethnic division and hostility, Paul's doctrine of justification by faith in Christ is essentially a peacemaking doctrine; for inter-ethnic reconciliation amidst identity conflict within the church is the immediate practical application of the doctrine. Paul's doctrine of justification implies that within the "one body" of the "new humanity" comprising diverse ethnicities there is only one status, being "in Christ." And this status is neither reckoned by human ancestry nor secured by human means — being "in Christ" is God's gift, not gained "by works" (Eph 2:8-9). It is precisely because the identity of and membership in the "one body" of the "new humanity" is founded solely and sufficiently upon the gracious work of God in Christ that the community of faith can be the place of reconciliation amidst the world's divisions and hostilities. D. M. Baillie remarks: "It [the church] was indeed a new kind of community: a society of sinners forgiven, with the Cross as its badge, and every member confessing: 'Not I, but the grace of God.' That breaks down the barriers between man and man. . . ."[1]

Now, because the status "in Christ by faith" in no way depends on anything human, those who are "in Christ" are no longer considered "in" or "out" on account of the merely human criteria that once counted for everything. So Paul writes:

> From now on, therefore, we regard no one from a human point of view [literally, according to the flesh]; even though we once knew Christ from a human point of view, we know him no longer in that way. So if anyone is in Christ, there is a new creation: everything old has passed away; see, everything has become new! (2 Cor 5:16-17)

1. D. M. Baillie, *God Was in Christ: An Essay on Incarnation and Atonement* (New York: Scribner's, 1948), p. 208.

Paul could thus write that, because "in Christ" the old marker of ethnic identity "according to the flesh" (circumcision) is annulled, all that remains that really matters now is "new creation": "For neither circumcision nor uncircumcision is anything; but a new creation is everything" (Gal 6:15). Paul's point is *not* that "the body of Christ" is *un*circumcised (in which case those who *are* circumcised would be excluded), but rather that "the body of Christ" is *neither* circumcised *nor* uncircumcised. The "body of Christ" includes *both* circumcised *and* uncircumcised, such that this old marker of identity and criterion of membership "according to the flesh" no longer counts at all. Again, Paul: "For in Christ Jesus neither circumcision nor uncircumcision counts for anything; the only thing that counts is faith working through love" (Gal 5:6).

The new identity of those "in Christ," and hence the criterion of membership in "the body of Christ," is defined not by "*who* we are" and "who we are *not*," but only by "faith in Christ" (Gal 2:16). And precisely because being "in Christ" does not *include* anyone on the basis of ethnic criteria, being "in Christ" does not *exclude* anyone on account of ethnic criteria; precisely because the "one body" is not identified by marks of ethnicity, this "new humanity" is free to embrace a diversity of ethnicity. The "one body" of the "new humanity" embraces *both* Jew and Greek, so that the new identity "in Christ" is not exclusive of either Jew-ness or Greek-ness. Jews by birth remain Jewish, Greeks by birth remain Greek; but in the "one body" of the "new humanity," *being* Jewish or *being* Greek no longer counts anyone "in" or "out" — all that counts is being "in Christ by faith." N. T. Wright draws out the social implications of Paul's doctrine:

> What Paul means by justification . . . is not "how you become a Christian," so much as "how you can tell who is a member of the covenant family." When two people share Christian faith, says Paul, they can share table-fellowship, no matter what their ancestry. And all this is based four-square, of course, on the theology of the cross. "I am crucified with Christ," he writes, "nevertheless I live; yet not I, but Christ lives in me" (Gal 2:19-20). The cross has obliterated the privileged distinction that Saul of Tarsus supposed himself to enjoy; the new life he has as Paul the apostle is a life defined, not by his old existence, but solely by the crucified and risen Messiah. . . . Justification, in Galatians, is the doctrine which insists that all who share faith in Christ belong at the same table, no matter what their racial differences, as together they wait for the final new creation.[2]

Paul's doctrine of justification implies that no one in the church enjoys any special or privileged status. As goes for ethnicity and race, so also goes for all other markers of identity and criteria of membership "according to the flesh."

2. N. T. Wright, *What Saint Paul Really Said: Was Paul of Tarsus the Real Founder of Christianity?* (Grand Rapids, MI: Eerdmans Publishing, 1997), p. 122.

Being baptized "into Christ" nullifies the significance of class and sex as much as it nullifies ethnicity and race: "As many of you as were baptized into Christ have clothed yourselves with Christ. There is no longer Jew or Greek, there is no longer slave or free, there is no longer male and female; for all of you are one in Christ Jesus" (Gal 3:27-28). The church is not to be divided along class or gender lines any more than it is to be divided along ethnic-racial lines. For the cross has nullified *all* the old demarcations of self-justifying, other-exclusive identity, rendering them of no account, so that in the "new humanity" of the church there is only one status — "in Christ by faith."[3] Baptism "into Christ" leaves Jews Jewish and Greeks Greek, slaves slave and freed free, men male and women female — such things "according to the flesh" are as they were. Nonetheless, justification by faith of those baptized "into Christ" nullifies the significance of all ethnic-racial, class, and gender distinctions and criteria regarding who belongs in the church. Because "we are justified by faith," all alike are freed "in Christ" for equal membership and full participation in Christ's "new creation."[4]

We may thus conclude: if only white, wealthy people are allowed to exercise the authority that Jesus conferred on the Apostles irrespective of race and class (Matt 18:15-20; 28:18-20), then the church frustrates the power of the cross to reconcile us as "one in Christ Jesus."[5] If only men are allowed to exercise the gifts of ministry, which have been bestowed by the Spirit on the members of the body irrespective of gender (1 Corinthians 12), then the church becomes a stumbling block to the liberating gospel of Jesus Christ.[6] Paul's doctrine of justification implies that the church, by its very identity "in Christ," is to be the embodiment of God's purpose to "reconcile all things in Christ" (Col 1:20; cf. Eph 1:10). Any church polity that nullifies or qualifies equality "in Christ," therefore, frustrates God's reconciling work in the world.[7]

---

3. For a more extended, in-depth discussion of Paul's "radical redrawing of traditional identity markers" in the church, see James D. G. Dunn, *The Theology of Paul the Apostle* (Grand Rapids, MI: Eerdmans Publishing, 1998), pp. 534-64.

4. Cf. Miroslav Volf, *Exclusion and Embrace: A Theological Exploration of Identity, Otherness, and Reconciliation* (Nashville, TN: Abingdon Press, 1996), pp. 43-50.

5. Regarding racial reconciliation in the church, see Spencer Perkins and Chris Rice, *More Than Equals: Racial Healing for the Sake of the Gospel*, revised and expanded ed. (Downers Grove, IL: InterVarsity Press, 2000).

6. Regarding Paul's teaching on women, see the excellent and accessible treatment by John Templeton Bristow, *What Paul Really Said about Women: An Apostle's Liberating Views on Equality in Marriage, Leadership, and Love* (New York: HarperCollins Publishers, 1988). Regarding the prominent role of women in the early church, see Rena Pederson, *The Lost Apostle: Searching for the Truth about Junia* (San Francisco: Jossey-Bass, 2006).

7. We add this note: Paul's doctrine of justification has two aspects. In Galatians, "justification" has the sense of "status *as* righteous," right standing in God's covenant community. In Romans, "justification" has the additional sense of "being *made* righteous," being "put right" and so enabled to live righteously, to do the works of righteousness that the covenant calls us to

33.2. Identity Conflict and Christian (Dis-)Unity: The Cross and Ecumenism[8]

33.2.1. *Intra-Christian Division and Hostility: Scandal to the Gospel*

Let us refocus our attention from the age-old problem of inter-ethnic conflict to the ongoing problem of *intra*-Christian conflict — enmity between fellow Christians — and consider the message of the cross for a divided church. No human conflict down the centuries and around the globe should concern Christians more than hostility between and division among fellow servants in the household of God. The divisive, and sometimes destructive, enmity between Christians, I believe, is *the* scandal to the gospel of Christ crucified. Such division enables ethnic identities and national loyalties to override Jesus' call to discipleship in the way of the cross (Mark 8:34) and so allows Christians to evade Jesus' prayer for unity in the body of Christ (John 17:20-21). The fact that many Christians of different nations at various times of war have chosen to obey their political leaders rather than Christ our Lord, and so slaughter one another as enemies on the field of battle, is an affront to and offense against the cross upon which Jesus gave his life in order to reconcile enemies. Intra-Christian enmity is, effectively, an anti-gospel, a counter-message to the enemy-loving, enemy-reconciling cross of Christ.

At least as important as Christian peacemaking in the midst of the world's wars, I am convinced, is ecumenical peacemaking within Christ's body, reconciling a divided church for the sake of the gospel. For directly at stake in intra-Christian conflict is the integrity of the message of the cross. Christians killing Christians is the gravest manifestation of the power of sin continuing to bear

---

do (Romans 6, 8). The first aspect (status as righteous) is, as we have shown above, directly relevant to the peacemaking question of identity conflict. The second aspect of justification (being made righteous), as we have emphasized at several points throughout this book, is relevant to our own justice-doing, which is made possible by the life, death, and resurrection of Christ. While we must be careful not to confuse these two aspects, we must also avoid pitting them against each other. In fact, each aspect of justification needs the other: having right standing by faith as a member of the covenant community is pointless apart from actually performing the works of righteousness that the covenant calls us to do, and vice versa. Or, as Paul and James agree, "the only thing that counts [in Christ] is faith working through love" (Gal 5:6), because "faith without works is dead" (Jas 2:17, 26). If the question is "Does justification' mean status *as* righteous or being *made* righteous?" then the answer is "both." Cf. Dunn, *Theology of Paul*, p. 344.

8. This section draws substantially upon two articles: "'Has Christ Been Divided? Was Paul Crucified for You?' — The Evangelical Imperative of Ecumenical Peacemaking and the Bridgefolk (Mennonite-Catholic) Movement," and "One Lord, One Baptism, One Body, One Table: A Reply to Penelope Adams Moon," published in *Mennonite Life*, Fall 2007 and Spring 2008 respectively. My thanks to the editor of this journal for permission to reuse this material.

592 "CHRIST IS OUR PEACE"

the fruit of death even within the body of Christ — and so is perhaps the surest indication that the "new creation" of Christ has not yet come to full realization even within the church. If Christians are not yet reconciled to one another within Christ's own body, how then can the church testify to the power of the cross to reconcile enemies in the world? We must never be ashamed of the gospel, for it is God's power of salvation, not ours, and no sin of ours can annul it; but in light of the gospel, we ought to be ashamed of Christian division and enmity.

Christian division and hostility is manifest in various forms of conflict. There are interest-driven conflicts within the church. We mentioned above the international conflicts that have divided the church along national lines during wartime. I'm sure most readers will be aware of power struggles among church leaders that result in the split of a local or denominational body. There are also ideology-driven conflicts within the church. The polarization of the political spectrum in the U.S., dividing the nation into "red states" and "blue states," is also manifest within the church. Congregations can readily split into partisan factions during election campaigns when parishioners appeal to the platforms of political parties rather than the witness of the prophets.

33.2.2. Christian Division as Identity Conflict

Christian division and hostility goes deeper than even Christians killing Christians, however. The Mennonite Central Committee has promoted "A modest proposal for peace: Let the Christians of the world agree that they will not kill each other." While much more than a "modest" proposal and surely necessary, this does not get to the root of the problem. For intra-Christian division and hostility, I think, is a manifestation of *identity* conflict, rooted in self-justifying self-definition — identity purged of the Other.

During the division of the Western church, commonly called the Reformation, the construction of self-justifying, other-exclusive self-definitions is evident in the very language of the various Protestant confessional statements.[9] Recall Lederach: "*First,* to construct an image of the enemy, I must *separate* myself from another. . . . Who I am is defined by who I am not. The origin of enmity lies in a self-definition built upon a negative projection about another. . . ."[10] As Volf observes, such self-definition serves "the pursuit of false purity" — "the enforced purity of a person or community that sets itself apart

---

9. My focus here is narrowed to division within the Western church. There is, we should not forget, that other and older division in the body of Christ, the "Great Schism" between East and West.

10. John Paul Lederach, *The Journey toward Reconciliation* (Scottdale, PA: Herald Press, 1999), p. 47, emphasis original.

from the defiled world in a hypocritical sinlessness and excludes the boundary breaking other from its heart and its world."[11] We see such self-definition in the Reformation-era confessional statements, by which various Protestant groups effectively sought to do in words what the hostile factions in the Balkan conflict sought to do by force — to cleanse the "unholy" Other from the "pure" identity and territory of "one's own."

Article I of the Schleitheim Confession (1527) purged the identity of the Swiss Brethren ("Anabaptists") of both Catholic ("popish") and Protestant ("repopish") association, naming "all popish and repopish works" (e.g., infant baptism and the mass) as belonging to "Belial" (Article IV).[12] The Augsburg Confession (1530) purged Lutheran identity of any association with the "radical reformers" by its several explicit condemnations of Anabaptist belief and practice (cf. Articles V, IX, XII, XVI, and XVII).[13] The Thirty-Nine Articles (1571) purged Anglican identity of Roman association, declaring the "Church of Rome" to be in error regarding matters of faith and ceremony (Article XIX) and denouncing "the Romish doctrine" of purgatory and invocation of saints (Article XXII). The Westminster Confession (1646) purged Presbyterian identity of Catholic association in no uncertain terms, naming the "Pope of Rome" as "that Antichrist, that man of sin and son of perdition, that exalteth himself in the Church against Christ, and all that is called God" (XXV) and denouncing "the Popish sacrifice of the mass" as "most abominable" (XXIX). And the Baptist confession (1689) followed suit, adding that the "Pope of Rome" is the one "whom the Lord shall destroy with the brightness of his coming" (26).[14]

11. Volf, *Exclusion and Embrace*, p. 74.

12. The Schleitheim Confession is accessible online at http://www.mcusa-archives.org/ library/resolutions/schleithiem/index.html. This sense of Anabaptist identity as a pure Christianity purged of both Catholicism and Protestantism endures today among the Mennonite descendants of the Anabaptist movement: see Walter Klaassen, *Anabaptism: Neither Catholic nor Protestant,* 3rd ed. (Kitchener, ON: Pandora Press, 2001).

13. These condemnations have recently begun to be addressed in Mennonite-Lutheran ecumenical dialogue. See *Right Remembering in Anabaptist-Lutheran Relations: Report of the Evangelical Lutheran Church in America–Mennonite Church USA Liason Committee* (Chicago: Evangelical Lutheran Church in America, 2004) and *Healing Memories: Reconciling in Christ — Report of the Lutheran–Mennonite International Study Commission* (Geneva: Lutheran World Federation; Strasbourg: Mennonite World Conference, 2010). According to the latter report: "these statements were not intended primarily to reflect or refute the theological positions held by specific Anabaptist leaders. Instead, they were meant to distance the reformers theologically and politically from a group with which their Roman opponents had falsely identified them and whose behavior could prima facie be construed as worthy of capital punishment" (p. 56). We thus see here a complex of identity conflict and interest conflict: the Augsburg exclusion of Anabaptist association from Lutheran identity served the political survival of the German reformation over against Roman opposition.

14. These Protestant confessions of faith can be accessed online at http://www.reformed .org/documents/index.html. Use of the Protestant confessions as instruments of Christian divi-

Such hostile words — and the violent deeds of official persecution of fellow Christians begotten by such words — are nothing less than crimes against the cross upon which Jesus gave his life to reconcile us to one another. They are sins needing atonement — confession, repentance, forgiveness, and cleansing.[15] John Paul II, on the Day of Pardon (March 12) in the Jubilee year 2000, set a precedent for all Christians, naming Catholic "sins which have harmed the unity of the body of Christ" during the second millennium as requiring confession and repentance.[16] He prayed:

> Let us pray that our recognition of the sins which have rent the unity of the Body of Christ and wounded fraternal charity will facilitate the way to reconciliation and communion among all Christians. Merciful Father, on the night before his Passion your Son prayed for the unity of those who believe in him: in disobedience to his will, however, believers have opposed one another, becoming divided, and have mutually condemned one another and fought against one another. We urgently implore your forgiveness and we beseech the gift of a repentant heart, so that all Christians, reconciled with you and with one another will be able, in one body and in one spirit, to experience anew the joy of full communion. We ask this through Christ our Lord.

Amen.

Given that the taproot of intra-Christian hostility is self-justifying self-definition, identity purged of the Other, the first step to ecumenical peacemaking, to healing a divided body of Christ, must be to confess and repent of the harmful (even hateful) words that we have used to depict and denounce fellow Christians. Such words not only became seeds that grew into noxious weeds of mutual hostility, but also nurtured negative images of the Christian Other that

---

sion prompts the question whether an ecumenical reclamation of the Nicene Creed might serve the cause of ecclesial unity. Concerning this, see S. Mark Heim, ed., *Faith to Creed: Ecumenical Perspectives on the Affirmation of the Apostolic Faith in the Fourth Century* (Grand Rapids, MI: Eerdmans Publishing, 1991), and Luke Timothy Johnson, *The Creed: What Christians Believe and Why It Matters* (New York: Doubleday, 2003).

15. The document *Called Together to Be Peacemakers: Report of the International Dialogue between the Catholic Church and Mennonite World Conference, 1998-2003,* resulting from the international dialogue between the Pontifical Council for Promoting Christian Unity (the ecumenical office of the Vatican) and Mennonite World Conference, addresses this issue, stating: "we agree that it is a tragedy when Christians kill one another" (¶175). I wish the document had used stronger language and so called this tragedy by its proper theological name: *sin.* The document is accessible online at http://www.bridgefolk.net/wp-content/uploads/2009/04/ctp_english.pdf.

16. John Paul II's prayer of confession on the March 12, 2000 Day of Pardon is accessible online at http://www.vatican.va/news_services/liturgy/documents/ns_lit_doc_20000312_prayer-day-pardon_en.html.

have persisted for centuries and justified division.[17] Ecumenical peacemaking thus requires, first, a "purification of memories" that addresses the past, and our remembering of the past, with honesty and humility.[18]

Second, because we have defined ourselves over-against the Other, Christians must reclaim their common identity "in Christ" through baptism, an inclusive identity that joins one-to-another: "As many of you as were baptized into Christ have clothed yourselves with Christ . . . you are all one in Christ Jesus" (Gal 3:27-28). Reclaiming our common baptismal identity "in Christ" will require reconfiguration of particular denominational identities to include baptized sisters and brothers of other denominations.[19] One of the most significant acts of the Second Vatican Council was to reclaim and rearticulate a common Christian baptismal identity, which reconfigured Roman Catholic identity to include all those "baptized into Christ." In its Decree on Ecumenism, the Roman Catholic Church affirms common Christian identity through baptism as a fundamental truth that no division of the church can annul: "it remains true that all who have been justified by faith in Baptism are members of Christ's body, and have a right to be called Christian, and so are correctly accepted as brothers by the children of the Catholic Church" (*Unitatis Redintegratio* 2). In order to make peace within the church, therefore, we must pay careful attention to *who* is the "we" of the church. When we say, "We are the body of Christ," does this "we" include "who we are *not*"? Is this "we" open to embracing the Other? Lutherans? Anglicans? Methodists? Presbyterians? Baptists? Adventists? Pentecostals? Mennonites? Catholics?

Now, in reclaiming the common identity of baptized believers, our oneness "in Christ," we need have no fear of a monolithic uniformity that erases differences and nullifies diversity. Unity is to be distinguished from uniformity. Paul

---

17. Persistent negative images of the Other, harbored unchanged for centuries, remains a significant obstacle to ecumenical relations between Mennonites and Catholics. See *Called Together to Be Peacemakers*, ¶¶23-29, 41-43, and 190-97. The negative images of Catholics harbored by Mennonites and Mennonite hostility toward Catholics have been sustained down the centuries by the martyrology preserved in *Martyrs Mirror*, a seventeenth-century compilation of the trials, tortures, testimonies, and executions of Anabaptist Mennonite Christians which is still read in Mennonite congregations and homes. An online version of *Martyrs Mirror* is accessible at http://www.homecomers.org/mirror/.

18. The theological foundations of "purification of memories" in ecumenical dialogue is set forth in the document "Memory and Reconciliation: The Church and the Faults of the Past," drafted by the Vatican's International Theological Commission for the Jubilee year 2000, available online at http://www.vatican.va/roman_curia/congregations/cfaith/cti_documents/rc_con_cfaith_doc_20000307_memory-reconc-itc_en.html#The%20Division%20of%20Christians.

19. In some Mennonite congregations, for example, this is happening in effect by recognizing the infant baptism of those raised, say, Catholic, Lutheran, Presbyterian, Methodist and thus not requiring adult baptism for church membership.

spells out what being "one in Christ" concerns: "one body and one Spirit . . . one hope . . . one Lord, one faith, one baptism, one God and Father of all" (Eph 4:4-5). As we saw with Paul's doctrine of justification, common identity in Christ is compatible with manifold diversity within the one body. Indeed, being "one in Christ" embraces a diversity of ethnicity/race, class, and gender, as well as a diversity of spiritual gifts and callings, theological understandings, and liturgical practices. James Dunn comments: "Paul's vision of the body of Christ is of a unity which consists in a diversity, that is, a unity which is not denied by diversity, but which would be denied by uniformity, a unity which depends on its diversity functioning as such — in a word, the unity of a body, the body of Christ."[20] Being "one in Christ" thus does not preclude believers joining together in and belonging to particular Christian communities, which are formed for the sake of common worship, fellowship, and mission and which express various gifts and callings within the one body, whether these be denominations, religious orders, or lay associations. In its Decree on Ecumenism, the Second Vatican Council emphasized an ideal that many Protestants will recognize — unity in essentials, diversity in non-essentials, and charity in all things:

> All in the Church must preserve unity in essentials. But let all, according to the gifts they have received enjoy a proper freedom, in their various forms of spiritual life and discipline, in their different liturgical rites, and even in their theological elaborations of revealed truth. In all things let charity prevail. If they are true to this course of action, they will be giving ever better expression to the authentic catholicity and apostolicity of the Church. (*Unitatis Redintegratio* 4)

Difference and diversity are not the problem, but disunity and division.

33.2.3. The Evangelical Imperative of Ecumenical Peacemaking

Far from being a recent movement, ecumenism is the original work of cruciform peacemaking. Ecumenism is rooted in the identity and mission of the church, ordained by Christ our Lord, motivated by the cross. Indeed, in his prayer on the night before his death, Jesus points to what might be called the evangelical imperative of ecclesial unity:

> I ask not only on behalf of these, but also on behalf of those who will believe in me through their word, that they may all be one. As you, Father, are in me and I am in you, may they also be in us, so that the world may believe that you have sent me. The glory that you have given me I have given them, so

20. Dunn, *Theology of Paul*, p. 564.

that they may be one, as we are one, I in them and you in me, that they may be completely one, so that the world may know that you have sent me and have loved them even as you have loved me. (John 17:20-23)

Notice, first, that Jesus prays not only for his disciples, but also for "those who will believe in me through their word" — that is, for all of us who have come to believe in Christ through the apostolic witness, who are now divided off from each other. Jesus prays simply, "that they may all be one." Jesus' final prayer with his disciples is for our unity, for the unity of the church. Not just a spiritual unity, but a unity that is visible to the world. And this because the very purpose of ecclesial unity is evangelical mission: "that the world may believe that you have sent me . . . that the world may know that you have sent me and have loved them even as you have loved me." I thus concur with John Paul II, who wrote concerning the Catholic Church's commitment to ecumenism (1995):

> Jesus himself, at the hour of his Passion, prayed "that they may all be one" (*Jn* 17:21). This unity, which the Lord has bestowed on his Church and in which he wishes to embrace all people, is not something added on, but stands at the very heart of Christ's mission. Nor is it some secondary attribute of the community of his disciples. Rather, it belongs to the very essence of this community. (*Ut Unum Sint* 9)

John Paul II puts the point simply, yet profoundly: "To believe in Christ means to desire unity." Ecumenical peacemaking aimed at restoring ecclesial unity is thus essentially and inescapably a matter of discipleship.

The visible unity of the church is to be a witness before a watching world, a proclamation of the good news that God has loved the world by sending the Son (John 3:16-17). Jesus thus prays: may the world come to know the love of God through the Son by seeing the love of Christians for one another in the church. We are to be united in love for one another, not only so that the world will know that we are Christians (13:34-35), but also so that the world will know that the gospel is true (17:20-23). We cannot be holy servants of the truth of the gospel (vv. 17-19) unless we are also dedicated servants of the unity of the church. By its disunity, the church betrays its service of the gospel. We might re-phrase: ecclesial disunity is bad evangelism, sending a counter-message to the good news that God so loved the world he sent the Son. The report of the official Catholic-Mennonite dialogue thus appropriately identifies the evangelical purpose of ecclesial unity as the chief motivation for ecumenical dialogue:

> But the basic inspiration for dialogue between separated Christians has been the realization that conflict between them impedes the preaching of the Gospel and damages their credibility. Indeed, conflict between Christians is a major obstacle to the mission given by Jesus Christ to his disciples. It is diffi-

cult to announce the good news of salvation "so that the world may believe" (*Jn* 17:21) if those bearing the good news have basic disagreements among themselves.[21]

This statement echoes the Decree on Ecumenism of the Second Vatican Council: "Such division openly contradicts the will of Christ, scandalizes the world, and damages the holy cause of preaching the Gospel to every creature" (*Unitatis Redintegratio* 1).

33.2.4. Ecumenical Peacemaking as Practical Atonement

The Apostle Paul attested that the church's mission as a light to the nations carries an imperative of unity in Christ; and this imperative of ecclesial unity turns on the cruciform identity of the church (Gal 3:27-28; 1 Cor 10:16-17; Eph 4:3-6). The church thus ought to see its mission of peace for the nations as hinging crucially upon unity in the body of Christ. For if the people of God from which the peacemaking mission radiates is not reconciled in Christ, then it is compromised in its offer of God's gift of peace to the nations. Let's review Paul's message of the cross.

By the grace of God, Christ has become our peace with God through the cross. This peace puts to death in Christ's crucified body the old enmity between human enemies and of humanity toward God, drawing us near to God through faith in Jesus as Christ and Lord (Rom 5:1-11).[22] God's reconciliation then extends through those reconciled to God in Christ, the church, to the world. The church has thus been given the task of carrying on Christ's ministry of reconciliation in the world by calling everyone to reconciliation with God in the name of Christ (2 Cor 5:18-20). God has made peace with humanity by creating his church on earth in the resurrected body of the crucified Christ. It is therefore the mission of the church in the world to make peace in Christ's name by calling the world to reconciliation with God through conversion to Christ's way of peace and incorporation into the body of Christ.

In order for the church to faithfully and effectively take up this mission of reconciliation in the name of Christ, however, the church itself must be reconciled in Christ through the cross. If the church is not reconciled in Christ, then

---

21. *Called Together to be Peacemakers,* ¶9.

22. Reta Haltemann Finger makes the case that the peace Paul mentions in Rom 5:1 is not only that of the individual reconciled with God but also that of Christians reconciled with one another in Christ. See "'Reconciled to God through the Death of His Son': A Mission of Peacemaking in Romans 5:1-11," in Mary H. Schertz and Ivan Friesen, eds., *How Beautiful upon the Mountains: Biblical Essays on Mission, Peace, and the Reign of God* (Elkhart, IN: Institute for Mennonite Studies, 2003), pp. 183-96.

its message to the nations of reconciliation to God in Christ is potentially both inauthentic and ineffective. The church's ministry of reconciliation in the world requires foremost that we be reconciled to one another in the body of Christ. Nothing less than the message of the cross is at stake regarding Christian unity: Christian division is a counter-cross reality.

The motivation for these thoughts is Paul's understanding of the message of the cross for inter-ethnic, class, and gender relations in the church (cf. Gal 3:26-28; 1 Cor 12:12-13). The historical distinction and conflict between Jew and Gentile — symbolized ritually and bodily by circumcision, realized socially through legal boundaries, and maintained physically by Temple barriers — are jointly nullified in Christ's body, so that both Jew and Gentile may be reconciled to one another and to God in Christ's body (Eph 2:14-16). The "dividing wall" that Christ "has broken down" was the legal barrier between clean and unclean, "circumcised" and "uncircumcised" that had separated Jews and Gentiles into two distinct social groups (cf. v. 11).

Until the Holy Spirit led Peter to transgress the legal boundary and cross the forbidden threshold into the house of Cornelius (an unclean, uncircumcised Roman!), Gentiles were categorically shut out of the early Jesus-community (Acts 10:1–11:18). With Jews and Gentiles unable to worship God together, unable to even break bread together around the same table much less share in the one bread that is Christ, there could be no church, no people of God redeemed from all nations, unless this question were resolved. At stake was the very identity of the "we" that the church has been created and is called to be. This hostility between Jew and Gentile, which presented a barrier to the church becoming one body unified in Christ, and hence a barrier to the mission of the church in fulfillment of the commission of Jesus to preach the gospel to all nations, was the very question addressed by the first ecumenical council at Jerusalem (Acts 15).

All this bears upon what God has purposed to do through the peacemaking cross of Jesus Christ. According to Paul (Ephesians 2), we receive reconciliation with God, and thereby enjoy membership in God's household and the blessings of God's covenant of peace, not individually, but corporately. The cross makes peace between Jew and Gentile by making them one people in Christ's body and reconciling them both to God as one body. The cross of Christ makes possible, first, a true spiritual and social unity of believers in Christ (see Chapter 27 above). This visible, corporate unity is to transcend racial-ethnic discord, geographic distance, social-economic-political division, cultural distinction, and gender difference (Gal 3:27-28). Paul thus charged the church to "make every effort to maintain the unity of the Spirit in the bond of peace" (Eph 4:3). Reconciling divisions in the church and restoring unity "in Christ," therefore, flows directly from God's purpose of salvation through the cross of Christ and from the identity of the church as the "new humanity" created "in Christ."[23] The message of the cross thus calls us to ecumenical peace-making.

33.2.5. *Christian Unity: One Lord, One Baptism, One Body, One Table*

Paul encountered the problem of division in the church not only between Jews and Gentiles but also among Gentile believers themselves. From the beginning, ecclesial disunity has been more than a matter of race and ethnicity. Within a generation, the believers at Corinth had splintered into factions caused by sectarian allegiances within the church that had come to supersede the allegiance of each believer and of the local church to Christ alone above all else. Common identity created by baptism "into Christ" had been supplanted by disparate and discordant partial identities — "Paulists," "Apollonians," and "Cephites" were conflicting with "Christians." These factions were fighting, disrupting the communion of the church. Paul implored them to be at peace with one another by being united in the mind of Christ and in the mission of the church:

> Now I appeal to you, brothers and sisters, by the name of our Lord Jesus Christ, that all of you be in agreement and that there be no divisions among you, but that you be united in the same mind and the same purpose. For it has been reported to me by Chloe's people that there are quarrels among you, my brothers and sisters. What I mean is that each of you says, "I belong to Paul," or "I belong to Apollos," or "I belong to Cephas," or "I belong to Christ." Has Christ been divided? Was Paul crucified for you? Or were you baptized in the name of Paul? (1 Cor 1:10-13)

Paul implies that such sectarian divisions in the church, depending as they do upon human wisdom and power, are counter-signs to the wisdom of God revealed through the cross of Christ (1 Cor 1:17ff.). It is the cross and resurrection of Christ, and baptism "into Christ," that create the common identity of Christians and constitute the basic unity of the church: one Lord, one baptism, one body (Eph 4:4-6). Any exclusive identity supplanting that common identity in

---

23. What we have expressed here in terms of reconciliation, N. T. Wright has expressed as well in terms of justification: "Paul's doctrine of justification by faith impels the churches, in the current fragmented state, into the ecumenical task. . . . The doctrine of justification . . . is itself the ecumenical doctrine, the doctrine that rebukes our petty and often culture-bound groupings, and which declares that all who believe in Jesus belong together in the one family. . . . The doctrine of justification is in fact the great *ecumenical* doctrine. . . . Justification declares that all who believe in Jesus Christ belong at the same table, no matter what their cultural or racial differences (and, let's face it, a good many denominational distinctions, and indeed distinctions within a single denomination, boil down more to culture than to doctrine)" (*What Saint Paul Really Said*, pp. 158-59, emphasis original).

Christ, any sectarian allegiance superseding that common allegiance to Christ, disrupts the peace of Christ within the church and frustrates the purpose of the cross to reconcile us in Christ, to one another and to God, "in one body." And when the peace among Christians is disrupted by exclusive identity and sectarian allegiance, the common good and common mission of the church is hindered (cf. 1 Corinthians 12). James Dunn:

> The identity of the *Christian* assembly as "body" . . . is given not by geographical location or political allegiance [or by race, social status, or gender, Dunn notes] but by their common allegiance to *Christ* (visibly expressed not least in baptism and the sacramental sharing in his body). The implication is clear that only when that common allegiance is given primacy in mutual relations can the potential factional differences be transformed into the necessary mutual cooperation for the common good.[24]

Sadly, the problem of faction and disunity persisted in the church at Corinth. Only forty years later (c. AD 96), Clement, Bishop of Rome, would also write to the Corinthians to address "the odious and unholy breach of unity among you, which is quite incompatible with God's chosen people" (*1 Clement* 1:1).[25] Clement knew Paul's letter to the Corinthians and the problem of factions that had divided the church generations earlier, and so he exhorts them to re-read Paul's call for unity among the believers (*1 Clement* 47). The problem of division that Clement addresses had been caused by a small faction ("a few hotheaded and unruly individuals") in the church that had ousted the local bishop, clergy, and deacon, who had been commissioned by the Apostles and had served faithfully for many years. This faction had then established their own leaders apart from the "apostolic succession" (chs. 37–44). Clement exhorts the believers in Corinth to respect the authority of the Apostles, who were commissioned by Christ himself, and to restore communion among themselves and with the rest of the body of Christ, which they have sundered by their insubordination to apostolic authority. Clement's exhortation to ecclesial unity echoes Paul's:

> Why must there be all this quarrelling and bad blood, these feuds and dissension among you? Have we not all the same God, and the same Christ? Is not the same Spirit of grace shed upon us all? Have we not all the same calling in Christ? Then why are we tearing asunder the limbs of Christ, and fomenting discord against our own body? (46:5-7)

24. Dunn, *Theology of Paul*, pp. 551-52.
25. Quotations from *1 Clement* are from Maxwell Staniforth and Andrew Louth, trans., *Early Christian Writings* (London: Penguin Books, 1987), pp. 23-50.

Clement concludes his call for unity by observing that ecclesial disunity is bad evangelism, a scandal to the gospel preached in the name of Jesus: "Even those who do not share our faith have heard this report, as well as ourselves; so that your thoughtlessness has brought the name of the Lord into disrespect" (47:7).

The problem of Christian disunity must not be misunderstood. The scandal here is no more about the diversity of denominations among Protestant Christians than it is about the diversity of religious orders among Catholic Christians. Diversity is not the issue, but disunity. The scandal of disunity is manifest chiefly in a divided communion table, the fact that Christian believers who have shared in one baptism are at present unable to gather with integrity as one body around the one table of the one Lord, Jesus Christ. Paul's concern for the church at Corinth (1 Cor 1:10-17) was precisely that factions had caused divisions at the communion table — the "Paulists," "Apollonians," "Cephites," and "Christians" were no longer coming together to celebrate the Lord's Supper as one body (11:17-34).

Paul's concern for a united communion table within the one body of Christ is reflected a couple generations later in the letters of Ignatius, Bishop of Antioch (c. AD 110). Ignatius repeatedly warned the churches of Asia Minor against all manner of partisanship and factions within the church and exhorted them to maintain sound teaching and ecclesial unity. The following citation is typical: "Allow nothing whatever to exist among you that could give rise to any divisions; maintain absolute unity with your bishop and leaders, as an example to others and a lesson in the avoidance of corruption" (*Magnesians* 6:2).[26] Ignatius was keenly aware that factions within the churches had led to divisions of the communion table. Some were excluding themselves from the one celebration of the Eucharist and were instead appointing separate leaders to celebrate a separate Eucharist at a separate communion table. Ignatius exhorted the churches to maintain a unified communion table, because it is an essential expression of unity in Christ under the authority of properly ordained leadership:

> Make certain, therefore, that you all observe one common Eucharist; for there is but one Body of our Lord Jesus Christ, and but one cup of union with his Blood, and one single altar of sacrifice — even as also there is but one bishop, with his clergy and my own fellow-servitors the deacons. This will ensure that all your doings are in full accord with the will of God. (*Philadelphians* 4:1)[27]

What concerned Paul and Ignatius is not at all foreign to us. If you have ever worshipped in a congregation of different denomination and found your-

26. *Early Christian Writings*, p. 72. Cf. *Ephesians* 4–5; *Magnesians* 1, 6–7; *Trallians* 6–7; *Philadelphians* 1–8; *Smyrnaeans* 8; *Polycarp* 1.

27. *Early Christian Writings*, p. 94. Cf. *Ephesians* 5; *Magnesians* 7; *Smyrnaeans* 8.

self in the pew wondering whether or not you could or should take communion with your brothers and sisters in Christ gathered around you, then you have experienced for yourself the very division that so concerned the Apostles and Apostolic Fathers. This division does not concern differences between denominations as such, but rather the question of *identity and belonging*. Notice how Paul describes the factions at Corinth: "'I am of Paul,' 'I am of Apollos,' 'I am of Cephas,' 'I am of Christ'" (1 Cor 1:12, my translation). When we sit in the pew wondering whether to take communion or not in a congregation of a denomination other than our own, we are asking implicitly, "Do I *belong* to this communion? Am I (a member) *of* this body?" The very fact that this question of identity and belonging arises in the mind at the invitation to communion is a symptom of the division within the church with which I am concerned.

The fullest visible expression of ecclesial unity, of mutual belonging to and with one another in Christ, is fellowship in the Lord's Supper — as one body, at one table. Community in Christ is expressed visibly by communion in the bread and cup, which is no less than a communal "sharing" *(koinonia)* in the body and blood of Christ (1 Cor 10:16). Partaking together of the one bread and the one cup both symbolizes and realizes our unity as a body: "Because there is one bread, we who are many are one body, for we all partake of the one bread" (v. 17). By communing in the bread and the cup, the body and blood of Christ, we commune in Christ; by the ritual action of partaking together in communion, we proclaim the truth sealed in our baptism, that we "are all one in Christ Jesus" (Gal 3:28).

The church's communion rite is not only an act of *thanksgiving* to God for the gift of grace through the life, death, and resurrection of Christ on our behalf, but is also an act of *peacemaking* among the members of Christ's body — the ancient Eucharistic liturgy includes an exchange of peace immediately prior to partaking of the bread and cup. The Lord's Supper is thus both sign and realization of our unity and peace with God and with our brothers and sisters who have been baptized "into Christ." If we Christians cannot approach one communion table as one body, then our exchange of peace with one another does not tell the whole truth despite our best intentions. That Christians cannot gather in unity at the communion table is the most telling sign of the "missing peace" in the body of Christ. The chief manifestation of ecclesial disunity is thus a divided table, which betrays to the world that Christians have failed to "maintain the unity of the Spirit in the bond of peace" (Eph 4:3). If the Christians of the world were to agree among themselves not to kill each other, it would be more than a modest contribution to world peace. Of what ultimate good would that peace be to the world, however, if Christians still cannot agree to fellowship in peace with each other at the communion table?

I cannot but agree with Walter Kasper, former President of the Pontifical Council for Promoting Christian Unity, that this division is both a painful wound in Christ's body and a scandal before a watching world that knows its own brokenness all too well. A divided communion table in the church is a counter-witness to the gospel of peace in a broken world and thus a stumbling block to faith in Christ. Cardinal Kasper writes:

> The reality in which we live is not a place of unshattered calm. The reality in which we live is characterized by conflicts, where unity is impaired and broken, and this reality cries out for healing and reconciliation.
>
> The biblical texts emphasize the connection between Eucharist and unity, Eucharist and church. The fact that fidelity to the truth makes it impossible in today's situation for all Christians to meet around the one table of the Lord and take part in the Supper of the Lord is a deep wound inflicted on the Body of the Lord, it is scandalous.[28]

Precisely because there is one Lord, one baptism, and one body, there is therefore to be only one table of communion. In light of Jesus' prayer "that they may all be one" (John 17:21), this present reality of division sets the ultimate aim and hope of ecumenical peacemaking — a single, all-inclusive table of communion with and in Christ. Given that "For the sake of the truth, it is not possible in today's situation for all Christians to gather around the one table of the Lord and partake of his one Supper," Cardinal Kasper appropriately sets the ecumenical hope of restored unity at the communion table against the eschatological horizon of God's salvation: "The goal of ecumenism, that all the disciples of Christ should assemble around the one table of the Lord, sharing in the one bread a drinking from the one cup, belongs to God's great plan of salvation."[29]

A church that would witness to the world concerning the gospel of God's salvation and peace in Christ must be *both* evangelical *and* ecumenical; indeed, we must be ecumenical in order to be evangelical. Through Christ and the message of the cross we are called to make peace with one another within the church for the sake of the gospel of Christ crucified. Through Christ and the power of the cross we are enabled by the gift of the Holy Spirit to break down walls of division between Christians before a watching world. Thus may the people of all nations — long divided by nationality, race, gender, and class — see a living, embodied sign of the reality of reconciliation with God through the peacemaking cross of Jesus Christ.[30]

---

28. Walter Cardinal Kasper, *Sacrament of Unity: The Eucharist and the Church* (New York: Herder & Herder, 2004), p. 9.

29. Kasper, *Sacrament of Unity*, pp. 143, 149.

30. Of course, many questions and obstacles remain to restoration of Christian unity, not least differing theological understandings concerning the Eucharist and differing conceptions of what institutional form a reunited church would take. For a clear presentation of the Roman Catholic position on such matters, see Kasper, *Sacrament of Unity*.

PART IV

"Redeemed for Good Works"

The Cross and Mission

CHAPTER 34

God's Purpose, Christ's Cross, the Church's Mission

You are worthy to take the scroll and to open its seals,
for you were slaughtered
and by your blood you ransomed for God
saints from every tribe and language and nation;
you have made them to be a kingdom
and priests serving our God.

REVELATION 5:9-10

We have sought to understand the cross in a way that integrates atonement, justice, and peace. Much of our study has proceeded by inductive examination and careful exegesis of biblical texts. Along the way, we have drawn implications for how we think about the cross of Christ as the revelation of God's justice-doing and peace-making — and, hence, how we should think about Christian justice-doing and peacemaking in light of the cross. As we approach the end of our study, we want to step back and take a wide-angle view of the cross of Christ in connection with the redemptive purpose of God and the evangelical mission of the church.[1]

34.1. God's Purpose: Redemption of the World

We seek to show how God's redemptive purpose, Christ's cruciform work, and the church's evangelical mission are an integral whole.[2] We might express this

---

1. What we seek to do here regarding the cross, N. T. Wright has done regarding the resurrection. See his *Surprised by Hope: Rethinking Heaven, the Resurrection, and the Mission of the Church* (New York: HarperCollins, 2008).

2. We thus follow the path of thinking found in Christian writers of earlier centuries —

point from any of three angles. God's purpose to redeem the world, worked in and through the life, death, and resurrection of Christ, continues in and through the mission of the church. The message of the cross concerns God's will to redeem humanity and the cosmos for the sake of God's love for his creation. The church, having been redeemed in Christ for God, is commissioned into service for God's purpose following Christ's cruciform example. We will unpack this angle by angle.

Several New Testament writers bear witness that God's redemptive purpose is the guiding aim of the Incarnation of Christ. According to John's Gospel, God, out of his great love for the world he created, sends Jesus into the world in order to bring about God's purpose of redeeming the world:

> For God so loved the world that he gave his only Son, *so that (hōste)* everyone who believes in him may not perish but may have eternal life. Indeed, God did not send the Son into the world to condemn *(krinō)* the world, but *in order that (hina)* the world might be saved through him. (John 3:16-17)

Jesus himself echoes this mission statement — "I came not to judge *(krinō)* the world, but to save the world" (John 12:47b). The purpose of God sending the Son into the world was neither that the Son might condemn sinners nor simply that the Son might die, John writes, but in order that a world in sin might be saved through the Son.

Paul proclaims a similar message: "God sent his Son, born of a woman, born under the law, *in order to (hina)* redeem those who were under the law, *so that (hina)* we might receive adoption as children" (Gal 4:4-5). Jesus is born, not just so that he might die, Paul writes, but in order that he might bring about God's purpose to redeem his covenant people. So also the writer of Hebrews:

> Since, therefore, the children share flesh and blood, he himself likewise shared the same things, *so that (hina)* through death he might destroy the one who has the power of death, that is, the devil, and free those who all their lives were held in slavery by the fear of death. (Heb 2:14-15)

Irenaeus, Athanasius, and Anselm. Peter Schmiechen, *Saving Power: Theories of Atonement and Forms of the Church* (Grand Rapids, MI: Eerdmans Publishing, 2005), contrasts views of atonement that consider only the relation between God and humanity (e.g., penal substitution) and views of atonement that consider the God-humanity relationship with respect to the purposes of God in the world: "when the purposes of God are introduced . . . there are three points for the theological framework: God, the world, and God's purposes. In this framework the question becomes: What is God doing in the world and how can I/we participate in that purpose for the glory of God? This is a radically different approach to the gospel and provides a broader vision for understanding the work of Christ" (p. 323).

Jesus shares flesh and blood, not for the sole purpose of dying, but for the purpose of destroying the power of death and setting humanity free from slavery to fear of death.

We should take careful notice here of the *motive* and the *means* of God's redemption. Both John and Paul testify that God's redemption of the world is *motivated* simply and solely out of love. John's gospel proclamation begins, "For God so loved the world . . ." (John 3:16). John writes again: "God's love was revealed among us in this way: God sent his only Son into the world so that we might live through him" (1 John 4:9). Where John writes of the Incarnation in general as God's expression of love for the world, Paul depicts the cross in particular as God's demonstration of love "for us." In Romans, Paul writes: "But God proves his love for us in that while we were still sinners Christ died for us" (Rom 5:8). In similar terms, Paul writes of redemption from sin and death through Christ: "But God, who is rich in mercy, out of the great love with which he loved us even when we were dead through our trespasses, made us alive together with Christ" (Eph 2:4-5). It is God's own steadfast love that moves God's action to redeem the world and humanity in Christ.

God's redemption, therefore, is not because of any legal requirement or divine deficit, as if God were not sovereign but subject to external necessity or internal need. God does not act to redeem the world in Christ because the law of retribution requires satisfaction or because the wrath of God demands propitiation. God acts freely to redeem the world in Christ on account of and for the sake of his own steadfast and abundant love for his creation and his creatures.

34.2. Christ's Cross: The Means of Redemption

The New Testament writers agree also that the cross of Christ is not the aim but the *means* of God's redemptive purpose. The writer of Hebrews: ". . . so that *through death (dia tou thanatou)* he might destroy the one who has the power of death . . . and free those . . . held in slavery by the fear of death" (Heb 2:14-15). Jesus' death is the *means,* not the aim, of his mission — the *aim* is victory and liberation. Paul uses similar phrasing three different times to make clear that Jesus' death is not God's aim but the means of bringing about God's purpose. In Romans, he uses parallel phrases: ". . . we have been justified *by his blood (en tō haimati autou)* . . . we were reconciled to God *through the death (dia tou thanatou)* of his Son" (Rom 5:9-10). Jesus' death ("his blood") is not the aim, but the *means* of God's demonstration of love — the *aim* is justification and reconciliation. In Ephesians:

> For he is our peace; in his flesh he has broken down the dividing wall, that is, the hostility between us. He has abolished the law with its commandments

and ordinances, that he might create in himself one new humanity in place
of the two, thus making peace, and might reconcile both groups to God in
one body *through the cross (dia tou staurou)*, thus putting to death that hostility in himself. (Eph 2:14-16)

Paul depicts the cross as the *means*, not the aim, of God's peacemaking — Jesus
makes peace *by means of* putting to death inter-human hostility in his own
body through the cross, but the *aim* is peace and unity. Again: "through him
God was pleased to reconcile to himself all things, whether on earth or in
heaven, by making peace *through the blood of his cross (dia tou haimatos tou
staurou autou)*" (Col 1:19-20). And again, Jesus' death on the cross is not God's
aim, but the *means* of God's purpose — God's redemptive *aim* is the cosmic
reconciliation of "all things."

The cross of Christ, therefore, is not an end in itself, as if Jesus were born
just so that he might die, as if Jesus' death, isolated from both his life-ministry
and his resurrection, were the entire point of the Incarnation. The Incarnation
— Jesus' birth, ministry, death, and resurrection — is an integral whole with a
single missional aim, God's redemption of the world. To suppose that Jesus'
death in itself is the aim of the Incarnation is to sever the cross from the overarching purpose of God and so empty it of redemptive meaning and saving
power.[3] Nor does being saved concern our receiving forgiveness of sin and
promise of life as an end in itself, as if Jesus dies on the cross just so that we
might have our sins forgiven and escape hell when we die (as popular evangelism presents the gospel).[4] Jesus dies "for us," but the cross is not all about "us."
God's redemption of humanity is ultimately about who God is and for the sake
of God's own purpose. God acts "for us and for our salvation" through the life,
death, and resurrection of Jesus in order to bring about God's redemptive purpose in a manner faithful to God's personal character. The upshot here is that
neither the cross of Christ *nor* the salvation of humanity through the cross is an
end in itself; rather, *both* are for God's purpose of bringing about the redemption of the world.

John and Paul thus emphasize that God's purpose does not end in either
the cross of Christ or the salvation of humanity, but aims toward the redemp-

---

3. Cf. David Brondos, *Paul on the Cross: Reconstructing the Apostle's Story of Redemption*
(Minneapolis, MN: Fortress Press, 2006), pp. x-xi: "what Paul *did* teach is that *by means of*
Christ's death God has saved and redeemed human beings and has reconciled them to himself.
This is not a matter of splitting hairs. . . . [F]or Paul, Jesus' death is certainly salvific and re-
demptive, but not *in itself*, and not through any 'effects' it has. Rather, *it is salvific and redemp-
tive only in that it forms part of a story*" (emphasis original).

4. Dallas Willard, *The Divine Conspiracy: Rediscovering Our Hidden Life in God* (San Francisco: HarperSanFrancisco, 1997), pp. 35-50, appropriately critiques the evangelical penal substitution doctrine in popular preaching as a "gospel of sin management."

tion of the *cosmos,* toward the reconciliation of *all things.* John proclaims that "God so loved the world *(ton kosmon)*" that he sent the Son "into the world," not in order to "condemn the world," but that "the world *(ho kosmos)* might be saved through him *(di' autou)*" (John 3:16-17). The Incarnation is all about God's plan of salvation for the entire cosmos, and Christ is God's way of cosmic salvation: Christ lived, died, and was raised so that the cosmos might be saved. Paul likewise proclaims that the cross of Christ and the salvation of humanity belong to God's "plan for the fullness of time, to gather up all things *(ta panta)* in him *(en autō),* things in heaven and things on earth" (Eph 1:10). The cross of Christ is the means of God's plan "to reconcile to himself all things *(ta panta),* whether on earth or in heaven" (Col 1:20). The cross of Christ is all about God's plan of pan-reconciliation, and Christ is God's way of pan-reconciliation: Christ lived, died, and was raised so that "all things" might be reconciled to God. These gospel proclamations, which echo the prophetic vision of the Old Testament (Isaiah 65–66), converge with the apocalyptic vision consummating the New Testament. In "the end," God's purpose in Christ is not only the healing of humanity from sin, suffering, and death, but the bringing forth of "a new heaven and a new earth" (Rev 21:1-4; cf. 2 Pet 3:1-13). God's redemptive purpose reaches its ultimate end in "making all things *(panta)* new" (Rev 21:5-6). Cosmic salvation, pan-reconciliation, new creation — this is the full gospel of God's purpose, the eschatological horizon of the life, death, and resurrection of Jesus Christ.[5]

34.3. The Church's Mission: Ransomed for Service

What, then, is our part in God's plan? We are redeemed in Christ so that, as was Christ, we also might be commissioned to serve God's purpose to redeem the world. God's redemptive purpose in Christ is now to be worked also in and through a holy people devoted wholly to God's work. Jesus "gave himself for us," Paul writes, not only "that he might redeem us from all iniquity," but also that he might "purify for himself a people of his own who are zealous for good deeds" (Tit 2:14). What Paul expresses here in terms of redemption, he expresses elsewhere in terms of new creation: "For we are what he has made us, created in Christ Jesus for good works, which God prepared beforehand to be our way of life" (Eph 2:10). God's purpose worked in and through the life, death, and resurrection of Christ is now to be worked also by our doing the work that God has prepared for us to do.

The "us" here is the church, the believing community whose members were formerly alienated from God and hostile toward one another but are now

---

5. Cf. Wright, *Surprised by Hope.*

reconciled "in Christ." The message of the enmity-destroying, enemy-reconciling cross reveals that God purposed to create the church in and through Christ to be a dwelling for God's presence and a servant of God's purpose (Eph 2:11–3:13). God's reconciling work in and through Christ is intended to continue in and through the church, to whom God has given "the ministry of reconciliation" and entrusted "the message of reconciliation" (2 Cor 5:18-20). The purpose of God's redemption of us in Christ is our participation in God's work of world reconciliation.

Paul expresses our "redemption in Christ" also with the phrase "you were bought *(ēgorasthēte)* with a price" (1 Cor 6:20; 7:23). The Revelation of John likewise uses this language to describe the redemption of the church: ". . . you were slaughtered and by your blood you ransomed *(ēgorasas)* for God saints from every tribe and language and people and nation; you have made them to be a kingdom and priests serving our God" (Rev 5:9-10). The verb *agorazō* ("buy" or "purchase") is market-place language, the *agora* being the central open market of a Greek city. In this context the word signifies the price one pays to purchase the rights to another person ("ransom") — Christ has "purchased" for God the "rights" to us at the price of his life ("by your blood").[6]

The implication of the metaphor is that, by Christ having redeemed or "purchased" us "for God," a transfer of ownership has taken place: we now belong to God. Who was our previous owner? In human pride, we would like to say that we were our own, that we were masters of ourselves but have now chosen to join ourselves to a new Master. Paul, however, depicts us as having been *slaves (douloi)* of sin needing to be freed (Rom 6:17-18). The metaphorical imagery of being "purchased" by God thus suggests a slave market: God "purchased" us at the slave market, thus setting us free from our previous master, sin. Christ did not "purchase" us "by his blood" and set us free from sin simply for our own sake, however, but "for God" (Rev 5:9). We have been redeemed from slavery, not so that we might now be masters of ourselves, but so that we might be the slaves of God (Rom 6:22). Having been redeemed in Christ from slavery to sin, God is now our Master, that we might serve not our own purpose but God's purpose: we are redeemed in Christ "to be a kingdom and priests

6. Because such language can be easily misunderstood by being taken in a too literal way, we repeat this caveat: language depicting Jesus' death as the "price" or "cost" of God's redemption of humanity is better taken metaphorically, not literally. We must be careful not to interpret Jesus' death as a "price" God "paid" to anyone or anything, as if God were under obligation to some higher law (the law of retribution) or in debt to some other power or personality (the devil) in the cosmos. The sovereign God does not "owe" anyone for anything; no one has "rights" to anything exclusive of God and to which God must secure by an "exchange." A literal interpretation of the cross as the "price" or "cost" of salvation undermines God's sovereignty: God-in-Christ freely and willingly, not out of any necessity or under any obligation or debt, bears the burden of our sin and accepts the cost of our redemption.

serving our God" (Rev 5:10). And we are to serve God our Master by becoming "slaves of justice" (Rom 6:18).[7]

In telling of "redemption in Christ," Paul depicts the purpose of Jesus' death "for us" in terms of our new life of service to God using two expressions, "so that" (or "in order that") and "therefore." Jesus dies "for us" in two senses: *in order to* set us free from sin and reconcile us to God, *so that* we might willingly take our part as obedient servants of God's purpose. Paul makes this point several times, perhaps no more clearly than this: "And he died for all, *so that* they who live might live no longer for themselves but for him who died and was raised for them" (2 Cor 5:15). Jesus gave himself "for all," not so that we might continue living a self-serving life, but so that we might live a self-giving life of service "for Christ." Peter expresses the same thought: "He himself bore our sins in his body on the cross, *so that*, free from sins, we might live for righteousness" (1 Pet 2:24). We are freed from sin through Jesus' death *so that* we might devote ourselves to God's justice. The purpose of being redeemed in Christ is that God's purpose in Christ might be our own. Jesus does not die "for us" as our substitute in God's plan, taking our place in God's work of salvation so as to make unnecessary our active participation. To the contrary, Jesus dies "for us" precisely so that we might take up our part in God's purpose.

Paul also uses the language of sacrifice to express this linkage between Jesus' death "for us" and our life "for Christ" in service of God's purpose. Jesus' dying voluntarily "for us" is the ground of Paul's instructing us "therefore" to give our lives sacrificially to God for the sake of others. He exhorts the believing community to offer up the very bodies of its members as a "living sacrifice" to God (Rom 12:1). The "living sacrifice" we are to present to God as our "reasonable worship," Paul writes elsewhere, is to be patterned after Jesus' own free-will sacrifice to God: "*Therefore* be imitators of God, as beloved children, and live in love, as Christ loved us and gave himself up for us, a fragrant offering and sacrifice to God" (Eph 5:1-2). We are to live and die as Jesus lived and died; as Jesus freely and self-sacrificially gave himself to God out of love "for us," so also are we freely and self-sacrificially to give ourselves to God through loving service for others.[8]

---

7. For a more extensive examination of the redemption/purchase motif in the New Testament, see John Driver, *Understanding the Atonement for the Mission of the Church* (Scottdale, PA: Herald Press, 1986), chapter 9.

8. Our previous remarks concerning necessity and God's action for our salvation need to be reprised here. Jesus offers his life to God, not out of external necessity as an obligatory sacrifice, but freely and willingly. Jesus sacrifices himself for our sake not because the law of retribution requires his death for "satisfaction" or because God's wrath demands his death for "propitiation." Rather, as the Gospels testify, Jesus freely lays down his life in self-sacrifice for us because of his whole-life devotion and surrender to God's will and, hence, his love for us whom God loves and desires to save.

Notice two things here concerning Paul's language of sacrifice. First, Paul exhorts us to present *our own bodies (sōmata)* as a living sacrifice to God (Rom 12:1). Rather than depicting Jesus as "taking our place" in the sacrificial offering that is "holy and acceptable to God," rather than exhorting us to present the body of a substitute as a sacrifice in our name, Paul emphasizes that our *bodily participation* is essential to the sacrificial service that God desires from us. Our living sacrifice to God, second, is to be patterned after the self-giving ministry of Jesus, who freely gave himself in whole-life service to God for our sake. Far from seeing Jesus' death "for us" as a substitution making unnecessary the sacrifice of ourselves to God, Paul sees Jesus' self-sacrificial life and death as the mandate and model for our self-sacrificial service to God and others. When Paul instructs us to (literally) "walk in love even as Christ loved us" (Eph 5:2, my translation), he uses the imperative mood: we are mandated to walk the way of whole-life, self-giving love that Christ walked and modeled for us in life and death.[9]

Jesus Christ is the one we are called to "follow" and to "imitate" (1 Cor 11:1). As we actively take our part in God's purpose, therefore, Jesus is our leader *(archēgos)* and exemplar, the one who goes before us in the way of the cross to show us the way of faith in which we are to go (Heb 12:1-3). The way of following Jesus is thus inescapably marked by the cross, as Jesus himself says (Mark 8:34). Peter also points to the cross of Christ as the example we are called to imitate, proclaiming that "Christ suffered for [us]" on the cross for the purpose of "leaving [us] an example" of how to "follow in his steps" (1 Pet 2:21-23). The Greek word "example" *(hypogrammos)* that Peter uses here means literally a "model" or "pattern" to be copied. Jesus' death "for us," as witnessed in Scripture, is the model or pattern for the holy mission to which God has called us.

Notice here which aspect of Jesus' cruciform example that Peter emphasizes — Jesus' refusal to pay back evil for evil and his trust in God for salvation and justice: "When he was abused, he did not return abuse; when he suffered, he did not threaten; but he entrusted himself to the one who judges justly" (v. 23). Peter thus implies that Jesus' non-retributive, non-retaliatory response to the injustice and violence he suffered through the cross is integral to his exemplary action. *The retribution-renouncing, God-trusting cross of Christ is the*

---

9. Regarding participation and imitation as key elements of Christian discipleship emphasized by New Testament writers, see John Howard Yoder, *The Politics of Jesus: Vicit Agnus Noster* (Grand Rapids, MI: Eerdmans Publishing, 1972), chapter 7; Stanley Hauerwas, *The Peaceable Kingdom: A Primer in Christian Ethics* (Notre Dame, IN: University of Notre Dame Press, 1983), pp. 72-81; Richard B. Hays, *The Moral Vision of the New Testament: A Contemporary Introduction to New Testament Ethics* (New York: HarperCollins Publishers, 1996), pp. 27-32; Luke Timothy Johnson, *Living Jesus: Learning the Heart of the Gospel* (San Francisco: HarperSanFrancisco, 1989); and Willard M. Swartley, *Covenant of Peace: The Missing Peace in New Testament Theology and Ethics* (Grand Rapids, MI: Eerdmans Publishing, 2006), chapters 13 and 15.

paradigm that God calls us to imitate. Peter then instructs us that to "follow in [Christ's] steps" and to live our holy calling entails, not only that we renounce retribution, but also that we transcend cycles of retaliation and act for reconciliation: "Do not repay evil for evil or abuse for abuse; but, on the contrary, repay with a blessing. It is for this you were called — that you might inherit a blessing" (3:9). And he goes on to explain that we receive the blessing of our calling by imitating Jesus — by speaking the truth, repaying good for evil, and seeking the way of peace and pursuing it (vv. 10-12).[10]

10. Regarding Jesus as "paradigm" for Christian ethics, see Hays, *Moral Vision*, pp. 208-9, 293-96, and 339-40, and Johnson, *Living Jesus*, pp. 45-51.

CHAPTER 35

─────────────

The Christian Commission to Holy Resistance

He it is who gave himself for us
that he might redeem us from all iniquity
and purify for himself a people of his own
who are zealous for good deeds.

TITUS 2:14

35.1. The Spiritual Discipline of Holy Zealotry

To put the point we have been developing succinctly and provocatively, God has redeemed us in Christ for *holy zealotry!* — to be "a people of his own who are zealous for good works" (Tit 2:14). The zealotry to which we are called and for which we have been set apart by God is whole-life commitment to God's redemptive purpose. As such, the holy zealotry of the redeemed of God is to be patterned after God's own covenant love and righteousness as demonstrated faithfully through the life, death, and resurrection of Jesus. Jesus Christ is the paradigm of holy zealotry. Redeemed for holy zealotry in the service of God's redemptive purpose, therefore, we are called to imitate Christ by following him in life and death, through cross and resurrection — in the way of faithful witness and suffering service, the way of doing justice and making peace, the way of victory and liberation. Christian mission should thus align in motive, means, and aim with God's work in and through Jesus Christ: the motive is love, the means is cruciform, and the aim is redemption.

Cruciform mission calls the church, therefore, to the spiritual discipline of moral discernment even as it calls us into the real-world struggle of good and evil. Christian mission must discern between the holy zealotry of Christ —

616

which is loving, cruciform, and redemptive — and the human zealotry that identifies and destroys enemies for the cause of "defending life" or "securing liberty" or "executing justice" or "making peace" or "saving the nation."[1] Human zealotry does not produce God's justice (Jas 1:20). We thus need to discern between the carnal warfare of the world, waged against human enemies with physical weapons, and the holy warfare of the church, waged neither against human enemies nor with physical weapons.

Paul emphasizes this crucial need for discernment in his exhortation that we prepare for holy warfare by armoring ourselves with the weapons and defense of God:

> Finally, be strong in the Lord and in the strength of his power. Put on the whole armor of God, so that you may be able to stand against the wiles of the devil. For our struggle is not against enemies of blood and flesh, but against the rulers, against the authorities, against the cosmic powers of this present darkness, against the spiritual forces of evil in the heavenly places. Therefore take up the whole armor of God, so that you may be able to withstand on that evil day, and having done everything, to stand firm. Stand therefore, and fasten the belt of truth around your waist, and put on the breastplate of righteousness [justice]. As shoes for your feet put on whatever will make you ready to proclaim the gospel of peace. With all of these take the shield of faith, with which you will be able to quench all the flaming arrows of the evil one. Take the helmet of salvation, and the sword of the Spirit, which is the word of God. Pray in the Spirit at all times in every prayer and supplication. To that end keep alert and always persevere in supplication for all the saints. (Eph 6:10-18)[2]

Notice, first, that Paul, in contrasting holy zealotry with human zealotry, depicts holy zealotry as nothing less than real *warfare*. Paul does not counsel the church to take up a "quietist" posture or exhort us only to "hold out" and "endure" until warfare has ended. The Greek verb "stand against *(antistēnai)*" (v. 11) is military terminology, meaning literally "fight" or "resist." The imagery of Paul's language is neither that of "a separate peace" apart from the conflict, nor that of a withdrawal from the conflict, nor that of entrenchment and defense against an assault, but rather offensive action — *advance* and *confrontation*.[3] We are called to

---

1. See my essay, "Tragic Zeal: The Spiral of Violence, Vengeance and Death," *The Mennonite*, September 7, 2004, pp. 16-17. Regarding Jesus and the Zealots of his own day, see John Howard Yoder, *The Original Revolution: Essays on Christian Pacifism* (Scottdale, PA: Herald Press, 1971), pp. 21-24, and "The Way of Peace in a World at War," in *He Came Preaching Peace* (Scottdale, PA: Herald Press, 1985), pp. 17-29.

2. My take on this text has been helpfully informed by Thomas R. Yoder Neufeld, *Ephesians* (Believers Church Bible Commentary; Scottdale, PA: Herald Press, 2002), pp. 290-316.

3. One might want to argue that Paul's intent here is defensive preparation, pointing to the

be *militant* — to stand against and resist the enemy, the "army of the Lord" vis-à-vis "rulers and authorities," "cosmic powers of darkness," and "spiritual forces of evil."

Notice, second, that we are to take up *God's* armor in this battle, not our own. And the injunction to take up the armor of God implies that this battle already belongs to God, not to us: it is God and God alone who gives victory. Nonetheless, this is our vocation, worthy of our holy calling in Christ (Eph 4:1). It is therefore a privileged duty of our citizenship in the household of God (2:19) to participate with God in the holy struggle for truth and justice (cf. Isa 59:1-20) and to do so with God's own armory. The church is thus not only called to be God's messenger of peace, but is also commissioned to be God's *holy warrior!* Hence, the church is to proclaim the gospel of salvation, justice, and peace, not only from the pulpit to the pews, but also in the streets and the public square, the very places where truth and justice have been trampled (Isa 59:14). The church is to pursue an active peace rather than a passive peace: a *wise* peace that confronts "rulers and authorities" with "the wisdom of God" (Eph 3:10; cf. Matt 10:16), a *truthful* peace that exposes "the unfruitful works of darkness" to the light of God's truth (Eph 5:11), a *just* peace that walks in the way of righteousness and holiness that we learned from Christ (4:17-24), and a *reconciling* peace that bears witness to God's purpose to "gather all things" in Christ (1:10).

35.2. Christian Resistance and the Powers of Evil[4]

Some readers may think that, by exhorting the church to wage a war of resistance against evil, Paul's ethic conflicts with that of Jesus. After all, Jesus calls his disciples to a way of non-resistant love of enemies (Matt 5:38-48). Indeed, Paul seems to command us to do exactly what Jesus commands us not to do: to "resist" or "fight" *(antistēnai),* while Jesus says "do not resist" or "do not fight" *(mē antistēnai).* Is this a contradiction? No, and that it is not will teach us something crucial for the mission of the church.

Jesus commands: "Do not resist an evildoer *(tō ponērō)*" (Matt 5:39). The Greek expression *tō ponērō* here implies a personal agent — "the one who does evil." The same expression appears in the Lord's Prayer: "rescue us from the evil

---

"shield of faith" as evidence. In ancient Greek warfare, however, the shield did not serve a merely defensive purpose. The armies of Sparta, for example, fought in phalanx formation, marching on enemy lines in companies of soldiers standing shoulder-to-shoulder, their body-length shields forming an overlapping wall enabling them to advance even under an onslaught of incoming fire.

4. This section is elaborated from my essay "How Can the Battle Be Won? War Rhetoric Makes False Assumptions about Good, Evil," *Mennonite Weekly Review,* March 10, 2003.

one *(tou ponērou)"* (6:13). That Jesus means to refer to personal agents is made clear in what follows: "But if anyone strikes you . . . and if anyone wants to sue you . . . and if anyone forces you . . ." (5:39-41). Jesus commands that we are not to "resist" or "fight against" human evildoers by returning evil "in kind." Paul also makes clear that "our struggle is not against enemies of blood and flesh." Rather, we are to "stand against" or resist ". . . the rulers . . . the authorities . . . the cosmic powers of this present darkness . . . the spiritual forces of evil in the heavenly places" (Eph 6:12).

Jesus and Paul are consistent, therefore. Taken together they teach non-retaliatory resistance — resistance without retaliation, resisting evil without reciprocating evil for evil. Do *not* fight against human evildoers, flesh-and-blood enemies, but pray for them and trust God for deliverance and vindication (Matt 5:44; 6:13; Rom 12:14-21; cf. Psalm 37).[5] Yet *do* put up a (non-retaliatory) resistance against the systems of violence, structures of oppression, powers of darkness, and forces of evil that really dominate humanity and the cosmos.[6] The ethics of Jesus and Paul are not only compatible, but complementary. We are not to fight with retaliatory resistance against human evildoers, flesh-and-blood enemies, but instead to pray for them, precisely because the real struggle is against "rulers and authorities," "cosmic powers of darkness," and "spiritual forces of evil," which exercise dominion over ourselves as much as over our putative enemies.[7]

Understanding how the respective ethics of Jesus and Paul are complementary requires seeing more deeply into the reality of evil than identifying human evildoers and naming individual evildoing. In the Pauline worldview, evil is not only individual human evildoing, but is manifest in manifold forms that can dominate humanity. Paul speaks not only of the sinful acts that individuals do ("injustice and impiety," Rom 1:18) but also of evil manifest in various forms that are: social, involving humanity collectively ("rulers and authorities," *archas* and *exousias*); cosmic, involving more than humanity ("cosmic powers of this

---

5. That we are not to resist evildoers by evil means prompts the perennial ethical question, "What would you do if . . . ?" See the excellent discussion in John H. Yoder, *What Would You Do? A Serious Answer to a Standard Question*, expanded ed. (Scottdale, PA: Herald Press, 1992). A consistent ethical practice of non-retaliatory resistance to evil certainly cannot stand apart from communal commitment and spiritual formation (see Chapter 31 above).

6. Concerning Jesus' command "Do not resist an evildoer" and active (non-retaliatory) resistance to evil, see Dorothy Jean Weaver, "Transforming Nonresistance: From *Lex Talionis* to 'Do Not Resist the Evil One,'" in Willard M. Swartley, ed., *The Love of Enemy and Nonretaliation in the New Testament* (Louisville, KY: Westminster John Knox Press, 1992), pp. 32-71 (esp. pp. 55-57), and Walter Wink, "Neither Passivity Nor Violence: Jesus' Third Way (Matt. 5:38-42 par.)," in Swartley, *Love of Enemy and Nonretaliation*, pp. 102-25.

7. Concerning Paul's distinction between resisting evil powers and resisting human beings, see Louise Schottroff, "'Give to Caesar What Belongs to Caesar and to God What Belongs to God': A Theological Response of the Early Church to Its Social and Political Environment," in Swartley, *Love of Enemy*, pp. 223-57.

darkness," *tous kosmokratoras tou skotous toutou*); and spiritual, involving more than material being ("spiritual forces of evil," *ta pneumatika tēs ponērias,* Eph 6:12).[8] Paul's gospel proclaims that God-in-Christ saves us from evil in all its manifold forms (Rom 8:38-39).

However we make sense of Paul's varied language of evil, I think we must acknowledge four things. First, Paul affirms that all realities and powers in the cosmos have been created by God through Christ — and thus that all realities and powers now hostile to God are ultimately to be conquered by Christ, brought into subjection to God under Christ, and reconciled to God in Christ (Col 1:15-20; 1 Cor 15:24-28). Second, Paul ascribes reality to the power of evil manifest in various forms; such forms of evil threaten to separate the faithful from the love of God and are the object of faithful struggle through the power of God (Rom 8:37-39; Eph 6:10-13). Third, Paul affirms (following the Genesis story) that sin enters the cosmos by way of humanity but then exercises dominion over humanity and the cosmos through death (Rom 5:12ff.). And fourth, Paul depicts evil manifest in creaturely sin as both an indwelling reality and an overwhelming power that can hold the body captive and so incapacitate the will (Rom 7:14-25).[9] Paul, as James Dunn puts it, thinks of sin as "a power bearing down upon himself and upon mankind generally."[10] Paul thus understands evil to be objectively real and manifest in individual and social, human and cosmic, material and spiritual forms. We do a disservice to Paul's thinking if we either deny objective reality to the various forms of evil or explain all evil as caused by the free-willed agency of individual creatures.[11] In Paul's view, Dunn writes,

8. Regarding Paul's varied language of evil, see James D. G. Dunn, *The Theology of Paul the Apostle* (Grand Rapids, MI: Eerdmans Publishing, 1998), pp. 104-10; Willard M. Swartley, *Covenant of Peace: The Missing Peace in New Testament Theology and Ethics* (Grand Rapids, MI: Eerdmans Publishing, 2006), pp. 223-28; and Paul S. Fiddes, *Past Event and Present Salvation: The Christian Idea of Atonement* (Louisville: Westminster/John Knox, 1989), pp. 114-25.

9. The "moral influence" theory of atonement is thus inadequate. A perfect example of divine love demonstrated through other-saving self-sacrifice might be sufficient to deal with sin were sin simply a matter of willful selfishness: having witnessed the good one might be persuaded to will the good and then actually do it. Insofar as sin dominates the whole person, however, we cannot free ourselves from our selfishness simply by choice of the will: "I can will what is right, but I cannot do it. For I do not do the good I want, but the evil I do not want is what I do" (Rom 7:18b-19). Freedom from sin, therefore, requires not only moral motivation but also freedom of will to act as one chooses, which in turn requires redemption of the body, which remains "a slave to the law of sin" (vv. 23-25) and awaits liberation from bondage to sin and corruption along with the rest of creation (8:18-25).

10. Dunn, *Theology of Paul the Apostle,* p. 112.

11. This discussion involves the philosophical question concerning the existence and essence of evil, which we cannot address at length here. We agree with Augustine that, according to the doctrine of creation, no thing is intrinsically evil and evil has no independent existence — and so concur in rejecting an ontological dualism of good and evil. It does not follow, however, that evil is only the privation of good, as Augustine thought (*Confessions,* III, VII; *City of*

"there are real forces for evil operative in the world" that "are not to be reduced simply to human willfulness or individual selfishness."[12]

As Paul sees the world, evil is not reducible to evil*doing*, sin is not reducible to sinning; there is more to sin than the evil deeds that creatures will to do. Because evil is more than an individual, volitional phenomenon, therefore, conquering evil is more than a matter of human willpower and, therefore, more than a matter of good-doers conquering evildoers. Against powers of darkness and forces of evil, retaliatory resistance is futile for it only feeds the very evil we fight and enhances our enslavement to it. Indeed, that the enemy we resist is not other human beings is the very reason that Paul enjoins us to equip ourselves with the armor of God (Eph 6:11-12). The physical weapons of merely human warfare are no good in the struggle against evil, then, because the real enemy we face is not merely human evildoers.

The church's calling to holy resistance thus requires careful discernment regarding good and evil. We must distinguish between evil and human evildoers, and ask: Who and what is the real enemy? The War on Terror provides a contemporary context for contrasting the world's way of carnal warfare and God's way of holy warfare concerning this question.

In his sermon from Washington National Cathedral in 2001, President Bush declared a crusade "to rid the world of evil." How does the War on Terror seek "to rid the world of evil"? By eliminating those identified as "terrorists," whether by killing or by capture. This war "to rid the world of evil" will end only when every last terrorist has been identified, hunted, and killed or captured. The protagonist-in-chief of the War on Terror thus conceives of evil itself primarily in terms of human, flesh-and-blood evil*doers*. That is, in the worldview of the War President, the primary source of evil to be fought is human beings that do evil deeds. This view has taken root in the American psyche. The day after U.S. forces killed the leader of al Qaeda in Iraq, the bold headline in my local newspaper read, "Evil Dead"[13] — as if killing him had eliminated evil itself and so brought salvation to the world (like killing off the "wicked witch" saved everyone in the Land of Oz).[14]

God, XI.9, 22). Nor need we analyze sin as a purely volitional phenomenon — a function only of free will, having no efficient cause (in the body, say) — as Augustine did (*City of God,* XII.6-8; XIV.13), to maintain human responsibility for sin and need of regeneration by God. Augustine's understanding of evil and sin, it seems to me, is inadequate to Paul's view of sin as a dominating power that indwells the body and so incapacitates the will, such that one might sin not on account of an evil will but on account of a sin-enslaved body (Rom 7:14-25). For a balanced appraisal and positive appropriation of Augustine's view, see Charles T. Mathewes, *Evil and the Augustinian Tradition* (Cambridge: Cambridge University Press, 2001).

12. Dunn, *Theology of Paul the Apostle,* p. 127.

13. *The Elkhart Truth,* June 9, 2006.

14. Such refrains were repeated after Osama bin Laden was killed by U.S. Navy SEALs and

If the battle of good and evil were merely a struggle only with flesh-and-blood enemies, with human evildoers, as the War on Terror envisions, then that would readily justify resort to violent force by physical weapons as the preferred option. The War on Terror's understanding of the struggle of good and evil, however, proceeds from a myopic view of reality. For it fails to recognize the reality of evil powers — social, cosmic, and spiritual — that might hold sway over us (the "good-doers") as over our putative enemy (the "evildoers"). We have only to remind ourselves of the ghastly photos from Abu Ghraib prison in Baghdad for evidence confirming that such powers of evil are not only real but *do* hold sway over "us" as well as "them."

If instead, with Paul, we acknowledge that in our real world there actually exist cosmic powers of darkness and spiritual forces of evil, then it becomes clear why employing physical weapons against human enemies, while doing so may bring some (temporary) useful result, does not take evil seriously or realistically enough. The reality of evil cannot be eliminated simply by killing off evil*doers;* the power of sin cannot be defeated simply by destroying sinners. Fighting evil with physical weapons against human enemies fails to adequately address the full reality of evil: violent force cannot ultimately save us because there is more to evil than evildoers and evildoing.[15]

If, moreover, death is the "last enemy" of God to be conquered and nullified through Christ "in the end" (1 Cor 15:24-28), then two things follow concerning Christian resistance against evil. First, in no way can we participate in Christ's defeat of evil by inflicting death upon our enemies. For death is itself the ultimate enemy in God's battle against evil; thus, the choice of the "lesser evil" in human warfare, killing in defense of good, always contributes to the

---

CIA operatives in 2011. One prominent national columnist described this "kill-mission" as "killing evil" (Maureen Dowd, "Killing Evil Doesn't Make Us Evil," *New York Times,* May 7, 2011). And one popular Christian commentator even invoked "Ding dong the witch is dead" from *The Wizard of Oz* to celebrate Osama's death (Cal Thomas, "Justice Has Been Done with bin Laden," *Washington Examiner,* May 2, 2011).

15. Echoing the "realism" of Reinhold Niebuhr in his Nobel Peace Prize acceptance speech (December 10, 2009) President Obama contrasted the nonviolent ideal of Gandhi and King with the violent reality of the world: "I know there is nothing weak — nothing passive — nothing naïve — in the creed and lives of Gandhi and King. But as a head of state sworn to protect and defend my nation, I cannot be guided by their examples alone. I face the world as it is, and cannot stand idle in the face of threats to the American people. For make no mistake: evil does exist in the world." Obama's statement implies three things concerning the "example" of Gandhi and King: they did not "face the world as it is," they "stood idle in the face of threats" to their people, and they were unrealistic about the world and idle in the face of threats precisely because they failed to acknowledge that "evil does exist in the world." Both Gandhi and King, I think, would repudiate Obama on all three points, especially the suggestion that they failed to face the reality of evil in the world. Indeed, they would insist that they were actively resisting evil by the only means capable of overcoming it.

"greater evil," the power of death. Second, to attempt to defeat evil by inflicting death upon our enemies is effectively to make an ally of death and so to put ourselves on the wrong side. When we take up death-dealing tactics in order to defeat evildoers, we not only adopt a self-defeating strategy, for thereby do we only strengthen the ultimate enemy; but by allying ourselves with God's ultimate enemy, we pit ourselves against God's purpose through Christ "in the end." We cannot conquer evil, therefore, by wielding the power of death against evildoers, even with good intention.

It is, really, the powers of evil that need to be defeated, not our putative enemies, and destroying enemies, even if they *are* evildoers, will not — cannot — contribute to the defeat of such powers, but can only extend their dominion. Evil is to be conquered, and we may participate in victory over evil, ultimately only through the power of "the love of God in Christ Jesus our Lord" and only by way of the death and resurrection of Jesus Christ (Rom 6:5-11; 8:37-39; 1 Cor 15:51-57).

35.3. Christian Resistance and the Weapons of War

When we take up physical weapons of merely human warfare, instruments designed to inflict destruction and death, furthermore, not only does our struggle fail to take stock of the full reality of evil, but we effectively place our very selves into the willing service of the evil we fight. Paul describes the "dominion of sin" that has invaded the world through humanity and enslaved humanity to its power (Rom 5:12–6:23). The power by which sin rules in the cosmos is death; under captivity to the power of sin, the end of our works is death (6:20-23). We have, however, been freed from the dominion of sin and death through the death and resurrection of Christ, in which we participate through baptism. Because "death no longer has dominion" over Christ, God having raised him from the dead, we who have been "baptized into his death" and resurrection are to regard ourselves as "dead to sin and alive to God in Christ Jesus" (vv. 1-11). Paul then writes:

> *Therefore,* do not let sin exercise dominion in your mortal bodies *(sōmati),* to make you obey their passions. No longer present your members to sin as instruments *(hopla,* literally "weapons") of wickedness, but present yourselves to God as those who have been brought from death to life, and present your members to God as instruments *(hopla)* of righteousness. (vv. 12-13)

While not depicting the body *(sōma)* as intrinsically evil, Paul makes clear that the body is the locus of the power of sin working death in us (cf. 7:21-24). Accordingly, in exhorting us to resist conformity to the pattern of this age, Paul calls us to present our "bodies" *(sōmata)* as a holy sacrifice to God (12:1-2).[16] Redemption in Christ, symbolized and realized by baptism into his death and resurrection (6:1-11), thus transforms the body from that by which sin works death in us into that by which we resist the power of sin to work death in the world.

Paul exhorts, first, that we are to no longer obey the "passions" that allow sin to "exercise dominion in [our] mortal bodies." These "passions" include not only the lust that leads into sexual impurity and the greed that leads to excessive consumption, but also the patriotic fervor that leads to taking vengeance on national enemies. Paul exhorts, second, that we are to "no longer present [our] members to sin as weapons *(hopla)* of wickedness," which produce only death. We are not to allow our bodies to become the very means by which sin does its death-producing work.[17] This includes not committing bloodshed with the hands as well as not committing deceit with the tongue. To be "dead to sin and alive to God in Christ Jesus," therefore, entails no longer submitting *either* the "inner" person (mind and will) or the "outer" person (body) to the death-producing power of sin.

Taking this text on its face, I think that human weapons designed for death and destruction should be regarded as instruments of sin — and, hence, that employing such weapons should be regarded as presenting our bodies to sin as servants of wickedness. The reign of sin brings death by and for all those enslaved to its power; death is the "payoff" of participation in sin (Rom 6:20-21). All that works death and destroys life in this world is subject to the dominion of sin — and so alienated from the reign of God and lordship of Christ. Human weapons are designed to deal out death and destruction; as such, they are instruments of the power of sin.[18] To take up such instruments of destruction, and to employ them according to their designed purpose of causing death, is thus to put oneself at the disposal of the power of sin. In effect, by taking up the sword or gun into our hands — whether in the name of "security" or "freedom"

16. Cf. Schottroff, "Give to Caesar," pp. 243-50.

17. With exception of Sparta, which maintained a professional military, ancient Greek city-states did not have standing armies but relied upon corps of civilian "reservist" soldiers, *hoplites,* that could be called into action when needed. These *hoplites,* so named for their standard equipment, were foot soldiers, commonly spearmen. We might thus hear Paul's exhortation: do not consent for yourselves to be foot soldiers of evil, "spearmen" of wickedness.

18. As noted above, I agree entirely with Augustine that no material thing is intrinsically evil, because all things have been created originally good by God. Nonetheless, I think that manufactured articles, which are human designs impressed upon created matter, do embody human intentions, just as natural objects embody the intentions of their designer and maker: whereas natural objects embody the good intentions of God, manufactured articles embody the intentions, whether for good or for evil, of humans. Weapons of war, while not intrinsically evil qua material things, embody the evil intentions of carnal warfare for which they were humanly designed and made.

or "justice" or "peace" — we take into our very bodily selves ("our mortal bodies") the power of sin that works death in and through us.

Recall the Amish elder Eli Lapp in the film *Witness* teaching his grandson to separate himself from bloodshed (see Chapter 31 above). Eli's grandson, Samuel, who has witnessed a murder, is fascinated with the handgun of the wounded police officer convalescing in the Lapp home. The boy is tempted to see the gun as an instrument of justice with which to fight the evil he has seen with his own eyes. Eli instructs the boy: "What you take into your hands, you take into your heart." By taking the gun to kill the "bad men," Eli warns, "you become one of them" — take killing into the heart and become captive to the same power of sin that worked death through the murderous actions of the men the boy witnessed. Citing Paul, Eli teaches his grandson that the way of holiness calls us to separate ourselves from evil — and so to separate ourselves from the instruments of violence that serve the end of sin, death: "Wherefore come out from among them, and be ye separate, saith the LORD, and touch not the unclean thing" (2 Cor 6:17 KJV). The commitment to nonviolence in the confrontation of evil, therefore, is a corollary of our calling from God to *holiness* (cf. 7:1).

When we take up and wield the physical weapons of human warfare, we place our very selves into the voluntary service of the army of death under the command of sin. The employment of weapons of death thus alienates us from the reign of God and lordship of Christ. This stark statement finds an early Christian precedent in Paulinus, bishop of Nola and contemporary of Augustine. In his *Letter* 25 to Crispinianus, a Christian in the Roman army, Paulinus exhorts the soldier to leave military service for the service of God. Paulinus writes:

> There is nothing, my blessed son, which can or ought to be preferred to Him who is the true Lord, the true Father, the eternal Commander. . . . Therefore do not any longer love this world or its military service, for Scripture's authority attests that "whoever is a friend of this world is an enemy of God." *He who is a solider with the sword is the servant of death.* . . . Let us follow Him, then. Let us be soldiers for Him.[19]

The carnal soldier, by habituating himself through training and fighting to the employment of weapons of destruction and death, surrenders himself to the rule of sin and, in effect, becomes in his own body and mind and will a "weapon of wickedness."[20] This is not just theological-philosophical abstrac-

---

19. Paulinus, *Letter* 25, to Crispinianus, in *Letters of St. Paulinus of Nola,* trans. P. G. Walsh (New York: Paulist Press, 1967), pp. 73-75 (emphasis added).

20. By habituating oneself to the employment of any material instrument — say, by learning to write with a pen or walk with a cane — the instrument becomes an extension of one's own embodied intention, such that one's consciousness effectively extends to the end of the instru-

tion or cinematic fiction, but worldly reality. In the recent documentary film "Soldiers of Conscience," Iraq War veteran Camilo Mejia describes killing an "enemy combatant" in terms that reflect the soldier's self — body, mind, and will — molded to the weapon's intention:

> Everything that I'm describing to you I'm looking through the rear aperture of my M-16 rear sight. So, it's a very, very, very intense moment. And, um, I don't remember squeezing the trigger and I don't remember seeing him go down. All I remember is that we shot him and that the next image that I have is two men came from the crowd and grabbed him by the shoulders and pulled him through a puddle of blood. And then I remember after that mission was over, you know, before we moved on to our next mission, I went into a dark room by myself and I pulled out my magazine and I counted the bullets and I realized that I had fired eleven bullets at him. And, um, it changes you.[21]

This phenomenon is not new. Ernie Pyle, the famous Army reporter during World War II, observed that ordinary soldiers, as they participated in daily combat, became habituated to the evil of killing. Where they had once been disposed to believe that "taking life is a sin," he reported, in war they came to adopt the "professional outlook" that "killing is a craft."[22] Mejia's personal tes-

---

ment: one's consciousness "touches" the world, not where the hand grasps the instrument, but where the instrument enacts one's intention. See M. Merleau-Ponty, *Phenomenology of Perception* (London: Routledge, 1962). The inverse is also true: the intention embodied in the instrument shapes one's consciousness through habitual use. This dialectical phenomenon was pointed out by Hegel and Marx. Marx observed that the mind of the laborer is shaped by the mode of his labor. Thus, as the factory worker, by habituating his body to the machine, becomes "machine-minded," so the soldier, by habituating his body to the weapon, becomes "weapon-minded." The general idea here, that technological tools are extensions of the outer/body-self that through habitual use remake the inner/mind-self such that the user of technology comes to embody the mentality of the tool, is the central thesis of Marshall McLuhan in *Understanding Media: The Extensions of Man* (1964), summed up in his catch-phrase "the medium is the message." See also the writings of philosopher George Grant, who argued that industrial and computer technology embody the "modern destiny" of manipulation of nature and homogenization of society that dictates the purposes and uses of technology, such that the users of technology become the instruments of that destiny.

21. "Soldiers of Conscience" (Luna Productions 2007), aired by Public Broadcasting Service on October 16, 2008. Mejia is describing here an incident in which his unit was observing a street protest from a distance. A man emerged from the crowd holding a grenade and advanced toward their position (hence, "enemy combatant"), but was too far away to do the soldiers any harm. Mejia killed the man, not because he posed a threat, but because of the inherent intentionality of the weapon and the war.

22. Quoted in Ken Burns's film documentary *The War,* episode 2, aired by Public Broadcasting Service on September 25, 2007. See the viewer's guide to the series at http://www-tc.pbs.org/thewar/downloads/thewarvgbroadcast0724.pdf.

timony and Pyle's combat-zone observation have been substantiated by the experience and research of Lt. Col. David Grossman (U.S. Army, Ret.). In *On Killing*, Grossman details how U.S. combat training changed during World War II to take into account the demonstrable fact that humans have a natural resistance to killing fellow humans. This psychological reality meant that combat training would have to overcome that resistance: the soldier must be habituated to killing, and the enemy must be dehumanized.[23]

Paul calls us to not habituate ourselves to evil by putting the members of our own bodies at the disposal of sin as instruments of death. Rather, having been raised from death to life in Christ, we are to put ourselves at the disposal of God, so that even our mortal bodies might be instruments of righteousness for the sake of God's peace. The church is to wage holy war by holy weapons with spiritual power:

> Indeed, we live as human beings, but we do not wage war according to human standards; for the weapons *(hopla)* of our warfare are not merely human, but they have divine power to destroy strongholds. We destroy arguments and every proud obstacle raised up against the knowledge of God, and we take every thought captive to obey Christ. (2 Cor 10:3-5)

Notice here that Paul does *not* say that Christians no longer wage war, but rather that "we do not wage war *according to human standards*." That is, Christians are not to wage war by human means for human ends, but rather are to wage war by holy means for divine ends: "the weapons of our warfare . . . have divine power . . . we take every thought captive for Christ." Louise Schottroff thus comments (with reference to Ephesians 6):[24]

> This *"militarized" language* does not mean that one now participates in the war of people against people, albeit with different means; rather, it means that Christian resistance comes from an endowment with power: with the power of the Spirit of God, which is *dynamis*, with the armor of God, where the swift feet of the messenger of peace take the place of the soldier's boots (Eph. 6:15).

35.4. Christian Resistance with the Armor of God

How, then, are we to prepare ourselves for battle? We are to take up only those weapons Jesus armed himself with as he went into the wilderness to resist Satan

---

23. David Grossman, *On Killing: The Psychological Cost of Learning to Kill in War and Society* (New York: Little, Brown & Co., 1995).

24. Schottroff, "Give to Caesar," p. 244, emphasis original.

and as he went to the cross to conquer death: truth, justice/righteousness, peace, faith, salvation, and the word of God (Eph 6:14-17; 2 Cor 6:7). These comprise "the *whole* armor of God," such that leaving out any one is an incomplete preparation for and an inadequate engagement in battle. There is no salvation (in the fullest sense) from evil without justice and peace as well as truth, faith, and the word of God. To seek salvation without a commitment to pursue justice and peace is to forfeit victory from the beginning. Likewise, to pursue justice in competition with peace is to obtain at best a half victory — and thus to incur at least a half loss. And because "the gospel of peace" is to be "shoes on your feet . . . to give you firm footing" (Eph 6:15 NEB), it is the component of God's armor that "steadies" all the rest. Without it, we risk losing our balance as we contend against evil. To take up the struggle without the full gospel of salvation, justice, and peace, therefore, is to fail to use the full power of God that enables us to "stand firm" in the face of evil.

Finally, we must not neglect a crucial aspect of the necessary spiritual preparation for the struggle against evil — prayer: "Pray in the Spirit at all times in every prayer and supplication" (Eph 6:18a). This preparation of prayer must be constant, lest we be caught off guard by the very powers against which we contend for the gospel: "To that end keep alert and always persevere in supplication for all the saints" (v. 18b). Our intercessory prayers in the name of Jesus may themselves become channels of justice-doing and peacemaking in this world. Far from being merely "the least we can do" or a weapon of "last resort," prayer is potentially an offensive spiritual weapon in the frontline struggle for truth, justice, and freedom.

An amazing contemporary example of this is the "revolution of the candles" in the former East Germany in September-December 1989 (described in Chapter 31 above). After weeks of peaceful prayer and nonviolent demonstration arising from weekly prayer services at the Nikolai Church in Leipzig — during which thousands suffered brutality, arrest, and interrogation — the authorities surrendered and opened the Berlin Wall, symbol and reality of the repressive state system. Said Christian Führer, a Leipzig pastor and co-organizer of the peace prayers: "They were ready for everything except candles and prayers."[25]

The day after the Berlin wall was opened, church leaders made this statement:

> Our society is changing from hour to hour. The opening of the borders, for which we have all waited, created a situation for which nobody was prepared. Today the Conference of Protestant Church Leaders cannot give an evaluation of the present or predictions of the future. But prayers and intercessory worship services are the most important things which we as Christians can

25. Andrew Curry, "Before the Fall," *Wilson Quarterly*, Autumn 2009.

do to fulfill our commitments to our society. No one else can do this for us. We will continue in prayer for peace, justice, and the preservation of creation. . . . Our prayers are based on the promise that God hears the one who is praying. We desire that His will be done.[26]

In January 1990, Dr. Werner Leich, a Protestant bishop and president of the Federation of Protestant Churches, spoke of the role of the church and Christians in shaping the future of East Germany: "We have discovered something special in the last months. Our service in the areas of prayer and preaching can change the political structure when God knows that the time is ripe."[27] I take the faithful witness and suffering service of the church in East Germany to confirm Walter Wink's bold claim: "History belongs to intercessors who believe the future into being. . . . The shapers of the future are intercessors, who call out of the future the longed-for new present."[28] Or, as I would rephrase it in the lyrics of the late singer-songwriter Rich Mullins: history belongs to the intercessors who believe that "God takes by its corners this old world and shakes us forward and shakes us free."[29]

26. Quoted from Jörg Swoboda, *The Revolution of the Candles: Christians in the Revolution of the German Democratic Republic*, ed. Richard V. Pierard and trans. Edwin P. Arnold (Macon, GA: Mercer University Press, 1996), pp. 70-71.

27. Quoted from Swoboda, *Revolution of the Candles*, p. 24. Swartley, *Covenant of Peace*, chapter 12, develops the connection between worship and nonviolent victory in the book of Revelation. Alan Kreider, Eleanor Kreider, and Paulus Widjaja, *A Culture of Peace: God's Vision for the Church* (Intercourse, PA: Good Books, 2005), chapter 6, also develop the connection between worship and peacemaking in the church.

28. Walter Wink, *The Powers That Be: Theology for a New Millennium* (New York: Doubleday, 1998), p. 185.

29. Understanding the possibility and efficacy of both intercessory prayer and divine intervention requires rethinking the relation between heaven and earth. See Walter Wink, *Engaging the Powers: Discernment and Resistance in a World of Domination* (Minneapolis: Fortress Press, 1992), pp. 3-10, and Wright, *Surprised by Hope*, pp. 109-17.

CHAPTER 36

Jesus Christ, Paradigm of Mission

For to this you have been called,
because Christ also suffered for you,
leaving you an example,
so that you should follow in his steps.

1 PETER 2:21

In this concluding chapter we organize the redemptive mission of the church around three pairs of motifs that the New Testament writers use to depict the life, death, and resurrection of Jesus Christ. We have already worked with each of these motifs in our exploration of the message of the cross: Jesus Christ is God's faithful witness and suffering servant, justice-doer and peacemaker, liberator and victor.[1] Because the New Testament writers depict Jesus Christ as the exemplar of the church's holy calling, these motifs also depict the mission of the church in parallel terms: the church is called to faithful witness and suffering (sacrificial) service, justice-doing and peacemaking, victory and liberation.

It has not been our goal throughout this book to construct a systematic theology of atonement as such. We have sought, rather, to explore the connections between atonement, justice, and peace, the implications of the message of the cross for the mission of the church. What follows is thus only an organizing scheme to help us see the mission of the church as motivated by the cross and as modeled and mandated by Jesus Christ. As such, it is not intended to be ex-

---

1. For an extensive examination of each of these motifs in the New Testament, see John Driver, *Understanding the Atonement for the Mission of the Church* (Scottdale, PA: Herald Press, 1986), chapters 3, 4, 6, 10, and 11. In *Images of the Church in Mission* (Scottdale, PA: Herald Press, 1997), Driver connects the several images of the church in the New Testament to the church's mission in the world.

haustive or fixed, much less a final analysis of either the message of the cross or the mission of the church. This paradigm pairs motifs that seem to us complementary and which, taken together, include much of the message of the cross and the mission of the church. As John Driver reminds us, however, the various atonement motifs are not mutually exclusive categories.[2] By depicting Jesus' death and the church's mission using one or several motifs, we neither deny other motifs nor paint a contradictory picture.

We might represent this cruciform paradigm of Christian mission as follows:

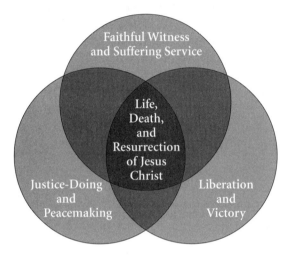

In what follows, we first expand briefly on each pair of motifs, reviewing how the various New Testament writers depict Jesus using those motifs. We then use the motifs to identify paradigmatic actions Christians are called to undertake in the imitation of Christ. And last we exhibit concrete examples of mission work that exemplify those paradigmatic actions (each of which, because the motifs overlap, might well be listed under one or both of the other headings).[3]

36.1. Faithful Witness and Suffering Service

The New Testament writers depict Jesus Christ as God's *faithful witness* and *suffering servant,* the one who endures faithfully in God's service, bearing witness to God's faithfulness and love. By his faithful endurance, Jesus Christ has be-

---

2. Driver, *Understanding the Atonement.*

3. I have chosen to highlight mostly Christian martyrs or ministries that have had a personal impact on me, to which I have had a personal connection, or in which I have personally participated.

come "the true martyr" (Rev 1:5), "the pioneer of [our] salvation" and "the per-fecter of our faith" (Heb 2:10; 12:1-2). Accordingly, Jesus Christ, in his life, death, and resurrection, is the One:

> who humbles himself in obedience to God's will, taking the position of the least and lowest, becoming a slave so that he might serve all (Mark 10:45; John 5:30; 13:1-17; Phil 2:5-8);
> who remains steadfast in undying trust in God and authentic loyalty to the covenant in the face of temptations to security and threats to life (Matt 4:1-11; 26:36-46; Luke 4:1-13; 22:39-46; Mark 14:32-42);
> who bears witness under trial to the truth and love of God in the face of lies and hostility (Matt 27:1-14; Mark 14:53-65; 15:1-5; Luke 22:66–23:12; John 18:19–19:12); and
> who endures innocent suffering for the cause of God's justice and freely sacrifices himself to God, offering his life for the sake of others, even sinners (Matt 26:26-28; Mark 14:22-24; Luke 22:19-20; Gal 1:4, 2:20; Eph 5:2; 1 Tim 2:6; Tit 2:14; Heb 5:7-10; 9:14; 1 Pet 2:21-25).

Serving God's purpose and following the example of Christ, we are called to:

> mourn loss of life and bear witness to truth (Matt 5:4; Luke 6:21b; John 11:32-35; 18:37; Acts 1:8; 1 Pet 3:15-16);
> speak truth to power and expose works of darkness, being wise in words and innocent in deeds (Matt 10:16-20; Mark 13:9-11; Luke 12:8-12; Acts 4:5-31; 5:29-32; Eph 3:10; 5:11);
> endure suffering and death for the sake of truth and justice with courage and hope (Matt 5:10-11; Luke 6:22-23; John 18:19-23; Acts 6:8–7:60; Rom 8:18-25; Eph 3:1, 6:10; Heb 12:3-11; 1 Pet 2:19-23, 3:8-22; Revelation 2; 6:9-11);
> live in vulnerable solidarity with the poor, weak, and defenseless, especially the victims of oppression, persecution, abuse, torture, and war (Matt 5:3; Luke 6:20-21a; John 1:10-14; Acts 2:43-47; 4:32-37; 1 Cor 12:12-13, 26; 2 Cor 8:1-15; Heb 13:1-3); and
> serve Christ by voluntary, self-giving (sacrificial) service to all, especially those whose rights are most vulnerable to exploitation — the hungry, homeless, sick, and imprisoned as well as widows, orphans, and immigrants (Mark 10:42-44; Matt 25:31-46; Acts 6:1-6; 1 Cor 9:19-23; Jas 2:14-17; 1 John 3:16-17).

Here are examples of the church living out its mission of faithful witness and suffering service, according to the pattern of Christ and for the sake of God's purpose:

Marcellus the centurion, martyr. Marcellus was a soldier and officer in the
Roman imperial army. After converting to Christ, he threw down his
sword during a religious festival in honor of the emperor's birthday,
saying, "I serve Jesus Christ the eternal King. I will no longer serve
your emperors." At his trial he testified that it is "not right for a Christian man, who serves the Lord Christ, to serve in the armies of the
world." He was executed as a faithful witness and suffering servant of
Jesus Christ on October 30, 298.[4]

Oscar Romero, martyr. After his elevation to archbishop of San Salvador in
1977, Romero served the poor and oppressed among his brothers and
sisters in military-ruled, war-torn El Salvador. He became the voice of
a people groaning under the yoke of their bondage, proclaiming the
gospel truth boldly, not only from the cathedral pulpit and over the radio waves, but also to "the powers that be" in the presidential palace.
He was assassinated in 1980 for his faithful witness in word and deed to
the gospel of Jesus Christ.[5]

Las Madres de Plaza de Mayo. During Argentina's "dirty war" of the 1970s
and 80s, mothers of the "disappeared" began a weekly demonstration
in front of the Government House in April 1977, calling for an accounting of those kidnapped, detained, interrogated, tortured, and
murdered by the military dictatorship. For thirty years, Las Madres
have persisted in their pursuit of truth and justice.[6]

The Chronicle of the Catholic Church in Lithuania. Suffering severe repression and persecution during a decades-long occupation by the Soviet
Union following World War II, the church established an underground journal in 1972 to document human rights abuses committed
against the faithful by the regime. This journal was smuggled to the
United States, where it was translated and published in English in Chicago under the auspices of the late Joseph Cardinal Bernardin.[7]

The Catholic Worker Movement. Since being founded by Dorothy Day and
Peter Maurin in New York City in 1933 during the Great Depression,
the Catholic Worker movement has been dedicated to "love in action"
by performing the "works of mercy" — feeding the hungry, giving

4. Learn more about Marcellus at http://www.catholicpeacefellowship.org/nextpage
.asp?m=2389.

5. Romero's homilies and radio addresses, *The Violence of Love,* is available for free download as an e-book from Plough Publishing at http://www.plough.com/ebooks/ViolenceOfLove
.html.

6. Learn more about the witness of the Argentine mothers in Peter Ackerman and Jack
Duvall, *A Force More Powerful: A Century of Nonviolent Conflict* (New York: Palgrave, 2000), pp.
267-79.

7. See http://www.jesuit.lt/modules.php?name=Content&pa=showpage&pid=52&cid=20.

drink to the thirsty, clothing the naked, sheltering the homeless, caring for the sick, visiting the imprisoned, and burying the dead — through houses of hospitality that welcome the forsaken.[8]

L'Arche. Founded in 1964 by Jean Vanier, L'Arche communities around the world bring together people with and without developmental disabilities to share everyday life in mutual relationships of vulnerability and support.[9]

Sant'Egidio Community. Begun in Rome in 1968 by a group of students, this world-wide Catholic lay association practices corporate prayer, friendship with the poor, and ecumenical dialogue. The original community in Rome has a ministry of solidarity with the outcast Roma people living in the outlying areas of the city.[10]

Jubilee Partners. This intentional Christian community based in Comer, Georgia, was begun by three families with a vision to welcome and help resettle refugees from conflict zones. Over three decades, Jubilee Partners has welcomed thousands of refugees from around the world and thousands of volunteers to live and work with them and their guests.[11]

Women's Care Center. This faith-based organization in Indiana draws on the resources of local parishes and congregations to maintain a network to support women facing unexpected or crisis pregnancies. It provides confidential services free of charge, including pregnancy testing, prenatal care referrals, parenting classes, baby food and clothing, and post-abortion counseling.[12]

The Simple Way. This intentional Christian community in inner-city Philadelphia was begun in the 1990s with the mission "to love God, love people, follow Jesus." They do this by feeding the hungry, planting urban gardens, playing with children, and advocating with and for their neighbors.[13]

---

8. Learn more at http://www.catholicworker.org/index.cfm. See also Dorothy Day's autobiography, *The Long Loneliness* (New York: HarperCollins, 1952).

9. Learn more at http://www.larche.org/home.en-gb.1.0.index.htm.

10. Learn more at http://www.santegidio.org/index.php.

11. Learn more at http://www.jubileepartners.org/. Read the story of this community in Don Mosley, *With Our Own Eyes: The Dramatic Story of a Christian Response to the Wounds of War, Racism, and Oppression* (Scottdale, PA: Herald Press, 1996).

12. Learn more at http://www.womenscarecenter.org/index.html.

13. Learn more at http://www.thesimpleway.org/. See also the book by community cofounder Shane Claiborne, *The Irresistible Revolution: Living as an Ordinary Radical* (Grand Rapids, MI: Zondervan, 2006).

36.2. Justice-Doing and Peacemaking

The New Testament writers depict Jesus Christ as God's *justice-doer* and *peace-maker,* the one who fulfills God's covenant righteousness and inaugurates God's peaceable kingdom on earth as in heaven (Matt 5:17; 6:10). Accordingly, Jesus Christ, in his life, death, and resurrection, is the One:

who proclaims good news to the poor and oppressed, the outcast and marginal (Luke 4:18-19; 6:20-22; 7:22; 14:15-24);

who calls the rich to have mercy on the poor and the oppressor to do justice for the oppressed (Luke 18:18-25; 19:1-10);

who prays for his enemies, does good to those who would harm him, forgives those who wrong him, and reconciles those who desert and deny him (Luke 22:51; 23:34; 24:3; John 21:15-19);

who gives his people peace and gives the Holy Spirit to empower his people of peace (John 14:27; 16:33; 20:19-23);

who makes peace between hostile parties by destroying walls of hostility and creating a new humanity (Eph 2:11-22);

through whom God demonstrates justice that redeems sinners (Luke 23:39-43; Rom 3:21-26);

through whom God "justifies" us (i.e., puts us in right relationship and makes us righteous) and is reconciling the world to himself (Rom 4:25–5:1; 2 Cor 5:18-19; Eph 1:10; Col 1:20); and

through whom God demonstrates his love for the weak and ungodly, for sinners and enemies (Rom 5:6-11; 1 John 3:16).

Serving God's purpose and following the example of Christ, we are called to:

show mercy to all and do justice for the poor and exploited (Matt 5:6-7; 9:13; 12:7; Luke 6:27-36; 10:29-37; Jas 2:1-13);

renounce retribution, pursue peace, and make peace (Matt 5:9; 5:38-42; Rom 12:17-18; 14:19; 2 Cor 13:11; Eph 4:3; Col 3:15; 1 Thess 5:13, 15; Heb 12:14; Jas 3:18; 1 Pet 3:9-12; 2 Pet 3:14);

love enemies, forgive those who wrong us, pray for them and do good to them (Matt 5:43-48; 6:14-15; 18:21-35; Rom 12:14-20; Eph 4:32; Col 3:13);

reconcile hostile parties (Matt 5:21-26; Acts 9–10; 16:27-34; 2 Cor 5:18-20);

seek redemption of both victims and offenders (Matt 18:15-20; Luke 15:11-32; John 8:1-11; Gal 6:1); and

build faith communities that cultivate the just and peaceable habits of prayer, patience, hope, compassion, gratitude, and generosity (Acts 2:3-47; 4:32-37; Col 3:12-17).

Here are examples of the church living out its mission of justice-doing and peace-making, according to the pattern of Christ and for the sake of God's purpose:

> *The Order of Saint Benedict.* Since its founding in the sixth century, the Benedictine monastic tradition has modeled for the whole church the way of Christian community that cultivates the peaceable habits of prayer, patience, hope, compassion, gratitude, and generosity.[14]
>
> *Saint Francis of Assisi.* In the early twelfth century, the young-adult Francis gave up a life of wealth and privilege for a life of poverty and service. Francis and his brothers and sisters (the Franciscan order) sought to follow Jesus in the way of the cross, preaching "peace and goodness" to all (including the birds!), practicing mercy for the poor, and making peace between enemies. One dramatic instance of the latter is most relevant for our time. During the Crusades, Francis risked his life in the midst of a war zone by crossing "enemy" territory to make peace between the Sultan commanding the Islamic army and the Cardinal commanding the Christian army. The Cardinal would not listen to Francis, but the Sultan was almost convinced by Francis's peaceable way to become a Christian: "If all Christians are like this, I would not hesitate to become one."[15]
>
> *Dirk Willems, martyr.* In Holland in 1569, Dirk was arrested, tried, and convicted, based on his own profession of faith, of being an Anabaptist. Dirk, having escaped from his prison, was pursued across a pond thinly covered by ice: he crossed safely, but the thief-catcher coming after him broke through. Hearing the man's cries for help, Dirk risked recapture and returned to pull the guard to safety. The thief-catcher wanted to let him go in gratitude, but the burgomaster ordered him to take back the prisoner. Shortly thereafter, Dirk was burned at the stake, a faithful witness to Jesus' love for enemies.[16]

14. For an excellent introduction to Benedictine monasticism by an "outsider," see Kathleen Norris, *The Cloister Walk* (New York: Riverhead Books, 1996). For an excellent introduction to Benedictine history and practice by an "insider," see Columba Stewart, O.S.B., *Prayer and Community: The Benedictine Tradition* (Maryknoll, NY: Orbis Books, 1998). For an insightful and practical introduction to and commentary on the Rule of Benedict in devotional format, see Joan D. Chittister, O.S.B., *The Rule of Benedict: Insights for the Ages* (New York: Crossroad Publishing, 1997).

15. The traditional stories of Francis are handed down in *The Little Flowers of Saint Francis of Assisi.*

16. Read Dirk Willem's martyrdom story in *The Martyrs' Mirror* at http://www.homecomers .org/mirror/dirk-willems.htm. For an insightful reflection on the communal faith formation that shaped Dirk's enemy-loving action, see Joseph Liechty, "Why Did Dirk Willems Turn Back?" at http://www.anabaptistnetwork.com/node/175, originally published in *Anabaptism Today* 6 (June 1994).

Desmond Tutu and the Truth and Reconciliation Commission. Archbishop Tutu chaired the unprecedented TRC, culminating the transition from a half-century of apartheid (white-supremacist) rule to democratic rule in South Africa that began in 1994. Although a legal process authorized by the South African government, the TRC was grounded in the Christian theology and spirituality of justice-doing and peacemaking. Developed as an alternative to the criminal justice system, the process addressed both victims and offenders and sought to establish a record of the crimes, abuses, and atrocities committed during the apartheid regime. Victims were offered a public telling and hearing of their story, an opportunity to forgive those who wronged them, and reparations for their losses. The guilty were called to an open and honest accounting of their crimes, expected to take responsibility for their actions, and offered an opportunity to confess publicly, repent of their sins, and request amnesty. While by no means a perfect process, the TRC contributed much to the healing of a nation.[17]

Murder Victim Families for Reconciliation. Founded in 1976, MVFR is an organization for those who have lost family members to murder or execution and are opposed to the death penalty.[18]

Center for Community Justice. Founded in 1978 in Elkhart, Indiana, CCJ has pioneered the field of "restorative justice" in the U.S. Based on gospel principles of justice-doing and peacemaking, CCJ seeks to "provide support and compensation for victims, aid restoration of offenders, and promote reconciliation among victims, offenders and the community." CCJ maintains the oldest Victim Offender Reconciliation Program (VORP) in the U.S., an alternative to the criminal justice system that seeks to address the real needs of victims and promote real accountability and responsibility for offenders.[19]

Dismas House. Founded in 1974 by Fr. Jack Hickey, O.P., and students from Vanderbilt University in Nashville, Tennessee, Dismas seeks "to facilitate the reconciliation of former prisoners to society and society to former prisoners through development of a supportive community." ("Dismas" is the traditional name given to the repentant criminal with whom Jesus died on the cross.)[20]

---

17. See Desmond Tutu's memoir, *No Future without Forgiveness* (New York: Doubleday, 2000). Learn more at the TRC website http://www.doj.gov.za/trc/ and by reading the TRC report at http://www.info.gov.za/otherdocs/2003/trc/.

18. Learn more at http://www.mvfr.org/.

19. The essential guide to restorative justice, both its gospel basis and practical application, is by Howard Zehr (who helped start the VORP program in Elkhart in 1978), *Changing Lenses: A New Focus for Crime and Justice,* 3rd ed. (Scottdale, PA: Herald Press, 2005).

20. Learn more at http://www.dismas.org/index.php.

Koinonia Farm. Begun by Clarence Jordan in the 1940s in Americus, Georgia, Koinonia Farm sought to directly address racial reconciliation in both the church and society at the same time as it developed sustainable methods of farming to enhance the southern agricultural economy. Jordan intended Koinonia Farm to be a "demonstration plot," an experiment in kingdom living.[21]

Voice of Calvary Ministries. Begun in the 1962 and located in Jackson, Mississippi, since 1975, VOCM is an intentionally interracial congregation and Christian community development organization. VOCM seeks "to rebuild people and rebuild communities through the gospel" in ways that promote racial healing in both church and society.[22]

Bridgefolk. Based at St. John's Abbey in Collegeville, Minnesota, Bridgefolk is a grassroots ecumenical movement of "sacramentally-minded Mennonites and peace-minded Roman Catholics" who seek to bridge the divide in the church through building friendships of faith and sharing gifts of the Spirit. Through annual conferences and local gatherings, Bridgefolk aims to "make Anabaptist-Mennonite practices of discipleship, peaceableness, and lay participation more accessible to Roman Catholics, and to bring the spiritual, liturgical, and sacramental practices of the Catholic tradition to Anabaptists."[23]

36.3. Liberation and Victory

The New Testament writers depict Jesus Christ as God's *liberator* and *victor,* the one who judges sin, conquers death, and sets free those captive to the power of sin and death. Accordingly, Jesus Christ, in his life, death, and resurrection, is:

the anointed herald whose Jubilee gospel proclaims release to the captives, restoration to the blind, and liberation to the oppressed (Luke 4:18-19);
the incarnate Son whose life condemns sin and whose word reveals the truth that sets us free from slavery to sin (John 8:2-11, 31-36; Rom 8:1-4);

---

21. Learn more at http://www.koinoniapartners.org/. The story of Clarence Jordan and Koinonia Farm is told in Ann Louise Coble, *Cotton Patch for the Kingdom: Clarence Jordan's Demonstration Plot at Koinonia Farm* (Scottdale, PA: Herald Press, 2002). Jordan's "cotton patch" parables are collected in Clarence Jordan and Bill Lane Doulos, *Cotton Patch Parables of Liberation,* 25th anniversary edition (Scottdale, PA: Herald Press, 2001).

22. Learn more at http://www.vocm.org/. The story of VOCM and the struggle for racial reconciliation is told in a powerful way in Spencer Perkins and Chris Rice, *More Than Equals: Racial Healing for the Sake of the Gospel,* revised and expanded ed. (Downers Grove, IL: InterVarsity Press, 2000).

23. Learn more at http://www.bridgefolk.net/.

the voluntary servant who gives his life as a ransom for many/all (Matt 20:28; Mark 10:45; 1 Tim 2:6);

the faithful servant who, through his life, death, and resurrection, "brings justice to victory" by peaceable means (Matt 12:18-21);

the crucified and risen Christ through whom God disarms, exposes, and triumphs over the rulers and authorities of this world and under whom God is bringing every ruler, authority, and power in the cosmos into subjection (1 Cor 15:24; Col 2:15);

the Son of Man who defeats the one who held the power of death and will destroy death as the last enemy of God, who holds the keys of death and hell and thus sets free all those held captive to the fear of death (1 Cor 15:26, 54-57; Heb 2:14-15; Rev 1:17-18);

the Lamb of God who was slain, who ransoms from sin a people for God, who conquers death and overcomes the world, and who is thus worthy of all power and honor and glory and praise (John 1:29; 16:33; 1 Pet 1:18-21; Rev 5:6–6:2); and

the interceding one in whom we are held secure by God's love and through whom we are enabled to conquer all powers of suffering and death (Rom 8:18-39).

Serving God's purpose and following the example of Christ, we are called to:

heal the sick and bind up those wounded in body and broken in heart (Matt 4:23; 9:35; Mark 1:23-34; 1:40–2:12; 3:1-6; 5:1-20; 5:25-34; 7:31-37; 8:22-26; 9:14-29; 10:46-52; Luke 4:18-19; 7:22; 10:9; John 5:2-15; Acts 3:1-10; 5:12-16; 16:16-18; 19:11-20; Jas 5:14);

liberate the oppressed and release the captives, freeing prisoners of conscience from their cells, freeing slaves from their masters, and forgiving the poor their financial debts (Matt 6:12; 18:21-35; Luke 4:18-19; 7:40-43; 13:10-17; Acts 5:17-21; 12:3-17; 16:19-40);

confront the fallen powers that be and overcome evil with good (Matt 5:38-42; John 2:13-17; Rom 8:37; 12:21; Eph 6:10-20); and

bring life out of destruction and ruin, both human and ecological (Mark 5:21-24, 35-43; Luke 7:11-17; John 11:1-44; Acts 9:36-42; 20:7-12).

Here are examples of the church living out its mission of liberation and victory, according to the pattern of Christ and for the sake of God's purpose:

Sister Maura Brannick Health Center. This clinic has been releasing the burden of illness from and restoring the blessing of health to the poor in South Bend, Indiana, since 1986. Following the mission of the Sisters of Holy Cross and relying on an all-volunteer staff of doctors, dentists, nurses, and counselors, the clinic makes a full range of affordable, quality health services accessible to the uninsured.[24]

Amnesty International and *Christian Solidarity Worldwide.* Founded in 1961, AI is dedicated to the defense of freedom of conscience and religion and seeks the liberation of prisoners of conscience around the world. AI mounts campaigns to confront regimes concerning their repressive policies, expose the works of darkness to the light, provide relief to prisoners and their families, and win release of prisoners from their cells. Founded in 1979, CSW "is a human rights organization specializing in religious freedom. CSW works on behalf of those persecuted for their Christian beliefs and promotes religious liberty for all." CSW has set up an international network of prayer, correspondence, advocacy, and reporting on behalf of prisoners of conscience.[25]

Military Counseling Network and *Catholic Peace Fellowship.* U.S. soldiers that come to the Christian conviction that all war is wrong or that a particular war is unjust often find themselves effectively imprisoned by military rules that forbid them to follow conscience. A project of the German Mennonite Peace Committee, MCN provides free information, counseling, and support to U.S. soldiers and their families stationed around the world who are questioning their participation in war. CPF does similar work in the U.S., supporting Christian conscientious objection to war through education, counseling, and advocacy. Both MCN and CPF help staff the GI Rights Hotline, which each year provides counseling and encouragement to thousands of soldiers who are struggling with the contradiction between their Christian faith and their military duty.[26]

Christian Solidarity International and *International Justice Mission.* There are more human beings enslaved now than at any other time in history, many of them child forced laborers and sex slaves. Founded in 1977 in Switzerland to promote religious freedom and encourage solidarity with persecuted Christians, CSI has renewed the biblical practice of redeeming slaves from captivity in the Sudan, citing Jesus' sermon in Luke 4. Founded in 1997 and motivated by Isaiah's call to "seek justice, rescue the oppressed, defend the orphan, plead for the widow" (Isa 1:17), IJM "is a human rights agency that secures justice for victims of slavery, sexual exploitation and other forms of violent oppression."[27]

24. Learn more at http://www.sjmed.com/medicalservices/community/brannick/.
25. Learn more at http://www.amnesty.org/ and http://www.csw.org.uk/.
26. Learn more at http://www.mc-network.de/ and http://www.catholicpeacefellowship.org/index.asp.
27. Learn more at http://csi-int.org/sudan_slavery.php and http://www.ijm.org/. See also "Slavery Lives Again: Evangelicals Once Led the Campaign to Abolish Slavery — It's Time to Do

Jubilee 2000. This global campaign is inspired by the Jubilee Year legislation calling for forgiveness of debts, release of slaves, and return of land every fifty years in order to break cycles of poverty and restore equality in the covenant community (Leviticus 25). Promoted by evangelical Christian and rock star Bono of U2, Jubilee 2000 seeks to break the chains of international indebtedness that bind the poorest countries to the will of the richest countries.[28]

Microfinance. Microfinance institutions support micro-enterprise development through micro-lending practices to the working poor of the world. A small loan to a business owner can liberate a family from bondage to debt, break cycles of poverty, and promote sustainable development and economic independence.[29]

Kryziu Kalnas. Drawing pilgrims from around the world, the Hill of Crosses in central Lithuania marks a significant place of faithful witness to Christ and nonviolent resistance to tyranny and oppression over the course of 150 years. The first crosses were placed on this small hill in the mid-nineteenth century to remember the peasants who had died resisting Tsarist Russian domination. During a period of independence between the World Wars, the Hill of Crosses was a place for Lithuanians to remember those lost to war and to pray for peace. Under Soviet occupation from 1944 to 1991, the Hill of Crosses became again a focal point for Lithuanian expression of faith in Christ and love of homeland as well as peaceable defiance of tyranny and oppression. Three times the Soviets bulldozed the site and scrapped the crosses; three times the people rebuilt the site and erected more crosses. It is fitting that atop the Hill of Crosses, amidst thousands upon thousands of crosses, a "peace pole" stands today.[30]

The Village of Le Chambon. During the Nazi occupation of France during World War II, this primarily Protestant (Huguenot) community, led by local minister André Trocmé, addressed the evil situation around them with suffering service and nonviolent resistance, seeking to overcome evil with good. In defiance of the Nazi occupation policy, the Christians of Le Chambon made their village a safe haven for Jews threatened with deportation and extermination. Villagers opened their homes to Jewish neighbors and refugees to save them from de-

It Again," *Faith Today: The Magazine of the Evangelical Fellowship of Canada*, January-February 2007, and "Free at Last: How Christians Worldwide Are Sabotaging the Modern Slave Trade," *Christianity Today*, March 2007.

28. Learn more at http://www.jubileeusa.org/ and http://www.jubileedebtcampaign.org.uk/.

29. Learn more at http://www.meda.org/web/ and http://www.kiva.org/.

30. Learn more at http://en.wikipedia.org/wiki/Hill_of_Crosses and http://sacredsites .com/europe/lithuania/hill_of_crosses.html.

struction, thus exposing themselves to risk of arrest and imprisonment or deportation. Trocmé himself was arrested and interrogated in an internment camp for several weeks.[31]

Martin Luther King, Jr., martyr, and the black freedom movement. Preaching and practicing the message of the cross — liberation of the oppressed, love of enemies, and overcoming evil with good — the Rev. Dr. Martin Luther King, Jr. led the movement to release black Americans from the last bonds of slavery, from the Montgomery bus boycott in 1955 to his martyrdom in Memphis in 1968. This nonviolent resistance movement brought thousands of ordinary Christians out of the pews and into the streets, carried into the struggle by the songs of freedom.[32]

The Revolution of the Candles. During the "revolution of the candles" in East Germany in 1989, hundreds of thousands of folks, led by prayers for peace and carrying lights of truth, marched from the churches into the streets of Leipzig and Berlin, rendering powerless the Communist regime and state security forces and returning power to "the people." The church played a leading role in this nonviolent revolution that released millions from captivity to repressive rule.

Christian Environmentalism/Creation Care. Evangelical Christians are now recognizing ecological ruin as a sin problem and are waking up to God's purpose to renew all of creation — and so are aligning their vision of church mission with God's purpose: because God's good news through Jesus Christ is for all creation, addressing the worldwide ecological crisis is an evangelical imperative.[33]

31. See Philip P. Hallie, *Lest Innocent Blood Be Shed: The Story of Le Chambon and How Goodness Happened There* (New York: Harper & Row, 1979). André Trocmé's book, *Jesus and the Nonviolent Revolution,* is available for free download as an e-book from Plough Publishing at http://www.plough.com/ebooks/nonviolentrevolution.html.

32. King's major sermons and speeches are collected in James M. Washington, ed., *A Testament of Hope: The Essential Writings and Speeches of Martin Luther King, Jr.* (New York: HarperCollins Publishers, 1986). I would also recommend Vincent Harding's essay collection *Martin Luther King: The Inconvenient Hero* (Maryknoll, NY: Orbis Books, 1996) and his historical reflection *Hope and History: Why We Must Share the Story of the Movement* (Maryknoll, NY: Orbis Books, 1990). For a helpful analysis of the movement's nonviolent strategy, see Ackerman and Duvall, *Force More Powerful,* pp. 305-33. The freedom songs of the movement are collected by Bernice Johnson Reagon on *Voices of the Civil Rights Movement: Black American Freedom Songs 1960-1966* (Washington, D.C.: Smithsonian Folkways Records, 1997).

33. Learn more at http://www.creationcare.org/ and http://www.careofcreation.net/.

Index of Modern Authors

Index of Subjects

Atonement: Anselm's theory of, 45-48, 78-79, 101-3, 196-97, 336-37, 384; basic principles of, 107-8, 332; Eastern Orthodox view of, 77-78, 348-51, 362-66; and ethics, 6-7, 611-15; and forgiveness, 192-208; and grace, 194-99; and justice, 45-50, 85-89; and nonviolence, 68-79; objective aspect of, 332-34, 343-47; and orthodox (creedal) tradition, 75-78, 95-101; in Reformation confessions, 101-4; and sacrifice, 171-91, 194-99; and sanctification, 177-80, 189-91, 203-4, 248; theories/models of, 106-8. *See also* Penal substitution

Capital punishment: and covenant law, 484-88; and cross of Christ, 373-76, 489-92, 497-501; and *lex talionis*, 493-97; and retributive paradigm, 27-28; and teaching of Jesus, 474-83

Christian ethics: and community, 517-18, 568-72; and discernment/discipline, 616-22; and eschatology, 563; and forgiveness, 505-7, 516-21; and holiness, 34, 408, 618, 623-27; and imitation of Christ, 262-64, 321-27, 613-15; and love of enemy, 32-36, 531-41; and love of neighbor, 32-36; and natural law, 42-43; and non-retaliation, 31-41; and realism, 560-65, 572; and resistance to evil, 616-29; and spirituality, 565-68, 627-29; and

(non-)violence, 71-73, 623-27; and worship, 452-53, 485

Christian/Church unity. *See* Ecumenism

Conflict: identity (inter-ethnic/inter-religious), 573-75, 577-86, 587-88; ideological (revolutionary), 576-77; interest (reactionary), 576-77; intra-Christian, 591-96

Covenant: benefits of through Christ, 164-65; as context of God's judgment/redemption of Israel, 410-14; as context of God's redemption in Christ, 129-34, 336-38; fulfilled in Christ, 17-19, 259-62, 369-72. *See also* Justice, covenant

Creation: and cross of Christ, 136, 448-49; and final judgment, 420-21, 432; and God's judgment of sin, 215-20; and God's purpose of redemption, 336-37, 343, 350, 359, 363-66, 428, 608-11; and human value, 484-86; and natural law, 435-36, 443-44, 445-47

Cross of Christ: as atoning sacrifice, 171-73, 190, 244-54; the believer's participation in by baptism, 313-21; as consistent with creation, 448-49; as destruction of enmity and reconciliation of enemies, 542-46; as God's conflict with and victory over evil, 18, 121-27, 526-30, 542-43; as God's demonstration of faithfulness, 259-61, 369-72; as God's demonstration of love, 139-40, 537; and

648

Index of Scripture and Other Ancient Writings